Sentencing and Criminal Justice

Now in its sixth edition, *Sentencing and Criminal Justice* has been extensively rewritten to reflect recent legislation, guidelines and judicial decisions. New material includes comparative sentencing research, which looks at models from other countries in comparison with the approach in England and Wales, and an additional chapter focusing on civil preventive orders and other ancillary orders. Written with clarity of expression coupled with critical analysis, this textbook offers an unrivalled combination of expertise, accessibility and coverage. This is the essential text for anyone interested in criminal justice.

Andrew Ashworth is Vinerian Professor of English Law Emeritus, University of Oxford and Fellow of All Souls College, Oxford. He was a member of the Sentencing Advisory Panel for eleven years and Chairman from 2007 to 2010.

The Law in Context Series

Editors: William Twining (University College London),
Christopher McCrudden (Queen's University Belfast) and
Bronwen Morgan (University of Bristol).

Since 1970 the Law in Context series has been at the forefront of the movement to broaden the study of law. It has been a vehicle for the publication of innovative scholarly books that treat law and legal phenomena critically in their social, political and economic contexts from a variety of perspectives. The series particularly aims to publish scholarly legal writing that brings fresh perspectives to bear on new and existing areas of law taught in universities. A contextual approach involves treating legal subjects broadly, using materials from other social sciences, and from any other discipline that helps to explain the operation in practice of the subject under discussion. It is hoped that this orientation is at once more stimulating and more realistic than the bare exposition of legal rules. The series includes original books that have a different emphasis from traditional legal textbooks, while maintaining the same high standards of scholarship. They are written primarily for undergraduate and graduate students of law and of other disciplines, but will also appeal to a wider readership. In the past, most books in the series have focused on English law, but recent publications include books on European law, globalisation, transnational legal processes, and comparative law.

Books in the Series

International Journal of Law in Context: A Global Forum for Interdisciplinary Legal Studies

The *International Journal of Law in Context* is the companion journal to the Law in Context book series and provides a forum for interdisciplinary legal studies and offers intellectual space for ground-breaking critical research. It publishes contextual work about law and its relationship with other disciplines including but not limited to science, literature, humanities, philosophy, sociology, psychology, ethics, history and geography. More information about the journal and how to submit an article can be found at http://journals.cambridge.org/ijc

Sentencing and Criminal Justice

Sixth edition

ANDREW ASHWORTH

Vinerian Professor of English Law Emeritus, University of Oxford

CAMBRIDGE
UNIVERSITY PRESS

CAMBRIDGE
UNIVERSITY PRESS

University Printing House, Cambridge CB2 8BS, United Kingdom

Cambridge University Press is part of the University of Cambridge.

It furthers the University's mission by disseminating knowledge in the pursuit of
education, learning and research at the highest international levels of excellence.

www.cambridge.org
Information on this title: www.cambridge.org/9781107057883

First published by Weidenfeld & Nicolson 1992
Second edition published by the Butterworths Division of Reed Elsevier 1995
Third edition published by the Butterworths Division of Reed Elsevier 2002
Fourth edition published by Cambridge University Press 2005
Fifth edition published by Cambridge University Press 2010
Sixth edition published by Cambridge University Press 2015
Reprinted 2016

Printing in the United Kingdom by Clays Ltd, St Ives plc

A catalogue record for this publication is available from the British Library

Library of Congress Cataloguing in Publication data
Ashworth, Andrew, author.
Sentencing and criminal justice / Andrew Ashworth. – Sixth edition.
pages   cm. – (Law in context)
ISBN 978-1-107-05788-3 (Hardback) – ISBN 978-1-107-65201-9 (Paperback)
1. Sentences (Criminal procedure)–Great Britain.   2. Punishment–Great Britain.   I. Title.
KD8406.A975 2015
345.41′0772–dc23   2015002314

ISBN 978-1-107-05788-3 Hardback
ISBN 978-1-107-65201-9 Paperback

Contents

Preface

The five years since the publication of the fifth edition have seen further changes in the form of the English sentencing system, although one of the key features (the size of the prison population) has seen little change, unfortunately. There are four major sources considered in this book – legislation, judicial case-law, sentencing guidelines, and scholarly research and writing – and I have tried to take account of materials available to me on 1 December 2014.

The pace of sentencing legislation has relented a little. There has been only one major statute, the Legal Aid, Sentencing and Punishment of Offenders Act 2012; several other statutes on criminal justice have been enacted, but without bringing major changes to the sentencing system.

Judicial case-law has continued to flow from the Court of Appeal (and, to a much smaller extent, from the Supreme Court), and full account is taken of judicial precedents in this new edition. A high proportion of case-law is now concerned with the application of sentencing guidelines, and that confirms the focus of the new edition.

Definitive sentencing guidelines from the Sentencing Council are now at the heart of sentencing in England and Wales, and are therefore central to this edition. From Chapter 1 through to Chapter 14, there is analysis of the applicable guidelines, and mostly those created in the last four years by the Sentencing Council.

Scholarly research and writing has also burgeoned, largely through the various initiatives of Julian Roberts, whom I am fortunate to have as a colleague. In the last few years he has edited and written in books of essays on a range of central topics in sentencing, and those essays – which have enriched analysis of the theory and practice of sentencing – are taken into account here, along with other recent writings.

There are some small changes to the format of the book. Chapter 11 formerly covered both ancillary orders and sentencing procedures, but those topics are now dealt with separately – Chapter 11 on ancillary orders and civil preventive orders, and Chapter 13 on sentencing procedures. The book concludes with a new Chapter 14, with more comparative materials than hitherto. A further change is that the statistical tables have been moved from the text into an appendix. There are now three appendices for reference purposes: Appendix A contains selected statutory provisions from the Criminal Justice Act 2003 and the Coroners and Justice Act 2009; the statistical tables will be found in Appendix B; and Appendix C sets out parts of two definitive guidelines, on assault occasioning bodily harm and on the importation of drugs. I am grateful to Keir Irwin Roger for assistance with Appendix B.

Finally, I must record my admiration for Von, whose support throughout this edition's intrusion into my semi-retirement has been unstinting and warmly appreciated.

A. A.

Oxford, December 2014

Table of legislative measures

Table of cases

1

An introduction to English sentencing

Contents

1.1 Courts and crimes

Although some common law crimes remain, most of the offences in English criminal law were created by statute and have a statutory maximum penalty. For the purposes of trial, offences were divided into three categories by the Criminal Law Act 1977 – offences triable only on indictment, offences triable only summarily, and offences triable either way. The most serious offences (e.g. murder, rape) are triable only on indictment, at the Crown Court. A large mass of less serious offences is triable only summarily, in magistrates' courts. The middle category of offences triable either way comprises most burglaries, thefts and frauds. The first question in these cases concerns the defendant's intended plea: if the defendant indicates a plea of guilty, the magistrates must assume jurisdiction and proceed to sentence, unless they decide that their sentencing powers are insufficient. If the intended plea is not guilty, the defendant will be tried at a magistrates' court unless either the magistrates direct or the defendant elects to have the case tried at the Crown Court.

The Crown Court sits with a judge and jury. There are three levels of Crown Court centre: first-tier centres, where both civil and criminal cases are tried and where High Court judges and circuit judges preside; second-tier centres, where High Court judges or circuit judges preside but only deal with criminal cases; and third-tier centres, where circuit judges or recorders deal with criminal cases, being mostly offences triable either way. The types of criminal offence are divided into four classes, according to their gravity, and some can only be tried by a High Court judge (of whom there are around 105), whereas others can be tried by circuit judges or recorders. Circuit judges (around 650) are full-time judges, although they may divide their time between civil and criminal work. Recorders and assistant recorders (around 1,200) are part-time judges, whose main occupations are barristers, solicitors or (in a few instances) academics; most full-time judges start their judicial careers in this way. Appeals against sentence from the Crown Court go to the Court of Appeal and, if there is no point of law involved, the appeal requires that Court's leave if it is to be heard. Applications for leave are dealt with by individual High Court judges.

Magistrates' courts deal with the least serious criminal offences. There are around 29,000 lay magistrates in England and Wales, divided into local benches, and a court normally consists of three magistrates. There are also some 140 full-time and 170 part-time District Judges (Magistrates' Courts) (DJMC), formerly known as stipendiary magistrates. A DJMC must be a barrister or solicitor of at least ten years' standing, and he or she sits alone – usually dealing with the longer or more complicated summary cases. The powers of magistrates' courts are limited to imposing a maximum of 6 months' imprisonment in respect of one offence (or a total of 12 months for 2 or more offences).[1] The maximum fine or compensation order that may be imposed by a magistrates' court was formerly £5,000, but since March 2015 is unlimited. Magistrates may, having heard the evidence in a case, commit it to the Crown Court for sentence, if they form the view that the offence was so serious that greater punishment should be inflicted than they have power to impose. As mentioned above, a defendant who indicates an intention to plead guilty to an either-way offence should be sentenced by the magistrates unless they decide that their powers are insufficient, in which case they should commit to the Crown Court for sentence. A person who has been sentenced in a magistrates' court may appeal against sentence to the Crown Court. The appeal takes the form of a complete rehearing of the case, before a circuit judge or recorder and two lay magistrates, and the Crown Court has the power to pass any sentence which the magistrates' court could have imposed, even if that sentence is more severe than the one the latter did in fact impose.[2]

Summary offences are little discussed in this book, although there are frequent references to sentencing in magistrates' courts (which also deal with many 'triable-either-way' offences). Most of the statistics quoted in part 1.3 of this chapter refer to 'indictable offences', which include those triable on indictment and those 'triable either way', whether tried in a magistrates' court or at the Crown Court.

---

[1] Section 154 of the Criminal Justice Act 2003 provided for the ordinary maximum to be raised to 12 months for one offence (15 months for two or more offences). But this increase was intended to accompany a new measure called 'custody plus' and, for reasons explained in ch. 9, this was never implemented.

[2] For fuller details on relevant aspects of criminal procedure, see Sprack (2012).

1.2 The available sentences

Recent years have seen frequent legislation on the sentencing powers of the courts, and three statutes are particularly important for present purposes. The first is the Criminal Justice Act 1991, which was the first major attempt for over 40 years to establish a coherent sentencing structure. After a series of further statutes in the 1990s, Parliament consolidated sentencing law in the Powers of Criminal Courts (Sentencing) (PCCS) Act 2000. This consolidation was a wonderful idea, since it promised the great convenience of bringing the various powers together in one place. Sadly, the statute had already been overtaken by new provisions by the time it came into force, and after three years large parts of it were replaced by the now principal statute, the Criminal Justice Act 2003. That Act, in turn, has been amended and added to by several subsequent statutes.

This part of the chapter gives a preliminary sketch of the courts' sentencing powers, referring also to the different sentences available in relation to young offenders. Most of these sentencing powers are discussed in detail in later chapters, and in part 1.4 of this chapter we examine the reasons why only a small proportion of the crimes committed in any one year result in offenders being sentenced in court.

1.2.1 Sentences for adult offenders

A court's duty in all cases involving injury, death, loss or damage is to consider making a *compensation order* in favour of the victim or, in a case of death, the victim's family: ss. 130–134 of the PCCS Act 2000. This forms part of a policy of increasing recognition of the needs, wishes and rights of the victims of crime, although it is subject to the means of the offender.[3] In 2013, over half of offenders convicted at magistrates' courts of indictable offences of criminal damage were ordered to pay compensation; as for those convicted of offences of violence, 30 per cent in the magistrates' courts and 9 per cent in the Crown Court were subjected to compensation orders.[4] A compensation order will usually be made as well as another order, but it may be made as the sole order against an offender.

The most lenient course which an English court can take after conviction is to order an *absolute discharge*, under s. 12 and Schedule 1 of the PCCS Act 2000. A conviction followed by an absolute discharge does not count as such for most future purposes. The power is used in fewer than 1 per cent of cases, and is generally reserved for instances where there is very little moral guilt for the offence.

---

[3] Victims of crimes of violence also have the possibility of applying to the Criminal Injuries Compensation Scheme: see below, ch. 10.4.

[4] Ministry of Justice (2014), Table A.17.

The power to grant a *conditional discharge* is also to be found in ss. 12–15 and Schedule 1 of the PCCS Act 2000, and once again the conviction does not count as such for most future purposes. The condition is that the offender must commit no offence within a period, of not more than three years, specified by the court. If the offender is convicted of an offence committed during that period, then he or she is liable to be sentenced for the original offence as well. As Tables 2 and 3 (see Appendix B) demonstrate, conditional discharges continue to be used in substantial numbers of cases, although there has been a decline in recent years to 46,000 adult males and around 15,000 adult females in 2013.

The *fine* remains the most used penal measure in English courts, largely because of its widespread use for summary offences. Its use for both summary and indictable offences has declined steeply. As Tables 2 and 3 demonstrate, the totals had declined to 478,000 adult males and 215,000 adult females by 2013. Maximum fines are usually unlimited for indictable offences tried in the Crown Court, and from March 2015 this is also applicable in magistrates' courts. The leading principle (in s. 164 of the Criminal Justice Act 2003) is that the fine should reflect the seriousness of the offence and the offender's ability to pay; and a court should give priority to a compensation order over a fine where the offender has limited financial resources and appears unable to pay both.

A court may only impose a *community sentence*, states s. 148 of the 2003 Act, if satisfied that the seriousness of the offence(s) is sufficient to warrant such a sentence. Having reached this decision, the court must then select the requirement(s) which (i) are most suitable for the offender and (ii) impose restrictions on the offender which are commensurate with the seriousness of the offence. There are now 15 possible requirements for adults, such as unpaid work and alcohol or drugs treatment, and the details are discussed in Chapter 10.6 below. In 2013 some 70,000 adult male offenders were given a community sentence and some 15,000 adult females, a decline probably attributable to the increased use of the suspended sentence order (below).

Next in ascending order of severity is *imprisonment*. Before imposing a custodial sentence, the court must be satisfied, according to s. 152(2), that the offence was 'so serious that neither a fine nor a community sentence can be justified', a formula that requires the court to dismiss all lesser alternatives before resorting to custody. If it decides on custody, s. 153(2) states that the sentence should be for the shortest term 'commensurate with the seriousness of the offence'. (These and other statutory provisions are set out in Appendix A, at the end of the book.) In determining the length of any custodial sentence, courts should apply any relevant guidelines, and take due account of aggravating and mitigating factors (see Chapter 5) and of previous convictions (see Chapter 6).

When the court has decided that a prison sentence is justified and has decided on its length, it may still have the choice between a suspended sentence order and immediate imprisonment. This applies where the court is minded to impose a sentence of between 14 days and 2 years (s. 189 of the 2003 Act, as amended). If it decides that there are grounds for suspending such a sentence, it should consider whether to order the offender to comply with one or more requirements taken from the list available for community sentences. Non-compliance may result in return to court and the activation of the whole or part of the prison sentence. Tables 2 and 3 show the sharp rise in the use of suspended sentence orders in recent years, with corresponding reductions in the use of imprisonment, community sentences and fines.

Parliament has introduced several mandatory and mandatory minimum sentences in recent years. For example, under s. 287 of the 2003 Act there is a minimum sentence of 5 years' imprisonment for various offences of possessing firearms, from which a judge may depart only in 'exceptional circumstances'. Already in place were the minimum sentence of 7 years for the third offence of trafficking class A drugs (s. 110 of the PCCS Act 2000) and 3 years for the third domestic burglary (s. 111 of the PCCS Act 2000), from which a judge may depart if the minimum sentence would be 'unjust in all the circumstances'. The provisions of the 2003 Act for dangerous offenders were repealed and replaced by the Legal Aid, Sentencing and Punishment of Offenders Act 2012 (LASPO). The two new sentences are the automatic sentence of life imprisonment for the second very serious offence, and an extended sentence on grounds of public protection. The discretionary sentence of life imprisonment is available for many serious offences, and the mandatory life sentence for murder remains in place.

Despite statutory provisions such as those in ss. 152 and 153(2) of the 2003 Act which prohibit courts from imposing a custodial sentence unless neither a fine nor a community sentence can be justified for the offence(s), and which require courts to impose the shortest custodial sentence commensurate with the seriousness of the offence(s), both the use of custodial sentences and their average length have shown general increases over the decade. As Tables 2 to 7 (see Appendix B) show, the proportionate use of prison sentences has increased by two-thirds in the last two decades, and the average length of immediate custodial sentences has increased significantly too, both at a time when the crime rate has decreased and the numbers of offenders for sentence has remained fairly stable. As the Tables show in detail, the use of immediate custody for males peaked at 103,000 in 2002 and stood at 85,000 in 2013; for females, the corresponding figures were 8,800 custodial sentences in 2002, falling to 7,125 by 2013. The actual meaning of custodial sentences depends on the operation of the system of early release under the Criminal Justice Act 2003. In broad terms, all prisoners are released after serving half their sentence, but are then on licence and subject to recall at any time until the expiry of the full sentence. The licence involves supervision only for sentences of 12 months or longer, but the Offender Rehabilitation Act 2014 will extend supervision to all released prisoners.

There is a whole list of ancillary and/or preventive orders which may be made by the courts in appropriate cases. These range from restitution orders and disqualification from driving, to the more recent flush of preventive orders – for example, serious crime prevention orders, sexual offences prevention orders and football banning orders. In some circumstances, such as drug trafficking and serious crime, a court is bound to follow the statutory procedure towards making an order for the confiscation of the offender's assets under the Proceeds of Crime Act 2002. Ancillary orders are discussed in Chapter 11.

1.2.2 Sentences for young offenders

The courts' powers for sentencing offenders aged under 21 fall broadly into two groups – first, those relating to offenders aged 18, 19 or 20, who have been termed 'young adults' and dealt with in adult courts; and secondly, those relating to offenders aged 10–17 inclusive, who are dealt with chiefly in the youth court.

There are now so few differences in the structure of sentencing for young adults that it may be questioned whether it constitutes a separate category. The small differences are set out in Chapter 12.2 below, where there is also discussion of whether this category should be revived, with separate and more constructive sentencing powers, and indeed whether it should be extended to the age of 25, as in some other jurisdictions. Tables 4 and 5 (see Appendix B) show sentencing trends for this age group.

For young defendants under 18 both the procedure and the sentencing powers differ considerably. Their cases are dealt with in youth courts, except when there is a charge of a particularly grave crime. Very young children charged with murder, manslaughter, and some other serious offences are tried in the Crown Court. However, where the defendants are as young as 11 or 12, special efforts must be made to ensure that the defendants can follow and participate in the trial: a Practice Direction on the appropriate procedures for such cases was issued in 2000,[5] but further changes were required by a subsequent decision of the European Court of Human Rights.[6]

However, cases of that kind are few. In practice, as we shall see in part 1.4 below, most offenders of this age have been dealt with by a reprimand or final warning under the Crime and Disorder Act 1998, and the system is described more fully in Chapter 12.1. Section 37 of the 1998 Act declares that 'the principal aim of the youth justice system [is] to prevent offending by children and young persons', but this has now been augmented by various reforms of youth justice in the Criminal Justice and Immigration Act 2008. For those who are prosecuted in court for the first time and plead guilty, the

---

[5] *Practice Direction: Young Defendants in the Crown Court* [2000] 2 All ER 284, applying the decision in *V and T* v. *United Kingdom* (1999) 30 EHRR 121.
[6] *SC* v. *United Kingdom* [2005] Crim LR 130.

court is under a statutory duty to make a referral order under s. 16 of the PCCS Act 2000. The consequence of the referral order, described more fully in Chapter 12.1.2, is the drawing up of a 'youth offender contract' requiring certain commitments. In other cases the youth court has the same range of powers as do the ordinary courts when dealing with young adults, with two noticeable exceptions. The first is that when a youth court is dealing with a child under 16, it must require the attendance of the child's parents unless this would be unreasonable, and it must bind over the parents to exercise control over the child unless it gives reasons for not doing so. The second difference concerns custodial sentences, which have been relatively rare for young offenders. Details of the law are given in Chapter 12.1 below, but essentially a 'detention and training order' may only be made in certain standard lengths, as consolidated in ss. 100–107 of the PCCS Act 2000 (i.e. 4, 6, 8, 10, 12, 18 or 24 months, and not intermediate lengths). The 2008 Act introduced the youth rehabilitation order, and the expressed intention was that this should be used instead of custody in many cases. The sentencing patterns in Tables 6 and 7 (see Appendix B) demonstrate a spectacular decline in the use of custody in recent years.

1.3 The general statistical background

In order to place the sentencing statistics in their criminal justice context, we must begin by examining 'the crime rate' and its variations. Apart from scrutinizing the concept of 'the crime rate', it is important to assess the sentencing decisions of the courts in relation to the many other decisions to be taken between reporting a crime and prosecuting an accused person to conviction. Thus, as will be argued in part 1.4 below, the numbers sentenced may reflect changes in police investigation priorities or changes in the policies of the Crown Prosecution Service, rather than any increase or decrease in 'the crime rate'.

How can the number of crimes committed each year be measured? The best that the official criminal statistics can offer is the annual total of crimes recorded by the police. It will be recalled that the second line of figures in Table 1 (see Appendix B), 'Offences recorded by the police', shows trends in recorded crime. The statistics in that table are more representative of the crime rate than the numbers of offences which are detected or which result in a conviction (i.e. all the figures lower down Table 1), but they still give only a small part of the picture. The police are informed about crimes mostly by victims, but not all victims report incidents to the police. Figures from the Crime Survey for England and Wales (CSEW, formerly the British Crime Survey) show that in 2010–11 some 38 per cent of victims reported the crime to the police. Of those crime victims who responded to the CSEW and who failed to report the crime to the police, some 72 per cent fell within the category of 'trivial/no loss/police would not (could not) do anything', and a further 16 per cent responded 'private/dealt with ourselves'.[7] Thus, although the figures for serious offences recorded by the police have been the most comprehensive set of statistics published regularly over the decades, they are not a reliable indicator of the number of crimes being committed, or of fluctuations in the crime rate.

Criminologists have attempted to estimate the number of unreported offences (sometimes called the 'dark figure' of crime) by two main methods. One is the self-report study, in which people are asked to divulge in confidence how many offences they have committed during a specified period of crime. An obvious defect of this approach is that some people may be reticent whereas others might exaggerate their deeds out of bravado. The second and more widely used method is to ask people to state in confidence the number of crimes of which they have been a victim during a specified period. If one then takes the results of such a study, known as a victimization study or crime survey, and compares them with the number of officially recorded crimes over the same period, an estimate of the proportion of crimes unrecorded can be made. This is the basis on which the CSEW (formerly the British Crime Survey) has proceeded since 1981. However, crime surveys are at their best when dealing with crimes with identifiable victims: the CSEW covers violence, sexual offences, burglary, robbery, theft, and damage. There is also a Commercial Victimization Survey, which estimated that in 2013 there were 7.3 million incidents of crime against businesses.[8] It is particularly hard to survey offences of which people are unlikely to think of themselves as victims, such as drug offences and consensual sexual crimes.

The CSEW consists of questions put to a large sample of citizens about crimes to which they have fallen victim in the past year. Although its scope is restricted to certain crimes, for the reasons just given, it does enable a comparison with the figures for crimes recorded by the police for those offences. It also enables comparisons of trends over time. What can be seen, from comparing the first line with the second line of figures in Table 1, is that 'Crime as measured by the British Crime Survey' peaked in 1991 and has been falling slowly but steadily since then. On the other hand, although the figures for 'Notifiable offences recorded by the police' also rose sharply during the 1980s, and then rose relatively slowly during the 1990s, they have recently begun to fall and to reflect the decline in numbers of offences found by the CSEW.

As the first line of Table 1 demonstrates, the amount of crime as measured by the CSEW in 2013 was less than half that of 1991. Some of the reductions recorded by the CSEW respondents are enormous. Thus in the 15 years from 1997, vehicle thefts declined by some 60 per cent; burglary declined by some 55 per cent; offences of violence declined by some 60 per cent; and so on.[9]

---

[7] Chaplin et al. (2011), p. 55.   [8] Office for National Statistics (2014).
[9] Chaplin et al. (2011), chs. 3 and 4.

It is evident that for robbery and serious wounding the decline has been less than for most other offences; but there is still a decline that contrasts with the considerable rise in such categories of offence recorded by the police. The CSEW figures are more reliable over time since they have been subject to fewer changes of recording practice. These statistics are particularly important as a corrective to arguments often advanced about crime rates and penal policy: the CSEW shows a consistent decline in the rate at which people are becoming victims of crime.

Enquiries made as part of the CSEW suggest that members of the public have not changed their approach to reporting crimes in the last three decades. This is important in ruling out one possible explanation for the rise and then decline in crimes recorded by the police, since around three-quarters of offences which come to the notice of the police are reported by members of the public rather than 'discovered' by the police themselves.[10] However, reporting habits do not merely relate to the offences against individuals with which the CSEW is concerned. Many organizations learn of offences of fraud or thieving committed by their employees, and deal with them by dismissing or disciplining the employee without reporting an offence. As for the offences which the police discover for themselves, the numbers will be affected by levels, styles and targets of policing. In general, the police are much more likely to 'discover' offences committed in public places than crimes committed in the home or in business or financial settings. Furthermore, fluctuations in the number of recorded offences of possession of drugs, possession of child pornography or possession of obscene articles for gain might largely reflect priorities in police deployment. Thus, discovery of many of these crimes may only loosely relate to variations in the actual rate of offending.

It is already clear, then, that the number of offences recorded by the police each year is a considerable underestimate; that the number includes proportionately more offences against individuals and public order offences than offences by and against companies; and that fluctuations from year to year may reflect changes in reporting or recording practices rather than changes in the true level of crime. The next stage in the process sees another major quantitative change. Only 28 per cent of offences recorded by the police in 2007–8 were detected (Table 1, line 4; no figures available for 2013). An offence is treated as 'detected' not only if a person is convicted or cautioned but also if a person was charged or summonsed, or cautioned or warned, or given a penalty notice for disorder, or had the offence 'taken into consideration' by the court on conviction for another offence.[11] The detection or 'clear-up' rate declined gradually from 38 per cent in 1981 to reach 23 per cent in 2001, but in the subsequent years – probably as a result of the 'closing the justice gap' initiative – it increased slightly to 28 per cent. The detection

---

[10] Bottomley and Coleman (1981), p. 44.   [11] This practice is discussed in ch. 8.1 below.

rate is certainly higher for the more serious offences. For many years about half of offences of violence against the person and a third of sexual offences have been 'cleared up', although these higher figures may owe as much to the fact that many victims recognize and can identify their attackers as to the greater efforts put into police work on these crimes. At the other end of the scale, only 13 per cent of recorded burglaries and 20 per cent of robberies were detected in 2007–8.

How do the courts use their sentencing powers? The detailed statistics for the last decade are presented in six separate tables. Tables 2 to 7 (see Appendix B) show the trends for all male and all female offenders for the years 1997–2013, showing the recent rise in suspended sentences, the decline in the use of the fine and community sentences, and the continuing high use of custody. Turning to young adult offenders, Tables 4 and 5 show how suspended sentence orders have tended to displace both custody and community orders in recent years, for both young men and young women. Tables 6 and 7 give the figures for offenders aged 10–17 inclusive. Community sentences have increased sharply throughout, largely at the expense of conditional discharges and fines, and the use of custody has seen a spectacular decline.

1.4 What is sentencing and where can it be found?

In the first three sections of this chapter, it has been assumed that the notion of 'sentencing' is unproblematic. It is what courts do to convicted offenders. However, we must now take the analysis further, and explore the concept of 'sentencing' in greater detail. Padfield, Morgan and Maguire (2012) refer to sentencing as 'the allocation of criminal sanctions', a definition that focuses on what is handed out ('criminal sanctions') but says nothing about the person or institution that is doing the handing out.[12] On this definition, therefore, a key question is what amounts to a 'criminal sanction'. Many regulatory bodies (such as the Competition Commission) have the power to impose swingeing fines on organizations that contravene the applicable rules: these are sanctions, but not *criminal* sanctions since they do not involve conviction of an offence and are part of a civil regulatory system. More contested is the category of civil preventive orders, of which there are now some 12 or more in English law: these orders can be made by a criminal court or a civil court, and are labelled 'preventive' (as distinct from punitive). The English courts have held that they are not 'penalties' as such,[13] and the Strasbourg Court has gone no further than to hold that confiscation orders are 'penalties' because of their punitive

---

[12] Freiberg and Murray (2012), in an article dealing with constitutional challenges to sentences in Australia, define a sentence as 'a dispositive order of a criminal court consequent upon a finding of guilt', focusing on the role of the court and excluding orders such as confiscation orders and civil preventive orders.

[13] *Clingham* v. *Kensington and Chelsea LBC* [2003] AC 787, criticised by Ashworth (2004).

elements.[14] The status of civil preventive orders such as sexual offences prevention orders, serious crime prevention orders and others remains to be litigated. They are further discussed in Chapter 11 below.

Closer to the boundary are the powers of bodies such as HM Revenue & Customs (HMRC), which is authorized to require payment of double the underpaid tax from those whom it finds avoiding tax, with enforcement powers in support. Such powers surely involve the imposition of 'criminal sanctions', imposed for an offence but not by a court. When we move to Penalty Notices for Disorder (PNDs), which are financial penalties for offences detected by the police, they may easily be included within the notion of a 'criminal sanction', not least because if the individual wishes to dispute the PND he can refuse to pay and invite the police to prosecute for the underlying offence. More details of PNDs will be given below, but the important point here is that there is a range of out-of-court disposals – in addition to PNDs' fixed penalty notices, simple cautions, conditional cautions and others – which clearly fall within the definition of a 'criminal sanction'.

What is different about those disposals is that they are not ordered by a court following conviction of an offence. Although access to a court is possible, in compliance with the right to fair trial (Article 6 of the European Convention on Human Rights), for practical purposes these out-of-court disposals are imposed and administered by the police, CPS or relevant agency (such as HMRC, the Environment Agency or the Department of Work and Pensions). So the question arises: should sentences only be imposed by courts? The issue is one of fairness and proportionality. The fairness requirement is that, under Article 6, an individual has a right to have a penalty imposed only after a fair and open hearing by an independent and impartial tribunal. This has not been interpreted to mean that a criminal sanction can only be imposed by a criminal court. Instead, the European Court of Human Rights has held that the requirements of Article 6 are satisfied if the individual has the right of access to a court, in order to challenge the imposition of the sanction.[15] Therefore, administrative fines imposed by officials, and various sanctions imposed by police or by public prosecutors, have been held to be Convention compliant so long as there is access to a court.

The driving force behind what may appear to be a compromise with normal standards of procedural fairness is the proportionality principle – in this context, the principle that court proceedings should generally be reserved for cases that are of moderate or greater seriousness or are contested. Under the banner of 'the simplification of criminal justice',[16] considerations of cost and speed which are pressing in all criminal justice systems have led to the

---

[14] *Welch* v. *UK* (1995) 20 EHRR 247; see ch. 2.7 below.
[15] *Ozturk* v. *Germany* (1984) 6 EHRR 409; Emmerson, Ashworth and Macdonald (2012), pp. 214–18.
[16] Council of Europe (1987).

development of various methods of diversion from the formal criminal process. In England and Wales, as will be discussed below, the police have long exercised the power to caution offenders rather than prosecuting them, and this has led to the various forms of out-of-court disposal now available. The idea is that, for non-serious offences, it is proportionate to allow a low-level sanction to be imposed by a non-judicial agent (provided, as always, that the right of access to a court is preserved). However, the fairness and proportionality of some such arrangements can be contested. The fact is that very few PNDs are refused and taken to court; PNDs are imposed by the police, and the blurring of their role as investigators and evidence gatherers with this power to impose a sanction may place the individual at a disadvantage; and although a PND does not give rise to a criminal record as such, most PNDs are given for recordable offences and are therefore placed on the Police National Computer and may be cited on future occasions.[17] To what extent this is fair and proportionate – even if it is known to the individual at the time the PND is accepted, which is not always the case – is open to debate.

There is thus an argument that the imposition of criminal sanctions by agents who also have the role of keeping order, investigating or preparing cases for prosecution (notably police, public prosecutors, and regulatory agencies) significantly compromises the principle of fairness. Sentences should be imposed by courts which are impartial and independent. Insofar as European criminal justice systems deviate from that 'gold standard', this is a matter for regret and is justifiable only on pragmatic economic grounds. But it is not only police, prosecutors, and regulatory agencies that are exercising what amounts to a sentencing function. Other non-judicial agents have substantial power over the quantum of punishment at a later stage in the process. For example, all prisoners serving sentences of between 3 months and 4 years are eligible for early release on Home Detention Curfew (HDC) unless they fall into one of the excluded categories (e.g. prisoners previously returned to custody, those serving extended sentences); but, even if eligible, a prisoner may not be granted early release by the responsible prison governor, particularly if the prisoner is a sex offender or a risk assessment is adverse. The HDC scheme, as administered in the prisons, is therefore capable of affecting the length of time actually served by most prisoners (HDC can extend for up to 135 days). Two further examples of administrative power over the quantum of a sentence are prison recalls and release of indeterminate prisoners. A prisoner who is released on licence after serving half the sentence (as is normal) and who breaches the terms of the licence will find that the decision to recall him or her to prison is an administrative one, and then the question of subsequent release from prison depends (in some cases, at least) on the decision of the Parole Board. Thus the initial loss of liberty does not require any appearance before a

[17] Padfield, Morgan and Maguire (2012), pp. 962–3; Larrauri (2014).

court. The Parole Board is a judicial authority (although not a court), and it also has power to determine the release of the 19 per cent of the English prison population who are serving indeterminate sentences (either life imprisonment, or sentences of imprisonment for public protection). After the expiry of the minimum term set by the court at sentencing, the indeterminate sentence prisoner will remain in prison until the Parole Board is satisfied that it is no longer necessary for the protection of the public that he should be detained. If released, the prisoner will remain on licence for the remainder of his life, subject to administrative recall.[18]

It is clear from the foregoing paragraphs that 'sentencing' is not a simple notion. While the paradigm of sentencing is the imposition by a court of a criminal sanction, we have seen that some criminal sanctions are not imposed by courts, and that some non-judicial agencies are able to alter significantly the length and impact of a sentence. Since the substance of most sentences involves a deprivation of certain fundamental rights – e.g. liberty of the person (imprisonment), freedom of movement (community sanctions), the right to personal property (fines, compensation) – strong justifications ought to be required before bestowing this power on non-judicial agents who are not 'independent and impartial' within the meaning of Article 6 of the European Convention. This book focuses on decisions of the courts in relation to criminal sanctions, but seeks also to take account of the effects of the other agencies that exercise power over sentences. In the remaining paragraphs of this section, therefore, attention is given to the several stages at which decisions are taken in a criminal process that begins with decisions such as reporting a crime or arresting a suspect, and goes through to decisions to release a prisoner on parole or to revoke a community order.

The effect of discretion is apparent from the very early stages of the criminal process. Thus, not all 'detected' offences result in a prosecution. In fact, both the police and the Crown Prosecution Service are urged to consider two factors, evidential sufficiency and whether prosecution is in the public interest. The police take no further action in some cases which are recorded as crimes but where the available evidence is considered weak – notably, no further action is taken in around 30 per cent of rape cases, largely because the complainant withdraws the complaint.[19] During the 1980s and early 1990s the police were encouraged to make greater use of formal cautions as an alternative to prosecution. However, different governments have tried to change cautioning policy at various stages, resulting in a fall in the cautioning rate in the mid- and late 1990s, followed by an increase to the peak of 363,000 in 2007, and a decline to 176,000 in 2013 (see Appendix B, Table 1).

A new form of diversion was introduced by the Criminal Justice Act 2003, the conditional caution. This may only be directed by a crown prosecutor,

---

[18] See further ch. 6.8 and ch. 9.5 below for further discussion of release arrangements.
[19] Harris and Grace (1999), ch. 3.

although the police retain their power to dispose of an offence by means of a 'simple caution'. Section 23 of the 2003 Act sets out five conditions to be met before a conditional caution is given, and they include sufficient evidence to bring a charge, an admission from the defendant, and the latter's signature to a document setting out the conditions to which consent is given. The conditions may include requirements to participate in some rehabilitative, reparative or restorative programme. Failure to observe the conditions may result in the bringing of a prosecution for the original offence. The Revised Code of Practice for Conditional Cautions (2009) lists certain criteria relevant to decisions to offer a conditional caution.

Not all criminal cases are handled by the police. Perhaps one-quarter of all prosecutions of adults for non-motoring offences are initiated by government departments, HM Revenue & Customs, the Post Office, the various inspectorates concerned with industrial safety and the environment, local authorities and their various departments (including trading standards) and, occasionally, private individuals. Indeed, it is not just that these bodies bring around a quarter of non-motoring prosecutions. Equally significant is their widespread practice of avoiding prosecution wherever possible. For example, HM Revenue & Customs has extensive powers of compounding, which enable it to exact compliance plus a financial penalty without bringing a case to court.[20] Research also demonstrates the emphasis of the Health and Safety Executive and other inspectorates on obtaining compliance with the required standards, and their general practice of using prosecution only as a last resort.[21] Since many of these offences are typically committed by people who have moderate or good financial resources, it follows that the figures for crimes recorded by the police and for persons prosecuted may tend to give greater prominence to crimes committed by members of the lower socio-economic groups.

Returning to the types of crime on which the police focus, the first point is that the police are empowered to deal with certain offences themselves by imposing a Penalty Notice for Disorder (PND). A PND can be issued not only for offences of disorder (including drunk and disorderly) but also for thefts from shops under £200 and low-level criminal damage. The PND is a fine of £40 or £80, but the ticketed person can elect to be prosecuted instead. The use of PNDs peaked at 207,544 in 2007, but since police targets for 'offences brought to justice' were abandoned in 2010 the number of PNDs issued has about halved, to 106,205 in 2012.[22] A review found that up to one-third of PNDs were not issued according to the guidance given to the police.[23]

In other cases, where the police wish to have a person charged, the file is shared with the Crown Prosecution Service under the 'statutory charging'

---

[20] Roording (1996).   [21] Hawkins (2003).

[22] See www.gov.uk/government/publication/criminal-justice-statistics-quarterly, Out of Court Disposals, December 2012.

[23] HMIC/HMCPSI (2011), and Padfield, Morgan and Maguire (2012), pp. 962–5.

scheme introduced by the Criminal Justice Act 2003. Police and prosecutors work together, but the CPS now has the power to determine whether and what to charge. The aim is that these arrangements will make for speed, better quality preparation and therefore fewer cases discontinued or dismissed by the courts.[24] In taking decisions either on initial charge or on later review, crown prosecutors are regulated by the *Code for Crown Prosecutors*.[25] In essence, they must take two related decisions. First, is the evidence sufficient for a prosecution? The code states that cases should only be brought where there is a 'realistic prospect of conviction'. Second, would a prosecution be 'in the public interest'? The code sets out a number of general criteria for and against prosecuting – most of them similar to the aggravating and mitigating factors in sentencing reviewed in Chapter 5 below. The two decisions are closely connected, and in practice there is considerable emphasis on pursuing serious charges and diverting less serious cases. The CPS has the power to alter the charge later or to discontinue a prosecution if this is thought to be appropriate.

The *Code for Crown Prosecutors* is not the only source of guidance for CPS decision-making. As is evident from their website, there is much available guidance on the proper approach to particular types of offence, and approved 'charging standards' for some offences.[26] No study of the effectiveness of this guidance has been published, and so it remains to be discovered whether it has brought about reductions in questionable practices. For example, s. 144 of the Criminal Justice Act 2003 gives legislative authority for a discount for pleading guilty. It is sometimes suggested that this gives an incentive to prosecutors to overcharge some cases, in the hope of inducing a bargain whereby the defendant agrees to plead guilty to a lesser offence (which may be the offence that should have been charged originally). On the other hand some cases may be undercharged, in order to have the case disposed of in the magistrates' court, where any plea of not guilty is less likely to succeed than it is in the Crown Court. Although it is not known how often these practices occur, they demonstrate that factors other than the intrinsic seriousness of the case may determine the charge brought and the way in which the evidence (or, on a guilty plea, the prosecutor's statement of facts) is presented. Moreover, the prosecutor's choice of charge may have a considerable effect on the sentence. The decision to charge a summary offence restricts the court's sentencing power. The decision to charge an offence triable either way, together with representations to the magistrates in favour of Crown Court trial, invariably results in the case being committed to the Crown Court, where the sentence may be much more severe than a magistrates' court's sentence.[27]

---

[24] See further Brownlee (2004) and Moreno and Hughes (2009).

[25] The latest version of the code was published in 2010: see www.cps.gov.uk.

[26] www.cps.gov.uk.

[27] Hedderman and Moxon (1992), in an earlier era, estimated that the sentence in the Crown Court would be, on average, seven times as severe as that in a magistrates' court.

The Crown Prosecution Service also has a role to play in any subsequent negotiations about the defendant's plea. Most cases end with a plea of guilty or a dismissal of the case: only 6 per cent of prosecutions in the magistrates' courts and 7 per cent in the Crown Court actually go to trial.[28] However, not all of the guilty pleaders began by pleading guilty: indeed, of those defendants in Hedderman and Moxon's study who had elected to go for trial in the Crown Court, no fewer than 82 per cent subsequently changed their plea to guilty.[29] Of those who thus changed their plea to guilty, some 51 per cent said that they 'expected some charges would be dropped or reduced, resulting in a lighter sentence', and a further 22 per cent now took the view that there was 'no chance of a not guilty plea succeeding'.[30] Since, as we shall see in Chapter 5, a plea of guilty should usually result in a significant reduction in sentence, these practices have implications for the powers of the courts as well as for the rights of the individual defendant. The finding of Baldwin and McConville (1978) that many such defendants felt under pressure from their lawyers to change their plea to guilty was hotly disputed by the legal establishment in the 1970s, but since then there has been a succession of cases in which judges were revealed to have played some part in negotiations, which would then have been relayed to the defendant by counsel.[31] Home Office research projects have confirmed the extensive influence of lawyers:

> The two most frequent reasons given for a change in advice on plea on the day scheduled for trial were 'a bargain with the prosecution' and 'information about probable sentence'. The most frequent forms of concession were that, in consideration of one or more pleas of guilty, the prosecution should offer no evidence, or agree to the defendant's being bound over, on other charges.[32]

Thus, even a matter of hours or minutes before a case is due to be tried, it can undergo changes which 'reconstruct' it. When it is presented to the court for sentence, the case may have been negotiated in certain ways so that it is qualitatively different from that originally brought by the police. One main purpose of enacting s. 144 of the Criminal Justice Act 2003 (requiring courts to consider a discount for a guilty plea) and s. 49 of the Criminal Procedure and Investigations Act 1996 ('plea before venue'), and of the institution of 'advance indications of sentence' in *Goodyear*,[33] was to place more pressure on defendants to plead guilty, and to do so at the earliest possible stage.[34] Unfortunately, that pressure falls upon the innocent as well as the guilty.

The main implication of this contextual discussion of the criminal process is that the cases which judges and magistrates have for sentence are

---

[28] Crown Prosecution Service (2013).   [29] Hedderman and Moxon (1992), p. 22.
[30] Hedderman and Moxon (1992), p. 24.
[31] A number of cases are discussed in Ashworth and Redmayne (2010), ch. 10.
[32] Riley and Vennard (1988), p. 20; also Hedderman and Moxon (1992), pp. 22–4.
[33] [2006] 1 Cr App R (S) 23, discussed in ch. 5.4.1 and ch. 13 below.
[34] The import of s. 144, and the guidelines attached to it, will be discussed in ch. 5.4.1 below.

quantitatively and qualitatively different from the 'real' amount of crime in society. This casts grave doubt upon pronouncements about crime, crime prevention and trends in crime which are based on the features of cases going through the courts. The differences stem from the several stages of selection, starting with the under-reporting of crimes in the home and crimes by and against businesses, continuing with the differential responses to crime by the police and the so-called regulatory agencies, taking in the differential diversion rates for juveniles and young adults, and ending with the plea negotiations which make some offences appear less serious than they were. The overall conclusion is that the types of case which come up for sentence are an imperfect reflection of the nature of crime in society.

The quantitative differences between the crimes actually committed and those coming up for sentence in court are immense. Taking the Home Office's own 1998 figures, compiled with the benefit of CSEW data, we start with the cautious assumption that some 45 per cent of offences were reported. Of those, only about 55 per cent were actually recorded by the police as crimes, for various reasons. That reduced the number of cases still within the criminal justice system to 24 per cent (i.e. 55 per cent of the 45 per cent reported). The detection rate for recorded crimes was less than a quarter, so the 24 per cent declined to 5.5 per cent of all offences detected. Of those offences, just over half resulted in a conviction or formal caution. This brought the figure to some 3 per cent of offences and, since about one-third of those resulted in a caution, sentencers probably dealt with just over 2 per cent of actual offences. (Around 0.3 per cent of offences result in a custodial sentence.) These figures would not have changed significantly in the last decade. The final figures would be higher for offences of violence, but lower for many thefts. Since the above figures come from the Home Office's own *Digest 4* (1999) of information on the criminal justice system, they can hardly be treated as exaggerated. What they demonstrate is that, if criminal justice policy-makers expect sentencing to perform a major preventive function, they are looking in the wrong direction. As Baldock put it, in the context of attempts to reduce the prison population,

> Prisons stand at the end of an elaborate process of selection by the public, police, courts and judges. Consequently, relatively small changes at any point in the process can have an amplified impact on the prison system. It is a mistake to seek the causes and remedies for the growth of the prison population by looking only at the very late stages of these processes, sentences of imprisonment. This is the tail end of the story and, as most of the attempts to 'reform' or counteract sentencing policy have shown, it is a tail which cannot easily be made to wag the dog.[35]

The argument, therefore, is that sentencing in the courts deals only with a small and selected sample of offences and offenders; that the preventive and

---

[35] Baldock (1980), pp. 149–50.

other general effects of sentencing in these cases should not be overestimated; that any assumption that crime rates stand in some hydraulic relationship to sentence levels, so that crime will go down if sentences go up and vice versa, seems wildly unrealistic; and, on the basis of the selection of offences they deal with, that judges and magistrates are likely to have a somewhat skewed view of the crime problem as a whole.

Alongside those important points must also be placed another. If we consider the sharp increase in the use of custody since 1993, the question arises whether it was a product of increases in the number of cases coming before courts for sentence, or of a change in the sentencing practices of the courts. As Table 1 (see Appendix B) confirms, there has been no significant increase in the number of cases coming up for sentence. That suggests that the explanation lies in the greater severity of sentencing practices. However, Hough, Jacobson and Millie's interviews of judges and magistrates yielded a trio of other explanations – that judges were responding to the more repressive climate of opinion in society, that the offenders coming before the courts had more previous convictions, and that the offences were more serious than in former years.[36] The first of these three explanations concedes the point that sentences have become more severe. The second and third were investigated by the researchers, who found that the available statistics do not confirm either that the offenders being sentenced have more previous convictions than formerly[37] or that their offences are more serious. However, as they conclude, sentencers clearly believe that these are major factors, and those perceptions may influence their behaviour.

Prominent at the various stages of the criminal process is discretion. The police exercise it, the regulatory agencies exercise it, the Crown Prosecution Service exercises it, and prison officials and the Parole Board exercise it at the stages of release and recall to prison. Now it may well be true that the many and varied elements which are relevant to these decisions tell in favour of discretionary rather than strictly rule-bound decision-making. This is often said to be true of sentencing to a certain extent, and may be no less true of prosecution decisions. However, discretion brings not only advantages, in the shape of flexibility to respond to different combinations of facts, but also disadvantages, in that it may allow the individual views of the decision-maker to influence (deliberately or otherwise) the approach taken, with unfortunate

---

[36] Hough et al. (2003), pp. 26–30.

[37] The authors find some evidence of an increased proportion of persistent offenders in the categories of theft and handling, which may be related to drug use (Hough et al. (2003), p. 29), but it is not of sufficient magnitude to explain the steep overall rise in the use of custody. Subsequent Ministry of Justice figures show that the proportion of indictable offenders with fifteen or more previous convictions has increased from 23 per cent in 2003 to 35 per cent in 2013: www.gov.uk/government/publications/criminal-justice-statistics-quarterly, Offending Histories Tables, June 2013.

consequences for consistency, equality, and social justice.[38] These values are further damaged by institutional relationships that ensure that certain types of offending such as 'white-collar crime' and so-called regulatory offences are unlikely to come to the attention of the police. Since the agencies dealing with those offences tend to regard prosecution as a last resort, the court system is likely to contain far more offenders of some kinds than offenders of other kinds.

Replacing discretion with rigid rules may eliminate its advantages as well as its disadvantages. A wiser course may therefore be to attempt to structure the discretion, in an attempt to ensure that it is exercised broadly in line with some coherent policies.[39] Steps have been taken in this direction, in the form of Home Office circulars to the police on cautioning, the *Code for Crown Prosecutors*, guidance to the police on the use of PNDs and guidance on the selection of prisoners for Home Detention Curfew. However, the principles contained in these documents are often fairly general, listing the relevant criteria rather than assigning them weight and outlining a decision process, and the guidance is not always supported by adequate training. Moreover, criminological research establishes that other influences – such as easing one's own job, maintaining good relations with others, and personal or local preferences – often enter into practical decision-making.[40] Drafting and promulgating guidelines is therefore not enough to ensure that discretion is exercised along the right lines. At least two further steps should be taken. One is to foster positive and constructive attitudes amongst the key decision-makers, so that they understand the reasons for policies and become committed to carrying them out. The other is to create structures of accountability, in terms of both internal monitoring and external scrutiny or audit.

1.5 The formal sources of sentencing decisions

The principal sources of English sentencing law are legislation, definitive sentencing guidelines and the common law (deriving from judicial decisions). In recent years the balance between the three has shifted. Legislation continues to dominate, in terms of both quantity and authority. But sentencing guidelines are so extensive that most of the cases in magistrates' courts and in the Crown Court now involve the application of a sentencing guideline. This means that the relevance of the common law of sentencing – appellate decisions on the 'going rate' of sentences for a certain crime, or on issues of general principle such as the guilty plea or the totality principle – has declined. Appellate decisions remain important, but their importance now lies in the interpretation of sentencing guidelines more than in the independent

---

[38] See further Gelsthorpe and Padfield (2003).
[39] See Galligan (1987) for a thoughtful discussion.
[40] For further discussion, see Ashworth and Redmayne (2010), ch. 3.

development of principles. Thus, volume 2 of the 2013 Criminal Appeal Reports contains 88 case reports: 49 relate to the application of guidelines, 20 to common law issues (general principles, offences without guidelines), and 18 to the interpretation of legislation.

To add to the three principal sources of English sentencing law – legislation, definitive sentencing guidelines, and judicial decisions – there is a fourth and less formal source: academic writings, or, to be more precise, the writings of D. A. Thomas of Cambridge University, a tireless collator of and commentator on sentencing decisions and legislation until his death in 2013. In his early writings Thomas shaped the nascent common law of sentencing, both through commentaries on Court of Appeal decisions in the *Criminal Law Review* and through a 1970 volume that structured the diverse decisions of the courts.[41] In more recent years, these commentaries have sometimes been cited with approval in the Court of Appeal, thus suggesting that they may be regarded as at least a secondary source of law.

1.5.1 Legislation

Statutes passed by Parliament establish the framework of English sentencing law, as will have been evident from parts 1.1 and 1.2 of this chapter. Statutes set a maximum sentence for almost every offence. Legislation (such as the Criminal Justice Act 2003) lays down the terms of the orders which a criminal court may make after conviction, and often imposes restrictions on the making of those orders. Legislation also defines the powers of magistrates' courts, and provides for the circumstances in which cases can be committed to the Crown Court for sentence. All this legislation has to be interpreted by the courts, providing a substantial amount of the Court of Appeal's caseload.

The role of legislation as a source of English sentencing law has therefore largely been one of providing powers and setting outer limits to their use. Within those outer boundaries, sentencing practice has been characterized by considerable discretion, subject (as we shall see) to the growing influence of sentencing guidelines and to the general superintendence of the Court of Appeal. One longstanding issue is the significance of the statutory maximum penalty: should the courts reserve it for the worst conceivable case, or is a more flexible approach possible? This issue is particularly pertinent where a maximum penalty is perceived to be low in comparison with other maxima, and not surprisingly the courts have chosen the more flexible interpretation. For example, in *Butt* (2006)[42] the Court of Appeal followed a statement of Lawton LJ three decades earlier in stating that the maximum does not have to be reserved for the very worst case but for a 'broad band' of cases of that type;

---

[41] Thomas (1970); see also Thomas (1979).   [42] [2006] 2 Cr App R (S) 304.

and in *Bright* (2008)[43] Lord Judge CJ stated that the statutory maximum 'is reserved not for the worst possible case which can realistically be conceived, but for cases which in the statutory context are identified as cases of the utmost gravity'.

In recent years two prominent characteristics of sentencing legislation have been its complexity and its relentless frequency. The much-needed consolidation of sentencing powers effected by the Powers of Criminal Courts (Sentencing) Act 2000 was overtaken within a year by significant further developments, and now has little relevance to current sentencing practice. In terms of frequency, almost every parliamentary session since 2000 has yielded a significant set of new provisions on sentencing. The most prominent remains the Criminal Justice Act 2003, but each subsequent year has brought more changes to the sentencing structure. In 1997 Thomas produced a devastating critique of the methodology of the typical legislative changes, highlighting the omissions and confusion resulting from late amendments, defective drafting, legislation by incorporation, staggered commencement dates, and ill-conceived transitional provisions.[44] All these criticisms are relevant to much subsequent legislation, and the practical difficulties for courts are increased by the dispersal of sentencing law across several statutes.

However, there are other arguments to be put – notably, that important policy objectives cannot be accomplished without legislation; and that fairer sentencing outcomes may not come about if maximum discretion is left to judges and magistrates, despite their claims to the contrary. Both of these arguments call for full consideration, before it is concluded that most new sentencing legislation is a bad thing, or that there should be a moratorium on sentencing legislation. It may well be possible to present good arguments of principle for encouraging Parliament to introduce new sentencing policies in some spheres. But one can still agree with Thomas that the manner in which new sentencing legislation is put forward, not to mention the frequent re-enactment of the same provision (committing offences on bail is an aggravating factor, pleading guilty is a mitigating factor), falls well below acceptable standards and is not designed to communicate clearly with either sentencers or the general public.

Not only the courts but also the Sentencing Council must work within the parameters established by the legislature. In recent years the legislature has increasingly made forays into the area previously left to judicial discretion. The high water mark of this is to be found in s. 269 and Schedule 21 of the Criminal Justice Act 2003: not only is life imprisonment the mandatory sentence for murder, but Parliament has now specified various starting points

---

[43] [2008] 2 Cr App R (S) 578, at pp. 588–9; for recent examples, see *Chowdhury* [2014] 1 Cr App R (S) 168 (maximum upheld) and *Wilson* [2014] 1 Cr App R (S) 490 (not the worst kind of case).

[44] Thomas (1997).

to which judges 'must have regard' when setting the minimum term to be served in a particular case. Although the Court of Appeal has softened the edges of this mandatory framework,[45] it continues to be a significant constraint on the judiciary. Two other forms of legislative constraint have also become prominent in sentencing law – prescribed minimum sentences and required minimum sentences. These are often referred to collectively as 'mandatory minimum sentences', but it is important to keep separate the two different forms. Prescribed minimum sentences have been enacted for the third class A drug trafficking offence, and for the third domestic burglary: the details (discussed in Chapter 6.7 below) are quite complex and the statutory requirements for qualifying burglaries are such that some repeat burglars qualify and some do not. There are definitive guidelines for both burglary and drug trafficking, and the correct approach is to apply the guidelines first and then use the prescribed sentence as a kind of 'cross-check'.[46] It is also relevant that both these prescribed sentences are subject to (a) a reduction of up to 20 per cent for pleading guilty, and (b) a judicial discretion to pass a lower sentence if there are circumstances that would make it 'unjust' to impose the prescribed minimum sentence. More constraining are required minimum sentences, e.g. for possession of a firearm, or for using a knife or other offensive weapon to threaten another in a school or public place.[47] The required minimum sentence is 5 years for the firearms offence and 6 months for the knife or offensive weapons offences. Both minima apply to all relevant offences, including a first offence. The firearms minimum is subject to 'exceptional circumstances',[48] and the other minima to an 'unjust to do so' proviso. The details of this sentence will be discussed in Chapter 3.5.1 below. The narrowness of the firearms exception and the absence of any reductions for pleading guilty (the only such provisions in English law) make required minimum sentences particularly severe, and capable of producing manifest injustices because of the very restricted discretion left to the courts.[49]

1.5.2 Definitive sentencing guidelines

Apart from the increase of legislation on sentencing, the other major development in recent years – and the other major constraint on sentencing decisions – has been the growth of guidelines. There are now definitive guidelines for the most significant offences sentenced in magistrates' courts, and also guidelines for most sentencing decisions in the Crown Court (as well as guidelines on general principles and on youth sentencing). The essence of offence guidelines is to provide ranges of sentence for different levels of

---

[45] In *Sullivan* [2005] 1 Cr App R (S) 308; for further discussion, see ch. 4.4.1 below.
[46] *Andrews* [2013] 2 Cr App R (S) 26, at [7].
[47] See the judgment of Lord Thomas CJ in *Gomes Monteiro* [2014] 2 Cr App R (S) 483.
[48] The minimum is 3 years where the offender is aged 16 or 17.   [49] Wasik (2014), pp. 482–3.

seriousness of each type of offence, and, within each range, to indicate a common starting point. The aim of the technique is to structure judicial discretion – not to take it away, but to provide a framework within which the court can locate the particular offence with which it is dealing, and then reflect the facts of that case (notably, the aggravating and mitigating factors) by placing it appropriately within or outside the relevant range. There are sound constitutional reasons for introducing such a framework. Sentencing decisions are of great significance to the public (insofar as they convey the degree of censure of the offender for the offence(s)), to victims, and to the offenders themselves. They may involve considerable deprivation of liberty, restrictions on liberty, or deprivation of money or other assets. It is therefore absolutely right that the rule of law should apply to them so far as possible: although passing sentence will always require an element of judgment, that judgment should be exercised within a framework of principles and guidelines set out in advance, so that court decisions are consistent in their approach and in their starting points, if somewhat different when the facts of the case have been taken into account.

The first guidelines were laid down in judgments of the Court of Appeal in the 1980s:[50] some of them are still in force, and they will be discussed at 1.5.3 (a) below. However, it was relatively rare for the Lord Chief Justice to deliver guideline judgments, and by the late 1990s they covered only a small proportion of offences. By ss. 80–81 of the Crime and Disorder Act 1998 two major changes were introduced: first, a Sentencing Advisory Panel was created to draft guidelines, consult widely on them, and then advise the Court of Appeal about the form that they should take; and second, the power of the Court of Appeal to give guideline judgments was restricted to offences on which it had received advice from the Panel, although it was not bound to accept the Panel's advice. This arrangement continued for some years, producing guideline judgments on racially aggravated offences[51] and on child pornography,[52] a revised guideline judgment on rape[53] and several others.

The 2003 Act changed the structure in major ways. The Sentencing Advisory Panel remained (s. 171) and continued to devise draft guidelines, to consult members of the public and its statutory consultees about them, and then to prepare its advice. However, that advice went not to the Court of Appeal but to a new body, the Sentencing Guidelines Council (SGC), which was empowered to issue 'definitive guidelines' (s. 170). The years between 2004 and 2010 gave rise to several guidelines, on offences such as theft, sexual offences, and assault, and on general principles and sentencing young offenders.

---

[50] The first guideline judgment issued by a Lord Chief Justice was that for drug offences in *Aramah* (1982) 4 Cr App R (S) 407. On the earlier efforts of Lawton LJ, see n. 118 below.

[51] *Kelly and Donnelly* [2001] 2 Cr App R (S) 341.

[52] *Oliver, Hartrey and Baldwin* [2003] 2 Cr App R (S) 64.

[53] *Milberry et al.* [2003] 2 Cr App R (S) 142.

The Coroners and Justice Act 2009 changed the sentencing guideline system again, creating a single body (the Sentencing Council) to undertake all the relevant tasks. The composition and duties of the Sentencing Council will be discussed in Chapter 2 below. The focus here is (a) on the format of the guidelines, and the emphasis on the process of guideline sentencing; and (b) on the departure test, and the way it has been implemented by the courts.

(a) Guidelines as process

The most conspicuous purpose of sentencing guidelines is to set sentence ranges and starting points for the sentencing of offenders. However, guidelines should also have the function of establishing patterns of reasoning among sentencers, and may serve as checklists for the many matters that must be taken into account when sentencing. In the offence guidelines introduced by the Sentencing Guidelines Council between 2004 and 2010, the guidelines typically established three or four levels or ranges of sentence, stating that they were based on a first offender pleading not guilty. The implication of this was that any previous convictions would require the sentence to be increased from the starting point, and that a guilty plea would require the sentence to be reduced. Each guideline also contained a page setting out 'The Decision Making Process', referring not only to the need to identify the appropriate starting point and to take account of aggravating and mitigating factors, but also to the identification of 'dangerous offenders', ancillary orders, the totality principle, and the formulation of reasons. Many guidelines in this format remain in force, unless and until they are replaced by guidelines issued by the Sentencing Council.

Offence guidelines issued by the Sentencing Council since 2010 are based on a remodelled format, and they incorporate the ranges and starting points within an eight- or nine-step process that is now so central as to embody the whole decision-making process from start to finish. In Appendix C the guideline for assault occasioning actual bodily harm is set out, that being an example of the Council's early style. That Appendix also contains part of the fraud guideline, as an example of a different approach. Other definitive guidelines, e.g. those on drug offences and on sexual offences, take a slightly different form again. However, common to them all is the eight- or nine-step process, and this must now be outlined and discussed.

Step One: determining the offence category

The first step requires the court to determine the offence category that best resembles the case at hand. The guideline provides an exhaustive list of the harm and culpability factors that may be taken into account in this initial categorization, and these are seen as the 'principal factual elements of the offence'. For example, for drugs offences the culpability factors relate to the role taken by the offender (leading, significant, lesser), and the harm factors divide the varying amounts of each drug into different categories or levels;[54] for an assault offence such as assault occasioning actual bodily harm,[55] the factors indicating greater harm include injury, repeated assaults, and vulnerability of the victim, whereas the factors indicating greater culpability include hate motivation, premeditation, use of weapon, leading role in a gang, and so on. That list also includes one factor indicating lesser harm, and five factors indicating lower culpability. For offences of assault occasioning actual bodily harm, the court should use these factors to place the offence in category 1 if it involves greater harm and greater culpability, in category 2 if it involves either greater harm and lower culpability or lesser harm and greater culpability, and in category 3 if it involves lesser harm and lower culpability. For drugs offences, the quantity of the relevant drug indicates the applicable category. For fraud, it is a combination of the amount of loss, the victim impact, and the culpability level.[56]

Step Two: starting point and category range

Having determined the offence category in Step One, the guideline now provides a sentence range for that category, and indicates the applicable starting point. The starting point applies to all offenders, irrespective of plea or previous convictions.[57] The task at Step Two is to determine how much the sentence should be raised or reduced from the starting point, by reference to a 'non-exhaustive list of additional factual elements providing the context of the offence and factors relating to the offender'. Roberts and Rafferty refer to this task as 'shaping the provisional sentence' and as fine tuning 'the calibration of harm and culpability'.[58] The list of 'factors increasing seriousness' includes previous convictions and a whole host of regular aggravating factors such as abuse of trust, attempt to dispose of evidence, offence committed whilst on licence, failure to heed warnings from others, etc. Among the list of 'factors reducing seriousness or reflecting personal mitigation' are isolated incident, remorse, serious medical condition, and mental disorder: this list is often shorter than the list of aggravating factors, and some have taken this as a sign that the Council's approach to personal mitigation is seriously underdeveloped.[59] There is a general guideline on *Overarching Principles: Seriousness*

---

[54] Sentencing Council, *Drug Offences: Definitive Guideline* (2013).
[55] Sentencing Council, *Assault: Definitive Guideline* (2011).
[56] Sentencing Council, *Fraud, Bribery and Money Laundering Offences: Definitive Guideline* (2014).
[57] This is no different in substance from the previous guidelines (because, insofar as the court should reduce the sentence for a guilty plea, that implies that the starting point assumes conviction after a trial; and if previous convictions take the sentence upwards, that implies that the starting point assumes someone with no significant prior record). But the Sentencing Council's model is much clearer, and prevents sentencers from suggesting that the guidelines are inapplicable because they apply only to first offenders – as was sometimes said of the SGC's guidelines.
[58] Roberts and Rafferty (2011), at p. 684.   [59] See the strong words of Cooper (2013).

(2004), but it is now a decade old and the time is ripe for the Council to revisit this topic. As it is, Council guidelines make it clear that in some cases a consideration of aggravating and mitigating factors (for example, a bad record) may render it appropriate to move outside the identified category range. The guidelines also remind sentencers that statutory tests have to be fulfilled before a community order is imposed or a custodial sentence handed down.[60] This is a welcome incorporation of these thresholds into the guideline, but it is not clear how often they are referred to in the courts.

Step Three: consider any other factors which indicate a reduction, such as assistance to the prosecution

Most of the work in determining the appropriate sentence is done at Steps One, Two, Four, and Six but Step Three is a reminder to ensure that all factors have been taken into account. The reference to assistance to the prosecution is connected to a special procedure, which will be discussed in Chapter 5.4.2 below.

Step Four: reduction for guilty pleas

This step ensures that the relevant reduction for a guilty plea is made after all the other factors have been taken into account. There is detailed discussion of the guilty plea discount in Chapter 5.4.1 below.

Step Five: dangerousness

For assaults and sexual offences, the court must at this stage consider whether a preventive sentence should be imposed, taking account of the statutory provisions on dangerous offenders (see Chapter 6.8 below). This step is inapplicable to property and drugs offences, and to other forms of offence that are not included in the statutory concept of dangerousness, and the guidelines for such offences have eight steps rather than nine.

Step Six: totality principle

When sentencing an offender for more than one offence, or where the offender is already serving a sentence, the court must consider 'whether the total sentence is just and proportionate to the offending behaviour'. This principle is discussed in detail in Chapter 8 below.

Step Seven: ancillary orders

This step alerts the court to the possibility of making ancillary orders, and to any compulsory provisions (e.g. on confiscation) requiring the court to impose or to consider imposing a particular order. Further discussion will follow in Chapter 11 below.

---

[60] These threshold tests, in ss. 148 and 152 of the 2003 Act, will be discussed in detail in chs. 10 and 9.

Step Eight: reasons

There are requirements to give reasons for the sentence, and to explain its effects, contained in s. 174 of the 2003 Act (as amended). These are discussed in Chapter 13.6 below.

Step Nine: consideration for remand time

The final step is for the court to consider whether it should give credit for time spent on remand, in accordance with s. 240A of the 2003 Act. The legislation is discussed at appropriate points in Chapters 9 and 10.

Three important aspects of this stepwise process may be highlighted. One is the element of progression through the various decisions that a court needs to take before settling on the final sentence. The stepwise process gives the proper structure to the decision-making sequence; even if it is thought to be no more than a checklist, it has significant value. The somewhat similar 'Decision Making Process' that accompanied the SGC's guidelines appeared not to be much used, perhaps because it was not a prominent part of the guideline.[61] Now there can be no doubt that the Sentencing Council is giving it prominence in each definitive guideline it publishes: judges are expected to pay attention to the eight or nine steps,[62] and this is a significant development.

Another significant development is that Step Two incorporates the statutory threshold tests that must be satisfied before a court imposes a community sentence or a custodial sentence. These statutory tests have rarely attracted much attention in Court of Appeal judgments,[63] and one wonders whether they exert much influence in everyday sentencing. But they embody criteria that are intended to be restrictive and to ensure proportionality and parsimony (see Chapter 3 below), and it is good to see them set out in the decision-making process.

A third significant development is the division of factors between Steps One and Two, and the amount of guidance accompanying them. It will be recalled that Step One is intended to include only the 'principal factual elements' of the offence, not all the factors bearing on the seriousness of the case, and that the list is exhaustive. The list focuses on harm and culpability, but it leaves some seriousness factors to be considered at Step Two (for example, abuse of trust, additional degradation of victim, etc.). At Step Two the list of factors that may be taken into account is non-exhaustive, to ensure that any feature of the offending that the sentencer feels to be relevant can be taken into account. However, the Council decided against giving any further guidance about how to assign weight to the various factors. One suggestion was that an offence

---

[61] Dhami points out that the SGC's 'Decision Making Process' was not placed next to each offence guideline, but was in an earlier part of the document: Dhami (2013), p. 173. For an example of this, see SGC, *Causing Death by Driving* (2008), p. 9.

[62] Dhami, one of the expert advisers to the Council, argues that the decision-making process should be presented as a flowchart rather than in text: Dhami (2013), p. 176.

[63] One exception was *Seed and Stark* [2007] 2 Cr App R (S) 436.

should only be placed in a certain offence category if it had two or more specified factors, but the Council decided against such an approach on the basis that it would be 'too prescriptive' and might give the impression that sentencing should be a 'numerical exercise'.[64] Dhami makes the point that failing to give guidance on the weight to be assigned to various factors is a recipe for inconsistency, but she adds that the sentencers whom she surveyed 'wanted more information, and to have that information presented in an easy to use way, but they did not want to be instructed on how to use that information'.[65] This is the view that evidently held sway in the Sentencing Council. Thus, for example, there is absolutely no guidance provided on decisions to be taken in Steps One and Two, not only in respect of weighing aggravating and mitigating factors, but also in taking account (as statute requires) of previous convictions. More will be said about this in Chapter 6 below, but it should be signalled here that Council guidelines say nothing about how a criminal record is to be interpreted and weighed. Apart from the statutory criteria of relevance and recency, the guidelines say nothing about the kind of criminal record that can justify raising the provisional sentence into a higher category range, even though they clearly indicate that this should be possible.[66] Nonetheless, there is evidence that the Council's guidelines on assault offences are being applied consistently across the Crown Court.[67]

The guideline format introduced by the Sentencing Council may be seen as an improvement on the previous format, but it remains to be seen what effects it has on the decision-making of sentencers. In relation to the matters aired in the previous paragraph, Dhami argues that:

> a lack of specification limits the ability of guidelines to improve consistency and transparency in sentencing, and to reduce the potential for biased decisions. It becomes more difficult to detect where along the decision process, and why, errors and inconsistencies have arisen ...[68]

Others may regard this 'decision science' perspective as demanding more precision than is possible without distorting the matters to be assessed. But it is important to keep two issues separate. It is one thing to claim that, even if an issue can be resolved or at least partly resolved at the level of principle, it is impossible to devise practical guidance that reflects the principles in an effective way. It is quite another thing to claim that key issues (e.g. the weight to be assigned to various previous convictions) cannot be determined in principle: the argument against this will be put in Chapter 6.

Finally, a troubling number of sentences are still imposed by trial judges without proper reference to the applicable guideline. Although it is now rare

[64] Sentencing Council, *Assault Guideline: Professional Consultation* (2010), p. 18.
[65] Dhami (2013), p. 180.
[66] Sentencing Council, *Assault Guideline: Professional Consultation* (2010), pp. 20–1.
[67] Pina-Sanchez and Linacre (2013).   [68] Dhami (2013), p. 181.

for the Court of Appeal to fail to refer to the relevant guideline (except for the totality guideline, which rarely receives a mention when the Court is dealing with totality issues),[69] a startling number of judges in the Crown Court appear to be able to pass sentence either without reference to the applicable guidelines or without stating or justifying their starting point, as is required by the decision-making process.[70] Since guidelines have been around for more than two decades, and definitive guidelines for ten years, this may be thought to raise some interesting questions about continuing education for advocates and for judges.

(b) The 'departure test' for guidelines

The 2003 Act imposed on the courts duties to 'have regard to any guidelines which are relevant' to a particular case (s. 172(1)), and to give reasons if they passed a sentence outside the range indicated by the guidelines. Section 174(2) (a) declared that, when stating in open court its reasons for passing sentence, 'the court must, where guidelines indicate that a sentence of a particular kind, or within a particular range, would normally be appropriate for the offence and the sentence is of a different kind, or is outside that range, state the court's reasons for deciding on a sentence of a different kind or outside that range'. Thus the departure test before 2010 was largely a question of giving detailed reasons.

The formal statutory requirements were considerably softened in practice, at least so far as the Court of Appeal was concerned. There were many authoritative statements that 'guidelines are no more than guidelines'.[71] In the same vein, Sir Igor Judge P (as he then was) sounded warnings against interpreting guidelines in a mathematical fashion, whereby each individual ingredient should increase or reduce the notional sentence by a prescribed amount:

> The reality, however, is that the sentencing decision requires the judge to balance all the ingredients of the case, whether aggravating or mitigating, in order to produce the appropriate sentence. There is no grid plan. There is no points system. Although consistency of approach is undoubtedly to be encouraged, guidelines, whether provided by this Court or the Sentencing Guidelines Council in accordance with its responsibilities, remain guidelines.[72]

---

[69] One rare occasion was *Dang* [2014] 2 Cr App R (S) 391, at [36–40].

[70] E.g. *Attorney General's Reference No. 72 of 2009* [2010] 2 Cr App R (S) 58, *Wells* [2010] 2 Cr App R (S) 512, *Sturgess* [2011] 1 Cr App R (S) 686, *Hoare* [2011] 2 Cr App R (S) 1, *Hume* [2011] 2 Cr App R (S) 268, *Fadare* [2012] 2 Cr App R (S) 412, *Finn* [2012] 2 Cr App R (S) 569, *Attorney General's Reference No. 40 of 2012* [2013] 2 Cr App R (S) 34, *Wade* [2013] 2 Cr App R (S) 52, *Hassan* [2013] 2 Cr App R (S) 170.

[71] E.g. Lord Phillips CJ in *Ismail* [2005] 2 Cr App R (S) 542, Latham LJ in *Attorney General's Reference No. 11 of 2007* [2008] 1 Cr App R (S) 26.

[72] *Martin* [2007] 1 Cr App R (S) 14, at [18]. An earlier example is *Attorney General's Reference No. 9 of 2005* [2005] 2 Cr App R (S) 664, at [11], 'no list of credit and debit' features.

The reference to a 'grid' is a reference to those US guideline systems that purport to constrain judicial sentencing through matrices or grids (see Chapter 14.2 below), and which appear to be the stuff of judicial nightmares in this country. While, on one reading, Sir Igor Judge's reference to 'balancing all the ingredients' may appear to come close to the notorious 'instinctive synthesis' idea,[73] this passage was in fact followed by a reference to the statutory provisions requiring judges to 'have regard to' guidelines and to give reasons if they depart from them. In *Oosthuizen*[74] the Court of Appeal considered whether judges were free not to follow the SGC's guideline on reductions for a guilty plea, and Rose LJ concluded that 'it is not open to [judges] to disregard what the Council says'. Similarly, the language of Lord Judge CJ in *Saw*[75] suggests that judges and magistrates would be expected to treat the 'normal ranges' in that 'guidance' judgment as binding too, although when the discussion turned to aggravating and mitigating factors Lord Judge held that 'what is required in reality is not compartmentalisation, but evaluation'.

As SGC guidelines increased in number – and perhaps as more members of the Court of Appeal gained experience of membership of the SGC – so the Court of Appeal came to engage more with the details of various guidelines and relevant starting points and ranges. A fine example of this is the case of *Attorney General's References Nos. 32, 33 and 34 of 2007* (2008),[76] where the Court of Appeal commented that both counsel and the trial judge had discussed the proper application of the relevant guidelines. Similarly in *Hurley* (2009)[77] the judge had given his reasons for sentencing outside (above) the relevant guideline range, and the Court of Appeal reached the same conclusion.

When the Gage Working Group reviewed the case for sentencing guidelines in its 2008 report, a majority of its members called for a revised departure test that would be 'sufficiently robust to provide the necessary consistency, transparency and predictability', as well as preserving judicial discretion to avoid any injustice that might be produced by rigid adherence to guidelines.[78] This led to s. 125(1) of the Coroners and Justice Act 2009, which provides that:

> every court must, in sentencing an offender, follow any sentencing guidelines which are relevant to the offender's case ... unless the court is satisfied that it would be contrary to the interests of justice to do so.

---

[73] Stemming from the Australian case of *Williscroft* [1975] VR 292; for a more recent endorsement by the High Court of Australia, see *Markarian* (2006) 228 CLR 357, discussed in ch. 14.2 below.

[74] [2006] 1 Cr App R (S) 375.   [75] [2009] EWCA Crim 1.

[76] [2008] 1 Cr App R (S) 187, per Hughes LJ at p. 192. See also *Attorney General's Reference No. 14 of 2008* [2009] 1 Cr App R (S) 360, *Adeojo and Mugambwa* [2009] 1 Cr App R (S) 376, *Shannon* [2009] 1 Cr App R (S) 551.

[77] [2009] 1 Cr App R (S) 568.   [78] Gage Report (2008), para. 7.18.

This seems to establish a two-stage departure test: first, a duty to follow or apply the relevant guideline; and secondly, a liberty to depart from it if it would be 'contrary to the interests of justice' to apply the guideline in this case. Reasons would need to be given for that decision. A court does have an obligation, when applying guidelines for an offence, to identify the relevant category range (s. 125(3)(b)); but that obligation does not apply if none of the category ranges sufficiently resembles the case at hand (s. 125(4)).

However, the departure test is far less demanding than it appears at first sight. This is because s. 125(3) makes it clear that what the sentencer 'must follow' is not the *category range* applicable to the facts of the particular case, but only the *offence range* applicable to all forms of the offence. A court therefore 'follows' the guideline when it passes any sentence between the lowest sentence in the least serious category and the highest sentence in the highest category. For most guidelines, that is an enormously wide range. Only if the court is minded to step outside this wide 'offence range' does it need to comply with the departure test and specify the grounds on which it finds that it would be 'contrary to the interests of justice' to follow the guideline. In practical terms, departures are very rare indeed – below 3 per cent on the Sentencing Council's figures[79] – but in one of the most high-profile cases of recent years, the Court failed to apply s. 125 properly.

This was the appeal against the sentences passed on certain offenders involved in the 2011 riots, *Blackshaw and others* (2011).[80] This was the first appeal that had specifically raised the question of departures from the guidelines, and the Court of Appeal consisted of Lord Judge CJ, Leveson LJ (then chairman of the Sentencing Council) and Thomas LJ (President of the Queen's Bench Division, subsequently Lord Chief Justice). Presumably a Court with such strong membership was convened in order to give guidance to lower courts, and it is therefore all the more regrettable that the judgment contains no proper analysis of the 'interests of justice' departure test, and no reasoning as to its application to each of the appeals. Moreover, there is no guidance about the Court's choice of sentences, once it has departed from the guidelines. Lord Judge said absolutely nothing about the appropriate starting point for those offenders who were sentenced outside the guidelines, yet it is important to know how far above the guidelines a court may go, and under what circumstances. Even if a court decides that a sentence at the top of the highest category is inadequate on the facts of the case – as it must, if it is minded to depart upwards from the guideline – it should continue to work through the various steps in the decision-making process, as Julian Roberts has tellingly argued.[81]

---

[79] Crown Court Sentencing Survey (2014): 3 per cent for assault offences (p. 36), 3 per cent for burglary offences (p. 38), and 2 per cent for drug offences (p. 40).
[80] [2011] EWCA Crim 2312.   [81] Roberts (2012).

Lord Judge in *Blackshaw* was right to state that the 'must follow' requirement does not require 'slavish adherence': the aim should be to foster consistency 'without sacrificing the obligation to do justice in the individual and specific case'.[82] The Court of Appeal has echoed the earlier judgment in *Oosthuizen*[83] in its more recent judgment in *Healey* (2013),[84] where Hughes LJ held that:

> the flexibility available to Crown Court judges … does not, however, extend to deliberately disregarding the guidelines, not on the grounds that the case has particular facts which warrant distinguishing it from the general level, but because the judge happens to take a different view about where the general level ought to be. The latter approach is demonstrably unlawful … Very few judges are fortunate enough to go through life without encountering rare occasions when they would prefer the law to be otherwise than that which it is. The judge's duty is nevertheless to apply it, whether at first instance or in this Court, just as it is the duty of the citizen to obey the law whether he happens to agree with it or not.

This approach confirms that there is a marked distinction between disagreement and departure. Disagreement with a guideline is not a sufficient reason for not following it,[85] whereas departures are possible if the appropriate test is satisfied.

One difficulty in relation to departures is that the Court of Appeal does not always, or often, refer to the 'interests of justice' test in s. 125(1).[86] As noted earlier, Lord Judge has never been slow to make the point that guidelines are merely guidelines, not tramlines, and his brethren have followed him in this. Thus, Hughes LJ has asserted that 'conscious clemency for good cause in an exceptional case, where justice requires it, remains within the armoury of any sentencing judge';[87] and there are many judgments in which the Court of Appeal has approved sentences above the top guideline level, i.e. above the offence range, although it is sometimes assumed that this requires 'exceptional circumstances'.[88] Before some examples of upward and downward departures are given, one more point should be made about appellate practice. It is this: although s. 125(3) states that 'following' a guideline means passing a sentence within the offence range, and not within any particular category range, it is now accepted that a judge who places an offence in the wrong category provides grounds for appeal. Thus there are many appeals to the Court of Appeal – most notably Attorney General's References, but also many

---

[82] [2011] EWCA Crim 2312, at [13–14].   [83] [2006] 1 Cr App R (S) 385.

[84] [2013] 1 Cr App R (S) 176, at [5].

[85] See also *Heathcote-Smith* [2012] 2 Cr App R (S) 133, and *Taylor* [2012] 2 Cr App R (S) 581.

[86] For three recent failures to apply the statutory test, see *Datsun and Rajak* [2014] 1 Cr App R (S) 137, *Stanton and Wildman* [2014] 1 Cr App R (S) 351, and *King* [2014] 2 Cr App R (S) 478.

[87] *Attorney General's Reference No. 6 of 2011* [2011] 2 Cr App R (S) 660, at [15]; cf. *Dodds* [2013] 2 Cr App R (S) 358 at [9–10], guidelines 'not a straitjacket'.

[88] E.g. *Makula* [2013] 2 Cr App R (S) 43, at [10].

others – the essence of which is to claim that the judge placed the offence in the wrong category and/or used the wrong starting point.[89] This is a development of great significance. It reduces the implications of the looseness of the departure test, which (as noted above) is linked to the 'offence range' as a whole. If appeals can be based on the court's choice of category range and/or starting point, this is a means of enforcing the guidelines properly despite the unsatisfactory statutory wording.

i) *Downward departures:* the next three paragraphs illustrate the types of case in which the Court of Appeal has taken the rare step[90] of approving, or disapproving, a downward departure from a guideline. Two examples of each will be discussed.

One of the best known is *Schumann* (2007),[91] where a depressed mother jumped off the Humber Bridge holding her 2 year-old daughter, then kept the child alive in the water for 45 minutes until rescued. The trial judge imposed an unusually lenient sentence for attempted murder (18 months' imprisonment), pointing to D's depressed state and her successful efforts to save the child's life. Although there were no definitive guidelines on attempted murder in place at the time, Lord Phillips CJ held that 'the one word that is not contained in the sentencing guidelines is "mercy." There are occasions where the court can put the guidelines and the authorities on one side and apply mercy instead.'[92] The Court held that this was such a case, and substituted a community sentence. Thus it is clear that the Court would not have followed guidelines even if they had existed; under the current guidelines for attempted murder,[93] the floor of the offence range is 6 years, and the Court would undoubtedly have held that it would be 'contrary to the interests of justice' to follow the guidelines.

In *Clarke* (2010)[94] D suffered a hypoglycaemic attack when driving, veered onto a footpath and collided with two boys, killing one of them. The judge concluded from expert evidence that D would have been aware of the onset of hypoglycaemia for some moments, and sentenced him to 3 years' imprisonment for causing death by dangerous driving. The Court of Appeal held that the appropriate category range was 4 to 7 years, but brought the case down below that because D's awareness of his condition (and opportunity to stop the car) would only have been momentary, there were delays in bringing the case to trial, and D suffered from complicated medical conditions which rendered imprisonment particularly onerous for

---

[89] Eight examples are *Pulido-Sanchez* [2011] 1 Cr App R (S) 641, *Attorney General's Reference No. 65 of 2010* [2011] 2 Cr App R (S) 209, *Harrison* [2012] 2 Cr App R (S) 449, *Blakeburn* [2013] 2 Cr App R (S) 500, *Jonsyn* [2014] 1 Cr App R (S) 438, *McDermott* [2014] 1 Cr App R (S) 502, *Blayden* [2014] 2 Cr App R (S) 447, and *McIntosh* [2014] 2 Cr App R (S) 503.
[90] See n. 79 above.   [91] [2007] 2 Cr App R (S) 465.   [92] Ibid., at 469.
[93] SGC, *Attempted Murder* (2008), p. 7.   [94] [2010] 1 Cr App R (S) 158.

him. The sentence was reduced to 12 months' imprisonment, well below the offence range (the floor of the lowest category range is 2 years),[95] referring to reduced culpability from 'highly exceptional circumstances' that took the offence 'significantly below' the range. This case, less dramatic than *Schumann*, demonstrates the way in which an accumulation of mitigating factors can combine to bring a case below the offence range for an offence.[96]

However, there are other cases in which attempts to persuade the courts to impose a 'merciful' sentence have been unsuccessful. In *Gibson* (2010)[97] D was charged with aggravated taking of a car, driving with excess alcohol and driving while uninsured. Having seen him crossing a red light, police signalled him to stop but he did not; the police chased him and he crashed the car. He pleaded guilty and was sentenced to 12 months' imprisonment. Account was taken of the aggravating effect of the excess alcohol, but on appeal the defence invited the court to quash the custodial sentence 'as an act of mercy' because any custodial sentence would result in D's discharge from the army. The Court of Appeal declined: D's military career should not deflect the court from passing an appropriate sentence for serious offences. In *McDade and Reynolds* (2010)[98] the appellants had pleaded guilty to misconduct in a public office and trying to smuggle prohibited items into prison. They were prison officers, and as a result of a relationship with a prisoner M was about to give birth to their child. M appealed against her sentence of 30 months' imprisonment, arguing that since her motive for the offences was not greed but love she should be treated mercifully. The Court of Appeal held that account had already been taken of the strong personal mitigation and of the effect on the young baby of being separated from its mother, concluding that the sentence was 'consciously compassionate' and could not be reduced further.

ii) *Upward departures:* Many offence guidelines are constructed in a manner that leaves a gap between the top of the offence range and the statutory maximum sentence. Thus in *P.* (2010)[99] the appellants had been involved in bringing girls and women to this country and forcing them to work as prostitutes. The relevant sentencing guideline for trafficking had 4–9 years as its highest category range.[100] This left a considerable gap beneath the statutory maximum of 14 years, and the guideline indicates that sentence lengths in that gap might be appropriate where aggravating factors such as 'a large-scale enterprise involving a high degree of planning, organisation or sophistication, financial or other gain, and the coercion

[95] SGC, *Causing Death by Driving* (2008), p. 11.
[96] Other examples of such reasoning include *Hussain and Hussain* [2010] 2 Cr App R (S) 399, *Foster* [2010] 1 Cr App R (S) 219, and *Wade* [2013] 2 Cr App R (S) 52.
[97] [2010] EWCA Crim 2813.   [98] [2010] 2 Cr App R (S) 530.
[99] [2010] 2 Cr App R (S) 7; see also *Dang* [2014] 2 Cr App R (S) 391.
[100] SGC, *Sexual Offences Act 2003: Definitive Guideline* (2007), p. 131.

and vulnerability of victims' are present. The sentences imposed here were 11 years for the first appellant and 14 years for the second appellant, who was convicted of offences relating to two women. The Court of Appeal concluded that the cluster of aggravating factors in this case – bringing a girl to this country under false expectations, exploitation of a child prostitute through coercion, commercial operations on a considerable scale – justified sentences above the highest category and therefore outside the offence range. One assumes that the decision would be the same under the 'interests of justice' test. However, as noted earlier, cases coming to the Court of Appeal appear not to address the 'interests of justice' test when departing upwards from a guideline, and the Court of Appeal itself seems to refer to the statutory test only rarely. This was one of the shortcomings of the disastrous judgment in the riots case of *Blackshaw*, discussed earlier,[101] and there is no shortage of other Court of Appeal cases that fail to refer to the statutory test when approving a departure.[102]

An example of the Court of Appeal disapproving of an upward departure may be found in *Shepherd* (2010),[103] where the offender was sentenced to 4 years' detention for causing death by careless driving after driving at excessive speed in a car that he knew to have defective brakes and tyres, losing control of the car and killing another driver. Since he had entered an early plea of guilty, this means that the trial judge must have taken the statutory maximum of 5 years as the starting point. Clearly the judge thought that the driver should have been prosecuted for the more serious offence of causing death by dangerous driving (whose sentence ranges go above those for causing death by careless driving). The highest category range for the offence charged has a ceiling of 3 years, and, while the Court of Appeal agreed that the driving was bad enough to go above that range, it reduced the original sentence:

> By placing this case at the statutory maximum, but for the plea, [the judge] left no room for the sort of case which might contain other aggravating features, or relevant previous convictions. It can be said on the other side of the coin that he cannot have given any weight to the appellant's young age and previous good character.[104]

Thus the facts were not thought to place the case in the group of cases of 'the utmost gravity' for this crime, and that was partly because of the presence of mitigating factors and the absence of previous convictions. This case was sentenced before the 2009 Act came into force, but conscientious application of the 'interests of justice' test would surely lead to the same outcome.

---

[101] Above, nn. 80–2 and accompanying text; see also *Bond* [2014] 2 Cr App R (S) 12, at [15–18].
[102] E.g. *Makula* [2013] 2 Cr App R (S) 43, *Roberts* [2013] 2 Cr App R (S) 84.
[103] [2010] 2 Cr App R (S) 370.
[104] Ibid., at p. 376; for the use of the statutory maximum sentence, see nn. 42–43 above.

In conclusion, it can be said that guidelines have now bedded down into sentencing practice in England and Wales. Whilst a small number of sentencing decisions fail to cite applicable guidelines, the vast majority do so, and indeed engage with the guidelines and with the stepwise decision process – the dreadful judgment in *Blackshaw* standing out as a failure in both respects, and as an example of rule-of-law values being compromised when they should have been upheld.[105] The Court of Appeal's handling of the 'interests of justice' test has been inconsistent, but the most significant step has been to treat as a ground of appeal the trial judge's selection of the wrong category or wrong starting point, giving the Court of Appeal the opportunity to superintend the use of the guidelines. There is some evidence that the Council's guidelines have improved consistency in Crown Court sentencing.[106]

1.5.3 Judicial decisions

Since the creation of the Court of Criminal Appeal in 1907, it has been possible for an offender to appeal against sentence. The Court formerly had the power to increase sentence on an appeal by a defendant, but this was abolished in 1966. However, since 1988 it has been possible for the Attorney General to refer to the Court of Appeal a sentence imposed by the Crown Court which is thought to be unduly lenient, and this is now done in around 100 cases per year. In such cases the Court has the power to increase the sentence if it concludes that this is appropriate. Further appeals to the House of Lords were extremely rare in sentencing cases between 1970 and 2000, but the amount of sentencing legislation means that some cases are now reaching the highest level (now, the Supreme Court) on points of sentencing law of general public importance.[107] However, the Court of Appeal remains the final appellate court in most sentencing cases.

The development of a worthwhile jurisprudence of sentencing would not have been possible in the absence of regular reporting of appellate decisions. This began in the *Criminal Law Review* in 1954, with brief reports, and gathered pace in 1979, when the publication of *Criminal Appeal Reports (Sentencing)* began. This series (inaugurated and edited by Thomas) is devoted entirely to sentencing decisions, and appears to have been one factor in the increased citation of previous decisions to the Court of Appeal by counsel and by the court in its judgments. The encyclopaedia *Current Sentencing Practice* (also inaugurated and edited by Thomas) builds on this series of reports by collating decisions and arranging them according to subject matter, providing judges and practitioners with a ready source of reference on most issues of

---

[105] See above, nn. 80–2.   [106] Pina-Sanchez and Linacre (2013).

[107] For recent examples, see *Varma* [2013] 1 Cr App R (S) 650 and *Waya* [2013] 2 Cr App R (S) 87, both interpreting the legislation on confiscation orders.

sentencing law.[108] Thus, just as the number of reported decisions on sentencing has increased exponentially in the last 35 years, so has the citation of previous decisions in the Court of Appeal. The most cursory glance through volume one of the *Criminal Appeal Reports (Sentencing)* in 1979, and then through the latest annual volumes, will quickly reveal the greater frequency of references to previous decisions.

Judicially created principles of sentencing have therefore gone through a case-by-case development, in the tradition of the common law. The reporting of decisions has increased, and with it references to earlier decided cases. A body of decisions worthy of being called a jurisprudence has grown up. From its earliest days, the Court of Criminal Appeal (now the Court of Appeal (Criminal Division)) established certain procedural principles. One was that the statutory maximum sentence should be reserved for the worst class of cases.[109] Another was that the Court should only alter a sentence if it is 'wrong in principle',[110] adapted latterly to Attorney General's references, so that a sentence will only be increased if it is 'outside the proper limits of a judge's discretion in cases such as this'.[111] A common law of sentencing has therefore developed, and examples of points on which a *jurisprudence constante* has developed will be found throughout the book. They include the principle that it is rarely appropriate to combine a compensation order with a custodial sentence,[112] the principle that courts should not give a financial penalty just because the offender is able to pay,[113] and the principles on adjusting the length of custodial sentences for offenders who are ill.[114]

The common law of sentencing continues to develop, even though the predominant function of the Court of Appeal is now to interpret and apply sentencing guidelines and sentencing legislation. In all of these matters the weight of particular Court of Appeal decisions varies. The pressure of work in the Court is considerable ('gruelling and relentless', according to one Lord Justice),[115] resulting in *ex tempore* judgments on the facts, put together at some speed. Where a judgment is intended to stand as a precedent, a court presided over by the Lord Chief Justice (or occasionally a Vice-President) will be convened. We have already noted that for the first major 'riots' judgment the Court of Appeal consisted of the Lord Chief Justice, the President of the Queen's Bench Division and the Chairman of the Sentencing Council.[116] For major judgments on more technical issues it is not unusual to convene a full Court of five judges.[117] Such judgments carry much more weight than ordinary sentencing appeals.

---

[108] See also Banks (2014) for a collation of sentencing legislation and judgments.
[109] *Harrison* (1909) 2 Cr App R 94; see nn. 42–3 above.   [110] *Gumbs* (1926) 19 Cr App R 74.
[111] *Attorney General's Reference No. 7 of 1989 (Thornton)* (1990) 12 Cr App R (S) 1, at p. 6.
[112] See *Panayioutou* (1989) 11 Cr App R (S) 535, and ch. 10.4 below.   [113] See ch. 10.5 below.
[114] See ch. 5.5 below.   [115] Darbyshire (2011), p. 328; see her ch. 14 generally.
[116] *Blackshaw et al.*, n. 80 above.
[117] E.g. *Sullivan* [2005] 1 Cr App R (S) 308 (Lord Woolf CJ, minimum terms for murder), *Attorney General's References Nos. 14 and 15 of 2006* [2007] 1 Cr App R (S) 215 (Lord Phillips

Particular attention should be paid to two distinct types of Court of Appeal judgment – guideline judgments, and guidance judgments.

(a) Guideline judgments

Of particular importance as precedents are guideline judgments from the period prior to the arrival of 'definitive guidelines' in 2004. A guideline judgment is a single judgment which sets out general parameters for dealing with several variations of a certain type of offence, considering the main aggravating and mitigating factors, and suggesting an appropriate starting point or range of sentences. This kind of judgment was pioneered in the 1970s by Lawton LJ,[118] and then taken over by Lord Lane when he became Lord Chief Justice. He developed the formulation of guideline judgments so that they set out a fairly elaborate framework within which judges should determine length of sentence. Lord Lane delivered around a dozen guideline judgments when presiding in the Court of Appeal, and in the 1990s both Lord Taylor CJ and Lord Bingham CJ continued to augment the stock of guideline judgments. These judgments acquired authority from the fact that the Lord Chief Justice laid them down: they were intended to bind lower courts, and were treated as doing so.[119] In strict terms it might be argued that the sentencing guidelines in all these cases are massive *obiter dicta*, since much of what is said is not essential to the decision in the particular case.[120] However, the key element is that they were intended and accepted as binding, in a way that most Court of Appeal judgments on sentence are not. The binding force of guideline judgments was enhanced between 1999 and 2004, since all of them were based (either entirely or to a large degree) on the advice of the Sentencing Advisory Panel, and their structure tended to be more definite than was typical of earlier judgments.[121] They also gained authority from the provisions in ss. 80–81 of the Crime and Disorder Act 1998 that created the Sentencing Advisory Panel and reconstituted the functions of the Court of Appeal.

CJ, increasing sentences in Reference cases), and *Oakes* [2013] 2 Cr App R (S) 132 (Lord Judge CJ, whole life terms for murderers).

[118] See e.g. *Willis* (1974) 60 Cr App R 146 on buggery, and *Taylor, Roberts and Simons* (1977) 64 Cr App R (S) 182 on unlawful sexual intercourse.

[119] For reassertions of the duty of courts to follow guideline judgments, see *Johnson* (1994) 15 Cr App R (S) 827, at p. 830, and *Attorney General's References Nos. 37, 38 and others of 2003* [2004] 1 Cr App R (S) 499, at p. 503.

[120] The Australian High Court has gone further, holding that the handing down of a guideline judgment is an act of a legislative character rather than the determination of a particular case: see *Wong* v. *R.* (2001) 207 CLR 584, and Freiberg and Murray (2012), pp. 344–5.

[121] See *Attorney General's References Nos. 37, 38 and others of 2003* [2004] 1 Cr App R (S) 499, per Kay LJ at p. 503.

(b) Guidance judgments

On the creation of the Sentencing Advisory Panel in 1998, the Court of Appeal lost its power to give guideline judgments without first referring the matter to the Panel.[122] However, that restriction was repealed without replacement by the 2003 Act, and so it may be inferred that the Court's power to create guidelines was restored. Indeed, Lord Judge CJ was at pains to

> emphasise that the jurisdiction of the Court of Appeal (Criminal Division) to amplify, to explain or to offer a definitive guideline of its own, to issue guidelines if it think fit, is undiminished.[123]

This seems to be something of an overstatement. The power to create a 'definitive guideline', with all the statutory implications, surely has to be conferred expressly by Parliament. Under existing law it has only been conferred on the Sentencing Council (and formerly the Sentencing Guidelines Council). Sir Brian Leveson P 'clarified' Lord Judge's assertion in a subsequent judgment:

> What Lord Judge was not saying was that this Court could issue its own guideline in conflict with the Definitive Guidelines issued by the Council; neither was he suggesting that it is appropriate to go back to the pre-guideline authorities and seek to argue that they, rather than the guideline, provide the approach that the court should follow. Amplification and explanation is precisely the function of this court, as is issuing guidelines in areas or circumstances not covered by a Definitive Guideline. If the interests of justice demonstrate that a guideline requires revision, the court will undoubtedly identify that fact: it will then be for the Council, pursuing its statutory remit, to revisit the guideline and undertake the necessary consultation which precedes the issue of all guidelines. Given the composition of the Council, we doubt that substantial differences of approach are likely ever to emerge.[124]

The Court of Appeal can certainly hand down a guideline judgment at common law, on the same basis as it did before 1998. However, given the statutory framework for Court of Appeal guidelines created between 1998 and 2004, it is probably more judicious to refer to any judgments of this kind handed down since 2004 as 'guidance judgments' rather than 'guideline judgments. Such judgments take their binding force from the general doctrine of judicial precedent, having due regard (as mentioned earlier) to the constitution of the particular Court of Appeal.

Why would the Court of Appeal feel the need to deliver a guidance judgment? Three sets of circumstances may be identified in answer to this question. The first is where there is concern about the interpretation of an

---

[122] Crime and Disorder Act 1998, s. 80(3).
[123] Per Lord Judge CJ in *Attorney General's References Nos. 73 and 75 of 2010 and No. 3 of 2011* [2011] 2 Cr App R (S) 555, at [5]; see also *Thornley* [2011] 2 Cr App R (S) 361, at [14].
[124] *Dyer* [2014] 2 Cr App R (S) 61, at [15].

existing guideline, or about sentences for a particular crime, and the Sentencing Council is known to have the topic on its agenda. The statutory framework obliges the Council to conduct a consultation on a draft guideline, and so it often takes between nine and twelve months to create a definitive guideline. Where there is concern in the meantime, or where Parliament introduces new legislation on sentencing, there may be a need to provide courts with guidance immediately, in the interim period before the Council guideline is laid down. Thus in *Saw* (2009)[125] Lord Judge CJ knew that revised guidelines for burglary of a dwelling were in preparation but, acknowledging the difficulty experienced by some judges in interpreting the existing guideline, he gave fresh guidance that effectively replaced most of the previous guideline judgment. Similarly in *Caley* (2013)[126] Hughes LJ (then Vice President of the Court of Appeal) responded to various uncertainties about the guilty plea guideline, in the light of changes in criminal procedure, by providing further guidance on some of the points in the existing definitive guideline. However, he stated that it would not be appropriate for the Court to attempt to make fundamental alterations to the guideline, because the Council was known to have the topic of guilty pleas on its agenda, and because the Court cannot conduct the same wide consultation as the Council.

A second set of circumstances in which the Court of Appeal may decide to lay down guidance is where the Sentencing Council does not have a topic on its agenda and there seem to be several appeals that betray uncertainties about the proper approach. This might be said of *P and Blackburn* (2008),[127] where the Court, with Sir Igor Judge presiding, gave guidance on sentencing in cases where the offender turned Queen's evidence, in the light of new provisions in the Serious Organised Crime and Police Act 2005. It can certainly be said of *Hancox and Duffy* (2010),[128] where Hughes LJ gave general guidance about the making of serious crime prevention orders, and of *Smith* (2012),[129] where Hughes LJ gave general guidance on the making of sexual offences prevention orders. Thus it seems that the Court will continue to give guidance, where none seems likely to come from the Sentencing Council, even though it does not receive the breadth of evidence that the Council is able to consider before creating definitive guidelines.[130]

A third set of circumstances is where the Court of Appeal believes that it is right to develop a particular line of reasoning. A prime example of this is that the Court, led by Lord Judge CJ, has taken the view that the statutory guidance on minimum sentences for murder that Parliament set out in Schedule 21 of the 2003 Act implies that all homicide offences should be revalued and the

---

[125] [2009] EWCA Crim 1.   [126] [2013] 2 Cr App R (S) 305.
[127] [2008] 2 Cr App R (S) 16, at p. 36.   [128] [2010] 2 Cr App R (S) 484.
[129] [2012] 1 Cr App R (S) 470.
[130] For an explicit attempt to give guidance (on the offence of encouraging or assisting suicide, which is not on the Council's to-do list), see *Howe* [2014] 2 Cr App R (S) 311.

sentence levels raised. This development will be examined in greater detail in Chapter 4.4.3 below, but the diminished responsibility case of *Wood* (2010) indicates the line of reasoning:

> There is no express statutory link between the guidance in Sch. 21 of the 2003 Act and the principles to be applied to sentencing decisions in diminished responsibility manslaughter ... accordingly when the sentencing court is assessing the seriousness of the offence with a view to fixing the minimum term, we can discern no logical reason why, subject to the specific element of reduced culpability inherent in the offence, the assessment of the seriousness of the instant offence of diminished responsibility manslaughter should ignore the guidance. Indeed we suggest that the link is plain.[131]

There are several other judgments with similar reasoning,[132] although whether this was Parliament's intention or is instead a judicial initiative remains to be determined.

Turning, finally, to the Court of Appeal's stock of judgments as a whole, it remains true that most of them deal with long custodial sentences or other orders imposed in serious cases. Thus the Court's precedents are richer as the seriousness of cases rises, and relatively poorer for cases at the lower end of the criminal calendar, where the bulk of the cases tried in the Crown Court lies. However, much of the guidance (perhaps most) now comes from definitive sentencing guidelines. Since these extend to most offences of theft and fraud and the majority of offences against the person and sexual offences, the Council's guidelines are well on the way to remedying any deficiencies of balance and range. The Court of Appeal's principal functions, in its routine cases, are to determine whether the judge selected the appropriate category range or starting point, and occasionally to determine the meaning of terms in a guideline.[133] This is the function of amplification and explanation to which Sir Brian Leveson referred.[134]

1.5.4 Magistrates' courts

The discussion so far has assumed that the most significant sentencing decisions are taken in the Crown Court. Certainly the most serious cases are dealt with there, but the vast majority of sentences are handed down by the magistrates' courts – which deal with well over 90 per cent of criminal cases. Most of these offences are triable summarily only, and have a fine as the maximum penalty. But there are many summary offences for which

---

[131] [2010] 1 Cr App R (S) 6, per Lord Judge CJ at [21], speaking for a full Court.
[132] Most recently in a medical case of manslaughter by gross negligence: *Garg* [2013] 2 Cr App R (S) 203.
[133] E.g. the concept of a 'vulnerable victim', on which see *De Weever* [2010] 1 Cr App R (S) 16, and *Sayed* [2014] 2 Cr App R (S) 318.
[134] Above, text at n. 124.

imprisonment is used with some frequency (common assault, driving whilst disqualified, assaulting a police officer, taking a conveyance without authority, etc.), and the magistrates' courts also pass sentence for more 'triable-either-way' offences than does the Crown Court.[135] Since the late 1980s there have been sentencing guidelines for the magistrates' courts, dealing with motoring offences and the most common non-motoring offences, but they have not had the force of law.[136] After extensive consultation, new definitive guidelines were issued by the SGC in 2008, the *Magistrates' Court Sentencing Guidelines*. These guidelines cover the most frequently sentenced offences, and they incorporate all other guidelines into an overall structure that presents a chart for each offence and combines this with a general commentary on the sentencing approach and the courts' powers. They are presented in a different format from guidelines intended for the Crown Court, in that they integrate the ranges and starting points into a structured decision-making process. The guidelines are updated regularly, to take account of new Sentencing Council guidelines. It is hoped that they will achieve national consistency in the approach to sentencing, but local traditions have a history of tenacity.

1.6 Informal influences on sentencing practice

The formal sources of sentencing law may be said to provide a kind of outer framework for sentencing decisions, and within that some internal rules, principles, and standards, but despite the spread of guidelines it is plain that a considerable amount of flexibility is still left in the hands of the court in many cases. When different combinations of facts present themselves, rules may prove too rigid and too crude to yield sensible decisions. Without discretion, unfairness results from treating as alike cases which are unalike. However, it is important to assess this reasoning with care. Speaking extra-judicially three decades ago, the then Lord Chief Justice Lord Lane declared that 'sentencing consists in trying to reconcile a number of totally irreconcilable facts'.[137] The reference to 'facts' is inaccurate in two respects. First, it omits the relevance of principles to the assessment of those facts, thus giving the false impression that 'facts' determine outcomes without reference to assessments of their relevance and salience. Secondly, it overlooks the influence of the working practices of judges and magistrates, which may be based on different views and different approaches developed over time. More will be said about the construction of 'facts' below. But, even though the amount of sentencing guidance is increasing all the time – more legislation, more definitive guidelines, the growing corpus of Court of Appeal decisions – there will continue to be cases in which new fact combinations raise new issues.

---

[135] See pp. 1–2 above for an outline of the different offence categories.   [136] See ch. 2.5 below.
[137] HL Deb., vol. 486, col. 1295.

This makes a strong argument for discretion, and is consistent with the thrust of the objections to prescribed minimum and mandatory minimum sentences. As the Halliday Report proposed, mandatory sentences can be removed when there is an operating system of guidelines.[138] Most supporters of what may be termed 'the guideline movement' accept the need for judicial discretion, since guidelines are not tramlines and should leave room for courts to depart from the guideline if new factors arise that give good reasons for doing so. This suggests that the structuring of the sentencing system should have two objectives: first, there are strong rule-of-law reasons for having guidelines, in order to ensure that sentencers are consistent in their starting points and in the weight attributed to major sentencing factors; and secondly, there are strong reasons of justice and equity for preserving an element of discretion, to enable sentencers to do justice in individual cases by giving effect to unusual combinations of facts. Both of these objectives have drawbacks: guidelines may be either too crude and over-prescriptive, or too broad and ineffectual, and to the extent that discretion exists it may allow personal preferences of the sentencers and other irrelevant factors (for example, race and other equality issues) to exert an influence.

Drawbacks of these kinds do not go unrecognized, of course. Judges are often keen to argue that Crown Court sentences are kept in check by the appeal system, and that unwarranted guideline departures and the intrusion of irrelevant factors can be controlled in this way. But appellate control is largely dependent on the system for giving leave to appeal, a 'system' that has never been subjected to research or independent scrutiny, and also dependent on the Court of Appeal's approach to the guidelines (already discussed in part 1.5.2 (b) above). We have also seen that the Court of Appeal has dealt with a number of cases in which judges either have misapplied or have been unaware of relevant guidelines.[139] This is a question of judicial training, and of recognizing that sentencing is not a question of responding to 'facts' but rather of applying guidelines and guidance to the varying facts of particular cases. The extent to which the Judicial College provides adequate training in the use of the guidelines is discussed in Chapter 2.4 below.

Practitioners are well aware of the predilections of certain judges, and problems of inconsistency of approach may not have been eliminated by the spread of guidelines. A small Crown Court survey in 2008 found that only around 52 per cent of sentences were within the relevant range, with 32 per cent above and 14 per cent below the ranges.[140] That was a small, snapshot survey. What is missing – and the Gage Report exposed this fully – is a reliable statistical foundation for understanding English sentencing. Data have not been collected on the matters needed to inform a proper appraisal of sentencing practice. The Sentencing Council has begun this task by inaugurating the

---

[138] Halliday Report (2001), ch. 8.   [139] Above, n. 70.   [140] SCWG (2008), pp. 16–17.

Crown Court Sentencing Survey, which since 2011 has required judges to fill out a form for each case, giving details of the case and indicating which factors the judge took into account at Step One, Step Two, Step Four (plea) and others. Important as this survey is, it leaves two important issues untouched. One is that reports on the CCSS data proudly announce that some 97 per cent of sentences fell within the offence range,[141] meaning that they fell between the lowest and the highest guideline sentences, and say nothing about the much more important question of whether they fell within the appropriate category range. The other vital development, not yet tackled, would be to carry out qualitative research into the working practices of judges in the Crown Court, so that the bare figures in the CCSS can be contextualized and brought to life. 'Whether judges actually follow sentencing guidelines, or simply refer to them orally and in writing, while they think something different in private, is a topic that has intrigued psychologists.'[142] The Sentencing Council is well placed to commission such research and to persuade judges to co-operate with it.

Are the prospects for legislation, definitive guidelines and Court of Appeal guidance any better in the magistrates' courts? Research in the 1980s suggested that magistrates believed that legislation has to be interpreted in the light of 'common sense', which tended to mean their own views and practices,[143] and that Court of Appeal principles were not consistently reflected in the sentencing practice of magistrates.[144] Local variations were found in both the Crown Court and magistrates' courts when the Home Office carried out detailed statistical research during the 1990s,[145] but recent quantitative research on Crown Court sentencing under the Council's guidelines suggests that consistency has improved.[146] Unfortunately the Sentencing Council has decided to terminate the CCSS, and this will take away an indispensible resource for understanding and monitoring the practical impact of the guidelines.

Until more well-targeted research is undertaken, it remains important to look into other probable determinants of sentencing decisions. One source of influence may be found in the working practices of others in the criminal justice system: in part 1.4 above we saw the influence of decisions by police, prosecutors, regulatory agencies, and others, and in Chapter 13 the influence of probation officers and counsel will be discussed. Another possible source of influence is the complex of attitudes and beliefs held by different sentencers. In areas where there is discretion, such attitudes are likely to shape the court's approach to sentencing. This will be explored tentatively in the paragraphs which follow.

What factors might be assumed to enter or influence a sentencer's thought processes when taking a decision in a particular case? Four groups of factors may be identified:

---

[141] Sentencing Council (2013).   [142] Goodman-Delahunty and Sporer (2010), p. 20.
[143] Parker, Sumner and Jarvis (1989).   [144] Henham (1991).
[145] Flood-Page and Mackie (1998), p. 128.   [146] Pina-Sanchez and Linacre (2013).

I. Views on the facts of the case.
II. Views on the principles of sentencing:
    (i) views on the gravity of offences;
    (ii) views on the aims, effectiveness and relative severity of the available types of sentence;
    (iii) views on the general principles of sentencing;
    (iv) views on the relative weight of aggravating and mitigating factors, previous convictions and the totality of sentences.
III. Views on crime and punishment:
    (i) views on the aims of sentencing;
    (ii) views on the causes of crime;
    (iii) views on the function of courts in passing sentence.
IV. Demographic features of sentencers:
    (i) age;
    (ii) social class;
    (iii) occupation;
    (iv) urban or rural background;
    (v) race;
    (vi) gender;
    (vii) religion;
    (viii) political allegiance.

It will be observed that groups I, II and III are expressed so as to emphasize the sentencer's *views* about the various factors: it is these perceptions, that may or may not correspond with authoritative or objective statements, which are likely to influence behaviour.

What is the relevance of the fourth group of factors? The argument must be that each of us projects into our daily decisions certain aspects of our personality which are traceable to one or more of the demographic features listed. Many of those who sit in the courts may maintain that they become accustomed to preventing their own personal preferences from influencing their decisions. However, there is no evidence of how successful they are in this, and in any event some sources of bias may be unconscious – a tendency to view matters from a particular perspective or to select certain kinds of information, which the sentencer does not realize he or she is doing. There is still much debate about the existence of racial bias in English sentencing: the evidence is reviewed in Chapter 7.2, which shows an over-representation of ethnic minorities in prison and an under-representation of ethnic minorities among sentencers. The possibility of age discrimination has been less widely discussed. Most sentencers are at least one generation older, and often two generations older, than most offenders, and they may fail to understand the context or meaning of certain behaviour by young people. Over 30 years ago Roger Hood found that the age of magistrates was related to the size of fine imposed in dangerous driving cases, with older magistrates being relatively severe in two of the cases involving younger drivers and relatively lenient in the three cases involving older drivers, as compared with the fines imposed by their younger colleagues:[147] might this still be true? In his Canadian study, Hogarth also found a relationship between specific beliefs and the age of the sentencer, with older magistrates tending to minimize sociological explanations of crime and generally to be more offence oriented than offender oriented in their approach to sentencing.[148]

By what process might the demographic features in group IV influence sentencing practices? What should be made of the repeated findings that about three-quarters of High Court judges, and a substantial proportion of circuit judges, have attended public school and then Oxford or Cambridge?[149] Penny Darbyshire argues that it is natural and fitting that 'judges in the highest courts are educated at elite universities', given the complex and unremitting work expected of them.[150] But there are consequential questions to be answered. Is it possible that one identified characteristic (high social class, or at least privileged education) might be associated with particular views? Could it be (see III (ii)) that judges with this background might tend to give less weight to social conditions or the effects of the criminal justice system itself as possible causes of offending?[151] Or that judges with this background might tend to take a more lenient view of income tax offences or fiscal offences by 'respectable' people, than they take of offences related to social security benefits or even of pickpocketing small amounts?[152] This fourth group of factors raises a number of hypotheses about the influence of demographic factors on sentencing which remain to be more fully tested in England. Hood's study found that magistrates' attributes exerted only a limited effect on their sentencing,[153] but there is a need for a broader, up-to-date study.

Turning to the factors in group III, it seems inherently likely that in a system which allows a fair amount of discretion, the views of sentencers on crime and punishment will exert some influence. Sometimes the views in group III may be the product of demographic features listed in group IV. Sometimes a more powerful source will be the bench which a magistrate joins. Thus Hood found that members of the same bench, determining a sentence at home without consulting colleagues, were still 'more likely to do something similar to their colleagues than we would expect by chance', and he found 'evidence that certain assumptions about penal policy are shared by magistrates on the same bench'.[154] Tarling's study of 30 magistrates' courts also found that bench tradition was a major factor in explaining sentencing patterns.[155] Darbyshire's study of justices' clerks in the early 1980s suggests

---

[147] Hood (1972), p. 140.   [148] Hogarth (1971), p. 211.

[149] See e.g. Oxford Pilot Study (1984), p. 32; Darbyshire (2011), ch. 3.

[150] Darbyshire (2011), p. 46.   [151] Oxford Pilot Study (1984), p. 27.

[152] Oxford Pilot Study (1984), p. 25.   [153] Hood (1972), pp. 140–3.   [154] Hood (1972), p. 145.

[155] Tarling (1979), and Tarling (2006).

that the tradition of some benches could be traced to the influence of their clerk, who took a major role in magistrates' training.[156] Although the system has now changed, local influences may still be considerable.

The same analysis cannot be applied to judges and recorders who sit in the Crown Court, since they sit alone. The Oxford pilot study in the early 1980s raised a range of questions about the relationship between the size of a court centre and the effects of colleagues on judges and recorders. For example, at very small court centres judges tended to be isolated, and at the larger court centres there may be so many different judges and recorders passing through (for a week or fortnight at a time) that little sense of collegiality could develop. Medium-sized court centres, with five or six judges taking lunch together, seemed to be the most collegial.[157] It is true that judges attend Judicial College refresher courses every three years, in addition to training days on their circuit, but it is not known to what extent this reduces any isolation.

Factor III(iii) raises the question of the functions which sentencers perceive themselves as having. A particular issue here is the extent to which they take account of public opinion in sentencing. Many of the judges interviewed in the Oxford pilot study regarded themselves as holding a balance between the more vociferous elements in the popular press and critics of other kinds, and aligned themselves more with 'informed public opinion' and the standards of 'right thinking members of the community'. There seemed to be a general assumption that these opinions and standards coincided with their own,[158] thus reinforcing Hogarth's finding that 'sentencers tend to define the operative constraints in a way which maximises concordance with their personal attitudes'.[159] The opinions and standards might well be associated with demographic factors such as social class and age. One difficulty with the notion of 'informed public opinion' is the repeated finding that many members of the public are ill-informed about crime trends in general and about sentencing practices in particular. There is evidence from the 1996 British Crime Survey to the effect that a majority of those surveyed made substantial overestimates of the proportion of recorded crime that involves violence, were unaware of the range of sentences available to the courts, and underestimated the use of imprisonment by the courts for offences such as rape, mugging, and burglary.[160] Other misperceptions include the murder rate in England and Wales.[161] Many sentencers in the survey by Hough, Jacobson and Millie recognized that much public and media opinion is uninformed;[162] yet many of them also conceded that general shifts in the climate of public opinion

---

[156] Darbyshire (1984).
[157] Oxford Pilot Study (1984), pp. 34–6; see more generally Darbyshire (2011), pp. 135–6 and ch. 9.
[158] Oxford Pilot Study (1984), pp. 30–4; see also Mackenzie (2005), pp. 143–5, on Queensland judges.
[159] Hogarth (1971), pp. 209–10.   [160] Hough and Roberts (1998).
[161] Hough and Roberts (2012), pp. 280–3.   [162] Hough et al. (2003), pp. 53–4.

affected sentence levels. Insofar as courts are tempted to increase sentences in response to public criticisms of leniency in sentencing, when it seems clear that those criticisms are based on misunderstanding, that is to allow error to breed error.

Turning to the factors in group II, one might expect that sentencers' views on the principles of sentencing would be closely related to their opinions on the aims of punishment. One old study found that magistrates' views on crime and punishment do not determine their sentencing practices,[163] but that study needs replicating in the contemporary environment. Under the Criminal Justice Act 2003 a sentencer is required to have regard to a whole range of possible sentencing purposes and, although proportionality is a primary factor in the definitive guidelines,[164] it is not known what effect, if any, the list of purposes in s. 142 of the 2003 Act has. Hood's research suggested that disparities in sentencing become wider as the facts of cases become more unusual, and he concluded that there is 'general support for an explanation of sentencing which sees differences in the way magistrates perceive and categorize offences as an important factor in producing disparate sentences'.[165] This was also a major factor for many of the sentencers interviewed by Hough, Jacobson and Millie – they perceived that offending was becoming more serious, and that they had to respond to this.[166]

Other influential factors might be found in group II(ii), sentencers' views of the aims, effectiveness and relative severity of the available forms of sentence. Perhaps the classic example here is sentencers' perceptions of the suspended sentence: the legislation makes it absolutely clear that this is a sentence of imprisonment, and that it should only be imposed after the court has decided that the case merits imprisonment of a certain length. But history shows some gross 'malfunctions' of the suspended sentence in England and Wales. The original 1967 law malfunctioned because many sentencers treated it as a non-custodial sentence with teeth, and used it where previously they might have used a community sentence; and sentences that were suspended tended to be longer. The same appears to have happened since the suspended sentence order was revived in 2005.[167] The term 'malfunction' has been adopted here, but in reality this is an example of sentencers' own perceptions overriding the letter of the law. Turning to imprisonment itself, the Danish study by Wandall shows how sentencers' views of the purpose and practice of imprisonment exerted an influence,[168] and this may well be true in other countries too. For some years certain sentencers have voiced disquiet about the organization of some types of community sentence, and may therefore have tended to use them less frequently. A variety of judicial opinions was uncovered in the

---

[163] Lemon (1974).   [164] See SGC, *Overarching Principles: Seriousness* (2004).
[165] Hood (1972), p. 141.   [166] Hough et al. (2003), p. 30.
[167] See the research by Bottoms (1981), discussed in ch. 9.4.5 below.   [168] Wandall (2008), ch. 8.

Oxford pilot study,[169] most of them stemming from personal or reported experience rather than from the results of research. There is no evidence on whether increased judicial training in recent years has reduced this diversity of approaches, but the research by Hough, Jacobson and Millie found many positive attitudes towards pre-sentence reports, drug treatment and testing orders, and other community-based developments.[170] Indeed, subsequent research by Jacobson and Hough demonstrates the way in which judges' views of personal mitigation worked in combination with their views of appropriate sentences (usually, in this respect, community sentences) to bring certain offenders below the custody threshold.[171]

Similar points could be raised in relation to views on the relative weight of aggravating and mitigating factors (group II(iv)). It is one thing to assess the weight of one factor alone, and quite another thing to reconcile combinations of aggravating and mitigating factors in a single case. In her US research, Shari Diamond found that 'when both aggravating and mitigating factors are present … there is evidence of greater disagreement among judges'.[172] In England, a simulated sentencing exercise with magistrates and justices' clerks led Claire Corbett to conclude that, at least in the reasons they give, different sentencers tend to place different values on the same factors.[173] These reflections probably apply no less to the weighing of previous convictions and the totality of sentences, on which sentencers may hold different views.[174] As Goodman-Delahunty and Sporer conclude from their review of psychological research:

> several other unanticipated sources of disparity that operate outside the conscious awareness of the judge can impinge on principles of equality in sentencing. The proportion of variability of sentencing attributable to unconscious extra-legal factors is substantially less than that attributable to the legally relevant factors, but these influences nonetheless produced significant differences in sentencing outcomes.[175]

In group I the only factor is the sentencer's view of the facts of the case. The importance of this is widely accepted, both by sentencers and by researchers. Sentencers are given to stating that 'no two cases are alike' and 'each case must turn on its own facts', or (in the contemporary version) that 'the fact-specific nature of the criminal activity involved in each offence remains the paramount consideration'.[176] Lord Lane CJ went so far as to assert that sentencing 'is an

---

[169] Oxford Pilot Study (1984), pp. 28–30. [170] Hough et al. (2003), pp. 46–9.

[171] Jacobson and Hough (2007), ch. 4; cf. Wandall (2008), ch. 3, on similar patterns of reasoning by Danish judges.

[172] Diamond (1981), p. 407. [173] Corbett (1987); see also Hood (1972), p. 124.

[174] For empirical findings on the relevance of criminal record, see Roberts (2008a), chs. 5 and 8.

[175] Goodman-Delahunty and Sporer (2010), p. 30.

[176] This was Lord Judge CJ's formulation in *Thomas* [2012] 1 Cr App R (S) 252, at [62]; one of many other examples is *Reeves* [2013] 2 Cr App R (S) 129, at [13].

art and not a science'.[177] We have already noted that such statements are often used as an argument against rules and guidelines for sentencing. Flexibility is needed, it is said, so that the court may reflect the particular combination of facts in each individual case. Similarly, there are those who argue that the legal analysis of sentencing decisions, in terms of offence-related and offender-related matters, and aggravating or mitigating factors, is never able to capture the uniqueness of the individual case. On this view, it is only by paying attention to the details of 'whole case stories' that it is possible to make sense of sentencing, not through the inevitably artificial categories and constructions of commentators.[178] Again, this argument is correct up to a point: cases do differ considerably in the combination of material facts. It justifies the view that rules cannot cater fairly for all eventualities, but it certainly does not justify the conclusion that rules and principles ought therefore to be kept to a minimum. Indeed, many of the judges who argue that each case depends on its own facts will also maintain that experience is of great value in the difficult task of sentencing. This reasoning contains the seeds of its own refutation, as Hood has pointed out:

> Magistrates and judges ... place particular value upon their experience in sentencing. Now, if this experience is to be of value, then all cases cannot be unique, they must be comparable at least in some respects; and even if it is agreed that all cases are unique in some sense, this cannot be decisive in the practice of sentencing, for frequently decisions are reached with the aid of 'experience'. There are, then, certain observable factors which magistrates will take into account in their consideration of the appropriate sentence.[179]

Thus the element of truth in the proposition that the facts of individual cases differ, and that sentencing must be 'fact specific', should not be allowed to obscure the importance of two other propositions – that facts do not determine cases, rather it is the approach of the court to those facts which is crucial; and that it is possible to identify certain factors which ought to have a major influence on sentence, even if other subsidiary factors vary considerably from case to case.[180]

However, investigation of the concept of 'the facts of the case' remains an important research question. Facts do not come ready-labelled as important or unimportant. The prosecution's statement of facts, or even the defence basis of plea, might influence the court's approach. But it may be the judge or magistrates who, in assessing the facts of the case, construct their picture of the salient facts by applying their own views on issues in groups II and III. An important element in this process of construction seems to be the court's impression of the defendant's character, gained from observation in court.

---

[177] The words of Lord Lane CJ when refusing to allow the continuation of a research project on judges' sentencing practices: Oxford Pilot Study (1984), p. 64.
[178] E.g. Tata (1997).   [179] Hood (1962), p. 16.   [180] On this last point, see Moxon (1988), p. 64.

It was apparent from observations during the Oxford pilot study that judges might be influenced by the defendant's appearance and attitude to the court.[181] Carol Hedderman's small study suggested that demeanour in court (such as appearing cocky, not doing as instructed, appearing calm rather than nervous and contrite) both influences the way in which magistrates react to a defendant and affects sentence severity, being one possible reason why women (who often appear more distressed than men) receive more lenient sentences.[182] Further support for this view may be derived from interviews with magistrates as part of a Home Office project on the sentencing of women, revealing that magistrates may react differently to those perceived to be deferential and those perceived to be arrogant, and that more women fall into the former category.[183] The research reviewed by Goodman-Delahunty and Sporer led them to conclude that 'judges can be unconsciously swayed by features of offenders that are readily observed, such as offenders' gender, baby-facedness, physical attractiveness and emotional displays'.[184] Judge Cooke came close to conceding the influence of these character assessments when ruminating on the possibility of sentencing by computer:

> At the end of the day, the exercise of discretion in sentencing must remain in human hands. You cannot program a computer to register the 'feel' of a case, or the impact that a defendant makes upon the sentencer.[185]

If, then, it is accepted that 'the facts of a case' are not an objective entity but to some extent a construction, certainly in respect of the weight assigned to different elements, the problem of achieving consistency and therefore equality before the law in sentencing practice is revealed as acute. This is not to suggest that authoritative guidance exerts no influence; rather, the suggestion is that it is not so strong as to exclude significant variations personal to the sentencer, especially where it leaves issues to the judgment of the court (as with aggravating and mitigating factors, previous convictions, and totality of sentence).[186]

This discussion then flows into the debate about the limits to which rules, principles and guidelines can go, before they become so rigid or complex as to be productive of more injustice than their absence. The judiciary has tended to defend broad discretion by arguing that sentencing is an art and not a science, and that it is essentially an exercise of judgment rather than a question of applying rules or guidelines. The most extreme form of this view is that espoused by the higher Australian judiciary – the idea that sentencing decisions consist of an 'instinctive synthesis' of the facts and principles relevant to

---

[181] Oxford Pilot Study (1984), pp. 20–4.   [182] Hedderman (1990).

[183] Hedderman and Gelsthorpe (1997), pp. 30–4; this study also questions the accuracy of perceptions of deference and arrogance, especially when interpreting the behaviour of members of ethnic minorities.

[184] Goodman-Delahunty and Sporer (2010), pp. 26–7.   [185] Cooke (1987), p. 58.

[186] See further the discussion of these issues in chs. 5, 6 and 8 below.

each case, and that any attempt to establish a starting point or guidelines for such decisions is bound to lead to distortion and injustice.[187] This goes too far, both practically and psychologically. In practice, the senior judiciary in England and Wales has acknowledged its untenability by embracing the development of guidelines, first as part of Court of Appeal judgments and then in the form of definitive guidelines. In terms of psychological research, there is a spectrum of decision-making styles running from the intuitive (fast and associative in its method, requiring little cognitive effort) to the analytic (slow and deliberative, and cognitively demanding), with 'quasirational' modes of cognition lying in the middle range of the continuum and containing elements of both intuition and analysis.[188] At the other end of the spectrum from the 'instinctive synthesis' lies the argument that sentencing could be reduced to a stable set of rules which allowed little or no discretion. This view is too extreme if and insofar as it allows no space for the sentencer to tailor the sentence to the particular offence and offender, thereby preventing the court from doing individualized justice. American systems of sentencing guidelines are sometimes depicted in these terms, although that may not be an accurate representation.[189] A more realistic target is mandatory or mandatory minimum sentencing, which constrains judges to a considerable degree.[190] However, both extreme ends of the spectrum can be rejected as unsuitable for sentencing – the 'instinctive synthesis' because it gives insufficient weight to rule-of-law values in sentencing, to principles, and to consistency of approach; a rule-bound approach because it leaves insufficient room for sentencers to use their judgment in reflecting unusual combinations of facts.

Rejecting the two extreme positions still leaves considerable scope for disagreement on the ideal amount of guidance to be given to judges, and on effective ways of suppressing the influence of factors that should not be taken into account, such as factors conducing to inequality of sentencing. Part 5 of this chapter has demonstrated that the English definitive guidelines impose a particular structure on the decision-making of judges and magistrates, but also leave considerable scope for individualized sentencing (e.g. in respect of aggravating and mitigating factors, previous convictions, and totality of sentences). This might be applauded as enhancing rule-of-law values while allowing 'space for the exercise of judgment'.[191] Some psychologists who have studied decision-making in sentencing argue that there is ample research 'highlighting the errors and biases that might result from intuitive judgment', and that therefore 'the balance may need to shift further towards a structured, analytic approach to sentencing'.[192] Thus any reference to individualized

---

[187] For elaboration, see the judgment of McHugh J in *Markarian* v. *R.* [2005] HCA 25, discussed in ch. 14.2 below.
[188] Dhami, Belton and Goodman-Delahunty (2014).   [189] For further discussion, see ch. 14.2.
[190] See ch. 1.5.1 above; for judicial opposition, see Mackenzie (2005), pp. 49–51.
[191] Hutton (2013), p. 102.   [192] Dhami, Belton and Goodman-Delahunty (2014).

sentencing risks importing the individual views of the sentencer, as well as an impression of the offence and offender that may be informed by unconscious preferences and beliefs. It will therefore be argued below that the Sentencing Council should do more to structure sentencers' assessments of aggravating and mitigating factors (Chapter 5), of the significance of the criminal record (Chapter 6), and of the totality of sentence (Chapter 8). Such developments could bring rule-of-law values into areas of sentencing where they currently appear to exert insufficient influence. Moreover, this is an argument that should be applied more broadly: as argued in part 4 of this chapter, there is a range of decisions that may fairly be described as 'sentencing', from various forms of pre-trial diversion through to discretionary release from custody, and the same principles should be adopted for them.

2

Sentencing and the constitution

Major changes in the sentencing field in recent years have raised several questions of a constitutional nature in this country and elsewhere. The position of sentencing in relation to the separation of powers has required clarification, particularly in the context of the legislative introduction of mandatory and mandatory minimum sentences. To what extent is the principle of judicial independence infringed by such developments? The advent of sentencing commissions charged with the creation of sentencing guidelines has raised questions about their place within the constitutional framework. The increasing prominence of fundamental rights has given rise to challenges to the compatibility of certain sentencing laws and procedures with those rights, notably those upheld by European Union law and by the European Convention on Human Rights. These and related constitutional issues are analyzed in this chapter, in the light of current controversies in England and Wales and elsewhere.

2.1 The separation of powers in sentencing

The doctrine of the separation of powers still has some relevance in British constitutional theory, but the place of sentencing has never been entirely resolved. In principle, the legislature has control over sentencing powers and policies – subject to the limitations of European Union law (see 2.6 below) and also the European Convention on Human Rights (see 2.7 below). The judiciary deals with the application of sentencing law and principles to individual offenders. The executive is responsible for carrying out the sentences imposed. But each of these propositions requires further discussion.

One clear starting point is that the legislature has superior authority to the courts: if Parliament passes legislation, the courts must apply it. Thus, when Sir Ivor Jennings identified three characteristics of the English courts, the first was 'their subordination to the legislature'.[1] To accept this as axiomatic is not to suggest that the judiciary should not develop policy on matters left aside by legislation. Thus Sir James Fitzjames Stephen went too far when he stated that, if the judiciary were to take upon themselves the task of formulating principles of sentencing, 'they would be assuming a power which the constitution does not give them'.[2] The statement is only trivially true: it is unhelpful because the British constitution does not explicitly 'give' the power to any organ. However, the High Court of Australia has held that if appellate courts lay down sentencing guidelines they are acting in a legislative character, and that this is an impermissible breach of the separation of powers.[3] This is doubtful, since guidelines are merely guidelines and do not have the legislative character of, say, a mandatory minimum sentence. Accepting the premise that the courts are subordinate to the legislature, the courts may surely guide the use of the judicial discretion left by the legislature, even though the realm of discretion delegated or simply left to the courts can be taken back by Parliament. Are there, then, any limits to the competence of either the legislature or the courts, bearing in mind that Parliament has superiority when it does decide to legislate?

If one looks at the history, then one finds that wide judicial discretion has only been a characteristic feature of English sentencing for the last hundred years or so. In the first half of the nineteenth century, there were two factors that considerably restricted judicial discretion. There were maximum and minimum sentences for many offences, and several statutes provided a multiplicity of different offences with different graded maxima. For much of the nineteenth century, judges were left with less discretion than their twentieth and twenty-first century counterparts,[4] and any claim that a wide sentencing discretion 'belongs' to the judiciary is without historical foundation. It gains its plausibility only from the legislature's abandonment of minimum sentences in the late nineteenth and early twentieth centuries, and from the trend at one time to replace the plethora of narrowly defined offences, each with its separate maximum sentence, with a small number of 'broad band' offences with fairly high statutory maxima.[5] That approach was adopted in the Theft Act 1968 and the Criminal Damage Act 1971, both of which replaced large numbers of separate offences dating from the nineteenth century with a few broadly defined crimes. These statutes broadened the discretion of judges in

---

[1] Jennings (1959), pp. 241–2.   [2] Stephen (1885).   [3] *Wong* v. *R.* (2001) 207 CLR 584.
[4] Thomas (1978); and Radzinowicz and Hood (1986), chs. 22, 23.   [5] Thomas (1974).

sentencing, but that approach has now been abandoned, and statutes such as the Sexual Offences Act 2003 return to the former approach of a multiplicity of offences with separate maximum sentences.

This is not to suggest, however, that judges in the later nineteenth century were tightly constrained in their sentencing. In fact, there was ample evidence of sentencing disparities, as Sir Leon Radzinowicz and Roger Hood have demonstrated.[6] There was concern in the Home Office, and even a proposal in 1889 for a royal commission with a view to bringing about uniformity through legislation. Opposing this successfully, the then Lord Chancellor, Lord Halsbury, relied on the (doubtful) proposition that sentencing is the province of the judiciary.[7] A few years later, in 1901, Lord Alverstone CJ and six Queen's Bench judges drew up a 'Memorandum of Normal Punishments', which sought to establish standard punishments for normal cases.[8] Thus, while it is often assumed that it was the creation of the Court of Criminal Appeal in 1907 which institutionalized judicial control over practical sentencing standards, the Alverstone Memorandum a few years earlier marked a significant step in this direction – albeit as a response to much public and official agitation about inconsistency in the closing years of the nineteenth century. Nonetheless, the gradual (and, in the fourth quarter of the twentieth century, rapid) accretion of sentencing decisions from the Court of Appeal must surely have strengthened the belief that this is a judicial province and that there was little need for detailed legislative provisions on sentencing.

That belief, widely shared in the judiciary, is a belief that judicial discretion supervised by the Court of Appeal is more likely to produce fair sentencing outcomes than greater statutory restrictions. This is an arguable proposition, discussed further in Chapter 14 below. But it is not the same as the principle of judicial independence, nor does it provide a basis for any principle that the legislature may not properly do more than set maximum sentences and introduce new forms of sentence. Thus when there was a fierce debate about the introduction of minimum sentences into English law, prior to the Crime (Sentences) Act 1997, senior judges abandoned the 'judicial independence' argument and faced the policy issues squarely. As Lord Bingham put it:

> There is room for rational argument whether it is desirable to restrict the judges' sentencing discretion in the way suggested or not. But even this is not a constitutional argument. As Parliament can prescribe a maximum penalty without infringing the constitutional independence of the judges, so it can prescribe a minimum. This is, in the widest sense, a political question – a question of what is beneficial for the polity – not a constitutional question.[9]

---

[6] Radzinowicz and Hood (1986), pp. 741–7.   [7] Radzinowicz and Hood (1986), p. 754.
[8] Radzinowicz and Hood (1986), pp. 755–8, and Advisory Council on the Penal System (1978), App. E.
[9] Bingham (1996), p. 25; see also Taylor (1996), p. 8, and Mason (2001), pp. 25–6.

When there was a constitutional challenge to an Australian statute which required a court to impose a specified penalty on conviction for a particular offence, the High Court of Australia dismissed it in these terms:

> It is both unusual and in general, in my opinion, undesirable that the court should not have a discretion in the imposition of sentences, for circumstances alter cases and it is a traditional function of a court of justice to endeavour to make the punishment appropriate to the circumstances as well as to the nature of the crime. But whether or not such discretion shall be given to the court in relation to a statutory offence is for the decision of the Parliament. It cannot be denied that there are circumstances which may warrant the imposition on the court of a duty to impose specific punishment. If Parliament chooses to deny the court such a discretion, and to impose such a duty, as I have mentioned the court must obey the statute in this respect assuming its validity in other respects. It is not, in my opinion, a breach of the Constitution, not to confide any discretion to the court as to the penalty to be imposed.[10]

The same argument may be applied to s. 269 of the Criminal Justice Act 2003, in which Parliament curtailed the judges' discretion to determine the minimum term to be served by a person convicted of murder, imposing a restrictive framework of judicial starting points.[11]

However, it is a different matter if the legislature purports to pass a law that mandates a certain sentence for a particular individual. This question was tested in Australia, where the Community Protection Act 1994 of New South Wales authorized and required the state's courts to impose a sentence of 6 months' preventive detention on a specific individual for the protection of the community. In *Kable*[12] the High Court of Australia held the legislation invalid, on the ground that it violated the separation of powers by requiring the courts to act as if at the behest of the executive. This and subsequent High Court decisions establish that legislation should not substantially impair a court's 'institutional integrity' or 'defining characteristics as a court'.[13]

The doctrine of the separation of powers therefore seems to confirm that the courts' sentencing powers can be created, regulated, and restricted by statute, even to the extent of requiring the imposition of mandatory or mandatory minimum sentences, so long as those requirements do not violate offenders' Convention rights.[14] The judiciary retains the power to deal with individual offenders, within the framework laid down by Parliament.

This leads into a final constitutional point related to sentencing – the true meaning of the principle of judicial independence. Although it has often been

---

[10] *Palling* v. *Corfield* (1970) 123 CLR 52, per Barwick CJ at p. 65; for recent constitutional challenges to mandatory sentencing provisions in Ireland, see O'Malley (2013), pp. 221–3.

[11] See below, ch. 4.4.1.   [12] (1996) 189 CLR 51.

[13] For discussion, see Freiberg and Murray (2012), pp. 339–40; see also O'Malley (2013), p. 221, for the constitutional importance of judicial selection of sentences.

[14] See part 2.7 of this chapter, and in Canada *Nur* 2015 SCC 15.

referred to rather extravagantly in the context of legislative sentencing reforms,[15] the true meaning of the principle is that when passing sentence in each case, a judge or magistrate should be in a position to administer the law without fear or favour, affection or ill-will.[16] No pressures upon the court to decide one way or the other should be countenanced. Within the framework laid down by Parliament, discretion should not be exercised on personal or political grounds: it should be an exercise of judgment according to legal principle. Appointments to the bench should not be politically motivated. Freedom from bias, from partiality and from undue influence is integral to any definition of the rule of law. This is surely the meaning implied by s. 3 of the Constitutional Reform Act 2005, entitled 'Guarantee of continued judicial independence'.

This principle is regarded as particularly important in those parts of the world where judges have been tightly restricted and, as political appointees, expected to follow approved paths.[17] However, it is worth remembering that in this country 'judicial appointments were influenced by party political considerations, as well as merits, until well into the twentieth century', and that 'it is to the post-war Lord Chancellorship of Lord Jowitt that we look for the establishment of the modern practice'.[18] In this sphere, as well as in respect of the role of the legislature, modern notions of judicial independence and the judicial function have a shorter history than many believe.

2.2 The constitutional position of the Sentencing Council

The constitutional arrangements for guidance on sentencing in England and Wales were altered three times in a decade, first by the appointment of a Sentencing Advisory Panel under ss. 80–81 of the Crime and Disorder Act 1998, secondly by the creation of the Sentencing Guidelines Council under ss. 169–170 of the Criminal Justice Act 2003, and thirdly by the replacement of those two bodies by the Sentencing Council in the Coroners and Justice Act 2009. The work of these bodies was introduced in Chapter 1.5.2, and we now turn to consider their constitutional position.

The Panel was constituted in July 1999 with eleven members, and soon attained its norm of fourteen members. Four of the members were sentencers (two circuit judges, a district judge and a lay magistrate), three were academics, four others had recent or current experience of the criminal justice system

---

[15] Proposals to create mandatory sentencing regimes are sometimes said to infringe the principle of judicial independence, but they do not. Cf. the response of the Magistrates' Association to the provisions of the Coroners and Justice Bill on the binding nature of sentencing guidelines, *The Times*, 26 February 2009.

[16] For an illuminating history, see Stevens (1993); see also the website of the Council of HM Circuit Judges, for diverse materials on the independence of the judiciary.

[17] See the UN Declaration of Basic Principles on the Independence of the Judiciary (1985).

[18] Munro (1992), p. 4.

(prisons, prosecutions, police, and probation), and the remaining three were laypeople with no connection to criminal justice. The Panel's principal functions were to examine the issues relevant to sentencing for a given offence, to consult with the professions and the public on its proposals for a guideline, and then to transmit an 'Advice' to the Court of Appeal. The Court was free to accept, reject, or accept in part the Panel's advice. The constitutional effect of these arrangements was that the laying down of guidelines was seen as part of the judicial function, to be carried out (as it had been at common law) by the Court of Appeal. Even though it amounted to policy formation, albeit within parameters established by the legislature, it remained under the direct control of the senior judiciary.

The arrangements were reviewed by the Halliday Report in 2001, which argued that steps must be taken towards the formulation of comprehensive sentencing guidelines and that a new machinery should be considered. The chosen machinery was that the Panel was to continue in operation, so as to carry out the preliminary work and to conduct its wide consultations, and a new Sentencing Guidelines Council (SGC) was to be created to take ultimate responsibility for the form and issuance of the guidelines. Thus the government's purposes in creating the SGC were a) to divorce the function of creating guidelines from that of deciding individual appeals (and therefore to take the function of creating guidelines away from the Court of Appeal), and b) to make provision for Parliament to have a voice in the creation of guidelines. It was assumed that for a) an entirely judicial body was needed, and so the Panel (with its diverse membership) would not be appropriate and instead an SGC composed entirely of judicial members would be introduced, fully recognizing 'the importance of an independent judiciary'.[19] Thus the Criminal Justice Bill presented to Parliament in 2002 provided for an SGC consisting of seven members – the Lord Chief Justice, two Lords Justice of Appeal, a High Court judge, a Circuit judge, a District Judge (Magistrates' Courts), and a lay magistrate.

Then, as the Bill was progressing through Parliament, the Court of Appeal received an Advice from the Panel on the sentencing of domestic burglars.[20] Lord Woolf CJ in the Court of Appeal gave a guideline judgment which accepted most of the Panel's advice but significantly lowered the starting points for first-time and second-time offenders who committed medium-level burglaries, proposing community sentences for them.[21] Although Lord Woolf took care to explain these changes by reference to various government policy statements, the popular press and subsequently the Home Secretary denounced the judgment as inappropriately lenient. The ensuing furore attracted extensive media attention, and the Home Secretary seems to have

---

[19] Home Office (2002), para. 5.15.
[20] Sentencing Advisory Panel, *Advice to the Court of Appeal – 8: Domestic Burglary* (2002).
[21] *McInerney and Keating* [2003] 2 Cr App R (S) 240; see further Davies and Tyrer (2003).

decided that an entirely judicial body could not be trusted with the important social function of creating sentencing guidelines. The government brought forward amendments to the bill which would add five non-judicial members to the SGC – persons experienced in, respectively, policing, criminal prosecution, criminal defence, the promotion of the welfare of victims of crime, and the administration of sentences. It was believed that the person with experience of the administration of sentences would be a civil servant from the Home Office, and a constitutional objection was taken to this in the House of Lords. To expand the SGC from an entirely judicial body to a body with wider membership was one thing; but to extend its membership so as to include a serving civil servant, a member of the executive who would be bound to put forward departmental views, was quite another thing. The House of Lords Select Committee on the Constitution took advice on the matter and, concluding that such an appointee might not appear independent, expressed its 'concern at the proposal that a serving civil servant should act as a member of the Sentencing Guidelines Council'.[22] This part of the amendment was therefore dropped, although a senior civil servant was allowed to attend and speak at SGC meetings.[23]

If the original assumption that the membership of the SGC should be entirely judicial was based on a belief that the creation of sentencing guidelines is a judicial function, that assumption has now been diluted and could apply only to a body with a judicial majority (as the SGC became). However, it has been argued in previous editions of this work[24] that it is desirable to have a body with diverse experience in broad matters of penal policy, not merely because many judges have a tendency to support existing arrangements rather than to favour change,[25] but also because other perspectives have a legitimate place in the deliberations.

This point was well taken in the Gage Report (2008), the report of a committee that was required within six months 'to examine the advantages, disadvantages and feasibility of a structured sentencing framework and permanent sentencing commission'. The report favoured an evolutionary approach to sentencing guidelines, rejecting American-style sentencing grids (see Chapter 14.2 below) and preferring an approach building upon the style adopted by the Panel and the SGC. The report made strong recommendations for improvements to the system of collecting data on sentencing and for thorough research into sentencing practice. One result of this was that the legislation – the Coroners and Justice Act 2009 – assigns to the Council various powers and duties that go well beyond those of its

---

[22] House of Lords (2003), para 6.   [23] CJA 2003, s. 167(9).

[24] See the final chapter of the first (1992) and second (1995) editions, containing proposals that may have had some influence on policy-making on this subject.

[25] This is the principal counter-argument of Tonry (2004), ch. 5. Cf. the review of the pre-2009 guideline system by Wasik (2008).

predecessor.[26] Those powers and duties raise constitutional issues, which are considered below as the fourth of four constitutional questions stemming from the creation of the Council – its membership, its relationship with Parliament, the degree to which its guidelines bind courts, and its wider policy remit.

First, the membership of the Council consists of eight judicial members, from all levels of criminal court, and six non-judicial members (having experience of one of seven specialties: criminal defence, prosecution, policing, sentencing policy and the administration of justice, victims of crime, relevant academic study, and the use of statistics). Substantial judicial representation is important in order to reflect judicial experience of sentencing, but a judicial majority is not required by any constitutional principle, as argued above. A judicial majority is defensible only insofar as it is necessary to ensure judicial acceptance of Council guidelines. Moreover, the list of non-judicial members fails to include any lay members, although the Gage Report commended their involvement in the Panel's work and saw them as 'key features' of the new body.[27]

The second constitutional issue concerns the relationship of the new body with Parliament. As argued in part 2.1 above, there is no reason of constitutional principle why Parliament should not pass detailed legislation on sentencing matters, and from the same standpoint there is no strong constitutional argument against the involvement of parliamentarians in giving approval to, or proposing amendments to, guidelines. At a political level, however, the danger lies in the vice of opportunism – the risk that politicians will be looking to either vote-winning or progress within the party rather than trying to take a considered and rounded view of the subject. The SGC was required to consult both the relevant ministers and the Justice Committee of the House of Commons; the responses were generally constructive and thoughtful, and party political points were not taken. The Gage Report explicitly considered the proposal that guidelines be laid before Parliament for approval. The majority rejected this, believing that it would lead to the politicization of the guidelines and either prolonged battles or stalemates. The minority thought that the guidelines should be subject to approval or disapproval as a whole,[28] and that the process would 'give the guidelines greater legitimacy'.[29] A significant issue is the working practices of the Council: the English guideline institutions have never contemplated issuing a whole set or system of guidelines at once, preferring an incremental approach. Party political interference would be more likely if specific offence guidelines

---

[26] For further discussion of issues raised during the passage of the Coroners and Justice Bill, see Roberts (2011a) and Ashworth (2010).

[27] Gage Report (2008), para 6.14.

[28] This is provided for in the New Zealand legislation: see Young and Browning (2008).

[29] Gage Report (2008), p. 30.

required parliamentary approval than if a whole set of guidelines were presented as a 'package', as envisaged in New Zealand.

The third constitutional issue concerns the tightness with which the guidelines should bind judges and magistrates. The Criminal Justice Act 2003 required them to 'have regard to' definitive guidelines, and to state their reasons if departing from a guideline. The Gage Report was divided on whether this is sufficient. The majority thought that there should be a presumption that the guidelines have to be applied, whereas the minority held that any tightening of the test in the 2003 Act would inhibit courts from passing the just sentence in some cases.[30] As we saw in Chapter 1.5.2(b) above, a version of the majority's proposal prevailed, so that courts must 'follow' the guidelines unless satisfied that it would be 'contrary to the interests of justice' to sentence within the offence range. It was argued in part 2.1 above that there can be no constitutional objection to this, and that it does not infringe the principle of judicial independence.

A fourth set of constitutional issues derives from the wide powers and duties of the Council. The Gage Report was rightly critical of the paucity of data on sentencing and on the effect of guidelines, and the Coroners and Justice Act set out to remedy this. Section 127 requires any draft guideline or definitive guideline to be accompanied by a resource assessment, indicating the likely effect of the guideline on prison and probation services. Section 128 imposes on the Council the duty to 'monitor the operation and effect of its sentencing guidelines', and to consider what conclusions can be drawn from this monitoring.[31] Section 129 requires the Council to publish data about local sentencing, and empowers the Council 'to promote awareness of matters relating to the sentencing of offenders by courts in England and Wales'. Sections 130 and 131 specify the contents of annual reports, but of particular interest is section 132, which imposes on the Council the duty to assess the impact on correctional resources of any government proposal on sentencing policy or legislation that the Lord Chancellor refers to it. This is closely related to the Council's duty, when formulating guidelines, to take account of 'the cost of different sentences and their relative effectiveness in preventing re-offending' (s. 120(11)(e)). Thus far the Council appears to have paid no attention to this duty. This may be connected with the fact that it is a chiefly judicial body (with a judicial majority); but, whether or not the Council as presently constituted has a taste for such inquiries, this is a statutory duty.

Beyond the position of the Sentencing Council under the 2009 Act, there are two broader issues that call for comment from a constitutional point of view. One concerns the propriety of the legislature delegating the function of creating and promulgating sentencing guidelines to a new, and not entirely

---

[30] Gage Report (2008), pp. 25–6.

[31] The Crown Court Sentencing Survey was implemented so as to provide the data required to discharge this duty, but the CCSS is now to be discontinued.

judicial, body. This question was tested before the Supreme Court of the United States in a constitutional challenge to the US Federal Sentencing Guidelines, which were formulated by the US Sentencing Commission pursuant to the Sentencing Reform Act of 1984. In denying the constitutional challenge by a majority of eight to one, the Supreme Court in *Mistretta* v. *United States* (1989)[32] maintained that, although at one time 'Congress delegated almost unfettered discretion to the sentencing judge to determine what the sentence should be within the customarily wide range', it remains the position that 'the scope of judicial discretion with respect to a sentence is subject to congressional control'. There was therefore nothing unconstitutional in a legislature taking back the wide discretion it had left to the courts and then delegating it, within statutorily defined limits, to an independent Sentencing Commission. This reasoning surely applies equally to the constitutional position in Britain, and supports the guideline-creating power conferred on the Council. Subsequently the Supreme Court's decision in *Blakely* v. *Washington* (2004)[33] raised questions about the constitutionality of US guideline systems. The precise holding in the case was that it was a denial of the appellant's constitutional right to trial by jury if his sentence was subjected to an enhancement, above the normal sentence range indicated by the guidelines, as a result of a decision by a judge and not a jury. However, *Blakely* proved to be the first in a line of judgments loosening the binding effect of sentencing guidelines. Thus in *United States* v. *Booker* (2005)[34] the Supreme Court effectively held that the Federal Sentencing Guidelines are advisory rather than mandatory. And in *Spears* v. *United States* (2009)[35] the Supreme Court held that a sentencing court may depart from the guidelines if it disagrees with the policy underlying them, in this case the ratio used to relate crack cocaine to powder cocaine. This particular controversy over cocaine has been resolved, to some extent at least, by the Fair Sentencing Act 2010.[36]

The final constitutional question concerns the 'definitive guidelines' that the SGC, and now the Council, has issued. What kind of law are these? They are not primary legislation, delegated legislation, or part of the judgment of a court. They have authority by virtue of the duty of sentencers to 'follow' definitive guidelines (unless the interests of justice indicate otherwise), but it is not clear in what other way their statutory authority is manifest. It is unlikely that an action for judicial review of a court that refused to follow a definitive guideline would be entertained: no doubt the applicant would be directed to use the normal channels of appeal against sentence. So, just as in the 1980s and 1990s judicial sentencing guidelines came to be treated as binding at common law even though in substance they were *obiter dicta* in relation to the judgment containing them, it also appears that definitive guidelines will acquire their authority partly through the legislative origin of

---

[32] (1989) 109 S. Ct. 647.   [33] (2004) 124 S. Ct. 2531.   [34] (2005) 543 U.S. 220.
[35] (2009) 555 U.S. 606.   [36] Steiker (2013).

the (qualified) duty to follow them, and partly through enforcement by the Court of Appeal. As a species of law, they remain *sui generis*.

2.3 The judiciary, the executive and sentencing policy

While the arrival of new sentencing guideline institutions has raised questions about their constitutional status, struggles between the judiciary and the executive over aspects of sentencing policy have continued. One longstanding feature is the royal prerogative power to commute sentences, the prerogative of mercy, which has come to be exercised by the Home Secretary (a member of the executive). At some times past it has been employed vigorously, as by Churchill during his short period as Home Secretary in 1910–11: so alarmed was he by disparities and by several instances of extraordinarily severe sentences that he used the prerogative to order the immediate release of several prisoners.[37] The exercise of the prerogative has usually come under scrutiny when the abolition of capital punishment has been debated,[38] but in recent times it has been used mainly in compassionate cases and other instances not related to general sentencing policy.[39]

Until 2003 the Home Secretary had a prominent role in determining how long prisoners sentenced to life imprisonment should spend in custody. However, recent case-law has confirmed that it is inconsistent with the Convention for decisions on the length of imprisonment to be taken by a member of the executive rather than by an 'independent and impartial tribunal'.[40] Similarly, life prisoners should be able to have access to a court which will determine the need for their continued detention (Art. 5(4) of the Convention), and it has been held that a 'court' for these purposes may be the Parole Board sitting with a judge as chair.[41]

Those authorities set the boundaries of executive power over individual sentences, but the rules and conventions are rather more fluid when it comes to executive attempts to influence the judiciary and judicial attempts to influence the executive in relation to sentencing policy. One firm principle must be that the courts are not obliged to defer to the executive. The House of Commons Expenditure Committee stated the position (albeit in rather dramatic fashion) in 1978:

[37] Radzinowicz and Hood (1986), pp. 770–5.   [38] Radzinowicz and Hood (1986), pp. 676–81.

[39] Smith (1983); for further discussion of the power to release on 'compassionate grounds', see the analysis of the judgments in *Vinter* v. *United Kingdom* [2014] Crim LR 81 and *Newell* [2014] Crim LR 471 in ch. 6.8 below.

[40] The crucial judgment was *Stafford* v. *UK* (2002) 35 EHRR 1121, applied in *R* v. *Home Secretary, ex p. Anderson* [2003] 1 AC 837; for further discussion, see ch. 4.4.1 below.

[41] The two principal Strasbourg decisions on this point are *Thynne, Wilson and Gunnell* v. *UK* (1989) 13 EHRR 666 (discretionary life imprisonment), and *Stafford* v. *UK*, above n. 40 (life imprisonment for murder).

The starting point of our discussion must be recognition of the constitutional position of the judiciary as independent of the executive arm of Government and the legislature. This means that it would not be appropriate for the Home Office to tell the judges what to do, even if the result of judicial activity were to threaten the breakdown of the prison system, which is very nearly what has happened.[42]

One step down from 'telling the courts what to do' is trying to persuade the courts to follow a certain course. One example of this was the Home Office's action in sending a copy of the interim report of the Advisory Council on the Penal System, *The Length of Prison Sentences*, to every judge and every bench of magistrates in 1977. This report offered evidence that longer sentences had no greater crime-preventive effect than shorter ones, and ended by 'inviting' the courts to 'make their contribution towards' solving the problem of prison overcrowding (i.e. by passing fewer and shorter prison sentences).[43] This was moderate, exhortatory language;[44] but one could see that frequent missives of this kind from the executive to the judiciary might be thought to overstep the mark, not least because there is another, judge-led body (the Judicial College) that has the task of keeping judges informed.

However, attempts to influence sentencing practice and policy have not all been one-way. Recent years have also seen a greater willingness among senior judges to give public addresses and to make use of the media to put over the judicial point of view. Lord Chief Justices such as Lord Taylor, Lord Bingham and Lord Woolf took full advantage of media interest in sentencing. Perhaps the most notable example of this was the day in 1996 on which the then Home Secretary, Michael Howard, announced his proposals for mandatory and minimum sentences. Obviously there had been prior discussions with the higher judiciary, and within the hour Lord Taylor had given a press conference to denounce the proposals, arguing (among other things) that mandatory sentences would not deter offenders because detection rates are so low. Both he and Lord Bingham accepted invitations to deliver public lectures at which the same views were presented with fuller argument.[45] They continued the attack in debates in the House of Lords, where Lord Taylor's comment was withering: 'Never in the history of our criminal law have such far-reaching proposals been put forward on the strength of such flimsy and dubious evidence.'[46]

---

[42] House of Commons Expenditure Committee (1978), para. 37; cf. Woolf (1991), para. 10.154.

[43] Advisory Council on the Penal System (1977), para. 12.

[44] For another example of an exhortatory statement, issued in 2002 by the Lord Chancellor and the Home Secretary jointly, see 5th edn of this work, pp. 62–3.

[45] Taylor (1996), Bingham (1996).

[46] HL Deb., 23 May 1996; in the same debate Lord Williams of Mostyn, who became Attorney General in the subsequent Labour government which supported the 1997 Act, criticized the Bill as 'a perversion of justice. It is an infinite shame that matters of this sort are dealt with on the basis of mottoes at party conferences. It demeans our society.'

More recently, in the debate preceding the creation of the Sentencing Council by the Coroners and Justice Act 2009, it was the Council of Circuit Judges that used the media to put over its objections to aspects of the government's proposals. However, on this occasion as in relation to the creation of the Panel and the SGC, neither the judiciary nor parliamentarians have actually opposed the very idea of placing power over sentencing guidelines in a non-judicial and non-parliamentary body. The judiciary seems to have been content so long as the guideline-giving body has a judicial majority, and parliamentarians seem content so long as the body has a duty to consult Parliament and Ministers on proposed guidelines. Neither the SGC nor the Council has been seen as a means of insulating sentencing from political issues:[47] improved consistency seems to have been the principal driver, with cost control as a significant element in the 2009 Act creating the Council.

While some policy conflicts between the judiciary and the executive are played out in public, it is likely that dialogue takes place more frequently behind closed doors. There were probable examples of this in the 1980s,[48] and the first decade of the new century also suggests instances of judicial representations leading to policy changes. Judicial opposition to the mandatory provisions for the ill-fated IPP sentence (imprisonment for public protection) was probably one reason why the mandatory elements were abolished in 2008,[49] although the unpreparedness of the prisons was another major factor. A more intriguing turn of events involves provisions in the same 2008 legislation, the Criminal Justice and Immigration Act, relating to the sentencing of young offenders. The Act was the first revision of sentencing powers relating to young offenders for a decade, and it required courts to have regard *inter alia* to 'the purposes of sentencing', which were stated in the following form:

(i) The punishment of offenders;
(ii) The reform and rehabilitation of offenders;
(iii) The protection of the public; and
(iv) The making of reparation by offenders to persons affected by the offence.[50]

Comparing this list of purposes with the corresponding list for adults in section 142 of the Criminal Justice Act 2003,[51] the absence of one purpose – 'the reduction of crime (including its reduction by deterrence)' – from the list for youths is striking. The Sentencing Advisory Panel pointed this out,

---

[47] This has been a prominent rationale in some other jurisdictions. On the USA, see Barkow (2005), p. 812.
[48] See 5th edn of this work, p. 63.
[49] See ch. 6.8 below, and Ashworth (2013), for further discussion.
[50] Section 142A(c)(c) of the Criminal Justice Act 2003, inserted by s. 9 of the Criminal Justice and Immigration Act 2008.
[51] Set out in ch. 3.1 below.

referring to the relevant empirical evidence[52] and citing the Supreme Court of Canada's decision to interpret the similar Canadian legislation as ruling out sentences for youths based on individual or general deterrence.[53] The Panel's advice was considered by the Sentencing Guidelines Council. Shortly afterwards, when the government made the commencement order for the 2008 Act, s. 142A(c) above was not brought into force, although the other parts of the legislation were. What happened here?

Two possible explanations suggest themselves. One is that the government realised of its own motion that it had made a mistake in excluding deterrence from the list of purposes for sentencing young offenders that was put before Parliament, and therefore decided not to implement the provision. The other is that senior judges, alerted by the Panel's advice, communicated to the government their concern about being deprived of the power to pass deterrent sentences on young offenders, and the government responded by excluding part (c) from its implementation of the 2008 provisions. There is no evidence to indicate which of the two explanations is true;[54] but if there is any substance in the second explanation, this is a further manifestation of judicial power, albeit power over a government that seemed to have little sense of direction on this particular issue.

Finally, it should be noted that s. 5 of the Constitutional Reform Act 2005 provides for the Lord Chief Justice to make written representations to Parliament on any matter of importance relating to the judiciary or to the administration of justice. It is possible that this power would be exercised if the Lord Chief Justice thought that the ability of judges and magistrates to do justice in their sentencing decisions was under threat.

2.4 The Judicial College

It is said that the first judicial conference devoted to sentencing matters was convened by Lord Parker CJ in 1963. In 1975 the Home Secretary, the Lord Chancellor and the Lord Chief Justice set up a committee under the chairmanship of Mr Justice (later Lord) Bridge, '(i) to review the machinery for disseminating information about the penal system and matters related to the treatment of offenders; (ii) to review the scope and content of training, and the methods whereby it is provided; and to make recommendations'. The committee's 1976 working paper used the term 'judicial training' in

---

[52] Sentencing Advisory Panel, *Sentencing Principles – Youths* (2009), paras. 53–6.
[53] *B.W.P.* 2006 SCC 27.
[54] Interestingly, when the Australian legislature removed general deterrence from the list of purposes of sentencing (following a recommendation of the Australian Law Reform Commission), the courts disingenuously held that this was a 'legislative slip' and held that general deterrence remained an important sentencing consideration: *DPP (Commonwealth)* v. *El Karhani* (1990) 52 A Crim R 123.

its title, a term to which some judges reacted strongly. As the committee put it in its 1978 report:

> It is said that 'training' implies that there are 'trainers' who can train people to be judges, and so long as this concept is capable of influencing the thought of those concerned with the provision of judicial training this must, despite all protestations to the contrary, represent a threat to judicial independence.[55]

This extreme sensitivity has largely dissipated over time.[56] The report of the Bridge Committee led to the establishment of a Judicial Studies Board (JSB) in 1979. From its original focus on Crown Court sentencing, the JSB was enlarged in 1985 and given much wider responsibilities which included training for magistrates and training for judges in criminal, family, and civil matters. Under the Constitutional Reform Act 2005 the Lord Chief Justice now has responsibility for the training of the judiciary, and the training of all judicial office-holders has since April 2011 been drawn into a single institution, the Judicial College.[57]

The College is committed to a programme of judicial training that involves both attendance at induction and continuation courses, and the use of e-learning. It seems that training is being distinguished from information and updating: 'the most effective judicial training is that which requires active participation by judicial office holders in a supportive environment and gives them the opportunity to practice and develop skills'.[58] This emphasis on judge-craft is important, but it leaves it to the judges themselves to ensure that they keep up to date with legislative changes, guidelines and developing case-law. Supplementary materials are available to judges on the website, and there are regular e-letters on developments in the law. However, given the scale of the changes to sentencing being introduced by the Sentencing Council, it is unfortunate that the College's strategy document does not say more about links between the Council and the College, or about the means by which judges are trained to use the sentencing guidelines.[59]

2.5 The position of the magistracy

Magistrates deal with the vast majority of criminal cases, but there are long-standing criticisms of the institution. The composition of the magistracy, and the relative failure of efforts to make the bench more representative, is often cited. While women now account for half of all lay magistrates, there is continuing under-representation of ethnic minorities and over-representation of (older) white people. The magistracy remains an essentially local institution:

---

[55] Bridge (1978), para. 1.6.   [56] See Darbyshire (2011), ch. 6.

[57] 'Strategy of the Judicial College, 2011–2014', at www.judiciary.gov.uk/about-the-judiciary/training-support/judicial-college.

[58] Ibid., para. 21.   [59] See Padfield (2013), pp. 49–50.

even though training is now overseen by the Judicial College and the sentencing guidelines are national, local cultures remain and there are still questions about the power of both local justices' clerks and local liaison judges, on which research is needed.[60] Moreover, magistrates' courts in many areas also have one or more District Judges (Magistrates' Courts) sitting, and this raises other issues.[61] Research in the mid-1990s found, for example, that provincial stipendiary magistrates (now DJMCs) used custody almost twice as frequently as metropolitan 'stipes'.[62] These matters call for more detailed research. The position of the magistracy, and the division of work between lay justices and DJMCs, were reconsidered in the Auld Review, but no structural changes were proposed.[63] The Judicial College provides guidance and training materials for local benches, and also runs courses for District Judges (Magistrates' Courts), for legal advisers, and for lay magistrates on chairmanship.

Particularly influential in the development of sentencing guidance has been the Magistrates' Association, a voluntary association to which the vast majority of some 27,000 magistrates belong. It represents the magistracy in national debates, commenting on policy proposals, responding to consultation papers and occasionally campaigning for or against a particular change in the law. Local branches of the Association hold regular meetings on issues of interest to the magistracy. At national level it has shown its concern for consistency in sentencing by offering its own guidance to its members. In 1966 the Association first circulated its *Suggestions for Road Traffic Penalties*, proposing starting points for all the common road traffic offences for which justices are called upon to pass sentence. The document was updated several times.[64] Some local benches adapted (i.e. altered) the national penalty scales. In the 1980s several local benches supplemented their own versions of the Association's *Suggestions* by adding 'starting points' or guideline penalties for a few other common crimes. The county of Cheshire developed a short booklet of guidelines, and in 1987 Lord Hailsham, as Lord Chancellor and president of the Magistrates' Association, commended the Cheshire guidelines and floated the idea of some national guidelines. The Association was already working on this, and in 1989 it issued its *Sentencing Guide for Criminal Offences (other than Road Traffic) and Compensation Table*. This provided starting points for some twenty frequent offences, prefacing them with some general principles.[65] The guidelines for road traffic cases were then incorporated in the general guidelines, which were reshaped and revised in 1992, 1993, 1997, 2000, and 2004 by a working group that included justices' clerks and stipendiary magistrates (later, district judges). However, from the outset there was a major

---

[60] Darbyshire (1997a, 1997b); see also Padfield (2008), ch. 6.   [61] Darbyshire (2011), pp. 167–72.
[62] Flood-Page and Mackie (1998), pp. 67–70.   [63] Auld (2001), ch. 4.
[64] The Association also commissioned research on its effect: Hood (1972), and the discussion in Ashworth (2003).
[65] For discussion of the controversy preceding the Association's decision to issue the guidelines in 1989, see Ashworth (2003).

difficulty with the guidelines: they had absolutely no legal authority, being the product of a voluntary association, and local benches, liaison judges, and justices' clerks knew perfectly well that they were under no legal obligation to follow them. Nonetheless, the Association performed an important function, in the absence of adequate guidance from any authoritative source, by showing leadership through its 'do-it-yourself' approach to sentencing consistency.

Those voluntary guidelines formed the foundation for what are now the *Magistrates' Court Sentencing Guidelines* (2008), a substantial loose-leaf folder devised by an ad hoc committee (including lay magistrates, District Judges, justices' clerks, and members of the Sentencing Advisory Panel and Sentencing Guidelines Council) and updated frequently by the Sentencing Council. This guidance was subsequently joined by the guideline on *Sentencing Young Offenders* (2009). Together these documents brought legally binding guidelines to the magistrates' courts for the first time. There is provision for even greater changes, since the Criminal Justice Act 2003 contains provisions that would double magistrates' sentencing powers for a single offence, from 6 to 12 months. This would inevitably have an effect on the types of case they try and they sentence, extending their jurisdiction to many cases now tried in the Crown Court. However, the relevant provisions have not been brought into force.

2.6 European Union law

EU law has a competence in matters of 'freedom, security and justice', and it pursues this through directives relating to enforcement of its own diverse activities and directives relating to issues of concern such as child pornography and environmental protection. Estella Baker has described EU sentencing law as 'deceptively rich, diverse and awkward to organize',[66] but a relatively straightforward example comes from the EU's right of free movement, which also enables member states to penalize those who fail to carry the required documentation permitting them to take advantage of that right. The European Court of Justice has insisted that sentences for breach must remain in proportion to the relevant right: any penalty 'which is so disproportionate to the gravity of the infringement that it becomes an obstacle to the exercise of that freedom' is inconsistent with Community law.[67] This has been reinforced by the provision, in the EU Charter of Fundamental Rights, that 'the severity of penalties must not be disproportionate to the criminal offence',[68] although it is

---

[66] Baker (2013), p. 260.

[67] *Casati* [1981] ECR 2595, para. 27; see also *Pieck* [1980] ECR 2171, and the discussion by Guldenmund, Harding and Sherlock (1995), pp. 110–17.

[68] Art. II.49(3), discussed by van Zyl Smit and Ashworth (2004); cf. Clayton and Murphy (2014).

not clear how the European Court of Justice will interpret and apply such a provision in the context of such divergent sentencing provisions in member states. However, EU law contains provisions on the level of maximum sentences for certain cross-border offences, including terrorist offences, money laundering, illegal entry, and currency counterfeiting, and Baker argues that the Sentencing Council has a duty to ensure that its guidelines are compatible with relevant European directives, a duty that will become more visible as the EU extends its areas of concern.[69]

2.7 European human rights law

Also of constitutional importance is the impact of European human rights law on sentencing. The United Kingdom allows an individual right of petition to the European Court of Human Rights in Strasbourg, and the Human Rights Act 1998 requires all public authorities in the United Kingdom (including courts, prosecutors, prisons, offender management services) to act in conformity with the Convention. While the Convention's main criminal justice impact has been on criminal procedure, its provisions have important effects on some sentencing matters. These are discussed more fully in the appropriate parts of the book, but it is convenient to mention six points of impact here.[70]

First, Article 3 of the Convention forbids torture and 'inhuman or degrading treatment or punishment': this rules out corporal punishment[71] and also, in conjunction with Protocol 6, capital punishment. If one considers the historical changes in the acceptability of forms of punishment, there has been a movement away from corporal penalties – those which affect the body, in the sense of the direct infliction of pain – towards punishments which affect the mind. Such measures as amputation, torture, and even corporal punishment are contrary to Article 3 of the Convention. The Strasbourg Court has held that imprisonment for life without the possibility of release ('life means life') is contrary to Article 3.[72] As Judge Power-Forde put it, 'to deny [prisoners with a whole life term] the experience of hope would be to deny a fundamental aspect of their humanity, and to do that would be degrading'. The Court of Appeal has taken issue with Strasbourg's interpretation of English law,[73] but there is an 'emerging consensus' in favour of the possibility, in all cases, of rehabilitation, release, and reintegration. Another issue is whether it is 'degrading' within Article 3 to have to share a small cell with two other prisoners, with or without integral sanitation, for many hours at a stretch and with little opportunity, for example, for exercise. After many years, modern sensibilities are now turning against this and are accepting that it shows insufficient respect for

---

[69] Baker (2013), pp. 273–9.
[70] For a recent US survey of constitutional rights at sentencing, see Hessick and Hessick (2011).
[71] *Tyrer* v. *United Kingdom* (1978) 2 EHRR 1 (use of birch as punishment violates Art. 3).
[72] *Vinter* v. *United Kingdom* [2014] Crim LR 81.   [73] *Newell* [2014] EWCA Crim 188.

human dignity.[74] Whether it will be held that wearing an electronic tag amounts to 'degrading punishment' remains to be tested.

Second, Articles 3 and 5 of the Convention may be invoked together or singly to rule out a disproportionate sentence. The Strasbourg Court has stated that life imprisonment for a small-value robbery might be so disproportionate as to amount to inhuman and degrading punishment, although it might be possible to justify it as a preventive sentence in certain circumstances.[75] Similarly, when holding in *Offen (No. 2)*[76] that the automatic sentence of life imprisonment for a second 'serious offence' should be made subject to a broader exception, Lord Woolf CJ drew upon Convention rights as part of his reasoning, noting that conviction of a 'serious offence' could result from a mere push that causes a fatal head injury:

> The offence is manslaughter. The offender may have committed another serious offence when a young man. A life sentence in such circumstances may well be arbitrary and disproportionate and contravene Article 5. It could also be a punishment which contravenes Article 3.

The result of this decision was to 'read down' the legislation creating the so-called automatic life sentence. Constitutional prohibitions on disproportionate sentences have been applied in Canada and South Africa, but they have been less successful in the United States.[77] In *Lockyer* v. *Andrade* the US Supreme Court held that a sentence of twice life imprisonment (with a minimum of 50 years) for two incidents of theft involving a total of 11 blank videotapes was not 'grossly disproportionate' and therefore not a 'cruel and unusual' punishment.[78]

Third, Article 5 has also had a considerable impact on the procedures relating to life imprisonment. The Strasbourg Court, applying Article 5(4), has insisted that there must be provision for regular judicial review of the need for continued detention, applying this first to discretionary life sentences[79] and eventually to life imprisonment for murder.[80] The effect of this is to transfer to the Parole Board, chaired by a judge, the task of deciding how long a life prisoner needs to be detained in order to protect the public.

Fourth, Article 6 declares the right to a fair trial, and this includes the sentencing decision. Article 6 and its safeguards will therefore apply wherever proceedings result in the imposition of a 'penalty' on a person.[81] One result of

---

[74] See the reports of the European Committee on the Prevention of Torture and Inhuman and Degrading Treatment, mentioned in ch. 9.1.3 below. See also *Napier* v. *Scottish Executive* [2004] UKHRR 881.

[75] *Weeks* v. *United Kingdom* (1987) 10 EHRR 293.   [76] [2001] 1 Cr App R 372.

[77] Van Zyl Smit and Ashworth (2004).

[78] (2003) 123 S Ct 1166; see also *Ewing* v. *California* (2003) 123 S Ct 1179.

[79] *Thynne, Wilson and Gunnell* v. *United Kingdom* (1989) 13 EHRR 666.

[80] *Stafford* v. *United Kingdom* (2002) 35 EHRR 1121, departing from its previous decision in *Wynne* v. *United Kingdom* (1994) 19 EHRR 333.

[81] For the meaning of 'penalty', see *Welch* v. *United Kingdom*, n. 84 below.

this is to hold that the Home Secretary cannot set the minimum term for an offender convicted of murder, since he or she is not an 'independent and impartial tribunal' as required by Article 6.[82] It has also been held that court proceedings must be specially adapted where the defendant is a child, so as to facilitate meaningful participation.[83]

Fifth, Article 7 declares that no person may be subjected to a greater penalty than the one applicable at the time of the offence. English law's classification is not determinative, since the Strasbourg Court held that a confiscation order is a 'penalty',[84] although it seems that most of the preventive orders are not regarded as penalties.[85] Of more general significance is the principle that changes to sentencing law may not operate retrospectively.[86] This is particularly relevant in view of the frequent changes in sentencing powers introduced by legislation in recent years.

Sixth, Article 8.1 declares each person's right to respect for his private and family life, his home and his correspondence, and Article 8.2 sets out the circumstances in which interference with that right may be justified. Even where it is held that interference is justified, any sentence resulting from conviction must remain proportionate to the rationale for the interference and must reflect the fact that a right is being compromised. Thus, in the sadomasochism case of *Laskey* v. *United Kingdom*,[87] the European Court showed its willingness to scrutinize the severity of the sentence on this ground (the sentence imposed at trial had already been reduced by the Court of Appeal, and no further adjustment was thought necessary). This line of argument was also accepted by the majority in the otherwise unsatisfactory case of *G*.[88]

These six points demonstrate the wide-ranging impact of the Convention on sentencing law,[89] and the need to keep the Convention in view throughout the chapters that follow. The Convention's effect on prisoners' rights has been more extensive, with a steady stream of decisions in Strasbourg and in the English courts, but they fall outside the scope of this work.[90]

2.8 Conclusions

Sentencing policy has in recent years become an increasingly political issue, and yet constitutional arguments are also raised from time to time, although

---

[82] As held by the House of Lords in *R* v. *Home Secretary, ex p. Anderson* [2003] 1 AC 837, reviewing the previous Strasbourg decisions.

[83] *V and T* v. *United Kingdom* (2000) 30 EHRR 121; *SC* v. *United Kingdom* [2005] Crim LR 130.

[84] *Welch* v. *United Kingdom* (1995) 20 EHRR 247.

[85] See e.g. *Ibbotson* v. *United Kingdom* (1999) 27 EHRR CD 332, holding that sex offender registration is not a penalty.

[86] Cf. *Ghafoor* [2003] 1 Cr App R (S) 428 on the application of the principle in juvenile sentencing.

[87] (1997) 24 EHRR 39.   [88] *G*. [2008] UKHL 37, *G* v. *United Kingdom* [2012] Crim LR 46.

[89] See more fully Emmerson, Ashworth and Macdonald (2012), ch. 20.

[90] See Livingstone, Owen and Macdonald (2008).

often (notably in relation to the principle of judicial independence) without a secure grounding. Probably the greatest constitutional limitation on sentencing stems from the Human Rights Act and the Convention rights, as just noted, although EU law also has the potential to impinge, as suggested in 2.6 above. Major institutional innovations such as the creation of the Sentencing Council have introduced constitutional novelties; and although we do not know what kind of law 'definitive guidelines' are, this obscurity does not appear to be a handicap. In terms of future developments, the most interesting possibilities lie in the statutory powers of the Sentencing Council. As we saw in 2.2 above, the Council has a wide range of powers in addition to its power to create definitive guidelines. It embarked with considerable enthusiasm on the task of compiling sentencing data and then abandoned the CCSS, but has shown much less interest in examining the effectiveness of various forms of sentence, and has never been called upon to advise the government on the implications of a proposed policy initiative. These broad powers could bring considerable influence to the Council, and indeed could (with some changes to its membership) constitute it as an independent body on penal policy, analogous to the Monetary Policy Committee of the Bank of England in relation to the interest rate. Both Nicola Lacey and the British Academy have put forward this model as a means of reducing the party political element in penal policy and placing it on more stable and rational foundations,[91] and such initiatives will be discussed further in the concluding chapter.

---

[91] Lacey (2008); see also British Academy (2014).

3

Sentencing aims, principles and policies

3.1 The aims of the criminal justice system

The 'criminal justice system' is not a structure which has been planned as a system. Nor is it so organized that the several interlocking parts operate harmoniously. In England and Wales, as in many other jurisdictions, the administration of criminal justice has grown in a piecemeal way over the years, with separate phases of development leaving their mark. To refer to a 'system' is therefore merely a convenience and an aspiration. It should not be assumed that the various arrangements were planned or actually operate as a system, although it remains necessary to recognize the interdependence of the different parts and to incorporate this into any planning.

It is important to distinguish the aims of the criminal justice system from the aims of sentencing, which merely relate to one element. As we saw in Chapter 1.4, the system encompasses a whole series of stages and decisions, from the initial investigation of crime, through the various pre-trial processes, the provisions of the criminal law, the trial, the forms of punishment, and then post-sentence decisions concerned with, for example, supervision, release from custody, and recall procedures. It would hardly be possible to formulate a single meaningful 'aim of the criminal justice system' which applied to every stage. It is true that one might gather together a cluster of aims: for example, the prevention of crime, the fair treatment of suspects and defendants, due respect for the victims of crime, the fair labelling of offences according to their relative gravity, and so on. But to combine these into some overarching aim such as 'the maintenance of a peaceful society through fair and just laws and procedures' would surely be to descend into vacuity, since it gives no hint of the conflicts that arise and the priorities that need to be determined. Thus the cluster of aims for different stages of the system needs to be stated in such a way as to maximize coherence and also to ensure compliance with international obligations such as the European Convention on Human Rights and the United Nations Convention on the Rights of the Child.

One aspect of this process should be to ensure that unrealistic aims are not set for individual stages of the criminal justice system. We saw earlier[1] that only a small proportion of crimes come before the courts for a sentencing decision – around 2 per cent on Home Office figures. Even granted that publicity may make it appear that the courts are dealing with a higher proportion than this, the potential of sentencing for altering the frequency and patterns of offending in society is severely handicapped by the fact that relatively few offences result in the passing of a sentence. However, it may be assumed that sentencing fulfils an indispensable public function within the criminal justice system: without the panoply of police, penal agents, and courts, there would surely be more crime. There is at least some evidence that law and order would break down in the absence of police,[2] and therefore that a sentencing system employing coercive sanctions is necessary as a standing deterrent. But it does not follow from any of this that increases in sentence levels will bring about increases in general crime prevention, as we shall see in the discussion of deterrence theory in part 3.3.2 below.

3.2 The role of the state

It is often assumed that the state's duty to punish crime is simply one aspect of the modern sovereign state, but (as we will see in 3.3.7 below) any such assumption is disputed by those who proclaim that victims and their families, or victims and communities (through restorative justice), ought to be central to responses to crime. However, our immediate concern here is with the wider obligations of the state – in particular, the role of the state in preventing harm and ensuring security. This is more complex than the duty to punish offenders because it is neither exclusive nor so well defined. Understanding what underpins the state's preventive function requires close attention to

---

[1] In ch. 1.4 above.

[2] Evidence for this might be derived from the spread of lawbreaking, mostly property offences, during the police strikes in Melbourne in 1923 (on which see Bagaric and Alexander 2011, pp. 280–2) and Liverpool in 1919, and during the immobilization of the Danish police force in 1944. It is argued by Mathiesen (1990), pp. 62–3, that these were such atypical situations that they leave the propositions in the text as unsupported assertions.

fundamental questions about the relationship between state and citizen, the role and remit of the state, and the obligations of citizens.[3]

Classical liberal conceptions of the relationship between state and citizen focus upon the obligations owed to the state by citizens and to citizens by the state. The citizen's obligation to obey the law is explained variously by reference to tacit consent to its authority; fair play to other citizens; submitting to reciprocal burdens when accepting the benefit of the services and protection provided by the state; or the consequentialist ground that, absent obedience to the law, the result would be chaos or a return to a Hobbesian state of nature.[4] What the state owes to citizens in return is less well defined, but seems always to include a duty to provide protection from the hazards and threats that they would otherwise face.[5] Thus, in exchange for the promise of the security of their persons and property, citizens are assumed to agree to renounce the right to self-government and to submit to the state's coercive force. Hobbes observed in the *Leviathan* that the purpose of this submission to state authority was 'the security of a man's person'. It follows that the state's primary task and indeed its very raison d'être is to secure for its citizens the conditions of order and security that are prerequisites of freedom. Two things follow from this characterization of the state's primary function. First, the protective or preventive function is written into the very fabric of state authority and imposes upon the state a duty to promulgate laws and pursue policies in order to provide security for its citizens. Secondly, citizens owe a *prima facie* duty to the state and to one another to abide by law and to accept state coercion as the necessary price of peace and good order.

The conscientious pursuit of crime prevention is thus a vital objective of a criminal justice system as a whole, and considerable developments have taken place in recent decades. There is a range of preventive approaches.[6] Some are developmental strategies, which may include family planning and parenting, through pre-school facilities to the identification and monitoring of children 'at risk' of offending.[7] Then there is situational crime prevention, which has been encouraged through a variety of initiatives, such as altering the designs of buildings or vehicles in order to reduce the opportunity for certain kinds of crime, 'target-hardening', access control, and so forth.[8] A major part of this approach is increased surveillance, e.g. the now widespread use of CCTV cameras in public places, on public transport, and in shopping centres and so forth.[9] A third approach is social crime prevention or 'community crime prevention': this is intended to include improvements to housing, social and

---

[3] See Ashworth and Zedner (2014), ch.1 and *passim*.
[4] For further analysis, see e.g. Knowles (2010).   [5] Ryan (2011), pp. 228–299.
[6] Note Ashworth and Zedner (2014), pp. 5–6, on the concept of 'prevention', which should not be taken to imply that all harms of a certain kind can be eliminated, just that they should be significantly reduced.
[7] Crawford and Evans (2012), pp. 781–3.   [8] Crawford and Evans (2012), pp. 773–81.
[9] Goold and Neyland (2009).

recreational facilities, education, and employment, as well as local preferences for the deployment of the police.[10] These initiatives are steered by local Crime and Disorder Reduction Partnerships, which are now working to a National Community Safety Plan.[11]

Some crime-prevention strategies have been shown to reduce crime and thereby reduce the load on the law enforcement agencies and minimise the labelling of people as offenders. The history of 'auto-crime' shows the considerable impact of introducing steering locks in the 1960s in reducing thefts and takings of cars – a far more significant reduction than could have been achieved by all but the most draconian sentencing policy – and in the 1990s motor manufacturers co-operated in improving car security as part of a renewed effort against these types of crime. However, although evidence-based crime-prevention strategies should be pursued with much greater vigour than at present, there are at least three drawbacks which must be borne in mind. One is that enthusiasm for small local projects may outstrip the amount of careful and rigorous evaluation. Schemes are often difficult to evaluate, and not just because one has to investigate possible 'displacement' effects, in the shape of lawbreaking of other kinds or in other areas. The political attractions of crime-prevention initiatives are sometimes allowed to run ahead of proper assessments of their effectiveness.[12] A second danger is that the schemes will be used to spread the net of social control, promoting so-called 'community' initiatives in a way which increases state control over individuals, families, and neighbourhoods and therefore brings other disadvantages. Insufficient attention has been paid to ethical issues in crime prevention, raised by a number of techniques (such as CCTV).[13] A third unwelcome consequence is that situational approaches might conduce the mentality of a 'fortress' society, surrounded by locks, bars, and unbreakable articles. This might heighten fear of crime, even if it reduces objective risk.[14] Despite these drawbacks, it remains the best policy to try to prevent crime before it occurs, so long as this can be achieved using evidence-based strategies within a rights-based framework.

In cases where prevention has not worked, the state must be prepared to respond to an offence that has been committed. However, there are well-documented reasons why sentencing cannot and should not be expected to function efficiently as a crime-prevention mechanism. Thus sentencing and crime rates may vary independently because (i) crime rates are affected by demographic factors such as the age profile of the population, and by changes in the availability of desirable and stealable goods (such as mobile phones); and (ii) fewer than half of all crimes are reported to the police, as we saw in

[10] Crawford and Evans (2012), pp. 784–8.
[11] See www.gov.uk/government/policies/reducing-and-preventing-crime-2 for key objectives.
[12] See Maguire (2004) on the then government's abandonment of over-ambitious targets.
[13] Cf. von Hirsch, Garland and Wakefield (2000).   [14] Zedner (2009).

Chapter 1.4 above.[15] When there is a formal response to an offence this does not always mean prosecution–conviction–sentence, since there are various methods of diversion available. For those cases that are brought to court, however, sentencing is a process that has considerable social significance in its own right. The sentencing decision can often be seen as the core of the public censuring or labelling process in that it gives a judgment of 'how bad' the offence was, and translates that judgment into the particular penal currency of this country at the time. Sentencing has an expressive function and, as Durkheim argued, 'the best punishment is that which puts the blame . . . in the most expressive but least costly form possible'.[16]

This expressive or censuring function is carried out by means of imposing coercive measures on convicted offenders. The imposition of punishment requires justification. We should not be satisfied with the proposition that anyone who commits any offence forfeits all rights, and may be dealt with by the state in whatever manner the courts decree. That would be to suggest that any convicted person is entirely at the disposal of the criminal justice system, and not a rights-bearing individual. Instead, we should seek strong justifications for contemporary sentencing practices, not least because of the increasing use of imprisonment and the greater restrictiveness of non-custodial sentences in many countries. But before turning to consider the possible rationales for sentencing, it is first necessary to say something about the institution of state punishment.

The importance of punishment being in the hands of state institutions rather than victims or other individuals resides in rule-of-law values. Decisions on punishment should be taken by an independent and impartial tribunal, not by individuals with an emotional involvement in the events. The outcome should not be dependent on whether the victim is vengeful or forgiving, but should be dependent on the impartial application of settled principles, notably principles that recognize the offender as a citizen capable of choice and that regard proportionality of sentence to offence as a key value.[17] As Thorburn has put it, developing a Kantian perspective, the justification for the state's monopoly over punishment 'flows from the fact that only the state has the standing to act in the name of the system of rights itself rather than in some narrower, partisan interest'.[18] The state therefore has the role of providing the institutions for an authoritative response to wrongs, which constitutes a public valuation of the offender's conduct.[19] Sometimes these notions are expressed in terms of the state and its courts being more 'objective' than victims and their families, but one must beware of the concept of objectivity here. Issues of crime and punishment have become intensely political in recent years and, even if sentences are objective in the sense that they are not chosen by victims

---

[15] See further Bottoms (2004), pp. 60–1.   [16] Quoted in Garland (1990), p. 46.
[17] Ashworth (2002b).   [18] Thorburn (2012), p. 282.
[19] See further von Hirsch and Ashworth (2005), ch. 2.

or their representatives, they are not objective in the sense of being free from the political posturing or vote-catching policies that have tended to shape sentencing legislation (and therefore judicial sentencing) in recent decades.

Thus whether one takes the justification for state punishment to reside in one variation on the social contract theme,[20] or (more pragmatically) in the displacement of individual revenge and retaliation by maintaining a social practice that constitutes an independent and authoritative response to crime,[21] there are problems in translating the justification to any particular criminal justice system. There are many signs of what David Garland has termed 'the decline of the sovereign State',[22] and, even if some of his analysis is less compelling than it might appear,[23] it is surely true that the simple model in which the state provides for the security of its subjects is not sustainable in many countries. Responsibility is being devolved to private entrepreneurs and to local authorities, and crime is perceived as a major social problem still. At some times in some countries, the legitimacy of the state and its institutions suffers collapse, and those dire circumstances force reconsideration of the basic principles.[24] Thus we might conclude with Antony Duff that, although there may be justifications for the state taking responsibility for criminal justice, they are contingent on the state fulfilling its side of the agreement,[25] and in many countries that is in doubt. This area of doubt makes it all the more important to scrutinize the justifications for sentencing policy in general, for the types of sentence that are used, and for the conditions that they impose on offenders.

3.3 The rationales of sentencing

3.3.1 The argument for declaring a primary rationale

When judges are discussing sentencing, one of the most frequent topics is discretion. As we saw in parts 1.5, 2.2 and 2.3 above, there is a constant tension between flexibility and the rule of law. There are many who would agree that sentencers ought to have sufficient discretion to take account of the peculiar facts of individual cases. So be it. But does that rebut the argument for bringing rule-of-law values as far into sentencing decisions as possible? The rule of law, in this context, means that judicial decisions should be taken openly and by reference to standards declared in advance.[26] It is one thing to agree that judges should be left with discretion, so they may adjust the sentence to fit the particular combination of facts in an individual case. It is quite another to suggest that judges should be free to choose what rationale of sentencing to adopt in particular cases or types of case. Freedom to select from among

---

[20] See n. 4 above and accompanying text.
[21] Gardner (1998); cf. the critical analysis by Thorburn (2012), pp. 278–84.   [22] Garland (2000).
[23] Zedner (2002).   [24] For references, see Ashworth (2002b), pp. 580–1.
[25] Duff (2001), p. 197.   [26] Raz (1979), ch. 11.

the various rationales is a freedom to determine policy, not a freedom to respond to unusual combinations of facts. It is more of a licence to judges to pursue their own penal philosophies than an encouragement to respond sensitively to the facts of each case.

It is often assumed that there are only two alternative courses to the problem of setting sentencing rationales: either (i) to declare a single rationale, or (ii) to allow sentencers a fairly free choice among several rationales. Critics of the first approach argue that it is too rigid, especially when there is such a wide range of crimes and criminals. It may then be assumed that the second approach is the only 'realistic' one, arguing that it is more 'balanced' or is 'multifaceted', and contrasting its practicality with the academic, even ascetic regime of a single rationale. Thus many judges and magistrates place great importance on the freedom to pursue whatever approach they think appropriate 'on the facts of the case'.[27] One notable decision of the Supreme Court of Victoria expresses what many judges may believe:

> The purposes of punishment are manifold and each element will assume a different significance not only in different crimes but in the individual commission of each crime ... Ultimately every sentence imposed represents a sentencing judge's instinctive synthesis of all the various aspects involved in the punitive process.[28]

The inscrutable idea of an 'instinctive synthesis' comes close to another under-specified notion, which is that the various aims of sentencing should be 'balanced' in each case. Yet it is fairly well established that a major source of disparity in sentencing is the difference in penal philosophies among judges and magistrates,[29] and that is likely to be enhanced by a 'free for all' approach to purposes of punishment. On this approach, then, no weight at all is given to rule-of-law values.

But there is a third possibility, which is both practical and consistent with the rule of law: (iii) to declare a primary rationale, and to provide that in certain types of case one or another rationale might be given priority. This approach has been operating in Sweden since 1989, with desert or proportionality as the primary rationale and other aims having priority in certain types of case.[30] It was also the approach embodied in the Criminal Justice Act 1991, with desert as the primary rationale and incapacitation having priority in certain types of case. And it received the approval of the Council of Europe in its recommendation on 'Consistency in Sentencing':

---

[27] See ch. 1.6 above on this concept.

[28] *Williscroft* [1975] VR 292, at pp. 299–300; cf. *Markarian* v. *R* (2005) 79 ALJR 1048 (High Court), and the Scots decision in *Murray* v. *HM Advocate* [2013] HCJAC 3.

[29] See Hogarth (1971), cited in ch. 1.6 above, and the wider review of research by the Canadian Sentencing Commission (1987), para. 4.1.2.

[30] For the text of the law in English, see von Hirsch and Jareborg (1989); for discussion, see Jareborg (1995).

A.1 The legislator, or other competent authorities where constitutional principles and legal traditions so allow, should endeavour to declare the rationales for sentencing.

A.2 Where necessary, and in particular where different rationales may be in
conflict, indications should be given of ways of establishing possible priorities in the application of such rationales for sentencing.

A.3 Where possible, and in particular for certain classes of offences or offenders, a primary rationale should be declared.[31]

However, the British government appears to have discarded this kind of
clearly structured approach. The scheme of the 1991 Act was abandoned in
2003, and in its place we have a law that seems to embody the worst of 'pick-
and-mix' sentencing. Section 142 of the Criminal Justice Act 2003 provides:

Any court dealing with an offender [aged 18 or over][32] in respect of his offence
must have regard to the following purposes of sentencing –

(a) the punishment of offenders,
(b) the reduction of crime (including its reduction by deterrence),
(c) the reform and rehabilitation of offenders,
(d) the protection of the public, and
(e) the making of reparation by offenders to persons affected by their offences.

Read as it stands, this section seems to invite inconsistency, by requiring
judges to consider a variety of different purposes and then, presumably, to
give priority to one. It is an approach that seems to have some political
popularity in Canada,[33] New Zealand,[34] and Australia, despite the low value
that it assigns to the rule of law.

However, it seems that the effect of s. 142 has been blunted by other
provisions in the 2003 Act, which the Sentencing Council has adopted as
the touchstone for its guidelines. Thus, having set out the terms of s. 142, the
former SGC went on to state that 'the sentencer must start by considering
the seriousness of the offence', and then quoted s. 143(1):

In considering the seriousness of any offence, the court must consider the
offender's culpability in committing the offence and any harm which the offence
caused, was intended to cause or might foreseeably have caused.

The remainder of the *Overarching Principles* guideline focuses on the proportionality principle in s. 143, without returning to s. 142.[35] It is clear that s. 143
underpins all the English guidelines, including those issued by the Council
since 2010. In addition to the terms of s. 143, there are two good reasons for

---

[31] Council of Europe (1993), p. 6.

[32] The section does not apply to younger offenders: there is a separate statutory framework of
aims for youth justice and sentencing, discussed in ch. 12.1 below.

[33] Canadian Criminal Code, s. 718.   [34] Sentencing Act 2002; see Roberts (2003).

[35] SGC, *Overarching Principles – Seriousness* (2004).

this. First, the idea of individual judges choosing which purpose to pursue is difficult to reconcile with the notion of sentencing under guidelines. Both the 2003 Act and the Coroners and Justice Act 2009 which created the Sentencing Council clearly contemplate that courts should generally follow any applicable guidelines. Secondly, the statutory thresholds for community sentences and for custodial sentences turn on 'the seriousness of the offence', which is linked to the concept of proportionality in s. 143.

Nonetheless, the enactment of s. 142 underscores the need to examine six contemporary rationales of sentencing: deterrence, rehabilitation, incapacitation, desert, social theories, and reparation or restoration. Each of these aims has a considerable philosophical background and penological context, which cannot be set out in full here. Readers are referred to an anthology of readings, with commentary and bibliography, for further study.[36]

3.3.2 Deterrence[37]

Deterrence is one of several rationales of punishment which may be described as 'consequentialist', in the sense that it looks to the preventive consequences of sentences. Thus deterrence is merely one possible method of producing crime prevention through sentencing: it relies characteristically on threats and fear generated by legal punishment, whereas rehabilitation and incapacitation adopt different methods of trying to achieve a preventive end, as we shall see below.

At the outset a distinction should be drawn between individual (or special) deterrence and general deterrence. The latter aims at deterring other people from committing this kind of offence, whereas individual deterrence is concerned with deterring this particular person from reoffending. A system which regards individual deterrence as the main goal would presumably escalate sentences for persistent offenders, on the reasoning that if non-custodial penalties fail to deter then custody must be tried, and if 1 year's custody fails to deter, 2 years must be tried, and so on. It is not the gravity of the crime but the propensity to reoffend which should be the main determinant of the sentence.[38] Individual deterrence relies on severity to give substance to its threats, but the evidence strongly suggests that using longer periods of imprisonment does not reduce recidivism.[39]

More significant is general deterrence. Jeremy Bentham was its chief proponent, and he started from the position that all punishment is pain and should therefore be avoided. However, punishment might be justified if the benefits (in terms of general deterrence) would outweigh the pain inflicted on the offender punished, and if the same benefits could not be

---

[36] Von Hirsch, Ashworth and Roberts (2009).   [37] Ibid., ch. 2; see also Brooks (2013), ch. 2.
[38] See the English law on previous convictions and sentencing, analysed in ch. 6.3.2 below.
[39] For a major meta-study, see Nagin, Cullen and Johnson (2009).

achieved by non-punitive methods. Sentences should therefore be calculated to be sufficient to deter others from committing this kind of offence, no more and no less. The assumption is that citizens are rational beings, who will adjust their conduct according to the disincentives provided by sentencing law. The same assumption leads to a belief in marginal deterrence – that increasing penalty levels by a certain amount will result in a decline in offending. Modern economic theorists such as Richard Posner adopt a similar approach, viewing punishments as a kind of pricing system.[40] Less sweeping is the rational choice perspective, adopted by criminologists such as Ronald Clarke as an explanation of certain types of offending and used to generate specific preventive strategies. The argument is that particular types of crime tend to result from a form of rational calculation (not perfect rationality but 'bounded rationality'), and that the responses to such crimes should take account of this and combat it.[41]

Criticisms of deterrence theory may be divided into the empirical and the principled. The main empirical criticism is that the factual data on which a deterrent system must be founded rarely exist. Reliable findings about the marginal general deterrent effects of various types and levels of penalty for various crimes are hard to find. A necessary element in research is a proper definition of deterrence, to establish that fear of the legal penalty was the particular factor that led to avoidance of the proscribed conduct. Deterrence must operate (if at all) through the potential offenders' minds, so it is essential that they know about the severity of the probable sentence, take this into account when deciding whether to offend, believe that there is a non-negligible risk of being caught, believe that the penalty will be applied to them if caught and sentenced, and refrain from offending for these reasons.[42] These subjective beliefs are vital components in the operation of deterrent policies, and all must therefore be investigated if research is to be reliable. Few studies satisfy these criteria, and they provide no basis for sentencing policies that simply involve increasing severity in the hope of reducing offending levels. This was the major finding of the Cambridge study, commissioned by the Home Office, although it did find that there was better evidence of the deterrent effect of a (believed) high risk of detection than of (believed) penalties.[43] The Halliday Report reviewed the evidence and also concluded that the limited evidence 'provides no basis for making a causal connection between variations in sentence severity and differences in deterrent effects'.[44]

Subsequent international reviews by Doob and Webster have recognized the intuitive attraction of the deterrent hypothesis but still found that the evidence

[40] Posner (1985), excerpted in von Hirsch, Ashworth and Roberts (2009), ch. 2.
[41] Cornish and Clarke (1986).   [42] See Bottoms (2004), p. 65.
[43] Von Hirsch et al. (1999), chs. 3 and 7; see also Bagaric and Alexander (2011), citing a German study by Entorf which found that certainty of conviction had significant deterrent effects, whereas increasing the length of custody did not.
[44] Halliday (2001), p. 129.

indicated 'that sentence severity has no effect on the level of crime in society'.[45] Bottoms and von Hirsch argue that this null hypothesis goes too far: there may be conditions in which the severity of potential penalties will have a marginal deterrent effect, if all the necessary subjective elements are present.[46] Thus Richard Harding found that robbers tended to desist from arming themselves with guns if there was a significant extra penalty for carrying a firearm.[47] This may be taken to bear out the proposition that general deterrence is more likely to be effective for planned or 'professional' than for impulsive crimes, although Harding notes that deterrent sentences need to be combined with publicity and appropriate 'social learning' opportunities if they are to have significant preventive effects. A counterpoint is provided by David Riley's study of drink drivers, in which he showed that the problems of a general deterrence strategy lie in drivers' optimism about the risk of being caught, ignorance of the penalty, and ignorance of the amount of alcohol consumption needed to commit an offence.[48] Another area in which the potential for legal deterrence appears not to be great is burglary: interviews with burglars suggest that most of them are not rational calculators but rather short-term hedonists or eternal optimists.[49] The chaotic lifestyle of some potential offenders, involving drugs or alcohol or both, may render them difficult candidates for deterrence strategies.[50] Particularly interesting is the finding of Burnett and Maruna that, although the majority of their convicted prisoners wanted to desist from crime after their release, only a minority succeeded in doing so and it tended to be a philosophy of hope that distinguished them. The notion of austere prison conditions as a deterrent was simply not enough.[51] Thus, although general deterrence can indeed work, given the necessary favourable circumstances,[52] the available research surely demonstrates the danger of generalizing from intuitions, or one's personal experience, as to the probable reactions of others.[53] Reliable and precise evidence of subjective perceptions is required.

Principled criticisms of deterrence theory would apply even if there were satisfactory evidence of general deterrent effects. One such criticism is that the theory could justify the punishment of an innocent person if that were certain to deter several others (who believe the person to be guilty): a simple utilitarian calculus would allow this injustice to be perpetrated, without any respect for the rights of the innocent person. A second, more realistic criticism is that the theory can justify the imposition of a disproportionately harsh sentence on one offender in order to deter several others from committing a similar

---

[45] Doob and Webster (2003), p. 143; Webster and Doob (2012).
[46] Bottoms and von Hirsch (2010).   [47] Harding (1990).
[48] Riley (1985); see also Weatherburn and Moffatt (2011).
[49] Bennett and Wright (1984), chs. 5 and 6. See also the more general findings of Kleck (2003), that there is generally no correlation between believed punishment levels and actual sentencing levels.
[50] Bagaric and Alexander (2011), pp. 271–2.   [51] Burnett and Maruna (2004).
[52] Nagin (1998).   [53] Mathiesen (1990), pp. 67–8, argues strongly on this point.

offence. This is the so-called 'exemplary sentence,' and its injustice lies in using one individual (violating his rights by imposing a disproportionately severe sentence) in the hope of achieving the goal of preventing further crimes by others.

Two well-known examples of exemplary sentences may be discussed briefly. One incident which has become part of judicial lore is the passing of exemplary sentences on certain offenders after the Notting Hill race riots in 1958. It is argued that such sentences may be justified by the consequences, which in this case were reductions in racial troubles in Notting Hill (although there were similar troubles in other cities in the following months). But who can assert that it was the exemplary sentences (4 years' imprisonment rather than 2) which caused the reduction in the number of offences which otherwise would have taken place? Might it not be the case that the police had arrested and charged the ringleaders, and without them there would be no continuation? Or that increased police patrols were thought to raise the risk of being caught? The Notting Hill case serves only to emphasize the formidable difficulties of gathering evidence on the effectiveness of exemplary sentences as short-term deterrents. Unless there are no other plausible explanations for the changes in people's behaviour, one cannot be confident of interpreting a sequence of social events correctly. Similar points emerge from the sequel to the Birmingham mugging case of *Storey* (1973).[54] A youth was ordered to be detained for 20 years for his part in the violent robbery of a drunken man. The sentence was widely publicized, both in Birmingham and in the national newspapers, as an exemplary sentence. Researchers were able to plot the rate of reported robberies in Birmingham and in two other cities during the months before and after the sentence was passed. The robbery rates seemed quite unaffected by the sentence in *Storey*: indeed, the rate of reported robberies in Birmingham had begun to rise before the trial and continued to increase before reaching a peak several weeks later. This calls into question the normal assumptions one would make about human behaviour, unless it is argued that the effect of *Storey* took several weeks to exert itself by reaching the ears of all potential robbers in Birmingham. The difficulty is that we do not understand the reasons, and this again shows the problems of firm assertions about general deterrent effects.

The real test of the second principled objection is this: even if one believes the Notting Hill anecdote, would this justify the extra-long sentences on the first people to be sentenced for the crime? Should, for example, an extra two years of one person's liberty be sacrificed in the hope of deterring several others? The objection to this is often expressed in the Kantian maxim, 'a person should always be treated as an end in himself [or herself], and never only as a means'. Respect for the moral worth and autonomy of the individual

---

[54] (1973) 57 Cr App R 240.

means that citizens should not be regarded merely as numbers, to be aggregated in some calculation of overall social benefit. It may be true that the fundamental justification for the whole institution of punishment is in terms of overall social benefit, in the same way as this is the justification for taxes. There are also plenty of other examples of compulsion 'for the greater good', such as quarantine, compulsory purchase of property, and so on. These measures do not, however, have the censuring dimension which sentences have. Exemplary sentences, by heaping an undeserved portion of punishment on one offender in the hope of deterring others, are objectionable in that they penalize an individual in order to achieve a social goal – and do so without any real criterion of how much extra punishment is necessary. A deterrent theory which incorporates no restrictions to prevent this invests great power in the state and the judiciary, with scant respect for individuals' autonomy.

English judges seem ambivalent about the defensibility of marginal general deterrence as a rationale for sentencing. When Lord Taylor, as Lord Chief Justice, was arguing against the introduction of mandatory minimum sentences into English law, he exposed the naïvety of the government's belief that such penalties would have a significant deterrent effect, referring to the evidence against this and the evidence that the risk of detection was more powerful.[55] Yet he and his successors as Lord Chief Justice have presided in the Court of Appeal when many sentences based on just such general deterrent reasoning have been upheld, some of them discussed in 3.6 below. Perhaps the most conspicuous recent example is the judgment in *Blackshaw et al.*,[56] relating to the 2011 English riots. Lord Judge CJ held that the devastation caused by those riots justified the courts in going above the sentencing guidelines in order to impose deterrent sentences, designed to prevent further disturbances of that kind. No reference was made to the lack of supporting evidence for such a strategy. No attempt was made to justify the amount by which the sentences were raised. Simply repeating the importance of having regard to the social context of offending and the 'need' for deterrent sentences was thought to be sufficient justification.[57]

A number of mixed theories of punishment have been advanced in an attempt to preserve some elements of deterrence theory (such as the need for a punishment system as a standing deterrent) while avoiding the principled objections. The most notable is that of H. L. A. Hart,[58] who argued that the general justifying aim of punishment must be found in the prevention and control of crime, but that in deciding whom to punish and how much to punish the governing principle should be desert. That is, only the guilty should be punished, and then only in proportion to the seriousness of their offences. This does away with deterrence as a rationale for particular sentences, but, on the other hand, it finds no place for desert in the basic justification for

---

[55] Taylor (1996), p. 10.   [56] [2012] 1 Cr App R (S) 679.
[57] Ibid., at [4], [75], [85–86], [91], and [125].   [58] Hart (2008).

punishment. There is a strong argument that in order to justify punishment there must be insistence on individual desert as well as overall social benefit.[59]

Sentences are not the only form of general deterrent flowing from the criminal justice system. In some cases it is the process that is the punishment – being prosecuted, appearing in court, receiving publicity in the local newspaper – rather than the sentence itself. Shame and embarrassment in relation to family and friends have long been said to have a more powerful effect than the sentence itself.[60] On the other hand, the deterrent effects of sentencing and of the process may be diluted considerably by enforcement policy, or at least by beliefs about the risk of detection. As we noted earlier, the evidence suggests that it is subjective beliefs about the probability of detection rather than about the quantum of punishment which are more likely to influence human behaviour.[61] However, there is little detailed know-ledge of the beliefs and thought processes of offenders and potential offenders, and the Cambridge study indicates a need for more focused research on these matters.[62] At a time when the detection rate for all crimes is around a quarter, and when burglary and robbery have detection rates of barely one-fifth, there are grounds for believing that any deterrent effect which sentence levels have upon the reasoning of potential offenders may be diluted considerably if the fairly low risk of detection is known. As noted earlier, there is much less research evidence in support of marginal deterrence by increasing the severity of penalties: few such effects have been reliably identified, and there are awkward questions such as how great an increase in severity is required, how that can be communicated to the target audience, and whether the severity of penalties has already reached saturation point.[63] Thus, all the indications are that it is naïve to assume the kind of hydraulic relationship between court sentences and criminal behaviour that some find intuitively appealing.

3.3.3 Incapacitation[64]

A second possible rationale for sentencing is to incapacitate offenders, that is, to deal with them in such a way as to make them incapable of offending for substantial periods of time. In its popular form of 'public protection' or 'community protection', this may be advanced as a general sentencing pur-pose.[65] Selective incapacitation focuses on particular groups of offenders, whereas collective incapacitation employs general increases in imprisonment levels. The debate has usually concerned lengthy periods of imprisonment and

---

[59] Lacey (1988), pp. 46–56; von Hirsch (1993), ch. 2.

[60] See the survey of young people by Willcock and Stokes (1963).

[61] See the review by von Hirsch et al. (1999), ch. 6.

[62] Von Hirsch et al. (1999), ch. 6; Bottoms and von Hirsch (2010).

[63] Von Hirsch et al. (1999), ch. 10; Bottoms and von Hirsch (2010).

[64] For fuller discussion and selected readings, see von Hirsch, Ashworth and Roberts (2009), ch. 3.

[65] As in s. 142(1)(d) of the Criminal Justice Act 2003.

of disqualification (e.g. from driving, from working with children, from being a company director). Some community measures, such as curfews, may also be included.

What has been claimed for selective incapacitation? This question receives detailed discussion below in the context of persistent and 'dangerous' offenders,[66] but two such strategies can be mentioned here. One is the imposition of long, incapacitative custodial sentences on offenders deemed to be 'dangerous'. It is claimed that one can identify certain offenders as 'dangerous', that is, as likely to commit serious offences if released into the community, and the risks to victims are so great that it is justifiable to detain such offenders for longer periods. The chief objection to this is over-prediction: even the former British coalition government has admitted that 'the limitations of our ability to predict future serious offending ... [call] into question the whole basis on which many offenders are sentenced to' indeterminate protective sentences.[67] This means that any portion of custody added to the proportionate sentence may be not only undeserved but also unnecessary to prevent that individual from committing a further serious offence.

The empirical basis of the second selective incapacitative strategy is likewise open to question. It was claimed by Greenwood in the United States that one can identify certain high-risk robbers and incarcerate them for substantial periods, achieving a reduction in the number of robberies and lowering sentence levels for other robbers.[68] The crime-preventive benefits of this are obvious, but the strategy has been shown to have major flaws. A subsequent report in the United States for the National Academy of Sciences demonstrated that Greenwood exaggerated the incapacitative effects and based his calculations on imprisoned robbers rather than robbers generally, and that a reworked version of his prediction method produced disappointing results.[69] More recent work has found that type of offence itself was not a significant predictor of the residual length of an offender's career.[70] The Halliday Report reviewed the research on incapacitation, and concluded that 'the available evidence does not support the case for changing the [sentencing] framework ... for the sole purpose of increasing an incapacitation effect'.[71] Despite these unpropitious findings, selective or none-too-selective incapacitative policies continue to have a political appeal: they underlie many 'three strikes and you're out' policies in the United States, and also the minimum sentences for third-time burglars and drug dealers introduced in England in 1997, the minimum sentence for possession of a firearm introduced by the Criminal Justice Act 2003, and the 'dangerousness' sentences discussed in Chapter 6.8 below.

---

[66] See ch. 6.7 and 6.8 below.   [67] Ministry of Justice (2010), para. 186.   [68] Greenwood (1982).
[69] Blumstein et al. (1986); see also Zimring and Hawkins (1995).
[70] Kazemian and Farrington (2006).
[71] Halliday (2001), para. 1.68; see the thorough review by Zimring and Hawkins (1995).

Apart from the empirical objections, there is also a principled objection to incapacitative sentencing, which parallels the objection to general deterrent sentencing: individuals are being punished, over and above what they deserve, in the hope of protecting future victims from harm. The moral objection is not merely to sacrificing one offender's liberty in the hope of increasing the future safety of others, but also to doing so on the basis of the offender's membership of a group with a certain probability score.[72] The force of such an objection is particularly strong where the successful prediction rate is low, and yet its high moral content is often submerged by seductive references to increased public protection and public safety. The more difficult question is whether the objection should be given absolute force if a fairly high prediction rate could be achieved. There are some cases where the prison authorities, doctors, and others feel sure that a certain prisoner presents a serious danger to others, in terms of violent or sexual assault. Should the Kantian objection be upheld even if there was an agreed high risk of serious offences? The Floud Committee thought that a just redistribution of risk should result in the prolonged detention of the high-risk offender rather than an increased danger to victims.[73] Some critics of their approach, who would wish to uphold an individual's right not to be punished more than is proportionate to the offence(s) committed, concede that in cases of 'vivid danger' it might be justifiable to lengthen detention for incapacitative purposes.[74] However, the better justification for doing so lies in the realistic prospect of a significant increase in public protection from doing so, rather than by comparing the offender's rights with the rights of potential victims.[75] The point is an important one, because the emphasis of liberal theories on individual rights does not necessarily lead to absolute rights which ignore the social context and the possibility of conflicting rights. Thus, even the staunchest advocate of individual rights might concede that there are exceptional circumstances in which it is the right of the convicted offender which should yield. All this would depend on an acceptably high rate of successful prediction and, even then, since the isolation from the rest of society would be purely on preventive grounds, it is strongly arguable that the detention should not be in a prison but in some form of civil facility.[76]

Practical examples of *collective* incapacitation are the sevenfold increase in the US prison population between 1973 and 2008,[77] and the doubling of the prison population of England and Wales between 1993 and 2011. The strategy is to introduce across-the-board increases in the imposition and length of custodial sentences, designed to reduce offending rates. As Bottoms and von Hirsch argue, there is no doubt that such a strategy has incapacitative effects,

[72] See Feeley and Simon (1974) on the 'new' penology.
[73] Floud and Young (1981), supported by Walker (1982).
[74] Notably Bottoms and Brownsword (1982).   [75] See von Hirsch and Ashworth (2005), ch. 5.
[76] Ashworth and Zedner (2014), ch. 7.
[77] On which see Travis, Western and Redburn (2014), ch. 5.

but their extent is contested, since this depends on assumptions about the frequency of offending. Moreover, the fact that there is an incapacitative effect does not necessarily mean that it is cost effective, either economically or socially (in terms of family disruption and social dislocation).[78] Crude assumptions about collective incapacitation should therefore be avoided.

3.3.4 Rehabilitation[79]

Like deterrence and incapacitation, the rehabilitative rationale for sentencing (sometimes termed 'resocialization') seeks to justify compulsory measures as a means of achieving the prevention of crime, the distinctive method involving the rehabilitation of the offender. This usually requires a range of sentences and facilities designed to offer various programmes of treatment. Sometimes the focus is on the modification of attitudes and of behavioural problems. Sometimes the aim is to provide education or skills, in the belief that these might enable offenders to find occupations other than crime. Thus the crucial questions for the sentencer concern the perceived needs of the offender, not the gravity of the offence committed. The rehabilitative approach is closely linked with those forms of positivist criminology which locate the causes of criminality in individual pathology or individual maladjustment, whether psychiatric, psychological, or social. Whereas deterrence theory regards offenders as rational and calculating, rehabilitative theory is aimed at those who are regarded as being in need of help and support. One key element in determining those needs is a report from an expert – for example, a pre-sentence report prepared by a probation officer or, occasionally, a psychiatric report. In England a diagnostic tool called OASys has been developed to assess offenders.[80] The resulting report will usually advise on the form of programme that matches the perceived needs of the offender, and the court may then make the appropriate order.

In their heyday, the operation of these 'treatment models' often led to sentences that were indeterminate, on the basis that a person should only be released from obligations when, in the opinion of the experts, a cure had been effected. This approach to sentencing reached its zenith in the 1960s, particularly in certain US jurisdictions. The 1970s are often said to have brought the decline of the rehabilitative ideal, but the decline was not terminal and rehabilitative elements have remained throughout. Why did faith in the rehabilitative ideal decline in the 1970s? Two major concerns can be identified. One was the criticism that few of these treatment programmes seemed to be better at preventing reoffending than ordinary, non-treatment sentences. There had been many studies of the effectiveness of particular programmes,

---

[78] Bottoms and von Hirsch (2010).
[79] For fuller discussion and selected readings, see von Hirsch, Ashworth and Roberts (2009), ch. 1; Brooks (2013), ch. 3.
[80] See Merrington (2004).

usually judging them on reconviction rates in subsequent years, and the conclusions of a widely publicized survey of the research by Martinson and others were represented as 'nothing works'.[81] In fact, Martinson disavowed such a totally negative conclusion,[82] and an English survey by Stephen Brody was more circumspect in pointing out that only a limited number of programmes had been tried and properly evaluated.[83] Moreover, it was increasingly recognized that it would be more sensible to look for 'interaction effects' than for overall reductions in reconviction – in other words, there might be sub-groups of offenders for whom a certain kind of treatment has markedly better or markedly worse results, but such effects might not be apparent by looking simply at reconviction rates for all offenders.[84]

The second objection to rehabilitative policies is that they considerably increase the powers of so-called experts and recognize no right in individuals to be regarded as worthy of equal respect and concern. Indeterminate or even semi-determinate sentences place the release of offenders in the hands of prison or probation authorities, usually without firm criteria, clear accountability, or avenues for challenge and reasoned decision-making. There is no question of recognizing an individual's right not to be subjected to compulsory state intervention which is disproportionate to the seriousness of the crime committed. Even if the crime is relatively minor, an offender who is assessed as needing help might be subject to state control for a considerable period. The motivation may be benevolent and 'in the person's best interests'. In effect the individual offender may be regarded more as a manipulable object than as a person with rights.[85]

The rehabilitative rationale has staged a revival in recent years. The response to the second, 'respect for personhood' objection has varied: some recognize that one route to successful rehabilitative programmes is for offenders to develop respect for the moral authority of those (notably probation officers) who are supervising their treatment,[86] whereas others (particularly, it must be said, in government circles) lay greater emphasis on notions of public safety and public interest that demand compliance by the offender within a chiefly punitive framework.[87] The response to the first, 'lack of evidence' objection has been to suggest that the 'meta-analysis' of large numbers of small rehabilitative schemes demonstrates that positive results can be obtained in favourable circumstances. Thus Mackenzie concluded that rehabilitation operates most effectively where there is substantial meaningful contact between treatment officers and participant and where the programmes use behavioural methods to develop skills.[88] Researchers warned of the need to implement schemes

---

[81] Martinson et al. (1974).   [82] Martinson (1979).   [83] Brody (1976).

[84] Early English research into intensive probation (Folkard 1976) did not yield impressive results from this point of view.

[85] See Allen (1981), excerpted in von Hirsch, Ashworth and Roberts (2009), ch. 1.

[86] For discussion see Rex (1998).

[87] E.g. the language pervading the National Standards, discussed in ch. 10 below.

[88] Mackenzie (2006), p. 385; see also McGuire (2002).

strictly if the positive outcomes are to be obtained. Unfortunately the Halliday Report failed to emphasize this sufficiently, and its claim that investment in cognitive-behavioural programmes could reduce offending 'by 5–15 percentage points'[89] was described by Bottoms as 'reckless'.[90] This is not to suggest that rehabilitative programmes should be abandoned, but that a more cautious and measured approach to them should be taken. As Raynor and Robinson concluded, the new rehabilitation movement in Britain 'tried to move too fast, too soon', and detailed evaluations are still awaited.[91]

The continuing support for rehabilitation in England and Wales may be connected with its reinvention as a means of risk management in an era when 'risk' is a buzzword; with the interest in desistance, and in programmes designed to help offenders to define their goals and to use their life skills to achieve them; and with the expressive quality that goes with the emphasis on offenders 'taking responsibility'.[92] Only in recent years has research begun to identify the factors or 'hooks' that help offenders to take steps towards desistance, and to devise community measures capable of responding to the offender's own decision to stop offending.[93]

Therefore, accepting that there are good reasons to devise and to evaluate new programmes, properly resourced and based on sound principles, several questions arise. Do we have rehabilitative programmes which could work for large numbers of offenders? Do we have programmes which could work for smaller numbers, but still significant groups of, offenders whose suitability could be identified in advance? Should these programmes be available to courts, even in cases where the duration of the programme exceeds the proportionate sentence? Even if all these questions are answered in the negative, there may be sound humanitarian reasons for continuing to experiment with rehabilitative programmes for offenders. However, respect for individual rights suggests that the duration of programmes should remain within the bounds set by proportionality,[94] and excessive claims of or targets for 'success in reducing reoffending' should be avoided. We return to these issues in the context of custodial sentences in Chapter 9, and of community programmes in Chapter 10.

3.3.5 Retributivism[95]

Retributivism (sometimes known as desert theory)[96] has various shades and hues. Its leading proponent is undoubtedly Andrew von Hirsch, the author of

---

[89] Halliday (2001), para 1.49.

[90] Bottoms (2004), p. 61; see now Bottoms and von Hirsch (2010), part IIIA.

[91] Raynor and Robinson (2009), p. 136.   [92] Robinson (2008).

[93] See Farrall, Hough, Maruna and Sparks (2011) for discussion and further references.

[94] Rex (1998).

[95] For fuller discussion and readings, see von Hirsch, Ashworth and Roberts (2009), ch. 4; Brooks (2013), chs. 1, 5, and 6.

[96] See Matravers (2010), who draws distinctions between forms of retributivism and desert theory.

the US report *Doing Justice* in 1976 and the writer of several subsequent articles and books.[97] He argues that punishment has two interlocking justifications. One element lies in the intuitive connection between desert and punishment: desert is 'an integral part of everyday judgments of praise and blame',[98] and state punishment institutionalizes this censuring function. Thus, sentences communicate official censure or blame, the communication being chiefly to the offender but also to the victim and society at large. However, censure alone is not enough: the fallibility of human nature makes it necessary to attach a prudential reason to the normative one. Thus, the second justifying element lies in the underlying need for general deterrence: without police, courts, and a penal system 'it seems likely that victimising conduct would become so prevalent as to make life nasty and brutish, indeed'.[99] This preventive element of the rationale is regarded as a (contingent) foundation for the sentencing system, but it does not justify severe penalties: on the contrary, if the punishment were severe, it would 'drown out' the moral quality of the censure.[100]

The essence of modern retributivism is thus that the sentence addresses offenders as moral agents, as having the capacity to assess and to respond to an official evaluation of their conduct. This evaluation is communicated by imposing a proportionate sentence, thereby respecting rule-of-law values (such as certainty and predictability) and placing limitations on state power over offenders. It is evident from this that the concept of proportionality is the touchstone, and two senses of the term must be distinguished. Ordinal proportionality concerns the relative seriousness of offences among themselves. The ordinal ranking of offences is a controversial matter, to which particular attention is devoted in Chapter 4.3 and 4.4 below. Cardinal proportionality relates the ordinal ranking to a scale of punishments, and requires that the penalty should not be out of proportion to the gravity of the crime involved. Different countries have different anchoring points for their penalty scales, often evolved over the years without much conscious reflection and regarded as naturally appropriate. It is sometimes alleged that the rhetoric of desert is likely to lead to greater severity of penalties, but in the jurisdictions that have embraced proportionality theory most fully – Finland, Sweden, and Minnesota – that has certainly not been the outcome. In some other jurisdictions, such as California, substantial increases in penalty levels did follow, but that was chiefly caused by the intrusion of incapacitative sentencing.[101] Leading writers on modern retributivism have insisted on restraint in the use of custody,[102] but in practice the implementation of policies depends on general political trends and judicial attitudes in the jurisdiction concerned.

---

[97] See especially von Hirsch (1993) and von Hirsch and Ashworth (2005).
[98] Von Hirsch (1986), p. 52.   [99] Von Hirsch (1986), p. 48.
[100] See further Narayan (1993); and von Hirsch (1993), ch. 2. Cf. the approach of Duff (2001), below.
[101] For further discussion, see von Hirsch and Ashworth (2005), ch. 6.
[102] Notably von Hirsch, e.g. in (1993), ch. 3.

Critics such as Norval Morris have called for a less prescriptive form of retributivism which recognizes that the concept of proportionality cannot be made sufficiently precise to indicate rankings of offences and punishments.[103] This is 'limiting retributivism', which rules out disproportionately severe and disproportionately lenient sentences but suggests that, within those outer boundaries, other guiding principles ought to determine the form and magnitude of the sanction. Rehabilitative and incapacitative principles would be allowed some space to operate, but there would be emphasis on the principle of penal parsimony.[104] One problem with limiting retributivism is that, since sentences do convey quantities of censure, any imposition of different levels of sentence for similar offences would be interpreted as inconsistent. While limiting retributivists are right to say that levels of cardinal proportionality and the anchoring point for a given punishment scale are contingent and therefore debatable, there is far more scope for principled assessment of ordinal proportionality and comparative offence-seriousness. Divergences at that level may give rise to greater injustices and should be avoided.

A different strain of retributive theory is that developed by Antony Duff.[105] He regards the proportionality principle as central, but the essence of his theory is that sentences are communicative. The punishment forces the offender's attention to the disapproval it conveys. The aim of the punishment is to bring the offender to repent of the wrongdoing, and to provide a means for the offender to 'work through' and express penitence. Punishment therefore has a significant psychological element, and the offender's response to the sentence may be seen as a kind of apology to the community wronged by the offence.[106]

Critics have attacked modern retributivism at various points.[107] It is said to be unsatisfactory to rest such a coercive response, even partly, on the mere intuition that punishment is an appropriate or natural response to offending.[108] Furthermore, exactly what is deserving of blame and punishment – culpable acts or dispositions?[109] It is also said to be unfair to rest desert partly on individual culpability when strong social disadvantages may be at the root of much offending.[110] One answer to this is to recognize grounds for mitigation of sentence for any offender who has suffered significant social deprivation,[111] while maintaining that the unequal distribution of wealth and opportunity in society ought to be tackled by means other than sentencing. Where social injustices are widespread, this 'does not

---

[103] See the restatement by Frase (2013), Introduction and ch. 1.   [104] See also Tonry (1994).
[105] See particularly Duff (2001).
[106] See Duff (2001) for the rich and detailed development of this theory. For some criticisms, see von Hirsch and Ashworth (2005), ch. 7.
[107] See Frase (2013), pp. 107–20.   [108] Cf. Lacey (1988), pp. 21–6, with Moore (1988).
[109] For this and other points, see Walker (1991).
[110] Mathiesen (1990), p. 121; and more broadly Lacey (1988), pp. 18–22.
[111] For the argument that this introduces incoherence into retributive theory, see Norrie (2014), ch. 12.

diminish … the harmfulness of common victimising crimes', although it strengthens the case for reducing overall punishment levels.[112] Critics have also argued that the key concepts of ordinal and cardinal proportionality are too vague and open to divergent interpretations, but this should be regarded as a challenge rather than a barrier.

The reasons for wishing to place principled limits on the state's power to punish are widely accepted. Thus it is significant that the Council of Europe's recommendation on *Consistency in Sentencing* (see part 3.3.1 of this chapter) states:

> A4. Whatever rationales for sentencing are declared, disproportionality between the seriousness of the offence and the sentence should be avoided.[113]

Similarly, Article 49(3) of the Charter of Fundamental Rights of the European Union (2000) declares:

> The severity of penalties must not be disproportionate to the criminal offence.

Likewise, critics of retributivism such as Michael Tonry[114] and Nicola Lacey[115] accept that disproportionate sentences cannot be justified, and therefore commit themselves to some form of desert reasoning. Support for a 'disproportionality' limit underlines the importance of retributivists working towards criteria for ranking offences for the purpose of ordinal proportionality,[116] and towards a principled approach to the awkward question of the relevance of previous convictions to sentence, rationalizing the concessions to first offenders in terms of human frailty and evaluating the relevance of various types of previous record (see Chapter 6.2). Many of the proposals require further refinement, but the strengths of proportionality theory are to be found in its apparent concordance with some widely held moral views, in its respect for the rights of the individual offender, and in its placing of limits on the powers of the state. Thomas Mathiesen has attacked desert theory for the implicit claims of precision and objectivity embodied in terms such as 'commensurate', 'ordinal and cardinal proportionality', 'culpability', and 'offence-seriousness'.[117] A different interpretation would be that it is a belief in the importance of these terms to the justification of punishment, and the concomitant rule-of-law concerns, that continue to motivate desert theorists towards further enquiries on these topics.

3.3.6 Social theories of sentencing

Several contemporary writers are dissatisfied with the tendency of the four 'traditional' theories of punishment, especially retributive theory, to deal with

---

[112] Von Hirsch (1993), pp. 107–8.   [113] Council of Europe (1993), p. 6.   [114] Tonry (1994).
[115] See part 3.3.6 below.   [116] See ch. 4.3 below.   [117] Mathiesen (1990), ch. 5 and *passim.*

sentencing in isolation from its wider social and political setting. Various theories are being developed which attempt to make the approach to sentencing more responsive to social conditions and community expectations. Three examples of this tendency may be described briefly.

In her work Barbara Hudson insisted that priority should be given to crime prevention and to reducing the use of custody by the penal system. Changes in social policy relating to employment, education, housing, and leisure facilities are far more important to justice than narrow debates about proportionality of sentence. And when it comes to sentencing, there should be greater concern with 'the problems of whole human beings' rather than with particular pieces of behaviour: the state should not 'privilege events over people' and should place more emphasis on the provision of rehabilitative opportunities. However, such developments at the sentencing stage should take place within a framework set by proportionality theory.[118]

Nicola Lacey likewise argues that the first step must be the state's recognition of its duty to foster a sense of community by providing proper facilities and fair opportunities for all citizens. Once this has been achieved in a community, punishment is justified as reinforcing the values that it has been decided will be protected through criminal law. The proportionality principle would remain important in sentencing, but so would the conflicting value of promoting the welfare of the community. Lacey disagrees both with desert theorists and with preventionists in their insistence on assigning general priority to a single value: for her, while the core of each value must be preserved, compromises have to be negotiated separately and sensitively, with due attention to the avoidance of gender and racial bias. However, Lacey recognizes that community determinations of these issues raise further questions of limits and of enforcement, and that vigilance must be maintained in order to ensure that 'community-based' arrangements remain inclusive and do not produce new forms of social exclusion.[119]

John Braithwaite and Phillip Pettit develop what they term a republican theory of criminal justice. Its central value is dominion, defined in terms of each citizen's ability to make life choices, within a social and political framework which each citizen has participated in shaping, and then to be protected in those choices. In its responses to offending, the criminal justice system should take the approach of minimum intervention, but may pursue policies of prevention through sentencing where appropriate. Proportionality of sentence is not a primary concern. Indeed, republican theory would decouple censure from sentencing. Censure might be achieved more effectively by shaming and other forms of social reaction, and a particular sentence might be lower if the prospects for shaming seemed good. Otherwise, while the authors gesture vaguely towards upper limits of proportionality, they seem

[118] E.g. Hudson (1995).   [119] Lacey (1998).

to accept that substantial sentences based on predictive and preventive rationales might be acceptable.[120]

These thumbnail sketches of complex theories should serve at least to demonstrate the continuing vitality of debate about the proper aims of sentencing. Moreover, even within a proportionalist framework, these concerns should be and can be taken seriously.[121] As with all the theories outlined in this chapter, it is necessary to go to the original texts in order to acquire an appreciation of the precise steps by which both theories and critiques are constructed. What is characteristic of theories that emphasize the social context of offending is that, to various extents, they assign greater importance to reducing overall levels of penalty and to removing wider social inequalities than to the relative fairness of individual sentences.

3.3.7 Restoration and reparation[122]

One of the major developments in criminal justice in the final quarter of the last century was the increasing recognition of the rights and needs of the victims of crime. This was clearly signalled by the United Nations in its *Declaration on the Basic Principles of Justice for Victims and Abuse of Power* in 1985, and in the government's *Victim's Charter* in 1990.[123] It has also been manifest in at least two different ways in sentencing theory. One is the increased attention to victims' rights in the criminal justice system, including the granting of the right to victims to make a statement to the court about the offence.[124] The second development will be the focus here – the growing number of restorative theories of criminal justice. The fundamental proposition is that justice to victims should become a central goal of the criminal justice system and of sentencing. This means that all the 'stakeholders' in the offence (the offender and the victim, their families, and the community) should become involved in discussions about the appropriate response to the offence. The aim would be to bring about an apology, to ensure that the offender compensates the victim and the wider community for the effects of the crime, and to take steps to ensure that the offence is not repeated. Thus, as Lucia Zedner puts it,

> criminal justice should be less preoccupied with censuring code-breakers and focus instead on the process of restoring individual damage and repairing ruptured social bonds. In place of meeting pain with the infliction of further pain, a truly reparative system would seek the holistic restoration of the

---

[120] Braithwaite and Pettit (1990); cf. Dagger (2008).   [121] See Lippke (2007), ch. 4.

[122] For fuller discussion, see von Hirsch, Ashworth and Roberts (2009), ch. 5; see also Dignan (2005), and Hoyle and Cuneen (2009).

[123] See now the Domestic Violence, Crime and Victims Act 2004, Part 3.

[124] *Practice Direction (Criminal Proceedings: Consolidation)* Part III.28 (2013). Some jurisdictions go further and permit victims to make submissions on sentence: see further ch. 13.7 below.

community. It would necessarily also challenge the claim of the state to respond to crime and would instead invite (or perhaps demand) the involvement of the community in the process of restoration.[125]

A considerable number of schemes of restorative justice are in place in different parts of the world. The first major initiative was that introduced in New Zealand by the Children, Young Persons and their Families Act 1989: young offenders are dealt with in 'family group conferences', in which a group including the victim and the offender and their families, together with a community representative as facilitator, formulate a plan for responding to the offence.[126] The best-known scheme in Australia was RISE in Canberra, in which persons charged with four types of offence (violence, property, shop theft, drunk-driving) were randomly allocated to court or to restorative justice. Interpretation of the results is problematic,[127] but it is claimed that victims who went to restorative justice conferences were much more satisfied with the procedure, and it appears that only violent offenders were less likely to reoffend following restorative justice, and not those who committed one of the other three types of offence.

Several restorative justice initiatives have begun in this country: a scheme of restorative cautioning started by Thames Valley police has spread to other areas,[128] and three schemes designed to include both adults and serious offences have been running for several years (previous schemes were limited to juveniles and non-serious offences).[129] However, assessing the research on restorative justice practices across Europe (including England and Wales), Carolyn Hoyle concludes that 'on current evidence it is far from clear that restorative justice is principally about victims'.[130] There is an abiding interest in its potential for reducing reoffending: thus Robinson and Shapland found that offenders who took part in restorative justice were significantly less likely to reoffend within two years, and they argue that restorative conferencing can facilitate or consolidate an offender's decision to desist from offending.[131]

Restorative justice has considerable attractions as a constructive and socially inclusive way of responding to criminal behaviour. But there remain various problems of principle which trouble critics.[132] One is to determine the objectives of restorative justice: many statements suggest that it can lead to the healing of victims, restore the community, and reduce reoffending, but there is no evidence that it can do all these things satisfactorily, and it seems likely that a focus on one may not enhance others. Moreover, the concept of restoring the community remains shrouded in mystery, as indeed does the identification of the relevant 'community'. If restorative justice is to be used for non-minor offences, then it is problematic to allow the victim and/or the victim's family to play a part in

---

[125] Zedner (1994), p. 233.   [126] See Morris (2002).   [127] E.g. Kurki (2001).
[128] See Hoyle and Young (2003).   [129] See Robinson and Shapland (2008).
[130] Hoyle (2012), p. 418.   [131] Ibid.
[132] For an enumeration of, and reply to, criticisms, see Morris (2002).

determining the response. In principle, such determinations should be made by an independent and impartial tribunal, and it is unconvincing to argue that offenders 'consent' to restorative processes in view of the pressures upon them.[133] If restorative justice is to be used, then at least there should be limits to the powers of conferences so as to ensure that proportionality constraints are not breached.[134] Advocates of restorative justice often complain that all these safeguards are unnecessary and that restorative justice is a positive experience which does not involve severity. However, the experience with rehabilitation in the 1960s warns of the dangers that the claims of enthusiasts might run ahead of the evidence and that the amount of control and coercion exerted over offenders might go beyond what is deserved for the offence.

3.3.8 The argument against s. 142 of the 2003 Act

We saw in 3.3.1 above that in English law s. 142 of the Criminal Justice Act 2003 requires courts, when sentencing an offender, to have regard to five purposes of sentencing. Two criticisms of s. 142 were put forward at that stage – that such an apparently unbridled discretion to select a rationale for sentencing is inconsistent with the requirements of the rule of law, and that it is manifestly inconsistent with a system of sentencing guidelines that requires courts to follow the guidelines (which are based on proportionality). To those criticisms we now add two further difficulties – that there are strong arguments of principle against some of the declared purposes, and that some of the declared purposes are not supported by empirical findings. For example, it has been argued that there are weaknesses of both kinds (principle, and empirical support) in the rationales of individual deterrence and general deterrence, and also in the rationale of incapacitation; and yet those rationales are the ones most frequently cited by legislators and judges. In view of the weight of criticisms of legislative declarations such as s. 142 (and its equivalent in other countries), it can be argued that they serve no useful purpose and should be abolished. Indeed, one can go further and argue that such declarations are confusing and unhelpful, inasmuch as they proceed without apparent awareness of the deficiencies of principle and of evidence affecting some of the declared purposes. Open debate, based on principle and on empirical evidence, should replace high-sounding but ultimately vacuous legislative statements.

3.4 Some principles and policies

The task of assessing the justifications for sentences and the sentencing system is not merely a matter of considering overall or ultimate aims. A number of discrete principles and policies may also have a normative claim on either

---

[133] See further Ashworth (2002b).
[134] On this and other matters, see von Hirsch and Ashworth (2005), ch. 9.

general sentencing policy or individual sentencing decisions. It would be extravagant to suggest that there is a settled core of these principles and policies, which can be drawn together and put forward as a coherent group. The reality is that they form a fluctuating body at different stages in penal history, and are invoked selectively as the tides of penal politics ebb and flow. The penal system may be regarded as one of the institutions of society (along with the family, religion, the armed forces, etc.), and in this context sentencing is an institution for the expression of social values as well as an instrumental means to a clinical penological end. An awareness of this wider context

> makes it easier to argue that the pursuit of values such as justice, humanity, tolerance, decency, humanity and civility should be part of any penal institution's self-consciousness – an intrinsic and constitutive aspect of its role – rather than a diversion from its 'real' goals or an inhibition on its capacity to be 'effective'.[135]

What might these values be, and how might they be expressed? Some attempt is made below to give brief descriptions of six principles and policies which have some contemporary relevance – the first by virtue of legal authority, the others on moral, social and political grounds. Clearly, they may conflict among themselves; each one has an element of indeterminacy; and some of them raise as many questions as they solve. Nonetheless, they may have a certain normative force and are therefore worth exploring.

3.4.1 The principle of respect for rule-of-law values and fundamental rights

This is a principle with both formal-procedural and substantive implications. In its purest form the rule of law may be taken to require 'rules which are fixed, knowable and certain':[136] however, there are limits on the extent to which certainty of definition can be required, and there are powerful arguments of justice for the preservation of some discretion in the sentencing process. Rule-of-law principles can claim to enhance liberty and reduce arbitrariness in the exercise of state power, but few would advocate the purest form of the rule of law and therefore there is much debate about the proper extent of discretion. Turning to respect for fundamental rights, this is now a matter of positive law in the United Kingdom, as well as one of international obligation. Thus the Human Rights Act 1998 requires all public authorities (including the courts, prosecutors, prison authorities, and so forth) to act in accordance with the rights set out in the European Convention on Human Rights. Relatively few of these rights impinge on the sentencing process, as we noted in Chapter 2.7 above, but they have a powerful effect when they do so. As a matter of principle, both the courts and the legislature should ensure that those rights are respected and not sidestepped or marginalized in the sentencing process.

---

[135] Garland (1990), pp. 291–2.   [136] Raz (1979), pp. 214–15.

3.4.2 The principle of restraint in the use of custody

In recognition that imprisonment is a severe deprivation of normal rights, there has been widespread formal acceptance that it should be used with restraint. Draft Resolution VIII of the Eighth United Nations Congress on the Prevention of Crime and the Treatment of Offenders recommended that 'imprisonment should be used as a sanction of last resort',[137] and the Council of Europe had also adopted a similar policy some years earlier when advocating the wider use of non-custodial sanctions.[138] But these formal statements largely disappeared from view in the closing decade of the twentieth century and the first decade of the twenty-first, with burgeoning prison populations in many countries, notably in the United States and latterly in England and Wales. Thus whereas a White Paper in 1990 had described prisons as 'an expensive way of making bad people worse',[139] and the principle of restraint had also been advocated strongly by the Woolf Inquiry into the prison disturbances of 1990,[140] the arrival of Michael Howard as Home Secretary in 1993 changed both the language and the substance of the official approach. Howard declared that 'prison works', and urged sentencers to make greater use of custody. In the following years the judiciary and magistracy found themselves unable to resist the political and media pressure for higher sentences, as Lord Bingham CJ subsequently admitted.[141] The change of government in 1997 brought no abatement of the punitive rhetoric from ministers, particularly in the years when David Blunkett was Home Secretary (2001–2004), but punitive rhetoric has been less prominent (although not entirely absent) in the coalition government since 2010.

Since the millennium it is fair to say that this 'populist punitiveness',[142] while often maintained in government publicity, has not been unmitigated. Detailed policies and pronouncements yield evidence of other concerns. The Criminal Justice Act 2003 had some reductivist aspects – tighter language on the threshold for custody, tighter language on the length of custody[143] – and the format of the sentencing guidelines since 2004 has included these requirements in the decision processes through which the courts must go before they decide to impose a custodial sentence.[144] The principle of restraint in the use of custody goes further than this. It emphasizes not just the deprivation of the core right to liberty, but also the high human and economic costs of imprisonment and its lack of effectiveness in preventing reconviction.[145] The principle

---

[137] United Nations (1990), para. 5(e).   [138] Council of Europe (1976), Res. 10.

[139] Home Office (1990), para. 2.7.   [140] Woolf (1991), discussed in ch. 9.1 below.

[141] 'Since 1993 the use of custody has increased very sharply, in response (it would seem likely) to certain highly publicized crimes, legislation, ministerial speeches and intense media pressure': *Brewster* [1998] 1 Cr App R (S) 181, at p. 184.

[142] The term coined by Bottoms (1995).   [143] See ch. 1.5 above.

[144] Sentencing Guidelines Council, *Overarching Principles: Seriousness* (2004), Part E.

[145] Nagin, Cullen and Jonson (2009); Durlauf and Nagin (2011), and Travis, Western and Redburn (2014), ch. 5.

therefore points in the direction of imposing fewer prison sentences, and making them shorter, than has recently become the norm in this country. Moreover, it also points to a rethinking of prison regimes so that they respect prisoners' rights and 'normalize' their lives so far as possible.[146]

3.4.3 The principle of parsimony

On the basis that all punishment is pain and ought therefore to be avoided or minimized where possible, Bentham argued for a principle of frugality in punishment:[147] in all cases the lowest sufficient punishment should be chosen. Norval Morris developed a similar principle of parsimony,[148] and this is urged in current debate by Michael Tonry.[149] It is, in effect, a more generalized version of the principle of restraint in the use of custody. What is not always clear is the level at which proponents are urging the principle. It could be regarded as a principle applicable to policy-makers – a broader version of the principle of restraint in the use of custody, perhaps phrased in terms of minimum intervention. This would recognize the punitive effects of the criminal process and publicity on many offenders, and would argue for the greater prominence of diversionary measures for less serious forms of crime. It would also support the approach of reserving community penalties for cases that are too serious for a fine or conditional discharge, an approach implicit in the Criminal Justice Act 2003. A more thoroughgoing 'decremental strategy' would involve a progressive reduction in penalty levels over time.[150]

Alternatively, or even additionally, the principle of parsimony could be regarded as a principle for the sentencer in individual cases. The question is how far this should be taken, if the court has two cases before it – both offences of stealing, one by a person of lowly status (e.g. from a 'criminal' family or neighbourhood), the other by a citizen whose background leads the court to believe it unlikely that he will ever offend again. If the court gives a lesser punishment to the second one, it may be following the principle of parsimony, but would this be fair? It would certainly breach the principle of equality before the law (below). The same would apply if the court gave a lesser punishment to an employed offender than to an unemployed offender, on the basis that it would be unfortunate if the former were to lose a job, bringing hardship to the family and so on. It is argued in Chapter 7 below that, while the principle of parsimony ought to be pursued at the general or legislative level, the principle of equality before the law should prevail in individual sentencing decisions. But Morris and Tonry decry this as producing 'equality of misery', and advocate the principle of parsimony in individual sentencing decisions too.[151]

---

[146] See e.g. Lippke (2007), Liebling and Crewe (2012).   [147] Bentham (1789), ch. xv, para. 11.
[148] Morris (1974).   [149] See e.g. Tonry (1994).
[150] See Braithwaite and Pettit (1990), and von Hirsch (1993), ch. 5.
[151] Morris and Tonry (1990), discussed in ch. 7.7 below.

3.4.4 Managerialism and the policy of controlling public expenditure

Governments always have an eye to public expenditure, but in the first decade of this century there was little evidence that economic constraints were a reason for controlling the prison population (as distinct from cutting the costs of running prisons). The government's 2008 review required the Ministry of Justice to 'make ambitious efficiency savings' and 'to achieve our goals with fewer resources',[152] not to reduce the numbers imprisoned or the length of their sentences. Indeed, the prison population rose to a record 88,179 in 2011, one year after the election of the coalition government, although it has fallen back since then. It is notable that the Sentencing Guidelines Council was required to have regard, when framing sentencing guidelines, to 'the cost of different sentences and their relative effectiveness in preventing reoffending',[153] and the Sentencing Council is likewise required to have regard to the cost and relative effectiveness of sentences, although there is little evidence that this is taken seriously.[154] No such requirements are imposed on government ministers; indeed, when the Labour government commissioned inquiries into the effectiveness of imprisonment and other penal measures,[155] it showed little interest in the consistent findings that the burgeoning custodial population was wasteful on so many grounds. Cost-effectiveness appears to be a low priority, despite the wider economic situation.

3.4.5 The principle of equality before the law

This is the principle that sentencing decisions should treat offenders equally, irrespective of their wealth, race, colour, sex, abilities, or employment or family status. English law now makes it a statutory aggravating factor if an offence is motivated or accompanied by hostility based on race, religion, sexual orientation, or disability.[156] More longstanding are the precedents stating that offenders with wealth should not be allowed to 'buy themselves out of prison' by paying large fines or compensation.[157] This principle of equality hardly needs justification, for it is surely unjust that people should be penalized at the sentencing stage for any of these reasons. Yet in practice there are difficulties. As we shall see in Chapter 7, there is evidence of discrimination according to wealth, some evidence of race and sex discrimination in certain respects, and clear evidence of discrimination on grounds of employment status. The last is a peculiarly difficult issue: courts often try to pass a sentence which ensures

---

[152] Ministry of Justice (2008), p. 5.   [153] Criminal Justice Act 2003, s. 170(5)(c).

[154] Coroners and Justice Act 2009, s. 120(11); s. 127 requires the Council to publish a resource assessment of each new guideline.

[155] See Moxon (1998), and also von Hirsch et al. (1999) for the Cambridge study of deterrence, carried out for the Home Office.

[156] Criminal Justice Act 2003, ss. 145–146.

[157] See *Markwick* (1953) 37 Cr App R 125 and other decisions discussed in ch. 7.5 below.

that a person who has a job is able to keep it, although the implication is that unemployed offenders are discriminated against, since that source of sentence reduction is not open to them. This leads into the question, already discussed in parts 3.3.5 and 3.3.6 of this chapter, of whether it is right to speak of 'just' or 'fair' sentences in a society riven with inequality.

3.4.6 The principle of equal impact

This principle argues that sentences should be so calculated as to impose an equal impact on the offenders subjected to them. Or, to phrase the principle negatively, the system should strive to avoid grossly unequal impacts on offenders with differing resources and sensitivities, because that would be unjust. The most obvious application of the principle is to fines, which ought to be adjusted to reflect the different financial resources of different offenders.[158] Another application may be to imprisonment for offenders who have some special mental or medical condition which may make custody significantly more painful,[159] although there may be an alternative justification based on compassion rather than equality of impact of sanctions.[160] Many of the questions raised by the principle of equal impact are discussed further in Chapter 7 below, where the problems of integrating it into a system of proportionate sentencing are examined.

3.5 Sentencing rationales in practice: deterrence

At the end of 3.3.8 it was argued that in practice some of the rationales for sentencing are used without reference to, and without apparent awareness of, their weaknesses in theory and in terms of evidence. This tendency is most obvious in relation to general deterrence, and examples of this are discussed in the paragraphs that follow.

3.5.1 General deterrence and mandatory minimum sentences

The sentence for murder in English law has been a mandatory sentence of life imprisonment, since capital punishment was abolished in 1965. Another longstanding mandatory sentence has been the minimum of 12 months' disqualification from driving, imposed (unless special reasons are found) on conviction for driving with excess alcohol. In recent years, however, governments have introduced several mandatory minimum sentences into English law. Prescribed minimum sentences relate only to offenders with previous convictions, and they will be analysed in Chapter 6.7 below. Mandatory

---

[158] See ch. 7.5 below for discussion.   [159] See Ashworth and Player (1998).
[160] Cf. von Hirsch and Ashworth (2005), App. C.

minimum sentences relate to the commission of a particular offence, irrespective of the presence or absence of previous convictions, and they are
discussed here.

The first of three prominent examples is the mandatory minimum sentence
of 5 years' imprisonment, unless exceptional circumstances are found, for
possession of a prohibited firearm or ammunition contrary to s. 51A of the
Firearms Act 1968 (inserted by the Criminal Justice Act 2003). A second
example is the offence of using someone to mind a dangerous weapon,
contrary to s. 29 of the Violent Crime Reduction Act 2006: this carries a
mandatory minimum sentence of 5 years (unless exceptional circumstances
are found) where the dangerous weapon is a prohibited firearm. A third
example is the offence of threatening another person with a knife or offensive
weapon, introduced by s. 142 of the Legal Aid, Sentencing and Punishment of
Offenders Act 2012 and carrying a minimum sentence of 6 months' imprisonment unless the court finds that it is unjust to impose that sentence.

While the last example contains considerable flexibility in the 'unjust to do
so' clause,[161] the first two examples only permit the court to go below the
minimum sentence in exceptional circumstances. The Court of Appeal has
noted the injustice that this may perpetrate in some cases, but has generally
kept faith with parliamentary intentions. The leading case on the s. 51A
firearms minimum is *Rehman and Wood* (2006),[162] where Lord Woolf CJ
began by affirming that Parliament intended deterrent sentences to be
imposed for these offences, to send out the message that the mere possession
of firearms can create dangers to the public. However, Lord Woolf insisted
that s. 51A should not be allowed to require a court to impose a sentence that
is 'arbitrary or disproportionate,' in human rights terms.[163] The proviso for
'exceptional circumstances relating to the offence or to the offender' is to be
interpreted in conformity with this human rights restriction. Thus Lord Woolf
noted that 'if an offender has no idea he is doing anything wrong, a deterrent
sentence will have no deterrent effect on him'. Thus ignorance of the law, a
feature of several cases, will usually be treated as an 'exceptional circumstance',[164] and personal factors such as old age or threats just short of duress
could also be so treated.[165] It is not necessary to find a single exceptional
circumstance: the cumulative effect of several mitigating factors (other than a
plea of guilty, which is not included) may suffice.[166] However, cases involving
exceptional circumstances seem to be relatively rare.[167]

---

[161] Lord Thomas CJ gave guidance on this in *Gomes Monteiro* [2014] 2 Cr App R (S) 483.
[162] [2006] 1 Cr App R (S) 404.
[163] Contrary to Articles 3 and 5 of the European Convention, as discussed in ch. 2.6 above.
[164] This was true of Rehman but not of Wood; see also *Ramzan* [2013] 2 Cr App R (S) 221.
[165] On threats, and related factors, see *Jones* [2012] 1 Cr App R (S) 151.
[166] *Jones*, ibid., applying *Rehman and Wood*, above n. 162.
[167] For examples of the minimum term being upheld, see *Wood*, ibid.; *Ocran* [2011] 1 Cr App
R (S) 223; *Attorney General's Reference No. 82 of 2012* [2013] 2 Cr App R (S) 406.

Can minimum sentences of this kind be justified? The usual justifications offered for minimum sentences are that they are transparent, even-handed, and deter people through the certainty of punishment they declare.[168] Each of these claims is dubious. The minimum sentence itself is transparent, but prosecutors may decide to bring a different charge and therefore considerable discretion is hidden by the decision to prosecute.[169] The claim that minimum sentences are even-handed means that they deal in the same way with substantially different cases: the absence of discretion produces injustice as well as a relatively valueless form of even-handedness. As for the deterrence claim, there is simply no supporting evidence on this. The most-researched minimum sentence regime is probably the Californian 'three strikes' law, and even the Californian legislature eventually recognized the clarity of the research findings of 'no effect'.[170] If English politicians claim deterrence as a justification for minimum sentences, therefore, they have no supporting English evidence and the international consensus goes against them.

3.5.2 General deterrence and the judiciary

The judiciary has had a long and ambivalent relationship with general deterrence as a sentencing aim. We saw in 2.3 above that, when the government first proposed to introduce mandatory minimum sentences in 1996, senior judges were swift to condemn the reliance of that policy on deterrence. Lord Taylor CJ argued, on grounds that many criminologists would recognize, that general deterrence may work through increasing the probability of being caught, but that the evidence of its effectiveness by raising the level of sentences was 'flimsy and dubious'.[171] This attack on the general deterrent premise of mandatory minimum sentences should be contrasted with the same judge's insistence that Parliament could not have intended to remove statutory authority from deterrent sentencing. Lord Taylor therefore (mis) interpreted s. 2(2)(a) of the 1991 Act as follows:

> The purposes of a custodial sentence must primarily be to punish and to deter. Accordingly, the phrase 'commensurate with the seriousness of the offence' must mean commensurate with the punishment and deterrence which the seriousness of the offence requires.[172]

This flagrant misreading of the statute – as is obvious from the White Paper that preceded the 1991 Act[173] – opened the way for the judges to continue to rely on general deterrent reasoning as a justification for some sentences, even

---

[168] See the leading article by Tonry (2009).

[169] See the discussion of s. 51A (minimum sentence) and s. 51B (no minimum sentence) in *Brereton* [2010] 2 Cr App R (S) 397 and *Ramzan* [2013] 2 Cr App R (S) 221.

[170] Tonry (2009), pp. 90–100.   [171] Taylor (1996): see ch. 2, nn. 45–6 and accompanying text.

[172] (1993) 14 Cr App R (S) 444 at p. 447.   [173] Home Office (1990), para. 2.8.

though the evidence in favour of its effectiveness is as 'flimsy and dubious' as Lord Taylor himself declared.

The judicial penchant for relying on deterrent reasoning, without reference to the principled objections and lack of empirical evidence (see 3.3.2 above), continues to this day. It was a major feature of the judgment of Lord Judge CJ in the English riots case of *Blackshaw*,[174] it is prominent in major cases involving firearms,[175] and it is also stated to be a reason in favour of insisting on imprisonment as a response to perverting the course of justice and kindred offences,[176] counterfeiting goods,[177] and passport offences.[178] However, there is an argument that the use of the language of deterrence does not actually mean that courts are adding a deterrent premium to the proportionate sentence. Some offences are so serious that they justify a substantial sentence on retributive grounds (e.g. serious offences involving violence or sexual assault), and the judge might refer to deterrence because there is a strong societal interest in reducing the numbers of such offences, without implying that the sentence is longer than would be proportionate.[179] This possible reading is supported by the judicial remarks in some serious cases, where the judge has identified five or six aggravating factors and then says that a deterrent sentence is called for.[180] Similarly, the appearance of 'deterrence' in the Council's guideline on environmental offences is rather obscure ('the objectives of punishment, deterrence and removal of gain'), in terms of whether it authorizes a court to go above the proportionate sentence.[181]

As noted in Chapter 2.3, Parliament passed a section in the Criminal Justice and Immigration Act 2008 that would have restated the purposes of sentencing for offenders under 18 without including deterrence. That section was not brought into force when the other sections relating to sentencing young offenders were implemented, largely (it seems) because the judiciary insisted on preserving deterrence as a rationale for sentencing young offenders in certain exceptional cases. Counsel argued against the imposition of a deterrent sentence on a 16-year-old in *Hagan* (2013),[182] but in the absence of an active statutory provision the Court of Appeal was able to rely on older common law authorities to justify this.

Since the argument here is that the judiciary has long been attached to the idea of deterrent sentencing, it is apposite to raise questions about a related

---

[174] [2012] 1 Cr App R (S) 679, above, n. 57.

[175] *Hagan* [2013] 1 Cr App R (S) 483, at [11–12]; *Cardwell* [2013] 2 Cr App R (S) 284, at [22–23].

[176] E.g. *Dittman and Anderson* [2013] 1 Cr App R (S) 113.

[177] *Wooldridge* [2006] 1 Cr App R (S) 72.

[178] *Attorney General's References Nos. 1 and 6 of 2008* [2008] 2 Cr App R (S) 557.

[179] See the interesting New Zealand discussion in *Graham* v. *R.* [2014] NZSC 55.

[180] E.g. *Howard* [2013] 1 Cr App R (S) 405 (armed robbery of corner shop), *Ekajeh* [2013] 2 Cr App R (S) 291 (identity fraud by employee), *Kasprzak* [2014] 1 Cr App R (S) 115, at [15].

[181] Sentencing Council, *Environmental Offences: Definitive Guideline* (2014), pp. 12, 18, and 21.

[182] [2013] 1 Cr App R (S) 483.

judicial favourite – the prevalence of the offence. Over the years courts have occasionally regarded the prevalence of an offence as a general reason for increasing sentence levels for it, but that is open to at least two major objections: there is rarely any firm evidence of prevalence, and if prevalence really were a key factor in sentencing, this would have the absurd consequence that theft from shops (and even illegal parking) would be projected sharply up the tariff.[183] The Sentencing Guidelines Council sought to lay down guidance on the use of the concept of prevalence to increase a sentence. In general, it states that sentences should not be increased on account of beliefs about the prevalence of a particular type of offence. But in 'exceptional local circumstances', and where there is 'supporting evidence from an external source' about the offence's prevalence, a court may impose a higher sentence than is proportionate to the seriousness of the offence. However, this would be 'exceptional', and 'sentencers must sentence within the sentencing guidelines once the prevalence has been addressed'.[184] This is a strong and restrictive guideline, and the Court of Appeal has insisted that the supporting evidence of prevalence should be detailed before the sentence can include an element of deterrence.[185] Thus it seems that considerations of prevalence are most likely to be raised where the offence is otherwise of low or moderate seriousness, whereas general deterrence itself is more usually cited in sentencing for serious offences.

3.6 The role of public opinion

The emphasis in this chapter has so far been on rationales for sentencing, considered from the points of view of principle and of evidential support. In practice, however, many decisions by governments on sentencing policy have tended to be based on a conception of 'public opinion'. What Bottoms has termed 'populist punitiveness' – i.e. politicians attempting to justify penal initiatives by reference to what they believe to be public opinion[186] – has played a major role in recent changes in English sentencing, mandatory minimum sentences (3.5.1 above) and the increased use of imprisonment (3.4.2 above) being two strong examples. A similar phenomenon has been observed in several other jurisdictions.[187]

In times when 'democracy' is widely regarded as a virtue, this prominence of 'public opinion' might appear to be a step in the right direction. But before any conclusions of that kind are drawn, it is necessary to assess exactly what is

---

[183] A fine judgment by Lloyd LJ in the Court of Appeal in *Masagh* (1990) 12 Cr App R (S) 568 spelt out these objections very clearly, but sadly it appears not to have lessened judicial references to the concept.

[184] SGC, *Overarching Principles: Seriousness* (2004), paras. 1.38–1.39.

[185] See e.g. *Oosthuizen* [2006] 1 Cr App R (S) 385, *Lanham and Willis* [2009] 1 Cr App R (S) 592, and *Moss* [2011] 1 Cr App R (S) 199, at [12].

[186] Bottoms (1995), p. 40.   [187] Pratt (2007).

being proposed. What counts as public opinion? If that question can be resolved satisfactorily, in what way should public opinion be streamed into sentencing? As for the first question, some invocations of 'public opinion' may simply be cynical calculations of what will win votes or what will gain support in the media. If we take the concept of 'public opinion' seriously on its own terms, there is an immediate problem. Research demonstrates that public knowledge of crime trends and of sentencing practices is generally low.[188] Not only is there little value in asking random members of the public broad questions such as whether sentencing is too harsh, too soft, or about right; but, even if a more targeted question is put, public attitudes will often be based on misconceptions, and they are therefore not a sound basis for influencing policy. Studies also demonstrate that it is possible to change attitudes by supplying information,[189] although how one could achieve this for the public at large (rather than for groups of people recruited for research purposes) is more problematic. However, it would be possible to assemble representative focus groups, to give them information about criminal justice and then to find out their opinions on possible policy options.

Assuming that a suitably informed 'public opinion' can be mobilised, for what purposes could it be used?[190] It could be one method of ascertaining crime seriousness rankings, which are an important element in any proportionality-based sentencing system, and they are considered in Chapter 4.2 below. It could also be a means of considering appropriate sentence levels for various forms of crime, and for considering whether particular factors should be accepted as mitigating or as aggravating. On these latter issues, an appropriate research methodology would also make it possible to discover the reasoning that underpins particular public attitudes. Paul Robinson is a strong advocate of what he terms 'empirical desert', i.e. a proportionality-based system that is informed by public assessments of offence seriousness and of sanction severity, and he claims that its closeness to public opinion would enhance the perceived legitimacy of the sentencing system.[191] Whether sufficient evidence could be assembled, and whether Robinson's various exceptions would reduce the claimed gains of legitimacy, are matters that require further debate.[192]

If well-informed opinions on key sentencing issues could be obtained, what would be the most appropriate ways of acting on them? The Sentencing Council (and formerly the Sentencing Advisory Panel) use relevant findings on public opinion to inform their development of sentencing guidelines. This is not to say that they have always adopted all the findings, but rather that informed public opinion and the reasoning on which it is based flow into the

---

[188] Hough and Roberts (2012), pp. 280–3.   [189] Hough and Roberts (2012), pp. 287–9.
[190] For extensive consideration of these issues, see the essays in Ryberg and Roberts (2014).
[191] Robinson (2008), relying in part on Tyler (2006).
[192] For critique and references, see Frase (2013), pp. 95–100, and Roberts (2011), pp. 110–12.

Council's discussions prior to the drafting of a guideline. This gives rise to two issues. First, the 'public opinion' on which reliance is being placed here is not a broad public or community view but rather the view of a small representative group to whom accurate information has been supplied. The upshot may still be unwelcome to the public in general, who are destined to remain relatively uninformed.[193] Secondly, it will be important to assess how the Council deals with the results of its own public opinion survey when it comes to draft a new guideline on sentence reduction for pleading guilty. This is a sensitive issue among politicians and among judges, and how much weight is assigned to any public opinion that does not accord with judicial opinion will constitute a stern test. As Julian Roberts argues:

> According to this model, sentencing policies do not simply track public opinion – the consequence would be unprincipled sentencing. However, when a specific policy or practice is clearly at odds with community values, this inconsistency should at the very least provoke an inquiry into the nature of these views, and possible modification of sentencing practice.[194]

The argument, therefore, is that informed public opinion should be regarded not as a trump card but simply as a significant factor in debate, the degree of significance being the crucial variable.

3.7 Conclusions

We saw in 3.2 above that English law, like that of some other jurisdictions, sets out a menu of 'purposes of sentencing'. This approach appears naïve, in that it pays no attention to the objections of principle and the deficiencies of evidential support that bedevil some of the listed purposes, as we saw in 3.3 Indeed, the sentencing purpose that many politicians and judges regard as particularly important is deterrence (on which see 3.5), probably the most contestable of the sentencing purposes. While this chapter has recognized that deterrence, public protection and conceptions of 'public opinion' drive some sentencing policies, the emphasis here has been placed on examining the principled and evidential foundations of the sentencing system. This task will be continued through subsequent chapters.

---

[193] De Keijser (2014).   [194] Roberts (2011), p. 121.

4

Elements of proportionality

Contents

This chapter investigates the practical application of the proportionality principle in English sentencing. After examining the relevant statutory provisions, we begin an exploration of the concept of proportionality in practice and in theory. Part 4.2 considers people's opinions about the relative seriousness of different offences, and part 4.3 discusses a possible theoretical framework for determining questions of offence-seriousness. Part 4.4 relates this framework to a selection of English offences: most of these are now the subject of guidelines, and one question will be how the guideline structure interprets proportionality. In part 4.5 we consider the variations in culpability, and part 4.6 presents some provisional conclusions on the elements of proportionality.

4.1 The proportionality principle

In 1990 the Home Office left no doubt that the intention behind the reforms which became the Criminal Justice Act 1991 was to introduce 'a new legislative framework for sentencing, based on the seriousness of the offence or just deserts'.[1] Arguing that both rehabilitation and deterrence have drawbacks as purposes of sentencing, the White Paper asserted that:

> If the punishment is just, and in proportion to the seriousness of the offence, then the victim, the victim's family and friends, and the public will be

---

[1] Home Office (1990), para. 2.3.

satisfied that the law has been upheld and there will be no desire for further retaliation or private revenge.[2]

As noted in Chapter 3.5 above, the 1991 Act failed to convey this message clearly, and led to some confusion. In the Criminal Justice Act 2003 the sources of confusion are much more plain to see, because, as noted in the previous chapter, s. 142 sets out five (conflicting) purposes of sentencing to which courts 'must have regard'.

However, other provisions of the 2003 Act appear to insist on proportionality of the sentence to the seriousness of the offence. Thus s. 143(1) states that 'in considering the seriousness of any offence, the court must consider the offender's culpability in committing the offence and any harm which the offence caused, was intended to cause or might foreseeably have caused'. That leads on to the question of when, under the 2003 Act, seriousness is a relevant matter. The statute indicates that it is relevant to three vital threshold decisions. First, s. 148(1) states that a community sentence must not be passed unless the offence 'was serious enough to warrant such a sentence'. Secondly, s. 152(2) states that a court must not pass a custodial sentence unless the offence 'was so serious that neither a fine alone nor a community sentence can be justified for the offence'. This formulation requires a court to relate its assessment of the seriousness of the offence to the possible penalty of a fine or community sentence. And thirdly, s. 153(2) states that, when a court does impose custody, the sentence 'must be for the shortest term that in the opinion of the court is commensurate with the seriousness of the offence'.

In its guideline on *Overarching Principles: Seriousness*, the Sentencing Guidelines Council deduced from these statutory provisions that the proportionality principle should be central to sentencing decisions. Thus '1.3 The sentencer must start by considering the seriousness of the offence . . .', and '1.4 A court is required to pass a sentence that is commensurate with the seriousness of the offence . . .'.[3] Similarly in its very first draft guideline, the Sentencing Council stated that its aim was 'to increase proportionality in sentencing across the range of assault offences'.[4]

How can a scale of ordinal proportionality be constructed? Some US systems have approached this by drawing up sentencing 'grids', which classify offences into various groups and then assign guideline sentences to them; this leaves the courts with more or less discretion, depending on the width of the ranges and the narrowness of the departure test.[5] In Finland, Article 6 of the Penal Code provides simply that 'punishment shall be measured so that it is in just proportion to the damage and danger caused by the offence and to

---

[2] Home Office (1990), para. 2.4.   [3] SGC, *Overarching Principles: Seriousness* (2004).

[4] Sentencing Council, *Assault Guideline: Professional Consultation* (2010), p. 5; see also the subsequent reference to 'the Council's aim for proportionality' (p. 8).

[5] See Frase (2013) for full discussion or, much more briefly, von Hirsch, Ashworth and Roberts (2009), ch. 6.2.

the guilt of the offender manifested in the offence'.[6] This leaves the court to do the calculation, using the legislative principles, as does Chapter 29 of the Swedish Criminal Code, introduced in 1989. This provides that sentences should be based on the penal value of the offence: 'The penal value is determined with special regard to the harm, offence or risk which the conduct involved, what the accused realized or should have realized about it, and the intentions and motives of the accused.'[7]

Apart from s. 143(1), mentioned above, the 2003 Act in England and Wales contains no elaboration of the term 'seriousness of the offence'. One possible problem is the structure of the criminal law. Some English offences are relatively narrow in the conduct they specify (e.g. murder and rape, although it is possible to distinguish degrees of each offence). Many other offences cover broad areas of conduct without legal differentiation: robbery can involve anything from a push to snatch a purse to an armed hold-up of a bank, and the offence of theft has no subdivisions according to the value of the property or the circumstances of the offender. In practice this may mean that the determinants of offence-seriousness are sometimes difficult to separate from the aggravating and mitigating factors. However, we shall devote Chapter 5 to the latter issue, and focus as far as possible on offence-seriousness itself here. The first task is to discover whether there are any shared opinions on the relative seriousness of offences. The next task is to examine the problem from the point of view of a theory which can be put into practice.

4.2 Opinions about offence-seriousness

Opinion surveys have been conducted several times in different countries in attempts to ascertain public views on the relative seriousness of offences. It is not proposed to discuss all of them here, even though some have achieved considerable sophistication.[8] The origin of modern surveys is the scale devised by Sellin and Wolfgang in 1964, which has been claimed to produce similar rankings when applied to subjects with different occupations and social standing and to subjects in different countries.[9] A recent survey by the Sentencing Advisory Council of Victoria (SACV), using focus groups of informed citizens, found that sexual penetration of a child under 12 was placed on a level with murder, whereas drug trafficking and robberies came lower down the scale. Whereas there was widespread agreement on the seriousness of violent offences, there was much less agreement on the relative seriousness of drug offences, of consensual sex with children aged 13–16, and of property offences generally.[10]

[6] Lappi-Seppala (2001).   [7] Jareborg (1995).
[8] For a summary see Roberts and Stalans (1997), ch. 4.
[9] Cf. Roberts and Stalans (1997) with the Introduction to Sellin and Wolfgang (1978).
[10] Sentencing Advisory Council of Victoria (2012).

To what extent do people from different backgrounds have different opinions? Analysis by Ken Pease of material from the 1984 *British Crime Survey* showed that there were no significant differences according to the social class of the person questioned, and that victims tended not to rate offences as more serious than non-victims.[11] The SACV found that punitiveness ratings tended to increase with age and to decrease with university education;[12] other international studies suggest that people with less formal education and living in smaller communities tend to regard all crimes as more serious.[13]

Notwithstanding these apparently high rates of agreement, certain reservations must be made. First, these surveys are usually based on very brief descriptions of different types of offence, and little may be known about the network of assumptions and beliefs which underlie the way in which subjects approach the task of ranking. Moreover, a crucial difference may be that between premeditated or planned offences and sudden or impulsive offences. These differences in culpability exert a powerful effect on sentencing practice, and may well influence people's judgments of crimes. Surveys which leave out this dimension are not only omitting a crucial element in the judgments but are also leaving that factor roaming 'loose', so it might enter into the assessments of different subjects in different ways. A survey by Leslie Sebba attempted to take account of the culpability dimension. He found not only that people's views of seriousness do differ according to the mental element specified, but also that when no mental element is specified they tend to regard the offence as intentional unless it is a 'regulatory' offence, where they tend to assume negligence only.[14] More recent studies such as SACV recognise and incorporate the dimension of culpability.

Secondly, the attitudes that are reflected in the rankings may often be based on false beliefs, for it is well-established that many members of the public have imperfect knowledge about the prevalence of crime, its effects on victims, and the level of sentences typically imposed by the courts.[15] Yet there must be explanations for the changes that have apparently taken place in the seriousness ranking of certain offences in recent years. Some offences have come to be regarded in a much more serious light in the last two decades. One is rape: greater publicity about the effects of rape, with research findings documenting this, has resulted in the police and the courts treating the offence as more serious.[16] Another such crime is causing death by dangerous driving: at one time this was treated as a 'mere' motoring offence, but increasing realization of the loss and devastation resulting and of the avoidability of such offences has led to public concern (to which Parliament and the courts have responded by

---

[11] Pease (1988).   [12] Sentencing Advisory Council of Victoria (2012), p. 38.
[13] Roberts and Stalans (1997), pp. 67–8.
[14] Sebba (1980); see also Roberts and Stalans (1997), pp. 61–2.
[15] Hough and Roberts (2012), pp. 280–3.   [16] See part 4.4.7 below.

increasing levels of sentence).[17] It is assumed that these increases reflect public opinion about the relative seriousness rankings of rape and of causing death by driving. But, again, it is not clear whether the shift in public opinion preceded or followed the legal changes, nor is it clear exactly why and how the opinions of large numbers of people changed – if, as it appears, they did. It therefore seems that the kinds of public opinion surveys carried out so far offer only broad pointers to any policy-maker pondering on the comparative seriousness rankings of different offences. It would take a large and carefully crafted survey, carried out on people who had a certain level of knowledge about the nature of the offences (and the culpability and harm involved in each), to supply robust evidence of this kind.

4.3 Developing parameters of ordinal proportionality

These examples of changes in the perceived seriousness of certain offences contain signposts to the difficulties ahead. The seriousness of rape may stem from the psychological as much as from the physical impact of the offence, and a scale of proportionality must take account of that. The same may be said of burglary, ostensibly an offence against property but which may have severe emotional effects. Causing death by dangerous driving is a homicide offence and therefore quite high on any scale. It is an offence of lesser culpability than murder or some forms of manslaughter, but how much should its seriousness be discounted from those crimes? There must be some way of comparing such offences with deliberate woundings and other non-fatal harms. Insider trading has no individual victim: it is a violation of the principles of the financial markets which may bring great profit to the offender without significant loss to any one individual (although perhaps loss of confidence in the market generally). Should the scale take account of profit gained, as an alternative to loss caused? Could the two be incorporated into a single scale? The same applies to social security frauds: it is more a question of gaining unfair financial advantage than causing felt losses.

The foremost modern attempt to establish some parameters for ordinal proportionality is that of Andrew von Hirsch and Nils Jareborg (1991).[18] Their approach, which deals only with crimes against individual victims, is to determine the effect of the typical case of particular crimes on the living standard of victims. The first question to be asked is what interests are violated or threatened by the standard case of the crime, and they identify four generic interests:

(i) physical integrity: health, safety and the avoidance of physical pain;
(ii) material support and amenity: includes nutrition, shelter, and other basic amenities;

---

[17] See part 4.4.4 below, where recent research on public opinion relating to serious motoring offences is discussed; but it does not rank those offences against other types of crime.

[18] For a recently revised version see von Hirsch and Ashworth (2005), App. A.

(iii) freedom from humiliation or degrading treatment; and

(iv) privacy and autonomy.

Additions could be made to this list, but their aim is to focus on paradigm cases of crimes with individual victims. They take the standard case in order to enhance the simplicity of the basic framework and in the knowledge that any non-standard features of the particular case can be taken into account when determining the offender's culpability and its effect on seriousness (did he know that the victim was elderly?), and when quantifying any compensation payable to the victim.

   Once the nature of the interest(s) violated has been settled, the second step is to assess the effect of violating those interests on the living standards of the typical victim. These effects are banded into four levels:

   (i) subsistence: survival with maintenance of elementary human functions – no satisfactions presupposed at this level;

  (ii) minimal well-being: maintenance of a minimal level of comfort and dignity;

 (iii) adequate well-being: maintenance of an 'adequate' level of comfort and dignity; and

 (iv) significant enhancement: significant enhancement in quality of life above the merely adequate level.

The differences between the four levels are couched in fairly general terms, such as 'adequate' and 'significant', but this is inevitable if the search is for general principles. The scale is to be applied to the offence and the harm which it penalizes, and one of its advantages should be to cut through the conventions which result in 'traditional' crimes such as wounding being regarded as naturally more serious than 'modern' crimes such as dangerous driving or the maintenance of unsafe working conditions. The scale does not itself yield an index of ordinal proportionality, but deals with one crucial step in that direction.

   Thus the violation of a protected interest is one key component of offence-seriousness, often expressed as harm or harmfulness but also including the concept of a wrong, since it is not merely the physical or psychological consequences but also the nature of the wrong done to a victim that is relevant in assessing seriousness.[19] A further step is to integrate into the calculation a judgment of culpability, which in some instances may have a considerable effect on the ultimate ranking of an offence. For example, manslaughter is usually thought to be a serious offence, and the harm involved is death, which ranks as a level (i) interest. But if the culpability involved is no more than the culpability for an ordinary assault (which is sufficient in English law), one

---

[19] For recent work on wrongs and harms, see Simester and von Hirsch (2011).

might expect that form of manslaughter to appear much lower down the scale than most other homicides.

A further component, in addition to culpability, is the remoteness of the offence from the occurrence of the harm. The law contains several offences which do not require the actual infliction of the harm concerned, such as offences of attempt (e.g. attempted robbery, attempted rape), offences of endangerment and risk-creation (e.g. dangerous driving, drunk driving, unsafe working conditions), and protective or preparatory offences (e.g. possession of an offensive weapon or of equipment for counterfeiting). A scale of offence-seriousness should discount the level of particular offences according to their remoteness from the resulting harm, but the extent of that discounting is likely to be a matter of controversy.[20]

The discussion so far has identified four main stages in the process of assessing offence-seriousness, following the von Hirsch–Jareborg principles. At the first stage it is a question of determining the interests violated. At the second stage there is a preliminary quantification of the effect of a typical case on a victim's living standards. At the third stage account is taken of the culpability of the offender. And at the fourth stage there may be a reduction in the level of seriousness to reflect the remoteness of the actual harm. The authors themselves demonstrate the application of their principles to a range of crimes, and show how effect might be given to the four stages by devising a harm scale. Once the second stage has been reached, there is a need to transfer those quantifications of effect on living standards on to some kind of harm scale. The authors recognize that this could be a more or less elaborate scale. It might, for example, be a 100-point numerical scale, but they reject this as evincing a 'misleading sense of precision'[21] and prefer a scale with five broad bands, each of them containing room for further differentiations of degree. Thus, the causing of a serious injury might be valued at level (ii) in terms of its effect on a typical victim's living standards, since it leaves the victim only with a minimal level of comfort and dignity; this might correspond to level (ii) on the harm scale, but it might then be reduced because the offender was merely reckless, or because the offence was merely an attempt.

Let us take stock of the argument so far. The previous paragraph has represented the von Hirsch–Jareborg principles in terms of four stages in gauging the seriousness of harms. One criticism might be that the parameters are vague and indefinitely expressed, with the result that they will allow room for inconsistencies in outcome between different users of the same scale. However, to concede this may be to suggest that a more precise scale is possible, whereas the authors rightly focus on establishing a methodology for determining these awkward questions. Another criticism might be that

---

[20] See further Ashworth and Zedner (2014), ch. 5.   [21] Von Hirsch and Jareborg (1991), p. 28.

the principles are far too complex to be of practical use. This should not be conceded, for much of the authors' enterprise has been to formalize the intellectual processes which sometimes take place, albeit impressionistically and even inconsistently, in the minds of the legislators and judges who have to decide these questions.

A more searching question is whether the authors' self-imposed restriction to crimes with individual victims does not impair the utility of their scheme. It is understandable that they should wish to construct some principles on firm ground before moving to the more intractable areas, but in the context of a pressing need to develop parameters of proportionality for English sentencing some additions and adaptations must be made. For example, the crime of theft covers a wide range of different situations, some involving individual victims and some not. Of those which do involve individual victims, some contain elements which have a wider significance. An example might be a theft in breach of trust, in which a solicitor misappropriates a client's funds. It is not just the effect on the typical victim's standard of living which determines the seriousness of the offence, but also the breach of trust by a solicitor on whom citizens tend to rely. This may be seen as a 'public' element in a crime with an individual victim. Nor can this be convincingly put aside as an aggravating feature rather than an integral feature of the crime, for it is questionable whether there is any such clear dividing line. Different legal systems incorporate different elements into the definitions of their crimes.

Moreover, many thefts are takings from companies. It would not seem fruitful to explore the 'living standards' of companies, because the effect of one particular theft on a corporate economy may not be large. The controversial question is whether the negligible effect on the victim makes the crime less serious, or whether it would not be better to focus on the gain to the offender. There is, perhaps, an argument for saying that, in general, it is slightly less serious to steal from a company than from an individual, because the offence is likely to have less of an impact on the victim, and also that the company may be said to have facilitated the offence through its method of trading. (Clearly there are exceptions, in the shape of individual millionaires and of small businesses with few reserves, but we are concerned with the typical case.) Is there any reason why a person who steals £10,000 from the company which employs him should be judged by the effect of that theft on the typical company, without any comparison of the seriousness of appropriating £10,000 from a non-corporate source? Surely it is at least relevant that the offender is £10,000 richer, whereas the person who steals smaller amounts from individual victims has gained far less. This chain of reasoning suggests that, at the second stage of the von Hirsch–Jareborg principles, it would be proper to introduce the notion of 'benefit to the living standards of the typical offender' as an alternative to the impact on the living standards of the typical victim. The receipt of £10,000 would significantly enhance the living standards of most people, and this suggests that an offence involving such a gain should be placed high in the fourth category – perhaps at level (iv) or (iii) of the seriousness scale, before culpability and mitigation are taken into account.[22]

How might a modified version of the von Hirsch–Jareborg scheme be presented? It could be characterized as a decision sequence along the following lines, and applicable to any conduct prohibited by the criminal law:

(i) four or more harm dimensions: physical integrity; material support and amenity; freedom from humiliation; privacy/autonomy; integrity of the administration of justice;

(ii) living standard impact or benefit in the typical case: subsistence; minimal well-being; adequate well-being; enhanced well-being;

(iii) map on to a seriousness scale of, for example, five levels;

(iv) culpability: planned, impulsive, knowing, reckless, negligent, and so on; adjust level on seriousness scale accordingly;

(v) remoteness: completed, attempted, risked, preliminary, or preventive offence; degree of involvement or participation in the offence; adjust level on seriousness scale accordingly;

(vi) aggravation and mitigation: assess the various factors, and adjust the level on seriousness scale accordingly; and

(vii) transfer from seriousness scale to commensurate sentence.

How can the 'transfer' envisaged by (vii) above be accomplished? The seriousness of offences forms one scale, and the severity of punishments another. There is no natural or inevitable relationship between them: the relationship can only be conventional and symbolic.[23] If there is a shared desire to alter the conventions, a change can be brought about: Dutch judges and prosecutors lowered their sentencing levels in the early 1950s,[24] and English juvenile courts did so in the 1980s,[25] whereas English courts in the 1990s raised their sentencing levels.[26] Despite this conventional or symbolic element, it can be argued that certain punishments would be excessive for certain crimes. If, for example, 3 years' imprisonment were the norm for theft from a shop, one could argue that this is not commensurate. For an offence that amounts to no more than a deprivation of property rights, it is difficult to justify depriving the offender of such a fundamental right as that to personal liberty. Because a typical shop theft causes only minor loss to the shop and only a minor gain to the offender, it cannot possibly justify the loss of a person's liberty and the associated pains of imprisonment, let alone for as long as 3 years.[27] Thus there surely is such a thing as utter disproportionality, even if there is no such thing as absolute proportionality.

---

[22] For fuller discussion, see the 5th edn of this work at pp. 109–15.

[23] Walker (1991), ch. 12; cf. Lacey (1988), pp. 20–1 with her later acceptance that 'proportionality to socially acknowledged gravity could serve a useful function in underlining community values', even if other functions would also be important (p. 194).

[24] Downes (1988).   [25] See ch. 12.1.1 below.   [26] As seen in ch. 1.3 above.

[27] See further Ashworth (2013b).

Within those outer limits, however, conventional modes of thought have tended to play a major part, together with the influence of the media and of politicians. Lord Bingham CJ acknowledged this strong political element:

> From 1987 to 1992 the use of custody generally declined, probably in response to legislation, ministerial speeches and the White Paper on 'Crime, Justice and Protecting the Public'. Since 1993 the use of custody has increased very sharply, in response (it would seem likely) to certain highly publicized crimes, legislation, ministerial speeches and intense media pressure.[28]

Detailed analysis of the issues of lengths of custody and degrees of restriction on liberty in the community will be left over to Chapters 9 and 10, where the specific policies bearing on them will be discussed. But there remain difficult questions about the numerical representation of differentials between offences and about the calibration of the punishment scale.

Catherine Fitzmaurice and Ken Pease (1986) raised various questions about this neglected aspect of sentencing. If it is decided that one offence is twice as serious as another, does it follow that it should attract double the penalty? Hypothetical exercises conducted with three judges suggested that there may be differences in the way in which incremental seriousness is reflected, with some judges having a steep and others a shallow slope.[29] There is no absolute reason why twice the seriousness should lead to double the sentence, especially when the experienced severity of a sentence might itself increase more steeply as months and years are added on.[30] Thus, criminological knowledge about the typical impact of sentences might be relevant to devising both a sentence severity scale and a ratio of commensurability. On the other hand, one might promote a scale which shows a degree of tolerance of minor crimes and a marked abhorrence of very serious crimes: the reasoning here would be that a typical rape is not twice as serious as the typical house burglary but, say, four times as serious. This would produce a ratio of commensurability which might be represented by a stepped upward curve: many minor crimes would receive minor penalties; in the middle range of crimes the increases in sentence severity are normal; but, for the most serious crimes, sentence severity increases steeply. This approximates to the twin-track or bifurcated policy, often associated with treating serious and violent crime severely while lowering the scale of response to most property crime. Whether this is truly an aspect of proportionality or rather a pragmatic compromise to appease the media by scapegoating certain offenders is a matter for debate.

This leads us to the calibration of the scale of punishment severity. How should the differentials between offences of varying seriousness be marked? It is well known that in nineteenth-century England the tendency had been to pass custodial sentences of the lengths previously used as periods of

---

[28] *Brewster* [1998] 1 Cr App R (S) 181, at p. 184.   [29] Fitzmaurice and Pease (1986), p. 87.
[30] See Kolber (2009).

transportation. Parliament tended to create maximum penalties by using the 'seven times table' – indeed, many offences still have maxima of 7 or 14 years – and the courts followed.[31] No less a figure than the 'supreme commander of the Victorian prison system', Sir Edmund du Cane, a man 'identified with stern discipline, rigidity . . . and faith in the deterrent force of penal discipline',[32] questioned whether these old conventions were not resulting in the infliction of unnecessary suffering. A further challenge came from the scientist Sir Francis Galton in 1895, in an article which showed how shorter sentences tended to cluster round 3, 6, 9, and 12 months, and how longer sentences tended to be rounded into years, with even larger gaps in the upper echelons. Galton argued that 'runs of figures like these testify to some powerful cause of disturbance which interferes with the orderly distribution of punishment in conformity with penal deserts'.[33] Those remarks are no less apposite today. The courts have their 'preferred numbers', and there is no reason of principle why a completely different mode of calibration could not be chosen. When a court wishes to make a 'just noticeable difference' from a 6-month sentence, the tendency is to give 9 months – not 7 or 8. When it wishes to signal a 'just noticeable difference' from a sentence of 8 years' imprisonment, it may go to 10 years instead of nine. These are preferred numbers, and their use 'probably protects sentencers from thinking about what a sentence means in practice'.[34]

Could a wholly different set of conventions be selected? One longstanding argument is that all terms of custody under 1 year should be expressed in weeks, and those above 1 year in months. This would lead sentencers to rethink their differentials, perhaps resulting in a more restrained use of imprisonment. A step in this direction was taken by s. 181 of the 2003 Act, which states that the term of a prison sentence of less than 12 months 'must be expressed in weeks'. This approach is now used in the *Magistrates' Court Sentencing Guidelines* (2008) and all other definitive guidelines where custodial sentences of less than 12 months are indicated. If this can be seen as belated statutory recognition that numbers have consequences, and conventions can produce extra pain, as du Cane and Galton showed a century ago, the question for research is whether it has had any effect on the length of sentences. Some of the preferred numbers relate to the previous structure (e.g. 26 weeks is much used), but if one aim is to question and then to reduce the lengths of sentences, the reasons for the use of terms such as 6 and 12 weeks should be scrutinised, and consideration given to using 5 and 10 or 4 and 8.[35]

---

[31] See Thomas (1978) and Advisory Council on the Penal System (1978), paras. 36–66 and App. K.

[32] The quotations are taken from Radzinowicz and Hood (1986), p. 747.

[33] See Fitzmaurice and Pease (1986), pp. 103–4.   [34] Fitzmaurice and Pease (1986), p. 113.

[35] The *Magistrates' Court Sentencing Guidelines*, pp. 42 and 68, includes starting points of 6, 12, and 18 weeks' custody; the Council's sexual offences guideline uses 13 weeks (at p. 77).

4.4 Offence-seriousness in practice

This examination of some of the problems of establishing a scale of ordinal proportionality and relating it to sentence severity has left us with few clear prescriptions, but it has raised many questions about current practices. The only modern committee of inquiry into English sentence levels, the Advisory Council on the Penal System in 1978, concentrated on levels of imprisonment without much discussion of relativities between offences. In the same decade Lawton LJ in *Turner* (1975)[36] attempted to map out the upper echelons of the sentencing tariff by taking average sentence lengths for murder as his starting point, and then working downwards to the serious armed robberies with which he was dealing. Major changes to the sentencing structure since 1975 – notably, the abolition of remission on prison sentences, and the lengthening of the effective period of detention of many murderers – render the numbers in *Turner* no longer reliable. But the *Turner* judgment is still relevant for at least one reason: to what extent, if at all, should sentence levels for other serious crimes be connected or pegged to the sentence for murder? Is it logical to 'steer by' sentence lengths for murder, when scaling the sentencing system, or does the oft-mentioned 'uniqueness' of murder as a crime suggest otherwise?[37]

The poignancy of these questions derives from Schedule 21 of the 2003 Act, in which Parliament set statutory starting points for the minimum terms for murder. The fact that these starting points are much higher than the previous ones places the relationship between minimum terms for murder and sentence lengths for other serious crimes under considerable strain, as we shall see in the pages that follow. Thus there has been anxious discussion in terrorist cases of the proper approach to sentencing, particularly where no actual harm has occurred. The longest determinate sentence in English law was upheld in *Hindawi* (1988).[38] The offender had placed a bomb in a bag carried by his pregnant girlfriend, who was about to embark on an aircraft carrying some 370 people. The bomb was timed to explode when the aircraft was in mid-flight, but was discovered at the airport. For the offence of attempting to place on an aircraft an explosive device likely to destroy or damage the aircraft, Hindawi was sentenced to 45 years. Stating that 'it is no thanks to this applicant that his plot did not succeed in destroying 360 or 370 lives', the Court of Appeal upheld the sentence as 'not a day too long'. This decision was considered in *Barot* (2008),[39] where the offender pleaded guilty to conspiracy to murder, admitting that he was involved in developing plans for terrorist attacks that would amount to mass murder. He had attended terrorist training

---

[36] (1975) 61 Cr App R 67, at pp. 89–91.
[37] See Lord Judge CJ in *Thomas* [2012] 1 Cr App R (S) 254, below, part 4.4.8 and n. 155.
[38] (1988) 10 Cr App R (S) 104.
[39] [2008] 1 Cr App R (S) 156; see also *Al-Banna* (1984) 6 Cr App R (S) 426 (35 and 30 years for attempted assassination of the Israeli ambassador); see also *Asiedu* [2009] 1 Cr App R (S) 420 (33 years upheld for conspiracy to cause explosions for terrorist purposes).

camps, but had not yet taken possession of any explosives, funding, vehicles, etc. He was sentenced to life imprisonment on grounds of his dangerousness, with a minimum term of 40 years. That (as we shall see in 4.4.1 below) is equivalent to a determinate sentence of 80 years. The judgment of Lord Phillips CJ recognizes that a more severe view of terrorism is now taken, and that this was a more professional and concerted set of plans than the attempt in *Hindawi*, although in this case the offender had not proceeded as far. Taking account of the massive scale on which the offender planned to kill innocent people, the Court of Appeal held that the appropriate minimum term was 30 years (equivalent to a determinate sentence of 60 years). These are exceptionally long sentences by any standard, but they must be assessed by comparison with sentences for murder, which we examine next in 4.4.1, followed by closely related offences such as attempted murder and manslaughter.

4.4.1 Murder

Since the Murder (Abolition of Death Penalty) Act 1969, the only sentence that a court may pass for murder is life imprisonment. The sentence for murder is divided into three portions. The first is now known as the minimum term (formerly, the tariff period), and is intended to reflect the relative gravity of the particular offence. It is a term that is served in full, and the early release provisions applicable to all determinate custodial sentences do not apply here. Once the minimum term expires, the second portion consists of detention determined by considerations of public protection: some may be released relatively quickly, whereas a murderer who is thought still to present a danger may be detained for many years longer. The third portion is release on licence, which endures for life and carries the possibility of recall to prison.

Until 2003 the determination of the first two portions of the mandatory life sentence was a matter for the Home Secretary, who would set the minimum term (having received the recommendation of the trial judge and the Lord Chief Justice on the matter) and later would set the release date (having received the recommendation of the Parole Board).[40] This system was attacked on human rights grounds, arguing that both these decisions amounted to sentencing functions and should therefore be carried out by an 'independent and impartial tribunal'. The Strasbourg Court eventually accepted this argument in *Stafford* v. *United Kingdom* (2002),[41] which removed the Home Secretary's right to determine release from the second part of the mandatory life sentence. It was not long before the English courts held, in *R* (*on*

---

[40] See Padfield (2008), ch. 10.

[41] (2002) 35 EHRR 1121, following the lead given in *V and T* v. *United Kingdom* (2000) 30 EHRR 121.

application of Anderson) v. *Secretary of State for the Home Department* (2002),[42] that it was incompatible with Article 6 for the Home Secretary to set the minimum period in murder cases because he is not an 'independent and impartial tribunal'.

Ministers from both major parties have always maintained that determinations of this kind should be under the control of an elected politician, and so Parliament moved swiftly to minimize the effect of these judgments through legislation.[43] Section 269 of the Criminal Justice Act 2003 essentially requires a court, when setting the minimum term to be served by a person convicted of murder, to have regard to the principles set out in Schedule 21 to the Act. The structure of that Schedule is to indicate three starting points:

- a whole life minimum term for exceptionally serious cases, such as premeditated killings of two or more people, sexual or sadistic child murders, or political murders;
- 30 years for particularly serious cases such as murders of police or prison officers, murders involving firearms, sexual or sadistic killings, or murders aggravated by racial or sexual orientation;
- 15 years for other murders not falling within either of the higher categories.

In 2010, at a time of anxiety about knife crime, the Minister for Justice exercised his power to introduce a further starting point of 25 years for murderers who take to the scene a knife or other weapon, intending to have it available for use and using it.[44] A further amendment in 2012 placed murders resulting from the targeting of a person on grounds of actual or perceived transgender identity in paragraph 5 of Schedule 21, alongside other murders aggravated by sexual orientation, effectively doubling the starting point from 15 to 30 years.

All the starting points in Schedule 21 are much higher than those previously in use, not least because these terms are served in full and therefore correspond to normal prison sentences of twice the length.[45] However, the language in Schedule 21 is not constraining. Although criteria are enumerated for the whole life and 30-year starting points, they are expressed as factors that would 'normally' indicate such a sentence. There is then provision for the court to take account of any further relevant factors, and an explicit statement that 'detailed consideration of aggravating and mitigating factors may result in a minimum term of any length (whatever the starting point)'. When Lord

---

[42] [2003] 1 AC 837; see also *Lychniak and Pyrah* [2002] UKHL 47.

[43] On the speedy (some would say, hasty) production of Sch. 21, see Jeremy (2010), pp. 595–600.

[44] The precise terms of the Order are analysed by the Court of Appeal in *Kelly* [2012] 1 Cr App R (S) 318.

[45] Thus a minimum term of 15 years means at least 15 years in prison, whereas a determinate sentence of 30 years means 15 years in prison (followed by 15 years on supervised licence: see ch. 9.5 below).

Woolf CJ discussed the effect of the Schedule in *Sullivan* (2005),[46] he emphasized that s. 269(3) states that the judge must specify the minimum term that 'the court considers appropriate', and indeed went on to say that so long as the judge bore in mind the principles set out in Schedule 21, 'he is not bound to follow them' – although an explanation for any departure should be given. He also drew attention to the inclusion in Schedule 21 of the discount for pleading guilty, although the Sentencing Guidelines Council has stated that the discount in murder cases should be roughly half that for determinate sentences, in order to achieve a similar effect in practice.[47]

There is considerable case-law on the proper calculation of the minimum term for murder, not least because of the great distance between the starting points of 15, 25, and 30 years and a whole life. In *Height and Anderson* (2009)[48] the Court of Appeal emphasised that the lists of factors in paragraph 5 of Schedule 21 are not exhaustive, and that the Schedule should not lead to an 'arithmetical' approach to sentencing. Similarly in *Griffiths et al.* (2013)[49] the Court of Appeal again stated that paragraph 5 is not exhaustive and that if a case does not fall within the express terms of paragraph 5 the judge is free to draw an analogy with the examples set out in that paragraph.

It remains uncertain whether 'whole life' minimum terms under Schedule 21 are compatible with Article 3 of the Convention. A full Court of Appeal was convened in *Oakes* (2013)[50] to consider the question, and the Court held that some murders may be so heinous that a whole life minimum term is justified, and that the Minister for Justice's power to release prisoners on compassionate grounds renders the whole life sentence 'reducible'. The Grand Chamber of the European Court of Human Rights in *Vinter* v. *United Kingdom* (2014)[51] held that a whole life minimum term may be justifiable, but that there must be the possibility of a review that allows consideration of whether the prisoner has undergone changes and made progress towards rehabilitation to the extent that continued detention may no longer be justified for penological reasons. The Minister's power to release 'on compassionate grounds' is at best ambiguous in this respect, and therefore does not clearly give prisoners the opportunity for hope. This judgment was considered by another full Court of Appeal in *Newell* (2014),[52] and the Court declined to follow the Strasbourg judgment, arguing that the Minister's power to release prisoners on 'compassionate grounds' should be read in a manner compatible with Article 3 of the Convention, as the Human Rights Act requires, and that it therefore provides the whole life prisoner with the hope or possibility of release in exceptional circumstances. This interpretation has now been accepted by the Strasbourg

---

[46] [2005] 1 Cr App R (S) 308.
[47] SGC, *Reduction in Sentence for a Guilty Plea: Revised Guideline* (2008), paras 6.5–6.6; see below, ch. 5.4.1.
[48] [2009] 1 Cr App R (S) 676.
[49] [2013] 2 Cr App R (S) 330; see also *Minto* [2014] 2 Cr App R (S) 301.
[50] [2013] 2 Cr App R (S) 132.   [51] [2014] Crim LR 81.   [52] [2014] Crim LR 471.

Court in Hutchinson v United Kingdom,[52a] even though the Court of Appeal's judgment stretches the term 'compassionate grounds' to an unconvincing extent.

The justifications for having a mandatory penalty for murder remain controversial. The offence has variable degrees of seriousness, and can sometimes be less serious than manslaughter.[53] The mandatory sentence does not require any finding of dangerousness,[54] and yet the three stages of the life sentence apply to all murderers. Previously the retentionist argument was that only a senior government minister can protect the public from danger, an argument of doubtful force aside from political populism. Now that the government minister's role has gone, sentences for murder should surely be put on the same footing as sentences for all other serious crimes. Indeed, the coalition government in 2010 referred to Schedule 21 as 'ill thought-out and overly prescriptive'.[55] Research by Kate Fitz-Gibbon found a body of practitioner opinion in favour of sentencing discretion so as to reflect the great variety of murders,[56] and research by Barry Mitchell and Julian Roberts indicates that members of the public would regard this as an acceptable alternative.[57] If the murderer fulfils the criteria for life imprisonment, on account of a finding of dangerousness, that will be the proper course.[58] In the absence of such a finding, the courts should impose determinate sentences.[59]

4.4.2 Attempted murder

We saw earlier, from the decisions in *Hindawi* and *Al-Banna*,[60] that very high sentences can be passed in cases which are either charged as attempted murder or amount to that in fact. The culpability required for attempted murder is an intent to kill, which (paradoxically) is a higher degree of culpability than is required for murder, where an intention to cause grievous bodily harm will suffice. Both those decisions adhere strongly to the view that the sentence should be based on the result intended by the offender, rather than the actual outcome of his efforts. This accords with the general principle endorsed by the Sentencing Guidelines Council for cases where the harm is much less than intended: 'the culpability of the offender ... should be the initial factor in determining the seriousness of an offence'.[61]

[52a] Judgment of 3 February 2015.

[53] Consider the case of *Inglis* [2011] 2 Cr App R (S) 66 (minimum term of 5 years).

[54] Cf. the reasoning in *Offen (No. 2)* [2001] 2 Cr App R (S) 44 in respect of the automatic life sentence.

[55] Ministry of Justice (2010), ch 4. No action followed this statement.   [56] Fitz-Gibbon (2013).

[57] Mitchell and Roberts (2012), ch. 6; they propose a new approach to murder sentencing in their ch. 8.

[58] See the discussion of this sentence below, ch. 6.8.

[59] For suggestions about how this might be done, see Wasik (2000), pp. 174–83, and Mitchell (2013), pp. 59–70.

[60] Above, nn. 38–9.   [61] SGC, *Overarching Principles: Seriousness* (2004), para. 1.19.

The result of the higher starting points for murder sentences introduced by the 2003 Act was to create a considerable gap between sentence levels for murder and for attempted murder. The issue was faced squarely by the Sentencing Guidelines Council: the SGC broadly accepted the Panel's advice in relation to other offences against the person, issuing a guideline in 2008,[62] but it held back the guideline on attempted murder for further consultation. The key question was whether attempted murder should be approached as the most serious of the non-fatal offences of violence, or rather as an inchoate form of murder. In its further consultation the SGC stated that it had 'determined that the consultation guideline should be based on a clear and obvious link with the approach to sentencing for murder enacted in Schedule 21 to the Criminal Justice Act 2003'.[63] The definitive guideline on attempted murder was published in 2009. Not only are its three sentence ranges set at levels linked to the starting points for murder in Schedule 21, but the text of Level 1 refers explicitly to offences which (if murder had been committed) would have fallen within paragraphs 4 or 5 of Schedule 21.[64] At each of the three levels, there are three degrees of harm to be taken into account – 'serious and long-term physical or psychological harm', 'some physical or psychological harm', and 'little or no physical or psychological harm'. These guidelines can be observed in operation in *Barnaby* (2013),[65] where the Court also had to consider the effect of paragraph 5A of Schedule 21, which introduced the 25-year starting point for murders with a knife taken to the scene. The Court of Appeal held that when sentencing for attempted murder a judge must take account of this amendment. This preserves the link with Schedule 21's calibration of murders, although the sentences indicated by the guideline are roughly 50 per cent of those for murder, since they are determinate sentences of which half is served in prison and half is served on licence.

4.4.3 Manslaughter

This is a single offence with several different legal bases. For present purposes, four types of manslaughter should be distinguished – manslaughter by reason of diminished responsibility, manslaughter by reason of loss of control, unlawful act manslaughter, and manslaughter by gross negligence. All forms of manslaughter involve the culpable causing of death, as does murder, and on the von Hirsch–Jareborg scale would be classified as attacks on physical integrity which affect (nay, obliterate) subsistence. Since the harm is the most serious of all, to what extent should lesser culpability reduce the seriousness of the offence? For the first two types of manslaughter, diminished responsibility

---

[62] SGC, *Assault and other Offences against the Person* (2008).
[63] SGC, *Attempted Murder: Notes and Questions for Consultees* (2007), para. 1.3.
[64] SGC, *Attempted Murder: Definitive Guideline* (2009), p. 7.
[65] [2013] 1 Cr App R (S) 302; see also *Kela* [2012] 1 Cr App R (S) 195.

and loss of control, all the requirements of murder are present but there are circumstances that lead to the reduction of the offence to manslaughter. For the second pair of manslaughters, there is no intent to kill or intent to cause grievous bodily harm: the culpability basis of the offence is much lower, deriving from a lesser intent or from gross negligence.

We observed in 4.4.1 above that the starting points for murder under Schedule 21 are a) much longer than previous minimum terms in murder cases, and b) very widely spaced, so that a single aggravating factor may make the difference between a 15-year and a 25-year or even 30-year starting point. That these differentials were not fully discussed in Parliament is now a matter of history.[66] The key question is the extent to which the introduction of the murder starting points indicates that sentences for other homicide offences should be raised. In the first major judgment to consider the question, Lord Judge CJ stated that 'a vast disproportion between sentences for murder and sentencing for offences of manslaughter which can sometimes come very close to murder would be inimical to the administration of justice'.[67] He continued:

> We derive some further, indirect support to our approach from the stark reality that the legislature has concluded, dealing with it generally, that the punitive element in sentences for murder should be increased. This coincides with increased levels of sentence for offences resulting in death, such as causing death by dangerous driving and causing death by careless driving. Parliament's intention seems clear: crimes which result in death should be treated more seriously and dealt with more severely than before. Our conclusion is not governed by, but is consistent with this approach.[68]

Thus Lord Judge's approach, which was to carry the day, was based not merely on Schedule 21 but also on other statutory changes. There seem to be five strands of reasoning here – the historical, the constitutional, the legal, the public reaction, and the logical – and they may be considered briefly. The historical argument is not clear-cut: whatever the Home Secretary's intentions, by the time the provisions came before the House of Lords the government did not agree that a consequence of Schedule 21 would or should be the 'ratcheting up' of sentence levels for other crimes, and the unique heinousness of murder was cited in support.[69] The constitutional argument fares no better, since the legislative intention behind Schedule 21 is unclear and therefore there is no clear path for the judiciary to follow. In the passage cited above, Lord Judge was at pains to state that his approach was 'not governed by' Parliament's intentions, whether he had them right or wrong.

The legal argument stems from s. 143(1) of the 2003 Act which requires courts, when considering the seriousness of an offence, to consider the offender's culpability and 'any harm which the offence caused, was intended to cause

---

[66] On which see Jeremy (2010), pp. 595–600.   [67] *Wood* [2010] 1 Cr App R (S) 6, at [22].
[68] Ibid., at [23].   [69] See the words of Baroness Scotland, quoted by Jeremy (2010), pp. 598–9.

or might foreseeably have caused'. Lord Judge described this subsection as 'new' and seemed to regard it as placing greater emphasis on harm and therefore on death.[70] However, it is not clear that it introduced, or was intended to introduce, any new principle. A fourth argument was that public confidence might be damaged if there were a large gap between murder sentences and those for other serious crimes. Whether or not this would have been so will never be known, but it can be questioned whether the large gaps between the different murder starting points are not equally hard to understand. Finally, there is the logical reason. This is at its strongest in relation to attempted murder (considered in 4.4.2), but may be applied also to manslaughter. Would it be logical to increase murder sentences substantially while leaving manslaughter sentences untouched? In particular, manslaughters by reason of diminished responsibility or by reason of loss of control are cases in which all the elements of murder are present, which surely indicates that Schedule 21 is the proper starting point for considering penalties for these 'mitigated murders'. How far this reasoning can be pursued for other offences depends on how much weight the belief in the 'unique heinousness' of murder can carry. Some senior judges have taken the view that murder is unique and that one should hesitate before reading across from murder to manslaughter.[71] On the other hand, if, as Lord Judge maintains, the real issue is the value of human life, then he is right to refer to the increased sentence levels for the various offences of causing death by driving (and the raised penalties for 'health and safety' offences) and to infer that Parliament has re-evaluated the significance to be placed on death. However, the increases for these 'causing death' offences are very small compared with the swingeing increases for murder, and so the question remains: to what extent should the very high starting points in Schedule 21 trickle down to related offences?

Let us pursue these questions in relation to the four types of manslaughter distinguished above. In manslaughter by reason of diminished responsibility, the case is essentially one of murder reduced to manslaughter because an abnormality of mind 'substantially impaired' the offender's ability to understand the nature of his conduct, to form a rational judgment, or to exercise self-control. The leading case of *Chambers* (1983)[72] set out three principal sentencing options, once the judge has reviewed the psychiatric report(s) on the offender. Where the psychiatric evidence points to a condition that requires treatment and falls within the relevant Mental Health Act

---

[70] *Attorney General's Reference No. 60 of 2009 (Appleby)* [2010] 2 Cr App R (S) 311, at [12]; similarly in *Mahil, Shoker and Peters* [2014] 1 Cr App R (S) 101 Treacy LJ referred to s. 143(1) as focusing direct attention on the harm actually caused by the offence, whereas its terms focus on harm no more than on culpability.

[71] E.g. May LJ in *Porter* [2007] 1 Cr App R (S) 706, and Latham LJ in *Attorney General's References Nos. 90 and 91 of 2006* [2007] 2 Cr App R (S) 177.

[72] (1983) 5 Cr App R (S) 190.

provisions, the court should make a hospital order, usually without limit of time.[73] If there is no recommendation in favour of a hospital order, and the offender is considered dangerous, the conditions for a life sentence may be met: a full Court of Appeal in *Wood (No. 2)*[74] held that the rare cases suitable for life imprisonment are likely to be particularly grave cases in which the offender's responsibility, though diminished, remains high, and that the minimum term should be set by reference to the statutory murder starting points, with appropriate reductions. In other cases the court may impose a determinate sentence of imprisonment – which may be as long as 10 years, but is more typically in the 3–5-year range. This is a clear compromise between punishment and treatment: the reasoning is that the length of sentence should reflect the portion of responsibility which is left after the mental abnormality has been deducted, a rather strange notion that has been little challenged.[75]

The only definitive sentencing guidelines relevant to manslaughter are the SGC guidelines on *Manslaughter by Reason of Provocation*, issued in 2005. They indicate that judges should assess the degree of provocation as shown by its nature and duration, and also the extent and timing of the retaliation. Post-offence behaviour is also relevant, but there is a warning that the use of a weapon to kill should not necessarily be treated as rendering the case significantly more serious, and should not necessarily move the case into a higher sentence range – this is to avoid discrimination, because women tend to use weapons to kill, whereas men can do so through physical strength. The guideline itself sets out three sentence ranges, each premised on provocation over a short period of time. Where there is a low degree of provocation, the starting point is 12 years and the range 10 years to life; where there is a substantial degree of provocation, the starting point is 8 years and the range 4 to 9; where there is a high degree of provocation, the starting point is 3 years and the range goes up to 4 years.

This guideline's continued authority has been questioned on two grounds – that it took no account of the Schedule 21 starting points for murder, enacted in 2003, and that it has been overtaken by a change in the law in 2009, when the partial defence of provocation was abolished in favour of the partial defence of loss of control. In *Thornley* (2011)[76] Lord Judge CJ took the view that, despite those two changes, the guideline remained authoritative and that any difficulty in a particular case could be met by invoking the 'interests of justice' ground for departure. Subsequent decisions have also relied on the SGC guidelines, whilst recognizing the two changes that need to be taken into

---

[73] See ch. 12.3 below. See, e.g., *Walton* [2004] 1 Cr App R (S) 234.

[74] [2010] 1 Cr App R (S) 6; for life imprisonment, see ch. 6.8 below.

[75] For examples, see *Slater* [2006] 1 Cr App R (S) 8, and (on calculation of the minimum term where life imprisonment is imposed) *Attorney General's Reference No. 83 of 2009* [2010] 2 Cr App R (S) 161.

[76] [2011] 2 Cr App R (S) 361.

account.[77] In both those cases the chosen starting point was 10 years before taking account of a guilty plea and other matters. The effect of this was to produce sentences a long distance below the minimum starting point of 15 years for murder, since a 10-year sentence is the equivalent of a 5-year minimum term. This raises again the question whether the mitigating effect of loss of control is too great: given that all the elements of murder are present, has the Court of Appeal taken due account of the two changes identified above? In approving sentences of around 6 years in those two cases, has it not raised questions about the relation of manslaughter sentences to sentences for, say, robbery and drug dealing?

The two other types of manslaughter, where death results from an unlawful act or from gross negligence, bring another awkward conflict to the surface. Unlawful act manslaughter varies widely in its seriousness, some of the cases being close to the borderline with murder and being sentenced accordingly.[78] Difficult problems of principle occur at the lower end of the scale, where the unlawful act is an assault or other relatively minor crime which happens to result in death. Reference is still frequently made to *Coleman* (1991),[79] where Lord Lane CJ gave guidance for sentencing in cases of death resulting from a fall caused by a single punch. He distinguished such cases from more serious ones in which the actual blow caused the injury, or where a weapon was used, or where a victim on the ground was kicked about the head. He held that 12 months' imprisonment on a guilty plea should be the starting point in cases where it was the fall that caused the death after a single blow: the sentence should be higher if the offender had a record of violence or if more than one blow was struck, and lower if the blow was unpremeditated and only of moderate force. Later, in *Furby* (2006),[80] Lord Phillips CJ reviewed some 19 previous appeals on 'one-punch manslaughter'. He concluded that the 12 months indicated in *Coleman* was still an appropriate starting point where there is a guilty plea and no aggravating factor, since the sentence should not be disproportionate if the consequences were not foreseeable. However, he indicated that the range could go up to at least 4 years for cases in which there was alcohol-fuelled violent behaviour in a public place. This last point was one of two issues highlighted by Lord Judge CJ, speaking for a full Court of Appeal in *Attorney General's Reference No. 60 of 2009 (Appleby)* (2010).[81] Lord Judge referred to 'gratuitous unprovoked violence' on the streets, and 'drunken yobbery', suggesting that where that was the context in which a punch was thrown a more serious view should be taken. He also referred to the passage in

---

[77] See *Bird* [2013] 1 Cr App R (S) 391, *Ward* [2013] 2 Cr App R (S) 233.

[78] E.g. *Hussain* [2004] 2 Cr App R (S) 497, where a sentence of 18 years was upheld for manslaughter by participating in the petrol bombing of a house, resulting in the death of eight people.

[79] (1991) 13 Cr App R (S) 508.   [80] [2006] 2 Cr App R (S) 64.   [81] [2010] 2 Cr App R (S) 311.

Wood, quoted above,[82] and to the various legislative provisions in recent years on the causing of death. He concluded that

> The increased focus on the fact that a victim has died as a result of an unlawful act of violence, even where the conviction is for manslaughter, should, in accordance with the legislative intention, be given greater weight.[83]

Lord Judge is drawing here on the increased maximum penalty for causing death by dangerous driving and other causing death offences, and less on the assertion that Parliament when enacting Schedule 21 was intending to initiate a revaluation of all manslaughter sentences. However, Lord Judge did cite s. 143(1), claiming that it was new and implying that it lent weight to the revaluation of manslaughter sentences when there is no evidence of such a legislative intent.

The conflict in unlawful act manslaughter is between sentencing based on the intrinsic gravity of the conduct itself, taking account of the offender's fault, and sentencing based to some extent on the unexpected and unfortunate result. Research findings suggest that public perceptions of conduct are heavily dependent on the harm actually resulting.[84] However, since the resulting harm is nothing more than a twist of fate, the fault-based approach is surely fairer. How much weight should be placed on the unexpected death rather than the offender's fault remains controversial, and it is important to avoid confusing the justice of a compensation claim with the justice of punishment. Many people inflict minor assaults without causing anything more than minor injuries, and there is really nothing other than misfortune to distinguish those thousands of cases from the few which happen to cause death. The proper approach, endorsed by the SGC, is that the sentence should be governed not by the vagaries of chance but by what the offender believed he was doing or risking, or at least what was reasonably foreseeable at the time of the conduct.[85] Thus the strength and circumstances of a single punch should be taken into account, and in *Duckworth* (2013)[86] a very strong blow delivered by a powerfully built man with a record of violence, causing the victim to fall and hit his head on the road, was held to justify a sentence of 6 years' imprisonment. Since the maximum for inflicting grievous bodily harm is 5 years,[87] this sentence demonstrates that there is a manslaughter premium. That is also

---

[82] Text at n. 68.

[83] [2010] 2 Cr App R (S) 311, at [22]; see also *Doblys* [2014] 2 Cr App R (S) 355, at [15].

[84] Cf. Mitchell (1998) with Robinson and Darley (1995).

[85] For further discussion and references, see Mitchell (2009); see also SGC, *Overarching Principles: Seriousness* (2004), para. 1.18: 'where unusually serious harm results and was unintended and beyond the control of the offender, culpability will be significantly influenced by the extent to which the harm could have been foreseen'.

[86] [2013] 1 Cr App R (S) 454; see also *Folkes* [2011] 2 Cr App R (S) 437.

[87] If the offender had been found to have caused gbh with intent, the crime would have been murder.

evident from the baby-battering case of *Burridge* (2011),[88] where a sentence of 10 years was imposed in a serious case.

The fourth type of manslaughter discussed here is manslaughter by gross negligence. Once again, the Court of Appeal has stated that sentence levels must increase for this kind of offence. In *Holtom* (2011),[89] where an employer was convicted of manslaughter for allowing an employee to work in unsafe conditions, the Court held that greater emphasis is now placed on the fatal consequences of a criminal act. In *Barrass* (2012),[90] where the offender had failed to call an ambulance for his dependent sister, the Court referred to 'a step change in the tariff' in manslaughter cases following the *Appleby* decision. These decisions have been followed in other cases, including medical manslaughter.[91]

4.4.4 Causing death by driving

This group of offences is both complex in its legislative structure and controversial in its sentencing implications. English law now has five offences of causing death by driving:

- causing death by dangerous driving, maximum 14 years;
- causing death by careless driving with excess alcohol, maximum 14 years;
- causing death by aggravated vehicle-taking, maximum 14 years;
- causing death by careless driving, maximum 5 years;
- causing death by driving while disqualified, unlicensed or uninsured, maximum 2 years.

Most frequently sentenced is the longest standing of these offences, causing death by dangerous driving. When the original guideline judgment for this offence was delivered, in *Boswell* (1984),[92] the maximum sentence was 5 years and one of the purposes of Lord Lane CJ's judgment was to persuade judges to increase the length of their sentences. In 1993 Parliament raised the maximum sentence from 5 to 10 years' imprisonment, and the 2003 Act further raised the maximum to 14 years.[93] The Court of Appeal gave a guideline judgment, based on the advice of the Sentencing Advisory Panel,[94] in *Cooksley* (2003),[95]

---

[88] [2011] 2 Cr App R (S) 148, discussed by Lord Judge CJ in *Attorney General's Reference No 125 of 2010* [2011] 2 Cr App R (S) 534, where the Court increased the sentence to 5 years.

[89] [2011] 1 Cr App R (S) 128.   [90] [2012] 1 Cr App R (S) 450.

[91] See particularly *Garg* [2013] 2 Cr App R (S) 203, and the discussion by Quirk (2013) of the distinction between momentary errors and knowing deviations from proper practice. Cf. *Kovvali* [2014] 1 Cr App R (S) 199.

[92] (1984) 6 Cr App R (S) 257.

[93] Criminal Justice Act 2003, s. 285; the maxima for causing death by careless driving with excess alcohol and for aggravated vehicle-taking causing death were also raised to 14 years by this section.

[94] SAP, *Causing Death by Dangerous Driving* (2003).   [95] [2004] 1 Cr App R (S) 1.

before the latest increase in maximum penalty came into effect. It was not clear whether the increase from 10 to 14 years was intended to apply only to cases in the highest range, or whether it should be reflected by increases to all the ranges. The Court of Appeal resolved this question in *Richardson et al.* (2007)[96] in favour of increases to all the ranges, but the matter is now subject to the SGC guidelines, *Causing Death by Driving* (2008).

In relation to causing death by dangerous driving, the guideline sets out a number of 'determinants of seriousness' that judges are expected to consider before classifying the offence in one of the three ranges. These factors include awareness of risk (including failure to heed warnings), effect of alcohol or drugs, inappropriate speed of vehicle, and seriously culpable behaviour (including aggressive driving, using a hand-held phone, and driving when deprived of sleep). There are also aggravating factors (including the causing of more than one death) and mitigating factors (good driving record, rendering assistance at the scene). All these matters must be considered and weighed when placing the offence on one of the three levels.

Level 1 is the highest category of seriousness, involving a deliberate decision to ignore the rules of the road and disregard of the danger to others. The starting point is 8 years, with a range of 7 to 14 years. In *Noble* (2003),[97] the Court upheld a sentence of 10 years (then the maximum) on an offender who caused six deaths by driving at excessive speed while two-and-a-half times over the drink-driving limit and who then claimed that someone else had been driving. Under the SGC guideline, and given the increase in the maximum to 14 years, this case would undoubtedly result in a longer sentence now. Slightly less serious but still in the highest category was *Barney and Barney* (2008),[98] where two brothers raced their cars along a long stretch of road, driving aggressively, overtaking on blind bends, and failing to stop after causing other cars to collide. Their sentences of 8 and 7 years, reflecting their (delayed) pleas of guilty and elements of remorse, were upheld.

Level 2 includes cases where the offender's driving created a substantial risk of danger to others. The starting point is 5 years, with a range of 4 to 7 years. A case at the top of this range was *Kuti and Cherry* (2008),[99] where the two offenders had been racing over about a mile, exceeding the speed limit, and one of them collided with a turning vehicle containing four women, three of whom died and the other suffered serious injuries. The case was placed at the very top of the range (there was no guilty plea), and the Court of Appeal reduced the sentences only slightly, to 6½ years, to reflect the good characters of the two offenders. Also into this category falls the very different case of

---

[96] [2007] 2 Cr App R (S) 211.   [97] [2003] 1 Cr App R (S) 312.

[98] [2008] 2 Cr App R (S) 208; see also the sentence on the co-defendant in *Attorney General's Reference No. 40 of 2012* [2013] 2 Cr App R (S) 34, at [15].

[99] [2008] 2 Cr App R (S) 369; cf. *Attorney General's Reference No. 40 of 2012* [2013] 2 Cr App R (S) 34.

Attorney General's Reference No. 158 of 2004,[100] where a lorry driver fell asleep towards the end of his day's work and crashed into another vehicle. The Court of Appeal held that the trial judge had erred in placing the offence at level 3 (see below). It should have been placed at level 2, because the offender must have known that he was deprived of adequate sleep and rest before he set out driving. This would qualify as 'seriously culpable behaviour', particularly for a professional driver. In *Wilson* (2011),[101] where a driver fell asleep and killed two pedestrians, the Court of Appeal held that she must have realised how tired she was, and it was only strong mitigating factors that reduced the sentence to 3 years' imprisonment.

Level 3 is for cases in which the offender's driving created a significant risk of danger to others. None of the determinants of seriousness would be expected to be found here, and these would typically be cases of momentary inattention or a single dangerous manoeuvre. Thus in *Hussain* (2008)[102] a minicab driver emerging from a junction failed to see an oncoming motorcyclist. He had an unblemished record, and for this momentary inattention the Court reduced the sentence from 30 to 15 months. Similarly in *Akujee* (2008)[103] a driver failed to notice a child on a pedestrian crossing. He had an unblemished record, and for this (unexplained) momentary inattention the Court reduced the sentence from 36 to 18 months.

The second of the 'causing death' offences is causing death by careless driving while under the influence of alcohol. Here the chief determinants of seriousness are the degree of intoxication and the degree of carelessness. Once again, the SGC guideline indicates three levels of seriousness, based on the interaction of these two axes. In practice, the average length of custodial sentence for this offence is somewhat higher than that for causing death by dangerous driving, at 61.3 months compared with 52.4 months in 2013.[104]

Turning now to the two offences introduced by the Road Safety Act 2006,[105] each of them generates controversy. The offence of causing death by careless driving combines the summary offence of careless driving (maximum sentence, a level 5 fine, no imprisonment) with the causing of death, to produce an offence for which Parliament has provided a maximum of 5 years' imprisonment. The maximum penalty is presumably to cater for cases that fall just below the threshold of dangerous driving (i.e. cases where the driving fell below, but not *far below*, the required standard): thus level 1 of the guideline provides for a starting point of 15 months, with a range from 36 weeks to 3 years, for cases falling just short of dangerous driving. If the case is close to dangerous driving, a judge may be justified in departing from the guideline

---

[100] [2006] 1 Cr App R (S) 274.   [101] [2011] 1 Cr App R (S) 11.   [102] [2008] 2 Cr App R (S) 485.
[103] [2008] 2 Cr App R (S) 188; see also *Attorney General's Reference No. 16 of 2008* [2009] 1 Cr App R (S) 138.
[104] Ministry of Justice, *Criminal Justice Statistics 2013* (2014), Table 8.1.
[105] The offence of causing death by aggravated vehicle-taking is not considered separately here: it is not frequently prosecuted, and was not included in the SGC guideline.

and going into the range above 3 years (but below the statutory maximum of 5 years).[106] Level 3, the lowest level, is for cases of momentary inattention with no aggravating features: the starting point is a medium community sentence, with a range from low to high community sentence. Between levels 1 and 3 comes level 2, for 'other cases of careless driving', with a starting point of 36 weeks' imprisonment and a range from a high community penalty to 2 years. Level 2 is particularly difficult for the sentencer, since there are few agreed examples and it also straddles the custody threshold. The Court of Appeal has pointed this out, but without being able to go further than the SGC in identifying any reliable indicators of the degrees of carelessness of driving.[107] There is a certain unease about this offence, given the wide gulf between the amount of fault (which may be low, and no more than many drivers succumb to from time to time) and the tragic consequences. As we shall see below, members of the public are ambivalent about the existence of the offence.

For the offence of causing death by driving while unlicensed, uninsured or disqualified, Parliament has set the maximum sentence at 2 years' imprisonment. No fault in the manner of driving is required for this offence: its rationale is that the offender should not have been on the road at the time of the offence, and should therefore bear responsibility even for an accidental causing of death (e.g. a child running out in front of a car). The government pointed to statistics showing that drivers in these categories are between three and nine times more likely to be involved in an accident. The SGC guideline identifies the disqualified driver as the worst of the three, since the disqualification will have been imposed for road safety reasons. Thus level 1 offences consist of those who kill when driving while disqualified, together with unlicensed or uninsured drivers with two aggravating features. The starting point is 12 months, with a range from 36 weeks to 2 years. Level 2 offences consist of unlicensed or uninsured drivers with one aggravating feature (starting point 26 weeks, range from high community order to 36 weeks).[108] Level 3 offences consist of unlicensed or uninsured drivers with no aggravating feature (starting point a medium community order, range from low to high community order).

As part of the consultation process when preparing its advice to the SGC, the Panel commissioned public opinion research on these offences. The research established that members of the public typically believe that the courts pass sentences well below the sentences they would prefer, although in fact court sentencing appears to be similar to what the public want.[109] This is consistent with much public opinion research. In general, over half of the

---

[106] As in *Shepherd* [2010] 2 Cr App R (S) 370, at [23–25].
[107] *Campbell* [2010] 2 Cr App R (S) 175; *Odedara* [2010] 2 Cr App R (S) 359; *Zhao* [2014] 1 Cr App R (S) 97.
[108] On the cumulative effect of aggravating factors, see *Headley* [2013] 1 Cr App R (S) 224.
[109] Roberts, Hough et al. (2008), pp. 530–2.

people in the focus groups or the survey would tolerate the starting points proposed by the Panel and issued by the SGC.[110] However, there was strong public rejection of the ranking of the offence of causing death by driving whilst disqualified: this offence was ranked almost as serious as causing death by dangerous driving and causing death by careless driving while under the influence of alcohol, and as distinctly more serious than causing death by careless driving. Whereas Parliament provided maxima of 5 years for causing death by careless driving and 2 years for causing death by driving while disqualified, public opinion strongly favoured the view that these are the wrong way round. This was partly because driving whilst disqualified is a deliberate illegal act, whereas careless driving involves the kind of lapse that most drivers will occasionally commit. The Panel was unable to act on this strong finding, however, since its proposals (and the SGC guidelines) have to be embedded within the statutory framework.

Is public opinion right on these issues? How serious are the four 'causing death by driving' offences just considered? On the von Hirsch–Jareborg scale the harm is at the highest level, since they violate the value of physical integrity and deprive the victim of subsistence. In principle the culpability is much lower than for an intentional causing of death or injury, but that point cannot be carried too far. The first two offences involve the culpable creation of an avoidable risk of death (or at least serious injury), and this may be thought to justify the recent raising of these offences in the scale of relative seriousness. On the other hand, Michael Hirst has argued that these two driving offences are now sentenced at a higher level than many offences of manslaughter, and that this is not warranted by either the substance or the definitions of the different offences.[111] He cites some decisions in support of this proposition, but the question is whether cases of causing death by dangerous driving at levels 1 and 2 do not exhibit greater culpability – often over a period of time – than the decisions he cites. In any event, there has been an increase in the level of most manslaughter sentences since 2009, as we saw in 4.4.3 above.

The third offence, causing death by careless driving, has such a slight culpability requirement that one may well question whether it should be sufficient to ground a homicide offence.[112] As for causing death by driving while disqualified, uninsured or unlicensed, the elements of deliberation and but-for causation are present – if the driver had not knowingly flouted his driving ban, the death would not have occurred – but there is no fault in the manner of the driving (otherwise it would be a more serious offence). The public's view of the seriousness of this offence seems to connect the element of deliberation with the harm actually caused, without much emphasis on the unforeseeability of the tragic event.

---

[110] Ibid., pp. 535–6.   [111] Hirst (2008).
[112] See generally the critique of the two new offences by Cunningham (2007).

4.4.5 Drug offences

Offences involving the importation or supply of prohibited drugs rank high in the current English scale of ordinal proportionality. They were the subject of the first of Lord Lane's guideline judgments, in *Aramah* (1982).[113] Parliament subsequently increased the maximum penalty for the importation, supply or production of class A drugs from 14 years to life imprisonment, and the *Aramah* guidelines were judicially revised in several judgments. The Sentencing Advisory Panel made proposals for definitive guidelines on drug offences just before its demise,[114] and the Sentencing Council, after carrying out further research, published definitive guidelines on *Drug Offences* (2012).

For each of the major drug offences – importation, supply, production, permitting the use of premises, and possession – the guideline takes the form of a two-dimensional grid. At Step One the sentencer has to decide on the offender's culpability as demonstrated by the role played (leading, significant or lesser), and on the category of harm (class and quantity of drug involved). At Step Two the initial categorisation is transferred to the two-dimensional grid, indicating the relevant category range and starting point. Step Two may look like a version of the widely criticised grids common in American guideline systems, and it is therefore not surprising that the Court of Appeal has been keen to emphasise that the drugs guidelines should not be treated as 'an arithmetical process'[115] and that 'the categories do not provide some kind of straitjacket into which every case must be squeezed'.[116] At both Step One and Step Two the sentencer is encouraged to be responsive to the particular facts of the case.

Thus in *Khan* (2014)[117] the offenders were convicted of a street-dealing operation that was on an unusually large scale, and the Court of Appeal approved the judge's decision to take the offence out of the indicated category range into the higher range. This case and several others show that appeals are often based on the sentencer's decision in respect of one (or both) of the two dimensions of the grid. There are two particular features of the Council's guidelines which deserve comment. The first is that, having carried out research into the circumstances of some 'drug mules' used as couriers to import drugs, the Council decided to reduce the sentence level for those couriers who are 'engaged by pressure, coercion, intimidation', and 'involved through naivety/exploitation'. Those features place the courier in the lowest culpability category of 'lesser role'. But this does not apply to all couriers, some of whom will rightly be placed in the higher category, 'significant role', because

---

[113] (1982) 4 Cr App R (S) 407.   [114] SAP, *Sentencing for Drug Offences* (2009).

[115] Per Hughes LJ in *Boakye* [2013] 1 Cr App R (S) 6, at [39].

[116] Per Hallett LJ in *Attorney-General's References Nos. 15, 16 and 17 of 2012* [2013] 1 Cr App R (S) 289, at [12].

[117] [2014] 1 Cr App R (S) 42.

they were 'motivated by financial or other advantage'.[118] The second feature is that the guidelines make it clear that 'where the operation is on the most serious and commercial scale, involving a quantity of drugs significantly higher than category 1, sentences of 20 years and above may be appropriate, depending on the role of the offender'. This wording appears at Step One, and for importation of class A drugs the highest sentence (category 1 offence, leading role) has a category range of 12–16 years with a starting point of 14 years. That category of harm has an indicative quantity of 5 kilograms of cocaine or heroin. In *Attorney General's References Nos. 15, 16 and 17 of 2012* (2013)[119] the imported drugs amounted to some 4 kilograms of cocaine and 70 kilograms of heroin, with a street value of some £4 or £5 million. The Court of Appeal increased the sentences, holding that this was importation 'on a massive scale', and approved a sentence of 20 years for the first offender. Whether this qualifies as a departure from the guideline is unclear – 20 years is higher than any category range, although encouraged by the Council's own statement – but presumably it would be regarded as being in the interests of justice.

This brings us to the key question: where should drugs offences be placed on a scale of ordinal proportionality? A number of arguments have been advanced. In *Aramah* Lord Lane said that rivalry between gangs 'may be a fruitful source of violence and internecine strife'. That may be true of some operations, but unless those offences are proved, it is wrong to allow such speculative and secondary consequences to raise valuations of the seriousness of drug offences. Lord Lane added another secondary consequence: that people addicted to the drugs imported by these offenders have to resort to crime in order to pay for the drugs. This leads to 'the most horrifying aspect': 'the degradation and suffering and not infrequent death which the drug brings to the addict. It is not difficult to understand why in some parts of the world traffickers in heroin in any substantial quantity are sentenced to death and executed'.[120] This hints at the argument that drug dealing is in effect a preliminary to homicide, since drug traffickers tempt addicts into a kind of physical and mental disintegration which may lead to death. However, this argument requires a large slice of paternalism, for those who use class A drugs must be supposed to have been rational citizens when they began, even if their addiction subsequently saps their free will. In other words, they cannot be said to be victims in the ordinary sense of unwilling participants; and, in terms of the von Hirsch–Jareborg scale, drug offences are remote from any danger to physical integrity, let alone death. Even if addicts' living standards have declined spectacularly, there may have been no force, fear, or fraud. At most, then, the analogy is with aiding and abetting suicide, not murder.

---

[118] See the discussions in *Boakye* [2013] 1 Cr App R (S) 6, at [34–37]; and in *Lopez-Sacido* [2013] 1 Cr App R (S) 440, at [18].

[119] [2013] 1 Cr App R (S) 289.   [120] (1982) 4 Cr App R (S) 407, at pp. 408–9.

While any connection with murder is therefore tenuous, a public opinion survey for the Council showed that members of the public in focus groups tended to favour very long prison sentences for drug traffickers who make high profits from their activities, even if they were less punitive for offences of medium or lower seriousness.[121] However, it is not clear that this presses the argument far enough. Sentences of imprisonment are not the only form of censure and deprivation for drug traffickers: the courts also have extensive duties and powers to order confiscation of their assets, consolidated in the Proceeds of Crime Act 2002, and there is good reason to place greater emphasis on this response to drug offending.[122] If and insofar as substantial prison sentences are to be imposed, how should they relate to sentences for armed robbery and multiple rape? We will see in 4.4.8 below that major robberies with the use of firearms tend to be sentenced within the 16–25 year range, reflecting the use of lethal weapons and the deliberate threats to others, as well as the financial gain. The highest category range for rape is 13–19 years, but the guideline notes that 'offences may be of such severity, for example involving a campaign of rape, that sentences of 20 years and above may be appropriate'.[123]

This confusion towards the top of the sentencing tariff is a further reason that indicates the urgent need for a reconsideration of drugs policy. Other European countries have begun to change their approach, and there have been evidence-based calls from across the world to discard the ultra-punitive approach to drugs.[124] This is not to suggest that there are any straightforward solutions, but rather to encourage the kind of root-and-branch rethinking that the Sentencing Council cannot undertake. Such rethinking would be focused on wider social and health policies, but would have an inevitable bearing on sentencing.

4.4.6 Serious woundings

We have already noted that some attempted murders lead to life-threatening injuries, and to considerable sentencing problems (4.4.2 above). We now move to consider cases where an intent to kill cannot be established – so that there can be no conviction for attempted murder – but where there is a wounding or serious injury. The Sentencing Council has issued a definitive guideline on *Assault* (2011),[125] which deals separately with six offences: wounding or causing grievous bodily harm with intent, unlawful wounding or grievous bodily harm, assault occasioning actual bodily harm, assault with intent to resist arrest, assault on a police constable, and common assault. Our focus here

[121] Jacobson, Kirby and Hough (2011).

[122] SAP, *Sentencing for Drug Offences* (2009), paras. 22–4.

[123] Sentencing Council, *Sexual Offences: Definitive Guideline* (2013), pp. 10–11.

[124] See [2013] Crim LR 271–2.

[125] This guideline replaced the SGC's *Assault and Other Offences Against the Person* (2008).

is on the two most serious offences in this group. Common assault will be discussed in the context of the *Magistrates' Court Sentencing Guidelines* later.

The most serious of these offences is that under s. 18 of the Offences Against the Person Act 1861, either wounding or causing grievous bodily harm with intent to cause grievous bodily harm. The Step One factors relevant to the choice between three categories of seriousness include the degree of injury, the vulnerability of the victim, premeditation, the use of a weapon or equivalent, leading role in group, and demonstrating hostility to the victim based on age, sex, gender, etc. Category 1 has a starting point of 12 years with a range of 9–16 years; category 2 has a starting point of 6 years with a range of 5–9 years; and category 3 has a starting point of 4 years with a range of 3–5 years. Thus in *Grubb* (2012)[126] D took part, with two men, in a revenge attack on a man suspected of abusing her child. Her role was to initiate the attack and to urge the others on. They inflicted serious injuries to the eye, the lung, a broken rib, a bruised kidney, and bleeding into the brain. D was convicted after a trial and sentenced to 11 years for a category 1 offence. The Court of Appeal agreed that this was a category 1 offence but reduced the sentence to 8 years to reflect her subordinate role and some personal mitigation.

One of the features of this part of English law is that the next lower offence – unlawful wounding or grievous bodily harm, contrary to s. 20 of the 1861 Act – has the considerably lower maximum of 5 years. If the prosecution accepts a plea of guilty to the s. 20 offence, or a jury convicts of this lesser offence, that decision necessarily has a significant effect on sentence. The guideline for s. 20 offences has three categories. Category 1 has a starting point of 3 years, with a range of 2 years 6 months to 4 years; category 2 has a starting point of 1 year 6 months, with a range of 1–3 years; and category 3 has a starting point of high-level community order, with a range of low-level community order to 51 weeks' custody.[127] In *Channer* (2011)[128] D pleaded guilty to a s. 20 offence, having attacked his former girlfriend by biting her, burning her cheek with a cigarette and punching her in the face on three successive occasions, breaking her cheekbone. The Court of Appeal agreed that this offence should be placed in category 1 (applying the former SGC guidelines, but the current Sentencing Council guidelines would yield the same result). The Court agreed that the starting point should be 4 years, at the top of category 1, with a 25 per cent reduction for pleading guilty. In *Lawrence* (2012)[129] D had run on to the pitch during a Sunday football match and struck a heavy blow to the head of a player who had just committed a foul, breaking his eye socket and cheek in four places. The Court of Appeal

---

[126] [2012] 2 Cr App R (S) 248.

[127] The next offence down, assault occasioning actual bodily harm, has the same maximum sentence of 5 years, but the ranges and starting points are somewhat lower than those for the s. 20 offence: see Sentencing Council, *Assault*, p. 12.

[128] [2011] 1 Cr App R (S) 464.   [129] [2012] 2 Cr App R (S) 243.

concurred in the placement of this offence in category 2, on the grounds of greater harm with lesser culpability (the Court did not explain why the culpability was lesser). The Court upheld the sentence of 9 months' imprisonment, beneath the 1–3 year range for category 2 offences, citing D's previous good character and the fact that a single blow was delivered.

These offences do harm to physical integrity and to autonomy, in von Hirsch and Jareborg's terms. Their effect is mostly in terms of minimal well-being rather than subsistence, and mitigation and aggravation again assume a critical role. The guidelines tend to focus on the degree of harm, including the use of a weapon, and on the offender's culpability. Since proof of an intention to cause gbh is sufficient culpability for murder, there might appear to be no less logic in linking s. 18 sentences to murder than in linking sentences for attempted murder to murder. Indeed, the Council stated its belief that 'the level of sentencing [for serious assaults] should be linked with that for murder',[130] although in the event its guideline for s. 18 cases is set no higher than the previous SGC guideline. More troublesome is the considerable distance between the offence ranges for s. 18 offences and for s. 20 offences (as required by the respective statutory maxima), with the result that serious violence may fall to be sentenced under s. 20. Moreover, it seems that the injuries inflicted in these assaults are often far in excess of the injuries in robbery cases sentenced at the same or a higher level, a point to be borne in mind when robbery is discussed in paragraph 4.4.8 below. The Crime Survey for England and Wales reported a 13 per cent decline in violence involving injury in the year 2012–13, continuing a longer-term trend that shows 2.4 million incidents of violence with injury in 1995 and 916,000 in 2012–13.[131]

4.4.7 Rape and other serious sexual offences

Rape is one of the offences whose known profile has changed considerably in the last 30 years. In 1985 there were just under 2,000 reported rapes, with stranger rapes, rape by intimates ('relationship rapes'), and acquaintance rapes in roughly equal proportions. In 1996 there were some 6,000 reported rapes: stranger rapes had not increased in number and thus now formed only 12 per cent of the total, whereas reported relationship rapes accounted for 43 per cent and rapes by acquaintances for 45 per cent.[132] Data from the British Crime Survey suggest that current partners are responsible for some 45 per cent of rapes, and strangers only for 8 per cent.[133] Police recorded rapes numbered 12,300 in 2002–3 and 18,300 in 2012–13, the rise being attributed partly to the reporting of historic offences, including those allegedly committed by

---

[130] Sentencing Council, *Assault Guideline: Professional Consultation* (2010), p. 8.
[131] Crime Survey for England and Wales (year ending September 2013), Figure 4.
[132] Harris and Grace (1999), p. 6.   [133] Myhill and Allen (2002), ch. 5.

celebrities. Other sexual offences recorded by the police stood at 44,400 in 2002–3 and 41,133 in 2012–13.[134]

The Sexual Offences Act 2003 expanded the definition of rape so as to include oral as well as vaginal and anal penetration by a penis, and also reformed many other sexual offences. The SGC issued a definitive guideline on rape and other offences in the 2003 Act,[135] and that has now been replaced by the Sentencing Council's definitive guideline on *Sexual Offences* (2013). The structure of the rape guideline involves three categories, each with two culpability levels. The category is to be determined by reference to the presence or absence of one or more of eight factors, including severe physical or psychological harm, pregnancy, additional violence or degradation, vulnerable victim, and uninvited entry into victim's home. If one or more of those factors is found in extreme form, that indicates category 1. If one or more of the factors is present, but not in extreme form, that indicates category 2. If none of the factors is present, that indicates category 3. There are then 11 culpability factors, including group offence, photographing incident, and abuse of trust. If one or more of those factors is present, the three ranges are: category 1, starting point 15 years with a range of 13–19 years; category 2, starting point 10 years with a range of 9–13 years; and category 3, starting point of 7 years with a range of 6–9 years. If none of the 11 culpability factors is present, there is a lower range for each category. The guideline makes it clear that 'offences may be of such severity, for example involving a campaign of rape, that sentences of 20 years or above may be appropriate'.[136]

When preparing its 2002 advice to the Court of Appeal, the Panel commissioned empirical research into views of rape among a sample of members of the public, including some rape victims.[137] One of the clear outcomes of this research was the view that relationship rape was no less traumatic and therefore no less serious than stranger rape, because, although the latter was frightening, the breach of intimate trust involved in relationship rape could have equally deep effects on the victim. The Panel therefore recommended, and the Court of Appeal accepted, that the starting points should be the same whether it was a stranger rape or relationship rape. This is retained in the SGC and Council guidelines, which draw no distinctions as to whether the victim is a woman or a man, and whether the rape was vaginal, oral, or anal.

How seriously should rape be ranked on the ladder of offences? Some two-thirds of rapes involve some violence or threat of violence, and many involve the infliction of other sexual indignities.[138] However, the fundamental interests violated by sexual attacks are autonomy and choice in sexual matters. It is not just that victims are wronged by the invasion of their right to respect for

---

[134] Kershaw et al. (2008), p. 67.

[135] SGC, *Sexual Offences Act 2003* (2007); the original rape guideline was created by Lord Lane CJ in *Billam* (1986) 82 Cr App R 347, and that was superseded by *Millberry* [2003] 2 Cr App R (S) 142, which was based on advice from the Sentencing Advisory Panel.

[136] Sentencing Council, *Sexual Offences* (2013), p. 10.

[137] Clarke, Moran-Ellis and Sleney (2002).   [138] Harris and Grace (1999), p. 19.

private life, of which sexual autonomy is a central feature.[139] The distinctly sexual element brings in other values and disvalues – self-expression, intimacy, shared relationships, shame, humiliation, exploitation, and objectification – which are often crucial to understanding the effects of sexual victimization.[140] In terms of the von Hirsch–Jareborg scale, then, there will usually be humiliation and deprivation of privacy and autonomy to a significant degree, often compounded by a threat to physical integrity. The typical effect on the victim is therefore likely to be at the level of minimal well-being. It is not thought that most rapes are planned, in the way that armed robberies often are, but the culpability will usually be high because the offender will know perfectly well what is being done.[141] This raises questions about the relationship of rape sentences to those for robberies of shops and off-licences, discussed below.

Down the scale from rape comes the offence of sexual assault, with a statutory maximum of 10 years. The Council's guideline indicates three categories of harm, with category 1 constituted by a) severe psychological or physical harm, b) abduction, c) violence or threats of violence, and d) forced/uninvited entry into victim's home, and category 2 constituted by e) touching of sexual organs, f) prolonged incident, g) additional degradation, and h) vulnerable victim. Culpability is divided into A and B, with a list of 11 factors any one of which places the offences within A. Category 1A has a starting point of 4 years, with a category range of 3–7 years; category 2A has a starting point of 2 years, with an overlapping category range of 1–4 years; and category 3A, for cases involving none of the factors in categories 1 and 2, has a starting point of 26 weeks' custody and a range of high-level community order to 1 year's custody. Lower ranges are provided for cases where the culpability level is only B. A case in which a man, using threats reinforced with a knife, forced a woman to masturbate him would presumably be in category 1.[142] A case in which D climbed onto a neighbour and held his penis two inches from her face, and subsequently tried to force her legs apart, would presumably be placed in category 2.[143] As cases of this nature demonstrate, these cases will invariably involve humiliation and deprivation of privacy and autonomy, on the von Hirsch–Jareborg scale.

4.4.8 Robbery

The definition of this offence is unusual.[144] The crime of robbery is made up of two elements, theft and the use or threat of force in order to steal. The amount

---

[139] This is emphasized by the jurisprudence on Art. 8 of the Convention – e.g. *Sutherland and Morris* v. *United Kingdom* (1997) 24 EHRR CD22, para. 57.

[140] For further discussion, cf. Lacey (1998) with Gardner and Shute (2000).

[141] For similar analysis see SAP, *Sexual Offences Act 2003*.

[142] *Attorney General's Reference No. 79 of 2010* [2011] 2 Cr App R (S) 333, sentence increased to 4 years under SGC guidelines.

[143] *Elliott* [2010] 2 Cr App R (S) 377, sentence reduced to 18 months under SGC guidelines.

[144] The argument here is elaborated more fully in Ashworth (2002a).

of force that turns a theft into a robbery may vary tremendously, from tugging at an arm in order to effect the release of a bag through to the use of firearms or other weapons coupled with threats to kill. As we saw in 4.4.6 above, when violence is threatened or used in other circumstances, the law offers a graduated scale of crimes, from murder through attempted murder, grievous bodily harm, unlawful wounding and assault occasioning actually bodily harm, and down to assault. Each of those offences against the person has its own sentence range. But robbery is robbery, a single undivided offence that leaves sentencers to make the appropriate assessments of the degree of force.

Sentencing practice for crimes of robbery can be divided into five gradations or levels. The SGC guideline covers the lowest three levels, leaving the top two levels to be developed through judicial guidance. The SGC guideline makes it clear that the element of violence is the foremost issue in sentencing – the seriousness of any injury inflicted, the nature and degree of any threat made, the amount of fear created, the use of a weapon, and so forth. The SGC's robbery guideline treats level 1 as the lowest category rather than the highest, and so that approach will be followed here. Level 1 robberies are typically street robberies or 'muggings', involving the threat or use of some force, causing bruising or pain. The starting point is 12 months' imprisonment, with a range going up to 3 years (no base for the range is specified). Many offences falling into this category will involve the taking of a mobile phone, wallet, or handbag, and it was in this context that Lord Woolf delivered a notorious judgment in 2002 calling for deterrent sentences.[145] The SGC's guideline replaces that judgment (and the SGC also created a separate guideline for young offenders for this offence).[146] An example of the application of the guideline is *Vuillermet* (2008),[147] where the principal offence involved D and another man aggressively approaching two women who were parking their car; D said 'give me your phone or I'll give you a black eye'; she gave it to him, and he then asked for her wallet; when she said she did not have one, he and the other man left. D, who had previous convictions, was sentenced to 4½ years. The judge had failed to refer to the SGC's guideline, and the Court of Appeal held that this was properly a level 1 case, for which the appropriate sentence was 2½ years. The Court of Appeal did not identify the features that took the case so far above the starting point of 12 months.

Level 2 consists typically of robberies of small businesses, although it includes other robberies with the use of a weapon to threaten or the application of significant force. The starting point here is 4 years, with a range of

---

[145] *Attorney General's References Nos. 4 and 7 of 2002, and Q* [2002] 2 Cr App R (S) 345, at p. 348; for an example of over-sentencing resulting from this decision, see *Attorney General's References Nos. 150 and 151 of 2002* [2003] 2 Cr App R (S) 658.

[146] The Youth Justice Board (2002) was particularly unhappy with the application of Lord Woolf's judgment to young offenders, since it seemed to rule out the use of community orders for this offence at a time when about one-half of them received a community order.

[147] [2008] 2 Cr App R (S) 204.

2–7 years. Thus in *Sykes* (2008)[148] the essence of the three robberies was that D entered small shops wearing a mask and wielding a kitchen knife, stealing money from the tills. The Court of Appeal allowed D's appeal against sentences of 7 years for the offences: the starting point should have been 5 years for each offence (higher than the level 2 starting point of 4 years because of the disguise and the knife), rising to 7 years for the three offences,[149] and reducing again to 5 years for the pleas of guilty. Also placed at level 2 was the rather different offence in *Morgan* (2008),[150] where D and another man seized a woman aged 73 returning home from shopping and forced her into a lift, the other man holding her tightly round the nose and mouth while D took £300 from her bag and rings from her fingers. The Court of Appeal held that, because of the force used on a vulnerable victim, resulting in pain to her face, the case fell properly within level 2. The sentence of 6½ years on a guilty plea was, however, too high for the secondary party to this brief though frightening robbery, and it was reduced to 4 years.

At level 3 come 'less sophisticated commercial robberies', typically involving the use of a weapon and significant force or serious injury. The starting point is 8 years, and the range 7–12 years. As with the two other levels, the aggravating factors include group offending, planning, wearing a disguise, and playing a leading role; the mitigating factors include remorse, fringe participant, and unplanned offence. A case held to fall within this category was *Howard* (2013),[151] where a robbery of an off-licence involved minor injuries but where there were serious threats reinforced by a metal bar and a long knife, plus some 28 previous convictions. A starting point of 12 years, with a one-third reduction for the guilty plea, resulted in a sentence of 8 years.

Two levels of robbery fall outside and above the SGC guidelines, although the SGC indicates their approximate ranges. Level 4 includes violent personal robberies in the home, for which a range of 13–16 years is mentioned by the SGC. A possible example is provided by *Attorney General's Reference No. 89 of 1999 (Farrow)* (2000),[152] where the offender forced his way into a house, threatened the elderly occupant with a knife, pulled a cable round his neck until he lost consciousness, and then stole some £120. The Court of Appeal stated that the proper sentence should have been 10 years' imprisonment on a guilty plea. In this group of cases, the violence is rightly regarded as more important than the theft.

Level 5 is the top category, referred to by the SGC as 'professionally planned commercial robberies' and formerly known as 'first division robberies'. The SGC refers to the old case of *Turner* (1975)[153] as providing an appropriate framework for sentencing at this level, but it seems that more recent decisions

---

[148] [2008] 2 Cr App R (S) 10; see also *Razack* [2009] 1 Cr App R (S) 17.
[149] See ch. 8 below on the principles of concurrent and consecutive sentencing.
[150] [2008] 2 Cr App R (S) 93.   [151] [2013] 1 Cr App R (S) 405.   [152] [2000] 2 Cr App R (S) 382.
[153] (1975) 61 Cr App R 67, at pp. 89–91; see n. 36 above and accompanying text.

have taken sentence levels significantly higher than the 15–18 years range indicated in *Turner*. Thus in *Jenkins et al.* (2009)[154] the Court of Appeal expressly stated that the *Turner* judgment was no longer a reliable guide to sentencing for the most serious armed robberies. The Court held that 25 years was an appropriate starting point for a series of five robberies in which sawn-off shotguns were carried and sometimes fired in attacks on security guards. The Court took the same view in *Thomas* (2012),[155] where a planned raid on a London jewellers' shop involved the taking of jewels worth £40 million, the use of firearms to frighten staff, hostage-taking and shots fired at members of the public. Lord Judge CJ held that, although the sentence levels set out in the *Turner* judgment were no longer to be relied on, the reasoning of that case remains relevant. There must be a relationship 'between the level of sentences for murder and for all serious cases involving violence'. Since the minimum terms for murder were now longer than in 1975, higher sentences for serious robberies were justified. In this case sentences in the range of 16–23 years were upheld on the facts.

How do offences of robbery stand in relation to the von Hirsch–Jareborg scale? The element of theft would not be greatly significant in many cases, especially at level 1, and the principal task would be to assess the gravity of the attack on the victim's physical integrity, including psychological harm. The SGC is therefore right to state, as the basis of its guideline, that 'it is the element of violence that is the most serious part of the offence of robbery', although other factors such as fear experienced by the victim are significant.[156] In pursuit of a consistent approach, it would therefore be preferable to set the ranges in terms of the levels indicated in the Sentencing Council's *Assault* guideline. That should be Step One, with other factors, particularly aggravating factors such as high financial yield (as in *Thomas*, for example) or the use of a firearm (unless separately charged), taken into account at Step Two. In October 2014 the Council issued a consultation document on robbery guidelines, proposing three categories of robbery to cover the whole range.[157]

4.4.9 Burglary

For sentencing purposes this offence is usually subdivided into two distinct types, domestic burglaries (of dwellings) and non-domestic burglaries (of commercial or industrial premises). The Criminal Justice Act 1991 confirmed this by reducing the maximum penalty for non-domestic burglary to 10 years, below the 14 years for domestic burglary. Domestic burglary is recognised as more than a mere property offence: the Sentencing Council commented that it is regarded as a serious offence 'because it involves an invasion of privacy and

---

[154] [2009] 1 Cr App R (S) 109.
[155] [2012] 1 Cr App R (S) 254; see also *Wynne* [2014] 1 Cr App R (S) 63.
[156] SGC, *Robbery*, pp. 4–5.   [157] Sentencing Council, *Robbery Guideline: Consultation* (2014).

can leave the victim with a sense of violation and insecurity'.[158] The possible effects were documented by Maguire (1982), who found that over a quarter of victims of residential burglary suffer quite serious shock as a result of the offence, and that the lives of some two-thirds of victims are affected for a period of weeks following the offence.

Sentencing practice in residential burglary cases has always been diverse, not least because the offence can vary from a quick walk-in theft to planned and targeted plundering. In 1997 Parliament introduced a presumptive minimum sentence for the third domestic burglary: in outline,[159] a court must pass a sentence of at least 3 years' imprisonment for the third domestic burglary unless it would be 'unjust in all the circumstances' to do so, but a burglary conviction only qualifies for this purpose if it relates to a crime committed after conviction of another qualifying burglary. The Sentencing Advisory Panel took the view that this required sentences for the first and second burglary to be ranged in steps up to that level. The Panel therefore proposed starting points of 9 months' imprisonment for the first domestic burglary and 18 months for the second.[160] The Court of Appeal in *McInerney and Keating* (2003)[161] declined to adopt the Panel's proposed starting points and held such prison sentences stood in the way of constructive efforts to break the cycle of offending.[162] This led Lord Woolf CJ to propose a starting point of a community sentence for the first, and even for the second, domestic burglary. He also pointed out that the presumptive minimum sentence 'gives the sentencer a fairly substantial degree of discretion as to the categories of situations where the presumption can be rebutted'.[163] This judgment resulted in a public furore about judicial leniency and in criticism of Lord Woolf by the Home Secretary.[164]

Ongoing confusion about the effect of the *McInerney and Keating* guidelines led Lord Judge, as Lord Chief Justice, to distance himself from Lord Woolf's judgment. In *Saw* (2009)[165] Lord Judge stated that the guidelines had proved 'controversial' and 'difficult of application', and required the giving of fresh guidance for courts until a definitive guideline could be issued. Much of Lord Judge's judgment spelt out the importance of viewing burglary as an invasion of the privacy and security of the home, and a long list of aggravating factors is discussed. However, both the *Saw* judgment and the Sentencing Council's subsequent burglary guideline preserve a non-custodial starting

---

[158] Sentencing Council, *Burglary Offences Guideline: Professional Consultation* (2011), p. 10.

[159] The provision was discussed in ch. 1.5.2 above, and is also discussed in the context of persistent offenders in ch. 6.7 below.

[160] SAP, *Domestic Burglary* (2002).   [161] [2003] 2 Cr App R (S) 240.

[162] Ibid., at paras. 38–9, quoting from the report of the Social Exclusion Unit (2002).

[163] [2003] 2 Cr App R (S) 240 at para. 16.

[164] For suggestions that Lord Woolf's guidelines were significantly lower than practice, see Davies and Tyrer (2003), although that research takes no account of the effect of mitigating factors.

[165] [2009] 2 Cr App R (S) 367.

point for category 3 offences. Thus the Council identifies six factors indicating great harm: significant degree of loss (economic, sentimental or personal); soiling, ransacking or vandalising; occupier at home or returning during burglary; serious trauma to victim; violence or threats; and context of general public disorder. Factors indicating lesser harm are that only property of low value was stolen, or there was limited damage or disturbance to property. Culpability factors are clustered around deliberation and planning. For category 1 offences the starting point is 3 years, in a range of 2–6 years; for category 2 (into which some 52 per cent of cases fall)[166] the starting point is 1 year's custody, with a range from high-level community order to 2 years' custody; for category 3 the starting point is a high-level community order, with a range from low-level community order to 26 weeks' custody. At Step Two the guideline states that cases of particular gravity, with multiple features of harm or culpability at Step One, could justify a starting point above the range for category 1 offences, referring to the gap between 6 years' imprisonment (the top of the offence range) and the statutory maximum of 14 years.[167]

The guideline for non-domestic burglary has similar harm and culpability factors at Step One, but lower ranges at Step Two. The range for category 1 offences is 1–5 years, with a starting point of 2 years; for category 2 the range is low-level community order to 51 weeks' custody, with a starting point of 18 weeks' custody; for category 3 the range is Band B fine to 18 weeks' custody, with a starting point of medium-level community order. These ranges reflect the generally less traumatic effect of commercial burglaries, although the overlapping nature of the ranges preserves the possibility of custody for a category 3 offence so long as the court applies its mind to the custody and community thresholds set out in the guideline.[168]

4.4.10 Theft

The SGC's guideline on *Theft and Burglary in a Building Other than a Dwelling* (2008) sets out guidelines for a number of forms of theft, including for theft in breach of trust, theft in a dwelling, theft from the person, and theft from a shop. English law has a single, undifferentiated offence of theft, and so these categories are for sentencing purposes only. There is no guideline for theft in general, and so sentencers are left to develop analogies with one of the existing guidelines when dealing with another kind of theft (e.g. theft by an employee not in a position of trust, or theft by finding).[169] We focus here on three of the guidelines.

We deal first with *theft in breach of trust*. Many of these cases involve solicitors, bank managers, building society cashiers, club treasurers, and others

---

[166] CCSS (2014), p. 18.
[167] Sentencing Council, *Burglary Offences: Definitive Guideline* (2011), pp. 8–9.   [168] Ibid., p. 13.
[169] Cf. *Jagintavicius* [2012] 2 Cr App R (S) 567.

who divert funds which are under their control. Post office employees who steal from the mail are sentenced on a similar basis.[170] Why should such offences be regarded as particularly serious? The answer, at least in relation to public officials and members of the professions, is that they are selected for their positions so that ordinary people can rely upon them. As Cox put it in the nineteenth century, professional people 'trade upon their honesty. They sell their trustworthiness.'[171] The Court of Appeal has commented that 'if people cannot deal with solicitors in absolute reliance on their honesty, the business of the country would be seriously affected in all sorts of ways'.[172] The same reasoning presumably underlies the readiness of HMRC to bring prosecutions against accountants found to have made false declarations for taxation purposes, which contrasts with their extreme reluctance to prosecute other taxpayers even where considerable sums have been underpaid.[173] What this seems to suggest is that the gravamen of theft in breach of trust stems not merely from the loss to the victim but also from the public significance of the breach of professional responsibility. It is not merely the effect on the victim's living standard, but the fact that the loss was inflicted by someone who is supposed to preserve and protect that living standard. The public element of breach of trust creates a difficulty for the von Hirsch–Jareborg framework, since there is no necessary impact on the living standard of the typical victim (who may be corporate, or simply one of many small depositors suffering small losses). If these cases are to be accommodated, some kind of public dimension must be added to the framework. There are also further factors which affect the seriousness of these offences: on the one hand, they usually involve planning and often continue over a substantial period of time, and on the other hand they are usually committed by people of previous good character who suffer many consequential deprivations (loss of job prospects, loss of pension rights) as a result of conviction.

Sentencing for theft in breach of trust was the subject of two Court of Appeal guideline judgments,[174] but it is the SGC guideline that is now definitive. This indicates starting points and ranges for four levels of offending. The highest level is for thefts involving over £125,000 (or over £20,000 if a high degree of trust), with a starting point of 3 years and a range of 2–6 years, all figures relating to a first offender convicted after a trial. The range is constrained by the maximum sentence of 7 years for this offence. In practice the courts occasionally have to deal with thefts of much greater sums by professional people in a high position of trust, and it is usual to bring a number of charges so that the court can pass consecutive sentences and reach a much higher total.[175] The second-highest level is intended for thefts of

---

[170] E.g. *Molcher* [2007] 1 Cr App R (S) 268.   [171] Cox (1877), p. 55.

[172] *Wooding* [1978] Crim LR 701.   [173] Roording (1996).

[174] *Barrick* (1985) 7 Cr App R (S) 142, amended in *Clark* [1998] 2 Cr App R (S) 95.

[175] See e.g. *Miles* [2007] 2 Cr App R (S) 19 (solicitor stole £1.3 million, 7 years upheld); *Fielding* [2007] 2 Cr App R (S) 117 (solicitor stole £5.8 million, 8 years upheld). Since there was a guilty

£20,000 to £125,000 (or £2,000 to £20,000 for a high position of trust), with a starting point of 2 years and a range of 1–3 years. The third level is for thefts of £2,000 to £20,000 (or under £2,000 for a high position of trust), with a starting point of 18 weeks and a range from a high community sentence to 12 months' imprisonment. The lowest level is for thefts under £2,000, with a starting point of a medium community sentence and a range from a fine to 26 weeks' imprisonment. In placing an offence within the appropriate range, the court should have regard to all the usual aggravating and mitigating factors, and also to particular aggravating factors such as a long course of offending, and deliberately throwing suspicion on someone else, and to particular mitigating factors such as the voluntary cessation of offending and reporting an undiscovered offence.

While the importance of taking breach of trust offences seriously was argued above, there are strong currents running in the opposite direction. First, there is the point that these offences are non-violent, non-sexual, and non-frightening. They are 'mere' property offences, although capable of causing great distress to those who suffer loss as a result. This raises the question of the relationship of the guideline to those for violent offences and for sexual offences. Secondly, almost all of the offenders in this category have impeccable previous records and suffer professionally and personally from their conviction. The guideline is quite clear in stating that 'other than in the most exceptional of cases, loss of employment and any consequential hardship should not constitute personal mitigation' for these offences. We will return below to the question of whether there is a fair relationship between sentences for theft in breach of trust and other theft sentences.

Another form of behaviour covered by English law's single theft offence is *theft from the person*. This usually takes the form of pickpocketing, and the SGC identifies as particular aggravating factors the use of force or intimidation, a confrontation with the victim, and a high level of inconvenience caused (as when stealing credit cards from a foreign tourist). The guideline indicates three levels for this offence. On the top level are thefts from a vulnerable victim involving force or intimidation, with a starting point of 18 months and a range of 1–3 years. The middle level deals with thefts from a vulnerable victim without intimidation, with a starting point of 18 weeks and a range from a high community sentence to 12 months. All other thefts from the person are at the lowest level, with a starting point of a medium community order and a range from a fine to 18 weeks' imprisonment.

What is the gravamen of these offences? They have been said to come close to burglary and robbery in their invasion of a person's privacy, and hence their 'offensive and frightening' nature.[176] The width of the sentence ranges allows

plea in both cases, this implies higher starting points of, say, 10 and 11 years (before reduction for guilty plea).
[176] James Committee (1975), para 92.

courts to respond to two further factors – the involvement of gangs and of 'semi-professional' offenders, and the fact that some offenders have lengthy criminal records. Nonetheless, in many cases the amount taken is low to moderate, and the offences are typically non-confrontational, non-violent, and non-sexual. The deliberation, planning, and repetition of these offences sometimes leads the courts towards sentences above the guideline range. Thus in *Gonzalez Ramirez and Padillo* (2012)[177] two Chilean nationals travelled to London and committed several offences of theft, usually by distraction, mostly of expensive items such as computers, jewellery, and mobile phones. They pleaded guilty to 6 such offences, and were sentenced to 3 years and 4 months in prison. This was equivalent to a sentence of 5 years after a trial, and the Court of Appeal held that sentences of this level were justified by the seriousness of the offences ('carefully planned multiple offending with high rewards'), with aggravating factors and no significant mitigation. However, the offences did not involve the 'force or intimidation' that characterises category 3 offences, and the sums involved were significantly less lucrative than breach of trust cases, so doubts must be registered about this decision.

The third type of theft case is *theft from a shop*, one of the most frequently sentenced offences in English courts.[178] All the general aggravating and mitigating factors apply to these offences, as to others, including deliberate planning and offending in groups. In addition, offences involving a child, the use of intimidation, and the offender's subjection to a banning order are all aggravating factors. The guideline indicates four levels of offending. At the top level come thefts in organized groups with intimidation, where the starting point (always for a first offender convicted at trial) is 12 months, with a range of 36 weeks to 4 years. At the second level are thefts involving either intimidation, or a high level of planning, or significant damage; the starting point is 6 weeks' imprisonment, with a range from a high community order to 36 weeks. In the third category come cases involving low-level intimidation or planning or damage, with a starting point of a low community sentence and a range from fine to high community sentence. The lowest level of theft from a shop consists of low-value cases with little planning, where the starting point is a fine and the range goes from conditional discharge to a low community order.

In the absence of intimidation this offence must rank very low on any scale of comparative seriousness. The sums involved are usually small and, while a case can be made that such offences increase prices for all of us and reduce the commercial viability of the shops on which we rely, such diffuse arguments cannot have great weight when it is considered that the offences are non-violent, non-sexual, non-frightening, and not lucrative. The major difficulty comes from the role of previous convictions. Research for the Sentencing Advisory Panel

---

[177] [2012] 2 Cr App R (S) 26; for pre-guideline decisions, see *Gwillim-Jones* [2002] 1 Cr App R (S) 19 and *McGhee and Hughes* [2004] 1 Cr App R (S) 399.

[178] Some such offences are dealt with by Penalty Notices for Disorder: see ch. 1.4 above.

revealed that the *average* number of previous convictions among those sentenced for theft from a shop was 42.[179] Many of the offenders were dependent on drugs, and were shoplifting in order to provide money to buy more drugs. Others were semi-professional, in the sense that they regularly stole from shops. Even if it is agreed that those on drugs should be offered a community order with a requirement of drug treatment, there will still remain many others to be sentenced, together with those who reoffend after being given a drug treatment order. The issue, which is confronted again in Chapter 6.3 below, is to what extent previous convictions should be allowed to augment the sentence for what is, in the scale of things, a relatively low-level offence. The guideline states that 'where an offender demonstrates a level of "persistent" or "seriously persistent" offending, the community and custody thresholds may be crossed even though the other characteristics of the offence would otherwise warrant a lesser sentence'.[180] That still leaves open the question of how far an offender's 42 previous convictions should be allowed to take the sentence for an offence with some planning, with a range (at the second-lowest level) rising only to a high community sentence. The justifications for imposing any custodial sentence in such a case call for close scrutiny, which they will receive in Chapter 9 below.

Let us now try to make some comparisons between theft in breach of trust, theft from the person, and theft from a shop. Breach of trust cases are characterized by the social importance of the position held by the offender, in terms of public reliance on probity; the sums involved are significantly higher, in most cases, than for pickpocketing or shoplifting. Yet for the second-lowest range for breach of trust, involving sums of £2,000 to £20,000, the starting point is 18 weeks – the same starting point as theft from a vulnerable person of what is likely to be a massively lower amount; it is also within the range for the second-highest category of shop theft, where again the amount taken is likely to be very much lower. All shop thefts and thefts from the person are surely in the lowest band of the von Hirsch–Jareborg scale, unless there is significant intimidation. Many thefts in breach of trust will also be at that level, albeit that they involve much greater sums of money. Whatever the proper place of breach of trust offences, therefore, there is a need to consider whether shop thefts and pickpocketing are sentenced too high – whether, in effect, it is the previous convictions rather than the nature of the offence that is driving the sentence towards custody. The Council has held a consultation on theft offences, and new guidelines are awaited.

4.4.11 Child pornography

In 2000 the maximum penalty for possessing an indecent photograph of a child was increased from 6 months to 5 years, and the maximum for making,

---

[179] SAP, *Sentencing for Theft from a Shop* (2006), para. 9.
[180] SGC, *Theft and Burglary in a Building Other than a Dwelling*, p. 16.

distributing, or publishing such photographs was increased from 3 to 10 years.[181] The Sentencing Advisory Panel delivered an advice which the Court of Appeal substantially incorporated into the guideline judgment in *Oliver* (2003).[182] That was subsequently embodied in the SGC's guidelines on sexual offences,[183] and it now appears in a less complex form in the Sentencing Council's definitive guideline on sexual offences.[184] The Council's guideline has three category levels: category A includes images involving penetrative sexual activity and images involving sexual activity with an animal or sadism; category B comprises images involving non-penetrative sexual activity; and category C is for all other indecent images not falling within A or B. Once the images are categorised, the other question at Step One is whether the offender's role was that of a possessor, distributor, or producer. These two elements – the category of images and the role of the offender – determine the category range and starting point. For example, where the seriousness of the images falls within category A, the starting points are 1 year for a possessor, 3 years for a distributor, and 6 years for a producer.

These are substantial prison sentences. Are they justifiable? On the von Hirsch–Jareborg scale, the actual making of indecent photographs of children may infringe two significant interests – freedom from humiliation or degrading treatment of the children, and their privacy and autonomy. In some cases, perhaps many, the photographed activities may have a lasting effect on their psychological adjustment.[185] However, to what extent should an offender who merely downloads images already available be sentenced on the basis of involvement in the exploitation of young children? The Panel's view, on which the guidelines are based, was that

> an offender convicted for possession of child pornography should be treated as being to some degree complicit in the original child sexual abuse which was involved in the production of the images. The level of sentence for possession should also reflect the continuing damage which is done to the victim or victims, through copying and further dissemination of the pornographic images.[186]

The argument in the first sentence is similar to that often applied to the offence of handling stolen goods, and its relationship to the original offence (burglary, robbery, or theft) whereby the goods were obtained.[187] The argument is either an expressive one – that the offender signifies his endorsement

---

[181] By s. 41 of the Criminal Justice and Court Services Act 2000.

[182] [2003] 2 Cr App R (S) 64, adopting SAP, *Offences Involving Child Pornography* (2002).

[183] SGC, *Sexual Offences Act 2003* (2007), pp. 108–14, followed in Scotland in *HM Advocate* v. *Graham* [2010] HCJAC 50.

[184] Sentencing Council, *Sexual Offences: Definitive Guideline* (2013), pp. 75–9.

[185] For such a case, involving the actual taking of photographs of very young children, see *Saunders* [2004] 2 Cr App R (S) 459.

[186] SAP, *Offences Involving Child Pornography*, para. 13.

[187] See the guideline judgment in *Webbe* [2002] 1 Cr App R (S) 82, at [15].

or support for the activities depicted by downloading the images – or a deterrent one – that if people did not download the images there would be no incentive for them to be made. The deterrent point is arguable, since there are certainly some people who take such photographs for their own use only.[188] The expressive point is stronger, for how could a person who knowingly downloads such an image protest that he does not condone the activities depicted? His downloading may be remote from the original making of the image, but in the absence of any plea of mistake he must to some extent be endorsing what was done. However, even if this explains why downloading such images of children cannot be decoupled from the making of them, it remains for discussion whether the guideline sentences for the possession offence are too low, about right, or too high.

4.4.12 The Magistrates' Court Sentencing Guidelines

Separate sentencing guidelines for the magistrates' courts have a lengthy history, as outlined in Chapter 2.5 above. Until recently all the guidelines were voluntary, having no legal standing other than commendations from the Lord Chancellor and Lord Chief Justice. However, the first set of definitive guidelines for the magistrates' courts was issued in 2008. A small working group, consisting of four members of the Panel together with some lay magistrates, justices' clerks, and district judges, prepared a new version of the guidelines for magistrates' courts, integrating all the specific SGC guidelines. After appropriate consultations, the *Magistrates' Court Sentencing Guidelines* (MCSG) were issued, and they have been updated ever since to take account of new definitive guidelines for specific offences.

The format of the MCSG is in transition, partly in its original form and partly in a new form. The original format was designed to integrate all existing SGC guidelines and to develop guidance for other common offences as well. The aim was to produce a looseleaf folder that would deal with each offence in two pages, the first setting out the maximum penalty and legal definition of the offence, and the second page setting out a decision sequence with three alternative starting points (tailored to the varieties of the offence commonly sentenced by magistrates). Many offences still have MCSG guidelines in that format, but all guidelines issued by the Sentencing Council appear in a separate part of the MCSG, and they are in the same form as the guidelines for all courts. Thus, for example, there is no guideline for common assault in the main body of the MCSG, because that is to be found towards the back of the folder in a special part devoted to Sentencing Council guidelines.

---

[188] E.g. *Saunders*, above n. 185.

4.5 Individual culpability

So far, this chapter has concentrated on one of the elements of proportionality – offence-seriousness – and on one of the components of offence-
seriousness – the harm done or risked by the offender's conduct. The other
principal dimension of offence-seriousness, the culpability of the individual
offender, has been mentioned at various points but not yet scrutinised.

> Harm refers to the injury done or risked by the criminal act. Culpability refers to
> the factors of intent, motive and circumstance that determine how much the
> offender should be held accountable for his act. Culpability, in turn, affects the
> assessment of harm. The consequences that should be considered in gauging the
> harmfulness of an act should be those that can fairly be attributed to the actor's
> choice.[189]

A number of the guidelines discussed in part 4.4 above turn on the degree of
offender's culpability. It is now time to explore the relevant principles.

In English law most of the offences discussed in part 4.4 require proof of an
intention to cause the prohibited harm, or proof of recklessness in that regard.
This is sometimes termed the subjective principle of criminal liability: for most
of the serious offences, criminal liability depends on the offender's choice or
awareness of what he was doing.[190] The concept of intention in English law is
wide enough to comprise a whole range of mental states, from planning,
through deliberation, to a hastily conceived intent, a 'spur of the moment'
decision and an impulsive response to a situation. Any of these mental
attitudes satisfies the definition of intention in English law: so long as the
offender realized for a split second the nature of the act, it is likely to be held
intentional. However, one might wish to argue that the premeditated offender
is more culpable than the one who acts on the spur of the moment. As
Bentham put it, the longer the offender continued under the influence of
anti-social motives, the more convincing is the evidence that he has rejected
social motives.[191] So there are degrees of culpability within the concept of
intention, running from the careful plan down to the sudden impulse.

Exactly the same might be said of the legal concept of recklessness. It is
usually defined in terms of awareness of risk, but the degree of culpability
surely varies according to the magnitude of the risk and the amount of
calculation involved. Although the term 'reckless' may be thought to suggest
a carefree act executed with abandon, there is a scale of recklessness running
along two dimensions: first, there is the anticipated degree of probability that
the harm will materialize, from a high to a low risk; second, there is a similar
scale to that within intention, running from a carefully calculated risk to
impulsive risk-taking. Once again, the decision on criminal liability does not

---

[189] Von Hirsch (1986), pp. 64–5.
[190] For fuller discussion see Ashworth and Horder (2013), ch. 5.
[191] Bentham (1789), ch. XI, para. 42.

supply the sentencer with the fine detail necessary for an estimate of culpability. It is possible that some of the more calculated forms of recklessness might be adjudged more serious than impulsive forms of intention. Tom Hadden argued that courts should be required to determine issues such as premeditation or impulse at trial:[192] he accepted that this would add considerably to the length and complexity of proceedings, which some would regard as sufficient to condemn the proposal, but his reasoning was that these decisions are no less important for the offender's sentence than the 'intention or recklessness' decision which the law now requires.

The two key legal concepts of intention and recklessness do not exhaust the factors which do, and should, influence judgments of culpability. Elements of negligence enter into some serious offences, most notably manslaughter by gross negligence (see 4.4.3 above). Moreover, most offences under the Theft Act 1968 and the Fraud Act 2006 require proof of dishonesty, a concept that draws in broader notions of moral turpitude. Beyond those offence elements, there is also a range of possible defences to criminal liability – insanity, duress, mistake of fact, and to some extent mistake of law and intoxication. English law confines each of these defences narrowly,[193] and does so partly because effect can be given at the sentencing stage to variations in culpability. As Martin Wasik has argued, there is a 'scale of excuse, running downwards from excusing conditions, through partial excuses to mitigating factors'.[194] Thus, provocation and entrapment do not constitute general defences in English law (though loss of control may reduce murder to manslaughter), but courts are expected to take them into account when assessing culpability for the purpose of sentencing. The important point is that culpability is a wider issue than cognition, as represented by the two legal terms of intention and recklessness, and that it extends to a wide range of volitional and situational factors.

Further and broader questions are raised by arguments, sometimes put by defence advocates, that an offender from a disadvantaged background is less culpable. Thus it has been argued that social deprivation should be recognized as diminishing the capacity of some offenders; that socially deprived people may find themselves under pressure to commit crime, or in a situation where crime is the 'lesser evil'; or that socially deprived people who have been abused and maltreated by others have already suffered and therefore should not be punished further, or at least fully, for their own crimes.[195] Thus in *Lockey* (2009)[196] the Court of Appeal reduced a sentence on the ground that insufficient mitigating effect had been given to the fact that D's past had been characterized by family dysfunction, bullying, abuse, lack of achievement, disability, and family tragedy. The small Crown Court survey found that

---

[192] Hadden (1968), pp. 534–5.   [193] Ashworth and Horder (2013), ch. 6.
[194] Wasik (1982), p. 524.
[195] See the critical assessments by Morse (2000), and Frase (2013), pp. 226–30.
[196] [2009] 1 Cr App R (S) 565.

'difficult/deprived background' was the second most frequently mentioned mitigating factor, and was regarded as relevant particularly in burglary and robbery cases.[197] In the same vein it could be argued that some people are trapped in a criminal lifestyle, with scarcely more capacity for free choice than the person subjected to direct threats, and that therefore they should not be held to the same normative expectations as others.[198] Critics suggest that this confuses explanation with excuse: research may demonstrate a strong association between social deprivation and offending behaviour, but this does not deny the capacity or a fair opportunity to behave otherwise,[199] and not all persons from these backgrounds commit crimes. Nonetheless, as Barbara Hudson warned:

> the notion of free will that is assumed in ideas of culpability ... is a much stronger notion than that usually experienced by the poor and powerless. That individuals have choices is a basic legal assumption: that circumstances constrain choices is not. Legal reasoning seems unable to appreciate that the existential view of the world as an arena for acting out free choices is a perspective of the privileged, and that potential for self-actualization is far from apparent to those whose lives are constricted by material or ideological handicaps.[200]

Thus there may be cases where a court is persuaded that a form of social deprivation has constrained an offender's choices to an extent significant enough to reduce their culpability.[201] In broader criminological terms, certainly, there is accumulating evidence that 'offenders differ from non-offenders in many respects, including impulsiveness, intelligence, family background and socio-economic deprivation'.[202] But the evidence on how such differences interact with the communities (and institutions) in which they live remains somewhat uncertain,[203] and in any event these differences will vary in degree from case to case. Whether they fall properly within reduced culpability (this chapter) or personal mitigation (Chapter 5) is less important, for there seems to be no firm dividing line between them at this point.

4.6 Proportionality and offence-seriousness

This chapter has considered ways of gauging the seriousness of the harm caused or threatened by various offences; the principal issues involved in assessing culpability; and the problem of 'discounting' seriousness to reflect remoteness from the harm. Issues of aggravation and mitigation have been left

---

[197] SCWG Survey (2008), pp. 14–15.
[198] For deeper discussion, see Lacey, Wells and Quick (2003), pp. 408–12.
[199] E.g. Moore (1985), Kadish (1987), pp. 102–6.
[200] Hudson (1994), p. 302; cf. Hutton (1999) for further discussion.
[201] On which see ch. 3.3.5 above.   [202] Farrington (2007), p. 629.
[203] Smith (2007), pp. 674–5; Frase (2013), p. 229.

over to Chapter 5. The effect of previous convictions is reserved for Chapter 6. The problems raised by proportionality in cases where the offender has to be sentenced for two or more offences will be examined in Chapter 8: these are difficult problems, since most discussions assume that it is two individual offences which are to be compared. Lastly, there is also the difficulty of achieving some kind of proportionality between the seriousness of the offence and the severity of the sentence, aired in part 4.3 of this chapter and discussed in Chapters 9 and 10. The present chapter is therefore little more than an exploration of one key concept in proportionality, the seriousness of the offence, and its practical instantiation in a particular criminal justice system.

In reality, all the elements of proportionality constantly come into play. The concepts of seriousness and of 'commensurability' are central to the scheme of the 2003 Act, being crucial to the threshold for community sentences and for custodial sentences as well as to determining the length of custodial sentences. In part 4.4 above we began to assess the offence-seriousness relativities that underpin the various sentencing guidelines that have been issued in the last decade. One of the Sentencing Council's tasks is to pay attention to the overall relativities between the offence ranges for the various types of offence. Several major issues stemming from the relativities discussed in this chapter have been identified, and three may be selected for further discussion.

The first is whether all the starting points can be defended on proportionality grounds, or whether it is necessary to rely on an alternative rationale (namely, deterrence) in some instances. This issue arises clearly if the sentencing approaches to rape and causing grievous bodily harm with intent are compared with those to robbery and drug dealing. In part 4.4 of this chapter a modified version of the approach proposed by von Hirsch and Jareborg was applied to these and other offences. It can be strongly argued that the starting points for armed robberies and drug importation fail to stand in a proportionate relationship to those for category 3 rapes (starting points of 5 and 7 years, depending on culpability factors) and for wounding or grievous bodily harm committed with a weapon carried to the scene (category 2, starting point 6 years). Whereas rape and grievous bodily harm strike at very basic elements in one's living standard, robbery and drug smuggling may often be more remote or diluted in their impact. Indeed, many of the robberies involve less injury than some offences of inflicting grievous bodily harm contrary to s. 20, as is evident from 4.4.6 and 4.4.8 above.

There has therefore been a tendency to justify the sentencing approach to robbery and drug smuggling on general deterrent grounds. This suggests that the English sentencing system attributes more importance to property than to physical safety. Drug smuggling is immensely profitable and, although attempts have been made to justify its high position on grounds of (remote) threat of harm to others, it seems that profitability is a central concern, buttressed of course by the planning and group elements. It seems unlikely that armed robbery would be ranked so highly if the two constituent parts were treated separately: the threats or use of force involved would not themselves attract substantial sentences if sentenced on the basis of the *Assault* guideline (see 4.4.6 above), and many building society robberies and street robberies yield fairly modest sums of money. If it is the deterrent rationale that gives these offences their high position on the tariff, then the evidence in its favour is not persuasive, as we noted in 3.3.2 above. Recent careful assessments of the general deterrence evidence demonstrate that there is no adequate empirical basis for believing that the marginal deterrent gains from increasing sentence levels above what is proportionate are likely to be significant.[204]

A second issue concerns the effect on sentence levels generally of the increase in severity when sentencing for offences involving death. As noted in 4.4.1 above, Parliament raised the minimum terms for murder by a significant amount in 2003, and also increased the maximum sentences for causing death by dangerous driving and for health and safety offences resulting in death. The question is whether this revalorization of certain offences resulting in death should a) result in increases in sentence levels for other offences resulting in death, and b) lead to more general increases in penalty levels for linked offences (such as attempted murder and causing grievous bodily harm) and for other offences. Lord Judge CJ led a movement towards increasing sentence levels for all linked offences, but it seems that the definitive guidelines have not reflected this increase whereas the homicide offences for which there are no definitive guidelines (notably manslaughter upon diminished responsibility, unlawful act manslaughter, and manslaughter by gross negligence) have seen significant increases in the sentences approved by the Court of Appeal. In discussion in 4.4.3 it was argued that the case for increasing sentence levels for linked offences such as manslaughter, attempted murder, and causing grievous bodily harm has some substance, but that any such argument weakens considerably as one goes lower down the scale of assaults, to robbery, and to drugs offences.

A third issue is the remoteness question. Those who justify high sentences for the importation, supply, or production of drugs sometimes argue that it leads to dependency, degradation, and death, but those consequences increase in remoteness as they do in seriousness. Moreover, they have to pass through some voluntary action(s) of the people who take the drugs, and voluntary acts are normally taken to sever the chain of causation.[205] Of course, once the dependency sets in, the degree of voluntariness may diminish; but there is still room for argument about whether the importer, supplier, or producer can be held liable to any significant extent for those consequences. Remoteness arguments are also found in relation to the crime of handling stolen goods (that the handler endorses the means by which the goods were obtained, i.e. endorses violence if they are the proceeds of a robbery), and in relation to the

---

[204] See Halliday (2001), p. 129, Bottoms (2004), pp. 63–6, and ch. 3.3.2 above.
[205] *Kennedy (No. 2)* [2008] 1 AC 269.

downloading of child pornography (that the viewer endorses the means by which the photographs were obtained, i.e. endorses the performing of sexual acts with the child). Some might consider these arguments overzealous, not least because the violent or sexual event has already taken place before the handler or downloader becomes involved. Others may prefer the response that if there were no market for what is produced by robbery or by photographing sex with children, then fewer people would commit those offences.

These three major issues are practical questions that require a principled answer. No system of sentencing guidelines can be expected to give adequate coverage to all variations of all offences. While there are compelling justifications for having a guideline structure that marks significant grades in the seriousness of each offence, there must be the possibility of departing from the guideline where it is in the interests of justice to do so. But the deeper questions of principle – such as what the ceiling should be for a non-violent, non-threatening, and non-sexual offence, and the question whether confiscatory or other mechanisms should be mobilized to deal with high-value but non-violent thefts – need to be confronted, both by government and by the Sentencing Council. Is the heavy reliance on long terms of imprisonment the most appropriate response?

5

Aggravation and mitigation

Contents

5.1 Some preliminary problems of principle

The factors recognized as aggravating or mitigating have often been thought to be uncomplicated or uncontroversial, or (in the terminology of the English judiciary) 'well known' and 'well established'. However, it will be argued in this chapter that many of them raise contentious issues. These issues assume particular importance for four reasons:

- several aggravating factors and one mitigating factor are statutory requirements under the Criminal Justice Act 2003, as we shall see;
- s. 166 of the 2003 Act reaffirms that the various statutory thresholds for imposing custodial sentences and community sentences should not be read as 'prevent[ing] a court from mitigating an offender's sentence by taking into account such matters as, in the opinion of the court, are relevant in mitigation of sentence'; and
- s. 174(2) of the 2003 Act requires the court in any case to 'mention any aggravating or mitigating factors which the court has regarded as being of particular importance'; and
- most sentencing decisions are now covered by guidelines; many guidelines indicate the significant aggravating and mitigating factors for the relevant offence(s), and the Sentencing Council's guidelines use some such factors at Step One when determining the appropriate category range.

For these four reasons, the analysis of the justifications for particular aggravating and mitigating factors becomes a more pressing task than may hitherto have been supposed. Moreover, the sentencing research by Hough, Jacobson and Millie shows that it was chiefly the influence of personal mitigating factors that often made the difference between a community sentence and a custodial sentence in cases 'on the cusp',[1] and the Crown Court Sentencing Survey (CCSS) confirms that even the crude number of aggravating or mitigating factors is related to the probability and length of a custodial sentence.[2]

The restatement in s. 166 of the power to mitigate sentence is broadly framed, and immediately it raises the question whether justifications for taking account of some personal mitigating factors may be found outside the fundamental rationale of sentencing – which, as argued in Chapters 3 and 4, is that the sentence should be proportionate to the seriousness of the offence. This would not necessarily be illogical: it was argued in Chapter 3.4 above that it is possible to defend a sentencing system which has a primary rationale and which then allows certain other rationales to have priority in respect of certain types of crime or types of offender. The key requirement is that the justifications be strong and specific. Similarly, the notion that all aggravating and mitigating factors ought necessarily to be linked to the primary rationale must be rejected as too astringent a view, particularly in the context of a branch of the law so closely entwined with social policy and so politically sensitive as sentencing. It would be odd and probably inconsistent if the central core of aggravating and mitigating factors were not linked to the primary rationale, but there is no reason why additional factors should not be recognized. Everything depends on careful examination of the justifications for these factors.

One reason why the main aggravating and mitigating factors should be related to the primary rationale is that their status as such might be purely adventitious. One legal system may have distinct offences of robbery and armed robbery, the latter defined so as to penalize robbery involving the use or threatened use of a gun. Another, such as England and Wales, might have a single offence of robbery, and might treat the use or threatened use of a gun as an aggravating factor. Similarly, some countries have various offences of theft, graded according to the amount stolen or perhaps the position held by the person who steals, whereas English law treats such matters as factors that aggravate the single offence of theft. It may therefore be a matter of legislative tradition whether such factors are part of the definition of the crime or are left to sentencing, but it should make no difference to the arguments needed to justify the factor as aggravating. Similarly, where a guideline lists certain factors as harm or culpability factors at Step One, this is merely an attempt to bring clarity to the guideline and does not remove the need to discuss the justifications for recognizing them as, in effect, aggravating or mitigating. However, it must be noted that many

[1] Hough et al. (2003), pp. 39–43.   [2] CCSS (2014), pp. 26–30.

guidelines list more aggravating factors than mitigating factors, tending not to mention some recognized mitigating factors and thereby leaving them even more at large.[3]

A further preliminary question concerns the practical relationship between aggravating and mitigating factors. It is often right to suppose that the opposite of a mitigating factor will count as aggravating (e.g. impulsive reactions may justify mitigation and premeditation may be aggravating), and this applies particularly where the two factors can be represented as extreme points on a spectrum. However, there may be other circumstances in which the absence of a mitigating factor should not count as aggravating. Consider the sentence 'discount' for pleading guilty: clearly, a person who pleads not guilty and is convicted cannot receive this discount, and so that person's sentence will be higher than for someone who pleaded guilty to a similar offence. But does that mean that pleading not guilty and putting the prosecution to proof is an aggravating factor? Pleading not guilty certainly has a potential cost that pleading guilty does not have; but in principle the person who is convicted after a not guilty plea should receive the normal sentence, not an aggravated sentence. In essence, therefore, there are three forms of response to factors in each case – aggravating, neutral, and mitigating. These may simply represent points on a spectrum (e.g. between impulsivity and premeditation). But where the factor relates to the presence or absence of a single element (e.g. pleading guilty or not guilty), there is a question as to how they should be characterized. The wrong approach is to assume that the opposite or negative of a mitigating factor is necessarily aggravating; it might be neutral, as demonstrated by the theory of the discount for a guilty plea. Similarly, it is widely accepted to be an aggravating factor if the offence is committed against an elderly or a very young victim, but it would be absurd to claim mitigation on the basis that the victim was aged between, say, 20 and 50. That is simply a neutral factor.

5.2 Aggravation as increased seriousness

5.2.1 Statutory aggravating factors

English law now requires courts to treat certain factors as aggravating. The Criminal Justice Act 2003 sets out three such factors, and one has been added subsequently. The first – previous convictions for relevant and recent offences – will be discussed fully in Chapter 6.3 below. The other three – offence committed on bail; hostility to a 'protected characteristic'; offences with a terrorist connection – are discussed here.

---

[3] See Roberts (2011a), pp. 9–10, Cooper (2013).

1. Offence committed on bail

Section 143(3) of the Criminal Justice Act 2003 states that 'in considering the seriousness of any offence committed while the offender was on bail, the court must treat the fact that it was committed in those circumstances as an aggravating factor'. This restates a principle recognized for some years,[4] but what is its justification? The fact that the offence was committed during a period when the offender was on bail does not increase the harm caused by the offence, nor does it increase the culpability of the offender in relation to that crime. Presumably the argument is that it constitutes an act of defiance of the court, or a breach of the trust placed in the offender by releasing him on bail pending the hearing of his case, or at least demonstrates that he has failed to heed the element of official warning implicit in the commencement of proceedings against him.[5] Since it is also a principle that the sentence for an offence committed on bail should be consecutive to the sentence for the original offence,[6] the aggravating effect of this factor ought to be relatively small. The consecutive principle will increase the sentence anyway, and the argument that aggravating the sentence is likely to have an additional deterrent effect is as unsubstantiated as most claims about deterrence.[7]

2. Hostility to a 'protected characteristic'

The Crime and Disorder Act 1998 introduced racially aggravated offences of wounding and assault (s. 29), criminal damage (s. 30), public order offences (s. 31), and harassment (s. 32). There are also two more general provisions, in ss. 145 and 146 of the Criminal Justice Act 2003 as amended, that where an offence demonstrates or is motivated by hostility based on the race, religion, sexual orientation, disability, or transgender identity of the victim, the court must treat that fact as an aggravating factor, and must state in open court that the offence was so aggravated.

The 1998 offences based on racial aggravation had an unusual structure of maximum penalties, and this was one reason that led the Sentencing Advisory Panel to propose guidelines for racially aggravated offences in 2000.[8] The Panel, noting the legislative intent of identifying racial crimes so as to mark them out for specific condemnation, proposed a scheme of enhancements to deal with this type of case. The Court of Appeal considered the Panel's advice in *Kelly and Donnelly* (2001),[9] and accepted it in part. It accepted the proposal

---

[4] It is substantially a re-enactment of s. 151 of the PCCS Act 2000 and s. 29(2) of the CJA 1991.
[5] It could be argued that the bringing of a prosecution implies censure (cf. Ashworth and Redmayne (2010), ch. 8); the analysis may depend on whether D intends to plead guilty or to contest guilt.
[6] See ch. 8.3.3 below.   [7] See ch. 3.3.2 above.
[8] SAP, *Racially Aggravated Offences: Advice to the Court of Appeal* (2000).
[9] [2001] 2 Cr App R (S) 341.

that courts should first state what the sentence would be without the racial (or religious) element, and then state the sentence including that element. As Rose LJ commented, 'this will lead to transparency in sentencing, which will be of benefit to the public and, indeed, to this Court if subsequently the sentence passed is the subject of challenge'.[10] The Panel had gone on to propose that the enhancement should normally be between 40 and 70 per cent of the sentence for the basic offence, but the Court of Appeal preferred to leave it to the judge to consider the appropriate overall sentence without any such guideline. The Court agreed with the Panel's proposed aggravating factors, including a pattern of racist conduct, membership of a racist group, deliberate humiliation of the victim, and repeated or prolonged expressions of racial hostility. Two factors that might make the behaviour less serious were identified as the relative brevity of the racist conduct, and cases where there was no evidence of racial motivation and any racial abuse was minor or incidental.[11] The same considerations now apply to aggravation based on the other four protected characteristics.

Increasing sentences for these reasons may be seen as generally justified on the ground of reaffirming and enhancing social values of toleration and respect for the variety of racial and religious groups, and more specifically as marking the humiliating effect on victims that such conduct often has. Whether or not Parliament was right to enact a handful of specific racially and religiously aggravated offences,[12] the general principle of aggravation of sentence on such grounds is surely correct, and one that coheres with the principle of proportionality in sentencing. The approach laid down in *Kelly and Donnelly* now needs to be considered in the light of the sentence enhancements for aggravation related to the other three protected characteristics, and the Law Commission has recommended that the Sentencing Council formulate a thematic guideline on sentencing for all such offences.[13] This, together with better recording of offences involving this kind of aggravating factor, would be an important advance.

3. Aggravation with a terrorist connection

Section 30 of the Counter-Terrorism Act 2008 states that, if the court determines that the offence had a terrorist connection, it must treat that as an aggravating factor when sentencing. This is a declaratory or expressive principle, which gives statutory reaffirmation of what courts would probably do anyway.

---

[10] Ibid., at p. 347. The Court thus reversed what it had held in the earlier decision in *Saunders* [2000] 2 Cr App R (S) 71.

[11] For a conscientious application of the *Kelly and Donnelly* process, see *Attorney General's Reference No. 78 of 2006* [2007] 1 Cr App R (S) 699, at pp. 704–5.

[12] On which see Law Commission (2014), ch. 4.   [13] Law Commission (2014), ch. 3.

5.2.2 General aggravating factors recognized in definitive guidelines

In its guideline *Overarching Principles: Seriousness*, the Sentencing Guidelines Council set out a number of general aggravating factors, or 'factors indicating higher culpability'.[14] The list is not intended to be exhaustive, and it includes the statutory aggravating factors already mentioned, but it may be useful to draw attention to the other factors:

> planning of an offence
> intention to commit more serious harm than actually resulted from the offence
> offenders operating in groups or gangs
> commission of the offence for financial gain (where this is not inherent in the offence itself)
> high level of profit from the offence
> attempt to conceal or dispose of evidence
> failure to respond to warnings or concerns expressed by others about the offender's behaviour
> offence committed whilst on licence
> offence motivated by hostility towards a minority group, or members of it
> deliberate targeting of vulnerable victim(s)
> commission of an offence while under the influence of alcohol or drugs
> use of a weapon to frighten or injure the victim
> deliberate and gratuitous violence or damage to property, over and above what is needed to carry out the offence
> abuse of power
> abuse of position of trust[15]

The Council's assumption is that these factors indicate greater harm or culpability, and are therefore compatible with the principle of proportionality. We may consider whether this is right, examining at least some of the factors listed.[16]

Targeting a vulnerable victim

Greater culpability is indicated where an offender commits a crime against a vulnerable victim: there is a widely shared view that it is worse to take advantage of a relatively helpless person, and so the offender is more culpable if aware that the victim is especially vulnerable (e.g. old, very young, disabled, etc.).[17] Thus in *Attorney General's References Nos. 38 and 39 of 2004 (Randall and Donaghue)* (2005)[18] the Court of Appeal regarded the robbery as

---

[14] A revised guideline is in the course of preparation.

[15] SGC, *Overarching Principles: Seriousness*, para. 1.22.

[16] Several similar factors are recognized in Swedish sentencing law: see von Hirsch and Jareborg (1989).

[17] For the definition of 'vulnerable', see *De Weever* [2010] 1 Cr App R (S) 16, *Sayed* [2014] 2 Cr App R (S) 318, and *Halane* [2014] 2 Cr App R (S) 375.

[18] [2005] 1 Cr App R (S) 267; see also *Attorney General's References Nos. 22 and 23 of 2005* [2006] 1 Cr App R (S) 286 (revenge attack on man with evident disability).

particularly heinous because the offenders had targeted the home of a man whom they knew to have learning disabilities. In *O'Brien* (2002),[19] D had tricked his way into the house of a woman of 81 by pretending to be an employee of a water company, and had then stolen £200, a watch, and a mobile phone. He had a record of committing similar offences, and the judge sentenced him to 9 years' imprisonment – very high on the scale for burglary, especially when the amount involved was so low.[20] The Court of Appeal reduced the sentence slightly to eight years on the ground that the original sentence did not adequately reflect the guilty plea, but the Court stated that the offender's

> speciality is vulnerable elderly people. He tricks them into allowing him into their homes and he steals their property. He serves his prison sentences and then very soon thereafter resumes his similar criminal activities. This type of burglary casts a shadow on the lives of elderly people: they begin to dread the unexpected knock on the front door.

The Court agreed with the sentencing judge's comment that 'society rightly reserves its deepest censure for those who prey on vulnerable groups such as the elderly'. The same point is emphasized in the leading case of *Attorney General's References Nos. 42, 43 and 44 of 2006*,[21] where Judge LJ elaborated on the rationale for treating these cases as aggravated:

> It may be difficult for those who are younger to understand how, in late years, the confidence that is built up over the years of decent ordinary living can be destroyed by offences of this kind. But it can be, and we have evidence to suggest that it has been in the case of many of these victims.

Martin Wasik, examining the relevant justifications, has argued that there is not only greater culpability but there may also be greater harm in these cases – and the quotation from *O'Brien* suggests that the harm may be to older people generally, not just to the victims in the particular case.[22]

These decisions, together with other judgments approving long sentences for conspiracies to defraud vulnerable people,[23] raise difficult questions about the power of this aggravating factor. Research in the 1980s suggested that having an elderly victim was the factor most strongly associated with the use of immediate custody, and with longer custodial sentences, in the Crown Court,[24] and the Crown Court Sentencing Survey shows that it is currently a frequent aggravating

---

[19] [2002] 2 Cr App R (S) 560; see also *Cooper* [2012] 2 Cr App R (S) 344.   [20] See ch. 4.4.9 above.
[21] [2007] 1 Cr App R (S) 493, at [47].   [22] Wasik (1998).
[23] See *Johnson* [2011] 1 Cr App R (S) 493 (9 years upheld for repeated targeting of vulnerable elderly people); *Field* [2012] 1 Cr App R (S) 395 (8 years upheld for conspiracy to defraud 28 vulnerable elderly people); *Attorney General's References Nos. 41, 42, 43, 44, and 45 of 2011)* [2012] 1 Cr App R (S) 589 (6 years for conspiracy to defraud 29 vulnerable elderly people); all sentences after guilty plea.
[24] Moxon (1988), p. 9; see also p. 31.

factor in sentences for robbery and sexual offences.[25] However, close scrutiny of the sentences approved in some of the cases suggests that the vulnerability of the victim may be a greater factor in the sentence than the underlying offence, and may propel the sentence to levels comparable with serious woundings and serious rapes. For example, in *Curtis* (2007),[26] by what calculation can a sentence of 5 years' imprisonment for a single distraction burglary (all stolen goods recovered quickly) be reached? The offender had several previous convictions, but the sentence was the equivalent of 7 or 8 years after a trial. Perhaps the answer in this case is that the burglary itself was 'worth' 3 years, and the targeting of elderly victims added 2 more years. In that case, the aggravating element almost equals the offence itself. Again, by what calculation can the sentence of 8 years' imprisonment on a guilty plea (perhaps 11 years after a trial) be reached in *O'Brien*? How long a sentence would be appropriate for a distraction burglary, yielding a few hundred pounds, by a man with several previous convictions? If the answer is, say, around 4 years, does that mean that the targeting of a vulnerable victim effectively doubled the sentence? These decisions raise two important questions – procedurally whether the power of certain aggravating (and mitigating?) factors operates entirely unconstrained by guidelines, and substantively whether the aggravating factor of targeting vulnerable victims is regarded as being (almost) as important to sentence as the offence itself, and, if so, whether that is defensible. The offence of burglary itself seems almost to be overshadowed by the focus on the targeting of the vulnerable victim (aggravated culpability) and the effects on such victims (aggravated harm).[27]

Offenders operating in groups or gangs

Where an offence is committed by two or more people, the justification for aggravating the sentence probably lies in the greater harm which it is believed to involve – although the Council's guideline suggests that 'offenders operating in groups or gangs' increases the culpability element. That may be so where a group of people come together in order 'by weight of numbers to pursue a common and unlawful purpose'.[28] In cases where two or more offenders confront a victim, a significant factor is that the victim is likely to be in greater fear and to feel a greater sense of humiliation and helplessness. These factors are likely to be relevant in cases of a) widespread public disorder, b) offences committed by groups, often organized, and c) offences committed in a gang context. The effect of a context of widespread lawlessness was said to be 'hugely' aggravating, by Lord Judge CJ in the leading case of *Blackshaw* (2012):[29]

---

[25] CCSS (2014), pp. 27–8; see also Pina-Sanchez and Linacre (2013).
[26] [2007] 2 Cr App R (S) 322.　　[27] See the discussion in ch. 4.4.9 above.
[28] *Caird et al.* (1970) 54 Cr App R 499, per Sachs LJ at p. 507; cf. Pina-Sanchez and Linacre (2013), suggesting that a gang element does not always aggravate sentence in practice.
[29] [2012] 1 Cr App R (S) 697, at [4] and [7].

those who deliberately participate in disturbances of this magnitude, causing injury and damage and fear to even the most stout-hearted of citizens, and who individually commit further crimes during the course of the riots are committing aggravated crimes.

As for offences committed by groups, one reason for aggravation in these cases might be that group pressure to continue may make such offences less likely to be abandoned, and that group dynamics may lead to greater harm or damage being caused.[30] Some group offences may be described as 'organized crime', when teams or systems operate so as to maximize profit. Whether they are charged as conspiracy or not, the courts treat even the organized theft of moderate sums as particularly serious where there is evidence of organization or selection of vulnerable victims.[31] Sentencers should, however, draw a distinction between the ringleader and fringe participants.[32] As for offences committed in a gang context, the Court of Appeal states that a deterrent element must be added to such sentences 'to demonstrate that society will not tolerate that type of culture and its associated violence',[33] although the commitment to violent gang warfare supplies a retributive reason for aggravation of sentence.

Planning of an offence

Elements of planning or organization may also be present in crimes committed by individuals. A person who plans a crime is generally more culpable, because the offence is premeditated and the offender is therefore more fully confirmed in his criminal motivation than someone who acts on impulse, since he is more considered in his lawbreaking. (An exception to this is where the planning is directed at minimizing the harmful results of the offence.) Planned lawbreaking betokens a considered attack on social values, with greater commitment and perhaps continuity than a spontaneous crime.[34]

Commission of an offence while under the influence of alcohol or drugs

There is a long history of treating intoxication as an aggravating factor, and it appears in the list of aggravating factors set out by the SGC[35] and also those set

---

[30] E.g. Lord Lane CJ in *Pilgrim* (1983) 5 Cr App R (S) 140, 'mob violence feeds upon itself'.

[31] See *Attorney General's References Nos. 42, 43 and 44 of 2006* [2007] 1 Cr App R (S) 493, and other cases cited in n. 23 above.

[32] As emphasized in decisions such as *Keys and Sween* (1986) 8 Cr App R (S) 444, and *Chapman* [1999] 2 Cr App R (S) 374.

[33] See *Thompson and Nelson* [2010] 2 Cr App R (S) 461, *Attorney General's Reference No. 106 of 2011* [2012] 2 Cr App R (S) 387, and *Hagan* [2013] 1 Cr App R (S) 483.

[34] For fuller discussion of this point, see ch. 4.5 above; cf. Roberts (2008a), pp. 80–3.

[35] SGC, *Overarching Principles: Seriousness* (2004), p. 6 ('commission of an offence while under the influence of alcohol or drugs').

out at Step Two of the Sentencing Council's guidelines.[36] Implicit in this approach is the judgment that offenders who voluntarily become intoxicated are more culpable, presumably because they realize (or ought to realize) that this may lead to uninhibited conduct with unpredictable results. Where the courts are dealing with repeated drunken violence the aggravating effect is most keenly felt,[37] since it can be maintained that an offender who knows of his propensity to turn violent when intoxicated is more to blame. Thus the Crown Court Sentencing Survey shows that intoxication is a frequent aggravating factor, featuring in 30 per cent of arson and criminal damage cases, 24 per cent of assault and public order cases, and 16 per cent of burglary cases, as well as 27 per cent of driving cases.[38]

However, as Nicola Padfield points out, this is at best a partial account of the significance of intoxication in sentencing decisions. Intoxication can aggravate, but it can also mitigate. Where there is an 'out of character' plea by someone with no history of drunken misbehaviour, the court may mitigate the sentence.[39] Moreover, where D can persuade the court that he is either undertaking or about to undertake a course of treatment, this may incline the court in favour of a rehabilitative sentence. This appears from the Crown Court Sentencing Survey, showing that 'determination/demonstration to address addiction/behaviour' was a mitigating factor in 15 per cent of cases of arson and criminal damage, 13 per cent of drugs cases and 9 per cent of burglary cases.[40] The Sentencing Council refers specifically to the possibility, where D has a propensity to misuse drugs and 'there is sufficient prospect of success', of making a community order with a drug treatment requirement as a 'proper alternative to a short or moderate custodial sentence'.[41] That applies to drugs and not alcohol dependency, and is not to be found in the subsequent guideline on sexual offences.

If intoxication may be aggravating or mitigating, according to the context and the prospects of future rehabilitation, how should sentencing guidance deal with the issue? Padfield asks:

> How is the court meant to distinguish remorseful drunks from dangerous drunks, one-off drunks from alcoholics, those who get drunk in order to commit their offences from those who did not know they were drunk?[42]

These are framed as evidential questions, and they point to practical problems of proof. But the normative question is what guidance courts should

---

[36] E.g. Sentencing Council, *Burglary Offences: Definitive Guideline* (2011), p. 9; Sentencing Council, *Sexual Offences: Definitive Guideline* (2013), p. 11.

[37] Cf. the analysis by Dingwall (2006), chs. 2 and 3.   [38] CCSS (2014), p. 28.

[39] Padfield (2011), p. 90, discussing *Trace* [2010] EWCA Crim 879 and other appellate cases.

[40] CCSS (2014), p. 31.

[41] Sentencing Council, *Burglary Offences: Definitive Guideline* (2011), p. 8, moving away from the position provisionally adopted in Sentencing Council, *Burglary Offences Guideline: Professional Consultation* (2011), pp. 16–17.

[42] Padfield (2011), p. 97.

be given,[43] and Padfield's three pairings make a good starting point. If D is remorseful, that may mitigate (see below). If it was a one-off occasion or D was unaware of the effects of intoxication, there may be grounds for mitigation. But for those who get drunk in order to commit the offence, or know of their propensity to offend when intoxicated, that is an aggravating factor. If the offence is not too serious, and there are good prospects of treatment for addiction, that may turn the court away from low-to-moderate custody towards a community sentence.

Failure to respond to warnings

Several offence guidelines also treat a failure to respond to warnings by others as an aggravating factor. This may evidence a callous indifference to the consequences of one's actions, a factor that has emerged in various different types of offence. Thus, where the offender has caused death by dangerous driving, it is an established aggravating factor that he ignored warnings or pleas from passengers to slow down.[44] Similarly, in relation to breaches of health and safety laws, 'inactivity in the face of previous incidents and previous complaints' was regarded as aggravating the seriousness of the offences.[45]

Abuse of position of trust

Where breach of trust or abuse of authority is an element in the crime, the force of aggravation comes more from the social context of the offence. The crime may be unplanned, committed by an individual and not involving any violence or threats. But trust is fundamental to many social relationships, as argued in Chapter 4.4.10 above, and one of the burdens of trust or authority is an undertaking of incorruptibility. As the Court of Appeal stated in a case involving a stockbroker, breaches of trust 'undermine public confidence, because the matters of financial dealing with which this man was involved cannot be carried out unless confidence is reposed in those who carry out these transactions on behalf of members of the public'.[46] The same applies to offences committed by police officers, as the Court of Appeal has stated:

> It is critical that the public retain full confidence in our police force. A feature of the trust that must exist is that the public can expect that they will not be assaulted by officers even if they are being a nuisance. Any erosion of that basic

---

[43] Cf. Padfield (2011), who is sceptical about the possibility of useful guidance, with Dingwall and Koffman (2008).

[44] As reaffirmed in SGC, *Causing Death by Driving* (2008), p. 11.

[45] *Firth Vickers Centrispinning Ltd* [1998] 1 Cr App R (S) 293.

[46] Per Stephen Brown LJ in *Dawson* (1987) 9 Cr App R (S) 248. See also the quotation from Cox in ch. 4.4.11 above.

but reasonable expectation will do profound harm to the good relationship that must exist between the public and the police service.[47]

The courts' reasoning has sometimes been based on deterrence: people in positions of trust or authority will inevitably have great temptation placed before them, and the law must match this with strong sentences for succumbing. But that is a doubtful argument in itself, since there will usually be other disastrous consequences of being caught offending in such a position (loss of job, loss of pension and other rights, inability to find comparable employment) which will render a strong sentence less necessary on deterrent reasoning.[48] The fundamental importance of networks of trust and authority for the smooth operation of society is surely sufficient explanation of the additional harm. A survey in the 1990s suggested that breach of trust was the factor most strongly associated with the imposition of custodial sentences in the Crown Court.[49]

Offences against public officials

It may be worth considering at this point the claims of a connected factor that is not included in the guideline list but which is often thought to be aggravating – that the offence was committed *against* a public official. Should an attack on a police officer be regarded as more grave than an attack on an ordinary citizen? One answer is that police officers are expected to place themselves in vulnerable positions sometimes, as part of their job, and that people who take advantage of this commit a worse offence. Probably this line of argument could be connected with that in the previous paragraph: society needs people to undertake policing and other positions of authority, and a person who knowingly attacks such an official is striking against a fundamental institution in a way that one who attacks a private citizen is not. Because of its great social significance, it should be regarded as more serious. Thus in *Attorney General's Reference No. 35 of 1995 (Hartley)* Lord Taylor CJ made it clear that the use of violence against a police officer 'who was merely acting in the exercise of his duty' was an aggravated offence;[50] the Court of Appeal also increased the sentence in *Attorney General's Reference No. 99 of 2003 (Vidler)* for similar reasons.[51]

From this brief consideration of general aggravating factors, it is evident that the courts have not always tended to justify them in terms of their effect in

---

[47] *Dunn* [2003] 2 Cr App R (S) 535 at p. 540. See also *Nazir* [2003] 2 Cr App R (S) 671, and, for an offence by a prison officer, *Mills* [2005] 1 Cr App R (S) 180. Similar considerations apply to the responsibility of social workers towards their charges: *Hardwick* [2007] 1 Cr App R (S) 54.

[48] The same applies where a sexual offence is committed by someone in a position of trust: e.g. *Cornwall* [2013] 1 Cr App R (S) 158.

[49] Flood-Page and Mackie (1998), p. 11.   [50] [1996] 1 Cr App R (S) 413, at p. 415.

[51] [2005] 1 Cr App R (S) 150; cf. Pina-Sanchez and Linacre (2013), suggesting that in practice this factor does not always aggravate.

increasing the seriousness of the offence. Instead, courts have often adopted the terminology of deterrence, probably without reflecting on the different rationales of sentencing. It is true that in a carefully constructed theory of deterrence the concept of proportionality is important, since Bentham devoted a whole chapter to it and included such injunctions as 'venture more against a great offence than a small one'.[52] However, the suggestion here is that each of the above factors is rightly regarded as increasing the seriousness of offences.

5.2.3 Specific aggravating factors

The number of aggravating factors specific to individual offences is enormous, and no purpose would be served by enumerating them here. Examples may be found in guideline judgments such as *Kelly and Donnelly* (2001),[53] where the Court of Appeal followed the Sentencing Advisory Panel in listing as aggravating factors in racially aggravated offences such matters as membership of a racist organization, deliberate humiliation of the victim, and impact on a particular local community. Examples may also be found in definitive guidelines. However, the Sentencing Council's approach to guidelines deploys as determinants of the offence category at Step One certain factors which would otherwise be treated as aggravating, and then deals with the remaining aggravating factors at Step Two. Thus the guideline on domestic burglary sets out, at Step One, factors such as 'soiling, ransacking or vandalism of property', 'violence used or threatened against victim', and 'member of group or gang', whereas at Step Two come other aggravating factors such as 'gratuitous degradation of victim' and 'child at home when offence committed'.[54] Similarly, the guidelines for importing and for supplying drugs take one would-be aggravating factor (whether D played a leading or a significant role) as a determinant of offence seriousness at Step One, leaving other aggravating factors to be taken into account at Step Two, such as 'sophisticated nature of concealment' and 'exposure of others to more than usual danger'.[55]

The discussion above has focused on the recognition of and rationale for various aggravating factors, but there is another major issue – their quantification – which remains at large. In view of the substantial effect that they can have on the determination of sentence, it is important to make further progress on the issue of quantifying or 'weighing' aggravating factors if the purpose of sentencing guidelines (in terms of establishing a common approach to sentencing) is not to be frustrated by a wide swath of unregulated discretion.[56] Questions of degree abound, of course, but the division of offenders

---

[52] Bentham (1789), ch. XIV, rule 2.
[53] [2001] 2 Cr App R (S) 341, at p. 348. Cf. the discussion in ch. 3.5.2 above.
[54] Sentencing Council, *Burglary Offences: Definitive Guideline* (2011), pp. 8–9.
[55] Sentencing Council, *Drug Offences: Definitive Guideline* (2012), pp. 4–14.
[56] See further Roberts (2008b).

into three roles in drug cases (leading, significant, lesser) marks an important beginning, even if there are a few offenders who cannot be fitted neatly into any category; further efforts in this direction are necessary.

5.3 Mitigation as diminished seriousness

The factors which have been recognized as mitigating sentences in England are a much more heterogeneous collection than the aggravating factors. There is only one statutory mitigating factor that courts are required to take into account, the plea of guilty, and that is independent of the seriousness of the offence (see part 5.4.1 below); so also is the provision in s. 73 of the Serious Organized Crime and Police Act 2005 stating that a court may take account of any assistance by the offender to the investigator or prosecution (see 5.4.2 below). Apart from those statutory factors, there is also the broad permissive provision in s. 166(1) of the Criminal Justice Act 2003, stating that the statutory tests for imposing custody or a community sentence should not prevent a court from mitigating a sentence by taking account of 'any such matters as, in the opinion of the court, are relevant in mitigation of sentence'. In this chapter, personal mitigating factors will be left for discussion in part 5.4 below, and here the focus will be on mitigating factors that reduce the seriousness of an offence. The distinction between general mitigating factors and those relevant only to particular types of offence will be adopted again, and it will be observed that some reflect the reduced harmfulness of the offence, and many more reflect the diminished culpability of the offender.

5.3.1 Specific mitigating factors

Just as most sentencing guidelines set out some offence-specific aggravating factors, so they also list some offence-specific mitigating factors (although usually fewer). Thus, the guideline on domestic burglary sets out two 'factors indicating lesser harm' ('nothing stolen or only property of very low value to the victim' and 'limited damage or disturbance to property') and three 'factors indicating lower culpability' ('offence committed on impulse, with limited intrusion into property', 'offender exploited by others', and 'mental disorder or learning disability, where linked to the commission of the offence'). Those factors are operative at Step One, whereas other factors reducing seriousness come in at Step Two, such as 'subordinate role in a group or gang' and 'age and/or lack of maturity where it affects the responsibility of the offender'.[57] By way of contrast, the guidelines on rape and other principal sexual offences include no reference to any factors indicating lesser harm or lower culpability; they do refer to a few mitigating factors at Step Two, but 'age and/or lack

---

[57] Sentencing Council, *Burglary Offences: Definitive Guideline* (2011), pp. 8–9.

of maturity' and 'mental disorder or learning disability' are on the borders between diminished seriousness and personal mitigation.[58]

5.3.2 General mitigating factors related to seriousness

We have noted that the seriousness of an offence may be analysed in terms of the harmfulness or potential harmfulness of the conduct, and the culpability of the offender. Into the former category fall such factors as the small amount of damage caused or property taken, or the minor role of the offender. But it is in the latter category that we find the core of mitigation – factors personal to the offender which are treated as reducing culpability. Thus, it is generally treated as mitigation where the offence was committed impulsively or suddenly:[59] this lies at the opposite end of the spectrum from planning and premeditation, which are treated as aggravating, whereas an intentional but unplanned offence might perhaps be neutral.

A frequent mitigating factor recorded in the Crown Court Sentencing Survey is 'age/lack of maturity affecting responsibility', which applies not only to youths but also to young adults aged 18–25. This factor appears in 43 per cent of robberies, 34 per cent of sexual offences, 31 per cent of offences causing death, 30 per cent of arson and criminal damage cases, and so on.[60] Other cases involving reduced culpability are those lying just outside the narrow confines of criminal law defences such as insanity, duress, necessity, or mistake of law. Indeed, many of those defences are restricted tightly in the expectation that courts will grant substantial mitigation of sentence where the circumstances fall just outside the legal requirements for a defence.[61] One example would be where an offender is suffering from a psychiatric disorder falling short of providing an insanity defence: thus in *Attorney General's Reference No. 37 of 2004 (Dawson)* (2005)[62] the Court of Appeal held that a community rehabilitation order with a condition of psychiatric treatment was not unduly lenient for attempted robbery by an offender suffering from clinical depression. Another example is where the offender was excusably ignorant of the law: thus in *Rehman and Wood* (2006)[63] the Court of Appeal had to decide whether there were exceptional circumstances that justified departure from the mandatory minimum sentence of 5 years for possession of an illegal

---

[58] Sentencing Council, *Sexual Offences: Definitive Guideline* (2013), pp. 10–24.

[59] 'Offence committed on impulse' was a mitigating factor in a quarter of the burglary cases in the small Crown Court survey, and about half of these resulted in a sentence reduction: SCWG Survey (2008), p. 15; see also Jacobson and Hough (2011), p. 149 on 'spontaneous offence'.

[60] CCSS (2014), p. 31.   [61] See Wasik (1983) for a full discussion.

[62] [2005] 1 Cr App R (S) 295; see also *Attorney General's Reference No. 83 of 2001 (Fidler)* [2002] 1 Cr App R (S) 588 (community rehabilitation order upheld for robber suffering from schizophrenia), but cf. *Jackley* [2013] 2 Cr App R (S) 521.

[63] [2006] 1 Cr App R (S) 404, at pp. 414–18, discussed in ch. 3.5.1 above. See also *Beard* [2008] 2 Cr App R (S) 232.

firearm, and the Court found such circumstances in the first offender's ignorance of the law (5 years reduced to 2), but not in the second offender's ignorance, since he was a collector of weapons and should have known to check the lawfulness of the particular gun.[64]

Turning to the entrapment of an offender by the police or an agent provocateur, the English courts have declared that it may be sufficiently fundamental to justify staying the prosecution for abuse of process,[65] but that lesser degrees of entrapment ought to be a matter of mitigation in appropriate cases. The Court of Appeal has reduced sentences where there has been a significant element of entrapment,[66] even when the 'sting' operation was carried out by journalists.[67] The Court has also approved sentence reduction in cases of threats of violence falling short of a defence of duress.[68] Finally, where the offender has been under exceptional stress or emotional pressure, this will generally be regarded as mitigation, on the basis of reduced culpability.[69] This is one of a number of factors regarded as insufficient to amount to a complete defence to liability but appropriate for mitigation, which may be substantial in an appropriate case. However, the effect of intoxication is different: often it aggravates (see 5.2.2 above), but an 'out of character' drunken episode may mitigate, as may a determination, or demonstration of steps taken, to address addiction to drugs or alcohol.

5.4 Personal mitigation

Research shows that in practice the range of factors advanced in mitigation is enormously wide.[70] An obvious mitigating factor is the previous good character of the offender: proportionality theory argues in favour of dealing more leniently with an offence that can be interpreted as an isolated lapse, recognizing human frailty and yet showing respect for the offender as a rational individual, capable of responding to the censure inherent in the sentence imposed. But this justification quickly evaporates as the offender gathers previous convictions, as we shall see in the detailed discussion of this issue in Chapter 6.2 below. We now step away from concepts of proportionality and offence-seriousness, to consider what other forms of mitigation might properly be admitted. The factors gathered together as 'personal mitigation' in the paragraphs that follow do not turn on diminished culpability or diminished harm: they range from a guilty plea and other factors contributing to the smooth running of the criminal justice system, to the offender's general social

---

[64] See also *Thomas* [2006] 1 Cr App R (S) 602, and *Wilson* [2012] 1 Cr App R (S) 542 (ignorance of change of law brought about by Sexual Offences Act 2003, some mitigation allowed).
[65] *Looseley* [2001] 1 WLR 2060.   [66] E.g. *Chalcraft and Campbell* [2002] 2 Cr App R (S) 172.
[67] *Barnett* [2008] 1 Cr App R (S) 354.   [68] *Hynes* [2009] 1 Cr App R (S) 535.
[69] As in some cases of violence against young children: e.g. post-natal depression in *Isaac* [1998] 1 Cr App R (S) 266.
[70] See the studies by Shapland (1981), (2011), and by Jacobson and Hough (2007), (2011).

contributions, to the impact of the sentence on the offender and others, and to the prospect of the offender's rehabilitation and desistance. In respect of each, it is important to examine the possible justifications – necessarily falling outside the theory of proportionate punishment – for reducing sentence on account of such extraneous considerations.

5.4.1 Statutory reduction of sentence for a plea of guilty

It was well settled in the English common law of sentencing that a plea of guilty should normally attract a reduction of sentence, and that the scale of the reduction should be greater, the earlier the plea was intimated.[71] However, in 1994 the government decided, following the report of the Royal Commission on Criminal Justice,[72] that what is usually known as the 'guilty plea discount' should be put into statutory form. In 2004 the Sentencing Guidelines Council handed down a definitive guideline on the reduction in sentence for a guilty plea, and a revised guideline was issued in 2007. The Council is to produce another revised guideline soon. Having explained the law and the SGC guideline, we go on below to discuss the available statistics, and the deep issues of principle raised by the guilty plea discount.

1. The statutory provision

The provision that originated in s. 48 of the Criminal Justice and Public Order Act 1994 is now to be found in s. 144 of the Criminal Justice Act 2003:

> (1) In determining what sentence to pass on an offender who has pleaded guilty to an offence in proceedings before that or another court, a court must take into account:
>   (a) the stage in the proceedings for the offence at which the offender indicated his intention to plead guilty, and
>   (b) the circumstances in which this indication was given.
> (2) In the case of an offence the sentence for which falls to be imposed under subsection (2) of ss. 110 or 111 of the Sentencing Act,[73] nothing in that subsection prevents the court, after taking account of any matter referred to in subsection (1) of this section, from imposing any sentence which is not less than 80 per cent of that specified in that subsection.

This must be read in conjunction with s. 174(2)(d), which provides that:

> where as a result of taking into account any matter referred to in s. 144(1), the court imposes a punishment on the offender which is less severe than the punishment it would otherwise have imposed, [it must] state that fact.

---

[71] See, e.g., *De Haan* [1968] 2 QB 108, and *Buffery* (1993) 14 Cr App R (S) 511. For a general criminal justice critique, see McConville and Marsh (2014).
[72] Royal Commission on Criminal Justice (1993), ch. 7.
[73] This is shorthand for the Powers of Criminal Courts (Sentencing) Act 2000.

The unqualified terms of s. 144 mean that the discount applies to all courts, both magistrates' courts and the Crown Court, and to all forms of sentence, not just custody. There is no reference to a different principle for murder cases, and therefore the calculation of the minimum term to be served by a person convicted of murder should take the discount into account, albeit in a somewhat diminished form.[74] Subsection (2) modifies the approach for the two prescribed sentences, the minimum of 3 years for the third domestic burglary and the minimum of 7 years for the third offence of dealing class A drugs.[75] Here the discount is limited to 20 per cent, presumably to emphasize the stringency of the minimum sentences while furnishing some encouragement to plead guilty. However, the Act includes no corresponding reference to the minimum sentence of 5 years for firearms offences,[76] and so the Court of Appeal has held that no discount may be given for pleading guilty to that offence.[77] This is the only occasion on which English law does not provide for a sentence reduction for pleading guilty, and it renders the minimum sentence comparatively more severe, without any compelling justification.

Since its inception, however, the legislation on discounts for pleading guilty has not been specific. Subsection (1) is drafted in a remarkably allusive manner. Not only does it fail to say anything about the scale of discounts, but it merely hints at the principle that the discount should be larger, the earlier the guilty plea is intimated. In the result, the Court of Appeal dealt with a succession of appeals on the subject between 1994 and 2004, and this underlined the need to establish guidance on the proper approach to sentencing in guilty plea cases.

2. The 2007 guideline

The SGC prefaced its guideline with a restatement of the purpose of the guilty plea discount in the following terms:

> A reduction in sentence is appropriate because a guilty plea avoids the need for a trial (thus enabling other cases to be disposed of more expeditiously), shortens the gap between charge and sentence, saves considerable cost, and, in the case of an early plea, saves victims and witnesses from the concern about having to give evidence. The reduction principle derives from the need for the effective administration of justice and not as an aspect of mitigation.[78]

---

[74] This was a controversial issue in the drawing up of the Council's guideline on the subject: see House of Commons (2004) for discussion of the issue and the public and government response to it. For an example of the application of the guideline in a murder case, see *Roberts and Mould* [2008] 2 Cr App R (S) 350, at p. 353.

[75] Discussed in ch. 3.5.1 above and ch. 6.7 below.   [76] See the discussion in ch. 3.5.1 above.

[77] *Jordan* [2005] 2 Cr App R (S) 267.

[78] SGC, *Reduction in Sentence for a Guilty Plea: Revised Guideline* (2007), para. 2.2.

The first three factors mentioned (speeding up the system, reducing time on remand, and cost) are all pragmatic reasons related to what the Australian courts have termed 'facilitating the course of justice'.[79] Some judges in the leading Scots decision of *Gemmell* argued that the judge should try to quantify the public benefits of the plea in the particular case,[80] but it is not clear where reliable information would come from or how much time this exercise would take, and it is surely preferable to have a standard scale.[81] The fourth factor – saving anxiety and distress for victims and witnesses – promises significant relief for those who would otherwise have to give evidence. Again, it could be argued that this should depend on the situation in the particular case – research indicates that some victims and witnesses insist that they would rather (if they had the choice) undergo the pains of giving evidence if it meant that the offender received a longer sentence (i.e. no discount)[82] – but since the rationale is that this is an incentive for defendants, it is surely preferable to base the sentence reduction on the predominant sparing of victims and witnesses.

Two points are missing from the Council's list of justifications. The first is any mention of remorse in this connection. Traditionally judges have cited remorse as a major justification for the guilty plea discount.[83] One difficulty with this is how courts can discern genuine contrition from the sheer realism of recognizing (often with legal advice) that pleading guilty leads to lower sentences. Remorse-based reasoning is surely implausible in cases where the guilty plea occurs at the last minute, or in the early stages of the trial.[84] Sentencers often refer to remorse as a factor that can tip them away from imposing a custodial sentence,[85] but at least some of them acknowledge the difficulty of assessing whether it is genuine (particularly where they only see the offender for sentence), and refer to 'demonstrated' remorse as the key to mitigation.[86] The Crown Court Sentencing Survey reveals that remorse is by far the most-cited mitigating factor, relevant in 37 per cent of arson and criminal damage cases, 34 per cent of assault cases, 29 per cent of sexual offences, 26 per cent of drug offences, and so on.[87] Even if a court can be sure that a particular offender is remorseful, ought that to be relevant to sentence? If the argument is that the offender's acceptance of his wrongdoing means that less punishment is needed to deter or to reform, that is questionable on two grounds – whether deterrent or rehabilitative considerations should be given

[79] E.g. *Cameron* v. *R.* (2002) 209 CLR 339; *Ironside* (2009) 195 A Crim R 483.
[80] *Gemmell* 2012 JC 223.   [81] As argued by Leverick (2014), pp. 342–3.
[82] This was a finding of the research on rape commissioned by the Panel: see Clarke, Moran-Ellis and Sleny (2002).
[83] E.g. *Fraser* (1982) 4 Cr App R (S) 254, *Archer* [1998] 2 Cr App R (S) 76.
[84] As in the former leading case of *De Haan* [1968] 2 QB 108.
[85] Jacobson and Hough (2007), ch. 2.
[86] Hough et al. (2003), p. 41; Jacobson and Hough (2007), ch. 3.   [87] CCSS (2014), p. 31.

such weight, and whether the assumption is in fact true.[88] The offender's culpability can hardly be diminished retrospectively by a show of remorse, but on desert grounds it is right to recognize that the offender has already responded in the way that moral agents are expected to respond.[89] There is public support for regarding remorse as a mitigating factor,[90] but some would argue that remorse is merely past-regarding and that a more secure basis for mitigation is a commitment to change.[91] The 2007 guideline states that courts should address both remorse and other mitigating factors separately from the guilty plea. This preserves the possibility of courts treating remorse as a general mitigating factor, but keeps it apart from the guilty plea discount.

Also missing from the 2007 guideline is any reference to the dangers of the guilty plea discount in terms of inducing innocent people to plead guilty. The Panel expressed some concern about this, and argued that a 40 per cent discount would be simply too much encouragement to plead guilty.[92] A government suggestion in 2010 that the discount be raised to 50 per cent was not pursued, on the grounds that it would not produce extra guilty pleas and would undermine public confidence.[93] The 2007 guideline makes no comment on these matters, but in the context of a study of the principles on which sentences are and should be based, this is a factor that must not be ignored (see further part 5.4.1.4 below). Moreover, the question of when 'too much encouragement' turns into pressure was revisited by the Court of Appeal in *Goodyear* (2006),[94] when it decided to give what it termed 'guidelines' on the circumstances in which a judge might give an 'advance indication of sentence' to a defendant who is pleading not guilty but wishes to know the likely sentence on a guilty plea. The Auld Report had recommended such a procedure, asking 'What possible additional pressure, unacceptable or otherwise, can there be in the judge, whom he has requested to tell him where he stands, indicating more precisely the alternatives?',[95] and the Criminal Justice Act 2003 introduced it (in Schedule 3) to the magistrates' courts. The Court in *Goodyear*, which included Lord Woolf CJ and Judge LJ, likewise stated that if the defendant seeks the judge's view, 'we do not see why a judicial response to a request for information from the defendant should automatically be deemed to constitute improper pressure on him'. The difference, of course, lies between defence counsel's prediction and the authoritativeness of the judicial indication: the roulette wheel has gone, but the judge's indication may impose enormous pressure on the defendant, particularly where the indicated sentence on a change of plea to guilty does not involve immediate

---

[88] Maslen and Roberts (2013), p. 125, cite evidence that remorse is a weak predictor of desistance.
[89] Maslen and Roberts (2013), pp. 126 and 134.   [90] Roberts, Hough et al (2008).
[91] Shapland (2011), discussed further in 5.4.4 below.
[92] SAP, *Reduction in Sentence for a Guilty Plea* (2004), para. 11 and paras. 21–4.
[93] Public views about the discount are discussed below, text at n. 123.
[94] [2006] 1 Cr App R (S) 23.   [95] Auld (2001), pp. 434–4.

imprisonment.[96] The *Goodyear* procedure is undoubtedly more transparent than secret meetings in the judge's chambers,[97] but there remains the fact that, in combination with the guideline of reduction of sentence for a guilty plea, it imposes considerable pressure on the guilty and innocent alike.[98] Whether it is more effective than the pre-*Goodyear* procedures in terms of producing guilty pleas appears not to have been the subject of research.[99]

Returning to the guideline, it states that the level of sentence reduction should be on a sliding scale from a maximum of one-third where the guilty plea was entered or intimated at the first reasonable opportunity, reducing to one-quarter if the trial date has already been set, and to one-tenth if the plea is tendered at the 'door of the court' or after the trial has begun.[100] The guideline gives illustrations of what may be regarded as the 'first reasonable opportunity' to intimate a plea, and this has been discussed and developed in a judgment of Hughes LJ in *Caley* (2013).[101] The guideline insists that, even for those who change plea at the start of a trial, there must always be some incentive or reward.[102] In cases where an early guilty plea is entered but then the offender's version of the circumstances of the offence is rejected in a *Newton* hearing, some of the normal reduction in sentence may be lost.[103] Thus procedurally the guideline recommends the following approach:

- decide on the sentence for the offence(s), taking account of aggravating and mitigating factors;
- select the amount of reduction for the guilty plea by reference to the sliding scale;[104]
- apply the reduction to the sentence decided on; and
- pronounce the sentence, stating what the sentence would have been if there had been no reduction as a result of the guilty plea.

Although there are references throughout the guideline to 'the sliding scale', this does not apply well to cases in which the discount has the effect of reducing a custodial sentence to a community sentence. The guideline states plainly that 'where a sentencer is in doubt as to whether a custodial sentence is appropriate, the reduction attributable to a guilty plea will be a relevant

---

[96] For a powerful critique, see McConville and Marsh (2014), chs. 3 and 4; see Flynn (2011) on sentence indications in Victoria.

[97] Darbyshire (2006).

[98] See further ch. 11.4.2 below. For the financial and other incentives to counsel in these circumstances, see Tague (2006 and 2007).

[99] As lamented by the New South Wales Law Reform Commission (2013), ch. 8, in its review of sentence indication systems.

[100] Essentially, this follows the lines of the proposal by Auld (2001), p. 441.

[101] [2013] 2 Cr App R (S) 305, at [9–22]; see also *Creathorne* [2014] 2 Cr App R (S) 382.

[102] See, e.g., *Attorney General's Reference No. 35 of 2010* [2011] 1 Cr App R (S) 711, at [26].

[103] Cf. *Caley* [2013] 2 Cr App R (S) 305, at [26–27].

[104] The guideline (see next note) proclaims a 'recommended approach', and judges may depart for good reason: see e.g. *Ward* [2014] 1 Cr App R (S) 466.

consideration. Where this is amongst the factors leading to the imposition of a non-custodial sentence, there will be no need to apply a further reduction on account of the guilty plea.'[105] This is a logical application of the discount, but (i) it is a crucial and momentous decision for the offender who is advised that the case is on or around the cusp of custody, capable of exerting considerable pressure to plead guilty; and (ii) such decisions cannot be based on the 'sliding scale' as such. Applying the logic of the guideline, only an early guilty plea could reduce a custodial sentence of, say, 12 weeks to a suspended sentence or community sentence; whereas a later plea might still be accorded the effect of reducing, say, a 2-week sentence in the same way.

At common law there was scattered authority allowing the discount to be withheld in certain circumstances, but the SGC reconsidered the proper approach. The 2004 guideline stated that there was no reason why credit should be withheld simply because the offender was caught 'red-handed' or otherwise had no defence to the charge. However, there was some judicial unease at this departure from previous practice, leading to what the chairman of the SGC referred to as 'concern about the extent to which the guideline has been consistently applied'.[106] If the purpose of giving credit is to encourage the guilty to enter their plea at the earliest opportunity and thus to spare victims and witnesses as well as to save money, some discount should be given in these cases too.[107] The revised guideline reaffirms this approach, and suggests that a 20 per cent reduction should then be the maximum available.

There was also some doubt at common law whether the discount should be given to offenders sentenced as dangerous: the guideline now states that the discount should apply to the proportionate part of the sentence (i.e. the minimum term) 'but not the public protection element of the sentence'.[108] The guideline goes on to emphasize that courts may not withhold the discount because they believe the maximum sentence for the offence is too low,[109] but a magistrates' court or any court dealing with a young offender may give the maximum permissible sentence if satisfied that a longer sentence (at the Crown Court, or a sentence of long-term detention for a youth) would have been justified in the absence of a guilty plea.[110]

Most of the issues of principle have been discussed by courts and law reform agencies in Scotland, Australia, and elsewhere,[111] although the English

---

[105] SGC, *Reduction in Sentence for a Guilty Plea* (2007), para. 2.3.

[106] Ibid., foreword; and see *Oosthuizen* [2006] 1 Cr App R (S) 385.

[107] For supporting discussion, see *Wilson* [2012] 2 Cr App R (S) 440, *Caley* [2013] 2 Cr App R (S) 305, at [23–25], and *Tarcuta* [2014] 2 Cr App R (S) 499; cf. the Australian decision in *Sutton* [2004] NSWCCA 225, and the Scots decision in *Gemmell* 2012 JC 223 (on which see Leverick (2014), pp. 346–7).

[108] SGC, *Reduction in Sentence for a Guilty Plea* (2007), para. 5.1. Cf. the divided Full Bench in Scotland in *Gemmell*, ibid.

[109] SGC, ibid., para. 5.6. For an example, see *Kirby* [2008] 2 Cr App R (S) 264.

[110] SGC, ibid., paras. 5.8 and 5.9; long-term detention of juveniles is discussed in ch. 12.1 below.

[111] See nn. 96, 98, 107 and 112 above; and now NSW Law Reform Commission (2013), ch. 9.

institutions have not yet drawn on the reasoning of these discussions. Whereas a sliding scale has been established in South Australia,[112] there has been a rejection of a formal 'sliding scale' in Victoria and in Scotland in favour of a discretionary case-by-case assessment of the issues and the appropriate discount. This is a recipe for inconsistency, and reduces any 'incentive' provided by a formal guideline.[113]

3. The statistics

Figures from the *Sentencing Statistics 2013* show that the overall differences in Crown Court custodial sentences between those who plead guilty and those who were convicted were considerable: thus, in 2013 some 72 per cent of those pleading not guilty who were convicted received immediate custodial sentences, compared with 56 per cent of those pleading guilty, and the average lengths of custodial sentences were 54 months and 24 months respectively.[114] Although these differences cannot be taken at face value because they are 'net' sentences which already reflect the impact of previous convictions or mitigating factors, they nevertheless raise questions about the size of the sentence reductions applied by the courts. Significant progress towards answering these questions has been made with the publication of statistics from the Crown Court Sentencing Survey (CCSS), reproduced as Table 10 in Appendix B. This table indicates a general compliance with the terms of the recommendations in the 2007 guideline, but there are anomalies to be explained. Most obvious are the discrepancies in late plea cases, suggesting 'a more generous interpretation of the appropriate reduction than envisaged by the guideline for offenders entering a guilty plea at the last opportunity'.[115] Almost a half of late guilty pleaders received reductions above the recommended figure of 10 per cent: whilst Roberts suggests that some of these cases involved the sparing of vulnerable witnesses or victims,[116] the fact is that this appears to be a long-standing practice which the guideline has not entirely dislodged.[117]

Welcome as the CCSS findings are, there are two issues which they do not yet deal with. One is the effect of the guilty plea reduction on the type, rather than merely the length, of sentence. The statistics and discussion seem to assume that sentence reduction is about shorter custodial sentences, whereas the 2007 guideline clearly recognizes that the guilty plea may be a significant factor in reducing a custodial to a non-custodial sentence.[118] These are the

---

[112] NSW Law Reform Commission (2013), para. 9.32.   [113] See also Leverick (2014), pp. 342–5.

[114] *Sentencing Statistics 2013*, Table A5.9. The average custodial terms do not include offenders sentenced to life imprisonment or imprisonment for public protection, but it seems unlikely that these would have a major effect on the differentials.

[115] Roberts (2013), p. 116.   [116] Roberts (2013), p. 118.

[117] See Flood-Page and Mackie (1998), pp. 91–2.

[118] SGC, *Reduction in Sentence for a Guilty Plea* (2007), para. 2.3; for empirical evidence, see Jacobson and Hough (2007), ch. 2.

cases where the greatest pressure may be felt by the defendant, and fuller data on them would be helpful. Secondly, as discussed in previous editions of this work,[119] there may be significant differences in the practices of sentence reduction between different types of offence. If it is still true that defendants pleading guilty to causing death by dangerous driving receive longer sentences, on average, than those convicted of this offence after pleading not guilty, the reasons for this need to be explored. One might speculate that those who plead guilty have committed the most serious offences, whereas those pleading not guilty are close to the borderline with the lesser offence of causing death by careless driving; but it would be good to have confirmation of the reasons for this and other apparent anomalies.

4. Is the discount justifiable?

What are the justifications for the guilty plea discount? The 2007 guideline states that the reduction principle is 'not an aspect of mitigation' but 'derives from the need for the effective administration of justice'.[120] This refers to the cost and administrative savings, and to sparing victims and witnesses from the anxiety of having to give evidence. However, the reference to public benefit in this context must be to a net calculation, in the sense that the benefits are thought to be worth forgoing any additional public protection that might accrue from passing longer sentences (and not giving any discount). This calculation is not evidence based, since there has been no attempt to determine how effective the sentence reductions are in producing guilty pleas. There is a strong lore that the administration of criminal justice would grind to a halt if the guilty plea discount were abandoned or even significantly reduced; but there is evidence that the 'tipping point' for defendants is when they realize they are probably going to be convicted, not the size of the discount,[121] and there is relevant American evidence too.[122] Surely it is unwise to make unqualified assertions about the need for the sentence discount without efforts to provide a sound empirical foundation for them.

Members of the public appear to be unenthusiastic about the sentence discount. Research for the Sentencing Council confirms that most people do not accept cost reduction as a strong reason, are more supportive of the importance of sparing victims and witnesses, but are opposed to discounts for late guilty pleas.[123] These public views should be taken as a further spur to empirical research, open calculations, and revisiting the foundations of the principle in relation to the purposes of sentencing.

In this process, account should be taken of other principles that the criminal justice system ought to respect – notably, the presumption of innocence and

---

[119] 5th edn, pp. 176–7.
[120] SGC, *Reduction in Sentence for a Guilty Plea* (2007), para. 2.2; cf. the critique by McConville and Marsh (2014), ch. 8.
[121] Dawes et al. (2011), ch. 5.   [122] E.g. Tonry (2004), p. 87.   [123] Dawes et al. (2011).

the principle of non-discrimination. Thus Article 6.2 of the European Convention on Human Rights declares the presumption of innocence. Is it not therefore a person's right to have the case against her or him proved beyond reasonable doubt? Is it proper that a person who insists on that should, as a result, be treated more severely at the sentencing stage if convicted? It seems a weak response to maintain that pleading not guilty is not an aggravating factor, but simply a neutral factor, whereas pleading guilty is a form of mitigation – although the European Commission on Human Rights accepted this view when examining the issue over 30 years ago.[124] Surely an inevitable consequence of the discount for pleading guilty is that a plea of not guilty has its price for defendants. Nor is this simply a matter of the length of custodial sentences: we have seen that the decision between custody and a non-custodial sentence can be influenced too. This serves to underline the pressures on defendants who believe, either as a result of what their lawyers have suggested or on an advance indication of sentence from a judge under *Goodyear*,[125] that a custodial sentence would follow conviction whereas a non-custodial sentence might follow a guilty plea.[126] There is evidence that some innocent defendants succumb to this pressure and decide to 'cut their losses' by pleading guilty: research carried out for the Royal Commission on Criminal Justice suggested that up to 11 per cent of guilty pleaders claim innocence,[127] and recent research by Stephen Jones illustrates the reasons why some women may decide to plead guilty while maintaining their innocence.[128] The Royal Commission concluded that the 'risk' of innocent defendants feeling pressure to plead guilty must be 'weighed against the benefits to the system and to defendants of encouraging those who are in fact guilty to plead guilty'.[129] This is a dreadful example of the 'balancing' metaphor, failing to assign special priority to avoiding the fundamental harm of convicting innocent individuals.[130] At the very least, the 'presumption of innocence' argument should lead to a reconsideration of the magnitude of the sentence reduction:[131] it is not merely a question of whether certain reductions are more effective, but of the extent to which they tempt defendants to sacrifice their rights.

It may be argued that the guilty plea discount is not only contrary to the spirit of the presumption of innocence declared by Article 6.2 of the European Convention on Human Rights, but also contrary to Article 14, which declares

---

[124] *X* v. *United Kingdom* (1972) 3 DR 10 at p. 16; a Commission decision of such antiquity has no great authority, and the issue would need to be argued afresh.

[125] Above, n. 94 and accompanying text.

[126] There is also pressure on advocates: see the judgment in *Re West* [2014] EWCA Crim 1480.

[127] Zander and Henderson (1993), pp. 138–42; McConville and Bridges (1993).

[128] Jones (2011).

[129] Royal Commission on Criminal Justice (1993), para. 7.44, criticized by Ashworth and Redmayne (2010), ch. 10, and by Darbyshire (2000).

[130] For another example, see *Ironside* (2009) 104 SASR 54.

[131] See further NSW Law Reform Commission (2013), paras. 9.32 and 9.41.

that all the rights in the Convention 'shall be secured without discrimination on any ground such as sex, race, colour . . .'. In his study of race and sentencing, Hood found that defendants from an Afro-Caribbean background tend to plead not guilty more frequently than whites (and tend to be acquitted more frequently), but that those who are convicted receive longer sentences largely, but not exclusively, because they have forfeited their 'discount'.[132] This can be regarded as a form of indirect discrimination: a general principle (the sentence discount) has a disproportionate impact on members of ethnic minorities simply because they more frequently exercise a right (the right to be presumed innocent until convicted). Hood argued that this supplies another reason to reconsider the discount. The Royal Commission stated merely that the policy of offering sentence discounts 'should be kept under review'[133] – an utterance of startling pusillanimity. The Auld Review did take this issue seriously, but favoured the view that the source of the injustice probably lay elsewhere than in the sentence discount,[134] whereas Michael Tonry argues persuasively that the sentence discount is a pillar of discrimination.[134a]

5.4.2 Assisting the criminal justice system

We have seen that the foremost rationale for the guilty plea discount is the offender's contribution to the smooth and cost-effective running of the criminal justice system. The same rationale underlies two other forms of personal mitigation. First, appellate decisions hold that an offender's conduct in admitting his offence before it is even discovered by others should be regarded as mitigation. In *R (on application of DPP)* v. *Salisbury Justices* (2003)[135] the offender, having taken drink, burgled the flat of an elderly lady and stole her handbag. The next day he walked into a police station and frankly confessed to the crime, saying that he had been drunk and very much regretted what he had done. He returned the property taken. Although he had many previous convictions for burglary, he had stayed out of trouble for over two years, and the circumstances of his voluntary admission of guilt without any prompting from the police were a major factor in the court's decision to order him merely to pay compensation to the victim. The Divisional Court declined to grant judicial review of the justices' decision, accepting that 'the very special facts' of the offence and of his reaction to committing it were sufficient reasons for the sentence. It greatly assists both the police and the victim to have a report and a full confession without the need for much investigation, and this assistance should be marked.

---

[132] Hood (1992), p. 125, stating that two-thirds of the 'race effect' in sentencing stems from the forfeiture of the discount by pleading not guilty.

[133] Royal Commission on Criminal Justice (1993), para. 7.58.   [134] Auld (2001), pp. 440–1.

[134a] Tonry (2004).

[135] [2003] 1 Cr App R (S) 560. For an earlier authority, see *Claydon* (1994) 15 Cr App R (S) 526. See also *O* [2004] 1 Cr App R (S) 130, which is on the boundary between an early guilty plea and an unprompted confession.

A second form of post-offence conduct applies the same reasoning directly: a person who assists the prosecution by giving evidence to the police and/or evidence in court which enables the detection and conviction of other offenders can expect credit for this at common law, particularly where the assistance is given before the offender is sentenced.[136] There is also a statutory scheme introduced by the Serious Organized Crime and Police Act 2005. In brief, s. 73 allows a court to reduce the sentence of an offender who has 'pursuant to a written agreement made with a specified prosecutor, assisted or offered to assist the investigator or prosecutor in relation to that or any other offence'. This power applies even where legislation prescribes a minimum sentence for the offence (s. 73(5)). Section 74 provides for a review process in cases where an offender gives assistance to the prosecution after being sentenced (and without having received a discount), and in cases where an offender fails to deliver on a promise to give assistance after receiving a discount. In his judgment in *P and Blackburn* (2008)[137] giving general guidance on the exercise of these powers, Sir Igor Judge pointed out that in order to take advantage of the discount an offender is required to reveal all his previous crimes. Where there was involvement in serious crime, the normal level of reduction should be between one-half and two-thirds of the total sentence that would otherwise be passed (only exceptionally could the reduction be greater), and a further reduction for pleading guilty should then be made, to reflect the stage at which that plea was entered. The Court recognized that for pragmatic reasons the size of the sentence reduction had to be considerable, in order to outweigh the considerable dangers to which such offenders were exposed (in prison and outside), but that much turns on the amount of assistance given.[138]

5.4.3 Worthy social contributions

A much-used mitigating factor is that the offence is 'out of character': good character (in effect, the absence of previous convictions) often has an effect on sentence, as the Crown Court Sentencing Survey shows.[139] However, in several decisions the Court of Appeal has upheld or advocated the practice of giving credit to an offender for 'good deeds' which are quite unrelated to the offence. For example, in *Reid* (1982)[140] the Court of Appeal reduced a custodial

---

[136] In *A and B* [1999] 1 Cr App R (S) 52, the Court of Appeal held that credit for assistance given after being sentenced was normally a matter for the prison and parole authorities, not the courts.

[137] [2008] 2 Cr App R (S) 16.

[138] See *H and D* [2010] 2 Cr App R (S) 104, *Bevens* [2010] 2 Cr App R (S) 199, and *Hankin* [2014] 1 Cr App R (S) 30.

[139] 'Offence out of character' appears in 21% of arson/criminal damage, 19% of driving offences, 22% of theft or fraud, and 18% of robberies; 'good character/exemplary conduct' appears in 16% of assaults and 17% of drug offences: CCSS (2014), p. 31.

[140] (1982) 4 Cr App R (S) 280.

sentence for burglary in the light of the offender's conduct, whilst awaiting trial, of attempting to rescue three children from a blazing house. That conduct, observed the Court, might justify the conclusion that 'the appellant was a much better and more valuable member of society than his criminal activities' would lead one to suppose. There are other decisions of a similar kind, concerning actions such as saving a child from drowning,[141] helping to foil an escape by prisoners,[142] and helping to arrest a criminal on a previous occasion.[143] In *Wenman* (2005),[144] an offender convicted of causing death by careless driving while intoxicated had, while awaiting trial, rescued another motorist whose car had skidded into a water-filled ditch and had saved his life. The Court of Appeal reduced the sentence from four to three years to reflect his 'bravery and high degree of responsibility' which suggested that 'he is a man whose natural instincts are caring and responsible'.

To grant mitigation on these grounds implies that passing sentence is a form of social accounting, and that courts should draw up a kind of balance sheet when sentencing. The offence(s) committed would be the major factor on the minus side; and any creditable social acts would be major factors on the plus side. Victoria and some other Australian jurisdictions adopt this approach, stating that the character of the offender is to be taken into account in sentencing, and that includes not merely previous convictions but also 'any significant contributions made to the community by the offender'.[145] English sentencing guidelines are more differentiated: whereas most guidelines include 'good character and/or exemplary conduct' as a mitigating factor at Step Two,[146] the guidelines for the more serious sex offences state that 'previous good character/exemplary conduct is different from having no previous convictions' and that, even so, for serious offences 'previous good character/exemplary conduct … will not normally justify a reduction in what would otherwise be the appropriate sentence'.[147] Where worthy social contributions may be taken into account, what is the justification? One argument is that good deeds, like remorse, suggest that the offender needs less punishment in order to reintegrate him or her into society. But even if it were justifiable to give preference to rehabilitative reasoning at this point, what is the evidence for asserting that those who do occasional good deeds are less likely to reoffend than those who cannot claim such 'social contributions'? In any event, is it a court's proper function to concern itself with these matters? The court is passing sentence for the particular crime(s) committed. There are civil awards for bravery and for outstanding service to the community. The only way to support the practice of taking these factors into account at

---

[141] *Keightley* [1972] Crim LR 272.   [142] *Dawn* (1994) 15 Cr App R (S) 720.
[143] *Alexander* [1997] 2 Cr App R (S) 74.   [144] [2005] 2 Cr App R (S) 13.
[145] Sentencing Act (Vic.) 1991, s. 6, discussed by Roberts (2011a), pp. 11–12.
[146] E.g. Sentencing Council, *Burglary Offences: Definitive Guideline* (2011), p. 9.
[147] Sentencing Council, *Sexual Offences: Definitive Guideline* (2013), p. 11.

sentence is by means of some modified Durkheimian concept of sentencing as a form of moral/social reinforcement, whereby courts which failed to recognize major social contributions of the offender might be taken symbolically to downgrade those contributions, and that might in turn be regarded as weakening instead of strengthening the collective conscience of society. If the public expects account to be taken of positive social contributions, it will have less confidence in a system that refuses to do so.

5.4.4 Voluntary reparation

Another source of mitigation deriving from events after the commission of the offence is where the offender has paid compensation or made reparation to the victim before the case comes to trial. In the context of a growing emphasis on compensation for victims, it might be thought that such conduct by an offender is meritorious and deserves some reward for its contribution to the goals of the criminal justice system. Indeed, for over thirty years there has been a statutory provision which allows a court to defer sentence for up to six months in order to have regard to an offender's conduct after conviction, including the making of reparation to the victim, and the Criminal Justice Act 2003 reaffirmed this.[148] Moreover, one of the statutory purposes of sentencing listed in the 2003 Act is 'the making of reparation by offenders to persons affected by their offences'. This suggests that, where the offender makes reparation without prompting by the court, this should be regarded as positive mitigation. An offender who voluntarily pays compensation makes public recognition of the wrong done, and may be taken to show genuine remorse and concern for the victim. However, as in guilty plea cases, this may or may not be so. In practice, both may be calculated responses to a system whose rules promise mitigation for guilty pleas and voluntary compensation, and any good legal adviser would surely inform a defendant of the probable benefits which might accrue from taking either or both of these courses.

Even if the court is satisfied that there is genuine concern for the victim, there are reasons of equity against reducing the sentence on this ground, as recognized in *Crosby and Hayes* (1974).[149] In that case two offenders had made efforts to pay compensation, but one had the financial capacity to do so and the other did not. The Court of Appeal held that to give them different sentences, for the sole reason that one had a source of finance which the other did not, was wrong in principle and 'not a firm foundation for the administration of justice'. The principle of equality before the law (see Chapter 7, below) therefore militates against this ground of mitigation. The point is obvious where there are two or more co-offenders in the same case, but it

---

[148] Criminal Justice Act 2003, Sch. 23, replacing ss. 1–2 of the Powers of Criminal Courts (Sentencing) Act 2000.
[149] (1974) 60 Cr App R 234.

should apply no less to any case where an offender claims credit for paying compensation to a victim voluntarily. Otherwise this is, in blunt terms, middle-class mitigation. As Joanna Shapland argues, it is preferable in principle and more acceptable to victims if offenders can show that they are 'trying to tackle those parts of their lives that were leading them to offend'. Thus what Shapland terms 'symbolic reparation', aimed at ensuring that further victimization does not occur, is to be preferred to a (retrospective) payment.[150]

5.4.5 The probable impact of the sentence on the offender

There is scattered support in the Court of Appeal's precedents for mitigation based on such factors as the age or physical or mental condition of the offender, the effect of a sentence on others and the effect of a sentence on the offender's career. These have some similarity with paragraph 5 of Chapter 29 of the Swedish Criminal Code, which provides that:

> [I]n determining the punishment, the court shall to a reasonable extent, apart from the penal value, consider:
>
> 1. whether the accused as a consequence of the crime has suffered serious bodily harm; . . .
> 5. whether the accused as a consequence of the crime has experienced or is likely to experience discharge from employment or other disability or extraordinary difficulty in the performance of his work or trade;
> 6. whether a punishment imposed according to the crime's penal value would affect the accused unreasonably severely, due to advanced age or bad health . . .

Let us examine the foundations for these supposed mitigating factors.

We saw earlier that serious injury to the offender is recognized as a mitigating factor in the offence of causing death by dangerous driving,[151] and there are other English decisions that accept this as a mitigating factor.[152] Why is this factor thought relevant? The reasoning may draw upon the kind of 'social accounting' criticized above, or the argument may be that the sentence will have a greater impact on the offender in view of her or his physical condition (see below). The Swedish approach seems to be that this should be regarded as a form of 'natural justice', in the sense that the offender has 'already been punished to some extent' by the injuries resulting from the offence. There are two weaknesses in this reasoning. First, the injuries are self-inflicted, stemming from the offender's own fault. Secondly, they are 'natural' punishment only in a

---

[150] Shapland (2011), pp. 76–7.
[151] SGC, *Causing Death by Driving* (2008), para. 22, cited in part 5.3.1 above; for an example, see *Revell* [2006] 2 Cr App R (S) 622.
[152] E.g. *Barbery* (1975) 62 Cr App R 248, sentence reduced because the offender's hand was severed during the commission of the offence.

(weak) metaphorical sense. Should courts attempt to regulate the total amount of pain to which an offender is subjected in consequence of an offence, or should they ignore these collateral matters? If they are to do the former, how far should they go – should an offender who is ostracized by the rest of his family after the offence receive a lesser punishment?

The Swedish law indicates that adverse consequences to the offender's employment or employment prospects may properly reduce sentence, whereas the Minnesota guidelines point to its discriminatory effect and prohibit courts from taking it into account.[153] The research by Jacobson and Hough suggests that English sentencers are divided on this issue, some regarding a good employment record as strong mitigation and others suggesting that having a steady job could be no mitigation for an acquisitive crime.[154] But these reasons are all at a pragmatic level. The question of principle is whether those fortunate enough to be in employment should be favoured by a source of mitigation that is not open to the unemployed. This looks like discrimination, and in principle it is objectionable. It sits alongside kindred principles such as not allowing wealthy offenders to 'buy themselves out of prison' by paying substantial financial penalties when a poorer offender would be sentenced to custody. The Sentencing Council has not yet taken a view on this, but it is an example of an issue of principle that should be tackled in a guideline system in order to foster consistency of approach.

At this point the argument merges into the next issue to be considered: what about the effect of the crime on the offender's career? The English decisions on collateral consequences of this kind seem to fall into two categories. Where the crime is unrelated to the offender's employment, there is sometimes a willingness to take account of such matters as the loss of a job and, with it, the loss of pension rights.[155] But where the crime arises out of the offender's employment and may be regarded as an abuse of a position of trust, it is well established as a matter of principle that no allowance should be made for these collateral matters.[156] Thus the definitive guideline on theft in abuse of trust is accompanied by the statement: 'Other than in the most exceptional of cases, loss of employment and any consequential hardship should not constitute personal mitigation.'[157] The guideline also makes it clear that a suspended sentence is within the permissible range of sentences only in the lowest category of case, involving a £2,000 to £20,000 loss and not a position of high trust. Guidelines for this particular type of offence appear not to have been followed faithfully in the past: although Lord Lane CJ held that 'it will not usually be appropriate

---

[153] See Ashworth (2011b), p. 30.
[154] Jacobson and Hough (2007), ch. 3; see also CCSS (2014), p. 31, reporting mitigation through 'loss of job or reputation' in 11 per cent of theft and fraud and 14 per cent of sexual offences.
[155] E.g. *Stanley* (1981) 3 Cr App R (S) 373, an army sergeant convicted of perjury; *Pearson* (1989) 11 Cr App R (S) 391, a young man hoping to join the army.
[156] *Barrick* (1985) 7 Cr App R (S) 142, updated in *Clark* [1998] 2 Cr App R (S) 95.
[157] SGC, *Theft and Burglary Other Than in a Dwelling* (2008), p. 11.

in cases of serious breach of trust to suspend any part of the sentence', the results of empirical research in the mid-1990s showed that only half of all thefts in breach of trust tried at the Crown Court resulted in immediate custody, and that the proportion of suspended sentences was much higher than for other offences (8 per cent compared with 3 per cent).[158] How the new guideline fares is a question for research.

Is there any merit in this source of mitigation? Once courts begin to adjust sentences for collateral consequences, is this not a step towards the idea of wider social accounting which was rejected above? In many cases one can argue that these collateral consequences are a concomitant of the professional responsibility which the offender undertook, and therefore that they should not lead to a reduction in sentence because the offender surely knew the implications. Moreover, there is a discrimination argument here too. If collateral consequences were accepted as a regular mitigating factor, this would operate in favour of members of the professional classes and against 'common thieves' who would be either unemployed or working in jobs where a criminal record is no barrier. It would surely be wrong to support a principle which institutionalized discrimination between employed and unemployed offenders.[159]

A more secure basis for mitigation is found in those cases where the normal sentence might have an exceptional impact on the particular offender. This may be relevant when the offender is very young, very old, or suffering from a life-threatening illness, for in such cases a substantial custodial sentence might be especially hard to bear. Insofar as there is a principle that sentences ought to have a roughly equal impact on offenders, this suggests that where an offender is likely to suffer from the sentence to a significantly different degree than most other people, there is a case for reducing its length.[160] In relation to the very young, the influence of this rationale was evident in the European Court of Human Rights in *T and V* v. *UK* (2000),[161] emphasizing that whether a punishment is 'degrading' depends to some extent on 'the sex, age and state of health' of the person.[162] In several cases the Court of Appeal has allowed some reduction in the length of sentences imposed on elderly offenders, particularly if the normally appropriate sentence 'would result in his release when he was well over the age of 80'.[163] A sentence of normal length on a person of such

---

[158] Flood-Page and Mackie (1998), pp. 85–6.

[159] On the other hand, it is important to ensure that any collateral orders made against white-collar offenders (e.g. disqualification from company directorship) are kept in proportion: see ch. 11.6 below.

[160] Cf. Ashworth and Player (1998) with von Hirsch and Ashworth (2005), App. C.

[161] (2000) 30 EHRR 121, paras. 70 and 99–100.

[162] See SGC, *Overarching Principles: Sentencing Youths* (2009), for this principle in action.

[163] The cases were reviewed in *Troughton* [2013] 1 Cr App R (S) 417, where a sentence was reduced to enable D's release at age 83. Cf. *Attorney General's Reference No. 38 of 2013* [2013] EWCA Crim 1450, where the CA noted that Stuart Hall, the convicted entertainer, was 83 but increased the sentence to 30 months' imprisonment.

advanced years might take most of his remaining days, but it may be argued that such a sentence on a young man in the flower of youth could be no less catastrophic in a different sense. There may be room for the alternative argument that prison is harder for a man of, say, 80; but perhaps that is a separate issue, to be dealt with on the principles that follow.

In relation to acute and/or terminal medical conditions, the leading decision of *Bernard* (1997)[164] yields two general principles. First, a medical condition that might at some unspecified future date either affect life expectancy or the prison authorities' ability to treat the offender satisfactorily is not a reason for a court to interfere with the sentence that would otherwise be appropriate, but it might be a matter which can be brought to the attention of the Home Secretary. Prisoners who are HIV positive fall into this category. Second, a serious medical condition, even when it is difficult to treat in prison, does not entitle the offender to a reduced sentence, although a court might impose a lesser sentence as an act of mercy. The second principle is unsatisfactory, inasmuch as it appears to leave the matter entirely at the discretion of the court.[165] The question should be resolved at the level of principle, in favour of such conditions being taken into account, and the degree of adjustment should reflect the nature of the condition and its implications.[166] A third relevant principle is that Article 3 of the Convention must be complied with, and so the courts must avoid sentences that consign D to inhuman or degrading treatment. However, there are arrangements in the prisons to cope with prisoners suffering from serious medical conditions, and it is only where the very fact of imprisonment might expose D to a real risk of an Article 3 breach that the court should not impose imprisonment.[167] As is evident from the case of an offender with multiple disabilities and illnesses,[168] only rarely will such action be regarded as necessary.

A more difficult group of cases is where the probable reaction of other prisoners makes it inevitable that an offender will serve much of the prison sentence in solitary confinement for his own protection, or where the offender has been attacked and victimized by other prisoners. The Court of Appeal has stated that 'a defendant's treatment by other inmates is not generally a factor to which this court can properly have regard', and that the defendant should rather proceed through official complaints procedures or by petitioning the Home Secretary for compassionate early release.[169]

---

[164] [1997] 1 Cr App R (S) 135, discussed by Ashworth and Player (1998).

[165] In *Stevens* [2003] 1 Cr App R (S) 32 the Court suspended a prison sentence on account of the offender's 'serious heart condition ... with a poor prognosis and the real probability of a custodial sentence causing many problems'.

[166] See also Piper (2007).   [167] *Qazi and Hussain* [2011] 2 Cr App R (S) 32, at [35].

[168] *Hall* [2013] 2 Cr App R (S) 434.

[169] *Nall-Cain (Lord Brocket)* [1998] 2 Cr App R (S) 145, at p. 150; see further Piper (2007), pp. 144–5.

Another group of cases consists of those where another person or persons may suffer abnormally as a result of the sentence imposed on the offender. It is rare for any reduction of sentence to be accorded on the ground that the offender's family will suffer,[170] because this is regarded as a normal concomitant of imprisonment, but the approach is different where a family member is suffering from a life-threatening disease. There are cases in which the Court of Appeal has reduced sentences on that account 'out of mercy'.[171] Perhaps the most frequent example of this line of mitigation is that of a mother caring for young children. Although there are some decisions in which mothers have had prison sentences reduced or suspended so as to allow them to care for their young children,[172] there are many others that take a harder line:

> This Court is always most reluctant to see a mother of young children sentenced to a term of imprisonment. Unhappily it is sometimes inevitable ... No one can fail to be moved by the children's plight but sadly the picture painted is all too familiar in cases where a young mother becomes involved in serious criminal activity. The circumstances which have been described to us are in no way exceptional.[173]

Some decisions suggest that, for an offence serious enough to merit 9–12 months' imprisonment, the courts are unlikely to suspend the sentence or to impose a community sentence out of compassion for the offender's children.[174] If the offence is more serious than that, it seems that a relatively small sentence reduction may be the most that is permissible, even taking account of the 'right to family life' in Article 8 of the Convention and the provisions of Article 3 of the UN Convention on the Rights of the Child.[175] Courts have sometimes been willing to avoid a custodial sentence where the offender is pregnant,[176] but, again, courts may find themselves unable to take this course where the crime is regarded as serious. Here as elsewhere, the courts tend to prefer the language of 'showing mercy' when the matter should be resolved at the level of principle. There is a strong argument that consequences of this kind should be alleviated by other means, and that departures from proportionate sentencing should not be permitted for reasons of this kind: as Susan

---

[170] Cf. *Grant* (1990) 12 Cr App R (S) 441.

[171] E.g. *Haleth* (1982) 4 Cr App R (S) 178, son suffering from kidney disease.

[172] E.g. *Whitehead* [1996] 1 Cr App R (S) 1, *Bowden* [1998] 2 Cr App R (S) 7.

[173] *Smith* [2002] 1 Cr App R (S) 258 at p. 261, upholding 12 months' imprisonment for conspiracy to evade customs duty of some £70,000. It is notable that a Home Office White Paper stated, under the heading 'What is not working', that 'prison can break up families ... 125,000 children are affected by the imprisonment of a parent each year': Home Office (2002), p. 85.

[174] *C* [2007] 1 Cr App R (S) 357, at para. 25; *Seepersad* [2007] 2 Cr App R (S) 34, at para. 7.

[175] See the full discussion by Hughes LJ in *Petherick* [2013] 1 Cr App R (S) 598; see also *Wilson* [2011] 1 Cr App R (S) 11, and *Spencer-Whalley* [2014] 2 Cr App R (S) 451.

[176] E.g. *Beaumont* (1987) 9 Cr App R (S) 342; the judges in the survey by Jacobson and Hough (2007, ch. 3) were divided in their approach to this issue.

Easton puts it, 'impact mitigation strikes at the heart of retributive theory'.[177] However, if it is thought that for pragmatic reasons the sentencing court should make some reduction on one of these grounds, or if one takes the view that the principle of equal impact can be accommodated within a retributive framework,[178] the questions should be faced squarely, without drifting into the blancmange of mercy.

One case which demonstrates unusual concern for the effects on third parties is *Olliver and Olliver* (1989),[179] where two brothers convicted of moderately serious offences of violence received suspended sentences and fines, rather than immediate imprisonment, largely on the basis that the livelihoods of some 23 employees in their carpentry business depended on their continued liberty. This, surely, is not a matter of mitigation of sentence properly so called; it is rather a case of adjusting the sentence so as to minimize the harmful consequences to uninvolved third parties. For the offender, it is a windfall. In *Attorney General's Reference No. 86 of 2006*[180] the Court of Appeal disallowed mitigation based on the effects on the job prospects of employees, since the offence involved the manslaughter of an employee by gross negligence through failure to take appropriate safety precautions.

5.4.6 Offender's present and future: 'ready to change'?

Most of the mitigating factors discussed in 5.4 have focused on the offence or the offender's past. However, there is no such restriction in s. 166(1) of the 2003 Act, which allows a court to take account of 'any such matters as, in the opinion of the court, are relevant in mitigation of sentence'. Furthermore, among the statutory 'purposes of sentencing' in s. 142(1) of the 2003 Act are some future-regarding aims, such as 'the reduction of crime' and 'the reform and rehabilitation of offenders'. Sentencers are keen to pursue these purposes when they have evidence that the offender is addressing the problems that led to the offending (such as drug or alcohol problems).[181] Thus Joanna Shapland argues that where the sentencer is pursuing the purpose of 'reform or rehabilitation', or in contemporary terminology 'a desistance paradigm', the key factor is 'for the offender to show agency – to move towards wishing to change their life'. Her research also shows that victims 'were enthusiastic about offenders trying to tackle those parts of their lives which were leading them to offend'.[182] Similarly, Jacobson and Hough's experimental sentencing

---

[177] Easton (2008), p. 116. See pp. 112–14 for the argument that it would be preferable to deal with the problem of imprisoning parents and carers by improving social support and prison conditions rather than by moving away from the appropriate sentence.

[178] Ashworth and Player (1998).   [179] (1989) 11 Cr App R (S) 10.

[180] [2007] 1 Cr App R (S) 621, at para. 36.

[181] On this, see Jacobson and Hough (2007), Table 2.2 and p. 10; Shapland (2011), pp. 68 and 75; Padfield (2011).

[182] Shapland (2011), p. 76.

scenarios revealed that 'motivated to get drug treatment' was placed second among mitigating factors in terms of importance.[183]

Nicola Padfield argues that sentencers try to determine whether an offender is 'ready to change', and 'should be allowed to take certain risks in sentencing in order to help an offender break their cycle of offending'.[184] The question is how these future-regarding factors fit into a framework of proportionality, and the answer is that a limited exception may be made where there is thought to be a real prospect of change. The exception is a limited one, and does not apply to serious offences. Thus the Sentencing Council's burglary guideline states:

> Where the defendant is dependent on or has a propensity to misuse drugs and there is sufficient prospect of success, a community order with a drug rehabilitation requirement may be a proper alternative to a short or moderate custodial sentence.[185]

The sexual offences guideline includes a similarly circumscribed reference to sex offender treatment.[185] These guideline statements confirm that sentencers have the discretion to make downward departures when they judge that there is a 'sufficient prospect of success' and the offence is not too serious.

5.5 Mitigation and aggravation in practice

This exploration of the sources of mitigation and aggravation has touched upon only some of the many problems they present in sentencing. What has emerged clearly, however, is the great power of aggravating and mitigating factors in two respects. First, as research shows, mitigating factors play a crucial role in deciding whether a case that is 'on the cusp' of custody can be dealt with by a form of non-custodial sentence. Hough, Jacobson and Millie found that, whereas the cases sent to custody turn on the seriousness of the offence or the offender's previous record, the key factors in bringing a 'cusp' case down to a community sentence were mitigating factors such as remorse, guilty plea, motivation to address personal problems, family responsibilities, or good employment record or prospects.[187] When the matter was investigated in more detail, it was found that in around a quarter of cases the effect of personal mitigation was to bring an offence that merited custody down below the custody threshold; in another quarter of cases personal mitigation had the effect of reducing the length of a custodial sentence, and there were further cases in which the guilty plea alone had that effect.[188] Sentencing guidelines are rarely prescriptive about the precise positioning of the 'custody threshold',

---

[183] Jacobson and Hough (2011), p. 155.   [184] Padfield (2011), p. 99.

[185] Sentencing Council, *Burglary Offences: Definitive Guideline* (2011), p. 8. It is unclear why this refers only to drug treatment and not to alcohol treatment.

[186] Sentencing Council, *Sexual Offences: Definitive Guideline* (2013), p. 18.

[187] Hough et al. (2003), pp. 36–7.   [188] Jacobson and Hough (2007), ch. 2 and Table 2.3.

and this appears to leave sentencers to engage in a kind of moral assessment of the offender and his or her prospects:

> This emphasis on the personal undoubtedly makes the sentencing process a highly subjective one, in which the individual sentencer (or group of sentencers, in the case of magistrates) has to assess the intentions and capabilities of the offender and his or her attitude towards the offence, and offending, such as the presence or absence of remorse and the determination to stop offending. These assessments feed judgements about responsibility and culpability. In other words, sentencers' decisions are framed within a set of explicitly ethical concepts.[189]

These moral assessments take place in a particular context, in which the defence advocate will attempt to construct the offender's character in a particular way, and in which the sentencer(s) may draw inferences from the offender's demeanour in court and other actions.[190]

The second respect in which aggravating and mitigating factors demonstrate their practical power is where their effect on the length of a custodial sentence seems (almost) to outweigh that of the offence itself. Thus a high degree of provocation can reduce the sentence considerably from the normal minimum for murder.[191] On the other hand, the targeting of an elderly victim can increase the sentence enormously for a moderate burglary, fraud, or theft, as we saw earlier.[192]

These strong effects of aggravating and mitigating factors take place within a system of legislation and definitive guidelines which establishes the legal effect of some aggravating and mitigating factors, but rarely give any indications about how a particular factor should be weighted. Before going on to discuss the approach of guideline systems to aggravating and mitigating factors, four questions of principle will be discussed. First, if a mitigating factor is present, is the offender entitled to a reduction in sentence or is this discretionary? Secondly, are there some kinds of offence for which normal mitigating factors may have only a negligible effect? Thirdly, how should courts deal with a mixture of aggravating and mitigating factors? Fourthly, when is it appropriate for a court to reduce a sentence out of 'mercy'?

5.5.1 Is mitigation an entitlement?

David Thomas, on the basis of a synthesis of early English decisions, argued that it is not.[193] Early cases suggested that judges might withhold mitigation when they wished to pursue some other penal objective such as deterrence, but the present sentencing framework ought not to allow the same flexibility. It is

---

[189] Hough et al. (2003), p. 41.
[190] See further ch. 1.6 above, and Jacobson and Hough (2011), p. 161.   [191] See ch. 4.4.1 above.
[192] See ch. 5.2.2 above.   [193] Thomas (1979) p. 47; see also pp. 35–7, 194.

true that there is only one statutory mitigating factor – the guilty plea discount – and that the terms of s. 166 of the 2003 Act are permissive. It is also true that s. 142 of the 2003 Act suggests that a court can pursue whatever penal aim it wishes, although the sentencing guidelines make it clear that this must be done within a proportionality framework. Most of the sentencing guidelines go no further than to indicate the relevant aggravating and mitigating factors, leaving the court to assign them the appropriate weight in each case. However, if a sentencer refuses to reflect a particular mitigating factor in the sentence, this would be a ground of appeal and of reviewable discretion. In principle, mitigation should be an entitlement where its factual basis is established.

5.5.2 Does the effect of mitigation vary according to the seriousness of the offence?

The discussion of the guilty plea discount shows that the reduction of sentence is intended to be proportionately the same, no matter whether the sentence is lengthy imprisonment or a mere fine (although there are, as noted above, policy-driven exceptions for mandatory minimum sentences and for murder). However, that approach does not apply to all mitigating factors, the most obvious example being previous good character. A first offender can expect to be dealt with much more leniently than a repeat offender. However, an offender whose first offence is rape or armed robbery cannot expect a significant discount: here, the gravity of the offence is held to overpower the usual claim to mitigation, and the 'concession to human frailty' reasoning looks rather thin when the wrong is so egregious. This appears to be the predominant view among sentencers,[194] and we noted in 5.4.6 above that the burglary and drugs guidelines restrict 'ready for change' treatment orders to cases of moderate seriousness.

5.5.3 Dealing with a mixture of aggravating and mitigating factors

In practice it is rare for a single mitigating or aggravating factor to appear on its own. In many cases there are two or more mitigating factors and, not uncommonly, two or more aggravating factors as well. How should a court gauge the overall effect of such elements? Research suggests that this is a source of considerable disparity in sentencing,[195] and that even where guidelines have been laid down for an offence the absence of clear guidance on weighting may produce manifest disparity.[196] The typical structure of English guidelines is to indicate various starting points, and then to say that certain

---

[194] Jacobson and Hough (2007), ch. 4.
[195] For English research, see Corbett (1987); for the United States, see Zeisel and Diamond (1977).
[196] Ranyard, Hebenton and Pease (1994), pp. 208, 216.

aggravating and mitigating factors can take the sentence up or down from that point – without proposing a weighting for individual factors, let alone suggesting which ones are typically more significant. One might accept that an arithmetical presentation of additions and reductions would be unduly mechanistic, but two limitations on that proposition must be acknowledged. First, far too little is known about the actual calculations of judges and magistrates in England. They have a tendency to retreat behind the 'no two cases are the same' argument or the 'mercy' approach, instead of identifying the issues of principle involved and the relative strength of the factors.[197] Secondly, both the guilty plea discount and the enhancement for racial aggravation (and other protected characteristics) have to be quantified, showing that some arithmetical clarity is possible.

5.5.4 Mercy

In a small number of cases the courts make a strong downward departure from the guidelines and take account of extraordinary factors relating to the offender's situation. In *Schumann* (2007),[198] discussed in Chapter 1.5.2(b) above, a woman suffering from clinical depression jumped off the Humber Bridge with her small child in her arms, intending to end both their lives. Lord Phillips CJ held that 'there are occasions where the court can put the guidelines and the authorities on one side and apply mercy instead', quashing the sentence of imprisonment in favour of a community sentence with a supervision requirement. Similarly in *Attorney General's Reference No. 11 of 2007*[199] part of the mitigation of an offender pleading guilty to a street robbery was that her sister was terminally ill, and her sister then died. The Court of Appeal declined to increase the sentence from 6 months, holding that mercy was appropriate. Mercy was also the reason for reducing and suspending the sentence of a householder who caused grievous bodily harm to someone who had burgled his house,[200] and for suspending the sentence of a man threatened and goaded by his step-son who wounded his step-son in an effort to resolve a desperate situation.[201] It is important that courts be allowed to reflect such extreme combinations of circumstances, but, as argued above in relation to *Bernard*,[202] where the offender suffered from a serious medical condition that was difficult to treat in prison, it is wrong that sentence reduction should be regarded as a matter for the discretion of the court. If the circumstances indicate a strong case for showing mercy, the court should give full reasons why 'the interests of justice' indicate a downward departure from the guideline, and should comment on the strength of the mitigating

---

[197] Jacobson and Hough (2007), ch. 5.   [198] [2007] 2 Cr App R (S) 465.
[199] [2008] 1 Cr App R (S) 26.   [200] *Hussain and Hussain* [2010] 2 Cr App R (S) 399.
[201] *Attorney General's Reference No 95 of 2009* [2010] 2 Cr App R (S) 535.
[202] N. 164 above and accompanying text.

factor and the reason for the quantum of reduction. The dispensation of 'mercy' is an important aspect of sentencing practice, but the use of that term should not be allowed to deflect courts from properly justifying their actions.

5.6 Conclusions

English sentencing guidelines say rather less about mitigating factors than about aggravating factors, and yet research by Jacobson and Hough confirms that personal mitigation may have a significant effect on the nature and the quantity of a court's sentence, at its most powerful either reducing an offence from a custodial starting point to a non-custodial outcome, or reducing the length of a custodial sentence.[203] Many of these factors are unrelated to proportionality, and the question is whether each of them can be justified. It was contended in part 5.4.2 above that offenders who, by their post-offence conduct, make a contribution to the smooth running of the criminal justice system or to its goals, ought to receive some mitigation. This recognizes that sentencing forms part of the criminal justice system in a society with certain values. But it was argued in part 5.4.1 that the same ought not to apply to the guilty plea discount as currently calculated, because reducing sentences significantly on that account goes too far towards undermining important rights of defendants, which are important social values (human rights) that should not be sacrificed. It was also submitted, in part 5.4.1 above, that courts should take account of any abnormal impact which the normal sentence would have on an individual offender. Bentham argued strongly for this principle of equal impact in the context of his deterrent theory of punishment,[204] and it is not inconsistent with proportionality theory.[205] However, it is merely a principle and not an absolute rule, and the possibility of its conflicting with other principles such as the principle of non-discrimination (equality before the law) will be explored more fully in Chapter 7.

Arguments were presented in part 5.4.5 above against the relevance of the collateral consequences of conviction as mitigating factors, and in part 5.4.4 above against any attempt at wider social accounting such as credit for saving someone from drowning. It is not merely that sentencers would not know where to stop if they purported to draw up a balance sheet of the offender's social contributions; it is that the arguments of policy or principle to support this approach seem insufficient, unless one adopts a modified Durkheimian view of the courts' function and places emphasis on what the public would expect a court to do. However, future-regarding factors may be more powerful

---

[203] Jacobson and Hough (2007), Table 2.3 and ch. 2 generally; see also Padfield (2011) and CCSS (2014).

[204] Cf. Bentham (1789), ch. XIV, para. 14.

[205] Cf. Ashworth and Player (1998) with von Hirsch and Ashworth (2005), App. C, and Easton (2008).

than past-regarding: it was argued in 5.4.6 that personal mitigation may rightly reduce a low or moderate custodial sentence to a community sentence where there is a good prospect that the offender will make an effort to change.

The least satisfactory aspect of aggravating and mitigating factors is that, in most instances, the English guidelines neither indicate the weight that they should bear (e.g. whether a particular factor can ever, or normally, take a case outside the category range) nor indicate how they should interact when there are both aggravating and mitigating factors in a case. The major exception to this is the sentence reduction for pleading guilty; there is also some guidance about the effect of previous convictions, as we will see in the next chapter. Now the traditional response would be to say that aggravating and mitigating factors vary in their strength and intensity from case to case, and so sensible guidelines are not possible. But that was often a response to the call for offence guidelines – the variations of this type of offence are so great that it is impossible to frame guidelines. That barrier has now been overcome, and it behoves the guideline-creating bodies to make an attempt to improve guidance on aggravating and mitigating factors, not least because research establishes clearly that they can exert a considerable effect on sentence. We saw in part 5.2.2 above that, where an elderly or disabled victim is targeted, the sentence may be far higher than that which the offence would normally attract – to the extent that the age and vulnerability of the victim overshadows the intrinsic seriousness of the offence. In some cases where an offence is planned or organized, such as pickpocketing, courts have also imposed sentences out of proportion to the amount stolen or distress caused, because the offender appears 'professional'.[206] It was argued above that there is no sufficient justification for according such an overpowering effect to an aggravating factor; this is an issue that the Sentencing Council should confront.

The whole purpose of guidelines is to foster consistency of approach to sentencing, and to the extent that the weight of aggravating and mitigating factors is left at large – let alone the very question whether it is right to take certain factors into account – then there will be a considerable deficiency in the guidelines. It is no answer to say that each case depends on its own facts and that therefore courts should have unfettered discretion in this matter: as has been demonstrated at various points in this chapter, there are issues of principle that can and should be resolved. Thus reasons have been given in this chapter for agreeing with the argument of Julian Roberts that it is not enough for the guidelines simply to provide a list of standard aggravating and mitigating factors, and that they should indicate the rationale for allowing each factor to have that effect; that some guidance should be given as to the different weight of the various factors, particularly in relation to the custody threshold; that it would at least be a step forward if factors were grouped, so that their

---

[206] See above, ch. 4.4.12, and below, ch. 6.4.

rationale could emerge more clearly; that personal mitigation should be more fully addressed in all guidelines; and that consideration should be given explicitly to certain controversial factors, such as mitigation for worthy social contributions or for a good employment record, with the aim of producing a list of non-mitigating (and of non-aggravating) factors.[207] For example, the report of the Australian Law Reform Commission deals with controversial factors such as the effect of a sentence on dependants,[208] and moves towards the grouping of factors to which courts should have regard. The Commission also discusses and determines factors that should not aggravate, factors that should not mitigate, and other factors not to be considered.[209] The Sentencing Council should follow this lead, and conduct its own assessment of these important issues. It should then consider in what form it is best to lay down guidance on these issues.[210] Unless these steps are taken, the objective of enhancing consistency of approach to sentencing cannot be attained.

---

[207] Roberts (2008b), Cooper (2013).   [208] ALRC (2006), paras. 6.121–6.127.
[209] Ibid., paras. 6.160–6.196.   [210] See further Shapland (2011).

6

Persistence, prevention and prediction

Contents

This chapter examines the controversial question of sentencing repeat offenders, including the sub-group of 'dangerous offenders'. After a brief historical introduction, part 6.2 explores four approaches to sentencing persistent offenders, and part 6.3 considers the relevant provisions of the Criminal Justice Act 2003. Parts 6.4 and 6.5 examine two specific problems, those of 'professional' criminals and of petty persistent offenders. In part 6.6 a different approach to repeated rule-breaking is examined – the use of civil preventive orders. Part 6.7 of the chapter turns to the question of selective incapacitation as a strategy for preventing crime, referring to the minimum 'three strikes' sentences in English law. In part 6.8 recent legislative attempts to provide suitable sentences for 'dangerous' offenders are assessed, and some concluding thoughts are found in part 6.9. Throughout these topics there are linking themes concerned with the promotion of security and the assessment of risk of future criminal behaviour. The invocation of such rationales amounts to a departure from the proportionality principle, and close attention will be paid to the justifications for this.

6.1 Historical introduction

The history of English measures aimed specifically at persistent offenders seems to be widely acknowledged as a history of failure. The judges have had sufficient discretion, for the last hundred years at least, to allow them to pass fairly long sentences on persistent serious criminals without invoking any special powers. But penal reformers and governments have invariably felt that no major set of reforms would be complete without making further special provision for persistent offenders. The Gladstone Committee in 1895 argued in favour of a special measure against persistent thieves and robbers, who would otherwise serve a succession of fairly short sentences and therefore return frequently to prey on the community. The Committee's proposals led, after much debate,[1] to the Prevention of Crime Act 1908. This empowered a court to impose, upon an offender with three previous felony convictions since the age of 16, a sentence of preventive detention of between 5 and 10 years, in addition to the normal sentence for the crime (a so-called 'double track' system). The practical focus of the Act was soon revised when Churchill became Home Secretary in 1910. He took the view that the Act, as it was being administered, concentrated unduly on mere repetition in lawbreaking, and he exposed the minor nature of some of the offences which had led to the imposition of preventive detention. He issued a new circular which declared that 'mere pilfering, unaccompanied by any serious aggravation, can never justify' preventive detention, and propounded the general test of whether the nature of the crime was 'such as to indicate that the offender is not merely a nuisance but a serious danger to society'.[2] The aim of preventive detention thus became that of 'protecting society from the worst class of professional criminal'. In fact, the courts often found their ordinary sentencing powers sufficient in such cases, and so the use of preventive detention declined.

A new form of preventive detention was introduced in the Criminal Justice Act 1948 for persistent offenders aged 30 or over, being a sentence of 5 to 14 years instead of (not in addition to) the normal sentence. The Dove-Wilson Committee in 1932 had proposed this as suitable chiefly for 'professional criminals who deliberately make a living by preying on the public',[3] but when the legislation was introduced in 1948 the government envisaged that it would also cover 'the relatively trivial [persistent] offender'.[4] Judges soon found themselves passing sentences of preventive detention on offenders whose records, while showing persistence, were not serious. In the late 1950s the judges increasingly set their faces against this, and in 1962 the Lord Chief Justice went so far as to issue a Practice Direction to restrict the use of preventive detention.[5] Following a gloomy report from the Advisory Council on the Treatment of Offenders (1963) and two other studies which demonstrated the minor nature of many of the offences committed by those subjected to preventive detention,[6] the sentence virtually fell into disuse.

---

[1] Radzinowicz and Hood (1986), pp. 265–78.   [2] Radzinowicz and Hood (1986), p. 285.
[3] Dove-Wilson (1932), para. 42.   [4] Hammond and Chayen (1963), p. 11.
[5] See [1962] 1 All ER 671.   [6] Hammond and Chayen (1963), West (1963).

The next measure to be introduced was the extended sentence: the Criminal Justice Act 1967 empowered a court to extend a sentence beyond the normal length or (in limited circumstances) beyond the statutory maximum where it apprehended the need, in view of the offender's record, to protect the public. The White Paper of 1965 had proposed the extended sentence for those offenders who constituted 'a real menace to society',[7] but a parliamentary amendment which would have required the court to have regard to the gravity of the current offence was not accepted by the government. Once again the courts soon found that those falling within the ambit of the sentence could hardly be described as real menaces, and at no stage did the extended sentence play a significant part in sentencing practice.

The Criminal Justice Act 1991 was the first statute to include a general provision on the sentencing of persistent offenders: although it was intended to restate the common law its drafting was obscure and it was repealed in 1993 in favour of a bland provision that was never, in ten years, the subject of authoritative consideration in the Court of Appeal (despite the large numbers of persistent offenders sentenced). The 1991 Act also included a provision, in s. 2(2)(b), permitting courts to pass a longer than proportionate sentence for a violent or sexual offence if it was of opinion 'that only such a sentence would be adequate to protect the public from serious harm from him'. However, the provision was vague on crucial issues and unacceptably wide in its scope as interpreted by the courts.[8] The power to impose longer than proportionate sentences was used relatively rarely, perhaps (again) because courts tend to give long sentences for serious offences anyway. The Criminal Justice Act 2003 changed the relevant law again, and its provisions are discussed in the remainder of the chapter.

This brief historical survey reveals two recurrent difficulties. First, legislation on persistent offenders has usually been framed in broad terms, often without clear and precise guidance about the types of offender to be included and excluded. Second, and more fundamentally, there has been little agreement about the group or groups of offenders who should be the target of special sentences. Terms such as 'professional criminals' and 'real menaces' have been used without much effort at precision, and when the law did eventually specify violent and sexual offenders (as distinct from property offenders, the most prominent recidivists), many of those included were at the lowest end of the scale.

6.2 Four approaches to punishing persistence

The differing views which have been expressed on the sentencing of persistent offenders do not always fall neatly into categories, but four paradigms are

---

[7] Home Office (1965).
[8] For the 1991 Act, see the discussions in the 3rd edn of this work, pp. 169–72 and 183–9.

(i) flat-rate sentencing, (ii) the cumulative principle, (iii) progressive loss of mitigation, and (iv) a moderate recidivist premium. What are the strengths and weaknesses of these approaches?[9]

6.2.1 Flat-rate sentencing

According to this approach, the sentence should be governed by the crime and not at all by the offender's prior record. This view has been advanced by a small group of desert theorists, most notably George Fletcher[10] and Richard Singer.[11] Their argument, in brief, is that an offender's desert should be measured by reference to the crime committed, in terms of its harmfulness and the offender's culpability in relation to it. Any previous offences cannot have a bearing on this. Indeed, not only are they irrelevant to the calculation, but to take them into account would be to punish the offender twice over – if sentence has already been passed for the previous offences, it is unjust to increase the sentence for a subsequent crime on account of a previously punished offence. Fletcher suggests that desert theorists who do take account of previous offences are indulging in a covert preventionist strategy. Since the increased sentence cannot be justified on desert grounds, says Fletcher, such writers are really trying to achieve a modest amount of individual prevention or incapacitation in such cases.

There are few practical examples of flat-rate sentencing schemes. Illegal parking of cars is one: the penalty does not increase according to the number of previous offences, and one could commit the offence every day without ever receiving more than the fixed penalty. Many other minor offences have fixed penalties or such low maximum fines that they may be viewed as flat-rate offences, although in practice a poor offender may be able to persuade a court to reduce the penalty.

6.2.2 The cumulative principle

Since at least the mid-nineteenth century there has been support for the cumulative principle of sentencing persistent offenders. The basic idea is that, for each new offence, the sentence should be more severe than for the previous offence. In this way sentences should be cumulative, with a view to deterring the individual offender from repeating the crimes. Perhaps the best-known exponent of the cumulative principle was the Gloucestershire magistrate Barwick Lloyd Baker. In 1863 he proposed that for a first felony conviction the punishment should be 1 week or 10 days' prison on bread and water; for the second conviction 12 months' imprisonment; for the third, 7 years' penal servitude; and for a fourth, penal servitude for life or for some very long period

---

[9] See now the discussion in Frase (2013), ch. 4.   [10] Fletcher (1978), pp. 460–6.
[11] Singer (1979), ch. 5.

which would allow surveillance on ticket-of-leave for the greater part of the criminal's life. He saw this as achieving protection through individual deterrence, and had no doubts about its fairness: 'if you tell a man clearly what will be the punishment of a crime before he commits it, there can be no injustice in inflicting it'.[12]

That harsh approach made no allowances for the fact that some offences were minor and some stemmed from human weakness or poverty rather than 'wickedness'. It met with considerable opposition, notably from Francis Hopwood, Recorder of Liverpool towards the end of the nineteenth century, who strenuously denounced heavy penalties for petty recidivists. The Lord Chief Justice of the time, Lord Coleridge, appeared to have had greater sympathy with Hopwood's approach, since he maintained that he would inflict punishment only 'for the particular offence for which the prisoner is being tried before me'. But even Lord Coleridge admitted that some of his colleagues had 'different guiding thoughts'.[13]

Although Baker's rationale was deterrence, incapacitation might also be invoked in support of the cumulative approach, especially in view of the contemporary emphasis on security and risk. However, Baker did not confine his approach to 'dangerous offenders': he argued that cumulative sentencing of habitual misdemeanants would reduce the incidence of petty offences by some 60,000 a year.[14] It is well known that reconviction rates increase sharply according to the number of previous convictions (45 per cent within two years for three to six previous convictions, 56 per cent for seven to ten, 76 per cent of those with ten or more previous convictions).[15] The problem is that most of these offences are towards the lower end of the scale of criminality: the high rates of recidivism are for lesser (usually, property) crimes, and a cumulative principle therefore tends to heap punishment on minor and relatively non-threatening offenders. This would be signally disproportionate.[16] The fairness of a cumulative principle restricted to violent and sexual offenders is discussed in part 6.7 of this chapter, where proposals for the selective incapacitation of certain types of offender are reviewed.

The more common rationale for cumulative sentencing is individual prevention. This was Baker's main argument: cumulative penalties would deter the offender or, if they did not, he would in effect 'with his eyes open deliberately sentence himself'.[17] Several questions are raised by this claim. Are all, or even most, persistent offenders the rationally motivated wicked offenders that it assumes? The historical evidence of measures against persistent offenders, reviewed briefly in part 6.1 of this chapter, suggests that many of

---

[12] See Radzinowicz and Hood (1986), pp. 237–8 and references.
[13] Radzinowicz and Hood (1979), pp. 1311–12.   [14] Radzinowicz and Hood (1980), p. 1330.
[15] Roberts (2008a), p. 31.
[16] Roberts also shows that disproportionate sentences would not command great public support, even though some enhancement would be insisted upon: ibid., p. 166 and pp. 171ff.
[17] Radzinowicz and Hood (1986), p. 238.

them are not.[18] Leaving aside the 'dangerous' offenders to be discussed in part 6.7 below, the bulk of persistent offenders contain significant numbers who are socially disadvantaged, or in personal turmoil, or substance abusers, or mentally disturbed. Thus the convicted recidivists interviewed by Julian Roberts referred both to repeat offenders being 'taught a lesson' and to the need for courts to examine why a particular recidivist was reoffending, arguing for a more individualized and less formulaic approach.[19] Thus for non-dangerous recidivists, an enquiry into the cause(s) of their offending may indicate that more constructive measures should be taken – an approach at odds with the cumulative principle.

Would the cumulative strategy be effective in preventing crime? This depends not only on such factors as knowledge of the penalties among offenders and the absence of countervailing considerations (e.g. low detection rate, absence of proper social provision for people in need), but also on the effectiveness of the penalty. English law has long had one form of cumulative sentencing – the penalty points system for road traffic offenders. When a court sentences an offender for certain traffic offences, it may (or must) impose a number of penalty points, and when an offender accumulates 12 points an immediate disqualification from driving follows. The justifications for having this system for motoring offences and not for other crimes have yet to be debated widely; but when it comes to a preventive system based on sentences of imprisonment, one objection was pointed out as long ago as 1932 by the Dove-Wilson Committee:

> the inference is that present methods not only fail to check the criminal propensities of such people, but may actually cause progressive deterioration by habituating offenders to prison conditions which weaken rather than strengthen their characters.[20]

Thus the repeated use of prison sentences may be counterproductive, making these offenders less able to live law-abiding lives and more likely to reoffend on release. If the cumulative principle is based on individual deterrence, and if the point of deterrence is to protect the public, heavy reliance on imprisonment for this purpose may not only go against the principle of restraint (see Chapter 3.4.2) but also be to a significant extent self-defeating.

On the basis of a review a decade ago of the available evidence on the typical characteristics of criminal careers, David Farrington argued that 'since a high proportion of offenders desist after the first or second offence, significant criminal justice interventions might be delayed until the third offence. Diversionary measures might be appropriate after the first or second offence.'[21] Reconviction rates show 13 per cent reconvicted after the first offence, and

---

[18] Radzinowicz and Hood (1986), chs. 8–12, on these debates in the nineteenth century.
[19] Roberts (2008a), pp. 148–52.   [20] Dove-Wilson (1932), para. 3.
[21] Farrington (1997), pp. 564–5.

30 per cent after one to two offences.[22] This drives a further wedge between cumulative sentencing and prevention. If prevention is to be the chief concern, it does not follow that cumulative sentencing is the most effective way of achieving this, particularly after two or three convictions, and particularly if incarceration is involved. Like many penal policies, it may have a superficial attractiveness to politicians and the media because it appears 'tough', but it relies on crude assumptions about the causes of offending, little understanding of desistance patterns, and a failure to grasp the criminogenic effects of the penal system itself.

6.2.3 Progressive loss of mitigation

This approach to the sentencing of persistent offenders differs from flat-rate sentencing in allowing some enhancement for previous record, and differs from the cumulative principle in placing strong limits on the influence of previous record in deference to an overall concept of proportionality. The principle of progressive loss of mitigation really consists of two parts: one is that a first offender should receive a reduction of sentence, and the other is that with second and subsequent offences an offender should progressively lose that mitigation. How soon all the mitigation is lost is a question for discussion later, but clearly the principle assumes a limit beyond which the sentence cannot go, no matter how many previous convictions the offender has. The gravity of the current offence(s) is taken to set a 'ceiling' for the sentence: a bad previous record should mean that the offender loses this source of mitigation, but the record should not be treated as an aggravating factor. As Thomas put it, a bad record 'will not justify the imposition of a term of imprisonment in excess of the permissible ceiling for the facts of the immediate offence'.[23]

What is the theory underlying progressive loss of mitigation? It is an approach characteristically adopted by desert theorists, who view proportionality to the seriousness of the offence as the chief determinant of sentence. Why would a desert theorist wish to incorporate into an offence-based system of sentencing (harm plus culpability) an element relating to the offender's past history? The argument, restated and refined by Andrew von Hirsch,[24] is based on the ideas of lapse and tolerance. Ordinary people do have occasional aberrations. Human weakness is not so unusual, especially in a context of peer pressure or multiple social disadvantage. The sentencing system should recognize not only this, but also the capacity of people to respond to formal censure, and to ensure that their future conduct conforms to the law. This is embodied in the idea of giving someone a 'second chance'.[25] So the justification for the

---

[22] Roberts (2008a), p. 31.   [23] Thomas (1979), p. 41.

[24] Von Hirsch and Ashworth (2005), pp. 148–55.

[25] Cf. Bagaric (2001), ch. 10.3.1, for the counter-argument that the moral notion of lapse is inappropriate for matters so serious as criminal convictions. However, it is questionable

discount for first offenders rests partly on recognition of human fallibility, and partly on respect for people's ability to respond to the censure expressed in the sentence. The justification for the gradual loss of that mitigation on second and third convictions is that the 'second chance' has been given and not taken:[26] the offender ought to forfeit the tolerance, and its associated sentence discount, because the subsequent criminal choices show insufficient response to the public censure.[27] In principle, therefore, the second offence deserves greater censure than the first (unless there is good reason to indicate otherwise), and the third offence may be censured fully. But the seriousness of the offence must remain the primary determinant of sentence, and therefore sentences imposed on repeat offenders should not cumulate so as to lead to sentences more onerous than the current offence could justify. This 'ceiling' principle also promotes the principle of parsimony and restraint in the use of custody.

One possible counter-argument is that the notion of lapse appears to take no account of the possibility that a first offender might have planned an offence meticulously and might have been fully aware of the gravity of the wrongdoing. However, the 'second chance' theory turns on the ability to respond to formal censure and punishment, not on mere awareness of wrong-doing.[28] A second counter-argument is that the justifications offered seem to assume that all offending is based on rational choice, and to ignore the findings of criminological research. Thus rational choice (of a kind) may be evinced by those who adopt a particular lifestyle, such as career burglars.[29] But some recidivism is largely a concomitant of going to particular places and associating with particular people, as with gang activities or the violence associated with drinking in certain public houses.[30] Some may stem from contacts made within penal institutions, where information is exchanged and alliances formed.[31] A large amount of recidivism may be associated with drug use.[32] And, more generally, some is part of a cycle of social deprivation and/or personal turmoil, which may or may not be deepened by the experience of imprisonment, as with the so-called petty persistent offenders.[33] Studies of

---

whether every criminal offence is sufficiently serious to remove the moral force of the argument from lapse. Bagaric also argues that the idea of a discount for first offenders is a subterfuge, and that in reality we are discussing the claim of previous convictions to operate as an aggravating factor. For contrary arguments, see ch. 5.1 above.

[26] See Lee (2009), for the argument that the true rationale is the repeat offender's culpable omission to address his offending behaviour.

[27] Roberts (2008a), p. 59, argues that this approach should be rationalized as a gradual loss of credit for law-abidance, and that the notion of lapse cannot meaningfully be employed more than once. *Sed quaere.*

[28] Cf. the critical exploration of what constitutes a 'lapse' by Ryberg (2010).

[29] E.g. Maguire (1982), Bennett and Wright (1984).   [30] Walmsley (1986), pp. 17–18.

[31] See ch. 9.2 below.

[32] 'Of social variables, drug misuse is most strongly linked with the likelihood of reconviction': Halliday (2001), App. 3, para. 11. See also n. 50 below and accompanying quotation.

[33] See this chapter, part 6.5.

desistance from crime, which focus on the circumstances in which offenders typically give up offending, have long indicated the relevance of stable relationships, a child, a job, and other prosaic factors in a person's life.[34] These are good reasons for the state not to give only one 'second chance', in recognition of the difficulty that some offenders have in complying with the law. In this context it is important to note two of the recommendations of the Council of Europe on sentencing:

D1 Previous convictions should not, at any stage in the criminal justice system, be used mechanically as a factor working against the defendant.

D2 Although it may be justifiable to take account of the offender's previous criminal record within the declared rationales for sentencing, the sentence should be kept in proportion to the seriousness of the current offence(s).[35]

Proposition D1 emphasizes the importance of considering the reasons for reoffending in each case. This does not present problems for desert theorists, for, as we saw in Chapter 4.5, they can accept grounds for mitigation based on diminished capacity, social deprivation, and so forth. Proposition D2 recognizes that, even in those countries where prevention is the primary rationale of sentencing, there should be a proportionality constraint in the sentencing of persistent offenders. The great merit of the 'second chance' idea is that a clear principle of fairness is accorded a central place.[36] Thus, progressive loss of mitigation assumes that a second and a third offence deserve greater censure, but it accords with the Council of Europe in leaving room for other responses if other explanations for reoffending seem persuasive and in insisting on a firm proportionality constraint.[37] This last point distinguishes it clearly from the cumulative approach, which may result in long sentences for persistent but non-serious offenders.

For many years the Court of Appeal claimed that progressive loss of mitigation was the proper approach to sentencing persistent offenders.[38] However, in practice there appeared to be a substantial recidivist premium for many persistent offenders. The disjunction between the Court's statement of principle and its application emerges clearly from *Bailey* (1988).[39] The offender stood convicted of two offences – one was theft of several ladies' nightdresses, which he had seized from a shop and taken to his solicitor's office nearby; the other was burglary of a hospital, in the form of taking four packets of frozen cod fillets from a hospital freezer. The trial judge imposed 2 years' imprisonment for the theft, and 18 months consecutive for the

---

[34] E.g. West (1963), Burnett (1994), Maruna (2001).

[35] Council of Europe (1993); to similar effect, see the Australian proposals in ALRC (2006), para. 6.179.

[36] Cf. Bagaric (2001), ch. 10, for the contrary argument that only by adopting flat-rate sentencing can bias against the poor and disadvantaged be reduced significantly.

[37] Roberts (2008a), p. 56; cf. Reitz (2010), p. 149 and ch. 8 *passim*.

[38] For an example, see *Queen* (1981) 3 Cr App R (S) 245.   [39] (1988) 10 Cr App R (S) 231.

burglary, totalling 3½ years. The offender's record was described by the Court of Appeal as 'truly appalling': it stretched back over 25 years, though most offences were 'comparatively petty thefts'. The trial judge evidently imposed the sentence in order to incapacitate Bailey for a lengthy time (a version of the cumulative principle), but the Court of Appeal held that this was wrong in principle. Stocker LJ stated:

> It is of course manifest that a convicted criminal's past record forms part of the matrix upon which he falls to be sentenced. Clearly no court would be likely to impose a sentence of imprisonment for a first offender of the same length that might be appropriate for a person with a substantial criminal record. To that extent the past record is a relevant factor to be taken into account. On the other hand, as has often been said by this court ... the sentence imposed must be related to the gravity of the offences in relation to which it is imposed ... Whilst fully understanding the motive which impelled the learned judge to impose a total sentence of three and a half years, we feel bound to say that those sentences bore so little relationship to the gravity of the offences that even having regard to the appalling background of this appellant, they cannot possibly be justified.[40]

The court went on to reduce the sentences to 15 months for the theft, and 3 months consecutive for the burglary which yielded the frozen cod fillets. By what benchmark was 15 months' imprisonment a proper ceiling for a rather feeble theft of nightdresses, which resulted in the recovery of the stolen property fairly soon after the event? The *Bailey* decision shows how the rhetoric of the courts was often different from the reality of their sentencing practice. However, as we shall see in 6.3 below, the principle has now vanished from English law.[41]

Even when the principle did form part of the law, however, it was not applied to all crimes. A different approach, more akin to flat-rate sentencing, applied to grave crimes. In his pioneering judgment in *Turner* (1975),[42] on sentencing levels for armed robbery and for grave crimes in general, Lawton LJ stated that 'the fact that a man has not much of a criminal record, if any at all, is not a powerful factor to be taken into consideration when the court is dealing with cases of this gravity'. The justification for this restriction must be along the lines that little concession to human weakness should be made where there is egregious wrong-doing. The usual 'concession to human frailty' implies that the offence can be seen as an unfortunate lapse, whereas there is less room for tolerance of those who succumb to the temptation to commit a grave crime, unless there is evidence of intense emotion or other strong mitigation.[43] This may suggest a kind of sliding scale, with the general 'concession to human frailty' approach to first offenders gradually giving way to a harder line towards egregious wrongs.

---

[40] Ibid., at p. 233.

[41] Progressive loss of mitigation is still the (official) approach in Ireland: O'Malley (2006), pp. 140–4.

[42] (1975) 61 Cr App R 67, at p. 91, discussed in ch. 4.4.8 above.

[43] On which see Roberts (2008a), p. 57.

6.2.4 A recidivist premium

A fourth approach to sentencing persistent offenders has been put forward by Julian Roberts. His work devotes considerable attention to the opinions of members of the public and also of convicted offenders on the subject, finding that the former seem to favour a substantial recidivist premium and that the latter, although taking a similarly hard line in some respects, also want a more individualized approach that distinguishes those persistent offenders who have problems that need addressing. However, he does not argue that popular views should determine policy, since he demonstrates how 'misperceptions about reoffending patterns help to explain support for the recidivist sentencing premium'.[44] His argument is that an offender with previous convictions has enhanced culpability which, on desert grounds, warrants a more severe response than would be appropriate for a first offender:

> Awareness of this previous legal censure should recall the individual to respect the law; the offender who re-offends is therefore similar to the offender who plans the offence. Both are worthy of a greater degree of moral reprobation to reflect their enhanced level of culpability. The conduct of the premeditated offender and the repeat offender both represent a more marked departure from acceptable conduct.[45]

This enhanced culpability, based on increased awareness of the wrongfulness of his behaviour, does not increase exponentially with each further conviction: the greatest increase is 'between a first offender and an individual with two priors', and a 'more multidimensional approach' is required to assess larger numbers of previous convictions.[46] The essence of his approach is its insistence that repeat offending is, generally speaking, more culpable and therefore deserving of a more severe sentence. For Roberts, the gradation of sentences from first offender to second, third, and fourth offender could be no different in practice than the gradation yielded by the doctrine of progressive loss of mitigation: the significant difference is that his approach refers not to mitigation and its loss (which he regards as strained and difficult for people to understand), but rather to a recidivist premium for second and subsequent offences, to reflect what he regards as the greater culpability. Roberts insists on a proportionality cap to the recidivist premium: although he is not precise about how this limit should be fixed, it could be similar to the proportionality cap or 'ceiling' that operates for progressive loss of mitigation. If so, it would be equally consistent with the principles of parsimony and restraint. However, the persuasiveness of the analogy with premeditation on which his approach

---

[44] Ibid., p. 189; cf. pp. 209–12.
[45] Roberts (2009), p. 154. A much less sophisticated statement is to be found in the US *Sentencing Guidelines Manual* (2008, para. 4A): 'a defendant with a record of prior criminal behavior is more culpable than a first offender and thus deserving of greater punishment'.
[46] Roberts (2008a), p. 89.

rests is significantly reduced for impulsive or drug-driven offenders, and others with personal problems, and in terms of recidivism they are likely to be more numerous (see 6.3.1 below) than the rational calculator who seems to be the focus of the Roberts analysis.[47]

Roberts insists, as do the supporters of progressive loss of mitigation, on the pivotal significance of formal legal censure. Conviction by a court is the key event, even if the offender has committed previous offences without being convicted of them (or has been given a formal caution of some kind). Others have agreed with the significance of the first formal legal censure, but have advanced alternatives to the premeditation rationale. Thus Youngjae Lee argues that when a person reoffends after a first conviction, that demonstrates the offender's omission to organize his or her life so as to prevent further offending.[48] On his view, the formal censure implicit in conviction by a court gives rise to an obligation on the offender to reflect on the conviction and then to make efforts to conform to the law – a special obligation, over and above the citizen's general obligation to obey the law.[49] The exact grounding of this obligation remains to be secured, but Lee is right to focus on what is implicit in the formal censure of court conviction. He also argues that, although the breach of obligation is an additional wrong, it is one that should not attract a great enhancement of the sentence. He is thus arguing for a restricted premium for repeat offending.

6.3 Previous convictions and the Criminal Justice Act 2003

The current law on the sentencing of repeat offenders is found in s. 143(2) of the Criminal Justice Act 2003. The discussion here begins by analysing official policy in respect of persistent offenders; it then examines the legislative provision in some detail; and finally it considers the impact of this provision on sentencing practice.

6.3.1 Framing the problem of persistent offenders

Sentencing policy for persistent offenders should be seen in the broader context of the criminal justice system. A good starting point would be some facts on the characteristics of the people under discussion:

> The 100,000 most persistent offenders share a common profile. Half are under 21 and nearly three-quarters started offending between 13 and 15. Nearly two-thirds are hard drug users. More than a third were in care as children. Half have no qualifications at all and nearly half have been excluded from school. Three-quarters have no work and little or no legal income.

---

[47] See von Hirsch (2009) and Tonry (2010), pp. 107–11, for similar critiques.   [48] Lee (2009).
[49] Bennett (2010), p. 80; Tonry (2010), pp. 104–6.

This important quotation comes not from a criminological textbook but from a major Home Office framework document.[50] It seems unlikely that the position has changed markedly in the years since it was written. Moreover the percentage of offenders sentenced for an indictable offence who have 15 or more previous convictions has increased from 23 per cent in 2006 to 33 per cent in 2013, demonstrating the need for the criminal justice system to focus on the response to persistent offenders (see Table 11 in Appendix B).

The predominant approach to this undoubted problem, encapsulated in the 2003 Act (to be discussed next), is to punish what appears to be defiance of the justice system. 'A continuing course of criminal conduct in the face of repeated attempts by the State to correct it calls for increasing denunciation and retribution.'[51] Admittedly the Halliday Report proposed that there should be 'more intensive efforts to reform and rehabilitate' within the more punitive sentences it recommended, but the question is whether this approach pays sufficient attention to the motivations and causes of reoffending indicated by the Home Office quotation above. Many repeat offenders are not rational calculators but people influenced by multiple disadvantages,[52] and the official response ought to take this into account if it is concerned with the prevention of crime. Criminological research shows that many criminal careers are short-lived, and mostly among males aged 15–25, and that there is a variety of personal and social-structural explanations of why offenders desist after a few years. The recent Sheffield desistance study of young male recidivists aged 19–22 shows that as they become older, the great majority say that they want to stop offending, and that they take steps towards desistance by holding on to various 'hooks' such as a partner, a job or family support.[53] However, they rarely stop offending all at once, and more usually reduce the frequency of their offending, often by taking decisions not to socialize with certain people or to avoid certain areas.

This can mean that when they appear in court they may look as if they remain persistent offenders. A repressive policy of escalating punishments may fail to take their efforts at desistance into account. The danger then is that any custodial sentence may delay desistance and have other negative effects.[54] What is required is a more differentiated approach, insisting on an

---

[50] Home Office (2001), App. B, para. B.7. Along similar lines, see the Joint Inspection Report (2004), para. 6.14, referring to the difficulties of prolific offenders, and offenders in general, in terms of 'problems with thinking skills, drug misuse, employment training and education, accommodation, lifestyle, attitudes and finance'.

[51] Halliday (2001), para. 2.7.

[52] Halliday did state that 'of social variables, drug misuse is most strongly linked with the likelihood of conviction': (2001), App. 3, para. 11.

[53] Bottoms and Shapland (2011).   [54] Farrall, Hough, Maruna and Sparks (2011), p. 17.

overall proportionality limit but facilitating rehabilitative programmes where there is evidence that they may be productive for particular offenders.[55]

Furthermore, while there is abundant evidence that the best predictor of reconviction is the number of previous convictions,[56] this proposition fails to take into account the relative seriousness of the individual offences. This is a faultline running through many discussions of risk. References to recidivism, reoffending and crime prevention often overlook the reality that repetition is at its greatest with the least serious offences. When the Prolific Offender scheme was launched a decade ago, and subsequently renamed the Prolific and Other Priority Offender scheme, its aim was to identify and catch prolific offenders and then to arrange for their resettlement after sentence. An early review of the scheme found that the most common offence by far was theft from shops, at 36 per cent of all those falling within the definition. Only 5 per cent of qualifying offences were burglary in a dwelling.[57] This demonstrates an abject failure to understand the lessons of history in respect of policy on persistent offenders, as described in part 6.1 above, and it is hardly surprising that the first recommendation made in the Joint Inspection Report was that the definition be narrowed so as 'to identify a more limited number of priority offenders'.[58] If resources are to be focused on one particular group, it is wise to target offences that are of particular concern – notably, the more serious ones.

However, the priorities in responding to persistent offenders became blurred in the statements of the former Labour administration. The Ministry of Justice stated that 'our starting point is that the public must be protected from those offenders who pose a threat. This is why prison is the right place for the most dangerous, serious and the most persistent offenders.'[59] Those final words seem to emphasize the persistence rather than the seriousness of the offending, and open up the possibility of long sentences for those repeating minor offences. A searching examination by the Justice Committee of the House of Commons condemned 'the Government's apparent acceptance of the use of short custodial sentences for repeat offenders' as 'disproportionate', and criticized 'a legislative framework that requires penalties to be ratcheted up'.[60] It is to that legislative framework that we now pass.

6.3.2 The current law

Section 143(2) of the Criminal Justice Act 2003 provides:

> In considering the seriousness of an offence ('the current offence') committed by an offender who has one or more previous convictions, the court must treat each

---

[55] Bearing in mind that the 19–22 year-old recidivists in the Sheffield study had difficult backgrounds, such as half had been excluded from school, 86% left school with no qualifications, 60% had not had a job in the previous 12 months, 47% were on drugs, etc: Bottoms and Shapland (2011).

[56] See, e.g., Halliday (2001), App. 3.   [57] Joint Inspection Report (2004), para. 6.13.

[58] Joint Inspection Report (2004), para. 7.8.   [59] Ministry of Justice (2008), p. 2.

[60] House of Commons (2008), paras. 107–8.

previous conviction as an aggravating factor if (in the case of that conviction) the court considers that it can reasonably be so treated having regard, in particular, to –

(a) the nature of the offence to which the conviction relates and its relevance to the current offence, and
(b) the time that has elapsed since the conviction.

The drafting of this provision creates an obvious tension. On the one hand, it indicates that a court is bound to ('must') treat each previous conviction as a factor that aggravates the current offence, and should do so each time the offender is sentenced.[61] This appears to require a cumulative approach, so that, for example, on sentencing a fifth-time offender, the court must treat each of the four previous offences as rendering this one more serious. On the other hand, the force of the mandatory words, 'must treat ... as an aggravating factor', appears to be softened by the later clause, 'if the court considers that it can reasonably be so treated'. Does that restore to the court a discretion to pursue a different policy on previous convictions if it does not agree with the cumulative approach? Surely not: the reasonableness of treating each previous conviction as an aggravating factor seems to be connected with the offender's previous conduct. Thus the court should have regard to each previous conviction's relevance and recency, as set out in (a) and (b), and perhaps to any other factor arising from those previous convictions. The Explanatory Notes to the Act stated baldly that recent and relevant convictions 'should be regarded as an aggravating factor which should increase the severity of the sentence', leaving no room for judicial discretion or for other factors.

What should be the criterion of whether prior convictions are *relevant* to the current offence? The Halliday Report noted that most persistent offenders have a mixed criminal record, and therefore argued that 'less weight should be given to whether previous and current offences are in the same category', so that 'the key point is whether the previous offences justify a more severe view'.[62] Insofar as this suggests that the seriousness of the previous offences is the crucial issue, that is quite different from s. 143(2) as drafted. 'Relevance' is surely to be taken as indicating a similarity of subject matter. Thus the practice in sentencing for offences of violence has been for courts to pay more attention to previous convictions for offences of violence than to others. This is borne out by the small Crown Court survey, which found that those previous convictions that led judges to move the sentence upwards tended to be those for offences related to the current

---

[61] Convictions from other jurisdictions may also be taken into account (sub-ss. (4) and (5)), but it is unclear whether a conviction followed by a discharge counts as a previous conviction in this context.

[62] Halliday (2001), para. 2.17; later in the same paragraph, however, the report states that 'completely disparate ... previous convictions should be given less weight'.

offence, especially where they disclosed an escalating pattern of offending.[63] Recent research by Roberts and Pina-Sanchez, using statistics from the CCSS, shows that English judges are discounting many previous convictions as irrelevant to the particular case, but it is not clear what criteria of relevance are being applied.[64] Offenders interviewed by Julian Roberts in earlier research thought that 'specialists' should be treated more severely.[65] Where there is a record of offences of dishonesty or burglary, courts may decide to treat the person as a 'professional' (see part 6.4 below). However, both Appendix 3 of the Halliday Report and Farrington's review of criminal career research lead to the conclusion that the typical pattern is a small degree of specialization 'superimposed on a great deal of generality or versatility in offending', and that the majority of offences of violent offenders are non-violent.[66] Thus specialization is rare, and one might question whether it is necessarily worse than versatility if the seriousness and number of previous convictions are similar.

Would the notion of lapse have any application here? Human weakness in losing one's temper momentarily and punching another may be regarded as different from human frailty in succumbing to the temptation of economic crime. There is therefore some ground for arguing that a first sexual offence by someone with previous property convictions should be treated as 'out of character', and should be mitigated to some extent.[67] But this argument cannot be pressed too far. It would be absurd to imply that everyone is entitled to one 'discounted' crime of violence, one 'discounted' fraud, one 'discounted' sexual offence, and so on. Thus Halliday suggested that the *seriousness* of the prior offences should be the primary determinant, in terms of 'whether there is a continuing course of criminal conduct'.[68] But, again, this is not what s. 143 (2)(a) says: it rests on the notion of relevance, presumably interpreted in terms of types or categories of offending.

The common law principle that a gap in offending should be taken to diminish the effect of previous convictions is restated in s. 143(2)(b), which requires courts to have regard to the time that has elapsed since each previous conviction. An old example of the principle is *Fox* (1980),[69] where the Court of Appeal reduced the sentence on a man aged 35 convicted of grievous bodily harm who had two previous convictions many years earlier: 'In our judgment,

---

[63] SCWG Survey (2008), pp. 10–11.

[64] Roberts and Pina-Sanchez (2014); see also CCSS (2014), p. 30, showing that the highest number of previous convictions taken into account is in burglary cases, and the lowest in sexual cases.

[65] Roberts (2008a), pp. 153–4.   [66] Farrington (1997), p. 380.

[67] See *Davies* [2006] 1 Cr App R (S) 213: D with 36 previous court appearances for 'more than 100 offences covering a wide variety of criminal activities' convicted of first sexual offence. Court of Appeal evidently did not regard previous convictions as aggravating, but no mention of 2003 Act.

[68] Halliday (2001), para. 2.17.

[69] (1980) 2 Cr App R (S) 188; see also *Bleasdale* (1984) 6 Cr App R (S) 177 (4 years without trouble for a man of 22 'is an important feature in his favour').

his previous record of violence when he was in his late teens and mid-twenties should have been left out of account in deciding what action to take.' Various justifications may be offered for this concession – for example the offender deserves credit for going straight, or the present offence is to some extent 'out of character' in terms of his recent behaviour, or the conviction-free gap makes it less likely that he will reoffend – but the most straightforward approach is to affirm the underlying principle of the Rehabilitation of Offenders Act 1974. Generally speaking, it is unnecessarily harsh if a person has to bear the burden of previous convictions indefinitely: after a number of years a person should be able to regain full rights as a citizen, and such a principle may even provide an incentive not to reoffend. Many US guideline systems provide for the 'decay' of previous convictions after ten years, and this has been adopted, for example, in the proposed South African sentencing code.[70] Although it appears that there is little public sympathy for this principle,[71] it forms part of English law and, applying the principle of decay, rightly so. However, the small Crown Court survey found divergences in judicial interpretations of recency, some going back only five years and others taking account of convictions up to ten years earlier.[72]

What is missing from s. 143(2) is any reference to an overall proportionality constraint, as recommended by the Council of Europe (see 6.2.3 above), adopted, for example, in Sweden.[73] The wording of s. 143(2) seems consistent with a cumulative approach that increases the severity of the sentence on each subsequent conviction, allowing sentences (e.g. for theft from shops) to ascend to 2, 2½ or 3 years' imprisonment as further convictions are recorded. Halliday insisted that 'the effects of previous convictions would always be subject to outer limits resulting from the seriousness of the current offences'.[74] At the time, Ministers stated that s. 143(2) merely 'modifies the proportionality principle so that previous, relevant convictions can act as an aggravating factor', and that it was not intended to lead to 'wildly disproportionate sentences'.[75] But the wording of s. 143(2) discloses no such constraint.

Finally, we should return to the use of 'must' in s. 143(2). Does the injunction to courts to 'treat each previous conviction as an aggravating factor' mean that Parliament intended to rule out the use of community sentences for repeat offenders? Judge Peter Jones put the case of offenders who commit frequent thefts of items such as toiletries, with a view to selling

---

[70] South African Law Reform Commission (2000), s. 42: 'where a period of 10 years has passed from the date of completion of the last sentence and the date of commission of any subsequent offence ... the last conviction and all convictions prior to that must be disregarded for the purposes of sentencing'.

[71] Hough, Roberts et al. (2009).   [72] SCWG Survey (2008), p. 11; see now Larrauri (2014).

[73] Von Hirsch and Jareborg (1989): see ch. 29.4, 'the court shall ... to a reasonable extent take the offender's previous criminality into account'.

[74] Halliday (2001), para. 2.20.   [75] Baroness Scotland, HL Deb. 24 February 2003.

them in order to raise money to buy drugs.[76] Such an offender may come
before the court with 30, 40 or more previous convictions. If the court wishes
to tackle what it regards as the underlying cause of offending (drug-taking)
by making a community order, would it be lawful to do so? Halliday himself
wanted to see community sentences used more widely in such cases, but that
was always in conflict with his proposed policy of 'increasing denunciation
and retribution' for persistent offenders,[77] which gave rise to the provisions
in s. 143(2). This is a practical problem: we have noted the increasing
proportion of indictable offenders with 15 or more previous convictions,[78]
but those figures also show that not all offenders with 15 or more previous
convictions are given custodial sentences. Both the Court of Appeal and the
Sentencing Council agree that a court can substitute a community sentence
with a treatment requirement for a low or moderate custodial sentence if it
judges this appropriate.[79] To make this compliant with s. 143(2), the court
would have to find that the relevant previous convictions cannot reasonably
be regarded as aggravating, and perhaps this would not be problematic if
those convictions are combined with a demonstrated intention to undergo
treatment for an underlying drug or alcohol addiction. Empirical evidence
indicates that judges are often prepared to reduce custody to a community
sentence if persuaded that a repeat offender has demonstrated a willingness
to change.[80]

These reflections on the law laid down by s. 143(2) appear to sit oddly with
practice. One recorder has stated that in the five years following the implementation of the 2003 Act he was not addressed by counsel once on the
wording of the section, even though many cases fell within its purview.[81] The
Court of Appeal has occasionally referred to s. 143(2),[82] but its normal
approach seems to be to deal with the issue without any specific legislative
reference.[83]

6.3.3 Sentencing guidelines and previous convictions

In most of the United States jurisdictions that employ sentencing guidelines,
there is a 'sentencing grid' with two dimensions, one being offence-seriousness
and the other being 'criminal history'. The Minnesota sentencing grid, for

---

[76] Jones (2002).   [77] Ibid., pp. 185–6, citing Halliday (2001), para. 6.6.

[78] See Table 13 in Appendix B.

[79] E.g. *Attorney General's Reference No. 64 of 2003* [2004] 2 Cr App R (S) 106; Sentencing Council, *Burglary Offences: Definitive Guideline* (2011), p. 8.

[80] E.g. Hough, Jacobson and Millie (2003), pp. 36–41; Millie, Tombs and Hough (2007), pp. 243 and 255.

[81] Wasik (2010), pp. 164–5.

[82] A rare example is *Howard* [2013] 1 Cr App R (S) 405, at [14], although the mention was not accompanied by any analysis.

[83] Of many such cases, four are *Sims* [2011] 1 Cr App R (S) 471, *Moore* [2012] 1 Cr App R (S) 19, *Mitchell and Kellman* [2012] 1 Cr App R (S) 387, and *Thomas* [2013] 2 Cr App R (S) 546.

example, has seven levels of criminal history score, from zero to six or more, and as an offender's criminal history moves upwards the impact on sentence length for a given offence is progressively more severe.[84] The calculation of a criminal history score is a complex and nuanced task in many US jurisdictions; but the result of the exercise is to indicate a presumptively more severe sentence as the score goes up.

Such apparent rigidity is rejected in England and Wales, where the approach to guidelines is more flexible. In respect of previous convictions, however, flexibility shades into the absence of real guidance. The style of the guidelines issued by the former SGC was to list previous convictions as an aggravating factor, and then to provide that:

> Where the offender has previous convictions which aggravate the seriousness of the current offence, that may take the provisional sentence beyond the range given, particularly where there are significant other aggravating factors present.[85]

This gave courts the liberty to go outside the indicated sentence range where previous convictions are treated as aggravating, but it offered no guidance on the extent to which previous convictions might aggravate sentence. The Gage Report identified previous convictions as a factor with considerable influence on sentence length, and proposed that greater guidance should be given. Predictably, 'many experienced judges expressed the view that there was no need for further guidance on this issue', since the relevant factors were well known and it was for the court to assess them in each case.[86] The Gage Report concluded that some further guidance was desirable, but added that it 'should not attempt to quantify the weight given to previous convictions in the sentencing process'.[87]

Just before its demise the Sentencing Advisory Panel consulted on the topic, and as a result commended five principles:

(i) The primary significance of previous convictions is the extent to which they indicate trends in offending behavior and the response to earlier sentences;
(ii) Previous convictions always will be relevant to the current offence if they are of a similar type;
(iii) Previous convictions of a type different from the current offence may be relevant where they are an indication of persistent offending;
(vi) Numerous and frequent previous convictions may indicate an underlying problem (for example, an addiction) that could be addressed more effectively

---

[84] This is well illustrated in Roberts (2008a), pp. 96–8.
[85] This wording is found in most SGC guidelines. See e.g. SGC, *Theft and Burglary in a Building Other Than a Dwelling* (2008), p. 8.
[86] Gage (2008), para. 7.9.
[87] Ibid., para. 7.10. Cf. ALRC (2006), paras. 6.176–9, arguing for a legislative statement in Australia that the fact alone that an offender has an antecedent criminal history should not be treated as aggravating.

in the community and will not necessarily indicate that a custodial sentence is necessary;

(v) The aggravating effect of relevant previous convictions will normally reduce with the passage of time; where a significant period of time has elapsed since the most recent relevant conviction, they may cease to have any effect at all depending on the nature of the offence and the reasons for the gap in offending.[88]

These principles reflect a mixture of consultees' responses, public opinion, and normative reasoning by the Panel (e.g. on the effect of serious but dissimilar previous convictions).

One of the Council's first moves was to abandon the SGC's insistence that guideline ranges relate to offences committed by first offenders, and that courts need to adapt the guidelines in order to take account of previous convictions. This approach was said to court unreality (very few people sentenced are first offenders) and to produce confusion (some sentencers thought that the guidelines did not apply at all to offenders with previous convictions). The Council rightly sought to establish clarity on the issue, and so announced that all its guidelines and ranges 'are applicable to all offenders, in all cases'. Once the starting point is established in a given case, the court should consider 'previous convictions so as to adjust the sentence within the range'.[89] The guideline continues: 'In particular, relevant recent convictions are likely to result in an upward movement.' In some cases, having considered these factors (i.e. previous convictions and other aggravating factors), 'it may be appropriate to move outside the identified category range'.[90] Unfortunately, this loose approach leads to judgments that fail to focus on the 'interests of justice' test when the court goes above the offence range, and which contain little reasoning relating to the quantum of the sentence.[91]

Does the Council's approach amount to 'guidance', or does it simply consign the whole issue to judicial discretion? It rejects the Gage Report's approach and is surely not compliant with the statutory requirement in s. 121 (6) of the Coroners and Justice Act 2009 that the Council's guidelines should '(c) include criteria, and provide guidance, for determining the weight to be given to previous convictions of an offender'? In its consultation on theft offences, the Council repeats its typical wording:

---

[88] SAP, *Overarching Principles of Sentencing* (2010), pp. 35–6.

[89] Sentencing Council, *Burglary Offences: Definitive Guideline* (2011), p. 2. One could maintain that logically the range must assume no previous convictions or some previous convictions, since sentencers are encouraged to mitigate for first offenders and to aggravate for repeat offenders. Probably the ranges assume one previous conviction, but this logical puzzle is not of great importance.

[90] Sentencing Council, *Burglary Offences: Definitive Guideline* (2011), p. 9.

[91] E.g. *King* [2014] 2 Cr App R (S) 478.

In particular, relevant recent convictions may justify an upward adjustment, including outside the category range. In cases involving significant persistent offending, the community and custody threshold may be crossed even though the offence may otherwise warrant a lesser sentence.

It then explains that this is not intended to alter sentencing practice substantially but to 'regularise' it, and goes on:

The wording on previous convictions is intended to provide sentencers with the discretion and flexibility to adjust sentences upwardly, including outside the category range, based on the individual facts before them, rather than prescriptively stating how sentencers should reflect this issue in every case.[92]

This seems to amount to a return to the 'no two cases are the same' and 'each case on its own facts' assertions, which were prevalent among judges before offence guidelines were first developed in the 1980s. Those assertions are no longer valid as an objection to offence guidelines, and they should not stand in the way of guidance on previous convictions either. As is evident from parts 6.2 and 6.3.1 above, and from the Panel's Advice, there are important issues of principle that need to be resolved. It is undeniable that many cases have different facts, and wise to leave judicial discretion to deal with that. But the issues of principle should be resolved at a general level, by the Council in its guidance, and then judges and magistrates should apply those principles as best they can to the varying facts of individual cases.

What are the issues of principle? We have identified several of them in the above discussions, and one obvious starting point would be the five principles enunciated by the Panel and set out above. Principle (v) would be widely accepted, but each of the others requires further discussion. If principle (ii) is accepted, is it possible to indicate how serious or frequent the similar offences need be if they are to take the sentence out of the category range, or even out of the offence range?[93] Is principle (iii) sound, and is it compatible with s. 143(2)? Should the guidance include a reference to avoiding total sentences that are disproportionate to the current offence – as urged by Halliday, and as stated by government ministers at the time, but without any basis in the wording of s. 143(2)?[94] Does the Council's decision to place previous convictions at Step Two rather than Step One constrain their influence, and is this (without any further guidance) a satisfactory approach?[95] Should the sentencer focus on

---

[92] Sentencing Council, *Theft Offences Guideline: Consultation* (2014), p. 22.

[93] E.g. *Howard* [2013] 1 Cr App R (S) 405, *Andrews* [2013] 2 Cr App R (S) 26, *Roberts* [2013] 2 Cr App R (S) 84.

[94] Cf. *Thomas* [2013] 2 Cr App R (S) 546, where the Court of Appeal held that proportionality to the current offence could not be a constraint when the criminal record was bad.

[95] See Roberts and Pina-Sanchez (2014), drawing on CCSS data to demonstrate that judges find relatively few previous convictions 'relevant' and that previous convictions appear to carry less weight since Council guidelines on assault came into force.

the number of court appearances, or the number of convictions?[96] How exactly should courts deal with high numbers of previous convictions, such as 40, 50, and 60, especially where the convictions are for relatively low-level offences? [97] If the court forms the view that the persistent offender is being defiant, though not committing offences in the first rank of seriousness, is that a good reason for going above the category range?[98] These and other issues of principle should not be left at the discretion of the particular sentencer, although there should be discretion in applying the principles to the facts of each case.

6.4 The problem of 'professional' criminals

In the past, as we saw in part 6.1 of this chapter, severe policies against persistent offenders have often been rationalized on the ground that they are aimed at 'professional criminals', even though they have often swept many minor offenders into the net. Courts still describe certain offenders as 'professional', raising questions about the justification for singling out this group, and questions of definition. It is fairly clear that the courts' aim is either deterrence or public protection. The argument seems to be that professional criminals set themselves deliberately against the rest of society and endeavour systematically to exploit opportunities for crime to reap the benefits. Thus, there is no question of human weakness in this group, no occasional succumbing to temptation, no underlying medical condition: they are perceived to be rational calculators, and the response should be a tough one.

But how is this group to be defined? It is one thing to affirm the existence of professional criminals ruthlessly and systematically exploiting law-abiding citizens. It is another to ensure that this group of offenders is so defined as to include only those who meet the description and to exclude others. As we saw in part 6.1 above, early in the last century Churchill 'was appalled to find that repetition was the criterion for imposing preventive detention, irrespective of the gravity of the offences committed'. There were long lists of offenders sentenced to preventive detention 'for such trivialities as stealing a pair of boots, or two shillings, or four dishes, or handkerchiefs, or fowls or slates or whatever'.[99] Is there a contemporary equivalent of this? The courts have tended to use the adjective 'professional' in relation to persistent pickpockets and bag-snatchers when justifying long sentences. Thus in

---

[96] See the discussion by Wasik (2010), pp. 168–70.

[97] SAP, *Sentencing for Theft from a Shop* (2008), para. 9, recording the results of research that found that the average number of previous convictions of persons convicted of theft from shops was 42.

[98] E.g. *Moore* [2012] 1 Cr App R (S) 19, *Jones* [2013] 2 Cr App R (S) 419, *Guminski* [2012] 2 Cr App R (S) 280, *Bond* [2014] 2 Cr App R (S) 12.

[99] Radzinowicz and Hood (1986), p. 283.

Freeman (1989)[100] the Court of Appeal upheld a sentence of 5 years on a persistent pickpocket who was described as a professional; in *O'Rourke* (1994)[101] the Court upheld a sentence of 3 years on a persistent handbag thief; in *Spencer and Carby* (1995)[102] similar sentences were upheld on offenders described as professional pickpockets; and in *Gwillim-Jones* (2002)[103] a sentence of 3 years was upheld on a professional handbag thief. Thus the adjective 'professional' appears to suggest that crime is the offender's principal source of income, or it is a regular source of income, or the offences are planned to maximize profit and minimize the risk of detection, or the offences are executed with great skill, or simply that the offender commits acquisitive offences frequently.[104] But are all offences committed in one of those sets of circumstances sufficiently serious to justify such long sentences? For example, it is sometimes said that 'the record of the offender is of more significance in the case of domestic burglary than in the case of some other crime',[105] but the reasoning behind this is not spelt out. Where the convictions are for theft of items of small value, or even for attempted theft, the guidelines indicate a starting point of a low community sentence; for theft from a person (not a vulnerable victim), the starting point is a medium community sentence.[106] Is it justifiable to impose a custodial sentence, because of a bad record thought to indicate professionalism, instead of a proportionate sentence? It is questionable whether custody is more likely to change the lifestyle of these offenders than targeted interventions under the umbrella of a community sentence.[107]

The concept of a professional criminal may trade on its association with organized crime, conjuring up images of entrepreneurs who meticulously plan their offences.[108] The two concepts must be kept separate when small-time thieves are being sentenced. There are some individuals whose criminality would seem to be clearly professional, in the sense that their skill, planning, and calculation of lucrative gains would bring them within most definitions – one example being the career of A. E. Brewster, who has repeatedly committed high-value burglaries at luxurious houses and flats in central London, serving long sentences (10 years and 9 years upheld in the two Court of Appeal cases) and then returning to the same occupation.[109] Evidence of involvement in

---

[100] (1989) 11 Cr App R (S) 398; see also *Whitrid* (1989) 11 Cr App R (S) 403, and the discussion in ch. 4.4.10 above.
[101] (1994) 15 Cr App R (S) 650; see also *Glide* (1989) 11 Cr App R (S) 319.
[102] (1995) 16 Cr App R (S) 482.   [103] [2002] 1 Cr App R (S) 19.
[104] Note also the varying definitions of 'professional' used by the judges in the study by Davies and Tyrer (2003); cf. *Daniels and Smith* [2012] 2 Cr App R (S) 532, at [12], 'experienced' offenders.
[105] *Brewster* [1998] 1 Cr App R (S) 181, endorsed in *Saw* [2009] 2 Cr App R (S) 367, at [24].
[106] SGC, *Theft and Burglary in a Building Other Than a Dwelling* (2008), pp. 15–17.
[107] See ch. 10.6 below.
[108] See the extensive discussion of definitions of organized crime by Levi (2012).
[109] *Brewster* (1980) 2 Cr App R (S) 191 and [1998] 1 Cr App R (S) 181; see also *Jenkins* [2002] 1 Cr App R (S) 22.

organized crime, for example through major armed robberies or trafficking in illegal immigrants, may warrant the term 'professional'. But the application of that term to pickpockets and handbag thieves, as a reason for imposing sentences in the same range as some rapes and serious woundings, cannot be justified. It is not clear how far above the relevant range a court may go:[110] and since the terms of s. 143(2) of the 2003 Act would seem to encourage rather than discourage long sentences for such offenders, it becomes all the more important to reconsider the use of the adjective 'professional'.

6.5 Persistent petty offenders

Prison surveys have revealed that a significant number of those in custody are there mainly because of their social rootlessness and the repeated commission of minor offences, often of a 'nuisance' or public order kind. One Home Office study expressed the point thus: 'the homeless poor may be persistently taken to court, and hence persistently returned to prison, because of a persistent failure to provide for them in any other way'.[111] A well-known survey by the Social Exclusion Unit referred to many prisoners (and particularly those serving short terms) as having 'experienced a lifetime of social exclusion', and commented that compared with the general population they were 'thirteen times as likely to have been in care as a child, thirteen times as likely to be unemployed, ten times as likely to have been a regular truant ...', and so forth.[112]

However, there are two sections in the 2003 Act which raise the possibility of disproportionately severe sentences for this type of offender. First, although s. 152(2) of the Criminal Justice Act 2003 should only permit the imposition of a custodial sentence if the offence is so serious that neither a fine nor a community sentence is an adequate sentence, this appears to run counter to the provision on persistent offenders in s. 143(2). The Home Office stated its support for 'diverting from prison minor offenders for whom a very short stay in prison serves little purpose',[113] without noting the contrary tendency of s. 143(2). But if s. 152(2) is to be given its proper force, courts should find themselves following the spirit of Lawton LJ's judgment in *Clarke* (1975),[114] where he declared (albeit in a case involving an element of mental disorder) that courts should not be used as 'dustbins for the difficult' and varied a sentence of 18 months' imprisonment, for damaging a flowerpot, to a fine of £2. This amounted to a strong declaration that most of these people are offenders only incidentally or symptomatically, and should properly be the concern of the social services. The provision of support and care for them

---

[110] See *Bond* [2014] 2 Cr App R (S) 12 for an example of unspecific reasoning.
[111] Fairhead (1981), p. 2.   [112] Social Exclusion Unit (2002), p. 6.
[113] Home Office (2004), para. 23.
[114] (1975) 61 Cr App R 320; see also *McPherson* (1980) 2 Cr App R (S) 4.

should not be the responsibility of the criminal justice system. It is a wider social problem concerning the provision of education, housing, training, and (where necessary) community care. But s. 143(2) may be taken to point in another direction.

Second, s. 151 of the Act empowers a court to impose a community sentence on an offender who has been fined on at least three previous occasions, and where (despite the effect of s. 143(2)) the court would not regard the current offence as serious enough to warrant a community sentence.[115] The court must decide that it is in the interests of justice to make such an order and to take the offender up-tariff in this way. The SGC's guideline emphasized that courts should only impose a community sentence in the lowest range of seriousness in these cases, and warned that:

> Where an offender is being sentenced for a non-imprisonable offence or offences, great care will be needed in assessing whether a community sentence is appropriate since failure to comply could result in a custodial sentence.[116]

However, the danger exists that petty offenders will be sent to prison if courts utilise this route.

6.6 Civil preventive orders as a response to persistence

The civil preventive order may be regarded as part of the strategy against persistent offenders. The basic model of this hybrid order is that a civil or criminal court may make a particular order, prohibiting a person from certain conduct, and then breach of the prohibition constitutes a criminal offence with a substantial maximum penalty (usually, 5 years' imprisonment). The range of civil preventive orders is discussed in detail in Chapter 11 below, but the prime example to be discussed now is the anti-social behaviour order (ASBO) and its 2014 replacements. It was in the same year as the Human Rights Act became law, 1998, that the ASBO was introduced by s. 1 of the Crime and Disorder Act.[117] It was a civil order, made by magistrates sitting as a civil court on application by the police, local authority, or landlord, and it imposed restrictive conditions on a person for at least 2 years. The magistrates had to be satisfied that the person had acted in a manner that caused or was likely to cause harassment, alarm, or distress to others, and that the order was necessary to protect local people from further such acts. The order could prohibit the person from doing anything that might expose people to further anti-social acts (not necessarily of the same type as already proved). It was also an order that could be made by a criminal court after convicting a person of an offence.

---

[115] This substantially re-enacts s. 59 of the Powers of Criminal Courts (Sentencing) Act 2000.
[116] SGC, *New Sentences: Criminal Justice Act 2003*, para. 1.1.10. 99.
[117] For discussion of the conflicting policies of the two statutes, see Ashworth (2004).

Breach of the order was a criminal offence with a maximum sentence of 5 years' imprisonment.

Why are ASBOs relevant here? The reason, in brief, is that courts could make them in respect of behaviour that could be non-criminal or criminal, and when they were made in respect of criminal behaviour, this was in reality a response to persistent offending. The ASBO will disappear with the implementation of the Anti-Social Behaviour, Crime and Policing Act 2014, and will be replaced by two new measures, the Injunction to Prevent Nuisance and Annoyance (IPNA) and the Criminal Behaviour Order (CBO). The injunction, details of which may be found in Part 1 of the Act, is a civil measure (with a power of arrest attached if there is a risk of violence or harm to others) to be enforced by the ordinary processes of contempt of court. A civil court (or the youth court) will be able to make an injunction if it is satisfied on a balance of probabilities that the subject has engaged in, or threatened, conduct capable of causing nuisance or annoyance to any person, and that an injunction is just and convenient for the purpose of preventing further such behaviour. It is apparent from this summary that the injunction will be a considerable extension of the ASBO, although only available in the county court and other civil courts (for adults) and the youth court (for those under 18). The targeted behaviour goes beyond 'harassment, alarm or distress'[118] so as to include 'conduct capable of causing nuisance or annoyance to a person in relation to that person's occupation of residential premises', an objective test that turns on the two very broad concepts of 'nuisance' and 'annoyance'. Further, making an IPNA does not have to be 'necessary', as with the ASBO, but only 'just and convenient', a very wide phrase. Moreover, the standard of proof may be lower unless the courts insist, as they did with the ASBO,[119] that the serious consequences that may attend breach of the injunction call for a higher standard of proof equivalent to that in criminal cases. Two serious consequences indicate the need for this higher standard: first, the injunction may include prohibitions or 'require the respondent to do anything', a move to positive obligations without the provision of support for those subjected to them; secondly, although breach of an IPNA will not amount to a criminal offence, it can result in imprisonment for contempt. Given that some 57 per cent of ASBOs were breached, and some 53 per cent of those in breach were given a custodial sentence,[120] it is not clear how the civil courts will resist the pressure to impose many more prison sentences for contempt. Thus the demise of the ASBO gives rise to deep misgivings.[121]

---

[118] See the criticisms of Cornford (2012).

[119] *Clingham* v. *Kensington and Chelsea Royal LBC; R (McCann)* v. *Crown Court at Manchester* [2003] 1 AC 787.

[120] Ministry of Justice, *Anti-Social Behaviour Order Statistics England and Wales 2011.*

[121] For critical reviews of the proposals in the 2013 Bill, see House of Commons Home Affairs Committee, *The Draft Anti-Social Behaviour Bill: Pre-Legislative Scrutiny* (2013); and Liberty,

Turning to the Criminal Behaviour Order, details of which may be found in Part 2 of the Act, this can only be made by a criminal court following conviction and sentence for an offence. The court must be satisfied that the offender has engaged in behaviour likely to cause harassment, alarm, or distress and that making the order will help in preventing further such behaviour.[122] However, the order can include any prohibition or requirement with the purpose of preventing the offender from engaging in anti-social behaviour. Breach of a prohibition is an offence carrying a maximum penalty of 5 years' imprisonment, but at least there are provisions for supervision of persons subject to an order (s. 24). There remains the question of why there should be a minimum duration of 2 years for the order: it is not clear why this should not be left to the court, as is its maximum duration.[123] There are doubts about the need for the CBO, given the court's extensive sentencing powers (including community sentences, with their range of requirements), and given the possibility of seeking an IPNA from the civil courts. The substantial maximum penalty for breach of a CBO – 5 years' imprisonment – will ensure that it remains thoroughly disproportionate, and likely to result in further custodial sentences simply for disobedience of a court order (and not necessarily for harmful behaviour).

The CBO is open to many of the objections to ASBOs, of which the first is the response to breaches. Some 57 per cent of ASBOs were breached,[124] far higher than the proportion of conditional sentences and licence provisions that are breached. Moreover, the penalties for breach may be out of all proportion to the conduct involved. The maximum is 5 years' imprisonment – well above that for many criminal offences, and of course a particularly severe measure for non-criminal behaviour or the commission of a criminal offence that is non-imprisonable – and, as noted, some 53 per cent of breaches result in immediate custody. The propriety of sentencing an offender for breach by taking account of the whole course of anti-social conduct, including the behaviour that led to the imposition of the original order, is debatable. Stuart Macdonald argues that this is consistent with the purpose of introducing the ASBO and that, if proper procedural protections were introduced into the original hearings, courts should be allowed to impose what he terms 'composite' sentences.[125] However, significant changes would have to take place if this approach were to be consistent with proper principles of sentencing, such as the principle that no person should be sentenced for wrongdoing which has not been admitted or been the subject of a conviction.[126] The SGC's guideline

---

Committee Stage Briefing on the Anti-Social Behaviour, Crime and Policing Bill in the House of Commons (2013).

[122] The legislation on the ASBO required that the order be 'necessary', and the guidance issued by the Judicial Studies Board (2007) usefully elaborated on this requirement.

[123] The minimum is 2 years for adults; for those under 18, there is a minimum (1 year) and a maximum (3 years): s. 25 of the Act.

[124] Above, n. 120.   [125] Macdonald (2006).   [126] See ch. 8.1.2 below.

on ASBOs stated that an offender should be sentenced for the conduct that constitutes the breach, but that 'the original conduct that led to the making of an order is a relevant consideration in so far as it indicates the level of harm caused and whether this was intended'.[127] This does not endorse the principle of composite sentencing, but treats the original conduct as relevant to the context of the sentencing decision.

A further difficulty has been the proper approach to sentencing when the breach constitutes a separate criminal offence. The SGC guideline stated that, whether the other offence is prosecuted separately or not, the proper approach is to sentence for both wrongs – for example, treating the breach of the ASBO (now CBO) as an aggravating factor if only the substantive criminal offence is charged. Dealing with a matter that has caused considerable controversy,[128] the guideline stated:

> Where breach of an ASBO also constitutes another offence with a lower maximum penalty than that for breach of the order, this penalty is an element to be considered in the interests of proportionality, although the court is not limited by it when sentencing an adult or youth for breach.[129]

This principle creates a difficulty when, as with begging and soliciting for prostitution, Parliament has taken a deliberate decision to reduce the offence from imprisonable to non-imprisonable.[130] Moreover, it is in this realm that the CBO may be seen as one of several possible responses to persistent offending. In its present form[131] it is a response with some especially severe components: wide-ranging prohibitions may be included, and breach of any condition constitutes a criminal offence and a custodial sentence often follows. The SGC's guideline emphasizes that 'the main aim of sentencing for breach of a court order is to achieve the purpose of the order', and indicates that a community order should be the starting point for breaches where no harm is caused or intended, i.e. no harassment, alarm, or distress caused or intended, and 'breaches involving being drunk or begging' or 'prohibited use of public transport or entry into a prohibited area'.[132] Unless this guideline is applied rigorously, there remains the danger that sentences for breaching CBOs will sweep into prison many people in the category of 'persistent petty offenders'

---

[127] SGC, *Breach of an Anti-Social Behaviour Order* (2008), p. 4.

[128] E.g. in *Morrison* [2006] 1 Cr App R (S) 488, and *H, Stevens and Lovegrove* [2006] 2 Cr App R (S) 453.

[129] SGC, *Breach of an Anti-Social Behaviour Order*, para. 22.

[130] Criminal Justice Act 1982, ss. 70–71. Cf. *Fagan* [2011] 1 Cr App R (S) 619, where the Court of Appeal failed to take this point sufficiently seriously.

[131] In a different form, it might be seen as a less serious and more constructive response to persistent offending than that embodied in s. 143(2), permitting an offender to take liberty on conditions. However, even for that, the grounds for making the order should be established in criminal proceedings, the order should be shorter, and the penalty for breach should be less draconian.

[132] SGC, *Breach of an Anti-Social Behaviour Order*, pp. 2 and 8.

considered in part 6.5 above. The Bradley Report draws particular attention to the danger of vulnerable people being swept into the criminal justice system by these means.[133] Insofar as CBOs are used for otherwise non-criminal conduct, the use of custody is even more disproportionate.

There will be more discussion of civil preventive orders in Chapter 11 below. Suffice it to say here that many of the above arguments apply to other civil preventive orders that are often used as a response to persistent offending or 'anti-social' conduct, such as the serious crime prevention order (SCPO) and the sexual offending orders. There is no doubting the importance of preventing serious crime or sexual offences. The question is whether it is justifiable to depart so signally from proper sentencing principles.

6.7 Minimum sentences and selective incapacitation

It was noted above that supporters of the cumulative principle for sentencing recidivists have regarded it as a significant measure of crime prevention, even though the evidence for this is unpromising. Moreover, the claim is weakened by its failure to distinguish serious from non-serious offenders. Thus, although the statistics indicate that a person with five or more previous convictions is 90 per cent likely to commit another offence within six years, and probably fairly soon,[134] they do not tell us what type of crime that will be. The historical evidence suggests that pursuit of the cumulative principle would result in severe sentences for minor offenders.[135] Serious offenders are likely to receive substantial sentences on proportionality grounds, which have the side effect of incapacitating them for a few years at a time.

In the early 1980s it was claimed that a policy of lengthening prison sentences for selected robbers and burglars would have significant benefits in preventing these lucrative and feared offences.[136] However, a reassessment of the data by the US National Academy of Sciences concluded that they did not provide a secure basis for an effective policy of selective incapacitation.[137] Moreover, the data took insufficient account of the rate at which such offenders would desist from crime voluntarily.[138] Even if the predictive techniques could be refined, would such a policy be justified? Selective incapacitation would involve the imposition of disproportionately long sentences on a few offenders, identified not just by reference to their prior criminal record but also (in Greenwood's model) by reference to lifestyle factors such as drug use and employment record. The latter criteria raise issues of equality before the law and unequal treatment of the disadvantaged, which are discussed further

---

[133] Bradley (2009), ch. 2.   [134] See e.g. Halliday (2001), App. 3.

[135] See part 6.1 of this chapter.   [136] Greenwood (1982).

[137] Blumstein et al. (1986); see also the readings in von Hirsch, Ashworth and Roberts (2009), ch. 3.

[138] On which see Burnett and Maruna (2006) and McNeill (2006).

in Chapter 7. A deeper question of principle is whether such an offender may justifiably be sentenced more severely than is proportionate to the current offence(s).

In the United States this question has been answered in the affirmative, for reasons that mix deterrence, incapacitation, and retributive arguments. In the 1990s several states introduced cumulative sentencing laws under the popularized banner of 'three strikes and you're out', providing for lengthy or indefinite imprisonment on the third conviction. The Californian 'three strikes' law introduced in 1994 is probably the broadest in its effects, mandating a doubled sentence on the second serious felony and 25 years to life on the third felony conviction. There is no restriction on the types of offence involved, and, although the first two convictions must be for 'serious felonies', that category includes burglary. In 1994 the US Congress introduced a 'three strikes' law for the federal jurisdiction: it provides for life imprisonment on the third 'strike', but all three convictions must be for drug trafficking or for violent crime (broadly defined). A careful examination of the effects of the California law by Zimring, Hawkins and Kamin (2001) shows that the mandatory 'three strikes' sentence was imposed in only about 10 per cent of eligible cases because of prosecutorial and other discretion,[139] that there is little evidence of a significant crime-preventive effect (and the Governor in 1999 vetoed a bill which would have funded research into the effects of the law), and that even the political legend of 'three strikes' laws as a new tough policy against crime is a falsehood, in that the previous laws were hardly less repressive.[140]

The rationales for minimum, mandatory or presumptive sentencing regimes are mixed: the reduction of crime by deterrence or incapacitation is a major aim. However, the Californian evaluation and others[141] create major doubts about the effectiveness of those sentencing regimes in achieving their goals. Tonry's major review of the research evidence indicates no proven deterrent effects.[142] In addition to the preventive goal, Tonry identifies two other goals of mandatory sentences – even-handedness in sentencing, and transparency of the process. Even-handedness tends not to happen because mandatory sentences are often circumvented by prosecutors and/or judges, leading to the return of the discretion that the mandatory provisions were intended to remove. Transparency is likewise compromised, since negotiations with prosecutors take place out of the public eye. Moreover, the notions of both even-handedness and transparency assume a concept of justice that overlooks significant differences between offenders that ought properly to lead to different sentencing outcomes.

---

[139] Spohn (2002) cites similar findings in New York, Massachusetts, and Michigan.
[140] Zimring, Hawkins and Kamin (2001).   [141] Ibid.; see also Tonry (2009) and Spohn (2002).
[142] Tonry (2009), pp. 95–100.

Notwithstanding the weakness of these rationales, mandatory sentences retain a significant expressive force in political terms – they give the appearance that tough action is being taken to deal with the problem – and many countries across the world have introduced one or more.[143] The most recent mandatory minimum sentences in England and Wales have been targeted at all those committing a particular type of offence, whether first-time or repeaters.[144] Earlier, English interest in such expressive and repressive policies for persistent offenders culminated in the Crime (Sentences) Act 1997, which introduced three minimum sentences. The most severe of these measures, the automatic life sentence (a 'two strikes' measure), was abolished by the Criminal Justice Act 2003 to make way for a new sentencing framework for dangerous offenders (see part 6.8 below). Here we will examine the two others, conceived as 'prescribed' sentences for third-time offenders.

Section 3 of the 1997 Act (consolidated as s. 110 of the Powers of Criminal Courts (Sentencing) Act 2000) requires a court to pass a sentence of at least 7 years' imprisonment on a class A drug dealer who has two previous convictions for similar offences, unless it would be 'unjust to do so in all the circumstances'. This is a presumptive (not mandatory) minimum sentence, designed to create the impression that Parliament was taking a firm stand against drug dealers, when in fact it would be normal for a third-time class A drug dealer to receive a higher sentence than 7 years in any event,[145] unless there were strong mitigating factors. The legislation does allow the court to give up to 20 per cent discount for a guilty plea, but the courts have been left to develop the 'unjust to do so in all the circumstances' exception. In *Turner* (2006)[146] the Court reduced the sentence on the ground that the offender was not a commercial dealer but merely a go-between for friends. In *McDonagh* (2006)[147] the Court reduced the sentence because the previous qualifying conviction was some ten years earlier, a substantial gap.[148]

Section 4 of the 1997 Act (consolidated as s. 111 of the 2000 Act) requires a court to pass a sentence of at least 3 years' imprisonment on a domestic burglar aged at least 18 who has two previous convictions for domestic burglary, each of them after 1 December 1999, and each of them in respect of an offence committed after the previous conviction.[149] Again, the court does not have to impose the 'prescribed sentence' if it would be unjust in all the circumstances to do so; and, of course, it is free to go above the prescribed sentence, on the normal proportionality principles. As with the prescribed sentence for drug trafficking, a discount of up to 20 per cent is available for a

---

[143] Warner (2007); for developments in Canada, see Manson, Healy et al. (2008), pp. 451–80.
[144] See ch. 3.5 above.   [145] As in *Willoughby* [2003] 2 Cr App R (S) 257.
[146] [2006] 1 Cr App R (S) 565.   [147] [2006] 1 Cr App R (S) 647.
[148] This 'gap' principle is consistent with the law on previous convictions (see ch. 6.3.2 above).
[149] The trial judge misunderstood the required sequence in *Hoare* [2004] 2 Cr App R (S) 261, and consequently thought himself bound by the minimum sentence legislation when he was not.

guilty plea.[150] In the former guideline judgment on domestic burglary,[151] Lord Woolf CJ gave three examples of circumstances in which it may be unjust to impose the minimum sentence:

> The sentence could be unjust if two of the offences were committed many years earlier than the third offence; or if the offender made real efforts to reform or conquer his drug or alcohol addiction, but some personal tragedy triggers the third offence; or if the first two offences were committed when the offender was not yet 16.[152]

It seems likely that the court would also follow the decisions on the prescribed sentence for drug dealing, mentioned in the previous paragraph. Given the presumptive nature of these sentences and the large numbers of repeat burglars coming before the courts, one might expect s. 111 to be invoked frequently. However, only about 600–700 cases per year[153] appear to fulfil the restrictive requirements of s. 111, notably that each offence must have been committed after the previous offence was sentenced. No research is available to show either the impact of this minimum sentence on the prison population or its impact on crime prevention. However, it must be admitted that this minimum sentence has less mandatory force than those of many other jurisdictions, since 'unjust in all the circumstances' is a potentially wide exception: it appears that fewer than half of those burglars who qualify for the minimum sentence actually receive a sentence of 29 months or more (29 months being the minimum sentence with a 20 per cent reduction for pleading guilty).[154] Moreover, when sentencing a repeat burglar, the correct approach is to calculate the sentence according to the burglary guideline and only then to cross-check with s. 111, rather than to use 3 years' imprisonment as the starting point.[155]

The primary rationale for the two prescribed sentences was deterrent –'severe deterrent sentences for those who deal in hard drugs are ... essential'[156] – and we have seen how vigorously that was attacked by Lord Taylor CJ on the ground that the low detection rate would weaken any deterrent effect.[157] But there was also an incapacitative element to the government's case. There is little doubt that the idea behind these prescribed or minimum sentences was borrowed from the

---

[150] This is not true of the two mandatory minimum sentences for firearms (see ch. 1.5.2 above), not discussed here because they apply to first offenders as well as recidivists.

[151] *McInerney and Keating* [2003] 2 Cr App R (S) 240, now superseded by *Saw* [2009] EWCA Crim 1 and by Council guidelines; see ch. 4.4.9 above.

[152] [2003] 2 Cr App R (S) 240, at p. 251. Note that the first example accords with the well-known principle of recency, whereby a gap in offending should tell in the offender's favour, but that principle was not applied in *Willoughby*, n. 145 above.

[153] See the 5th edn, p. 227, Table 14, for earlier figures: the statistics appear to have been discontinued.

[154] *Sentencing Statistics 2007*, Table 6.12. This table records 491 eligible burglars given a custodial sentence, and Table 6.11 refers to a further 90 who were not sent to custody at all.

[155] *Andrews* [2013] 2 Cr App R (S) 26, [7–10].   [156] Home Office (1996), para. 11.2.

[157] See ch. 2.1 above.

United States, but it was borrowed without proper attention to the evidence on their operation. As noted earlier, the American research casts doubt on the effectiveness of minimum sentences. They should therefore be seen as a form of political symbolism designed to bolster the political fortunes of the government, and they are unworthy of any government that purports to engage in evidence-led policy-making.[158]

In the United States mandatory minimum sentences have been attacked on the principled ground that they may lead to disproportionate and therefore 'cruel and unusual punishment' contrary to the US Constitution. In *Lockyer* v. *Andrade* (2003)[159] the offender had been sentenced to twice life with a minimum of 50 years' imprisonment, consisting of two sentences of life imprisonment (each with a minimum term of 25 years) for two incidents of theft involving a total of 11 blank video tapes. The majority of judges in the Supreme Court held that this did not violate the 'gross disproportionality' test under the Constitution. The minority commented that 'if Andrade's sentence is not grossly disproportionate, the principle has no meaning'.[160]

6.8 'Dangerous offenders' and the 2012 Act

Many legal systems contain a special set of provisions aimed at protecting the public from offenders deemed 'dangerous'. English law has changed its 'dangerousness' provisions several times in recent decades. Some of the earlier statutory regimes remain relevant to the release of detained offenders, and some are relevant insofar as people are being convicted now of serious offences committed many years ago. For present purposes, the last three sets of 'dangerousness' provisions will be outlined briefly, before turning to the current provisions under the Legal Aid, Sentencing and Punishment of Offenders Act 2012.

For offences committed between 1997 and 2005, the sentencing structure under the Criminal Justice Act 1991 as amended by the Crime (Sentences) Act 1997 was in force – the automatic life sentence for the second life-carrying offence,[161] longer than proportionate sentences for sexual and violent offenders,[162] the original version of the extended sentence and the discretionary sentence of life imprisonment (which had survived from the common law). In the next phase, lasting from 2005 to 2008, the governing provisions were to be found in Chapter 5 of Part 12 of the Criminal Justice Act 2003. Sections 224–236 were headed 'Dangerous Offenders', and they introduced an entirely new regime for the sentencing of offenders classified as dangerous. The main feature was a mandatory framework for the sentencing of 'dangerous

---

[158] Cf. the powerful argument of Tonry (2004), ch. 1, with the analysis by Warner (2007).
[159] (2003) 123 S. Ct 1166, discussed by Van Zyl Smit and Ashworth (2004).
[160] Ibid., at p. 1179, per Souter J.   [161] On which see the 3rd edn of this work, pp. 193–6.
[162] See ibid., pp. 183–9.

offenders', requiring courts to impose one of three levels of sentence – imprisonment for life, imprisonment for public protection (IPP), or an extended sentence. However, the mandatory framework led to large numbers of offenders being subjected to IPP sentences: the range of qualifying offences was so wide that courts were frequently imposing IPP sentences for offences so low down the scale that the minimum term for some of them (calculated according to the seriousness of the offence of conviction) was only 12 or 18 months – after which they were liable to be detained indefinitely until they satisfied the conditions for release.

The injustice of subjecting so many non-serious offenders to indeterminate sentences was manifest and troubling, not to mention the effects on the prisons of this unexpected surge of offenders. In response, the government loosened the structure of the 2003 Act by means of amendments contained in the Criminal Justice and Immigration Act 2008. The main difference was that from 2008 to 2012 courts had the power but not the duty to impose one of the three levels of protective sentences where the qualifying conditions were met, and there was no longer a presumption of dangerousness for certain offenders.[163]

Most of the previous regime, and most obviously the IPP sentence, disappeared with the enactment of Part 3 of the Legal Aid, Sentencing and Punishment of Offenders Act 2012 – although over 5,000 IPP prisoners remain in prison past their minimum term, unable to persuade the Parole Board to release them.[164] This is notwithstanding the fact that for the first time a government acknowledged the shaky foundations of indeterminate sentences for public protection, stating that 'the limitations of our ability to predict future serious offending . . . [call] into question the whole basis on which many offenders are sentenced to IPPs'.[165] The new scheme retains the mandatory sentence of life imprisonment under the 2003 Act and retains life imprisonment at common law, and introduces two new dangerousness sentences – an automatic sentence of life imprisonment for the second very serious conviction, and a revised version of the extended sentence.

6.8.1 Mandatory life imprisonment

The most severe sentence that can be imposed on a dangerous offender remains life imprisonment. Section 225 of the 2003 Act is unaffected by the 2012 Act, and *requires* a court to impose life imprisonment if it is of the opinion that there is

---

[163] For analysis of the law under the Acts of 2003 and 2008, see the 5th edn of this work, pp. 228–35.
[164] See *James, Wells and Lee* v. *United Kingdom* (2013) 56 EHRR 399.
[165] Ministry of Justice (2010), at [186].

> - a significant risk to members of the public of serious harm occasioned by the commission by him of further specified offences

and the court has considered that

> - the seriousness of the offence, or the offence and one or more offences associated with it, is such as to justify the imposition of a sentence of imprisonment for life.

Thus, if the conditions are met, it is mandatory for the court to impose life imprisonment. The second condition is not clear about the level at which the bar must be set: at common law the offence itself always had to be of a certain gravity before life imprisonment could be imposed, but it was never clear where the line should be drawn (although there was some authority suggesting that the current offence(s) had to be worth at least a sentence of 7 years' imprisonment).[166] This question was less pressing between 2003 and 2012 when the courts had the IPP sentence available, since that was also indeterminate and in some respects indistinguishable from life imprisonment. Thus in *Kehoe* (2009)[167] the Court of Appeal quashed a sentence of life imprisonment in favour of an IPP sentence for manslaughter on grounds of diminished responsibility. The minimum term was set at 3 years (less the period held on remand). The Court stated that life sentences 'should be reserved for those cases where the culpability of the offender is particularly high or the offence itself particularly grave'. However, the Court of Appeal has now decided that life imprisonment may be imposed in cases that would previously have attracted an IPP sentence,[168] arguing (doubtfully) that this is what Parliament intended. This makes it all the more important to determine the minimum sentence level at which life imprisonment may properly be imposed.

At common law there was often mention of a further requirement – evidence of mental instability, or some imponderable element that indicated the appropriateness of an indeterminate sentence. However, in *McNee, Gunn and Russell* (2008)[169] the Court of Appeal accepted this as the general principle, but went on to hold that instability of that kind is not necessary in all cases. This was a decision on the common law, not the 2003 Act, and Sir Igor Judge P stated that the imposition of life imprisonment 'did not require medical evidence suggesting irrationality, or instability of the personality, for this purpose. The danger could be represented by a wholly rational individual.' The judge was entitled to make his own judgment. In this case, the calculating manner in which the offenders had planned the

---

[166] *Gray* [1983] Crim LR 691.   [167] [2009] 1 Cr App R (S) 4.

[168] *Saunders* [2014] 1 Cr App R 258, followed in *Burinskas; Attorney General's Reference No. 27 of 2013* [2014] 2 Cr App R (S) 359, esp. at [8].

[169] [2008] 1 Cr App R (S) 108. To the same effect, see the judgment of Lord Phillips CJ in *Barot* [2008] 1 Cr App R (S) 156, also on the pre-2005 law.

revenge killing of two people (which was carried out by unknown hitmen) was held a sufficient basis for concluding that the offenders constituted 'a continuing risk for the indefinite future'.

Where the conditions are satisfied and the court decides that the offence(s) justify life imprisonment, the court must specify a minimum term – by taking the determinate sentence that would be proportionate to the current offence (s), halving it to take account of normal release provisions, and then subtracting any period spent on remand.[170] In *Hogg* (2008),[171] it was held inappropriate for the trial judge not to have set a minimum term, on grounds of the extreme danger of further child abuse by an unrepentant offender, and the Court of Appeal set a 10-year term. In *McNee, Gunn and Russell* Sir Igor Judge P held that in a case of conspiracy to murder it was proper for the court to have regard to Schedule 21 of the 2003 Act (minimum terms for murder), and, given the facts of that case, upheld minimum terms of 25, 35 and 30 years for the offenders.[172] Those are to be taken to reflect determinate sentences of double that length. Similarly in *Barot* (2008),[173] the Court of Appeal held that a minimum term of 30 years was appropriate for a terrorist involved in a conspiracy to commit mass murder, reducing it from the 40 years (equivalent to a determinate sentence of 80 years) set by the trial judge. Once the minimum term has expired, the offender's release is a matter for the Parole Board, which should order release on licence only when satisfied that detaining the offender is no longer necessary for the protection of the public (see s. 28 of the Crime (Sentences) Act 1997).

Thus far in this discussion we have been focusing on the legislative framework in the 2003 Act for the imposition of life imprisonment. Although the discussion is entitled 'Discretionary Life Imprisonment', the wording of s. 225 of the 2003 Act is mandatory – a court 'must' impose life imprisonment if the conditions are fulfilled. However, one logical consequence of this wording is that it does not abolish the genuinely discretionary sentence of life imprisonment that was available at common law. So, as argued by Thomas and accepted by the Court of Appeal in *Saunders*,[174] there remains a discretion to impose life imprisonment even where the conditions in s. 255 are not fulfilled. This is life imprisonment at common law, and its requirements are as stated already.

Finally, what determines release from life imprisonment? The judge will have specified a minimum term and, provided that it is not a whole life term,[175] the expiry of that term is the first condition for release. After that, the Parole Board should direct the release of the lifer when it is satisfied that it

---

[170] *Marklew and Lambert* [1999] 1 Cr App R (S) 6; *Attoney General's Reference No. 3 of 2004 (Akuffo)* [2005] 1 Cr App R (S) 230, at p. 240.
[171] [2008] 1 Cr App R (S) 99.   [172] See n. 170 above and accompanying text.
[173] [2008] 1 Cr App R (S) 156.
[174] See the commentaries on *Cardwell* [2013] Crim LR 508 and on *Saunders* [2013] Crim LR 930.
[175] On which see *Vinter* v. *United Kingdom* [2014] Crim LR 81, and the discussion in ch.4.4.1.

is no longer necessary for the protection of the public that the prisoner should be confined.[176] This is a predictive decision, and the Parole Board has naturally been cautious in its release policy.[177] A released lifer remains on licence for the remainder of his life, and is subject to recall if there are any risk factors that give reasonable cause for regarding him as a risk to the public – meaning that he can be returned to prison indefinitely on account of something that it is thought he might do.[178]

6.8.2 Life imprisonment for a second listed offence

Part 3 of the 2012 Act introduces, by way of amendment of the 2003 Act, a new sentence of mandatory life imprisonment. The formal title is life imprisonment 'for a second listed offence', and the list is to be found in a revised Schedule 15B inserted into the 2003 Act. The list contains 44 offences plus murder, some of the offences not carrying life imprisonment. If the offender is aged at least 18 and committed a listed offence after the commencement of this Part of the 2012 Act, he must be sentenced to life imprisonment (unless the court finds 'particular circumstances' that would make it unjust to impose the required sentence) if two further conditions are satisfied. Those two conditions are the 'sentence condition' and the 'previous offence' condition, set out in the new s. 224A as follows:

(3) The sentence condition is that, but for this section, the court would, in compliance with sections 152(2) and 153(3), impose a sentence of imprisonment for 10 years or more, disregarding any extension period imposed under section 226B;

(4) The previous offence condition is that (a) at the time the offence was committed, the offender had been convicted of an offence listed in Schedule 15B ('the previous offence'), and (b) a relevant life sentence or a relevant sentence of imprisonment or detention for a determinate period was imposed on the offender for the previous offence.

The effect of the sentence condition is to narrow down the range of application considerably, since the current offence must have otherwise warranted a final sentence of at least 10 years – which means, for example, that if the offender had received full credit for an early plea of guilty, the offence would need to have been 'worth' 15 years in order to produce a final sentence of 10 years. Very few offenders will fulfil this condition. The effect of the 'previous offence' condition is that the offender must have received either a determinate sentence of at least 10 years, or a life or IPP sentence with a minimum term of at least 5 years (leaving out of account any credit for time spent awaiting trial). This is the meaning of a 'relevant' sentence, and once again its effect is significantly to

---

[176] Crime (Sentences) Act 1997, s. 28(6)(b).   [177] See Padfield, Morgan and Maguire (2012).
[178] Appleton (2010), p. 36.

narrow down the pool of available offenders. Where this sentence is imposed, the conditions of release are as for discretionary life imprisonment (above).

The narrow focus of the new sentence of life imprisonment for a second listed offence is to be welcomed. Whereas the IPP sentence was over-broad and therefore unjust in its scope, this new sentence is defined so as to capture only people who have committed two very serious offences (of the kinds listed in the new Schedule 15B). Indeed, whereas the 'automatic life sentence' introduced in 1997 was mandatory save for the court's finding of 'exceptional circumstances', this new sentence is not mandatory, and if the court decides that there are particular circumstances that make it unjust to impose life imprisonment, it is not bound to do so.

The main drawback of the new arrangements is the continued availability of the discretionary life sentence – that is, if the courts fail to insist on a sufficiently high threshold for imposing that sentence, the consequence may be the imposition of indeterminate sentences on a significant number of those previously sentenced to IPP. This would be unjust for the reasons given above. Indeed, the then government conceded that IPP sentences perpetrated an injustice on many of those receiving the sentence, and it would be unfortunate if the judges were to reinstate the source of that injustice.

6.8.3 Extended sentences

The extended sentence applies to all 'specified offences' listed in a new Schedule 15B. This new Schedule is one of the few changes of substance introduced by the Legal Aid, Sentencing and Punishment of Offenders Act 2012, which replaces s. 227 of the 2003 Act with a new s. 226A. The four conditions are:

- the offence of conviction is a specified offence, within Schedule 15B,
- life imprisonment is either unavailable or not justified,
- the court considers the offender 'dangerous', in the sense that there is a significant risk to members of the public of serious harm occasioned by the commission by him of further specified offences,
- either the offender has a previous conviction for an offence listed in Schedule 15B, or the current offence justifies a custodial term of at least four years.[179]

The distinctive element of extended sentences is that the court must also fix the extension period to be applied to the offender. Section 226(a) states that the extension period should be 'of such length as the court considers necessary for the purpose of protecting members of the public from serious harm occasioned by the commission by him of further specified offences', although the extension period is limited to 5 years for specified violent offences and 8 years for specified sexual offences. In the guideline judgment

---

[179] Criminal Justice Act 2003 (as amended), s. 227(2B).

on the pre-2005 form of extended sentences (which is of no more than persuasive value post-2005), the Court of Appeal pointed out that there is nothing inconsistent in having an extension period longer than the appropriate custodial sentence, since the criteria are different. The latter should be proportionate to the seriousness of the current offence(s), whereas the former is determined by predictions of future behaviour. Even though the offender may actually serve some or most of the extension period in prison if the licence conditions are violated, 'it would be illogical to require strict proportionality between the duration of the extension period and the seriousness of the offence', although proportionality does 'have some relevance' to the overall sentence.[180] The aggregate of the custodial term and the extension period must not exceed the maximum penalty for the offence.

The effect of an extended sentence was altered by the 2012 Act: whereas previously release was automatic after serving half the custodial term, the general principle now is that release is automatic after serving two-thirds of the sentence. However, there are two exceptions to this: if either the appropriate custodial term is 10 years or more, or the extended sentence was imposed for an offence listed in Part 1 of Schedule 15B, release is a matter for the Parole Board. Release should only be ordered if the Board is satisfied that it is no longer necessary for the protection of the public that the extended sentence prisoner be detained. Release is on licence for the full extension period, subject to recall if the conditions are not observed. As with release from life imprisonment and any subsequent recall, immense power is bestowed on the Parole Board without any of the detailed guidance now provided for sentencers in the Council guidelines.[181] Admittedly the Parole Board is dealing with risk and prediction, whereas most guidelines are concerned with proportionality and relative seriousness, but this strengthens rather than weakens the case for principled guidance on the practical decisions to be taken. This will be more urgent when s. 4 of the Criminal Justice and Courts Act 2015 comes into force, placing all decisions on release after two-thirds in the hands of the Parole Board.

6.8.4 Dangerousness – the trigger condition

It is apparent that, before a court imposes either discretionary life imprisonment, life imprisonment for a second listed offence, or an extended sentence, it must make certain predictive findings about the offender. Essentially, as the guidance provided by the Court of Appeal makes clear,[182] the focus of this element in the decision is upon prediction and protection, and there are

---

[180] *Nelson* [2002] 1 Cr App R (S) 565.
[181] Padfield (2008), p. 464; Ashworth and Zedner (2014), pp. 157–61.
[182] See particularly Rose LJ in *Lang* [2006] 1 Cr App R (S) 13 and Sir Igor Judge P in *Johnson* [2007] 1 Cr App R (S) 674.

two linked points on which the court must be satisfied. First, is there a significant risk of the offender committing further specified offences? Secondly, is there a significant risk that such offences will cause serious harm to members of the public?

The assessment of dangerousness in this context is now a question for the judgment of the court: the 2003 Act had created a presumption of dangerousness for some offenders (those with a previous conviction for a specified offence), but that presumption was over-inclusive and was abolished by the 2008 amendments. The court should reach its judgment on the basis of all the available information about the nature of the current offence, the nature and circumstances of any other offence of which the offender has been convicted in any part of the world, and any information about the offender and about any pattern of behaviour of which the offence forms part.

Turning to the first point on which the court must be satisfied, is there a significant risk of the offender committing further specified offences? Those offences may be either offences of violence or sexual offences, as set out in Schedule 15B. The risk must be 'significant': Parliament could have selected the adjective 'substantial' but it did not, and it may therefore be argued that 'significant' means not insignificant, or more than minimal. The Court in *Lang* thought it appropriate to take account of D's social circumstances, thinking, emotional state, and attitude towards offending (so far as those appear from a pre-sentence report).[183] The Court in *Johnson* added that the existence or non-existence of previous convictions does not determine dangerousness. The judge must consider the whole offending history, particularly the facts of the current offence and any previous offences. The Court also stated that previous offences do not have to be 'specified' (in terms of Schedule 15B) in order to be relevant, and that a series of minor previous offences of gradually escalating seriousness may be particularly relevant.[184] The court must assess future risk at the time of sentence, and not attempt to assess the risk the offender might pose on release.[185]

The second, linked and more important point on which the court must be satisfied is whether those predicted offences create a significant risk of serious harm to members of the public. The issues here are not merely the degree of risk, 'significant', but also the nature of the predicted harm, 'serious'. Section 224 defines 'serious harm' as meaning 'death or serious personal injury, whether physical or psychological'. Thus a prediction of further repetitive low-level offending will not meet the seriousness threshold. The fact that the predicted offences are 'serious offences' within the meaning of the Act does not mean that they necessarily create a risk of causing serious harm.[186] Thus in *McGrady* (2007)[187] the judge had formed the view that there was a high risk of

---

[183] [2006] 1 Cr App R (S) 13, at [17]; see also *Cheshire* [2014] 2 Cr App R (S) 430.
[184] [2007] 1 Cr App R (S) 674, at [10].   [185] *MJ* [2012] 2 Cr App R (S) 416.
[186] *Lang* [2006] 1 Cr App R (S) 13, at [17].   [187] [2007] 1 Cr App R (S) 256.

further robberies by D, but the current robbery was essentially a bag-snatch and the Court of Appeal held that robberies without the use of a weapon or significant force did not necessarily give rise to a significant risk of serious harm. However, in *Johnson* Sir Igor Judge P put the point that a court may find such a risk even though the current offence or previous offences resulted in no actual harm. Thus if an offender was carrying a weapon but did not use it, the court may still conclude that he presents a significant risk of causing serious harm.[188] It also seems that the court may treat an old offence as relevant, even if it was committed many years previously.[189]

The 2003 Act (as amended by the 2012 Act) provides a parallel to the extended sentence for offenders aged under 18. The guidance published by the Sentencing Guidelines Council urges that 'the court should be particularly rigorous before concluding that a youth is a dangerous offender', and refers to Youth Justice Board guidance that anticipates that such a finding would only be made where a pre-sentence report finds a 'very high risk' of serious harm or, 'in a small number of cases and due to specific circumstances, a high risk of serious harm'.[190]

6.8.5 The empirical evidence

The difficulties of predicting whether a particular person will constitute a danger to others are well documented in the criminological literature. The Floud Committee's survey of the available studies three decades ago revealed that no method of prediction had managed to do better than predicting one false positive for every true positive, that is a 50 per cent success rate in predicting 'dangerousness'. Indeed, many of the prediction methods had only a one-third success rate.[191] Part of the problem is that really serious crimes are rare events, and therefore particularly hard to predict with accuracy. The Floud Report also confirmed that actuarial methods of prediction, based on selected objective characteristics of the offender, were generally more reliable than clinical predictions, based on the judgment of experienced diagnosticians – an important finding, since there is a natural tendency in the courts to respect the judgments of experienced psychiatrists, despite this evidence of fallibility. Around the same time there was a Home Office study by Brody and Tarling, which involved clinicians reviewing the records of over 700 prisoners and selecting those who might be termed 'dangerous' on certain criteria. Of those who were so classified, 48 had been released and their records were examined for the 5 years following release. It was found that 9 of them committed 'dangerous' offences during that period. This means that, if all of

---

[188] [2007] 1 Cr App R (S) 674, at [10], discussing *Shaffi* [2006] 2 Cr App R (S) 606.
[189] Cf. the reference to recent and relevant convictions in s. 143(2), discussed in ch. 6.3 above.
[190] SGC, *Overarching Principles – Sentencing Youths* (2008), p. 18.
[191] Floud and Young (1981), App. C.

them had been detained for an additional 5 years on the basis of the prediction of dangerousness, there would have been 9 true positives and 39 false positives – a successful prediction rate of around 20 per cent only. It is also noteworthy, since public protection is often said to be the aim here, that 9 of the 700 non-dangerous offenders who had been released had also committed a 'dangerous' offence during the 5-year period.[192] In other words, the risk of being the victim of one of these serious offences was as great from the large number of 'non-dangerous' as from the small number of 'dangerous' offenders.

It is also true that, even if the current offence is one of violence, this does not suggest that any subsequent offending will be of the same kind.[193] As Skeem and Monahan conclude, 'clinicians are relatively inaccurate predictors of violence'.[194] Hood and Shute have pointed out the difficulty of using offences of conviction (or previous offences) as the main index of 'high risk'.[195] And Hood et al. have also shown that fewer than 10 per cent of serious sexual offenders released from prison commit another sex offence within six years, and that Parole Board members tend to overestimate considerably the risk presented by sex offenders. As they comment, 'attempts to predict reconviction when the "base rate" is low inevitably produce a high rate of "false positives"'.[196] Other research on the risk assessment of offenders believed to be 'dangerous' gives few grounds for optimism:[197] there is little research into the effectiveness of predictions of serious harm by offenders who are not diagnosed as mentally disordered. Predictions for those who are so diagnosed still do not have a high rate of success,[198] and the Bradley Report recommended a close study of the relationship between IPP sentencing and mental disorder and disability.[199] It bears repeating that in 2010 the government stated that 'the limitations of our ability to predict future serious offending ... [call] into question the whole basis on which many offenders are sentenced to IPPs'.[200]

6.8.6 Arguments of principle[201]

Despite the poor prospects for accurate predictions at even a 50 per cent rate, the imposition of disproportionate sentences on offenders believed to be dangerous remains attractive to politicians and legislators, and to some extent to members of the judiciary, in the hope of improving the protection of the public. How, if at all, can such disproportionate deprivations of liberty be

[192] Brody and Tarling (1981), pp. 29–30.   [193] See Farrington (1997).
[194] Skeem and Monahan (2011), p. 39.   [195] Hood and Shute (1996).
[196] Hood, Shute, Feilzer and Wilcox (2002).
[197] Brown (1998); Brown and Pratt (2000); Harcourt (2007).   [198] Monahan (2004).
[199] Bradley (2009), ch. 4.
[200] Ministry of Justice (2010), at [186]; in similar vein, House of Commons (2008), paras. 39–85.
[201] See further Ashworth and Zedner (2014), chs. 6 and 7.

justified? The Floud Committee concluded that the question is really a matter of the just redistribution of risk, between a known offender and a potential victim of a predicted offence. It is a moral choice between competing claims: who should bear the risk? Generally, they argued, everyone is presumed to be harmless. But once a person has manifested, by committing a serious crime, the capacity to be harmful to others, that presumption no longer applies. It may therefore be justifiable to redistribute the risk of future harms by protecting the potential victims (who are unlikely to have lost the presumption of harmlessness) and by burdening the known offender (who has lost the benefit of that presumption). Although they proposed various procedural safeguards for defendants before a protective sentence could be imposed, the Committee concluded that the redistribution of risk should favour potential victims.[202]

However, reliance on a previous offence to rebut the presumption of harmlessness cannot safely be regarded as sufficient evidence of a continuing disposition to wrongdoing in the future. An alternative approach is suggested by Walen who contends that convicted offenders 'have, at least for a while, lost the moral basis for claiming the right to benefit from the respect that grounds the immunity to LTPD' (long-term preventive detention).[203] He argues that whereas the state ought normally to accord its citizens the presumption that they will be law-abiding 'as a matter of basic respect for their autonomous moral agency',[204] conviction for a very serious crime or string of serious crimes demonstrates 'that they do not deserve the presumption that they will be law-abiding'.[205] Yet here too it is unclear for what period this loss of status should persist or how it might be regained. Walen avers that his approach preserves the presumption of innocence in respect of future charges and thus avoids vulnerability to undeserved punishment, though his claim relies upon the ability and willingness of the courts to observe this fine distinction in practice. It relies also on acceptance of the claim that preventive detention is not punishment because it is not intended by the court as such and does not express censure for wrongs done (of which more below).[206] It is difficult to escape the objection that for the state to take such power over individuals is an unacceptable incursion into their autonomy. It denies that they can be trusted to make the right choices in given situations, endowing them (on the basis of one or more previous offences) with a character trait of which they are deemed incapable of ridding themselves. Of course there are many acts of the state that curtail individual autonomy, from taxation onwards. Floud and her followers take the view that there must be some balancing of the offender's right to liberty (certain to be lost if the sentence is lengthened for preventive reasons) against the potential victim's freedom from harm (of unspecified magnitude, at an unspecified rate of probability). The resolution of this conflict is by no

---

[202] Floud and Young (1981), chs. 3 and 4.   [203] Walen (2011), p. 1231.   [204] Ibid., pp. 1230–31.
[205] Ibid., p. 1231.   [206] See Ashworth and Zedner (2014), ch. 7.1.

means straightforward, but the fallibility of predictions and the already pre-ventive effect of proportionate sentences should weigh heavily.

6.9 Conclusion

Both persistent offenders and those predicted to be dangerous present difficulties for the theory and practice of sentencing. As this chapter shows, the current trend for sentencing persistent offenders (evident in s. 143(2) of the 2003 Act) is in the direction of a cumulative principle, and tends to neglect the work of criminologists and practitioners on desistance from crime. Unless clear guidance to the contrary is given, courts will (continue to) concentrate on the offender's record rather than the current offence, at least after two or three convictions. This is objectionable because the offence is then used as a mere peg on which to hang allegedly preventive (and sometimes severe) measures, with little regard for the seriousness of the current offence. As the Justice Committee of the House of Commons argued, this approach to non-serious persistent offenders should be abandoned as ill-founded and unjust.[207] The same objection can be levelled at criminal behaviour orders, which seem unlikely to differ significantly in practice from anti-social behaviour orders, which had both a high breach rate and a high custody rate for breach, even when the behaviour in question was either non-criminal or non-imprisonable.

It has been noted that some kind of incapacitative or 'public protection' sentence is found politically attractive in many jurisdictions. However, the British government came to recognize that the 2003 Act's regime of three mandatory 'dangerousness' measures of ascending severity – extended sen-tences, imprisonment for public protection, and life imprisonment – was an over-repressive mistake. It swept far too many offenders into the prisons for indeterminate sentences that were not justified either by predictive accuracy or by the seriousness of the latest offence. In the 2010 Green Paper the incoming coalition government confronted the point that dangerous offender provisions such as the IPP were (and were well known to be) based on theoretically and criminologically doubtful foundations.[208] Yet successive governments have failed to invest resources in rehabilitative programmes by which over 5,000 IPP prisoners might tackle the causes of their supposed dangerousness. In *James, Wells and Lee* v. *UK*, the European Court of Human Rights found that the period of post-tariff detention served by the applicants was 'arbitrary and therefore unlawful within the meaning of Article 5 § 1' ECHR.[209] It heard evidence that, despite the fact that IPP had been premised on rehabilitative treatment being made available to prisoners, there had been considerable

---

[207] House of Commons (2008), paras. 107–8.
[208] Ministry of Justice (2010), at [186]; in similar vein, House of Commons (2008), paras. 39–85.
[209] *James, Wells and Lee* v. *UK* (2013) 56 EHRR 399, at [221].

delays in its provision, such that the applicants 'had no realistic chance of making objective progress' towards parole.[210] The Court accepted that 'any review of dangerousness which took place in the absence of the completion of relevant treatment courses was likely to be an empty exercise'.[211] These difficulties have not been remedied in the three years since the judgment in *James, Wells and Lee*. Some comfort may be taken from the fact that the dangerousness sentencing framework introduced by the 2012 Act is much more restrained, although that depends on the way in which the mandatory and discretionary life sentences are used. It remains the case that England and Wales have far more prisoners serving indeterminate sentences than any other West European country, amounting to almost 20 per cent of their relatively high prison population. Governments have tended to use the political irresistibility of the claim of public protection to promote repressive measures with weak evidential foundations. There is no political constituency of support for persons labelled 'dangerous', but there remain strong arguments based on principle and on human rights for continuing to press home criticisms of these measures.

---

[210] Ibid., at [220].   [211] Ibid., at [212].

7

Equality before the law

7.1 The principle and its challengers

The constitutions of many countries proclaim a principle of equality before the law or non-discrimination, or at least a general principle of equality.[1] There is no British Constitution as such, but (as we saw in Chapter 2.7 above) the Human Rights Act 1998 brings into UK law most articles of the European Convention on Human Rights. Article 14 declares that the enjoyment of all the rights declared in the Convention shall be secured 'without discrimination on any ground such as sex, race, colour, language, religion, political or other opinion, national or social origin, association with a national minority, property, birth or other status'. This is not a general principle of non-discrimination, since it applies only to discrimination in respect of rights declared in the Convention, but it is nevertheless important.[2]

In English law the Equality Acts 2006 and 2010 establish a general legal anti-discrimination framework, monitored by the Equality and Human Rights Commission. The protected characteristics are age, disability, gender, gender reassignment, pregnancy and maternity, race, religion or belief, sex, and sexual

---

[1] See von Hirsch, Ashworth and Roberts (2009), p. 343.
[2] Protocol 12 to the Convention includes substantive and broader protection against discrimination, but it has not been ratified by the UK: Wintemute (2004).

orientation. Section 149(1) of the 2010 Act requires public authorities to a) eliminate discrimination or harassment on any of these grounds, b) advance equality of opportunity for those with a protected characteristic, and c) foster good relations between those persons and others. While duty a) is negative, duties b) and c) require public authorities to take positive action – an important feature of the law, since the criminal justice system alone cannot hope to bring about changes in social attitudes or opportunities.[3] It can be argued that a sentencing system that places emphasis on proportionality should leave no room for discrimination, since courts should focus on the seriousness of the offence in each case. However, we have seen in Chapter 3 that s. 142 of the Criminal Justice Act 2003 appears to allow courts to pursue other purposes apart from proportionality; in Chapter 5 that some of the recognized aggravating and mitigating factors are not linked to proportionality principles; and in Chapter 6 that previous convictions and predictions of dangerousness can play a prominent part in sentencing. Moreover, although there are sentencing guidelines for many offences, a margin of discretion has been preserved, especially in respect of mitigation and aggravation, and discretion raises the possibility of discriminatory practices.

This chapter therefore seeks to examine both issues of principle and evidence of sentencing practice, in order to pursue certain thematic questions. Does English sentencing practice give grounds for believing that discriminatory factors are present in some cases? Even if discriminatory elements are not evident as primary reasons for sentence, do they exert an indirect influence through other factors such as unemployment, previous record, or previous remand in custody? And, if so, should the principle of non-discrimination always be accorded greater weight than other relevant principles?

The first and second questions are matters for empirical inquiry, and the evidence will be reviewed briefly below in relation to race, gender, employment status, social status, and other factors. The focus here is on sentencing but, as argued in Chapter 1.4, sentencing is merely a single stage in a sequence of decisions in the criminal process, and practices at earlier stages might exert a considerable (though perhaps unrecognized) influence on sentencing. On some of the points the available evidence is inconclusive, and definitive studies are awaited.

The third question goes to the foundations of sentencing policy. It is sometimes presented as the issue of whether the sentencing system should simply try to avoid discrimination in its own decisions, or whether sentences should be calculated in an effort to counteract discriminatory forces which are known to operate more widely – leading in some instances to a kind of positive discrimination. This important issue is also linked to more specific issues. For example, how should the principle of parsimony be related to the

---

[3] See Player (2012), pp. 245–7.

principle of equality before the law? Norval Morris and Michael Tonry take a strong line: 'To insist that criminal A go to jail or prison because resources are lacking to deal sensibly with criminal B is to pay excessive tribute to an illusory ideal of equality.'[4] They are content to see a white or employed person receive a non-custodial sentence in the same circumstances in which a black or unemployed person would be incarcerated. This furthers parsimony, in the sense that fewer people would be incarcerated by subordinating the principle of equality before the law in such instances. Morris and Tonry would rather have the system discriminatory than uniformly punitive. Others would argue that equality before the law is simply not negotiable: it is a principle which should not be compromised, and any concerns about over-punitiveness should be tackled through the overall system rather than by discriminating between individual offenders.[5]

Another aspect of this argument is that available statistics tend to suggest that those who suffer from certain social disadvantages (e.g. unemployed, no fixed address, no close family ties) are more likely to be reconvicted than those who are socially well-established. A preventive sentencing strategy might therefore lead to the imposition of more onerous sentences on the disadvantaged, and correspondingly less onerous sentences on the well-established. This, however, would be to pursue prevention at a fairly superficial level. Prevention at a deeper level requires a social strategy which tackles housing, employment, community facilities, and related matters. To pursue preventive strategies through sentencing is as short-sighted as it is unjust. Thus Elaine Player argues that 'the equality legislation could exercise an important restraining influence over the tyranny of risk assessment and the increasing punitiveness of sentences deemed necessary for public protection'.[6] References will be made to these themes in various parts below, and the arguments of principle will be reviewed in a concluding discussion.

7.2 Race[7]

The clearest application of the principle of equality before the law is that no person should be sentenced more severely on account of race or colour. Is there evidence that blacks, Asians or any other ethnic group are treated more severely than whites?[8] In 2013 some 26 per cent of people in prison were non-white. Just over a third of these were foreign nationals.[9] Among the non-white British nationals, by far the largest group was 'Black or

---

[4] Morris and Tonry (1990), p. 33.

[5] However, this should not rule out pilot schemes and local experiments for new measures.

[6] Player (2012), pp. 264–5.   [7] Bowling and Phillips (2002); Phillips and Bowling (2012).

[8] The term 'blacks' is used here to refer to people from an African-Caribbean background, the term 'Asians' includes both people from a background in the Indian sub-continent and those of south-east Asian origin. Neither term is ideal.

[9] Berman and Dar (2013), pp. 10–11.

Black British',[10] with an imprisonment rate of about ten times that of white people.[11] Does this indicate discrimination in sentencing?

Apart from the fact that the prison population statistics include remand prisoners and others, it must be recalled that the offenders who come up for sentence in the courts are a selected group, resulting from various patterns of reporting, investigating, and filtering in the pre-trial stages. The importance of regarding the sentence of the court as merely one stage in a lengthy process, signalled in Chapter 1.4, must be emphasized here.[12] It can be shown, for example, that of persons stopped and searched by the police in 2009, 15 per cent were black and 9 per cent Asian.[13] A wider power to search without suspicion under s. 60 of the Criminal Justice and Public Order Act 1994 is now used more frequently: compared with white people, 'black people [were] nearly 27 times more frequently stopped and searched. Asians were more than six times as likely to be searched.'[14] The charges brought against black people show a relatively high rate of victimless, preparatory and public order offences,[15] and a high rate of charges of robbery.[16] The extent to which these differences reflect real offending patterns or the influence of racial stereotypes on reporting and investigation remains to be examined. However, they certainly have consequences in the criminal process, inasmuch as a higher proportion of blacks appear at the Crown Court rather than the magistrates' courts[17] – notably because robbery is triable only in the Crown Court and not because more blacks elect to be tried there – and, partly in consequence, a higher proportion of blacks are remanded in custody.[18]

It would therefore be a mistake to point to the sentencing statistics for black and white offenders or, even worse, the numbers of black and white offenders in prison, and to argue that the racial imbalance demonstrates discrimination in sentencing. Even if the courts pursued an absolutely impartial sentencing policy, the results would appear discriminatory because of the already skewed group of offenders coming before them. The need, therefore, is for research into those earlier processes; and, at the sentencing stage, for research which takes proper account of all the major variables in sentencing (e.g. type of offence, previous convictions, and so forth), which distinguishes at least between blacks, Asians, and whites (rather than grouping blacks and Asians together), which distinguishes between the Crown Court and magistrates' courts, and which has sufficiently large numbers of non-whites in its sample. The study carried out in the West Midlands by Roger Hood (1992) meets most

[10] The Ministry of Justice statistics (ibid.) also show that over a quarter of the women in prison are black, and a majority of these are foreign nationals (often, drug couriers); see ch. 7.3 below.
[11] Phillips and Bowling (2012), p. 386.
[12] See further Fitzgerald (1993) and Bowling and Phillips (2002).
[13] Phillips and Bowling (2012), p. 381.   [14] Ibid., p. 382.
[15] Hood (1992), pp. 144–5. This category included drug offences.   [16] Hood (1992), ch. 8.
[17] Ibid., p. 442; Hood (1992), p. 51; Fitzgerald (1993), p. 21.   [18] Hood (1992), pp. 148–9.

of these desiderata, although it was confined to Crown Court cases, was unable
to examine the pre-trial processes, and is now over two decades old.

Hood's sample comprised 2,884 males, of whom half were white and half
non-white (the latter including roughly twice as many blacks as Asians), and
443 females. It was therefore one of the largest samples of Crown Court
sentencing ever processed, and it produced a number of familiar findings
apart from racial issues. Thus custody rates varied among the courts studied,
and this sentencing inconsistency persisted even after account had been taken
of the different offence mix and offender mix of the various courts. Hood's
methodology included the calculation of expectancy scores for sentencing,
based on the characteristics of offences and offenders apart from race, in an
attempt to show whether race did exert an independent effect. One result
of this exercise was to show that a higher proportion of blacks fell into the
high-risk (of custody) category, whereas a higher proportion of Asians fell into
the lowest risk category.[19]

Comparing expected custody rates with actual custody rates, Hood found a
'residual race difference' of the order of a 5 per cent greater probability of a
black offender's being sent to prison, which was greater at one court and lower
at another.[20] The origins of this appeared to reside in the tendency
of particular judges to deal relatively harshly with some blacks with low or
medium expectancies of custody. The two characteristics of black offenders
most highly correlated with severity were being aged 21 or over, and being
unemployed.[21] If, therefore, we return to the fact that the proportion of
black males in prison is many times higher than that in the general population,
what causal inferences can be drawn from Hood's study? He estimated that
the bulk of the difference, some 70 per cent, was accounted for by the number
of blacks appearing at the Crown Court for sentence: this, in other words,
reflects the influence of all the pre-trial decisions and filters discussed above.
This should not be represented as a cumulative bias: the research suggests
discrimination at several stages, but not at every stage.[22]

What of the remaining 30 per cent of the difference? Hood estimated that
some 10 per cent was accounted for by the more serious nature of the
offences of which black offenders were convicted. No research has yet
determined the extent to which blacks are disproportionately involved in
more serious types of crime, or the extent to which the figures merely reflect
stereotyping, labelling, and deviancy amplification by the public and law
enforcement officers.[23] A further 13 per cent was attributable to the

---

[19] Hood (1992), pp. 68, 197; cf. Flood-Page and Mackie (1998), who, in a smaller study with less
sophisticated analysis, found that custody rates for white, black, and Asian offenders were
broadly similar in both magistrates' courts and the Crown Court.

[20] Hood (1992), p. 78.   [21] Ibid., p. 86 and ch. 6 generally.

[22] Indeed, black and Asian defendants have higher acquittal rates: Phillips and Bowling (2012),
p. 385.

[23] See Cook and Hudson (1993), pp. 9–10.

imposition of longer sentences on black offenders, which was traced almost entirely to the greater propensity of black defendants to plead not guilty and, therefore, the unavailability to them of the sentence discount for pleading guilty.[24] The remaining 7 per cent was accounted for by the greater use of custody than expected. If the same analysis is carried out for black offenders under 21, some 92 per cent of the difference was attributable to the numbers appearing for sentence and the seriousness of their cases. Hood states that these estimates 'must be regarded with a degree of caution',[25] and in respect of sentencing decisions he argues that 'in most respects Asian offenders did not fare worse than whites, nor did all Afro-Caribbeans'.[26] Nonetheless, 20 years on, this remains Britain's most careful and wide-ranging examination of race and the sentencing of male offenders,[27] and it makes a powerful case for vigilance rather than complacency about the existence of racial discrimination in sentencing.

In some jurisdictions the issues take on a more fundamental significance because they concern indigenous racial groups who are now minorities but who are over-represented in the prisons, notably aboriginal people in Canada and in Australia. In its judgment in *Gladue* (1999)[28] the Supreme Court of Canada gave its interpretation of Canadian legislation designed to redress this imbalance, requiring courts to take notice of the social and other background factors that result in aboriginal people committing offences. The arguments cannot be set out in detail here, but they point up three broader issues of principle for sentencing. One is whether judges should be expected, when sentencing individual cases, to redress the overall racial balance in the prisons or whether it should be recognised that this is a broader system-wide concern, going well beyond criminal justice. Another issue is whether factors such as social disadvantage or the harsher impact of prison on people from remote communities should be linked specifically to aboriginal offenders or should be available generally to offenders. A further question is whether such factors should be allowed to mitigate sentences for serious violence, a question already discussed in Chapter 5.

Returning to England and Wales, the problem of race in sentencing must be seen at three different levels, at least. First, there is the broadest level of social policy: unless there is an end to racial discrimination in society, it is likely to manifest itself in criminal justice no less than elsewhere. But, despite legislation and the work of the Equality and Human Rights Commission, change is difficult to bring about – not least when race issues are woven into public concern about gangs, immigration, asylum seekers, and terrorism.

---

[24] Hood (1992), pp. 124–5; issues around the guilty plea discount are discussed in ch. 5.4.1 above.
[25] Hood (1992), p. 130.   [26] Ibid., p. 183.
[27] Ch. 11 of Hood's book discusses the sentencing of women, but the numbers of blacks and Asians in the sample were relatively small.
[28] [1999] 1 SCR 688; for discussion and references, see Stenning and Roberts (2001) and Warner (2011).

In terms of social policy, many of the issues cannot and should not be isolated from more general inequalities in matters of wealth, employment, and housing. This point is taken further in part 7.7 below.

Second, there is the level of criminal justice administration, where the proportion of minority ethnic officers is variable. At the top come youth offending teams (16 per cent), probation officers (13 per cent) and the Crown Prosecution Service (12 per cent), whereas at the bottom come the police (4 per cent), prison officers (5 per cent), and judges/recorders (5 per cent).[29] Racial awareness training of judges and magistrates has increased in recent years, through the work of the Equal Treatment Advisory Committee (known as ETAC). Under the auspices of the Judicial College, ETAC advises on the structure of the sentencing and procedure exercises that judges are asked to discuss during their seminars. Training of this kind may help to remove prejudices of which sentencers may be unaware – for example, one study found evidence that magistrates were influenced by demeanour in court and might misinterpret the body language of some defendants as 'arrogance', leading to an unsympathetic response.[30] A study by Hood, Shute and Seemungal found that there were no major differences in the proportions of whites, blacks and Asians who felt unfairly treated in the criminal courts. They did find that one-fifth of black defendants in the Crown Court believed that they had suffered unfair treatment as a result of racial bias (as did one in eight Asian defendants), proportions that are lower than some might expect but which are still unacceptably high.[31]

Third, there is the level of criminal justice policy. Various initiatives, policies or targets may have impacts that amount to at least indirect indiscrimination. Thus, in the context of US criminal justice, Michael Tonry has argued that the 'war on drugs' has had racially discriminatory effects, and has resulted in the sacrifice of black youths (imprisoned at an extraordinarily high rate) in pursuit of a drug-control policy with no better prospects of success than certain less repressive and less discriminatory alternatives would have.[32] He applies the same analysis to the guilty plea discount in this country, arguing that its abolition would advance racial equality.[33] A similar analysis of sentencing could be pursued here, not only for drug offences but also for robbery. It could be argued that the label 'robbery' has an inflationary effect on sentences that might disappear if the offence of robbery were abolished, leaving prosecutors and sentencers to focus on the theft and any offence against the person committed.[34]

---

[29] Ministry of Justice figures in Phillips and Bowling (2012), p. 390.
[30] Hedderman and Gelsthorpe (1997), pp. 33–4.   [31] Hood, Shute and Seemungal (2003).
[32] Tonry (2011), Garland (2014), pp. 60–3.
[33] Tonry (2004). Cf. the debate between Tonry and Brownlee, in von Hirsch, Ashworth and Roberts (2009), pp. 354–65.
[34] Ashworth (2002b).

7.3 Gender[35]

The combined effect of the Equality Acts 2006 and 2010 is to impose a detailed 'Gender Equality Duty' on all public authorities.[36] How should this duty be discharged? Is there any evidence of discrimination against, or for, women in the sentencing system? One-fifth of persons convicted and sentenced are female, although in the Crown Court, where the more serious offences are tried, it is one in eight. As Tables 2 and 3 in Appendix B demonstrate, adult women are much more likely to receive a discharge than adult men, more likely to receive a community sentence than adult men, but significantly less likely to be sentenced to immediate custody. The appearance given by these statistics is that women are favourably treated at the sentencing stage. However, these figures cannot be taken at face value for three reasons.

First, different types of offence are typically committed by men and by women. A far higher proportion of women than of men are sentenced for theft and related offences. For burglary and drug offences, the positions are reversed.[37] The general position is that women are convicted of less serious offences than men. A second variable is the court in which an offender is sentenced: a higher proportion of women are sentenced by magistrates' courts, and the research evidence shows that the Crown Court tends to pass significantly more severe sentences in comparable cases.[38] A third variable is criminal record: in 2011 some 26 per cent of women in prison had no previous convictions, more than double the rate for men (12 per cent).[39]

Relatively little is known about sentencing practice on these matters, but a study by Lizanne Dowds and Carol Hedderman found that, taking account of the usual variables, women shoplifters were less likely than men to receive a custodial sentence, whether as first offenders (1 per cent and 8 per cent respectively) or as repeat offenders (5 per cent and 15 per cent).[40] Women were more likely to receive a community sentence and to receive a discharge, but this seemed to be because sentencers were often reluctant to fine a woman in circumstances where they would fine a man.[41] Insofar as this is true, it may mean that some women receive a more severe sentence (a community sentence) than some men, because they are thought unsuitable to be fined.

However, it has long been suggested that the whole orientation of sentencing for women is different: the emphasis in pre-sentence reports, speeches in mitigation, and sentencing is often on their multiple disadvantages.[42]

---

[35] For detailed discussion see Heidensohn and Silvestri (2012) and Player (2012).

[36] See n.3 above, and accompanying text.   [37] Flood-Page and Mackie (1998), p. 134.

[38] Hedderman and Hough (1994), drawing on Hedderman and Moxon (1992).

[39] Prison Reform Trust (2013), p. 32.   [40] Dowds and Hedderman (1997), p. 11.

[41] Magistrates interviewed by Gelsthorpe and Loucks (1997), ch. 4, were often reluctant to fine women because they had no independent means and/or because taking money from them might make their childcare responsibilities more difficult.

[42] Gelsthorpe and Loucks (1997), ch. 3, recording the tendency of the magistrates they interviewed to regard women offenders as 'troubled' rather than 'troublesome'.

This might be a separate strand of explanation for the higher use of community sentences, particularly those involving supervision. Thus, David Farrington and Allison Morris found that divorced and separated women received relatively more severe sentences than married women, as did women regarded as 'deviant' (e.g. unmarried mothers with no employment) rather than as 'normal'.[43] The other side of this coin is that the traditional family unit is adopted as the centre of normality. Where women do have family responsibilities, these sometimes militate in their favour;[44] but Mary Eaton has argued that 'by judging both female and male defendants in the context of their families, the court displays not impartiality, or equality of treatment, but its role in preserving differences based on sexual inequality'.[45] Moreover, this may confirm the suggestion that women with less conventional lifestyles tend to be viewed unsympathetically, as may those who fail to exhibit expected female responses in court (tearful, apologetic, respectful).[46] We return below to the question of how to promote equality in the sentencing of women.

There is evidence that when dealing with female offenders some magistrates give much greater weight to mitigating factors and, in particular, strive harder to avoid a custodial sentence than when sentencing a male.[47] However, there was a great upward surge in the average female prison population between 1992 and 2002 (an increase from 1,577 to 4,299, around two-and-a-half times the 1992 figure) and, although there has been some steadying since then, the figure remains around 4,000. A government survey confirms that women offenders in general, and certainly those sent to prison, constitute a group with 'multiple needs' stemming from 'complex problems':

> Women offenders experience high rates of mental health disorder, victimization, abuse and substance misuse, and have low skills and rates of employment. Their specific needs are distinct from those of male offenders.[48]

Moreover, prison is harder for women because they are likely to be held further away from their home (there being fewer women's prisons), and are more likely to lose their children to care and to lose their accommodation.[49] These are strong reasons for the minimal use of prison sentences for women, not least when it is considered that almost two-thirds of women sentenced to imprisonment receive a sentence of six months or less. Such sentences afford little public protection and cannot be rehabilitative – indeed, they may be thought to create problems of resettlement rather than to resolve any difficulties. It seems that most of these short sentences are imposed as

---

[43] Farrington and Morris (1983).
[44] On the mitigating effect of such factors, see ch. 5.4.5 above.   [45] Eaton (1986), p. 98.
[46] See the remarks of the magistrates quoted by Gelsthorpe and Loucks (1997), pp. 30–4.
[47] Gelsthorpe and Loucks (1997), ch. 4.   [48] Social Exclusion Task Force (2009), p. 3.
[49] See further Prison Reform Trust (2000), and Corston (2007) ch. 5.

'last resort' punishments for persistent offenders, or for breaches of licence, bail or community sentence; but there are no clear data.

There needs to be further enquiry into the routes by which such high proportions of non-white prisoners arrive in English prisons, and a corresponding scrutiny of the justifications for imprisoning women in these and other cases. The Sentencing Council's study of 12 women imprisoned for trying to import drugs explored the circumstances and pressures that led them to commit the offence, depicting several of the women as desperate and naïve.[50] As a result, the guidelines on sentencing for drug offences place offenders who were 'engaged by pressure, coercion or intimidation' or who had 'very little, if any, awareness or understanding of the scale of the operation' at the lowest culpability level.[51] However, the Council has not followed up this initiative when dealing with other offences such as fraud and theft from shops, where women offenders are imprisoned in significant numbers. The report of the Committee on Women's Imprisonment made a strong case for wider use of diversion to respond to the needs of women offenders.[52] While some measures were taken in response to this report, the imbalance has not been reversed, or indeed convincingly explained.[53] In 2007 Baroness Corston's *Review of Women with Particular Vulnerabilities in the Criminal Justice System* was published, calling for clearer leadership in dealing with women offenders, dedicated forms of community sentence, and radical changes in the approach to sentencing. Those changes would include a principle that prison should be reserved for women who are 'serious and violent offenders who pose a threat to the public', a principle that 'women should never be sent to prison for their own good, to teach them a lesson, for their own safety or to access services such as detoxification', and a loosening of the restrictions on sentencers dealing with breaches of orders.[54] Despite a broadly positive response from the then government, introducing leadership changes such as a new cross-departmental group and a ministerial 'champion' for women in the criminal justice system,[55] the first two Corston recommendations on prison sentences for women have reached neither the statute book nor the Sentencing Council, and the women's prison population remains unacceptably high. A review of the Corston recommendations six years on, by the House of Commons Justice Committee, found that the equality duty has exerted little effect, and that NOMS is not designing or commissioning its new measures by reference to women (designing for men, then considering adaptations for women).[56] The Justice Committee was critical of the

---

[50] Sentencing Council (2011).
[51] Sentencing Council, *Drug Offences: Definitive Guideline* (2012), p. 4.
[52] Prison Reform Trust (2000); see further ch. 9.6.2 below.
[53] See Heidensohn and Silvestri (2012).   [54] Corston (2007), ch. 5.
[55] Ministry of Justice (2007).
[56] Justice Committee (2013a); on 25 October 2013 the new Minister for Female Offenders, Lord McNally, announced new resettlement measures for women prisoners.

number of women being imprisoned for short periods, but failed to mention the Sentencing Council's role in this.

There remains a debate about what the gender equality duty means in sentencing – whether women should be dealt with on the same principles as men, or whether there should be special principles applicable to women. One approach is that the same principles should be applicable to both. This should mean that women receive prison sentences less frequently and for shorter periods than men, inasmuch as their crimes are less serious and their previous records better: there is a strong argument that adherence to the proportionality principle might assist women offenders, by avoiding the assumption that women's offending has pathological causes.[57] It should also result in women more frequently having the benefit of certain mitigating factors connected with family responsibilities, even if the same principle is capable of operating in favour of men. This approach would be quite compatible with, for example, the development of special forms of community sentence for women: its focus would be on proportionate sentencing, taking account of the seriousness of the offence and the normal aggravating and mitigating factors. However, some argue that 'treating women like men' is the wrong approach, insofar as it accepts the male world-view and fails to adopt different responses to different circumstances.[58]

An alternative approach would be to develop some separate principles for the sentencing of women, principles that take account of their typically different backgrounds and of the typically different effects of imprisonment on them. Just before its demise, the Sentencing Advisory Panel took some steps in this direction in its advice on *Overarching Principles of Sentencing*. It proposed that gender differences be taken into account in three particular respects: i) in the identification and meaning attributed to personal mitigation when assessing culpability; ii) in considering the different punitive impact of sentences on women; and iii) in responding to the differential provision of services for men and for women in both custodial and non-custodial sentences. In particular, the statutory restriction on imprisonment should be given special force when sentencing women because of the greater effects of imprisonment; a pre-sentence report should always be obtained before sentencing a woman to custody; custody should never be imposed simply because an appropriate community sentence placement cannot be found; and the fact that a woman is on a low income or on state benefits should not prevent the court from imposing a fine if this is the proportionate sentence.[59] While it can be argued that these proposals do not go far enough in fulfilment of the positive obligations flowing from the gender equality duty,[60] it is more unfortunate that the proposals have not been taken up, or even commented upon, by the Sentencing Council. All recent enquiries into the treatment of women

[57] See Player (2005), pp. 424–6.   [58] Eaton (1986), p. 11; Hudson (1998), pp. 246–8.
[59] SAP, *Overarching Principles of Sentencing* (2010), pp. 67–80.   [60] Player (2012).

in the criminal justice system have led to similar recommendations, but, as the Justice Committee concluded,[61] action on them has been patchy and lacking in commitment.

7.4 Employment status

We have already seen, in Chapter 5.4.5 above, that a good work record may constitute a powerful factor in mitigation. Understandable as it is that courts should wish to avoid passing a sentence which will result in an offender losing a job, one result of this approach may be that unemployed offenders suffer discrimination. This ground of mitigation is unavailable to some two-thirds of sentenced offenders.[62] Particularly interesting, in the light of the discussion in part 7.2 above, was the finding that in magistrates' courts 75 per cent of black offenders were unemployed, compared with 64 per cent of white offenders and 48 per cent of Asians; the figures for the Crown Court were somewhat similar, at 77 per cent, 65 per cent, and 64 per cent respectively.[63]

The research evidence is clear: a higher percentage of unemployed offenders are imprisoned, whereas a higher proportion of employed offenders are fined or given a community sentence.[64] The study by Hough, Jacobson and Millie on sentencers' decision-making in cases on the cusp of custody shows that having a job or good employment prospects would often militate in favour of a community sentence. 'An existing job and home, family support, or family responsibilities, are likewise viewed as encouraging aspects of an offender's life', leading to the inference that they are less likely to breach a community sentence because they have 'more to lose'. This emphasis on having a job suggests, the authors comment, that 'offenders who are already socially and economically disadvantaged are likely to suffer further disadvantage in the sentencing process'.[65] The study by Jacobson and Hough confirms the mitigating effect of a 'steady job', with some judges reluctant to damage an employed offender's prospects by imposing a prison sentence or taking account of loss of job as a mitigating factor.[66] However, judicial views of the relevance of having a job were not uniform, with some sentencers arguing that offenders in employment are more culpable because they have no excuse for committing a property offence.

---

[61] Justice Committee (2013).

[62] Flood-Page and Mackie (1998), pp. 117–19, reporting a study in the mid-1990s. The Social Exclusion Unit (2002, p. 53) found that 'over two in three prisoners are unemployed at the time of imprisonment, around 13 times the national unemployment rate'.

[63] Ibid. The study of race and sentencing by Hood (1992) showed that being unemployed was a significant factor in producing greater sentence severity for black offenders aged 21 and over, although not for whites or Asians.

[64] E.g. Moxon (1988), Crow and Simon (1989), and Flood-Page and Mackie (1998).

[65] Hough et al. (2003), p. 42.   [66] Jacobson and Hough (2007), ch. 3.

These surveys yield some strongly suggestive evidence of discrimination on grounds of employment status, but it is different in nature from discrimination on grounds of race or sex. Recalling the analysis of aggravating and mitigating factors in Chapter 5 above, a factor may be aggravating, neutral, or mitigating. Being unemployed is not treated as an aggravating factor: the true position is more likely to be that being employed is often a mitigating factor, whereas being unemployed is neutral. That still means, however, that an unemployed offender is not eligible for this source of mitigation, and therefore receives a more severe sentence on this ground. Is there a social justification for this? Lord Lane CJ argued that there is

> [a] desire if possible to keep people out of prison who can be dealt with otherwise, and that is much to be applauded, because as we know, prison places at the moment are extremely valuable, and if people can be dealt with properly by means of non-custodial sentences, and fines are possibly the best of all the non-custodial sentences, then that should be done.[67]

The reasoning can be strengthened by adding that it is not only the expense but also the negative effects of prison which justify restraint in its use. But is the general argument sound? The case in which Lord Lane spoke these words concerned two brothers who had committed fairly serious offences of violence. The trial judge imposed suspended sentences of imprisonment combined with large fines. One reason was that the brothers were in employment. Another (with which we are not concerned here)[68] was that the jobs of some 23 others depended on the continuation of the brothers' business. By thus discriminating in their favour because they were in employment, were the courts not in effect discriminating against the unemployed? Tony Bottoms has pointed out that suspended sentences were sometimes used for persons of 'education and intelligence' and for 'white-collar' offenders when they would not be used for people without those characteristics, and he argued that this amounts to 'the suspension of terms of imprisonment for middle-class offenders'.[69] Hough, Jacobson and Millie identified a good employment record as a factor that sentencers might treat as tipping a borderline case away from a custodial disposal.[70] In the small Crown Court survey the second most frequently mentioned mitigating factor was 'currently in work/training or prospects of'.[71] The upshot of these findings is that the principle of parsimony is given priority over the principle of equality before the law. Lesser punishments are given to one group on grounds of parsimony, although other offenders who are similarly placed in terms of offence and criminal record receive no such concession. However, that approach should be challenged: if the principle of parsimony is regarded as

---

[67] *Olliver and Olliver* (1989) 11 Cr App R (S) 10, at p. 13.   [68] See ch. 5.4.5 above.
[69] Bottoms (1981), p. 18.
[70] Hough et al. (2003), p. 42 and ch. 4 generally. See also Jacobson and Hough (2007), ch. 3.
[71] SCWG Survey (2008), p. 14.

more powerful, it should lead to the reduction of sentence lengths for all offenders, not just for a sub-group supported by no compelling justification.

The only way to pursue equality before the law here is to offer no concession at all based on employment.[72] Thus the Minnesota Sentencing Guidelines state that employment status is not to be taken into account in sentencing. Just as Eaton attacks the emphasis placed on the conventional family by sentencers of women, so one might criticize the influential role that the work ethic seems to play in sentencing.[73] It is certainly true that there should be no direct inference from the status of being employed, resulting in the ascription of moral or social superiority to employed people over unemployed people. There is no general link between, for example, unemployment and personal culpability or unemployment and lack of respect for family responsibilities. As recent experience demonstrates, unemployment rates tend to result more from changes in government economic policy or world trading conditions than from outbreaks of inadequacy among employees.

7.5 Financial circumstances

The principle of equality before the law indicates that poor offenders should not, on account of their poverty, be treated less favourably than wealthy offenders. In practice, it may be less that courts aim to penalize those without financial resources, and more that courts find themselves able to take a lenient course with an offender who has financial resources. In terms of sentencing principles, however, this route to leniency has long been declared to be wrong. In the well-known case of *Markwick* (1953),[74] a wealthy member of a golf club had been fined £500 for stealing two shillings and sixpence from a golf club changing room, in circumstances which had cast suspicion on others. He appealed against this sentence to the Court of Criminal Appeal, which responded with a rare exercise of its power (since removed) to increase the severity of sentences on defence appeals. Sentencing Markwick to 2 months' imprisonment, Lord Goddard CJ remarked that in such a case a high fine 'would give persons of means an opportunity of buying themselves out of being sent to prison ... There should be no suggestion that there is one law for the rich and one for the poor.'

The same principle has been applied to compensation. Thus, in *Copley* (1979)[75] Lane LJ observed that 'it is not open to persons who participate in crime and plead guilty to try to buy their way out of prison, or to buy shorter sentences, by offering money in the way of compensation'. Some defence lawyers still advance pleas in mitigation based, explicitly or implicitly, on the

---

[72] Cf. Warner (2012), pp. 239–41.

[73] Almost six out of ten female offenders identified unemployment and skills deficits as factors contributing to their offending: Social Exclusion Task Force (2009), p. 11.

[74] (1953) 37 Cr App R 125.

[75] (1979) 1 Cr App R (S) 55; see also the discussion of the *Inwood* judgment in ch. 10.4 below.

offender's ability to pay a substantial fine or substantial compensation. Such attempts to persuade a court to act contrary to principle may succeed occasionally, but they may also misfire. Far from persuading a court to suspend a sentence and impose a financial penalty, the court might give both immediate prison and a financial penalty.[76]

There is also some judicial authority for the converse principle, that an offender should not be given a more severe penalty simply because the court regards him or her as incapable of paying a sufficient fine.[77] In practice, however, there have been distinctly different patterns of disposal according to whether or not the offender is unemployed, as the findings set out in part 7.4 above demonstrate. Unemployed offenders are less likely to be fined and more likely to receive other sentences, particularly discharges and community service orders.

No research project has set out to examine the relationship between financial resources and sentencing as such, but there has always been a strong suggestion that defendants with means may receive better treatment. It has been argued that class differences exert considerable influence in the courtroom, whether or not the defendant is legally represented.[78] Perhaps the greatest influence, however, occurs before cases come to court. From the outset there is a greater probability that 'white-collar' offenders will be dealt with outside the formal criminal process. Offences committed by companies and their officers are likely to be processed by statutory agencies such as the Health and Safety Executive and the various industrial inspectorates, for whom prosecution is a last resort.[79] Those who commit income tax offences are unlikely to be prosecuted, since HM Revenue & Customs focus on civil measures of recovery;[80] and even those who commit benefit fraud are likely to be subjected to administrative penalties and various claw-back provisions by the Department of Work and Pensions.[81] However, such imaginative approaches are not available for 'ordinary' thefts and frauds, with the result that some offenders (often wealthy ones) receive more lenient responses than others committing offences of the same gravity. The egalitarian principles declared by the Court of Appeal in relation to sentencing are right in principle, but they need to be applied to the criminal justice system as a whole – particularly in respect of property offences.[82]

Moderating inequalities in the system as a whole is, however, a worthy goal of sentencing. The principle of equality before the law points in this direction. So too does the principle of equal impact: where a court decides to impose a financial penalty, such as a fine or compensation order, it should ensure that it is adjusted to the means of the offender. In the present context the most

---

[76] Cf. *Olliver and Olliver* (1989) 11 Cr App R (S) 10, discussed in ch. 10.5.5 below, with *Fairbairn* (1980) 2 Cr App R (S) 284.

[77] E.g. *Myers* [1980] Crim LR 191, *Ball* (1981) 3 Cr App R (S) 283.   [78] McBarnet (1981).

[79] See Hawkins (2003), and ch. 1.4 above.

[80] www.hmrc.gov.uk/prosecutions/crim-inv-policy.htm.   [81] See www.gov.uk/benefit-fraud.

[82] Ashworth (2013).

important aspect is that the size of the fine be reduced for an offender of limited means, a principle long established in the law. The courts resisted the corollary that fines should be increased for the wealthy, but since 1991 there have been legislative provisions embracing the principle of equal impact and stating that the fine should reflect the means of the offender, whether the effect is to increase or reduce its amount.[83] Recent years have seen a revival of official interest in the kind of 'day-fine' system used in other European countries, discussed in Chapter 10.5.3 below, and if there is to be a reversal of the decline in fining and adherence to the principle of equality of impact, some such system must be adopted again.

At a theoretical level, does the principle of equal impact conflict with the proportionality principle? Could it be said that a fine of £7,000 for a theft in breach of trust involving property valued at £700 is disproportionate?[84] The answer is to be found in a separation between the gravity of the offence and the means of the offender. Proportionality should govern the process of estimating the gravity of the offence, taking account of aggravating and mitigating factors. Only when the relative seriousness of the offence has been assessed should the court turn to the offender's financial resources and strive to achieve equal impact. To say, 'a fine of £7,000 is disproportionate for an offence involving £700', is to make the wrong comparison. The £7,000 ought to be compared with the relative seriousness of the offence and the offender's means; it should not be related directly to the amount involved in the offence, since that is only one of the factors relevant to its seriousness (breach of trust being another). Under the kind of day-fine system used widely in other European countries and some US jurisdictions,[85] the point is made much clearer by announcing the fines, not in terms of the actual sum ordered to be paid, but in terms of the number of 'days' or 'units' (which represent the seriousness of the offence). There is thus no inconsistency between the proportionality principle and the principle of equal impact.

The latter principle is, however, compromised for reasons of administrative efficiency in at least two situations. One is the standardized nature of some of the calculations which form part of any system of unit fines or day fines. They sacrifice maximum accuracy in individual cases in order to achieve a relatively rapid processing of large numbers of cases in the lower courts. Such systems can therefore claim greater equality of impact, not perfect equality. So long as the compromise is relatively generous to those least able to pay, it may be acceptable. The second form of compromise is inherent in the fixed penalty system: a large number of motoring offences and an increasing number of other offences have a fixed financial penalty,[86] which does not vary

---

[83] Fully discussed in ch. 10.5 below.
[84] As argued unsuccessfully in *Fairbairn* (1980) 2 Cr App R (S) 315.   [85] Greene (1998).
[86] E.g. the Penalty Notice for Disorder, a standard penalty of £40 or £80 for certain non-serious offences.

according to the means of the offender. It is true that any offender has the alternative of going to court rather than accepting the fixed penalty, but there are obvious uncertainties and other disincentives attendant on this course. Some magistrates maintain that anyone who can afford to run a car can afford a penalty of this size, but that is too simplistic an approach, and there is a case for re-examining the impact of fixed penalties on the economically disadvantaged.

7.6 Social status

The principle of equality before the law requires that offenders should not be sentenced more favourably because of their social status or 'respectability'. In practice, social status is sometimes closely linked to other factors already discussed, such as employment and financial circumstances.[87] But there are a few cases in which the Court of Criminal Appeal considered the proper approach to sentencing someone who, until the offence, held a high social position. Both in *Cargill* (1913)[88] and in *Fell* (1963)[89] it was held that the proper approach is to pass sentence according to the seriousness of the offence. In *Attorney General's Reference No. 38 of 2013 (Hall)*[90] the Court of Appeal held that 'the offender's successful career provides no mitigation. On the contrary, it was the career that put him in a position of trust which he was then able to exploit and which contributed to his image as a cheerful, fun-loving and fundamentally decent man.' Thus, where the offence involves a breach of trust, the gravity of that breach will generally be greater if the offender's position was higher.

The fact that there is appellate authority for the application of the principle of equality before the law in sentencing does not exclude the possibility that other factors may operate at earlier stages. As with race and financial resources, it remains probable that social status is sometimes influential at the stage of deciding whether or not to prosecute, or even whether or not to report, certain cases. 'Young people' in one part of a city might receive an informal warning for 'rowdiness' or 'high spirits', whereas 'youths' in another area might be prosecuted or formally cautioned for similar behaviour interpreted as 'disorder'.

7.7 Equality, parsimony and risk

Inequality in sentencing is sometimes linked with inconsistency, a frequent battle-cry of those who attack English sentencing practice. It is a fundamental principle that like cases should be treated alike, and different cases differently.

---

[87] See Wandall (2008), p. 150.
[88] (1913) 8 Cr App R 224 ('prominent citizen of Hull': 'the sentence is harder but the offence is correspondingly greater').
[89] [1963] Crim LR 207 (senior civil servant: 'the higher one's position, the greater one's responsibilities').
[90] [2014] 1 Cr App R (S) 394, at [75].

The practical significance of this principle depends, however, on authoritative agreement on which resemblances and which differences are to count as relevant or irrelevant. This is where the principle of equality before the law has its application, in arguing that certain differences should be excluded and rendered irrelevant to sentencing decisions. On a proportionality rationale, equality before the law at the sentencing stage is assured *if* the proportionality principle applies throughout sentencing, and *if* there are no significant amounts of unaccountable discretion in practical sentencing. Neither of these conditions seems to be satisfied by English sentencing. For example, the development of mitigating factors has largely been left to the courts themselves, with little guidance in sentencing guidelines – so that, as we have seen in this chapter, parts 7.3 and 7.4, domestic responsibilities and employment record may sometimes act as mitigating factors and sometimes not, a vital difference on the cusp of custody.[91]

There is good reason to pay renewed attention to the practical application in sentencing decisions of the principle of equality before the law, but this chapter has shown the complexity of doing so. Equality before the law is not the only principle or policy which may be relevant here, and so there are conflicts to be resolved. One obvious conflict is that between equality before the law and efficiency in the administration of justice: to what extent, and under what circumstances, might it be acceptable to forgo maximum equality of impact in fines in order to expedite the processing of cases in magistrates' courts? Are the supposed effectiveness and administrative efficiency of on-the-spot fines (Penalty Notices for Disorder) sufficient reasons to outweigh the principle of equal impact? Another conflict is that between equality before the law and the principle of parsimony, or restraint in the use of imprisonment. There are strong arguments for imposing lesser punishments when they seem likely to be no less effective than the greater punishment; but should that be done if it results in giving preference to an employed over an unemployed offender, or a white over a black offender? Is this not discrimination? Should it be absolutely forbidden, or does parsimony have stronger claims?

Before these questions are debated, it is worth discussing further the concept of discrimination. As argued above, the effect of taking account of a positive factor in mitigation of sentence – e.g. that the offender has a steady job, or that the offender has paid compensation to the victim – may be to discriminate against others who are less fortunate. In exactly similar cases, the unemployed or poor offender would receive a more severe sentence. We saw earlier that this does not amount to using unemployment or poverty as an aggravating factor: it is a neutral factor, while the good employment record or payment of compensation is a mitigating factor. The motivation behind the mitigation of sentence may be laudable, but the effect is discriminatory.

---

[91] See Hudson (1998), p. 231.

If these grounds of mitigation are to be justified, then, it must be by reference to values which are regarded as superior to equality before the law. Can such a justification be found?

As we saw in part 7.1 of this chapter, Norval Morris and Michael Tonry argue that the principle of parsimony ought to be accorded greater weight than the principle of equality before the law. In their view, proportionality merely sets loose outer limits to the severity and leniency of punishments for particular crimes. They argue that the concept of cardinal proportionality is so uncertain in its application that this undermines the whole basis of desert theory. There are no criteria for determining the anchoring points of the scale, they say, and therefore there can be no compelling reason why judgments of ordinal proportionality should be accorded absolute priority. Reasonable people may differ about the appropriate levels of punishment for different types of crime, and the avoidance of manifest disproportion is all that can be achieved.[92] It is therefore preferable to allow the principle of parsimony to lead to lower sentences in suitable cases, so long as the sentences are not disproportionately low:

> A developed punishment theory requires recognition that precise equivalency of punishment between equally undeserving criminals in the distribution of punishments is in practice unattainable and in theory undesirable. We argue that all that can be achieved is a rough equivalence of punishment that will allow room for the principled distribution of punishments on utilitarian grounds, unfettered by the miserable aim of making suffering equally painful.[93]

The utilitarian aim to which Morris and Tonry refer is the principle of parsimony. They apply it particularly to certain prison sentences:

> Imprisonment is expensive and unnecessary for some convicted felons who present no serious threat to the community and whose imprisonment is not necessary for deterrent purposes, and yet whose crime and criminal record could properly attract a prison sentence. Are we to allow an excessive regard for equality of suffering to preclude rational allocation of scarce prison space and staff?[94]

Morris and Tonry make it clear that one result of their approach would be that a white, middle-class offender is likely to receive a more lenient sentence than a black offender living on state benefits, if there are community treatment facilities in the first locality which are unavailable in the second.[95] They characterize the principle of equality before the law as a principle of equality of suffering, since it refuses to allow more lenient sentences for certain offenders if the result would be to discriminate on improper grounds against others. They oppose equality of suffering because their utilitarian concern is the

---

[92] This aspect of their theory was discussed critically in ch. 3.3.5 above.
[93] Morris and Tonry (1990), p. 31.   [94] Morris and Tonry (1990), p. 90.
[95] Morris and Tonry (1990), p. 33.

reduction of suffering wherever possible. They deny that this will infringe the principle of equality before the law *in the long run*, because they argue that one result of their scheme will be to produce more community sanctions for offenders of all races and social classes.[96] If intermediate punishments were seen to work for white, middle-class offenders, they might then be expanded so as to be available for all. Inequality of treatment in the short run should be tolerated in order to bring greater equality in the longer term.

Considering their approach on its own terms, is it more likely that the overall amount of suffering generated by their approach (discrimination in the short term, in order to show that community sanctions perform acceptably) would be less than the suffering generated by an approach which insisted on equality before the law, but yet which involved efforts to introduce more community sanctions which the courts would use? Much depends on the political system, on the attitudes of sentencers, on government funding, and so on. The difficulty in the United States, as Morris and Tonry describe it, is to gain acceptance for community sanctions for offenders now sent to prison. Many states have no fines, and relatively few other sanctions. The position in this country is different: there is a wide range of available alternatives, and the problem is to ensure that they are used in a more extensive and more principled way. The problem is probably less one of discrimination than of a general reluctance to use fines, and to use community sentences for offenders now sent to prison.[97] It is hard to be confident that Morris and Tonry's approach would reduce overall suffering in England and Wales, whatever the probabilities elsewhere.

On theoretical grounds, however, their analysis cannot be accepted. To caricature equality before the law as equality of suffering is unconvincing. Equality before the law is a fundamental value which cannot simply be cast aside: it stands for propositions about respect for human dignity, and impartiality in the administration of criminal justice. This is not to say that it should be regarded as absolute and inviolable. But the principle should be recognized as fundamental in most modern societies, not simply to be traded for gains in efficiency and so forth. If there are situations in which it has to be weighed against other principles such as parsimony, the two principles should be considered not only in their intrinsic strength but also in their wider social effects. Discrimination in the criminal justice system may alienate sections of the community and contribute to racial tensions or class divisions, as well as undermining respect for the administration of criminal justice. Moreover, Morris and Tonry's approach is not the only possible one. They seem to assume that the principle of parsimony entails the reduction of individual sentences wherever possible; another interpretation is that it requires a general

---

[96] Morris and Tonry (1990), p. 33.
[97] See the findings of Hood (1992), p. 141, on the disinclination of probation officers and courts to contemplate community sentences for black offenders.

lowering of punishment levels and expansion of community sanctions,[98] and not discriminatory distinctions among individual offenders. On the same reasoning, there should be no individual-case pleading for women offenders: 'feminist criminologists and legal theorists are not asking for special-case leniency, but ... are challenging the present assumption that the male penal norm is generalisable'.[99] Reducing penalty levels for males too would be a splendid application of the principle of parsimony.

Commitment to the principle of equality before the law may appear empty when there is so much inequality evident in society. Social unfairness may be largely the product of the social structure, and its roots are likely to be found in institutional arrangements rather than in the actions of a few individuals.[100] There is also the argument that remedying social inequality in such fields as housing, employment, and education is likely to be a more potent means of crime reduction than specific measures taken through the criminal justice system. It is trite to say that the criminal justice system can have little effect on crime unless the social system is altered in certain ways. Since the sentencing system can only deal with those offenders who are prosecuted to conviction, it should be recognised that, dealing with only a small proportion of offences each year, sentencers can be expected to have far less influence on patterns of lawbreaking than certain strategies of crime prevention, whether situational or social. There may be social or even constitutional arguments for sentencers to mark certain differences symbolically, but should this kind of symbolism ever be preferred over respect for equality before the law?

In the absence of a fairly adjusted social system and criminal justice system, notions of proportionality and desert in the allocation of punishment are placed under strain. Desert theorists can respond to that strain in two ways – first, by advocating a decremental strategy so as to achieve greater parsimony; and secondly, by requiring an equality impact assessment for every legislative or sentencing innovation. Andrew von Hirsch is right to argue that:

> The sentencing of convicted persons cannot wait until underlying social ills are remedied, nor can it be abandoned until they are addressed ... Addressing fundamental social ills (desirable and, indeed, essential as this is) cannot constitute a substitute for trying to make sentencing policy more coherent and fair.[101]

However, at least two measures should be insisted upon. Adopting a decremental strategy means reducing sentence levels across the board in order to promote penal parsimony, rather than adopting the opportunistic variety of parsimony advocated by Morris and Tonry. Insisting on an 'equality impact assessment' of all penal developments, adapting the 'racial impact statements' advocated in the United States,[102] should lead to a public exploration of the

---

[98] See ch. 3.4 above.   [99] Hudson (1998), p. 248.   [100] Cook and Hudson (1993), pp. 9–10.
[101] Von Hirsch (1993), p. 98; see also von Hirsch and Ashworth (2005), ch. 6.
[102] For a brief discussion and references, see Frase (2013), pp. 221–4.

direct and indirect discriminatory effects of various measures. This should accompany every consultation of the Sentencing Council and every legislative proposal by the Ministry of Justice.

Finally, it is important to signal the dangers to the principle of equality before the law that flow from the increasing emphasis on risk assessment. We have seen in Chapter 6 how significant the idea of prediction is in sentencing law, and we shall see in Chapter 12 how prominent a place is coming to be given to risk assessment in the social response to offending by young people and by the mentally disordered. The greater the focus on risk, the greater the focus on what might be termed 'non-legal' variables – that is not just previous convictions, but upbringing, family size, income, and housing. Reliance on these factors is highly likely to lead to direct and indirect discrimination. The direct discrimination would be against the poor and unemployed. The indirect discrimination would be against those who fall disproportionately within the categories of high risk, such as certain ethnic minorities and single mothers. The threat to equality before the law in the 'risk society' is therefore a real one, and righteous pronouncements on 'community safety' must be scrutinized closely from this point of view.

8

Multiple offenders

Contents

This chapter, like Chapter 6, deals with some of the problems posed by the sentencing of persistent offenders. Its focus, however, is on offenders who come before the courts in a different context. In Chapter 6 the main concern was with the sentencing of recidivists – those who are convicted repeatedly, despite the fact that they have experienced criminal sanctions. The main concern here is with offenders who commit a number of offences before they are detected and convicted, so that the court has to sentence them on one occasion for multiple offences. Not all these multiple offenders could be described as 'persistent offenders', for in some cases the offender has been involved in a single incident which gives rise to a number of charges and convictions. But many 'multiple offenders' are people who have been committing offences over a period of weeks, months, or even years before they appear in court, and they then face a number of charges. The criminal record of such multiple offenders may vary: some of them will be recidivists too, having experienced a number of criminal sanctions in the past, whilst others will fall into that seemingly incongruous category of 'persistent first offenders' – those who, when they are convicted for the first time, are convicted of several offences which show that they are accustomed to lawbreaking, if not to the criminal process.

The focus of this chapter, then, will be on multiple offenders, some of whom are being sentenced for a number of offences arising from a single incident, but most of whom are being sentenced for offences committed at different times during the period before their court appearance. It seems that around half of all Crown Court cases and about a quarter of magistrates' court cases involve two or more convictions, so there is no doubting multiple offenders' centrality to sentencing.[1] They give rise to difficulties both theoretical and practical, particularly in relation to proportionality. It is one thing to compare a residential burglary with a rape; it is quite another thing to draw comparisons of gravity between two, four or six residential burglaries and a single rape. Before tackling these problems, however, the various procedural methods of dealing with multiple offenders must be briefly explored.

8.1 Charging the multiple offender

What approach should the police and prosecutors take when it emerges that a suspected offender may have committed more than one offence? A full answer to this question would import a mass of technical detail; for present purposes, a sketch of the four main avenues open to the prosecution should provide a sufficient basis for the remainder of the discussion.

8.1.1 Charge all offences

The straightforward approach is to charge all the offences of which the prosecution have sufficient evidence. This has the disadvantage that the indictment could be so long as to make it very difficult for the court to deal fairly and accurately with the various charges against the defendant. If there is a plea of not guilty, the task of a jury dealing with a lengthy indictment may be formidable and beyond what it is reasonable to expect of them. For this reason, it has long been accepted that, although the prosecution must ensure that all outstanding matters against the defendant are dealt with at the same time,[2] no charge ought to be brought in respect of relatively minor incidents where the defendant already faces a number of more serious charges.[3] To some extent it remains in the prosecution's interest to bring a number of charges against a defendant, since they may then agree not to proceed with some of the charges in exchange for the defendant's agreement to plead guilty to the others. Where a defendant does plead guilty to some charges and it appears to the prosecution that he is likely to receive a broadly appropriate sentence for those offences, it will usually be right for the prosecution to drop any further charges to which he pleads not guilty.[4] This requires, and will usually receive, the trial judge's consent.[5]

---

[1] Moxon (1988), p. 9, found that 62 per cent of cases in his Crown Court research involved two or more offences; the Crown Court Sentencing Survey has 48 per cent of Crown Court cases in this category.
[2] *Bennett* (1980) 2 Cr App R (S) 96.   [3] E.g. Lawton LJ in *Ambrose* (1973) 57 Cr App R 538.
[4] *Code for Crown Prosecutors*, available at www.cps.gov.uk, paras. 4.12.a and 4.12.f.
[5] *Broad* (1979) 68 Cr App R 281.

8.1.2 Charge specimen offences

Where the prosecution have evidence of a course of offending over a considerable period, usually but not necessarily against the same victim (e.g. sexual
offences against one or more children, thefts from an employer), they may
decide to charge only a few incidents as 'specimen counts'. The chosen
'specimen counts' should relate to the most serious of the alleged offences,
and the purpose is to avoid complicating a single trial with too many charges
and to avoid the need for several trials, while giving the judge a sufficient basis
for a proportionate sentence. This is obviously easier for the prosecution, since
it spares them the burden of adducing evidence in relation to each one of a
long series of offences. But if the defendant is unwilling to admit to the
offences not charged, can the court sentence as if they were proved, simply
because the prosecution described its charges as specimens (of a longer course
of offending)? In the leading decision of *Canavan and Kidd* (1998),[6] Lord
Bingham CJ declared that:

> A defendant is not to be convicted of any offence with which he is charged
> unless and until his guilt is proved. Such guilt may be proved by his own
> admission or (on indictment) by the verdict of a jury. He may be sentenced
> only for an offence proved against him (by admission or verdict) or which he
> has admitted and asked the court to take into consideration when passing
> sentence. If, as we think, these are basic principles underlying the administration
> of the criminal law, it is not easy to see how a defendant can lawfully be
> punished for offences for which he has not been indicted and which he has
> denied or declined to admit.

He added that 'prosecuting authorities will wish, in the light of this
decision ... to include more counts in some indictments', and expressed the
view that this would not be unduly burdensome. However, some prosecutors
and trial judges have found the implications of the *Canavan* principle burdensome, and on various occasions – notably in *Tovey and Smith* (2005)[7] and in
Hartley (2012)[8] – the Court of Appeal has had to reassert the principle.[9] If the
offender can be said to have agreed to the court taking account of other
offences, the *Canavan* principle does not apply.[10]

    If the prosecution wishes to prefer specimen charges, s. 17 of the Domestic
Violence, Crime and Victims Act 2004 provides for the prosecution to apply to
a Crown Court judge to have some of the counts in an indictment tried by
judge alone, while others are tried by jury. This means that the prosecution
may charge a considerable number of offences, and then satisfy the judge that

---

[6] [1998] 1 Cr App R (S) 243.   [7] [2005] 2 Cr App R (S) 606.   [8] [2012] 1 Cr App R (S) 166.
[9] As in *BDG* [2013] 1 Cr App R (S) 134.
[10] *Powell and Hinkson* [2009] 1 Cr App R (S) 30; cf. the position in many US jurisdictions, where
    the judge is allowed to take account of non-conviction offences in calculating the sentence,
    known as 'real offence sentencing' (Reitz 2010, pp. 236–43).

some of them may fairly be regarded as samples of the others. If the judge decides that trial by jury of every count would be impracticable, that the counts to be tried by jury are a sample, and that it is in the interests of justice to proceed in this way, the judge may make an order for trial of the other counts by judge alone. The jury trial then proceeds, and if the defendant is convicted 'on a count which can be regarded as a sample of other counts to be tried in those proceedings', the judge may then try the defendant on the other counts, giving a reasoned judgment (s. 19). In most cases the defendant will probably change the plea to guilty of these other offences, but the new procedure gives the prosecution an opportunity to circumvent the problems of practice and principle presented by *Canavan and Kidd*.[11]

8.1.3 Prefer a general charge

Another approach, when there is evidence of a course of offending over a long period, is to frame a general charge, such as fraudulent trading or cheating the revenue. If two or more people have been involved, a charge of conspiracy may have procedural advantages for the prosecution and open the way to higher sentences, especially if more than one conspiracy is involved.[12]

8.1.4 Offences taken into consideration

The prosecution may invite a defendant to ask the court to take other offences into consideration when sentencing him for the crimes charged. The House of Lords has laid down that a defendant should be informed explicitly of each offence and asked to consent to the court taking each one into consideration when sentencing.[13] The offences thus taken into consideration do not rank as convictions, but the court is likely to increase the sentence in order to take account of them, and the procedure is a relatively informal and expeditious way of disposing of a long series of offences which are not especially serious in nature. The Sentencing Council has issued guidelines on TICs.[14] These begin by stating that the court must be able to pass a total sentence that reflects all the offending behaviour, and sets out six sets of circumstances in which it is undesirable to allow TICs. Various procedural safeguards are laid down. When the court comes to pass sentence, it is urged to treat the TICs as aggravating factors, noting that it may be appropriate to move outside the category range so long as the totality principle (below) is observed.[15]

---

[11] See the Criminal Practice Direction [2013] EWCA Crim 1631, para. 14A.4–13.

[12] E.g. *Attorney General's References Nos. 120 and 121 of 2004* [2006] 1 Cr App R (S) 44.

[13] *DPP v. Anderson* [1978] AC 964.

[14] Sentencing Council, *Offences Taken into Consideration and Totality: Definitive Guideline* (2012).

[15] The CCSS (2014), p. 28, records that offences of burglary which involve TICs have sentences on average 1 year longer than cases without TICs.

8.2 The problems of sentencing multiple offenders

At the outset, the limitations of any theoretical discussion of the sentencing of multiple offenders must be openly avowed. The wide variety of combinations of offences in particular cases, and the equally wide variations in the timespan of the offending with which the court has to deal, are sufficient to test any general philosophy of sentencing. Kevin Reitz has pointed out the inconsistency in most systems' treatment of persistent offenders (a recidivist premium of some kind, arising from sequential sentencing) and their treatment of multiple offenders (some kind of discount for bulk offending, arising from simultaneous sentencing), and he argues that one searches in vain for a persuasive rationale.[16] In an important recent essay Martin Wasik has challenged the logic on which the current English approach is constructed.[17] Is it possible to identify some general principles, or do the case-by-case variations allow nothing more than an untidy pragmatism?

Just as the straightforward approach to prosecuting is to bring a charge in respect of each offence of which there is prima facie evidence, so the straightforward approach to sentencing is to impose a sentence for each offence of which there is a conviction. The offender who is convicted of one crime receives one sentence; the offender who is convicted of three crimes receives three sentences, each one additional to the others. The logic of this approach, however, is far from perfect. There are two problems with the straightforward approach. First, in certain instances the law may provide (and the prosecution charge) a number of offences where in theory one would suffice, and in other instances the law may provide (and the prosecution charge) one offence where it would be natural to think of two or three. For example, the offence of aggravated burglary contrary to s. 10 of the Theft Act 1968 is apt to cover a case where a person commits burglary and has with him a firearm, an offensive weapon or an explosive; therefore it is not necessary to charge such a person on one count with burglary and on a separate count with the offence of possessing a firearm, offensive weapon, or explosive substance. The law provides a single offence, aggravated burglary, and the court will naturally take account of both elements of the crime (the burglary and the possession offence) in its calculations. On the other hand, crimes such as manslaughter and robbery do not specify the use of a weapon; whilst prosecutors will usually add a charge under the Firearms Act 1968 if the accused was carrying a firearm, this is strictly unnecessary because the robbery guidelines make provision for the use or carrying of a firearm as an aggravating factor, and the whole matter can be dealt with on conviction for robbery.

From the point of view of calculating the total sentence, it should be immaterial whether a firearms charge is added in such a case or not. The sentencer has

[16] Reitz (2010); the sequential/simultaneous terminology is that of Frase (2013), ch. 4.
[17] Wasik (2012).

all the facts, the maximum sentence for manslaughter or robbery is sufficiently high to allow full account to be taken of any such aggravating factor, and it is highly unlikely that these features of the case would be overlooked. But there would be a choice as to how the sentence is expressed. If only manslaughter or robbery were charged, obviously there would be a single sentence. If there were an additional conviction under the Firearms Act, in theory the sentencer has a choice: if the decision is that, say, 9 years is the appropriate total sentence, this total may be expressed in terms of two consecutive sentences (e.g. 6 years for robbery, 3 years for the firearm) or in terms of two concurrent sentences (e.g. 9 years for robbery, with 3 years concurrent for the firearm). The straightforward approach (one crime, one sentence) cannot deal with this kind of problem, since it overlooks the vagaries of prosecutorial discretion and of the shape of English criminal law. In some fields of activity the law provides several separate offences, in other fields a single encompassing crime. Merely to add a sentence for each conviction ignores these quirks of history and convention.

The second problem with the straightforward approach is the powerful intuition that it conflicts with proportionality principles. Simply to add up the sentences for the separate offences might lead to a total wildly out of proportion to sentences for other offences. The overall sentence would violate ordinal proportionality, placing several less serious offences (e.g. seven burglaries) alongside a much more serious offence (e.g. rape). In order to avoid this, the courts developed a principle which David Thomas called 'the totality principle', which requires a court to consider the overall sentence in relation to the totality of the offending and in relation to sentence levels for other crimes. Section 166 of the 2003 Act preserves the principle by stating that nothing in the Act should prevent a court, 'in the case of an offender who is convicted of one or more other offences, from mitigating his sentence by applying any rule of law as to the totality of sentences'. Early authority may be found in an unreported judgment in 1972:

> When cases of multiplicity of offences come before the court, the court must not content itself by doing the arithmetic and passing the sentence which the arithmetic produces. It must look at the totality of the criminal behaviour and ask itself what is the appropriate sentence for all the offences.[18]

The application of this principle produces what is in effect a discount for bulk offending. The court is expected to impose a sentence which is lower than the total which has been reached by a correct assessment of the gravity of each individual offence. The offender would certainly receive a lower total sentence than he would have received if he had been before the court on a number of separate occasions for the same number of offences – indeed, as Reitz points out, the recidivist would often receive increasingly severe sentences for the

---

[18] *Barton* (1972), cited by Thomas (1979), pp. 56–7.

subsequent offences, by contrast with the multiple offender for whom the totality principle delivers decreasingly severe sentences. This is strikingly demonstrated in cases where an offender asks the court to take numerous other offences into consideration (see 8.1.4 above), although some might justify the discount in those cases as an incentive for the offender to confess and thereby to enable the crimes to be 'cleared up'. In most cases where a multiple offender is sentenced, however, the offender is being given a discount because his total sentence appears excessive when compared with sentences for graver individual crimes, and that is because he managed to commit so many offences before being caught.

Implicit in the principle is a rather different sense of proportionality than that commonly used. The point is not whether one type of offence is *ceteris paribus* more heinous than another; it is a question of how a series of offences, sometimes all of the same kind and sometimes of different kinds, can be brought into a conceptual scheme which relates principally to single offences. The problem is illustrated by the Court of Appeal's remarks in *Holderness*, a case described by Thomas in the following terms:

> The appellant received sentences totalling four years' imprisonment for a variety of charges, primarily motoring offences. The court stated that the sentencer had failed to 'take the step . . . of standing back and looking at the overall effect of the sentences', and that if he had done so, 'he would have at once appreciated that he was imposing the kind of sentence which is imposed for really serious crime'. The sentence was reduced to twenty-seven months.[19]

The total sentence of 4 years passed by the trial judge was not impugned as an aggregate of the sentences appropriate for each individual crime. What the sentencer had failed to do was to consider that total sentence in relation to other crimes which would attract such long terms of imprisonment – perhaps a single serious wounding or a rape. It was argued in Chapter 4 that some progress can be made towards criteria of proportionality between different types of offence. We can give reasons why a single middle-range rape is *ceteris paribus* more serious than a single middle-range burglary or a single offence of driving while disqualified. But what reasons can be given for saying that a middle-range rape is more serious than four burglaries or nine cases of taking cars? Assuming there is agreement on what constitutes a middle-range burglary,[20] it still seems implausible merely to 'do the arithmetic' and to rest content with that. 'Doing the arithmetic' might mean that a rape is given 5 years, that 4 burglaries at 12 months each amount to 4 years, and that 9 offences of theft from shops at 4 months each amount to 3 years. There is an intuition that any calculation which results in such a close approximation of sentences between a

---

[19] Thomas (1979), p. 58.

[20] In the guideline decision of *McInerney and Keating* [2003] 2 Cr App R (S) 240, above ch. 4.4.10, the court (following SAP) described a 'standard burglary' and used this as a marker.

rape (5 years) and a moderate number of burglaries or of thefts from shops goes against common sense. This intuition suggests that ordinal proportionality is the driving force behind the totality principle – an extended notion of ordinal proportionality that places the seriousness of individual offence types above the seriousness of repeat minor offending. We return to the normative problems after a critical survey of current English law, based on the sentencing guidelines.

8.3 Guidelines on sentencing multiple offenders

The Sentencing Council was placed under a statutory duty to prepare a guideline 'about the application of any rule of law as to the totality of sentences'.[21] It issued a definitive guideline in 2012, and we have already referred to its approach to offences taken into consideration (see 8.1.4 above). On the issue of multiple offenders and totality, the guideline states two general principles:

1. All courts, when sentencing for more than a single offence, should pass a total sentence which reflects *all* the offending behaviour before it and is just and proportionate. This is so whether the sentences are structured as concurrent or consecutive. Therefore, concurrent sentences will ordinarily be longer than a single sentence for a single offence.
2. It is usually impossible to arrive at a just and proportionate sentence for multiple offending simply by adding together notional single sentences. It is necessary to address the offending behaviour, together with the factors personal to the offender as a whole.[22]

The guideline goes on to set out the circumstances in which either concurrent or consecutive sentences will ordinarily be appropriate, but it insists that there is no inflexible rule on this and that 'the overriding principle is that the overall sentence must be just and proportionate'. The totality principle is therefore rendered as the principle that the sentence must be 'just and proportionate', but no guidance is given as to how the court should achieve such a sentence.

Should the totality principle be used as the finishing point or the starting point of a court's reasoning when sentencing a multiple offender? It is usually presented as having a limiting or restraining effect on normal sentencing principles, and therefore as a finishing point. However, there is some evidence that, in practice, judges do not always proceed by first calculating the appropriate sentence for each offence, then adding them together, and then reducing the total so as to arrive at a fair overall sentence. Marianne Wells, in her detailed study of sentencing for multiple offences in Western Australia, argued that many cases show a 'top-down' approach which starts with the totality principle rather than ending with it.

---

[21] Coroners and Justice Act 2009, s. 120(3)(b).
[22] Sentencing Council, *Offences Taken Into Consideration and Totality: Definitive Guideline* (2012), p. 5.

The totality principle becomes the primary determinant of whether the total sentence is appropriate; considerations of whether the individual sentences are correctly calculated and rightly made cumulative [i.e. consecutive] are subsumed in the general question of whether the total sentence is appropriate.[23]

This led her to suggest that on some occasions the principle drives the sentence rather than limiting it. Austin Lovegrove, in his detailed study in Victoria, also concluded that the totality principle is determining as well as limiting in its effects.[24] The English guidelines set out four steps for sentencing multiple offenders, of which the third is 'Test the overall sentence(s) against the require-ment that they be just and proportionate', to be applied only after the court has calculated concurrent or consecutive sentences. However, the guideline begins with 'general principles' 1 and 2 set out above, and they focus on the totality principle, making it clear that the concurrent/consecutive question is a mere presentational matter. This emphasis on totality may lead sentencers to focus on that rather than on the individual sentences for the various offences. There is considerable attraction in Wasik's suggestion that totality should function 'as a reference point for the judge throughout the whole sentencing exercise, rather than as something that comes just at the beginning, or just at the end'. The Sentencing Council purported to reject this characterization of the process, even though Step Two of its guideline requires the court to 'reflect the overall criminality involved' and to 'consider if the aggregate length is just and proportionate'.[25]

Turning to the four steps in the guideline, the first step is to consider the sentence for each offence, referring to the relevant sentencing guidelines. The second step is to determine whether the case calls for concurrent or consecu-tive sentences (it already having been stated that this is less important than the overall question of totality). Concurrent sentences will be discussed first, followed by consecutive sentences in 8.3.3.

8.3.1 The idea of concurrence

Where a court has to pass sentence for two or more offences, the sentences might in theory be made concurrent or consecutive. Taking the question at the level of principle, what does the notion of concurrence imply?[26] Its most obvious reference is temporal: offences committed concurrently ought to receive concurrent sentences. Of course, concurrence in time is not a precise

---

[23] Wells (1992), p. 43.

[24] Lovegrove (1997). See also Lovegrove (2004) for detailed analysis of the reasoning of judges in Victoria when sentencing multiple offenders.

[25] Cf. Wasik (2012), p. 291, with Sentencing Council, *Overarching Guideline Professional Consult-ation: Allocation, Offences Taken Into Consideration and Totality* (2011), p. 17. See also the Victorian Sentencing Manual, which emphasizes the role of totality as a 'guiding principle': Judicial College of Victoria (2014), s. 6.4.1.

[26] For a learned analysis of the continental law, see Jareborg (1998).

concept: if one offence follows immediately upon another, or even rapidly upon another, one might be tempted to refer to them as occurring at the same time and to treat them as parts of the same incident. On the other hand, the longer an incident continues, the more serious it usually is; therefore, irrespective of the procedural issue of whether a continuing series of offences is thought to call for concurrent or consecutive sentences, it is surely right that such a series of offences should be regarded *ceteris paribus* as a more serious manifestation of criminality than a single such offence and as justifying a greater total sentence.

Even where there is exact temporal concurrence, however, there might be other reasons for arguing that concurrent sentences would be inappropriate. Consider a case of burglary in which the offender enters the house, begins to steal items and to pack them into a bag, is surprised by the occupier and strikes the occupier in order to make good his escape. It would generally be said that the offence of violence was committed at the same time as the burglary;[27] in principle an offence of burglary accompanied by violence ought to be regarded as more serious than burglary without violence; the crime of burglary is not sufficiently broad to encompass all cases of violence;[28] therefore, it could be both logically and morally appropriate to pass consecutive and not concurrent sentences. Although the offences were concurrent in point of time, they violated different kinds of legal prohibition (i.e. offences against property, offences against the person). The offender ought to be labelled both as a property offender and as a violent offender, and his criminality should be viewed more seriously than if he had committed the property offence alone.

8.3.2 Concurrent sentences

The Council's guideline states that 'concurrent sentences will ordinarily be appropriate where

a) Offences arise out of the same incident or facts, or
b) There is a series of offences of the same or a similar kind, especially when committed against the same person.

Proposition a) reflects the longstanding principle that where two or more offences are separately charged and they form part of a 'single transaction', the court should generally impose concurrent sentences. Sometimes this refers to offences committed within a short space of time, sometimes it refers to a single incident that gives rise to two or more charges. Thus in *Attorney*

---

[27] Technically, if the burglary were charged under s. 9(1)(a) rather than s. 9(1)(b) of the Theft Act it would be complete at the time of entry. But the time difference would still be small.
[28] Burglary contrary to s. 9(1)(b) includes the infliction of grievous bodily harm, but no lesser form of violence. Aggravated burglary (s. 10) involves the carrying, not the use, of a weapon.

General's Reference No. 57 of 2009 (2010)[29] the offender was given concurrent sentences in respect of the possession of several firearms found when his house was raided. The Court of Appeal was asked to increase the overall sentence by imposing some of the sentences consecutively, largely in order to circumvent a maximum penalty that was regarded as too low. The Court refused to do this, on the basis that sentences arising from a single transaction should be concurrent. A similar stance has been taken in other judgments.[30] The guideline itself gives the example of 'robbery with a weapon where the weapon offence is ancillary to the robbery and not distinct and independent of it'.[31] The guideline goes on to say that the robbery sentence 'should properly reflect the presence of the weapon' and that the separate sentence for the weapons offence should run concurrently 'in order to avoid the appearance of under-sentencing in respect of the robbery'.

However, it is very difficult to construct a workable definition of a 'single transaction': Wasik demonstrates the elasticity of the concept in the hands of the Court of Appeal, citing several decisions that seem to make the timeframe narrower or broader without explanation, let alone justification.[32] The problem is that there is an indisputable core of meaning, so that in some cases there can be no doubt that the offences arise out of a single transaction since there is temporal concurrence; but there is a penumbra of uncertainty in which no firm guidance can be given to courts and which is open to manipulation. In these penumbral cases, the 'single incident' principle seems to be little more than a pragmatic device for limiting overall sentences rather than a reflection of a sharp category distinction. Wasik, in the same vein as Jareborg, concludes that the 'single transaction' principle is 'too malleable and vague to form a useful basis for distinguishing concurrent from consecutive sentencing'.[33] We will return to the question of principle later. For the moment, the 'single incident' principle forms part of the definitive guideline; in some decisions the Court of Appeal applies it faithfully,[34] whereas in others it exploits the penumbra of uncertainty that the guideline makes no attempt to clarify.[35]

The justification for proposition b) is more difficult to discern. If all other factors are held constant – a given number of offences committed over a given period; the nature and circumstances of violence, or the amounts involved in theft or fraud, or the degree of sexual violation – it is hard to see why the mere fact that the offences were committed against the same victim or, as the case may be, against different victims should make a substantial difference to the seriousness of the case. It is equally hard to see why the probably slight difference in overall gravity should be reflected in a decision to impose

---

[29] [2010] 2 Cr App R (S) 190.   [30] E.g. *Whittingham et al.* [2011] 2 Cr App R (S) 96.
[31] Sentencing Council, *Offences Taken Into Consideration and Totality: Definitive Guideline* (2012), p. 6, citing *Celaire and Poulton* [2003] 1 Cr App R (S) 610.
[32] Wasik (2012), pp. 294–7.   [33] Wasik (2012), p. 296, citing Jareborg (1998), p. 131.
[34] See nn. 29–30 above.   [35] See the cases cited by Wasik, above, n. 32.

concurrent rather than consecutive sentences. The guideline itself seems to regard this as a presentational matter. The first example given is 'repetitive small thefts from the same person, such as by an employee': the guideline contemplates that the sentence 'would be properly considered in relation to the total amount of money obtained and the period of time over which the offending took place'. In other words, length of sentence should be determined on the totality principle, and the sentences should then be expressed as concurrent, 'each one reflecting the overall seriousness'. Thus the totality principle appears to be the primary determinant of the sentence, rather than a limiting principle.

The guideline refers to circumstances in which concurrent sentences 'will ordinarily be appropriate'. It says nothing about possible exceptions, but there is established common law authority for at least two. The first is that the carrying of a firearm should be marked not only by the separate conviction but also by a consecutive sentence. A longstanding authority is *Faulkner* (1972):[36] the offender was seen on the roof of a warehouse and chased by the police, and was subsequently convicted of various offences including conspiracy to steal, assault, and offences contrary to the Firearms Act. He was sentenced to 3 years' imprisonment for the firearms and 3 years consecutive for the other offences. On appeal it was argued that the offences formed part of a single transaction and ought to attract concurrent sentences. The Court, dismissing the appeal, held that if an offender carried a firearm with intent when pursuing a criminal enterprise, a consecutive sentence should be imposed in order to discourage such conduct. This is deterrent reasoning, but a similar result can be reached by referring to the need to mark the special seriousness of firearms offences. Although the sentence should be consecutive, the judge should ensure that the 'totality of sentences is correct in all the circumstances of the case', so that the offender 'is not sentenced twice over for carrying a gun'.[37] There is also authority that sentences for assaults on the police or others attempting a lawful arrest should be consecutive. As the Court of Appeal remarked in *Kastercum* (1972),[38] consecutive sentences are generally preferable to emphasize the gravity of assaulting the police as a means of escape. The arguments in favour of these two exceptions seem strong, but one could follow Wasik in questioning whether, granted the social importance of these policies, it is necessary to mark them with consecutive sentences. Why not impose separate sentences which are concurrent, allowing the court to mark the overall seriousness of the conduct and to register a separate sentence for the firearms or the attempt to evade justice?

---

[36] (1972) 56 Cr App R 594.
[37] To the same effect, *Kent* [2004] 2 Cr App R (S) 367: judge correct to pass consecutive sentence for firearms offence when sentencing for manslaughter, but total sentence reduced from 15 to 12 years.
[38] (1972) 56 Cr App R 298, followed in *Wellington* (1988) 10 Cr App R (S) 384.

8.3.3 Consecutive sentences

The Council's guideline states that 'consecutive sentences will ordinarily be appropriate where

a) Offences arise out of unrelated facts or incidents, or
b) Offences that are of the same or a similar kind but where the overall criminality will not sufficiently be reflected by concurrent sentences,
c) One or more offence(s) qualifies for a statutory minimum sentence and concurrent sentences would improperly undermine that minimum.'[39]

Proposition a) is the mirror image of proposition a) on concurrent sentences: it is the necessary implication of the 'single transaction' principle. As such, it has similar strengths and weaknesses to those pointed out in 8.3.2 above. Thus the distinction between a 'single incident' and an 'unrelated incident' is far from clear-cut. There are plenty of indisputable cases – not merely those with a lengthy and manifest time difference, but also the second example from the previous paragraph (assaulting the police in order to escape arrest). Offences committed while on bail could also be added. A decision that falls clearly within this category is *Hartley et al.* (2012),[40] where a group of men set up machinery for producing counterfeit £20 notes; they were detected and charged with conspiracy, and while on bail for that they set up another counterfeiting operation elsewhere, which became the subject of a separate conspiracy charge. The Court of Appeal dismissed the argument that concurrent sentences were appropriate for the two conspiracies, and held that the sentence should be consecutive, subject to overall totality. Not only were the two offences separated by some four months, but the second was committed while on bail for the first. The notion of 'unrelated facts or incidents' may be applied to some clear cases, but it also leaves some penumbral cases of doubt,[41] which remain with no more guidance than was available in respect of concurrent sentences.

Proposition b) is intended to operate by way of an exception to proposition b) in respect of concurrent offences. Thus a series of offences of the same or a similar kind should be sentenced concurrently, 'especially when committed against the same person', unless the offences involve domestic violence or sexual crime, in which case some consecutive sentences may be called for. Presumably the aim of this is to mark the special seriousness of offences of those kinds; but just as it was not clear why offences against the same victim should be treated as less serious than offences against different victims, so it is also unclear why offences of these two kinds are singled out. Properly sentenced, such offences are already treated seriously, and so are various other kinds of offence.

---

[39] *Offences Taken Into Consideration and Totality*, p. 7.   [40] [2012] 1Cr App R (S) 431.
[41] On which see Wasik (2012), p. 296.

Proposition c) reaffirms that the concurrent/consecutive distinction should not be allowed to have the effect of circumventing the policy of minimum or prescribed sentences, or indeed the effect of circumventing a maximum penalty that is thought to be too low.[42] Thus the distinction between concurrent and consecutive sentences may be used not only presentationally but also to ensure respect for other sentencing policies.

8.3.4 The totality principle

The guideline sets out four steps, of which the third is to 'test the overall sentence(s) against the requirement that they be just and proportionate'. This is an attempt to establish the totality principle as the ultimate reference point of all sentences imposed for multiple offences. There are two difficulties with this. The first is that the guideline gives no guidance whatsoever on the way in which a judge or magistrates' court should approach the matter. How is totality to be assessed? At the consultation stage the Council showed no appetite for linking the calculation of totality to the guidelines for particular types of offence: the formulation by Thomas, that the aggregate sentence should not exceed the top of the range for the most serious of the offences, was dismissed for the rather thin reason that the range for some offences comes close to the maximum sentence – a reason that in any event only applies to a small number of offences.[43] As a result, the calculation of totality seems to be left to 'instinct' and 'feel', creating a most unsatisfactory hole in a system of guideline sentencing.

The second difficulty with Step Three of the guideline, which compounds the first difficulty, is that the totality principle has already made two appearances at Step Two, raising doubts about the schematic process of the guideline. Thus at Step Two, when the court has decided to impose concurrent sentences, 'the sentence should reflect the overall criminality involved. The sentence [by which is meant, the total sentence] should be appropriately aggravated by the presence of the associated offences.' The Council is concerned here to ensure that, where its propositions indicate concurrent sentences, the level of those concurrent sentences should be sufficient to reflect the fact that multiple offences were involved, usually by treating the other offences as aggravating the sentence for each offence. This means that the court must form an opinion about the level of sentence that would be 'just and proportionate' in order to calculate the appropriate concurrent sentences. Thus the totality principle is engaged at Step Two. The point is even more obvious when the Step Two propositions indicate consecutive sentences: 'where consecutive sentences are to be passed, add up the sentences for each offence and consider if the aggregate

---

[42] See *Raza* [2010] 1 Cr App R (S) 56, and the cases in nn. 30–1 above.

[43] Sentencing Council, *Overarching Guideline Professional Consultation: Allocation, Offences Taken Into Consideration and Totality* (2011), p. 18.

length is just and proportionate'. The guideline then goes on to suggest ways in which the overall sentence can be reduced. Thus the totality principle is wholly engaged in these calculations.[44] There is no objection to its being used as what the Council terms a 'stand back and look' test applied 'towards the end of the decision-making process', at Step Three;[45] but it is wrong to suggest that it is not involved at earlier stages, and Wasik's suggestion that it should be regarded 'as a reference point throughout the sentencing process' is more realistic.[46]

Returning to the first difficulty with the Council's use of the totality principle, the guideline's failure to go beyond the phrase 'just and proportionate' means not only that sentencers are furnished with no guidance but also that the Court of Appeal needs to give no particular reasons for its assertions about totality. The opacity of English sentencing practice on this point may be illustrated by two decisions. In *Jenkins et al.* (2009)[47] the offenders were being sentenced for five armed robberies of security guards over a period of six months. The Court of Appeal discussed what the starting point should be, and decided that 25 years was appropriate 'for a number of armed robberies where violence is actually used'. The Court went on to decide that 21 years was the appropriate starting point for these five robberies, and so calculated the proper sentence from that. Clearly this was an application of the totality principle; but no hint was given as to how this figure was reached and, more particularly, how the actual number of robberies impacted on length of sentence. Similarly in *Hartley et al.*, mentioned earlier,[48] the Court of Appeal agreed that the sentences should be consecutive, but concluded that the trial judge 'did not make a proper reduction for totality'. The Court then reduced the overall sentence from 12 years 2 months to 10 years 8 months, without disclosing any reasons for the amount of the adjustment. Further examples of this opacity are plentiful, and it should be added that recent judgments dealing with totality fail even to mention the Council's guideline[49] – hardly surprising, in view of its declared purpose of summarizing current practice, but nevertheless procedurally defective.

8.3.5 Other applications of totality

The discussion so far has been limited to sentencing for multiple offences as applied to determinate custodial sentences. The guideline goes on to indicate the preferred approach to a number of other sets of circumstances, such as where the offender is being sentenced to indeterminate custodial sentences or to extended sentences, or is already serving a custodial sentence, or is in breach of a licence. The details will not be discussed here.

---

[44] Judicial College of Victoria (2014), p. 1.   [45] Ibid., p. 17.   [46] Wasik (2012).
[47] [2009] 1 Cr App R (S) 109.   [48] N. 40 and accompanying text.
[49] See e.g. *May* [2014] 1 Cr App R (S) 58, *Wynne et al.* [2014] 1 Cr App R (S) 63, *Williams* [2014] 2 Cr App R (S) 464.

In principle it is right that courts should adopt the same approach when dealing with a multiplicity of less serious offences which result in either community orders or fines. The guideline indicates that consecutive community orders (e.g. unpaid work) will be rare. It indicates a preferred approach to fines for multiple offences, starting with the proposition that 'the total fine is inevitably cumulative' (i.e. there are no concurrent fines). A relevant decision is *Chelmsford Crown Court, ex p. Birchall* (1989).[50] Between 12 July and 19 July one year, the offender was driving his lorry between a quarry and some roadworks, fulfilling a contract. Investigators found that on ten of these journeys the lorry had been overweight. Sentencing him for ten offences, a magistrates' court simply added together the fines for each of the offences, producing a total fine of £7,600. The Crown Court dismissed his appeal against sentence. The Court of Appeal held that the sentence was 'truly astonishing', in that the lower courts had simply 'applied a rigid formula to each offence' and had then added up the resulting fines to produce a total. The main point in the decision to reduce the fine to £1,300 was that proper account had not been taken of the offender's means, but the Court of Appeal also deprecated the failure to have regard to the totality principle.

8.4 Totality: time for a fresh start?

The English sentencing system, with or without guidelines, is in a ragged state when it comes to dealing with multiple offenders. It has few defensible principles, and its central concept is the nebulous notion of totality. In this final section, the discussion begins with some reflections on the core concepts in this branch of English sentencing law, moves on to some deeper questions of principle, and then finally proposes some ways of introducing structure and consistency to this vexed issue.

8.4.1 Reappraising the concurrent/consecutive distinction

It was argued in 8.3.1 and 8.3.2 above that there are some central cases where there can be no dispute that the offences form part of a single incident or transaction, and thus where concurrent sentences make perfect sense; and equally there are some cases where there can be no dispute that the offences were not part of a single incident. The problems are that i) some single incident cases might justify consecutive sentences on the ground that two different wrongs have been committed at the same time and they should be signaled appropriately, and ii) there is a penumbra of uncertainty where reasonable people could disagree about whether or not the offences form part of a single incident. These difficulties, particularly the second one, have led

---

[50] (1989) 11 Cr App R (S) 510.

Wasik and others to argue for a reappraisal of the concurrent/consecutive distinction. One approach would be to abolish consecutive sentences, leaving only concurrent sentences. Sentence length would be determined by the most serious offence, with the other offences treated as aggravating factors. A second approach would be to introduce a presumption in favour of concurrent sentences, allowing consecutive sentences for presentational purposes.[51] Richard Frase argues for this approach, drawing on various US systems. The presumption would be in favour of concurrent sentences; consecutive sentences would be permissible for certain limited purposes, e.g. marking out the seriousness of firearms offences or offences against law enforcement officers; but there would be an overall limit, which might be twice the guideline sentence for the leading offence.[52] A third approach would be to continue to allow courts to present the sentences as they wish, using concurrent or consecutive sentences, so long as the overall sentence complies with the totality principle. In all these calculations the totality principle would be the most powerful element, and any legislative change would not affect the overall severity of sentences, just their presentation (in terms of effective communication to the offender, the victim(s), and the wider public). However, there is a fourth option – to leave courts to use concurrent or consecutive sentences where the facts clearly point in one or other direction, but to emphasize that in cases of doubt the court may present the sentences as it wishes so long as totality is observed and there is no double-counting or under-sentencing. The concurrent/consecutive distinction does make good sense in clear cases, but Wasik is right to argue that fundamentally the question is one of presentation and that calculating the total sentence is the most important task.

8.4.2 The foundations of the totality principle

What arguments support the totality principle? It seems to have some resonance with public opinion: research by Robinson and Darley into popular assessments found that most people intuitively adopted a model similar to the English, so that sentences for multiple offenders were increased but the approach was to add 'a decreasing increment for each additional offence'.[53] There is also plenty of evidence in judicial reasoning that the totality principle has strong intuitive appeal, but where are the principled arguments?

One argument is that the principle is supported by the exercise of mercy at the sentencing stage. Thus Thomas identified a judicial principle that the total sentence should not be such as to impose a crushing burden on an offender

---

[51] This is similar to the law in the Australian state of Victoria, which lays down a general presumption that sentences should be concurrent, although the Victorian Sentencing Manual, s. 6.4.9.1, states that in practice consecutive sentences are frequently imposed: Judicial College of Victoria (2014).

[52] Frase (2013), pp. 144 and 149, and ch. 4 generally.

[53] Robinson and Darley (1995), p. 193, and comments by Roberts (2008a), pp. 180–2.

whose prospects are not hopeless.[54] In Lovegrove's study in Victoria it seemed to be concern for the crushing effect of the sentence on the offender rather than concern about the proportionality principle that led judges to consider the totality of the sentence.[55] Thus the Victorian Sentencing Manual states that sentencers should avoid, whenever possible, sentences that will have a 'crushing effect' either by provoking a feeling of helplessness or by destroying any reasonable expectation of useful life after release.[56] In a sophisticated discussion of the totality principle, Anthony Bottoms argues that the principle might be supported as a rational exercise of mercy.[57] However, the terms in which such exercises of mercy are justified must be carefully expressed. In the formulations by Thomas and Lovegrove (above), it is the crushing effect of a very long sentence (to which Thomas adds, 'on an offender whose prospects are not hopeless') that justifies some reduction. But if we are to be faithful to the argument of Bottoms that the exercise of mercy must be rational, this means that mercy must also be exercised where similar (undefeated) reasoning applies. What about very long prison sentences in general? In Chapter 4 we noted the use of very long sentences not only for homicide offences but also for robbery, drug importation, and rape. If an offender receives a very long sentence for a single bad offence of this kind, should the same reasons of mercy operate to reduce the length of the sentences? The Victorian Sentencing Manual does apply the principle generally, although it also states that some offences are so serious that a 'crushing' sentence will be appropriate. Thus, if this kind of exercise of mercy is to be confined to multiple offenders, on what grounds should they be singled out? Most tellingly, why is the same reasoning on mercy not applied to the repeat offender, who is convicted several times and receives a longer sentence on each occasion? As Reitz has argued,[58] the persistent offender who is convicted frequently may have the same number of convictions as the multiple offender, or even fewer, but sentencing principles tend to offer no mercy to him or her – indeed, many sentencing systems increase rather than decrease the severity of the applicable sentences.

If the mercy rationale does not seem to be convincing, where else should we look? There seems to be an impression that cumulative sentences for multiple offenders may be viewed as disproportionate unless reined in by something like the totality principle. There seem to be two different senses of proportionality at work here. As Wells argued,

> it is one thing to say that, even though all the sentences are appropriate and proportionate to the individual offences and rightly made cumulative, the total is excessive by reference to a more serious offence; it is quite another to say that, in the same circumstances, the total is excessive in relation to the total conduct

---

[54] Thomas (1979), p. 9.   [55] Lovegrove (2004).   [56] Judicial College of Victoria (2014), s. 6.6.
[57] Bottoms (1998), pp. 63–70.   [58] Reitz (2010), pp. 145–7.

involved. If the sentence is reduced because it exceeds the normal range of sentences for a more serious offence, it does not necessarily follow that the reduced sentence is proportionate to the total conduct.[59]

This ambiguity between what might be called 'inter-offence' and 'intra-offence' proportionality is evident in the English sentencing guideline, which requires a total sentence 'which reflects all the offending behaviour and is just and proportionate' – thus encompassing both forms of proportionality.[60] As Wells argues, it is possible for the sentence to satisfy one form of proportionality without satisfying the other. One might wish to say that the sentence for 14 indecent assaults on children should remain below the normal sentence for rape,[61] but what if there were 24 or 34 indecent assaults on children? In that eventuality it could be argued that the overall sentence should remain below the level for rape (perhaps, the starting point for level 2), but it might be thought that the sentence was disproportionately low in terms of the serial sex offending involved. Which kind of proportionality should prevail? The predominant answer to this question is that it should be the first, 'inter-offence' sense of proportionality that should be uppermost. As will be evident in 8.4.3 below, attempts to 'capture' the totality principle tend to start from the appropriate sentence for the most serious of the offences committed, so as to preserve proportionality between types of offence. The result is that multiple offenders being sentenced for 20 or 50 offences are subjected to only small and barely existent increments for the large number of offences, thereby sometimes failing to satisfy the intra-offence sense of proportionality. Thus Reitz objects that:

> It is implausible to say that one robbery plus ten burglaries cannot surpass the maximum seriousness threshold of one robbery, or that six sexual assaults upon different 14 year-old victims may never exceed the gravity of the most aggravated rape of a single 10 year-old.[62]

The plausibility may depend on the width of the sentence ranges provided by the applicable guidelines, but in general Reitz's point is well taken, not least if one compares the sentences for the multiple offenders with those for recidivist offenders who are convicted after each burglary or sexual assault. However, the point being made in this paragraph is a point about intuitions: there seems to be a powerful public and judicial intuition that inter-offence proportionality should be the principal driver.

One possible ground for taking a different approach to sentencing recidivists and multiple offenders is that the former have continued to offend despite

---

[59] Wells (1992), p. 38.
[60] Sentencing Council, *Offences Taken Into Consideration and Totality: Definitive Guideline* (2012), p. 5.
[61] E.g. *Attorney General's References No. 38 of 2013(Hall)* [2014] 1 Cr App R (S) 394.
[62] Reitz (2010), p. 146.

being formally censured. As we saw in relation to previous convictions in Chapter 6.2.4 above, official censure by conviction should be expected to bring an offender to adjust his conduct.[63] Insofar as the multiple offender has not had such a conviction during the period of the offences for which he is now being sentenced, this situation is different in principle from that involving previous convictions. However, it is doubtful whether the significance of the public censure involved in conviction is sufficient to support the wide difference between the mitigating effect of the totality principle and the aggravating effect of the recidivist premium. Thus the 'official censure' argument has some, but not enough, resonance.

8.4.3 Totality operationalized

It has been manifest throughout this chapter that the most powerful concept is that of totality. However, the English guideline states the test, 'that the total sentence should be just and proportionate', without saying anything about the method of achieving this. There is a strong argument that the Sentencing Council has failed in its statutory duty: the Gage Committee called for 'narrative guidance' on totality to 'assist transparency and consistency and possibly improve predictability',[64] but the 2012 guideline cannot be said to have achieved that, or even to have adopted it as a goal.

What should be done? It has already been observed that the Council declined, on rather weak grounds, to adopt the principle formulated by Thomas, that 'the aggregate sentence should not be longer than the upper limit of the normal bracket of sentences for the category of cases in which the most serious offence committed by the offender would be placed'.[65] Some such approach would be a step towards inter-offence proportionality, and is fairly similar to that proposed by the Advisory Council on the Penal System.[66] The approach of German law is also similar, taking the most serious of the offences and treating the other offences as aggravating factors, but all the time insisting that the sentencer makes a comprehensive judgment of the offender's person and of the individual offences. This resembles the English guideline on taking offences into consideration (see 8.1.4 above). The practical results of the German system may be seen in the research by Hans-Jörg Albrecht, as presented by Nils Jareborg:

> The average 'cost' for one burglary was 7.9 months, for three burglaries 15.6 months (97 per cent added for two more crimes), for five burglaries 22.9 months (47 per cent), for seven burglaries 24.6 months (7 per cent), and for 9 burglaries

---

[63] Cf. also the argument of Lee (2009) that a moral obligation to desist from reoffending arises from the fact of conviction, which would also indicate a distinction between multiple and recidivist offenders.

[64] Gage (2008), para. 7.13.   [65] Thomas (1979), p. 9, cited above, n. 42.

[66] ACPS (1978), para. 219.

26 months (6 per cent added for two more crimes). A rough norm resulting from the data indicates that the total sentence is found halfway between the punishment for the most serious crime and the sum of punishments for all the crimes. It was also apparent that the upper limit of the scale of penalties used in practice (not the statutory maximum) had a steering effect.[67]

The details of the German system are less important than its general approach. In a system such as the English, the crucial step would be to create a definite link between the particular offence guidelines and the totality principle for multiple offences. Without this, the purpose of sentencing guidelines is likely to be undermined, so frequent are multiple offences.

In order to sketch a possible approach, we should return to the discussion of persistent offenders in Chapter 6 above. We noted that offence guidelines tend to list recent and relevant previous convictions as the first aggravating factor at Step Two, and to add that such relevant convictions may make it appropriate 'to move outside the identified category range'.[68] That formulation was criticized for its vagueness, since it offers no guidance on the types of previous record that might justify going above the category range. However, it would be a major step if the approach to sentencing for multiple offences were placed on the same footing – as an aggravating factor in relation to the most serious offence of conviction, which might in appropriate circumstances result in going above the category range. That would have the great advantage of tying the total sentence for the multiple offences to the offence range for the most serious of the offences, and of achieving a measure of inter-offence proportionality, so long as the guidelines indicated the proper approach to the quantum of the aggravation. Thus the offence guidelines should be developed by giving examples of practical problems in multiple offence sentencing, with recommended solutions. Among the examples might be cases with large numbers of multiple offences, multiple offences against multiple victims, and so forth.

There would undoubtedly be judicial resistance to such an approach, arguing that this is *par excellence* a proper realm for discretion and judgment, and that 'a mathematical approach is liable to produce an inappropriate answer'.[69] However, a reconsideration of sentencing multiple offenders should be based on research carried out by the Sentencing Council, both statistical and involving discussions with judges about their approach to totality. Linking the totality principle to the offence guidelines would not be more 'mathematical' than the rest of guideline sentencing. Currently there must be some rule of thumb that judges themselves use. No doubt senior judges would say that it is a question of judicial experience. But, as pointed out in Chapter 1, if 'experience' is to be valuable then all cases cannot be unique, and there must

---

[67] Jareborg (1998), p. 135.

[68] E.g. Sentencing Council, *Burglary Offences: Definitive Guideline* (2011), p. 9.

[69] Per Judge P in *P and Blackburn* [2008] 2 Cr App R (S) 16, para. 39.

be discernible factors that are given particular weight. We have seen in this chapter that the totality principle is pragmatic, with shaky theoretical foundations but a strong intuitive attraction. The aim should now be to ensure that it has a consistent structure that judges can apply in individual cases. No less important is empirical research into how judges make these calculations, in order to capture the factors that influence judges in practice and that constitute their 'experience'.

9

Custodial sentencing

Contents

This chapter presents a critical appraisal of the law and practice on custodial sentences. Imprisonment involves deprivation of liberty and is the most onerous and intrusive sentence available in this and other European countries, engaging several rights declared in the European Convention. Deprivation of liberty and incarceration in a punitive institution therefore require special justification. To begin that process, it is necessary to understand the practical meaning of custodial sentences. This depends on the various provisions for calculating the proportion of the nominal sentence that the offender will spend in custody, on the conditions in which prisoners are held, and on the terms on which they are later released. While the sentence handed down in court establishes the framework, there are exercises of discretion in the prisons and by the Parole Board that have powerful effects in determining the time actually served.[1]

The chapter begins with an outline of the state of English prisons. It then considers principles and policies for the use of custodial sentences, and moves on to an analysis of the statutory tests for imposing custody, and also the prevailing approach to long custodial sentences. The chapter concludes with a brief discussion of various groups of prisoners who raise particular issues of principle.

---

[1] See Padfield, Morgan and Maguire (2012), pp. 967–981.

9.1 The state of the prisons

What have been the conditions in English prisons in recent years, and what are they likely to be in the foreseeable future? The brief survey below looks at trends in the prison population, at the prison estate and at recent problems in the prisons.

9.1.1 The prison population

The size of the prison population is determined, to a considerable extent, by sentencing law and practice. However, there are other significant influences: we saw in Chapter 1.4 above that practices in reporting, recording, and prosecuting may vary, and this affects convictions and sentences; the use of remand in custody, and recalls to prison for breach of conditions, both have an effect; and there are exercises of discretion by the prison authorities and the Parole Board in relation to the timing of release of sentenced offenders. The ebbs and flows of these various influences have produced significant changes in the prison population in England and Wales during the last three decades. In 1980 it stood at a little over 42,000; by 1988 it had reached almost 50,000, but it then fell again, to a low of 40,606 in December 1992; from 1993 it rose steeply, reaching 66,000 at the end of 1999, and peaking at 88,000 in 2011 before falling back slightly to 85,000 in 2014. It must be borne in mind that prisons do not only hold sentenced offenders, and that the figures for the prison population include prisoners held on remand. However, the steep rise in the prison population since 1993 is almost entirely attributable to an increase in the numbers of sentenced prisoners held. In round figures, some 11,000 of the average number of 43,000 prisoners held in 1993 were on remand, whereas in 2013 the figure was some 11,000 out of some 84,000 (see Appendix B, Table 8). Thus, an increasingly high proportion of the prison population – over five-sixths – consists of offenders sentenced to custody by the courts.

9.1.2 The prison estate

When an offender is sentenced to custody in England and Wales, there are two administrative but critical decisions to be taken by the Prison Service. The first decision is to place the offender in one of the security classifications, from A (high risk) to D (suitable for open conditions). The security classification of each prisoner is a 'continuing responsibility' of the Prison Service,[2] and so it should be reconsidered from time to time. It is important not only because it determines the restrictiveness of the regime to which the prisoner will be subject, but also because it governs the second decision – the allocation of the prisoner to a particular establishment. There is a list of factors that should

[2] *R v. Home Secretary, ex p. Duggan* [1994] 3 All ER 271.

be taken into account in this allocation decision,[3] but inevitably a significant amount of discretion is exercised, often purely on grounds of administrative convenience (i.e. available space).

According to their security classification, female offenders are sent to open or closed women's prisons or, if under 21, to a young offender institution. Male young offenders go to young offender institutions, whereas adult male prisoners may be sent to open or closed prisons, according to their security classification. Prisoners sentenced to 18 months or less may serve the whole sentence in a local prison, if they are not considered suitable for open conditions. Prisoners serving longer sentences are likely to be sent to a 'training prison'. Regimes differ considerably between local and training prisons, with fewer activities and more time locked in cells at the former. This is partly because local prisons usually hold remand prisoners, whose stay in prison may be relatively short and may involve frequent trips to and from court, and partly because local prisons tend to be overcrowded, with a consequent difficulty of providing adequate supervision, work, etc. for all inmates. These observations are taken further in part 9.1.3 below.

Since the early 1990s there has been a substantial expansion in the prison estate. By building new prisons, extending existing institutions, and contracting with private operators, governments have increased the 'certified normal accommodation' (CNA) of prison service establishments to around 76,000 in mid-2014. But the number of prisoners has continued to outstrip the supply of places, and therefore the building programme has not solved some of the endemic problems of English prisons. While the Carter Review (2007) recommended that the prison estate be brought up to 96,000 places by 2014, governments fortunately did not follow this advice. But by falling so far short of what is necessary to house prisoners in decent and humane conditions, governments have perpetuated a situation in which about of a quarter of prisoners are accommodated in overcrowded conditions.

9.1.3 The problems of the prison system[4]

If sentences of imprisonment are to be justified, the justifications must extend not simply to depriving an offender of liberty for a certain period of time but also to incarcerating the offender in the particular conditions that obtain in the relevant prison system – including subjection to the extraordinary social order constituted by the prison, and to relative powerlessness and to violence. Even if England and Wales had a prison system that complied fully with all international standards and with the targets set for the Prison Service itself,

---

[3] See Livingstone, Owen and Macdonald (2008), ch. 4, on classification and allocation of prisoners.
[4] For fuller discussion, see Liebling and Crewe (2012), and Cavadino, Dignan and Mair (2013), chs. 6 and 7.

each custodial sentence and each month or week of it would still require strong justification. This is a crucial point to be borne in mind when assessing the various rationales for sentencing outlined in Chapter 3 above: an English sentence of imprisonment involves loss of liberty under certain adverse conditions and, insofar as these amount to infringements of basic human rights, they call for clear and convincing justification.

Many of the endemic problems stem from the single fact of overcrowding. At the beginning of July 2014 the five most overcrowded prisons were Swansea, Leicester, Lincoln, Exeter, and Wandsworth, all operating at around 170 per cent of their official capacity (certified normal accommodation). Many establishments (chiefly local prisons) have been operating at well over their CNA for several years, with a consequent strain on officers, prisoners, and the regime itself. Insufficient progress has been made since the European Committee for the Prevention of Torture, Inhuman and Degrading Treatment (CPT) visited four prisons in England and Wales in 2001. As it observed then, 'much remains to be done to achieve the objective of holding all prisoners in "a safe, decent and healthy environment"',[5] and it specifically criticized the conditions under which some inmates were held two to a cell measuring 8.5 metres square or less, sometimes without properly partitioned lavatories.[6]

The reasons for the persistent overcrowding seem to involve a complex mixture of geographical demands, an excess of accommodation in open institutions, the need to close wings of some prisons in order to refurbish them, and, of course, the fact that the prison-building programme (although considerable) has not kept pace with the number of people sent into custody. The effects of overcrowding are felt in a variety of ways, and the implications are well documented. Thus in his examination of the causes of the disturbance at Strangeways Prison, Manchester, a quarter of a century ago, Lord Woolf found that:

> A large proportion of the inmates were sympathetic to the instigators of the disturbance and antagonistic towards the Prison Service because of the conditions in which they were housed at the time at Strangeways ... As the inmates repeatedly told the Inquiry, if they were treated like animals they would behave like animals. The prison was overcrowded, and the inmates provided with insufficient activities and association.[7]

The effects of overcrowding and allied problems remain a theme of reports by HM Chief Inspector of Prisons. In its annual report for 2012–14, the Inspectorate applied a safety index to the 39 prisons inspected: while most of the training prisons and open prisons were found to be 'good' or 'reasonably good' on safety, 7 of the 12 local prisons were 'not sufficiently good' on safety;[8] it is local prisons, as already stated, that bear the brunt of overcrowding.

---

[5] CPT (2001), p. 19.   [6] CPT (2001), p. 23; see also p. 45.   [7] Woolf (1991), para. 3.432.
[8] HMCI Prisons (2014), p. 25.

The Inspectorate also applied a 'respect' index to the 39 prisons, and here the results (relating to the treatment of prisoners and the quality of staff-prisoner relationships) were more mixed and were less differentiated between training and local prisons. In the 12 locals 'respect' was 'not sufficiently good' or 'poor' in 5, and the same unsatisfactory results were found in 9 of the 15 training prisons.[9] Research suggests that safety may be connected with the culture of an institution and the regime: where the authorities exert greater control, the opportunities for predatory violence are diminished; while many prisoners prefer a relaxed regime, this allows the staff more discretion and also offers more opportunities for violent attacks.[10] Assessing the 'legitimacy' of given prison regimes is therefore no easy matter, but perceptions of fairness (particularly in dealings with staff) are crucial, and seem to have an effect on the wellbeing of prisoners.[11]

One well-known concomitant of overcrowding is a lack of activity for prisoners, and the latest Chief Inspector's report follows many previous ones in highlighting this deficiency. Just under half of the 39 prisons visited (18) were 'not sufficiently good' or 'poor' on purposeful activity, including 8 of the 12 local prisons inspected. Some 29 per cent of prisoners in local prisons spent less than 2 hours a day out of their cells. It is not just a question of absence of work; there is also a lack of education and skills courses in many establishments, particularly local prisons. It is hardly surprising that research indicates that prisons have an overall negative effect – often destabilizing family ties, disrupting employment opportunities, stigmatizing ex-prisoners, and causing difficulties for the communities that the prisoners come from and return to.[12] Whether the Ministry of Justice's 'Transforming Rehabilitation' Strategy succeeds in altering this dismal trend remains to be seen. The Inspectorate reported that 'offender management and resettlement work were still uncoordinated and inconsistent' in 2013–14.[13] The Ministry's new policy has laudable ideals: 'establishing a nationwide "through the prison gate" resettlement service to give most offenders continuity of support from custody into the community'.[14] However, the method will depend to some extent on tendering for contracts to provide the required service (to be discussed in Chapter 10.8). Moreover, conditions in the prisons are not propitious. In 2014 the Chief Inspector of Prisons twice issued public warnings about the deteriorating state of the prisons, with more overcrowding and staff shortages.[15] His 2014 report records that 'overcrowding continued to be a problem in more than 60% of prisons inspected, with prisoners

[9] Ibid., p. 32.   [10] Liebling and Crewe (2012), pp. 902–3.

[11] E.g. Sparks, Bottoms and Hay (1996), Liebling (assisted by Arnold) (2004).

[12] For a review of US research, see Travis, Western and Redburn (2014), chs. 8, 9, 10 and 11.

[13] HMCI Prisons (2014), p. 47.

[14] Ministry of Justice, www.justice.gov.uk/transforming-rehabilitation (4 June 2014).

[15] See www.bbc.co.uk/news/uk-27847007 (14 June 2014) and www.bbc.co.uk/news/uk-28233294 (9 July 2014).

sometimes living in squalid conditions'.[16] These are poor conditions in which to achieve a 'rehabilitation revolution'.

Two further reflections on the experience of imprisonment concern mental health and religion. On the first point, it is important to keep in mind the characteristics of prisoners. Not only are many of them disadvantaged in various ways (e.g. upbringing, education, employment), but a relatively high proportion have suffered from mental disorder before they are imprisoned, and the prison regime has strongly negative effects on the mental health of some prisoners. The high rate of suicides in prison bears testimony to this, and half of prison suicides take place during the first month of entering prison.[17] As for religion, recent surveys of prisoners reveal that substantial numbers are converting to Islam, and that this is not only having a polarizing effect on some other prisoners but also presenting staff with new challenges relating to alleged discrimination.[18] These concerns demonstrate the extraordinary tensions within prisons, which have their effect on staff and prisoners alike.

9.2 The use of imprisonment

Before examining the law relating to custodial sentencing, it is instructive to consider the evidence on the use of imprisonment by the courts of England and Wales. How does the overall imprisonment rate relate to that of other similar countries? What kinds of offender are imprisoned, and for how long, in English prisons?

9.2.1 International comparisons

The traditional way of comparing the relative severity of different sentencing systems has been to refer to the current table of prisoners per 100,000 of population in various countries. The *World Prison Population List* is not an utterly reliable indicator, because different countries compile their statistics in different ways.[19] However, at least within Western Europe, the figures show fairly consistent patterns across time from jurisdiction to jurisdiction. While there is a need for more searching work on the proper basis for international comparisons, it is surely legitimate to draw attention to some longstanding differences. Thus the statistics consistently suggest that some countries, particularly those in Scandinavia, succeed in using custody distinctly more sparingly: in 2013 the relevant rates were 58 for Finland, 67 for Sweden, 72 for Norway, and 73 for Denmark – all below one-half of the rate in England and Wales, which stands at 148. The two countries with which the

---

[16] HMCI Prisons (2014), p. 32.
[17] Liebling and Crewe (2012), pp. 918–20; HMCI Prisons (2014), pp. 28–9.
[18] For a summary of the evidence, see British Academy (2014), pp. 57–61.
[19] See Nuttall and Pease (1994), and Walmsley (2013), p. 1.

UK is often compared economically and socially have also tended to use imprisonment at distinctly lower rates: 79 for Germany and 98 for France.[20] Moreover, as the Carter Review (2007) reported, in the years from 1995 to 2006 the prison population in England and Wales rose by 60 per cent, compared with 16 per cent in Germany and 1 per cent in France.[21] There are therefore serious questions about whether the use of imprisonment in England and Wales (almost double that in Germany, and 50 per cent higher than in France) might be reduced without increasing the risk of victimization, particularly at a time when crime rates are falling.[22]

In a major study, Nicola Lacey has examined the reasons for the significant differences in imprisonment rates, particularly across Europe but also including the United States. Going beyond the useful typology and information set forth by Cavadino and Dignan (2006), Lacey argues that account must be taken of the institutions of different kinds of country, including 'welfare states, professional bureaucracies, electoral systems and labour market and training structures'. Deploying this sophisticated socio-economic framework, Lacey suggests that:

> The relatively disorganized, individualized 'liberal market economies' such as the USA and the UK could be shown to be particularly vulnerable to the hold of 'penal populism', while the 'co-ordinated market economies' of Northern Europe and Scandinavia, with their proportionally representative political systems and economies focusing on long-term investment in specialist skills providing a reliable bridge to employment, were better placed to resist pressures for penal expansion.[23]

Thus Lacey argues that social and economic policy may have more to do with crime rates than sentencing policy. The corporatist approach in Germany means that there is little political or legal discussion of sentencing reform, and moderate sentencing levels are sustained by institutional features such as the form of German legal education (inculcating certain values) and the selection of career judges from the top law school graduates.[24] More broadly, towards the end of his recent study, Tapio Lappi-Seppala contrasts the effects of different kinds of political system:

> Consensual politics lessen controversies, produce less crisis talk, inhibit dramatic turnovers and sustain long-term consistent policies. In other words, consensual democracies are less susceptible to political populism. While the consensus model is based on bargaining and compromise, majoritarian democracies are based on competition and confrontation. The latter sharpens distinctions, heightens controversies and encourages conflicts. This affects the stability

---

[20] Walmsley (2013), p. 5.   [21] Carter (2007), p. 5.

[22] Much higher rates of imprisonment can be found in Eastern European countries; the world 'leader' is the USA (716): Walmsley (2013).

[23] Lacey (2008), pp. 115–16.   [24] Hoernle (2013).

and contents of policies, as well as the legitimacy of the political system as a whole. There is more crisis talk, more criticism, more short-term solutions, more direct appeals to public demands, and a higher risk of exclusive populist penal policy.[25]

This emphasizes the social and political locus of criminal justice in general and sentencing in particular. Any assertion of a causal connection between crime rates and imprisonment rates must be based on a thorough assessment of other social and political forces. It is tempting to argue that the decline in crimes recorded by the British Crime Survey (now CSEW) since 1995, which roughly corresponds to the increasing imprisonment rate, demonstrates that England and Wales has successfully deployed a greater use of prison to bring down rates of crime and of victimization, perhaps through incapacitation. This would be a particularly important argument in these times of economic austerity, because it might furnish some reason for thinking that the vast sums spent on prisons are producing a safer society. But the argument does not work: in common with almost all other European countries, France and Germany, which have not had a significant increase in the use of imprisonment, have also experienced declines in their crime rates in recent years.[26] Moreover, any assertion that deterrent or incapacitative effects are being achieved needs to be investigated thoroughly. If the claim is that 'prison works' through deterring potential offenders, it would have to be found, for example, that potential offenders are aware of an increasing risk of conviction and of imprisonment for longer and that this has affected their decision-making. In fact, what the well-known Farrington and Langan studies show is that there is a significant link between the certainty of punishment and offending rates, but not between the severity of punishment and offending rates.[27] If the claim is that 'prison works' through incapacitating a considerable number of offenders, it is important to examine that claim in the context of the fact that only some 3 per cent of offenders in any one year go to court, and an even smaller percentage go to prison. None of this is to deny that there may be a small causal link; rather it is to indicate the complexity of establishing even a modest effect, as shown by the detailed examination of the evidence in the recent report on *The Growth of Incarceration in the United States*.[28]

---

[25] Lappi-Seppala (2013).

[26] Various sets of relevant statistics may be found at epp.eurostat.ec.europa.eu/statistics_explained.

[27] See the searching discussion of Farrington and Langan (1992) by von Hirsch et al. (1999), pp. 25–8.

[28] Travis, Western and Redburn (2014), ch. 5. The Halliday Report (2001, p. 130) cited Home Office estimates that around 10,000 more prisoners would be needed to reduce the incidence of crime by 1 per cent. The Carter Review (2003, p. 16) concluded that the increase in the prison population since 1997 might have reduced crime by 5 per cent, adding: 'the fall in the number of young people over the same period is estimated to have reduced crime by a similar amount'.

Once it is accepted that crime rates are affected by social and economic factors as much as by sentencing choices, it becomes evident that political change is necessary if the prison population is to be reduced. The 'tough on crime' message that has been at the core of most party political pronouncements in recent years seems to be welcomed by many sections of the press. The media remain a powerful influence, or at least threat, on this subject. The strategy for change therefore requires a 'replacement discourse' that has a wide popular appeal, but which is likely to require a great deal of political courage from the government in the first place. Indeed, Lacey argues that major aspects of criminal policy ought to be removed from bipartisan politics in the same way as monetary policy has been transferred to an independent committee at the Bank of England, in order to insulate decisions from the media and from politicians.[29]

9.2.2 The changing profile of the prison population

In a study entitled *Story of the Prison Population 1993–2012* the Ministry of Justice sets out to identify the main drivers of the almost doubling of the English prison population between 1993 and 2012, from some 44,000 to around 86,000. Not surprisingly, the study found that some 85 per cent of the rise stemmed from increases in the use and length of sentences of immediate custody. However, it is significant that most of the remaining increase (13 per cent) was attributable to the steep increase in recalls to prison of prisoners released on licence. Release policies, such as parole and home detention (discussed below), were said to have been more or less neutral, and the remand population has been fairly stable.[30]

The study finds that the increase in determinate sentences chiefly took effect between 1997 and 2002, and that since then most of the increases in the prison population are attributable to the growth in the breach and recall populations, and to the delayed effect of the longer sentences handed down in those years together with the period during which the indeterminate sentence of imprisonment for public protection (IPP), discussed in Chapter 6.8 above, was in force. If we focus on determinate prison sentences, we find that the custody rate rose from 16 per cent in 1993 to 28 per cent in 2002, around which point it has settled (27 per cent in 2012). Average determinate sentence lengths went up from 14.3 to 16.4 months for indictable offences between 1999 and 2004, and then steadied before increasing to 17.4 months in 2011.[31] This increase is all the more remarkable because many of the more serious offenders were receiving indeterminate sentences of IPP between 2005 and 2012, and IPP and life sentences are outside the calculation of average sentence lengths.

---

[29] Lacey (2008), pp. 190–6; see also British Academy (2014), pp. 87–90.
[30] Ministry of Justice (2012), p. 1.   [31] Ibid., p. 11.

Although the sentence of IPP was abolished as from 2012, over 5,000 prisoners are still serving IPP sentences. Table 15 in Appendix B shows that IPP prisoners and lifers now form a significant part of the adult male sentenced custodial population, almost one-fifth. Numbers nearly doubled between 2002 and 2007, and these are offenders who will remain in prison (and therefore forming part of the prison population) for many years. The table also shows that the number of offenders in prison sentenced to under 12 months has begun to decline for men, with the growth taking place in all the longer sentences, with increases even in recent years of sentences in the 4 years plus range.

9.3 Principles for the use of custodial sentences

We have noted in 9.1.3 above that the conditions in which English prisoners may serve their sentences sometimes (or often) fall short of international standards. Where this is so, custodial sentences are hard to justify – they knowingly condemn offenders to 'inhuman and degrading' treatment. Such sentences should not be imposed; or, if for public policy reasons this is thought 'necessary,' the principle of restraint in the use of custody should be strictly construed.[32] As noted in Chapter 3.3.2, there is now widespread international assent to the principle of restraint in the use of imprisonment. Resolution VIII of the Eighth United Nations Congress on the Prevention of Crime and the Treatment of Offenders (1990) states in paragraph 5(e) that 'imprisonment should be used as a sanction of last resort'. The Council of Europe has likewise declared a policy of encouraging the use of non-custodial sentences and reserving custodial sentences for the most serious types of offence.[33] However, the international survey by Dirk van Zyl Smit and Frieder Dünkel demonstrates the continuing centrality of imprisonment to the sentencing policy of most nations:

> The sentence of imprisonment remains the backbone of the system of penal sanctions – in spite of repeated proclamations at international congresses and in resolutions of the United Nations and the Council of Europe and other regional bodies that imprisonment should be seen solely as an *ultima ratio*. Alternatives to imprisonment continue in most countries to derive their credibility from the residual function of imprisonment, which, in as far as the death penalty has been abolished, is the most serious reaction to conduct that is seen as particularly dangerous to society or that repeatedly contravenes the law. This is strikingly demonstrated by the threat of imprisonment being used as the primary sanction for infringement of conditions of probation or the failure to pay a fine.[34]

---

[32] See Kleinig (1998) on related issues.   [33] Council of Europe (1992).
[34] Van Zyl Smit and Dünkel (2001), p. 796.

Increases in the use of imprisonment are policy choices, and in 9.2.1 above we noted the fragility of the evidence on the effects of such increases on crime rates. Moreover, the policy choices may be those of other agencies (such as the police and prosecutors) rather than the government or the courts. In England and Wales government policies have been somewhat diverse (some would say, confused). During the second part of the 1990s Michael Howard, as Home Secretary, pronounced that 'prison works', and his successors, Jack Straw and David Blunkett, continued an expansionist prison policy.[35] However, there were also official statements and policies favouring restraint in the use of custody in some less serious cases. The coalition government of 2010 to 2015 began with some strongly reformative statements, including a denunciation of the foundations for the IPP sentence,[36] and it has continued with the Offender Rehabilitation Act 2014, which seeks to reduce offender reconvictions. However, the coalition government has also introduced strong measures and has certainly not explicitly pursued a policy of reducing the prison population. In broad terms, it seems to follow the bifurcated policy of its predecessors.

9.3.1 Justifying restraint in the use of custody

The true principle of restraint in the use of custody is one which argues for the use of non-custodial sentences instead of custodial ones, and which argues for shorter custodial sentences instead of longer ones. The UN declaration that 'imprisonment should be used as a sanction of last resort', and its Latin form *ultima ratio*, is a problematic formulation: it seems to imply that custody may justifiably be used for someone who persistently commits minor offences, and for whom all other measures have been tried, whereas that justification is questionable; on the other hand, it contains

> the important truth ... that not too much should be expected of the criminal law or of criminal punishment, and that it should always be asked whether there are other less costly and more promising methods for trying to achieve the social ends that criminal law is often ill-equipped to serve.[37]

This reasoning, grounded in the realities of English imprisonment set out in 9.1.3 above, points in the direction of restraint in the use of custody, or a 'presumption against imprisonment'.[38] Brief consideration is given here to three arguments in favour of restraint – doubts about the preventive effects of imprisonment, human rights and humanitarian concerns, and the importance of an inclusionary and secure society.

---

[35] For the politics of 'prison works', see Windlesham (1996), ch. 4; see further Downes and Morgan (2007), p. 214.

[36] Cited in Chapter 6.8 above.   [37] British Academy (2014), p. 78.

[38] British Academy (2014), Part II.

(i) Doubts about the preventive effect of custody

When Michael Howard was Home Secretary, from 1993 to 1997, he proclaimed that 'prison works'. This could hardly stand as a reference to deterrence or to rehabilitation, since the reconviction figures within two years remain over 50 per cent for adults released from prison and are significantly higher for young offenders – similarly the figures for desistance from crime in the ten years following release.[39] It may be true to say that 'prison works' in that it succeeds in incapacitating almost all prisoners (except the very few who escape) for the duration of their sentences. But this hardly seems a convincing basis for penal policy, since (i) it is a short-sighted kind of effectiveness when so many of the prisoners then reoffend on release; (ii) it is also short-sighted if there is little possibility of innovative schemes for prisoners, especially given the considerable overcrowding in local prisons; and (iii) the impact of keeping these offenders in prison is slight in terms of additional security for the ordinary citizen since, as we saw in Chapter 1.4, fewer than 3 per cent of offences result in conviction, and many of those are not sentenced to imprisonment. The evidence suggests that the threat to a citizen's safety and security is not likely to be diminished significantly by imprisoning 70,000 rather than 40,000 people. When in the United States the National Academy of Sciences investigated the incapacitative effect of imprisonment on the crime rate, they found it to be marginal. The Halliday Report reached the same conclusion,[40] as did the recent US survey by Travis, Western and Redburn.[41] There is also little evidence of any general deterrent effect from greater use of custody.[42]

Turning to rehabilitation, in the 1930s Alexander Paterson, one of the most influential of Prison Commissioners, declared that 'it is impossible to train men for freedom in a condition of captivity'. This sceptical position has occasionally been repeated in government statements, most plainly in the Thatcher government's 1990 assertion that prison 'can be an expensive way of making bad people worse'.[43] Whether and to what extent the experience of imprisonment makes offenders worse may be difficult to establish;[44] but such consequences as loss of employment, loss of housing, loss of contact with family, increased financial problems, and possible deterioration in physical and mental health must all be taken into account.[45] Moreover, the people sent

---

[39] See Burnett and Maruna (2004), tracing the careers of some 130 offenders released in 1992, on whose reactions to prison Mr Howard had originally placed reliance.

[40] Halliday (2001), App. 3.   [41] Travis, Western and Redburn (2014), ch. 5.

[42] Von Hirsch, Bottoms, Burney and Wikstrom (1999); Halliday (2001).

[43] Home Office (1990), para. 2.7; for a similar earlier statement, see Home Office (1977), para. 17. Cf. the coalition government's statement that '[t]he criminal justice system cannot remain an expensive way of giving the public a break from offenders, before they return to commit more crimes.' Ministry of Justice (2010), p. 1.

[44] See Nagin, Cullen and Johnson (2009).   [45] Social Exclusion Unit (2002).

to prison tend to have high rates of social disadvantage. In 2002 the Social Exclusion Unit reported that:

> Many prisoners' basic skills are very poor. 80 per cent have the writing skills, 65 per cent the numeracy skills and 50 per cent the reading skills at or below the level of an 11-year-old child. 60 to 70 per cent of prisoners were using drugs before imprisonment. Over 70 per cent suffer from at least two mental disorders. And 20 per cent of male and 37 per cent of female sentenced prisoners have attempted suicide in the past.[46]

Given these characteristics of prisoners, and the conditions in many prisons (particularly local prisons), it is hardly surprising that reconviction figures for released prisoners are poor. Indeed, a comparative survey of reconviction rates following various types of sentence, which took account of age, type of offence and previous record, found that custodial sentences performed slightly worse than expected for all offenders other than the few first offenders. In general terms, the proportion reconvicted within two years of release was 54 per cent for prison, 49 per cent for community service, 42 per cent for 'straight' probation and 63 per cent for probation with additional requirements.[47]

Greater optimism has been generated by enthusiasts for the What Works movement, which has led, inter alia, to the introduction of programmes for prisoners aimed at reducing reoffending. The Halliday Report claimed that there was evidence that these programmes could bring about a 5 to 15 per cent reduction in reoffending, whether the programmes were delivered in the community or in prison.[48] This claim was described by Tony Bottoms as 'reckless', and he showed it to have been ill-founded.[49] A detailed review by Colin Roberts of three evaluations of offending behaviour programmes in prisons shows that the promising results of the first phase, in the mid-1990s, were not maintained in later years, and that there were mixed results in one-year and two-year reconviction studies. Roberts suggests that, if there has been a downturn in effectiveness, this may be explained by the enthusiasm of the staff and the volunteers in the early programmes compared with the more generic approach of the much-expanded programmes now delivered.[50] Several thousand prisoners per year are being put through the various programmes: on the one hand the Carter Review stated that reoffending by ex-prisoners had been reduced by 4.6 per cent between 2000 and 2006,[51] whereas on the other hand the Chief Inspector continues to warn of the restrictive effects of overcrowding in many prisons.[52] In the prison conditions that currently obtain in England and Wales, therefore, doubts about the rehabilitative potential of penal institutions are well-grounded.

---

[46] Ibid., Summary, para. 12.   [47] Lloyd, Mair and Hough (1994).
[48] Halliday (2001), para. 1.49. See also p. 130, where para. 30 repeats the claim but para. 31 states that 'the actual impact of these programmes has yet to be validated through proven results'.
[49] Bottoms (2004), pp. 62–3.   [50] Roberts, C. (2004), pp. 136–42; see also Wilkinson (2005).
[51] Carter Review (2007), p. 5.   [52] HMCI Prisons (2014), pp. 32–3.

The coalition government has introduced a scheme aimed at improving the support of prisoners on release, particularly short-term prisoners, under the Offender Rehabilitation Act 2014. Important as this initiative is, it has to work against the negative effects of imprisonment on those who experience it, and the fractured relationships and difficulties over housing and employment that await many prisoners on release. All these realities point in the direction of reducing reliance on prison sentences in the first place.

(ii) Human rights and humanitarian concerns

It is simply not acceptable for state institutions to operate in violation of human rights. There is already plenty of evidence, in reports from the CPT and academic research,[53] that some English penal establishments fall below international standards in several respects. Insofar as particular prisons do not attain the minimum standards required internationally, this may be a reason for closing them. It is certainly a strong argument for reducing the number of people sent to prison and the length of their sentences.

Greater weight is sometimes placed on a related argument, that imprisonment should be used less because the prisons are *overcrowded*. There is some logic in this: a given number of months incarcerated in overcrowded conditions may be as punitive as a longer period in less unpleasant conditions.[54] But it shares with the human rights argument a temporary dimension. Overcrowding could be removed by a massive programme of prison building. This, however, would be the opposite of restraint in the use of custody. If, for example, the government were to commit itself to provide in the next year 100,000 prison places in conditions that fulfil international standards, the human rights arguments would be met but the principle of restraint in the use of custody would be undermined rather than advanced. In practice, the human rights and overcrowding arguments ought to have considerable purchase in England and Wales at present because there is no immediate prospect of significant improvement. But their limitations should not be overlooked.

A more durable line of reasoning stems from the inevitable pains of imprisonment. Custody entails a deprivation of personal liberty, which is one of the most basic rights, and often involves considerable 'hard treatment'.[55] Loss of liberty takes away the freedom to associate with one's family and friends, and separates one from home and private life as well as from open society. Prison is therefore a severe restriction on ordinary human rights, far above those imposed by most non-custodial sentences, and its negative effects

---

[53] Above, nn. 10–13 and accompanying text.

[54] See the reasoning in *Mills* [2002] 2 Cr App R (S) 229 at p. 233 ('in a borderline case . . . it is very important that those who have responsibilities for sentencing take into account the overcrowding in women's prisons'), and *Kefford* [2002] 2 Cr App R (S) 495 at p. 497 ('the courts must accept the realities of the situation', i.e. overcrowding).

[55] Kleinig (1998).

on the prisoner's capacity for autonomy and responsible citizenship should be recognized.[56] Moreover, the restriction of rights impinges not just on the offender but also on the offender's family and dependants. These considerations suggest that custody should not be used without some strong justifications, and should be reserved for the most serious cases of lawbreaking. In particular, they suggest that custody should not simply be seen as the top rung of a ladder which starts with discharges and runs upwards through fines and community penalties. The imposition of a custodial sentence restricts liberty to a far greater degree than any other sentence, and for that reason should require special justification.

(iii) The importance of an inclusionary and secure society

The arguments in the preceding paragraph can and should be taken further.[57] Undoubtedly the state has a duty to protect the security of its citizens, and the punishment of offenders is one way of doing that; but any regime of state punishment should be faithful to the basic values of the society. Prominent among the values of British society are personal liberty (which imprisonment takes away); autonomy, dignity, and solidarity – values that are fundamental to individual and social life but which must also be respected by the punishment system (imprisonment seriously compromises them); social inclusion (which non-custodial sentences may help to emphasize, but which imprisonment – as a form of social exclusion – seriously compromises); and security, not an illusory subjective security but an objectively grounded reduction of risks (the difficulties in English prisons were explained in preceding paragraphs (i) and (ii)). These are central values for democratic societies. They should be reflected in all social institutions, including those of state punishment. They point to a reduction in the use of imprisonment from the current immoderate level, renouncing its use as a default punishment, and demanding strong justifications for each prison sentence and for each month and week of imprisonment.

9.3.2 Government policy on imprisonment

For at least 15 years, government policy has appeared consistent with the idea of bifurcated responses to offending, commending long sentences for serious offenders and a reduction in sentence severity for minor offenders. Thus in December 2008 the Ministry of Justice made this statement of policy:

> Our starting point is that the public must be protected from those offenders who pose a threat. This is why prison is the right place for the most dangerous, serious and the most persistent offenders. We are increasing prison capacity to ensure that we always have enough places for these offenders ... But we need

---

[56] Lippke (2007), esp. chs. 5, 6 and 7.
[57] The arguments in this paragraph are based on British Academy (2014), Part II.

both prison places and effective community punishments to achieve the best outcomes for victims and the public. For less serious offenders, tough community sentences can be more effective in punishing and reforming them than a short custodial sentence.[58]

While this passage is consistent with a bifurcated approach, the difficulty is that it explicitly includes within the upper track (prison) 'the most persistent offenders', without any reference to the seriousness of their offences. Either this is a casual use of language, or it suggests that the government wishes those who persistently commit credit card frauds and thefts from shops to be sent to prison, once they have experienced non-custodial sentences. However, as argued in Chapter 6 above, this is often to sentence such offenders disproportionately severely, in view of the scale of their depredations.

It is not only in relation to persistent offenders that bifurcated policies give rise to controversy. Prison is said to be reserved for those committing serious offences, but where is the line to be drawn? Controversy on this point arose when Lord Woolf departed from the Sentencing Advisory Panel's proposed sentencing levels on domestic burglary by calling for the greater use of community sentences for certain first- and second-time burglars.[59] That judgment drew strong criticism from Mr Blunkett as Home Secretary, from sections of the media and from some sentencers.[60] Less publicity was accorded to the fact that the foundation stone for Lord Woolf's argument that public protection would be improved rather than reduced by giving fewer custodial sentences to first- and second-time burglars was a report from the government's own Social Exclusion Unit that spelt out the shortcomings of imprisonment as a form of public protection, criticizing it as expensive and counterproductive.[61] What this public disagreement shows is that the positioning of the two tracks of bifurcation policy is open to debate, and that often politicians may be more interested in making political capital out of an issue than in spelling out the reasons and the details of their policy. It is perhaps not surprising that several of the sentencers interviewed by Hough, Jacobson and Millie complained about 'mixed messages' from both politicians and the senior judiciary.[62]

Although the then Home Secretary was prominent in the reaction to Lord Woolf's burglary judgment, the mass media played their part in condemning, even lampooning, the Lord Chief Justice. Interestingly, a research project by Bottoms and Wilson into public attitudes was able to include a question directly about Lord Woolf's burglary guidelines, and some 70 per cent of the

---

[58] Ministry of Justice (2008), p. 2; for an earlier example, see Home Office (2002), paras. 5.6–5.7.
[59] *McInerney and Keating* [2003] 2 Cr App R (S) 240.
[60] Charted in Davies and Tyrer (2003). See further ch. 4.4.10 above.
[61] *McInerney and Keating* [2003] 2 Cr App R (S) 240, at pp. 256–8, quoting from Social Exclusion Unit (2002); see also text at n. 46 above.
[62] See above, ch. 6.3.

responses supported his approach.[63] The research was conducted in Sheffield, the city often referred to by the then Home Secretary, David Blunkett, as his barometer on crime. Once again, careful research demonstrates differences between the true opinions of the public, and those voiced by politicians and the media.

In 2010 the coalition government's Green Paper, *Breaking the Cycle: Effective Punishment, Rehabilitation and the Sentencing of Offenders*, struck a different note. Its theme was that the prisons were not doing their job: 'The criminal justice system cannot remain an expensive way of giving the public a break from offenders, before they return to commit more crimes.'[64] 'Recent reform has been dominated by increases in the prison population rather than tackling reoffending … Nearly 50% of offenders released from prison reoffend within a year.'[65] The message of expenditure cuts was combined with that of rehabilitation: 'Our proposals will achieve this [sc. reducing spending] through a greater focus on protecting the public by rehabilitating criminals and turning them away from a life of crime.'[66] Despite a change of Justice Secretary and a toughening up of some rhetoric, the coalition government has continued to develop its emphasis on rehabilitation, by introducing post-release supervision for short-term prisoners and by piloting privatized 'payment for results' schemes to turn offenders away from crime. These, and a small reduction in the prison population from its peak of 88,000 in 2011 to 85,000 in 2014, open up the possibility of a distinct change of emphasis. So far, it has been a matter of 'too little, too slowly', and without a real determination to re-examine the use of imprisonment.

9.4 On the cusp of custody: short custodial sentences and suspended sentences

In 2002 a government White Paper stated that 'for those who are not serious, dangerous or seriously persistent offenders, we need to provide a genuine third option to sentencers in addition to custody and community punishment'.[67] This strategy was to be realized in the 2003 Act by providing, in addition to a new 'customized community sentence' (see Chapter 10 below), three new forms of short custodial sentence for those offenders for whom 'short prison sentences will continue to be appropriate'. The motivating force behind the new sentences was that the pre-2003 Act regime of short sentences included no element of supervision: prisoners serving less than 12 months were released after serving half the nominal term, but without proper support. The new strategy was to emphasize 'our overall aim of reducing reoffending' by ensuring that offenders on short sentences 'have proper support, supervision and follow-through of education programmes, drug treatment and anger

[63] Bottoms and Wilson (2004), pp. 394–5.   [64] Ministry of Justice (2010), p. 1.
[65] Ibid., paras. 6–7.   [66] Ibid., para. 25.   [67] Home Office (2002), para. 5.7.

management schemes in the community'.[68] This was to be achieved by creating three new forms of sentence – the suspended sentence, intermittent custody, and custody plus.

The provisions of the 2003 Act on intermittent custody and on custody plus were never brought into force. Intermittent custody was given a trial in a few parts of the country, but the courts did not find many cases for which it was ideal, and some of the doubts set out in a previous edition of this work seemed to be borne out.[69] Custody plus was one of the flagships of the 2003 reforms: every sentence of under 12 months was to take effect with a short custodial period followed by a licence period of up to 26 weeks, with supervision and other requirements aimed at reducing reoffending. Not only would custody plus require considerable resources to provide the community supervision, but there were obvious dangers of overuse, leading to fears that the system would quickly become overwhelmed and unable to deliver the intended benefits. Although sentencing guidelines were created in order to try to prevent the anticipated misuse,[70] the government recognized the dangers of introducing custody plus (five of which were set out in a previous edition of this work).[71] Of the three reforms for which the 2003 Act legislated, only the suspended sentence was introduced, and its subsequent history may be thought to confirm the fears of what might have happened if custody plus had been implemented.

Before examining the suspended sentence, we must discuss the statutory tests for custodial sentences, and the way in which the courts now tend to use short custodial sentences, and the provision of supervision and support for short-sentence prisoners.

9.4.1 The statutory tests for custodial sentences

Section 152(2) of the Criminal Justice Act 2003 provides:

> The court must not pass a custodial sentence unless it is of the opinion that the offence, or the combination of the offence and one or more offences associated with it, was so serious that neither a fine alone nor a community sentence can be justified for the offence.

Thus a court that is thinking in terms of custody ought first to consider whether a fine or a community sentence could be justified. Only if the court concludes that the case is too serious for either of those measures is a custodial sentence lawful. Once the court reaches this stage, a second statutory test in s. 153(2) requires it to ensure that the custodial sentence it passes is 'for the shortest term (not exceeding the permitted maximum) that in the opinion of the court is commensurate with the seriousness of the offence'.

---

[68] Home Office (2002), paras. 5.22–5.23.   [69] 4th edn (2005), pp. 277–8.
[70] SGC, *New Sentences: Criminal Justice Act 2003* (2005).   [71] 4th edn (2005), pp. 278–81.

In practice, neither of these statutory provisions is widely referred to. Mention of them in Court of Appeal judgments is rare, although there are some prominent judicial pronouncements on the need to reserve custody for serious cases and, where it is thought inevitable, to make sentences as short as possible, particularly for women and for those convicted of 'economic' offences.[72] Lord Lane CJ originally made such a pronouncement in the context of high levels of prison overcrowding,[73] and that theme was also emphasized by Lord Phillips as Lord Chief Justice. In *Seed and Stark* (2007)[74] Lord Phillips set out ss. 152 and 153 of the Act, and continued:

> In times of prison overcrowding it is particularly important that judges and magistrates pay close regard to the requirements of both these provisions. In particular, when considering the length of a custodial sentence, the court should properly bear in mind that the prison regime is likely to be more punitive as a result of prison overcrowding.

He added that, unless imprisonment is considered necessary for public protection, a court should always give consideration to a community sentence – a far-reaching proposition. The Sentencing Guidelines Council sought to reinforce the purpose of s. 152(2) by emphasizing two principles:

- the clear intention of the statutory test is to reserve prison as a punishment for the most serious offences;
- satisfying the custody test does *not* mean that a custodial sentence should be deemed inevitable, and custody can still be avoided in the light of personal mitigation or where there is a suitable intervention in the community which provides sufficient restriction (by way of punishment) while addressing the rehabilitation of the offender to prevent future crime. For example, a prolific offender who currently could expect a short custodial sentence ... might more appropriately receive a suitable community sentence.[75]

In previous editions of this work, and in several appellate judgments, there are frequent references to the 'custody threshold'. However, Nicola Padfield has argued that this is an unhelpful term, since there is no demonstrable threshold and no bright line, and in practice much depends on the various factors in each case.[76] Whether Padfield is right to suggest that reference to a custody threshold is a barrier to imposing community sentences is more doubtful; but, in order to avoid giving a false impression of sharp distinctions, reference is now made here to 'satisfying the statutory test for custody'.

---

[72] See e.g. *Mills* [2002] 2 Cr App R (S) 229, at p. 233, and *Kefford* [2002] 2 Cr App R (S) 495, at p. 497.

[73] In *Bibi* (1980) 2 Cr App R (S) 177; see also *Upton* (1980) 2 Cr App R (S) 132.

[74] [2007] 2 Cr App R (S) 436, at p. 440; see also *Attorney General's Reference No. 11 of 2006* [2006] 2 Cr App R (S) 705, at p. 711, for similar remarks.

[75] SGC, *Overarching Principles: Seriousness* (2004), para. 1.32.   [76] Padfield (2011).

As Padfield recognizes (and as research shows),[77] even in cases that do satisfy the statutory test, mitigating factors may have the effect of bringing the sentence back 'below the line'. This was the message of the leading case under the 1991 Act, *Cox* (1993),[78] where the offender's relative youth and the fact that he had only one previous conviction combined to bring the sentence for an offence that satisfied the custodial test down to a community penalty. It is also clear from the guideline on reduction of sentence for guilty plea that a timely plea of guilty may, in appropriate cases, be accorded the effect of reducing a custodial sentence to a non-custodial one.[79] Further reflections on the courts' treatment of the custody test may be found in the sentencing research by Hough, Jacobson and Millie. They found no consistent differences in the types of offence that fell either side of the 'custody threshold', but they did find particular factors that 'tipped the decision one way or the other'.[80] For decisions resulting in custody, in some cases it was the intrinsic seriousness of the offence and in others the offender's record of convictions or breaches that appeared to dominate. For cases resulting in a non-custodial disposal, a whole range of mitigating factors seemed capable of swaying the decision – remorse, guilty plea, motivation to address underlying personal problems, family responsibilities, good employment record or prospects, and a previous good record. Often the assessment of these mitigating factors came down to a moral judgment of the offender, making the sentencing process 'highly subjective'.[81]

There are some types of offence for which a custodial sentence is said to be 'unavoidable' because of their intrinsic seriousness, whatever the mitigation. Some of these offences are reviewed in the next section, before turning to the relationship between the statutory tests and sentencing guidelines.

9.4.2 The notion of 'unavoidable' custodial sentences

The purpose of this section is not to cast doubt on the use of imprisonment for really serious offences, but rather to explore certain types of case for which custody is said by the judges to be 'unavoidable'. One set of such cases is where the offender has many previous convictions or breaches of conditional sentences and, although the current offence is not particularly serious, the bad criminal record propels the offender into custody. This is where courts often say that custody is regrettable but is a 'last resort' (see 9.3.1 above) in order to

---

[77] Hough, Jacobson and Millie (2003); Jacobson and Hough (2007).
[78] (1993) 14 Cr App R (S) 479.
[79] SGC, *Reduction in Sentence for a Guilty Plea* (2007), para. 2.3, discussed in ch. 5.4.1 above.
[80] Hough et al. (2003), pp. 36–8. This finding is significant when interpreting the study by Davies and Tyrer (2003), which suggests more punitive attitudes but leaves mitigating factors largely out of account.
[81] Hough et al. (2003), p. 41; cf. the discussion in ch. 5.5 above.

give society a rest (see 9.3.1(i) above). The use of imprisonment for persistent non-serious offenders was discussed in Chapter 6.3 above.

The main interest here is in types of offence for which custody is said to be 'unavoidable'. Probably the highest profile offence of this kind is perverting the course of justice. The offence may be committed in diverse situations, but courts tend to regard it as deserving custody, in principle, and irrespective of mitigation. One group of cases is where one person agrees to pretend that he or she was driving in order to take the speeding fine and penalty points of the real driver. Thus in *Henderson and Metcalfe* (2012)[82] the offenders, both men of previous good character, were imprisoned for four months. The statutory test in s. 152(2) was satisfied because 'offending of this sort strikes at the heart of the criminal justice system'. A second group of cases is where a person falsely reports that he or she has been the victim of a crime. False allegations of rape, for example, have tended to attract substantial sentences of up to two years' imprisonment. This was the sentence upheld in *Day* (2010),[83] even though the offender had mental and alcohol problems. She had named her alleged attacker, and he was detained by police for 10 hours.[84] In cases where no person is named as the alleged attacker, levels of sentence tend to be lower but prison is still said to be unavoidable.[85] A third group of cases is where an offence is committed by or against a juror. Thus prison was said to be unavoidable when two women followed jurors onto a bus and spoke about the case in loud and intimidating ways: in *Curtis and Medlan* (2013)[86] the two young women of previous good character were imprisoned for 5 and 3 months respectively for contempt of court. In *Chapman* (2013)[87] a juror was imprisoned for 2 months for contempt of court for lying in order to absent herself from court to take a holiday. Somewhat similar is *Dittman and Anderson* (2013),[88] where two women of previous good character were sentenced to 2 months when one of them impersonated the other in order to take part of the driving test. All these cases involve or are analogous to the offence of perverting the course of justice. When judges refer to custody as 'unavoidable' in these cases, they are testifying to a belief that only a custodial sentence can mark the degree of censure required for such an offence. Most of the offenders have strong mitigation, often including previous good character and childcare responsibilities, which might otherwise bring an offence that has

[82] [2012] 1 Cr App R (S) 95; see also *Huhne and Pryce* (2013), www.standard.co.uk/news/crime/huhne-and-pryce-jailed-the-judges-sentencing-remarks-in-full, the imprisonment of a former government minister and his former wife.

[83] [2010] 2 Cr App R (S) 73.

[84] Compare *Weiner* [2012] 1 Cr App R (S) 24, where D planted indecent images of children on another man's computer and then reported him to police; man suspended from work, and not exonerated for 18 months; sentence of 12 years reduced to 10 years, still a very heavy sentence.

[85] E.g. *England* [2011] 1 Cr App R (S) 335 (false allegation of rape, 12 months); *Brustenga-Vilaseca* [2012] 1 Cr App R (S) 13 (false allegation of rape, 6 months); *Afford* [2014] 1 Cr App R (S) 4 (false allegation of assault, 8 months).

[86] [2013] 1 Cr App R (S) 147.   [87] [2013] 1 Cr App R (S) 117.   [88] [2013] 1 Cr App R (S) 113.

admittedly satisfied the custody test down below the 'custodial threshold' to a community sentence or substantial fine. But the judgments cited in this paragraph do not allow that to happen. Custody is the only suitable currency of censure and condemnation, according to the courts.

Turning away from offences of perverting the course of justice, similar reasoning can be found across a wide range of offence types. Thus in *Kidd and Bianchy* (2008)[89] the Court upheld sentences of 12 months on a mother and daughter who had forged a will in order to get their hands on an estate of some £142,000: the Court followed previous authority to the effect that forging a will requires custody, but, even accepting that as the starting point, one might argue that the sentence should be brought below the 'custody threshold' by the mitigation appropriate for a woman of 70 with no previous convictions, or at least that the sentence was surely not the shortest period commensurate with the seriousness of the offence. In *French* (2008)[90] the offender had pleaded guilty to holding himself out as a veterinary surgeon and supplying veterinary products (including antibiotics) which were not authorized. The Court of Appeal upheld the sentence of 12 months' imprisonment, despite the man being 69 and in poor health, on the basis that his illegal operations jeopardized strict controls imposed for good health reasons. In *Noonan* (2010)[91] a man pleaded guilty to several counts arising from illegal trading in elephant tusks and sperm whale teeth. Upholding the sentence of 10 months' imprisonment, the Court of Appeal drew attention to the global effects of the destruction of animal species, and the deliberate nature of the offences. In *Crosskey* (2013)[92] a young man of 20 (no previous convictions) hacked into a celebrity's Facebook account, changed the password, and invited the site administrator to discuss how to stop him going further. The Court of Appeal held that the custody test was satisfied because the violation of privacy rendered it 'inevitable', and that 8 months was appropriate. As a final example, in *Adeyimi* (2013)[93] a landlord of previous good character was sent to prison for 4 months for failing to comply with fire regulations. Two tenants died in a fire at the house, and it was held that the offender had deliberately put profit ahead of safety by ignoring warnings and lying to the authorities.

These short accounts of only some of the 'unavoidable custody' decisions do not do justice to the full facts of each case, but they are sufficient to raise questions about what is going on here. Two issues stand out. First, the judgments suggest that judges have a fixed idea that only immediate imprisonment is capable of marking the seriousness of certain offences. It is the only currency of censure, the only coinage of condemnation. A community sentence or a suspended sentence order would simply not convey an adequate message. This notion seems to be particularly strong in relation to offences against the administration of justice, notably perverting the course of justice,

---

[89] [2008] 1 Cr App R (S) 471.   [90] [2008] 2 Cr App R (S) 81.   [91] [2010] 2 Cr App R (S) 229.
[92] [2013] 1 Cr App R (S) 420.   [93] [2013] 1 Cr App R (S) 126.

but questions should be asked about the justifications for this. In some judgments this retributive sentiment is found alongside assertions about the need for deterrence – the idea that, if the sentence were not custodial, many people would take advantage and commit these offences. As with most assertions about deterrence, they are founded on a notion of 'common sense' rather than evidence, and the limitations of 'common sense' in this sphere were discussed in Chapter 3.3.2 above. Some of the offences amounted to deliberate flouting of the law, usually for profit, and this seems to be a major factor driving the court towards custody. The second issue is that very few of these 'unavoidable custody' judgments engage with the custody test in s. 152(2) or with the implications of s. 153(2). Whether the outcome would have been different if the Court of Appeal had focused on these statutory tests before reaching their conclusions is difficult to say, but the statutory tests are a direct challenge to their reasoning. Why cannot these cases be dealt with by substantial fines, or by community sentences?[94] And if the custody test is satisfied, why are the mitigating factors not sufficient to support the suspension of the custodial sentence? Probably the number of these offences is not great, by comparison with the high numbers in prison. But the argument here is about justice, fairness, and proportionality, not about saving money or reducing overcrowding. Finally, the custodial sentences upheld in these cases cannot be justified by reference to the interests of victims. There were indeed real victims in some of these cases, but the custodial sentences did nothing to compensate them or improve their position.

9.4.3 Sentencing guidelines and the custody test

How do the sentencing guidelines deal with the statutory tests for custody? Different styles are evident. In the early guidelines there was rarely any explicit mention of the statutory tests, although the guideline for handling stolen goods contains a paragraph explaining that the custody threshold will be passed where the offender has 'a record of offences of dishonesty' or engages 'in sophisticated law breaking'.[95] In the second phase of guidelines, the SGC developed a seven-step 'Decision Making Process' to guide courts through the application of the various guidelines, but that did not include any mention of the statutory tests in ss. 152 and 153.[96]

The Sentencing Council's guidelines vary. The guideline for common assault refers explicitly to the custody threshold (and to the community order threshold) at Step Two, without citing the relevant sections or their terms,[97] and the

---

[94] For a stark example, see *Vaiculevicius* [2013] 2 Cr App R (S) 362 (sex in a public park, 3 months' imprisonment, no reference to statutory tests).
[95] *Webbe* [2002] 1 Cr App R (S) 82, at [28].
[96] See e.g. SGC, *Breach of an Anti-Social Behaviour Order* (2008), p. 7.
[97] Sentencing Council, *Assault: Definitive Guideline* (2010), p. 25.

guidelines for burglary take the same approach.[98] However, the fraud guideline neglects the whole issue: the tables of category ranges and starting points include several which straddle custody and community sentences, but there is no reference to the statutory tests at all.[99] This is an unfortunate change. However, even where the guideline does refer to the statutory tests (as does that on cannabis cultivation), the relevant tests do not always form part of judicial reasoning: two Court of Appeal judgments in which custodial sentences were held to be unnecessary make no mention of the statutory wording.[100]

9.4.4 The dilemma of short prison sentences

Of some 80,000 male sentenced prisoners received into prison in 2012, some 36,000 had been sentenced to 6 months or less. For females the total was 7,600, but the number sentenced to 6 months or less was 4,400. Those who are sent to prison for short periods are, by definition, not major offenders. They may have committed a single bad act (see 9.4.2 above) or, more often, are persistent minor offenders for whom the courts see themselves as having 'run out of options'. It may be argued that prison, as our most serious form of punishment and as involving a loss of personal liberty, should be reserved for serious cases in which there is a significant danger to the community, rather than imposed on people who may be social casualties who present no real danger to others.[101] For those who regard the prisons as having rehabilitative responsibilities, short sentences are to be avoided because they allow too little time for any programmes or courses to be undertaken. At worst, they introduce offenders to prison and to other prisoners, without any counterbalancing influences. For those who regard a 'short, sharp shock' as justifying the use of short prison terms, there is a question of evidence: do they not rather 'deepen criminal justice entanglement'?[102] Arguments of this kind can be deployed in favour of a policy of abolishing short prison sentences, or creating a presumption against their use save in exceptional circumstances, or requiring courts to suspend short sentences. However, the evidence on the effect of such policies is mixed: Scotland's presumption against sentences of 3 months or less appears to have reduced their number, but has increased the number of slightly longer sentences.[103] On the other hand, the requirement to suspend sentences under 6 months appears to work reasonably well in Germany.[104]

Many European countries with a much lower use of imprisonment than England and Wales use short sentences frequently. The major difference

---

[98] Sentencing Council, *Burglary Offences: Definitive Guideline* (2011), pp. 9 and 13.
[99] Sentencing Council, *Fraud, Bribery and Money Laundering: Definitive Guideline* (2014), pp. 8–10.
[100] See *Wood* [2013] 1 Cr App R (S) 492 and *Burke* [2013] 1 Cr App R (S) 499, applying Sentencing Council, *Drug Offences: Definitive Guideline* (2012), pp. 18–21.
[101] See Scotland's Choice (2008), pp. 22–3.   [102] Ibid., p. 23.   [103] Scottish Government (2012).
[104] For discussion, see British Academy (2014), pp. 96–7.

between the English prison population and that of Nordic countries is the use of long prison sentences rather than short ones. Thus there is nothing intrinsically objectionable about short prison sentences, if they form the lower end of a proportionate use of prison sentences that reserves sentences of 3, 4 and 5 years for really serious offenders. The English system uses much longer prison sentences and indeterminate sentences with far greater frequency than any other Western European country, and consequently uses short sentences for offenders who would probably not go to prison elsewhere. It is this issue, rather than short sentences intrinsically, that is the problem. We saw in 9.4.2 above that many offenders of good character are subjected to immediate rather than suspended prison sentences on the ground that prison was 'unavoidable'. We have also referred to the problem of using short prison sentences for 'persistent' but non-serious offenders: the SGC guideline on theft stated that the community and custody thresholds may be crossed 'even though the other characteristics of the offences would otherwise warrant a lesser sentence'.[105] This is in accordance with the relevant statutory provision, s. 143(2) of the 2003 Act, but it means that persistent minor offenders will be sent to prison in considerable numbers. Even though their offences are below (or well below) the custody threshold, mere repetition is regarded as sufficient to satisfy the test in s. 152(2). The Justice Committee rightly concluded that many such offenders receive sentences disproportionate to their offending, and added:

> We are disappointed at the Government's apparent acceptance of the use of short custodial sentences for repeat offenders. There is no evidence that a short prison term will tackle recidivism. We recommend that the Government should instead produce a range of sentencing options, based on suitable evidence, after consulting sentencers, probation and other services, on what successfully removes offenders from a cycle of crime and repeat offending.[106]

This suggests both that the present statutory framework is inadequate and that more resources for new schemes are required.

9.4.5 Suspended sentence orders

Before the 2003 Act it was only possible to suspend a sentence of imprisonment in 'exceptional circumstances'. That restriction was abolished by the 2003 Act, allowing a court to impose a suspended sentence order where it passes a sentence of imprisonment of between 14 days and 12 months (or 6 months in the case of a magistrates' court). In 2012 the maximum length of a sentence that may be suspended was increased from 1 to 2 years.[107] When a court imposes a suspended sentence it may[108] order the offender to comply, during

---

[105] SGC, *Theft and Burglary in a Building Other Than a Dwelling* (2008), p. 16.
[106] House of Commons (2008), para. 107.
[107] Legal Aid, Sentencing and Punishment of Offenders Act 2012, s. 68.
[108] The 2012 Act (ibid.) replaced the word 'must' with the permissive 'may'.

the 'supervision period', with one or more specified requirements from those listed in s. 190 of the Act[109] – essentially the same list of 14 possible requirements as applies to community sentences.[110] The operational period (i.e. of the suspension) should be between 6 months and 2 years, and the supervision period (within which the requirements take effect) must not be longer than the operational period. The offender is liable to be ordered to serve the term of imprisonment if either there is non-compliance with a requirement during the supervision period, or the offender commits an offence during the operational period. An offender who breaches a community requirement should normally be given a warning on the first occasion, and then brought to court on the second. There are detailed provisions for dealing with breaches of suspended sentences in Schedule 12 of the 2003 Act. Essentially, paragraph 8(2) provides that the court must order the custodial term to take effect, either in whole or in part, unless it concludes that it would be unjust to do so, in which case there are powers to amend the order in various ways and a power to impose a fine.[111]

The suspended sentence has been part of English sentencing law since 1967, in some shape or form, and its history is not one of unmitigated success. One longstanding complaint is that it has been regarded as a let-off, with no serious consequences for many offenders: this was tackled by the 2003 Act, which stated that the court must (now, may) add community requirements to the order, and so it constitutes a demanding sentence in its own right, even apart from the suspension of the prison sentence. Among the SSOs imposed in 2013, the four most frequent requirements were unpaid work, supervision, supervision plus unpaid work, and supervision plus an accredited programme; other requirements and combinations of requirements were made in smaller numbers.[112] On the other hand, the SGC in its guideline warns that the requirements should not be too onerous:

> Because of the clear deterrent threat involved in a suspended sentence, requirements imposed as part of that sentence should generally be less onerous than those imposed as part of a community sentence. A court wishing to impose onerous or intensive requirements on an offender should reconsider its decision to suspend sentence and consider whether a community sentence might be more appropriate.[113]

The last suggestion is important, since one of the rationales behind the 2003 framework was that the community sentence should be regarded (with

---

[109] In *Lees-Wolfenden* [2007] 1 Cr App R (S) 730 the trial judge had suspended a sentence of 21 months (above the then 12-month limit) and had failed to add any requirements. The Court of Appeal confirmed that the sentence was unlawful on both grounds.

[110] For this reason the details are discussed in ch. 10.6 below.

[111] Added by s. 68 of the Legal Aid, Sentencing and Punishment of Offenders Act 2012.

[112] Criminal Justice Statistics Quarterly, December 2013, at www.gov.uk/government/statistics/criminal-justice-statistics-quarterly-December-2013, Table 3.4.

[113] SGC, *New Sentences: Criminal Justice Act 2003* (2004), para. 2.2.14.

all its requirements) as a serious measure that can be made where an offence has satisfied the custody test.

Another longstanding criticism of the suspended sentence has been the tendency to use it in cases where an immediate custodial sentence would not be justified. As Bottoms showed, ever since its introduction there has been a conflict between the official aim of the suspended sentence, avoiding prison, and the way in which many sentencers regard it – the sword of Damocles.[114] In other words, there has always been a body of opinion among sentencers to the effect that the suspended sentence is merely another non-custodial sentence with a sharper threat to it, and not in any real sense a custodial sentence. Against this background, it is hardly surprising that in the early days suspended sentences were imposed in large numbers, some of them were breached, and in the event the hoped-for reduction in the prison population failed to occur. The SGC guideline seeks to tackle this 'malfunction' of the suspended sentence by reiterating the sequence of decisions implicit in the statutory framework:

(a) Has the custody threshold been passed?
(b) If so, is it unavoidable that a custodial sentence be imposed?
(c) If so, can that sentence be suspended (sentencers should be clear that they would have imposed a custodial sentence if the power to suspend had not been available)?[115]

This wording is followed closely by the Sentencing Council (except where it neglects the statutory tests, as in the fraud guideline),[116] but the statistics suggest that it is not much followed in practice.[117]

One problem with suspended sentences is that the logic may be thought imperfect. No doubt it is true that sentencers regard the SSO as an important part of their sentencing toolkit. As Martin Wasik states:

> They [SSOs] allow judges to reflect the seriousness of the offence by passing a custodial sentence, but at the same time to take account of personal mitigation and the prospects for rehabilitation by suspending it.[118]

But how does that account of the reasoning process fit with the statutory tests? In taking step (b) above, and deciding whether a case which satisfies the custody test can be brought below the threshold, so that a community sentence can be imposed, the court must take account of all mitigating and aggravating factors – once. Then in deciding (c), whether there are factors justifying the suspension of a sentence that cannot be brought below the custody threshold,

---

[114] Bottoms (1981).   [115] SGC, *New Sentences: Criminal Justice Act 2003* (2004), para. 2.2.11.
[116] See nn. 97–9 above and accompanying text.
[117] For a rare example, see *Morgan* [2014] 2 Cr App R (S) 57. Cf. Frase (2013), pp. 52–7, on the apparently more structured approach in Minnesota.
[118] Wasik (2014), p. 482.

the court must consider the same aggravating and mitigating factors – again. If a plea of guilty, or having only one previous conviction, or having a young dependent child, is thought insufficient to bring a case below the custody threshold, can it then be held sufficient to justify suspending? If there is to be a positive answer to this question, it must consist of two elements – one, that in theory it is possible to think of a given set of mitigating factors being not quite strong enough to justify bringing a custodial sentence down to a community sentence but having sufficient strength to justify suspending the custodial sentence; and the other, an admission that the line is necessarily a fine one. Moreover, the line has become even more fine now that courts are able to suspend sentence of up to 2 years. To quote Wasik, this change 'stretches credulity with the idea that an offender requires a sentence as long as two years but nevertheless need not serve it'.[119] Does this not suggest that the logic of the suspended sentence is flawed entirely?

All the indications are that this malfunction (using the SSO in place of community sentences, and not always in place of immediate custody) has re-emerged. The statistics in Table 2 in Appendix B demonstrate the enthusiasm with which the relaunched suspended sentence order was greeted by the courts. For adult males, suspended sentences went from 2,000 in 2004 to 25,000 in 2006 and 37,000 in 2013. While the number of adult male indictable offenders sent to prison remained fairly constant at 75,000 throughout that period, the numbers given community sentences declined from 98,000 in 2004 to under 70,000 in 2013. It is clear that suspended sentences have replaced community sentences much more than custodial sentences.

If a community requirement of an SSO is breached, the court has the power to activate the prison sentence in whole or in part, or to make the community requirements more onerous. However, it does not have the power to revoke the SSO and to re-sentence for the original offence:[120] that is possible with a community sentence, and some may see it as an advantage of community orders. The proper approach on breach of SSO requirements is, first, to decide whether or not it is unjust to activate the sentence (the court must activate unless it is 'unjust to do so'), and secondly, if the sentence is to be activated, to consider taking account of any part performance of community requirements by the offender.[121]

Is the SSO a worthy addition to the sentencer's range of options? It seems that sentencers like using the SSO, but that they are not always using it for the

---

[119] Wasik (2014), p. 482; cf. the state of Victoria, which has removed the availability of suspended sentences from 'serious' and 'significant' offences.

[120] *Phipps* [2008] 2 Cr App R (S) 114 confirms this.

[121] The general proposition was applied in *Kavanagh* [2011] 1 Cr App R (S) 395. If the requirement was not unpaid work but merely attending a course, the court may not credit part performance (*Collins-Reid* [2013] 1 Cr App R (S) 504) unless completion of the course was a real achievement (*Pash* [2014] 1 Cr App R (S) 14). A persistent offender may get no credit for part performance: *Finn* [2012] 2 Cr App R (S) 569.

intended purposes. The evidence suggests that the SSO has displaced community sentences more frequently than immediate custodial sentences – or, at least, that its arrival has caused a ripple effect, so that fewer offenders receive down-tariff measures and more receive either community order, SSO, or custody. Thus the SSO might result in offenders going to prison sooner than they would in a sentencing system without it: this was one of the conclusions of the New South Wales Sentencing Council in its background report on *Suspended Sentences*.[122] If no SSO were available, a few offenders would receive immediate custody, but perhaps rather more would receive a community sentence, which leaves a court with a wider range of options in the case of breach. In Germany, the law requires all prison sentences of 6 months or less to be suspended unless the court finds special circumstances, an approach that has been followed conscientiously by the judiciary.[123] When the conditional sentence was introduced in Canada, albeit with some different features, a significant reduction in the use of custody followed.[124] This suggests that the judiciary in Canada have been following the official guidance, whereas that has plainly not happened in this country. The small Crown Court survey found that almost half of SSOs imposed were above the appropriate SGC guideline, raising 'further questions about sentencers' interpretation of guidance on the use of SSOs'.[125]

9.4.6 Supervision and short-to-medium prison sentences

As noted at the beginning of 9.4, one of the central planks of the 2003 Act's reforms was a new sentence called 'custody plus', which was intended to introduce compulsory supervision as part and parcel of all sentences under 12 months. Probably because of the resource implications, this sentence was never implemented. Those serving prison sentences of 12 months and less have not had any compulsory supervision, unlike those serving longer terms. Support and supervision could form part of a community sentence, and of a suspended sentence order, but not of a short prison sentence. However, the Offender Rehabilitation Act 2014 will change this. For all prison sentences up to and including two years, offenders will be released at the halfway point, as is the case now, and they will be on licence for the remainder of the sentence and subject to a period of compulsory supervision. The period of licence and supervision must total 12 months: thus a 6-month sentence means release after 3 months, a further 3 months on licence, and then 9 months of supervision, whereas a sentence of 18 months means release after 9 months, a licence period of 9 months, and then 3 more months of supervision. This new regime will require an injection of resources, and the government is hoping that a scheme of 'payment by results' for supervision will be both more effective and

---

[122] NSW Sentencing Council (2011), ch. 3.   [123] British Academy (2014), p. 96.
[124] Roberts (2003, 2004).   [125] SCWG Survey (2008), p. 22; see also pp. 30–1.

more economical. More will be said about this scheme in Chapter 10 below. The 2014 Act should be welcomed for its provision of supervision for those short-term prisoners, many of whom should benefit from the support from which they were hitherto excluded. An implementation date for the Act has not yet been announced.

9.5 Medium-to-long custodial sentences: release on licence

The discussion in Chapter 4 explored some of the parameters of proportionality in English sentencing, drawing on definitive guidelines and appellate judgments. However, there is a difference between the custodial sentence announced in court and the time actually served. This difference also applies to sentences of up to 2 years, discussed in 9.4.6, and it must now be explored. Once a court has decided to impose custody and has calculated the appropriate length, it is the judge's duty to specify how much of any time spent on remand should be deducted from the sentence pronounced;[126] it is also possible to order time spent on curfew to be deducted from a custodial sentence.[127] Once the court has completed that calculation, the practical impact of the sentence depends on three factors – the statutory release provisions, the application of executive early release, and any recall to prison. These factors will be discussed in relation to medium-to-long determinate sentences, leaving indeterminate sentences for discussion later.

9.5.1 Statutory release provisions

The statutory provisions on release from sentences of imprisonment have been changed several times in recent decades, and the current provisions stem from the Criminal Justice Act 2003 as amended by the Criminal Justice and Immigration Act 2008.[128] All prisoners serving determinate sentences are automatically released after half the sentence, with the exception of those serving extended sentences imposed under the Legal Aid, Sentencing and Punishment of Offenders Act 2012, who cannot be released until the two-thirds point. Release is on supervised licence for the remainder of the nominal sentence, under the supervision of the National Offender Management Service (NOMS). Courts have the power to recommend certain licence conditions at the time of sentencing,[129] but the precise terms of the licence are set by the Ministry of Justice on advice from the prison governor and from NOMS. Supervision is organized by NOMS, and will be subject to the new 'payment by results' scheme to be introduced under the Offender Rehabilitation Act 2014 (see Chapter 10.8).

---

[126] CJA 2003, s. 240.
[127] The details are in the Criminal Justice and Immigration Act 2008, s. 21.
[128] For a helpful review, see Padfield (2009).   [129] Criminal Justice Act 2003, s. 238.

9.5.2 Executive early release

We have seen that determinate sentence prisoners have a right to be released after serving one-half of their sentence. However, the period served may be further reduced in practice by the operation of one of two forms of executive early release – Home Detention Curfew (HDC) and Release on Temporary Licence (ROTL). Brief mention will also be made of the now defunct End of Custody Licence (ECL).

Home Detention Curfew was introduced in 1999 as a form of executive release of certain prisoners earlier than their normal release date, subject to curfew restrictions which are electronically monitored. Offenders thus released therefore have to be 'tagged'. Most prisoners serving sentences of 3–12 months (excluding sex offenders and some others) are presumptively to be released on HDC unless an assessment in prison yields 'exceptional and compelling reasons' to refuse it.[130] HDC is also available to prisoners serving sentences of 12 months and under 4 years, with certain exclusions of sex and violent offenders. There is a risk assessment process within the prison, and the decision to release is that of the prison governor. The maximum period of HDC was raised to 90 days in 2002 and then to its present 135 days in 2003; the minimum period is 2 weeks. The regulations provide for recall to prison for non-compliance with the terms of the licence or, more broadly, if the offender is considered to represent a threat to public safety. The rationale for HDC has always been ambiguous, with some claims that it assists resettlement and therefore rehabilitation, and other suggestions that it is merely a back-door way of relieving overcrowded prisons. The number of releases on HDC has been declining in recent years (a total of 6,400 in July to December 2012, against a total of 5,200 in April to September 2013).[131] The effect of HDC release can be considerable, however. For an offender serving 12 months, the statutory release date of 6 months can be halved again to 3 months if he or she is fortunate enough to be granted HDC release.[132]

Release on Temporary Licence is chiefly used to allow prisoners to work outside a prison during the daytime, but it can be used to enable a prisoner to make a home visit in order to finalize arrangements for accommodation, work, etc. on release. In that respect it can be an important step towards release, but in June 2014 the government was embarrassed when some prisoners on ROTL went missing. There may be calls for a more restrictive approach, although the Chief Inspector is positive about ROTL.[133]

End of Custody Licence was available between 2007 and 2010, enabling release 18 days before the end of the sentence. It had the same dual aims

---

[130] For an analysis of the relevant regulations, see Livingstone, Owen and Macdonald (2008), pp. 287–94.
[131] Criminal Justice Statistics Quarterly, December 2013, at www.gov.uk/government/statistics/criminal-justice-statistics-quarterly-December-2013, Table 3.3.
[132] For discussion of the possibility of challenging adverse decisions, see Padfield (2009).
[133] HMCI Prisons (2014), pp. 51–2.

(or ambivalence) as HDC, resettlement and relief of prison overcrowding. There was a presumption in favour of ECL for prisoners serving between 4 weeks and 4 years; but, since ECL did not apply to prisoners given HDC, its greatest use was for sentences of less than 4 months. The government always said that ECL was to be a temporary measure, and its abolition was one of the last acts of the Labour administration.

9.5.3 Recalls to custody

We have seen that most prisoners are now released on some form of licence, be it HDC or the normal licence after release from a determinate sentence. Breach of a licence can lead to recall to prison, and three aspects of this merit brief discussion here. First, the decision to recall is an executive decision, taken by the probation and prison services. This means that a released prisoner can be deprived of liberty again, without recourse to a court. There are rights of appeal to the Parole Board in certain circumstances,[134] and there is always the possibility of challenge by way of judicial review.[135] But these avenues take effect after the event, and the system provides no judicial input at the time of deprivation of liberty. Secondly, there are complicated provisions for release after recall. In essence, some prisoners will be released automatically after a further 28 days if considered suitable (known as Fixed Term Recalls or FTR), but excluded from this are sexual or violent offenders, those on HDC, and those previously recalled. Prisoners in the excluded groups, plus those considered unsuitable for automatic release, can only be released by the Parole Board. The whole system of recall and subsequent release is deficient in fairness and respect for human rights.[136] Thirdly, we have already noted the significance of the growing number of recalls for prison overcrowding and prison management. Thus recalls contributed 13 per cent of the increase in the prison population between 1993 and 2012,[137] because of both the greater number of recalls (reflecting the greater number of prisoners released on licence, including HDC) and longer stays in prison for recalled prisoners. No fewer than 16,591 prisoners were recalled to prison during 2011–12.[138] Sections 8–11 of the Criminal Justice and Courts Act 2015 will bring changes, including the appointment of 'recall adjudicators' and increasingly tough conditions for re-release.

9.6 Long custodial sentences

The clearest distinguishing factor of English sentencing compared with that of other European countries is the greater length of sentences in England and

---

[134] CJA 2003, ss. 254–255; see generally Padfield and Maruna (2006).
[135] See the discussion by Padfield (2009, pp. 169–71) of challenges to HDC.
[136] See further Padfield (2009), p. 178, and Padfield and Maruna (2006), pp. 343–6.
[137] Ministry of Justice (2013), p. 16.   [138] Ministry of Justice (2014b), Table 5.01.

Wales, including a greater number of indeterminate sentences. How has this come about? What determines the length of these sentences? Is continual escalation unavoidable?

9.6.1 Longer determinate sentences

The Ministry of Justice's *Story of the Prison Population 1993–2012* records that determinate sentences increased in length by 2.1 months between 2000 and 2004, and again by 2 months between 2007 and 2011 – averages that are truly underestimates because of the increasing number of offenders given indeterminate sentences rather than determinate sentences.[139] Three offence groups have had a particular impact: longer sentences for violence against the person, for drug offences, and for sexual offences. The steep increase in drug offenders came in the 1990s, whereas for sexual offences the steep rise followed the revision of the law and maximum penalties by the Sexual Offences Act 2003. Between 2004 and 2011 the average length of custodial sentences for sexual offenders rose by over 13 months, an enormous increase.[140]

In general, determinate sentence prisoners are released automatically after one-half of their sentence, and are on licence for the second half. However, prisoners serving determinate sentences of 4 years or more that were handed down before 2005 are still subject to discretionary conditional release by the Parole Board. The numbers in this category are dwindling, but the Parole Board also deals with the release of prisoners on extended sentences (see Chapter 6.8.3 above).

9.6.2 Indeterminate sentences

The proportion of the sentenced prison population serving indeterminate or life sentences increased from 9 per cent in 1993 to 19 per cent in 2012,[141] by far the highest proportion of any European country. Much of the increase stems from IPP sentences, introduced as mandatory in 2005, made discretionary in 2008, and abolished in 2012.[142] There remain three forms of life imprisonment available to the courts, as explained in Chapter 6.8 above, but it is unlikely that they will be imposed as frequently as were IPP sentences. In the meantime, there remains the scandal of over 5,000 prisoners detained under a sentence (IPP) that is widely recognized as a penal mistake,[143] and the continued (unlawful) detention of over 3,000 IPP prisoners who have gone beyond their minimum term. There is an overwhelming argument for the urgent review of the case of each IPP prisoner who has served his minimum

---

[139] Ministry of Justice (2013), p. 11.   [140] Ibid., p. 2.   [141] Ibid., p. 15.
[142] Discussed in ch. 6.8 above.
[143] Its progenitor as Home Secretary, David Blunkett, has now apologized for the whole saga: see Wasik (2014), p. 478.

term, with a view to release.[144] Also, as argued in Chapter 4.4.1 above, fresh scrutiny of the mandatory sentence for murder is long overdue, despite the longstanding political reluctance even to open the topic for public discussion.

9.6.3 The Parole Board

The role of the Parole Board is to determine which eligible prisoners should be released and which ones recommended for transfer to open conditions, and it has tended to become more risk-averse.[145] The caseload of the Board has changed in recent years, with the introduction of automatic release for all determinate sentence prisoners sentenced after 2005 (reducing its caseload significantly) and the burgeoning of indeterminate sentence prisoners (increasing it significantly). The Board also decides on the release of those serving Extended Determinate Sentences, and those recalled to prison for breach of licence. In all cases, the question is whether the prisoner no longer poses a significant risk of serious harm to the public. In 2013–14 there were about 20,000 paper hearings and about 5,000 oral hearings,[146] but in *Osborn, Booth and Reilly* v. *Parole Board* (2013)[147] the Supreme Court held that oral hearings should be held in a wider range of cases than hitherto. Where there were disputes about important facts (such as mitigating factors and reports about the prisoner) or where there had been no oral hearing for a long while, and particularly where the sentence was indeterminate or the prisoner had been recalled, it was unsatisfactory that a paper hearing should terminate the matter. Prisoners have a right to participate in a hearing, as a matter of natural justice and fairness, even in cases where there is no prospect of early release. This judgment will increase the number of oral hearings, which is of concern to the Board for administrative reasons. More important is the Supreme Court's recognition that these review and release decisions are crucial to the determination of effective sentence length, especially for indeterminate sentences and those recalled to prison, and that therefore full, fair, and open consideration should be given to them by the Parole Board. When an offender is sentenced, we expect proper judicial consideration of the issues, and guidelines are provided for most of those decisions. The sentence provides the legal framework, and real decisions about the actual time to be spent in custody – no less important than setting the framework, and arguably more important – ought to be taken by a tribunal with appropriate procedural safeguards and according to guidance or guidelines. It is unsatisfactory that only the Minister of Justice has the power to issue directions to the Board, and not helpful that those previously in force have been withdrawn without replacement.[148] There is a strong case for the Parole Board to be replaced

---

[144] An argument set out by the British Academy (2014), p. 103.   [145] Gage (2008), para. 2.7.
[146] Parole Board (2014), p. 6.   [147] [2013] UKSC 61.
[148] See www.gov.uk/government/organisations/parole-board (accessed 1 December 2014).

by a judicial body,[149] and to undertake joint work with the Sentencing Council on guidelines for the release of eligible prisoners.

9.6.4 Alternatives to long sentences

The gradual lengthening of prison sentences over the last two decades has occurred as a response to political posturing on law and order and to a media-driven view of public opinion (which is different from actual public opinion).[150] Its high water marks were the steep increase in minimum terms for murder and the IPP sentence, both introduced by the Criminal Justice Act 2003. The former appears to have had an upwards effect on other sentences for violence;[151] the latter has now been repealed, but its effects continue to be felt. In the meantime, judges and others are becoming sensitized to longer prison sentences, to the extent that any proposal for reducing sentence lengths may appear as a plea for patently inadequate responses to serious offences. Consider, for example, the position in Germany:

> The upper limit for all offence types is set at 15 years, except for murder and a few other felonies involving the death of another. Currently, there are just over 100 life sentences per year. It does not matter what kind of felony or how many felonies the offender has committed: be it numerous aggravated robberies, awful kidnappings, a series of most humiliating rapes, or acts of particularly harmful arson, the maximum sentence is 15 years' imprisonment.[152]

In this country, changing ingrained patterns of thought and winning acceptance for a less prison-heavy sentencing system would be a difficult and probably slow task, requiring a broad consensus within the criminal justice system (including judges and magistrates) and leadership from politicians. Maximum sentences would have to be reviewed, rationalized, and reduced, minimum sentences abolished, and the murder guidelines reassessed. Unless there is a cross-party agreement to place sentencing policy in the hands of an independent agency, as was done with fiscal policy and the Monetary Policy Committee,[153] the prospects for change are remote.

9.7 Demographic features of the prison population

The composition of the prison population is largely the result of decisions taken by the legislature, the Sentencing Council, the courts, by the executive

---

[149] Padfield, Morgan and Maguire (2012), pp. 979–80.   [150] On which see ch. 3.6 above.

[151] On which see ch. 4.4.1 above.

[152] Hoernle (2013), p. 198. It should be acknowledged that Germany has a form of preventive detention for particularly dangerous offenders, which is imposed as an additional form of detention after serving the sentence; but the numbers are relatively small (see Hoernle, p. 205).

[153] As proposed by Lacey (2008) and the British Academy (2014), pp. 87–90.

(NOMS) and by the Parole Board. A major contribution to the almost doubling of the prison population since 1993 has been made by Parliament, by means of mandatory and minimum sentences, particularly the IPP sentence between 2005 and 2008, and higher maximum sentences for sexual offences and for causing death by driving. The Sentencing Council has seen its role chiefly in terms of devising guidelines that maintain current sentencing levels. The courts have retained a fair amount of flexibility, notably around the custody 'threshold', in relation to suspended sentences, and in passing longer sentences for serious offences. The executive has contributed through its decisions on release (HDC), its decisions on licence conditions for released prisoners, and its recall decisions. The Parole Board also plays its part, through its release decisions. One pertinent question is whether all or any of these decisions impact disproportionately on particular groups. Thus we examine below whether there are particular problems in prison for women, ethnic minorities, and mentally disordered offenders. First, however, mention must be made of prisoners who have not been convicted – the remand population.

9.7.1 Remand prisoners awaiting trial

While the total prison population increased from some 44,000 in 1993 to 86,000 in 2012, the number of those on remand remained fairly stable at around 12,000.[154] The numbers rose temporarily in the aftermath of the 2011 riots, but have declined since the introduction of the presumption that a defendant should not be remanded in custody if there is no real prospect that he or she will receive a custodial sentence.[155] It is projected that numbers will remain around 11,500 for the next four to five years.[156] Although this represents a lower proportion of the prison population than a decade ago, because of the steep rise in the numbers of sentenced prisoners, it remains a cause for concern. Putting the matter bluntly, those awaiting trial have not been convicted and should receive the benefit of the presumption of innocence; and yet they are not only deprived of their liberty but also, in many cases, subjected to the worst conditions in the English prison system (i.e. in local prisons). Although there are some new, purpose-built remand prisons, most of the overcrowding occurs in local prisons, as we saw in parts 9.4.1 and 9.4.2 of this chapter. The conditions are particularly inappropriate for those remandees who are acquitted at their trial or have their case discontinued – one-fifth of both male and female remand prisoners.[157] It also bears particularly harshly on women, for the reasons elaborated in part 9.7.2 below. A quarter of a century ago the Woolf Report placed strong emphasis on the special rights of

---

[154] Ministry of Justice (2013), p. 19.
[155] Legal Aid, Sentencing and Punishment of Offenders Act 2012, Sch. 11, para. 25.
[156] Ministry of Justice (2013).
[157] See the discussion in Ashworth and Redmayne (2010), ch. 8, and by Duff (2013).

remand prisoners and called for improved and separate facilities for them, describing the present situation as 'a travesty of justice'.[158] There has been some progress since then, but in essence the problem remains.

9.7.2 Women prisoners

Table 3 in Appendix B demonstrates the rapid increase in the female prison population, which trebled from 1,500 in 1992 to 4,500 in 2002, falling slightly since then to 3,900 in 2013, still two-and-a-half times the 1992 figure. The increases have been spread across the range of custodial sentences, but it is remarkable that some 63 per cent of women entering prison are sentenced to 6 months or less, mostly for theft or handling.[159] Three strands of explanation for the rise of the women's prison population are usually put forward – a rise in the number of women being prosecuted and convicted, a rise in the proportion of women being sentenced to custody, and an increase in the average length of custodial sentences.[160] The first factor appears not to be borne out, since the number of women found guilty of indictable offences stood at 47,300 in 1998, peaked at 50,200 in 2003, and had fallen to 45,300 in 2007.[161] The last two factors apply to men also, as we saw in part 9.2 above, and yet the increase in women prisoners far outstrips the percentage increase in male prisoners in recent years.

There have been several enquiries into women in prison,[162] and all of them have concluded that there are far more women in prison than necessary. But what is the yardstick of necessity here? Baroness Corston wrote that she was:

> dismayed to see so many women frequently sentenced for short periods of time for very minor offences, causing chaos and disruption to their lives and families, without any realistic chance of addressing the causes of their criminality ... we must find better ways to keep out of prison those women who pose no threat to society.[163]

In her report on Scotland, Dame Elish Angiolini took this argument further, observing that:

> short-term prison sentences have little or no impact on offending, with 70 per cent of women offenders who received a sentence of three months or less reconvicted of an offence within two years.[164]

The Angiolini Report goes on to make the economic point that such sentences are largely a waste of money. These and other reports acknowledge that most women in prison do not present any danger to public safety, but this worthy

---

[158] Woolf (1991), para. 10.55.   [159] Cabinet Office (2009), p. 8.
[160] Prison Reform Trust (2000), p. 2.   [161] Ministry of Justice (2008), Table 3.7.
[162] E.g. Prison Reform Trust (2000), Corston (2007), and Angiolini (2012).
[163] Corston (2007), pp. i and 5.   [164] Angiolini (2012), p. 3.

sentiment plays out into two very awkward problems. One is that many of women offenders who present no danger are imprisoned for drug offences, a major issue of much broader proportions.[165] The other awkward problem is that most of the short-term women prisoners have persistently committed property offences. There is a need for commitment to tackling this kind of offending in the community, leaving prison out of the equation. This means devising more supportive community sentences, and being less punitive about breaches, a point made strongly in the Corston Report with reference to the disadvantaged and unstable characteristics of many of the women in this group.[166]

This feeds into the argument, set out in Chapter 7.3 above, that a sentence of imprisonment for a woman is correspondingly harsher than for a man: the existing prison estate for women means that, too frequently, they are held a considerable distance from their home and family; women are more likely than men to have childcare responsibilities; women are more likely than men to have problems of mental disturbance and/or of substance misuse; women prisoners are more likely to self-harm and to attempt suicide. All of these constitute extra sources of deprivation. Without repeating the points made in Chapter 7.3 above, there are compelling reasons for an urgent review of the pathways by which women are sentenced to custody since, to put the matter neutrally, they represent a far lower risk to the public than male offenders. The Sentencing Advisory Panel made cogent recommendations on this,[167] but they have not yet been taken further by the Sentencing Council.

9.7.3 Ethnic minority prisoners

The sentencing of ethnic minority offenders was discussed in Chapter 7.2 above. In 2012 some 26 per cent of people in prison were non-white. Among the non-white British nationals, by far the largest group was 'Black or Black British', representing over 13 per cent of the prison population compared with less than 3 per cent of the general population. The category 'Asian or Asian British' represents 7.9 per cent of the prison population compared with 5.8 per cent of the general population.[168] Whether these proportions are evidence of discriminatory practices in the criminal justice system was discussed in Chapter 7.

A somewhat related issue in the prisons is the number of foreign nationals held. In 2013 almost 11,000 foreign national prisoners were among the prison population.[169] Foreign nationals present obvious problems of communication within the prisons, as well as suffering additional hardships concerned with isolation from their families, some discriminatory treatment, and a lack of

---

[165] See ch. 4.4.5 above.   [166] Corston (2007), p. i and ch. 5.
[167] Sentencing Advisory Panel (2010), pp. 67–80.   [168] Berman and Dar (2013), pp. 10–11.
[169] Berman and Dar (2013), p. 10.

preparation for release. In 2009 the Chief Inspector drew attention to the very high percentage of foreign nationals in certain women's prisons, and to many practical problems such as the high cost of telephoning home.[170] However, important as these issues of fairness, rights, and management are, there is a need for renewed focus on the pathways by which ethnic minority men and women come to be imprisoned at such a disproportionate rate compared with the general population.

9.7.4 Mentally disordered prisoners

Successive studies have found that a significant proportion of the prison population is suffering from mental disturbance, and that some prisoners – possibly as many as one-third – might be classified as mentally disordered. In a survey by Gunn, Maden and Swinton, some 37 per cent of the sentenced prisoners were diagnosed as mentally disordered, including 3 per cent whose conditions were severe enough to require hospital treatment.[171] A survey of the custodial remand population by Brooke, Taylor, Gunn and Maden put at 63 per cent the proportion suffering from mental disorder.[172] Whereas the proportion of the sentenced prison population suffering from a psychosis was put at 2 per cent, it rose to 5 per cent among remandees. A subsequent study by Singleton, Meltzer and Gatward found that as many as 78 per cent of male remand prisoners, 64 per cent of sentenced males and 50 per cent of sentenced females had some form of personality disorder, and also that 10 per cent of male prisoners and 20 per cent of female prisoners had been mental hospital patients at some time.[173] It may be assumed that the situation has not changed markedly since then. The prevalence of mental disorder among prisoners is definitely much higher than in the general population.[174]

Policy in this sphere has not been coherent, as we shall see in Chapter 12.3 below. The Mental Health Act 1983 sought to restrict the use of hospital orders for offenders classified as mentally impaired or psychopathic, by requiring evidence that the condition is treatable. This was effective in reducing the number of offenders admitted to mental hospital, but one consequence has been that mentally disordered offenders continue to be sentenced to custody, even though it is clear that prison is not a suitable place for many mentally disordered people. Section 157 of the Criminal Justice Act 2003 imposes a duty to obtain and consider a medical report before passing any custodial sentence on a person who appears to be mentally disordered (although s. 157(2) qualifies that duty), and also requires the court to consider any other information bearing on the offender's mental condition and the likely effect of a custodial sentence on that condition and on any possible

---

[170] HMCI Prisons (2009), p. 62.   [171] Gunn, Maden and Swinton (1991).

[172] Brooke, Taylor, Gunn and Maden (1996).   [173] Singleton, Meltzer and Gatward (1998).

[174] Peay (2014), pp. 6–9 and 19. For US evidence, see Travis, Western and Redburn (2014), ch. 8.

treatment for it.[175] This is an important provision, but courts are often constrained by restrictive admissions policies in hospitals.

The Bradley Report (2009) called for several changes in the approach to mentally disordered persons and imprisonment, including diversion from prison where possible (and the transfer of acute cases from prison to hospital within 14 days), and improved support for those mentally disordered persons who are held in prison, including a fresh evaluation of treatment options for prisoners with personality disorder.[176] Implementation has been slow, but there is now a commitment to act on Bradley's proposal to place mental health nurses in police stations and courts.[177] In relation to prisons specifically, their unsuitability for many mentally disordered people[178] and the higher than normal risks of self-harm and suicide suggest that a greater number of mentally disordered people should be transferred from prison to hospital.[179] However, the numbers (perhaps 2–3,000) are such that this is highly unlikely to happen in the near future, because the necessary resources are unlikely to be forthcoming.[180] These and other issues relating to the sentencing of mentally disordered offenders will be revisited in Chapter 12.3.

9.8 Conclusions

This chapter has pointed out the strengths of the argument for restraint in the use of custody – arguments of principle, of effectiveness in preventing crime, and of economics. These arguments received some degree of acceptance at the beginning of the 1990s, at least in one part of the then government's twin-track approach to sentencing policy and among some members of the judiciary. But during that decade they lost virtually all political force, as the rhetoric of penal repression began to spiral upwards. The first decade of the new millennium brought no change in the political rhetoric, although the Labour government's policy did appear to be one of bifurcation (prison for 'serious, dangerous and seriously persistent offenders') and not of unmitigated severity. The coalition government's policies have been variable: its rapid abolition of IPP sentences contrasts with its unwillingness to deal fairly with the thousands of IPP prisoners still in prison; its 'rehabilitation revolution' has fine aspirations, particularly in relation to short-term prisoners, but it is marred by its chosen method ('payment by results') and by its occasional resort to minimum sentences and to increased maximum sentences without taking an overall view.

---

[175] The section re-enacts s. 4 of the Criminal Justice Act 1991; see also s. 166(5) of the 2003 Act, preserving the courts' power to mitigate sentence in the case of mentally disordered offenders.
[176] Bradley (2009), ch. 4.   [177] Peay (2014), pp. 19–20.
[178] Peay (2014) argues that some mentally disordered offenders may fairly be sentenced to imprisonment, whilst accepting that for others this is unjust both in principle and in relation to actual prison conditions.
[179] See, e.g., the recommendation of the British Academy (2014), p. 102.   [180] Peay (2014), p. 25.

Overcrowding and poor regimes remain major practical concerns in relation to the prison system. Overcrowding continues to be acute in certain prisons, and inmates are forced to endure unsatisfactory conditions in their cells for long hours, without adequate exercise or provision for employment or programmes – conditions that could be found to violate Article 3 of the Convention. Evidence that prisons have significant negative effects on their inmates is powerful,[181] and the current expenditure cuts are more likely to worsen than to improve conditions in the prisons.[182] The radical remedial step advocated in the Woolf Report – declaring that no prison shall admit prisoners above the number for which its certified normal accommodation provides[183] – remains the most conscientious advance towards the protection of rights and the promotion of a civilized approach. An alternative would be to adopt a 'resource management' approach of the kind used in several US jurisdictions and commended by the Carter Review:[184] sentence levels would be adjusted so as to ensure a 'fit' between sentencing and correctional capacity. A fair system of punishment should not involve the infliction of deprivations that erode a prisoner's capacity for autonomy and responsible citizenship.[185]

Much attention has been paid in this chapter to the drivers of the increase in the prison population – the roles of the legislature, the Sentencing Council, the courts, the executive, and the Parole Board; the impact of IPP, of recalls to prison, of increased numbers of foreign nationals, and so forth. What is important here is the connection between those trends and the sentencing system. The steep rise in the prison population leads to overcrowding, and that produces impoverished prison regimes, all of which increase the deprivations of imprisonment and make each unit of it harder to justify. In this context, the Sentencing Council should take a lead in reassessing the use of custodial sentences, as its predecessor did.[186] Some aspects of the statutory framework point in the right direction, with the tests set out in ss. 148, 152, and 153 of the 2003 Act. But the custody threshold in s. 152 needs to be made even more demanding, and the provision on previous convictions in s. 143(2) should be abandoned. Thus we noted in part 9.4.1 above how the courts regard prison as 'unavoidable' in a number of cases (e.g. forging wills, perverting the course of justice), which should be urgently reassessed. The imprisonment of those who persistently commit non-serious offences is a longstanding issue in English sentencing law and practice, and the allegedly restraining principle of using prison 'as a last resort' has absolutely no impact on such cases. Even for those serious

---

[181] E.g. Lippke (2007), ch. 5, and Travis, Western and Redburn (2014), ch. 9.
[182] See British Academy (2014), pp. 54–61.   [183] Cf. Woolf (1991), para. 1.190.
[184] Carter (2007), p. 15; Reitz (2013), pp. 185–91.   [185] Lippke (2007), esp. ch. 5.
[186] SGC, *New Sentences: Criminal Justice Act 2003* (2004), paras. 2.1.5–2.1.10; there is no evidence that these exhortations had any effect on sentencing practice.

offenders who go to prison in all European countries, there are questions of duration. English sentence lengths have increased in recent decades:[187] the absolute and comparative lengths of prison sentences cries out for re-evaluation, as does the use of indeterminate sentences. Unfortunately, all these issues require more political courage, to raise and to argue through, than is likely to be forthcoming unless there is some cross-party agreement to remit issues of sentencing policy to an independent body.[188]

---

[187] Ministry of Justice (2013), p. 13.   [188] See the proposal in ch. 9.6.4 above.

10

Non-custodial sentencing

Contents

In Chapter 9 the close connection between custodial and non-custodial sentencing was often evident, particularly when discussing the statutory test for custody. The present chapter aims to examine the principal non-custodial measures available to English courts when sentencing offenders aged 18 or over.[1] The discussion begins with so-called 'third tier' sentences (absolute discharges, conditional discharges and bind-overs, compensation orders and fines), and then moves on to the community sentence, as reshaped by the Criminal Justice Act 2003. First, it is necessary to consider the route by which the English system arrived at its present position.

10.1 A brief history

Successive governments between the 1960s and the early 1990s stated a policy of reducing the use of custodial sentences, and regarded the provision of new forms of non-custodial sentence as a key element in this strategy.[2] Community service orders (and compensation orders) formed part of the 1972 Criminal Justice Act. New forms of probation order were

---

[1] Non-custodial measures for young offenders are dealt with in ch. 12 below.

[2] For an analysis of policy changes, see Bottoms (1987); Bottoms, Rex and Robinson (2004).

introduced by a Schedule to the 1982 Act, the Act which also legislated for curfew orders on young offenders. The result was that courts in England and Wales had available a wider range of non-custodial measures than the courts of most European countries, most states in the United States and probably most countries in the world. What might be described as the policy of proliferation was not a conspicuous success. Simply widening the range of available non-custodial sentences did little to deflect courts from their use of custodial sentences. Changes in sentencing practice did take place, but these did not impinge significantly on the use of custody.

It was lack of progress in that direction, combined with concern among sentencers about laxity in the enforcement of non-custodial sentences, that led to changes in the 1991 Act. The notion of 'alternatives to custody' had not been found convincing or even comprehensible by many sentencers: there was, they would say, nothing equivalent to prison, and certainly nothing in the available options. Major changes of direction were proposed in the 1990 White Paper: restraint in the use of custody for non-serious offences, a toughening of community sentences, more rigorous enforcement of community measures, and greater use of financial penalties. Perhaps the most important change was the abandonment of the 'alternatives to custody' rhetoric, and its replacement with the idea of punishment in the community, focusing on restrictions on liberty. Thus the Criminal Justice Act 1991 separated out six sentences (i.e. probation, community service, combination orders, curfew orders, attendance centres, and supervision) and termed them 'community sentences'. A seventh community sentence, the drug treatment and testing order, was added by s. 61 of the Crime and Disorder Act 1998. These were reinforced by the drawing up of National Standards, specifying the form that each community sentence should take, the contents of the order, the enforcement of the order, and so forth. The suspended sentence, which had no equivalent restrictions of liberty, was confined to exceptional cases.

What was the effect of these major changes? The proportionate use of community sentences increased significantly for both male and female offenders, but these increases were not accompanied by reductions in the use of custody, which also rose steeply. Thus community sentences rose from 18 per cent in 1992 to 25 per cent in 2002 for adult men at the same time as the proportionate use of custody rose from 18 per cent to 30 per cent for that age group. For adult women the rise in community sentences was from 22 per cent to 33 per cent at the same time as custody for this group increased from 6 per cent to 17 per cent. Overall, therefore, the displacement was, not from custody to community sentences, but rather from suspended sentences and fines to community sentences and custody. The aim of increasing courts' use of fines was not realized, the abolition of the unit fine system by the Criminal Justice Act 1993 amounting to an abandonment of that policy.

Thus, through their greater demands and tougher enforcement, community sentences contributed to an increasingly punitive sentencing system.[3]

The Criminal Justice Act 2003 introduced the single, generic community sentence, in an attempt to simplify the law and to achieve a more productive relationship between the powers of the court and the powers of the Probation Service. The resulting structure is mostly still in place, as discussed in part 10.6 below, but under the coalition government there have been changes motivated partly by what it terms a 'rehabilitation revolution' and partly by a renewed insistence on punitive elements. Before those changes are discussed, the various 'third tier' sentences are examined.

10.2 The absolute discharge

This is the least severe order which a court can make on conviction. It requires nothing from the offender, and imposes no restrictions on future conduct. The statutory provisions on discharges are consolidated in ss. 12–15 of the Powers of Criminal Courts (Sentencing) Act 2000. For many purposes an offence followed by an absolute discharge does not count as a conviction (s. 14 of the 2000 Act), but s. 134 of the Sexual Offences Act 2003 provides that a conviction followed by a discharge does count for the purpose of requiring sex offender notification.

Absolute discharges are relatively uncommon, being granted in under 1 per cent of cases, mostly in magistrates' courts. They are generally reserved for the most venial of offences, committed in circumstances of little moral blame. We saw earlier that one criterion for cautioning or discontinuing a case is that the court 'would be likely to impose a purely nominal penalty'.[4] If that test is conscientiously applied, most of the absolute discharge cases ought not to be prosecuted, and one might regard those that do end in an absolute discharge as 'failures' of the prosecution system. In his study, however, Martin Wasik argues that this might not always be so. He discusses three main reasons for granting an absolute discharge: where the offence is venial; where the offender had low culpability or high motivation, but the law does not provide a defence; and where the offender has suffered collateral losses or 'indirect' punishment as a result of the offence. Cases in the last category do not suggest any failure of prosecution policy: whether they should result in mitigation of sentence was discussed earlier.[5]

---

[3] Brief reference should be made to an inglorious but short-lived chapter in penal history. In 2000 the government decided that the familiar names of community sentences should be changed: the Criminal Justice and Court Services Act 2000 changed probation orders to community rehabilitation orders, community service orders to community punishment orders, and so forth. These names were abandoned in 2003, when, as we shall see in 10.6 below, a further change in nomenclature took effect.

[4] Ch. 1.4 above.   [5] Cf. Wasik (1985), pp. 229–33, with ch. 5.4.5 above.

10.3 Conditional discharges and bind-overs

The conditional discharge has a similar legal framework to the absolute discharge. The condition which forms part of the discharge is that the offender should commit no further offence during the specified period, which may be up to 3 years. If a further offence is committed during the specified period, the court may sentence the offender not only for that offence but also for the original offence which gave rise to the conditional discharge. The statutory provisions on discharges are consolidated in ss. 12–15 of the PCCS Act 2000. Section 134 of the Sexual Offences Act 2003 provides that a conviction followed by a conditional discharge does count for the purposes of sex offender notification and other orders under Part 2 of that Act.

The essence of the conditional discharge is therefore a threat or warning: the court is prepared to impose no sanction for the present offence, on condition that there is no reoffending within the specified period. This is different from the suspended sentence of imprisonment, which should only be imposed where the present offence is so serious as to justify custody, and under which the second court has a qualified duty to activate the suspended sentence, whereas the second court has a wide discretion on breach of a conditional discharge.[6] David Moxon's 1988 survey showed that in the Crown Court over half the conditional discharges were granted in theft cases, mostly involving little or no loss, often committed by people of fairly good character.[7] In their mid-1990s survey, Flood-Page and Mackie give no details on discharges granted by the Crown Court, but they report that in the magistrates' courts conditional discharges were given to 11 per cent of men and 21 per cent of women. Stress, mental health problems, and being a first offender were associated with decisions to grant a conditional discharge, and their interviews with magistrates revealed that it was often regarded as a difficult choice between a fine (immediate bite, no lasting effect) and a conditional discharge (no immediate bite, but a 'sword of Damocles' for a year or more).[8]

The use of conditional discharges has drifted downwards in the last decade. For adult males, the numbers peaked at 60,000 in 2003 before declining to 46,000 in 2013; conditional discharges for adult females peaked at over 18,400 in 2003 before declining to 15,400 in 2013 (Appendix B, Tables 2 and 3). Nonetheless, the Halliday Report had referred favourably to conditional discharges, commenting that 'the evidence shows that they are an effective disposal, attracting better than predicted reconviction rates'.[9]

---

[6] The suspended sentence was discussed in ch. 9.4.5 above; cf. *Watts* (1984) 6 Cr App R (S) 61 for an example of the Court of Appeal replacing a suspended sentence with a conditional discharge.

[7] Moxon (1988), pp. 47–8.

[8] Flood-Page and Mackie (1998), pp. 53–4; it should be pointed out that many fines have more than an immediate bite, since many offenders pay by instalments over several months.

[9] Halliday (2001), para. 6.19, showing that the two-year reconviction rate was 2 per cent below expectation.

The power to 'bind an offender over' is a flexible creature of statute and common law, which may be applied to offenders, witnesses, and indeed anyone involved in proceedings.[10] The former power to bind over an offender to be of good behaviour is no longer available, since it was declared insufficiently certain,[11] but there remains the power to bind over an offender to do or not to do a specified act. Some courts make considerable use of the 'bind-over' as a sentence, whereas others do not. In a survey 20 years ago for the Law Commission, almost three-quarters of bind-overs were for purposes other than sentencing.[12] As a sentence, the bind-over may amount more or less to a suspended fine. Under the Justices of the Peace Act 1361 an offender may be bound over in a certain sum to keep the peace for a specified period, on which there appears to be no limit. Breach leads to forfeiture of the sum. At common law an offender may be bound over in a certain sum to come up for judgment, apparently subject to almost any condition – in *Williams* (1982)[13] a condition of going to Jamaica and not returning for five years was not held unlawful. Despite the Law Commission's recommendation that the power was unnecessary, too broad, and ought to be abolished, it remains and is governed by paragraphs in the Criminal Procedure Rules that attempt to regulate its exercise.[14]

10.4 Compensation orders

Although the idea of making offenders pay compensation to their victims has a long history,[15] it is only since the 1970s that it has become a regular and significant element in English sentencing. The Criminal Justice Act of 1972 introduced the compensation order for injury, loss, or damage. In the Powers of Criminal Courts Act 1973 it took its place alongside other measures such as the confiscation order for property used in the commission of crime (s. 43) and also the restitution order (s. 28 of the Theft Act 1968). One of the objectives of the 1982 Criminal Justice Act was to increase the use of compensation orders by courts, and among the changes it introduced were the possibility of making a compensation order as the only order in a case, and the principle that the compensation order should have priority over a fine where an offender has limited means. The strongest measure is that introduced in 1988 and now consolidated in s. 130 of the Powers of Criminal Courts (Sentencing) Act 2000, which requires a court to consider making a compensation order in every case involving death, injury, loss, or damage, and to give reasons if it makes no compensation order in such a case.[16] The maximum

---

[10] For review and reform proposals, see Law Commission (1994).
[11] Law Commission (1994), and *Hashman and Harrup* v. *United Kingdom* (2000) 30 EHRR 241.
[12] Ibid., para. 4.3.   [13] (1982) 4 Cr App R (S) 239.   [14] Criminal Procedure Rules, part III.31.
[15] For debates in the nineteenth and early twentieth centuries, see Radzinowicz and Hood (1986), pp. 654–5.
[16] Reinforced by s. 63 of the Legal Aid, Sentencing and Punishment of Offenders Act 2012.

order in magistrates' courts was £5,000 until 2013, but now that maximum only applies to offenders under 18;[17] for adults there is no statutory limit in the Crown Court or the magistrates' courts.

Systems of criminal justice ought to be concerned to assist victims no less than to deal fairly with offenders. Crime is no less 'about' victims than it is 'about' offenders. Indeed, the explanatory memorandum of the Council of Europe's Convention on Compensation for the Victims of Violent Crimes includes the proposition that states have a duty to ensure that crime victims receive compensation, because the state is responsible for maintaining law and order, and crimes result from a failure in that duty.[18] There was, however, considerable reluctance to accept a state obligation in this country, although it was among the first to have an *ex gratia* state scheme for criminal injuries compensation.[19] That has now developed into the Criminal Injuries Compensation Scheme: its legislative framework is found in the Criminal Injuries Compensation Act 1995, but it was changed in major ways in 2012 in order to reduce expenditure. The details of the scheme raise a number of important issues which cannot be pursued here,[20] but it is relevant to note that the minimum claim which the Criminal Injuries Compensation Authority will entertain is £1,000, and that the scheme is confined to crimes of 'violence'. Until 1996 the quantum of awards reflected civil damages, but now there is a reduced tariff-based scheme.

Criminal justice systems rely heavily on victims for information about crimes and about offenders, and for evidence in court. It is only fair that, in return, the system should ensure that they receive the proper help and support. Apart from the Criminal Injuries Compensation Scheme, recognition of this is evident in government assistance for the spread of victim support schemes, to bring help, support, and advice to the victims of burglary, rape, and other crimes. Beyond that, there is a Code of Practice for Victims, issued under s. 32 of the Domestic Violence, Crime and Victims Act 2004 and now in its third edition (2013). The Code does not create a right of legal action, but it is admissible in legal proceedings generally. As well as giving information about the Criminal Injuries Compensation Authority and about Victim Support, it provides for victims to be informed about progress in dealing with their crime, including any arrest and court proceedings; for the right to a family liaison officer for bereaved families; and for the right to enhanced support for vulnerable or intimidated victims. These rights arise from obligations imposed on various criminal justice agencies. The 2004 Act also created the office of Commissioner for Victims and Witnesses: the current Victims' Commissioner is Baroness Newlove,

---

[17] Crime and Courts Act 2013, Sch. 16; general provisions are in ss. 130–134 of the PCC(S)A 2000.
[18] Council of Europe (1984), Preamble.   [19] Rock (1990), p. 273.
[20] For a brief history and full analysis of the 2012 'reforms', see Miers (2014).

whose objectives include promoting the interests of victims and holding agencies to account for their implementation of the Code.[21]

Whenever a person is sentenced for an offence committed after 1 April 2007, the court must order the offender to pay the Victim Surcharge, a levy used to fund the improvement of services for victims of crime. Since 2012 there is a sliding scale of surcharges: £15 for a conditional discharge, 10 per cent of the value of a fine (minimum £20, maximum £120), £60 for a community sentence, £80 for up to 6 months' custody (suspended or immediate), £100 for up to 2 years' custody, and £120 for longer custodial sentences. Offenders under 18 pay much less.

Returning to the compensation order made by a criminal court, this sits rather uncomfortably with other forms of sentence and order. It has a dual function: in many cases it operates simply as an ancillary order, to ensure some compensation to the victim in addition to the state punishment contained in the principal sentence; in other cases it becomes a central feature, as where it takes priority over a fine or accompanies a conditional discharge, and particularly where it is the sole order in the case. In the 'ancillary' cases it can be justified as a reparative element which accompanies the proportionate sentence. But some have found the task of justification harder when the compensation order is the principal or sole order in the case. How can this be regarded as sentencing when, in effect, the court is merely making a relatively 'rough and ready' award of damages to the victim? The offender would have been civilly liable to the victim in almost all cases and therefore, the argument goes, the court's order amounts to nothing in sentencing terms – no punishment, but rather a kind of civil award made by a criminal court.[22] One counter-argument to this is that, in practice, very few victims sue their offenders; therefore, in practice, the compensation order does transfer from the offender to the victim money which the offender would not otherwise have been made to pay. It may therefore be realistic to regard the compensation order as punitive in its effect on the offender, as well as reparative in relation to the victim. Another counter-argument would be that orders do not have to be punitive anyway: the compensation order should be applauded as a form of reparative justice,[23] or at least as recognition that our system ought to be multifunctional rather than limited to punitive responses.

How ought compensation orders be used by the courts? Section 130 of the PCCS Act 2000 (as amended) requires a court to consider an order in every case involving death or injury, damage or loss. It is well established that an order can be made in a case where the offence causes distress and anxiety.[24] Courts are empowered to make a compensation order for 'such amount as the

[21] Commissioner for Victims and Witnesses (2014).   [22] See *Barney* (1989) 11 Cr App R (S) 448.
[23] Thereby fulfilling purpose (g) in s. 142(1) of the 2003 Act, 'the making of reparation by offenders to persons affected by their offences'.
[24] *Bond* v. *Chief Constable of Kent* (1982) 4 Cr App R (S) 314, *Godfrey* (1994) 15 Cr App R (S) 536.

court considers appropriate', but appellate courts remain reluctant to uphold orders unless the amount of the loss is agreed or proved,[25] and unless the grounds for liability are clear and not complex.[26] Where the victim provoked the violence, the compensation order should be reduced by an appropriate amount.[27] It is the prosecution's duty to ensure that such evidence is available in court, and if there is no up-to-date evidence it would be wrong for the court to calculate the compensation on the basis of long-term effects which have not been proved.[28] The court should be satisfied that the offender caused the harm for which compensation is ordered,[29] although in public order cases where several offenders are convicted courts have not required proof that the particular offender actually inflicted the harm.[30]

Section 130 requires the court to have regard to the means of the offender when deciding whether to make a compensation order and when deciding on its amount. It will be apparent that the characterization of compensation orders as essentially civil measures breaks down at this point, because awards of damages are not reduced to take account of the means of defendants. Compensation orders are enforced as if they were fines, and imprisonment is the ultimate sanction for non-payment. This blurring of the civil and the criminal continues when we consider what assets of a defendant may be used to pay a compensation order: a court may be justified in ordering the sale of a moveable asset such as a car to pay compensation, so long as it has reliable evidence of the car's value,[31] but it is usually regarded as wrong to order the sale of a family home in order to compensate the victim, unless the home was purchased substantially out of the proceeds of the offence.[32] No such indulgence would be granted by the civil courts, but the criminal courts prefer the interests of the offender's family over those of the victim, presumably on the grounds that to impose too severe a burden might encourage further crime or might lead to the offender's being imprisoned for default. The payment period for a compensation order out of income should normally be no longer than one year, but where the offender has a regular income and can afford to pay, the period may be two, three, or (exceptionally) eight years.[33] More generally,

---

[25] *Vivian* (1978) 68 Cr App R 53; however, if a certain minimum loss is beyond dispute and a greater loss is contested and difficult to assess, the court should make the compensation order for the minimum loss: *James* [2003] 2 Cr App R (S) 574.

[26] *Horsham Justices, ex p. Richards* (1985) 7 Cr App R (S) 158; *Stapylton* [2013] 1 Cr App R (S) 68.

[27] *Flinton* [2008] 1 Cr App R (S) 575.   [28] *Smith* [1998] 2 Cr App R (S) 400.

[29] *Graves* (1993) 14 Cr App R (S) 790.   [30] *Taylor* (1993) 14 Cr App R (S) 276.

[31] See e.g. *Martin* (1989) 11 Cr App R (S) 424, a case where the offender was also sentenced to custody.

[32] Cf. *Holah* (1989) 11 Cr App R (S) 282, also a case where the offender was imprisoned, with *McGuire* (1992) 13 Cr App R (S) 332; cf. *Carrington* [2014] 2 Cr App R (S) 337 on payment by taking out a loan.

[33] *Olliver and Olliver* (1989) 11 Cr App R (S) 10, below, part 10.5.6; see also *Ganyo and Ganyo* [2012] 1 Cr App R (S) 652, upholding an 8-year repayment period by D who had obtained money by fraud to fund a training course, and who now had a steady job that enabled repayment (like a student loan).

it is regrettable that governments have not acted on the proposal that the court should pay the full amount of the awarded compensation order to the victim immediately out of court funds, and should then recover it from the offender in the ordinary way.[34]

Soon after the introduction of compensation orders, the question of their relation to other sentences was raised. The words of Scarman LJ in *Inwood* (1974)[35] remain apposite:

> Compensation orders were not introduced into our law to enable the convicted to buy themselves out of the penalties for crime. Compensation orders were introduced into our law as a convenient and rapid means of avoiding the expense of resort to civil litigation when the criminal clearly has means which would enable the compensation to be paid.

It therefore follows that an offender's swift payment of, or ability to pay, compensation should not be allowed to deflect the court from imposing a custodial sentence or a community sentence, if that is what the offence justifies.[36] If this were not so, the law would permit wealthy offenders to receive reduced sentences, which would infringe the principle of equality before the law (see Chapter 7.1). However, there is also the principled argument that an offender who makes reparation swiftly is giving some public recognition of the fact that he has wronged the victim – and that, if voluntary (rather than prompted by a legal adviser), deserves to be marked. It may be said that for less serious offences the law accords precedence to reparative over punitive elements, in that a compensation order has priority over a fine. But the priority is reversed for serious offences: thus, in *Jorge* (1999)[37] the Court of Appeal, reviewing the authorities, confirmed that it is generally wrong to impose a compensation order with a custodial sentence unless 'either the defendant has assets from which to pay it, especially no doubt the proceeds of his crime, or he is reasonably assured of income when he comes out from which it is reasonable to expect him to pay'.

How frequently do courts make compensation orders? The trends are broadly downwards for indictable offences and upwards for summary offences. Thus in the Crown Court some 21 per cent of offenders in 1989 and 1990 were ordered to pay compensation, but this had fallen to 7 per cent in 2002 and to 3.5 per cent in 2013. One possible reason for this is that the rise in the use of custody has precluded the making of a compensation order in some cases. Thus, for example, in 2013 the Crown Court only made a compensation order in 9 per cent of cases of violence and 7 per cent of fraud cases.[38] There has been a decline and slight revival in the use of compensation orders by magistrates' courts for indictable offences, from

---

[34] See the prevarication in Home Office (1990), para. 4.25.   [35] (1974) 60 Cr App R 70, at p. 73.
[36] E.g. *Copley* (1979) 1 Cr App R (S) 55.   [37] [1999] 2 Cr App R (S) 1.
[38] All statistics from Ministry of Justice (2014), Table A5.17.

29 per cent in 1990 down to 15 per cent in 2002 and up to 20 per cent in 2013. An order was made in some 30 per cent of cases of violence and 52 per cent of criminal damage cases in 2013. Turning to summary-only offences (including, of course, common assault and most offences of criminal damage), there was a sharp increase in the number of compensation orders from some 48,000 in 1997 to 113,000 in 2007, settling back slightly to 105,000 in 2013.

The mid-1990s study by Flood-Page and Mackie showed that legal procedures were not being carried out in some cases: a magistrates' court is required to give reasons if it does not make a compensation order, but in over 70 per cent of cases this was not done; in some cases magistrates said that they did not award compensation because the victim did not request it, a clear breach of the statutory requirement to consider it in every case of harm.[39] However, the most common reason for not making a compensation order was that stolen goods were recovered, and in some cases the offender's income was thought too low to make an order. Some courts regarded it as pointless or counterproductive to make an order against an offender in the same household as the victim.

Although the theory behind compensation orders is right, there is a significant practical drawback from the victim's point of view: an order can only be made if the offender is detected, prosecuted, convicted, and not penniless. Since only around one-quarter of all reported offences are 'cleared up', and since around two-thirds of defendants are unemployed, a victim's prospects of receiving compensation from this source are hardly bright. However, one condition that should normally be considered for inclusion in a conditional caution is that the offender pays some compensation to the victim; although only 1,200 conditional cautions were imposed in 2012–13, three-quarters had compensation as the condition.[40] There remains the problem that many offenders (whether cautioned or prosecuted) lack financial resources, and there may be a danger that an emphasis on paying compensation will discriminate against some offenders. However, it is important to recall that surveys of victims have shown that they set particular store by receiving some money, even if not full compensation, from the offender rather than from any other source.[41]

10.5 Fines

10.5.1 Introduction

The fine is the standard penalty for summary offences, and may be imposed for almost all indictable offences. Maximum fines for summary offences are ranged on five levels according to the seriousness of the offence. For indictable

---

[39] Flood-Page and Mackie (1998), pp. 60–4.   [40] CPS (2014).
[41] Shapland, Willmore and Duff (1985).

offences the Crown Court has long had no limit, and recent legislation has swept away the former normal maximum of £5,000 for magistrates' courts, giving them an unlimited power to fine for offences triable either way and other offences with a previous maximum of £5,000 or more.[42] Over 80 per cent of all cases in magistrates' courts result in a fine, mostly summary offences. Looking at indictable offences tried in magistrates' courts or the Crown Court, around 60 per cent of adult male offenders were fined in the mid-1970s, but the figure has declined to just over a third of that rate during the first decade of the twenty-first century. Fines are the normal response to offences committed by companies and organizations, and the attendant difficulties are discussed in part 10.5.6 below.

The fine is often presented as the ideal penal measure. It is easily calibrated, so that courts can reflect differing degrees of gravity and culpability. It involves no physical coercion and is non-intrusive, since it does not involve supervision or the loss of one's time. It is largely reversible, in the event of injustice. Indeed, it is straightforwardly punitive, 'uncontaminated by other values',[43] which also indicates that it has no affirmative rehabilitative value.[44] Fines are used extensively for regulatory offences, and the fine is one of the few sentences that can be used on corporate offenders. But it is the use of the fine for indictable offences by individuals that remains a focus for controversy. Fines seem to be relatively effective for such offenders, since surveys show that they tend to be followed by fewer reconvictions than other sentences. The assertion of superior efficacy has been doubted, since Bottoms rightly pointed out that courts tend to select for fines offenders with a certain stability in their lives (job, family) which would in any case indicate a lower risk of reoffending.[45] Justifiable as this is as a criticism of most studies of comparative effectiveness, it remains true that fines have emerged well from almost all of them. This is no reason to claim *superior* efficacy, but neither does it suggest that the decline in fining should be applauded. As one Home Office survey put it, 'reconviction rates for fines compare favourably with community penalties. There is thus no evidence that the switch from fines to community penalties that has occurred over the last twenty years has achieved anything by way of crime reduction.'[46]

The 1990 White Paper promoted the twin aims of greater use of fines and greater justice in fining: 'Setting fairer fine levels should lead to the greater use of fines and less difficulty in enforcing them.'[47] However, as will be explained in part 10.5.3 below, the provisions of the Criminal Justice Act 1991 aimed at greater justice in fining were abandoned within a few months of their introduction, and the overall use of fines has continued to decline. In recent years there has been a revival of government interest in fines. The Courts

---

[42] Legal Aid, Sentencing and Punishment of Offenders Act 2012, s. 85.   [43] Young (1989).
[44] See generally O'Malley (2009).   [45] Bottoms (1973).   [46] Moxon (1998), p. 98.
[47] Home Office (1990), para. 5.2.

Act 2003 made provision for the Court Service to focus on the enforcement of fines, but the Criminal Justice Act 2003 did little to advance the Halliday Report's support for the fine. Halliday argued that fines should be used 'at all levels of seriousness, both in isolation and in combination with [other] non-custodial penalties'.[48] He was aware that adding a financial penalty to a community sentence should not be allowed to take the 'punitive weight' of the sentence above the level proportionate to the seriousness of the crime, and he also argued that 'substantial fines in quite serious cases might be enough to meet the needs of punishment'.[49] However, little of this found its way into the White Paper of 2002. Instead it was Rod Morgan, then Chief Inspector of Probation, who demonstrated that low-risk offenders were increasingly being given community sentences instead of fines, taking those offenders more quickly up-tariff and also 'silting up' the probation service with offenders who did not really need their intervention.[50] The Carter Review (2003) took this argument forward and returned fines to the main agenda of sentencing reform. Carter argued that:

> Fines should replace community sentences for low risk offenders. 30 per cent of community sentences are given to offenders at low risk of reoffending.[51]

Carter then went on to recommend the introduction of a day-fine system – along similar lines to the system abandoned in 1993. In its reply, the government cited the fall in the use of fines as a principal reason for the 'increased severity in sentencing' and rising use of prison.[52] It accepted the recommendation that 'revitalized fines should replace a very substantial number of the community sentences that are currently given to low risk offenders', and promised to explore the feasibility of legislation to introduce day fines.[53] However, since then there has been little concrete action towards this goal. The coalition government has promoted the use of higher fines instead of community sentences, and the combination of fines with community sentences; it applauds increases in the average size of fines without detailed discussion of the financial resources of most offenders.[54]

10.5.2 Fines and fairness

As we saw in Chapter 7.5, the fine may raise questions related to the principle of equality before the law and the principle of equal impact. Equality before

---

[48] Halliday (2001), para. 6.15. Earlier (para. 6.5), he stated that 'the "serious enough" threshold [for imposing a community sentence] may have unintentionally created an impression that fines should be reserved for the least serious cases, which is not the case'.

[49] Halliday (2001), para. 6.16.   [50] Morgan (2003).   [51] Carter (2003), p. 27.

[52] Home Office (2004), para. 19.

[53] Home Office (2004), paras. 34–5. See also Coulsfield (2004) for a similar proposal.

[54] Ministry of Justice (2012), paras. 87–109. Sch. 16, Pt 7 of the Crime and Courts Act 2014 empowers bodies such as HMRC to give courts details of an offender's recorded income.

the law is relevant in two ways. One is that courts should not fine a wealthy offender when the offence justifies a more severe measure which they would have imposed on a less wealthy offender. The striking decision in *Markwick*[55] was cited in support. The other aspect is that courts should not impose a more severe penalty on an offender who lacks the means to pay what is regarded as an adequate fine. In the past, the Court of Appeal struck down several suspended sentences on this ground:[56] the proper course, if a court declines to impose a fine, is to move down to a conditional discharge and not up to a more severe measure. There is no ready way of assessing how faithfully the principle of equality before the law is followed in practice.

The principle of equal impact points to another aspect of social justice in relation to fines. It has long been established that a court should have regard to the means of the offender when calculating the amount of a fine, but this principle had been somewhat blunted in practice in three ways – the old rule that fines should not be increased for the rich, the difficulties in obtaining accurate information about an offender's financial situation, and courts' reluctance to impose fines that appear derisory to them and to newspaper readers.

10.5.3 The rise and fall of unit fines[57]

In an endeavour to achieve more and fairer fining, the 1991 Act introduced the unit fine. Day-fine systems operate in other European countries, such as Germany and Sweden, and it was decided to adapt them for use here. An experiment in the late 1980s showed that, after initial scepticism among local magistrates, the courts had quickly become accustomed to calculating fines in units; that fine levels were more realistic; and that fine enforcement was improved, with less resort to the sanction of imprisonment for non-payment.[58]

The success of these schemes not only persuaded the then government to provide for their introduction into all magistrates' courts under the 1991 Act, but also led several benches to introduce them of their own accord, in advance of the legislation. In outline, the scheme introduced by the 1991 Act was that magistrates' courts, when dealing with an individual (not a company), should calculate the fine by deciding how many units, on a scale from 1 to 50, represented the relative seriousness of the offence. This would be the judicial or judgmental part of the decision. Then the court would turn to the more administrative task of deciding how much the offender could afford to pay. The Act, combined with rules made by the Lord Chancellor's Department, instructed courts to calculate each offender's weekly disposable income, to make some standard deductions to reflect ordinary living expenses, and then

---

[55] (1953) 37 Cr App R 125, discussed in ch. 7.5 above.
[56] E.g. *McGowan* [1975] Crim LR 111; *Ball* (1981) 3 Cr App R (S) 283.
[57] See Warner (2012), esp. pp. 233–9.
[58] See Gibson (1990), and Moxon, Sutton and Hedderman (1990).

to move towards the decision of how much the offender should pay per unit. The minimum was set at £4 per unit, which was regarded as possible for an offender whose only income came from state benefits, and the maximum was £100 per unit.

The statutory unit fine system came into force on 1 October 1992, and was abolished in the summer of 1993 by the Criminal Justice Act 1993. What were the problems? First, the amount of unit fines under the statutory scheme was far higher than in the experimental schemes. It is said that this was at the insistence of the Treasury, but it resulted in a scheme with a quite different flavour: few of the experimental courts went above £25 per unit, whereas the statutory scheme went up to £100 per unit. Second, the scheme emphasized income to the exclusion of capital and other indicia of wealth – an approach aimed at simplicity, but productive of some injustice. Third, the statutory scheme became extremely complex, particularly in the regulations for calculating weekly disposable income. Since the scheme was never intended to be precise, but merely to mark a significant step towards equality of impact, this complexity was regrettable. Fourth, a vocal group of magistrates, particularly some stipendiary magistrates, felt that the scheme was misconceived because it was too rigid and overlooked the practical problems of determining the income of certain types of offender, such as prostitutes and foreign tourists.

However, it was a fifth difficulty that was probably the major factor in the decision to abolish unit fines. The system resulted in particularly high fines for offenders who might previously have received relatively low fines, especially middle-class motoring offenders with moderately or well-paid jobs. This, of course, was one of its aims: the 1990 White Paper referred to the need to impose substantial fines on 'an increasing minority of offenders with greater resources'.[59] If courts had routinely announced fines in terms of the number of units imposed, rather than the total payment, this element in the new scheme might have been less open to misinterpretation. As it was, the press, and particularly one newspaper group, began assiduously to collect examples of different levels of fines being imposed on people who had committed similar offences. One newspaper headline ran: 'Two cases, minutes apart, but with very different penalties. For a Mr Rothschild, a £2,000 fine; for a man named Bell, an £84 fine.'[60] No mention was made of the principle of equal impact that lay behind the new scheme, or of the fairness of differentiating between rich and poor. The journalists almost seemed to be assuming that the two men should have received the same fine, despite the vast difference in their incomes. The widely publicized case of a man who was fined £1,200 for dropping an empty crisp packet in the street increased the pressure on the government to 'do something about' the new scheme, even though it quickly

---

[59] Home Office (1990), para. 5.5.   [60] *Daily Mail*, 28 October 1992, p. 5.

became evident that the reason why the magistrates had fined this offender at £100 per unit was that he failed to disclose his income to the court.

In May 1993, at a time when the Magistrates' Association had put together some proposals for alterations to the scheme, the then Home Secretary, Kenneth Clarke, made the politically extravagant gesture of announcing the abolition of unit fines entirely. Over two decades later it remains politically awkward, apparently, to reverse that decision. Yet unit fines or day fines operate perfectly well in several other European countries. The Carter proposals, if thin on details, were clear about the desirable direction of change – 'fines rebuilt as a credible punishment' – but there has been no significant policy initiative to make this happen.

10.5.4 Fines in magistrates' courts

The legislation on fines as sentences was substantially re-enacted in the Criminal Justice Act 2003. Section 164(2) provides that the amount of the fine should reflect the seriousness of the offence. Section 164(3) provides that in fixing the amount of the fine a court should take account of the offender's financial circumstances. Section 164(4) adds that this applies whether it has the effect of increasing or reducing the amount of the fine. These provisions ought to be applied step-wise: first, the court should determine the level of fine that represents the seriousness of the offence; second, it should make the appropriate adjustment to reflect the offender's means. Section 164(1) requires a court to inquire into the offender's financial circumstances before fixing the amount of a fine. Section 162 empowers a court to make a financial circumstances order, requiring the relevant person to provide the court with such financial details as it requests.

This legislative framework was first introduced in 1993 to replace unit fines. Whereas the effect of unit fines had been to lower fines for the unemployed and to increase fines for the employed, the immediate effect of the greater flexibility of the 1993 framework was that fines for the unemployed rose again and fines for employed offenders began to reduce.[61] Different magistrates' courts were adopting different approaches to, and interpretations of, the legislative framework. Research by Charman, Gibson, Honess and Morgan (1996) demonstrated the considerable differences between courts, and sentencing exercises carried out by magistrates from various courts showed some divergent approaches to fining some fairly typical road traffic cases.[62]

Research by Robin Moore at the turn of the century revealed a failure of many benches to grasp the financial circumstances of some offenders.[63] There appear to be two major barriers to fairer fining – a reluctance to fine unemployed people amounts which look small through middle-class eyes, and

---

[61] Charman et al. (1996).   [62] Ibid., p. 4.   [63] Moore (2003).

a reluctance to impose on offenders with substantial incomes fines which look high in relation to the offence. As to the first barrier, Staughton LJ lamented:

> What troubles me about these cases is not the remedies which the magistrates had to choose from as means of enforcement, but the size of the fines which people on income support were expected to pay out of resources which are said to be only sufficient for the necessities of life.[64]

As to the second barrier, Flood-Page and Mackie concluded from their mid-1990s research, in which they questioned magistrates about their willingness to increase fines for the wealthy, that 'these contrasting opinions meant that wealthy offenders could receive very different fines at different courts as the size of the fine imposed depends largely on the views of the magistrates at that court'.[65] Section 164(4) makes it clear that wealthy offenders should be fined more, but there appeared to be a barrier to translating the principle of equality of impact into practice.

Fining in magistrates' courts is now governed by the definitive *Magistrates' Court Sentencing Guidelines* (2008). For each offence for which a fine is a guideline sentence, the guideline indicates fine Band A, B, or C as the starting point. Band A represents 50 per cent of 'relevant weekly income', within a range from 25 to 75 per cent; Band B represents 100 per cent, within a range from 75 to 125 per cent; and Band C represents 150 per cent, within a range from 125 to 175 per cent. Once the court has decided on a fine, and has identified the appropriate Band (according to the guideline for the offence), the court should move up or down from the starting point in order to reflect aggravating or mitigating factors relevant to the seriousness of the offence. Offender mitigation should then be taken into account, and the court will have arrived at a provisional fine level, in percentage terms. Then the court should turn its attention to the financial circumstances of the offender, requiring a statement of means to be produced and then assessing the 'relevant weekly income'.[66] While no account should be taken of tax credits, housing benefit, child benefit, etc., the court may take account of extraordinary expenses or of unusually low outgoings. The guideline indicates various other reasons for departing from the basic formula, but the aim is to foster a common approach. Once the court has completed its calculation of the fine, it must apply the reduction for a guilty plea as appropriate.

The guideline makes provision for two higher fining bands, Band D (where a community sentence would otherwise be warranted), and Band E (where the test for custody has been passed). Such cases will be rare, but it remains possible that, for example, an offence is serious enough to warrant a community sentence but that the offender is not thought to need any of the

---

[64] *Stockport Justices, ex p. Conlon* [1997] 2 All ER 204, at p. 214.
[65] Flood-Page and Mackie (1998), p. 53.
[66] For the details, see SGC, *Magistrates' Court Sentencing Guidelines* (2008), pp. 148–9.

requirements of a community sentence.[67] This may be seen as a small attempt to revive the use of the fine and to avoid the unnecessary 'silting up' of community sentences. The danger is that it may be used only for offenders with money, leaving the less well-off to face the greater demands of a community sentence.[68]

The MCSG approach to fines is an attempt to combine structure with flexibility. Strong supporters of unit fines will still find it too woolly,[69] whereas those who think that courts should be left with maximum discretion may regard it as too formulaic. In their trials of the MCSG approach, Raine and Dunstan noted misunderstandings of the methodology (which have presumably now been cured) but also a powerful tendency of some magistrates to regress towards their local conventions if the MCSG indicated otherwise.[70] The urgent need is for research and monitoring, to discover how the guideline is being applied, particularly in relation to the unemployed and the better-off – for example, nearly 650,000 deduction of benefits orders were made in 2010–11, more than twice the number two years earlier, and the government expects the maximum weekly deduction for those on benefits to rise from £5 to £25 with the advent of universal credit.[71] Moreover, the research should also examine the borderline between fines for prosecuted offences and fines levied by the police using Penalty Notices for Disorder (see Chapter 1.4 above). Armed with that information, it may be possible to refine the approach in order further to improve its fairness.

10.5.5 Fines in the Crown Court

The unit fine scheme was never applicable to the Crown Court, which has continued to be subject to the general statutory framework on fining, including the principle that fines should be increased for the wealthy as well as reduced for those of limited means.[72] Section 163 empowers the Crown Court to impose a fine (not subject to any limit, other than the offender's means) 'instead of or in addition to' any other way of dealing with the offender. Fines are imposed relatively rarely in the Crown Court (only around 1,400 per year from 2011–2013),[73] but questions remain about the extent to which the Crown Court adjusts fines according to the income of offenders. Thus, Flood-Page and Mackie found that the average fine for an unemployed man was £340

---

[67] This is advocated in Ministry of Justice (2012), paras. 87–8.

[68] This problem was not mentioned by Halliday (2001), para. 6.5, when advocating wider use of fines up-tariff.

[69] Cf. Moore (2003), who argues for a different structure based on payments for a set number of weeks.

[70] Raine and Dunstan (2009), at pp. 29–31.   [71] Ministry of Justice (2012), para. 106.

[72] Section 164(4) of the 2003 Act. In these cases there must still be some element of proportionality to the seriousness of the offence: *Jerome* [2001] 1 Cr App R (S) 316.

[73] See Tables 2–7 in Appendix B.

(which would take 16 months to pay at £5 per week, then thought to be the maximum for those on state benefits), and that just under one-fifth of unemployed men who were fined had to pay over £500.[74] Section 152(2) of the 2003 Act requires courts to impose custody only where it is satisfied that 'neither a fine alone nor a community sentence can be justified for the offence', and that may be taken to indicate a need for courts to consider imposing a substantial fine in cases approaching the custody threshold. The ensuing difficulty (as suggested above, in relation to fine Bands D and E in the magistrates' courts) is that courts may fine those who can afford to pay large amounts and imprison those of lesser means.

A possible example of this and other difficulties is *Olliver and Olliver* (1989).[75] Two brothers were convicted of wounding and of assault occasioning actual bodily harm to a police officer. Such offences would often result in immediate custodial sentences, but the court imposed suspended sentences of 2 years and 18 months, combined with fines and compensation orders totalling over £5,000 for one of the brothers, and somewhat less for the other. The reason for taking this course was that the brothers ran a carpentry business on which the jobs of 23 others depended, and to imprison them would put the business and the jobs in jeopardy. The Court of Appeal dismissed an appeal against the fines, Lord Lane remarking that it is 'desirable if possible to keep people out of prison' and that 'if people can be dealt with properly by means of non-custodial sentences, and fines are possibly the best of all the non-custodial sentences, then that should be done'. This case was supremely difficult, involving as it did a conflict between the principle of equality before the law, the principle of restraint in the use of custody, and the avoidance of harmful consequences to innocent third parties. However, it is important that the last-mentioned point be emphasized. Surely it was the consequences to the 23 employees which turned the case:[76] restraint in the use of custody should not so easily outweigh the principle of equality before the law in general Crown Court sentencing.

10.5.6 Repayment periods

A fine is payable on the day on which it is imposed, but courts should always be prepared to allow time to pay. The MCSG states that fines should normally be payable within 12 months, and warns that 'it may be unrealistic to expect those on very low incomes to maintain payments for as long as a year'.[77] Time for payment may be adjusted subsequently, by way of administrative

---

[74] Flood-Page and Mackie (1998), p. 106.

[75] (1989) 11 Cr App R (S) 10; compare *Ganyo and Ganyo* [2012] 1 Cr App R (S) 652.

[76] See the discussion in ch. 5.4.5 above.

[77] SGC, *Magistrates' Court Sentencing Guidelines* (2008), p. 152. It also states that 'the maximum weekly payment by a person in receipt of state benefit should rarely exceed £5'.

decisions which may differ from court to court.[78] The normal maximum repayment period of one year was set by judicial decisions in the 1980s,[79] but some commentators have assumed that the effect of *Olliver and Olliver* (1989)[80] was to overturn this. What the Lord Chief Justice said in that case was that there is nothing wrong in principle in the payment period being longer than one year, provided that it was not an undue burden or too severe a punishment. Two years would seldom be too long, and three years might be acceptable in an appropriate case. Care must surely be taken in ensuring that these longer periods are not used too readily, particularly since they apply to compensation orders as much as to fines. If the burdens are too great, the orders may be prison sentences in disguise;[81] but there may be cases involving offenders in work where a repayment period of eight years might be appropriate.[82]

10.5.7 Fining companies and organizations

A company which is convicted of, or pleads guilty to, an offence may be sentenced in one of a number of ways – a compensation order, or an absolute or conditional discharge, would be possible. But fines are the most frequent penalty, and this immediately raises the issue of how such fines should be calculated. In the leading cases on environmental offences, the Court of Appeal rightly emphasizes the importance of assessing the degree of the company's culpability, especially where the offence is one of strict liability. But, when summarizing the issues in *Anglian Water Services Ltd* (2004),[83] nothing was said about the relevance of the economic standing of the company to the size of the fine, although in *Thames Water* (2010)[84] the Court of Appeal held that account should be taken of money pledged in compensation. In the leading decision on fines for breaches of the health and safety legislation, *F. Howe & Son (Engineers) Ltd* (1999),[85] the Court of Appeal took account of the fact that this was a small company with limited financial resources. The judgment sets out the main factors relevant in assessing culpability for health and safety breaches, and then adds that the state of the company's finances is a relevant factor. For larger companies, however, the discussion of financial standing is often rather brief, and the size of the fine seems to be calculated by reference to fine levels in similar cases.[86] For very large

---

[78] Moore (2003).   [79] *Knight* (1980) 2 Cr App R (S) 82, *Nunn* (1983) 5 Cr App R (S) 203.
[80] Above, n. 75 and accompanying text.
[81] As recognized by Staughton LJ in the quotation above, text at n. 64.
[82] *Ganyo and Ganyo* [2012] 1 Cr App R (S) 652.
[83] [2004] 1 Cr App R (S) 374; cf. now *Pyranha Mouldings Ltd* [2014] 2 Cr App R (S) 349.
[84] [2010] 2 Cr App R (S) 567.
[85] [1999] 2 Cr App R (S) 37; on obtaining financial information, see *Criminal Practice Directions* (2013), VIIQ.
[86] E.g. *Avon Lippiatt Hobbs (Contractors) Ltd* [2003] 2 Cr App R (S) 427, reviewing the size of fines in earlier cases; *FJ Chalcroft Construction Ltd* [2008] 2 Cr App R (S) 610.

companies, fines running into several million pounds have been imposed: thus in *Balfour Beatty Rail Infrastructure Ltd* (2007)[87] the Court of Appeal reduced the fine from £10 million to £7.5 million (in order to prevent disparity with the fine imposed on Railtrack) for health and safety offences that caused the Hatfield rail crash, in which four people died.

In principle, the approach to fining companies and other organizations should be the same as for individuals: s. 164(2) states that the fine should reflect the seriousness of the offence, s. 164(3) states that the court should take account of the financial circumstances of the offender ('whether an individual or other person'), and s. 164(4) states that this may have the effect of increasing or reducing the amount of the fine. Adjusting fines to the means of individuals is difficult enough: how can courts adjust fines to the means of companies and organizations? The Sentencing Council in its guideline on environmental offences has sought to apply the statutory principles by dividing the size of the 'turnover or equivalent' of companies into four levels – large (£50 million or more), medium (£10 million to £50 million), small (£2 million to £10 million) and micro (below £2 million). The offences are then divided into four category ranges, and the court moves towards the fine by locating the appropriate category range for the size of company involved.[88] This particular guideline reminds courts that compensation has priority over fines, but its approach to the calculation of fines is preferable to the virtual abandonment of the statutory principles by the Sentencing Guidelines Council in its guideline on corporate manslaughter.[89]

10.5.8 The enforcement of fines[90]

In recent years there has been a concerted and successful effort to reduce the number of fine defaulters sent to prison. Over 22,000 fine defaulters were received into prison in 1993 and in 1994. More than three-quarters of these were unemployed, and were on state benefits, some two-thirds had been in prison before, and 80 per cent had more than one set of fines outstanding. The most frequent reason for default given by those interviewed in a small survey was that they could not afford to pay the fines; clearly it is important to distinguish between those who cannot pay and those who can but will not.[91] Another survey found that some magistrates were reluctant to consider some alternative enforcement measures, such as money payment supervision

---

[87] [2007] 1 Cr App R (S) 370.

[88] Sentencing Council, *Environmental Offences: Definitive Guideline* (2014), pp. 7–10.

[89] SGC, *Corporate Manslaughter and Health and Safety Offences Causing Death: Definitive Guideline* (2010), p. 7. See the poor judgment in *Parker and McClane* [2013] 1 Cr App R (S) 189, where the fine on a company was simply described as 'somewhat too large', with absolutely no reference point.

[90] For thorough recent reviews see Moore (2003), 2004), and Raine, Dunstan and Mackie (2004).

[91] Moxon and Whittaker (1996); Moore (2004).

orders.[92] In the late 1990s courts were urged to make much greater use of alternative means of enforcement, both by guidance from the Lord Chancellor's Department and by the landmark decision in *Oldham JJ, ex p. Cawley*,[93] which requires courts to give active consideration to all alternatives before committing a young fine defaulter to prison and to state those reasons in open court. The provisions relating to the committal of adult fine defaulters to prison are less exacting, as the Divisional Court pointed out in *Stockport JJ, ex p. Conlon*,[94] but the court in that case nonetheless scrutinized the reasoning of the magistrates and remitted one case for reconsideration.

As a consequence of these developments, of a 'best practice' guide issued by the Lord Chancellor's Department, and of new enforcement powers introduced by the Courts Act 2003, the number of fine defaulters received into prison has dropped sharply – from its peak of 22,000 in 1994 to around 6,000 in 1997 and to around 1,000 in recent years (1,100 in 2012).[95] A court may instead impose a community service order, a curfew with electronic tagging, or disqualification from driving as a means of dealing with unpaid fines. Findings from two pilot areas showed that over three-quarters of the orders made were community service orders; that, although it remains possible for a fine defaulter to terminate the default order by paying off part or the whole of the fine, this rarely happened; and that both magistrates and fine defaulters seemed content with the new arrangements.[96] Effective enforcement involves understanding the reasons why offenders default. In Moore's sample, over three-quarters of fine defaulters were unemployed, and there was little prospect of their paying the sums required.[97] Moore argues for a more sensitive approach that focuses on better decision-making by courts at the stage of imposing the fine, and then careful enquiries in cases of default, leading to properly targeted methods of ensuring payment.[98] Similarly, Raine, Dunstan and Mackie show that it is wrong to assume that non-payment is simply the fault of wilful or feckless offenders, and argue that it is preferable to consider a range of reasons for non-payment (including decisions of the court and its staff) which then require a range of appropriate responses.[99] That these research findings have been influential is shown by the fact that the payment rate of fines has increased significantly. The payment rate by value, excluding administrative cancellations, increased from 71 per cent in 2008–09 to 80 per cent in 2010–11.[100]

Both these improvements and the significant move away from imprisonment for fine default are to be welcomed, particularly because the offences for which fines are imposed are usually well short of custody in their seriousness. But if the fine is to become more widely used again, care must be taken to

---

[92] Whittaker and Mackie (1997).   [93] [1996] 1 All ER 464.   [94] [1997] 2 All ER 204.
[95] Ministry of Justice (2013), Table 6.1.   [96] Elliott, Airs and Webb (1999).
[97] Moore (2003), p. 16.   [98] Moore (2004).
[99] Raine, Dunstan and Mackie (2004), at pp. 523–34.   [100] Ministry of Justice (2012), para. 105.

ensure that initial decisions and subsequent enforcement are properly grounded. There should also be active consideration of whether custody should be regarded as a proper sanction for default: in principle it should not, and some European countries manage without it.[101]

10.6 The community sentence

10.6.1 Introduction

We now move away from discharges and fines and begin a lengthy consideration of community sentences. While the Criminal Justice Act 1991 appeared to place community sentences one level above fines, the Sentencing Guidelines Council's guideline on the 2003 Act states that 'even where the threshold for a community sentence has been passed, a financial penalty or discharge may still be an appropriate penalty'.[102] Moreover, in cases where the court is considering a custodial sentence, it must only impose such a sentence if satisfied that 'neither a fine nor a community sentence can be justified for the offence'.[103] The structure of the 2003 Act stemmed mostly from recommendations in the Halliday Report:[104] the Act replaced the range of separate community sentences with a generic community sentence which could contain one or more of several requirements.

There have been some distinct trends in the content and aims of community sentences in recent decades, although often they have intermingled. In the late 1980s and early 1990s the emphasis was on 'punishment in the community', the idea that community sentences should be seen as a form of punishment, in terms of restrictions on liberty (e.g. through curfews or unpaid work). In the early 2000s a further dimension received emphasis, with the emergence of risk management as a central part of community sentences, in furtherance of public protection. Probation officers became 'offender managers', and the multi-agency public protection arrangements (MAPPA) formed the leading edge of efforts to protect the public from reoffending by persons known to present a considerable risk.[105] Throughout this period, however, there had also been developments in rehabilitative techniques under the broad umbrella of the What Works movement. Among these were the pathfinder projects[106] and the RNR model, which focused on 'risks-needs-responsivity' in terms of the application of cognitive behavioural interventions and improving compliance by ensuring the engagement of the offender in the strategy.[107] The latter point ties in with the desistance movement, another strand of

---

[101] Shaw (1989), and Council of Europe (1993).
[102] SGC, *Overarching Principles: Seriousness* (2004), para. 1.36.
[103] Section 152(2) of the 2003 Act, discussed in ch. 9.4.1 above.
[104] For discussion, see the 5th edn of this work at pp. 338–40.   [105] Kemshall (2008).
[106] For a summary, see Raynor (2012), pp. 936–41.
[107] Raynor and Robinson (2009); Canton (2013), pp. 584–6.

probation work that places emphasis on providing support for the offender's efforts to desist from crime.[108]

The coalition government has proclaimed a 'rehabilitation revolution', which emphasizes the benefits to victims and the wider public of rehabilitating offenders. In the context of community sentences the coalition government's objective has been to develop a diverse system of service providers, i.e. private and voluntary sector providers as well as the National Probation Service, and to introduce payment by results.[109] More will be said about these initiatives in part 10.8 below.

10.6.2 The statutory tests for imposing a community sentence

There are two separate sets of circumstances in which a community sentence may lawfully be imposed. The first and more widely applicable threshold test is that created by s. 148(1):

> A court must not pass a community sentence on an offender unless it is of the opinion that the offence, or the combination of the offence and one or more offences associated with it, was serious enough to warrant such a sentence.[110]

The purpose of this provision is to ensure that community sentences are not used for minor cases, which should generally be dealt with by way of a discharge or fine.[111] The key judgment here is one of relative seriousness, and it is very difficult to offer concrete guidance – this is one of those issues on which the spirit or disposition of the courts will always be more influential than any attempt at guidance. However, all definitive guidelines issued divide community sentences into three bands – low, medium, and high – and express starting points and ranges in that way. For example, the starting point for the category 3 of domestic burglary is 'High Level Community Order', and the range is from 'Low Level Community Order to 26 weeks' custody'. The Annex to the guideline gives indicative examples of low-, medium-, and high-level community orders.[112] A pre-sentence report should indicate the degree of risk presented by the offender, and the SGC's original guideline contains a gentle nudge in the direction of restraining the use of community sentences for low-risk offenders:

> Where an offender has a low risk of reoffending, particular care needs to be taken in the light of evidence that indicates that there are circumstances where

---

[108] Farrall and Calverley (2006).   [109] Ministry of Justice (2010), paras. 128–58.

[110] Broadly speaking, an offence is 'associated with' the current offence if it is one for which the court is passing sentence on the same occasion: *Baverstock* (1993) 14 Cr App R (S) 471, *Godfrey* (1993) 14 Cr App R (S) 804.

[111] The wording also permits the use of a fine in serious cases that satisfy the community sentence threshold: see Bands D and E, discussed in 10.5.4 above.

[112] Sentencing Council, *Burglary Offences: Definitive Guideline* (2011), pp. 9 and 15.

inappropriate intervention can increase the risk of reoffending rather than decrease it. In addition, recent improvements in enforcement of financial penalties make them a more viable sentence in a wider range of cases.[113]

This guidance is based on risk of reoffending, whereas the point at issue is the different one of avoiding a disproportionate response to a relatively minor offence. But its general thrust communicates to sentencers the need for restraint.

The second and less frequently used threshold is to be found in s. 151 of the 2003 Act.[114] This empowers a court to impose a community sentence on a person who has been fined on three or more occasions since the age of 16, whose current offence is not serious enough to warrant a community sentence (even taking account of previous convictions under s. 143(2)), and where the court concludes that it would be in the interests of justice to impose a community sentence. The SGC's guideline warns that in these cases 'great care will be needed in assessing whether a community sentence is appropriate since failure to comply could result in a custodial sentence'.[115] There may be some cases where an element of supervision will help some such offenders to overcome underlying problems, but the danger is that a number of minor offenders will be taken up-tariff and hence subjected to more severe sanctions than their minor crimes properly warrant.

10.6.3 The range of requirements

The 2003 Act provided twelve forms of requirement that a court may make as a community order (s. 177) that constitutes a community sentence for the purpose of the Act. In recent years five new requirements have been added, and two (including the supervision requirement) have been abolished, changes that will be discussed in the appropriate places below.

This list of requirements applies only to offenders aged 18 and over: a different list applies to younger offenders, and is discussed in Chapter 12 below. The principles that should guide a court when determining which requirements to impose are discussed in part 10.6.4 below. Here, the focus is upon the meaning of and legal framework for each of the requirements. The legal framework is reinforced by *National Standards for the Management of Offenders* (2011), which include (but extend beyond) the supervision and management of offenders on community sentences. These standards no longer contain details of what should be provided, but focus on the issues of risk assessment, the 'tiering' of offenders according to the risk they present, the frequency of contacts between supervisor and offender, and so forth.[116]

---

[113] SGC, *New Sentences: Criminal Justice Act* (2004), para. 1.1.9.
[114] It substantially re-enacts s. 59 of the PCCS Act 2000, and was discussed in ch. 6.5 above.
[115] SGC (above, n. 113), para. 1.1.10.   [116] NOMS (2007).

1. Unpaid work requirement

Section 199 of the 2003 Act states that an offender may be required to perform between 40 and 300 hours of unpaid work, provided that the court is satisfied that the offender is a suitable person to perform such work. The work must be carried out within 12 months 'at such times as he may be instructed by the responsible officer' (s. 200(1)). When proposing orders of this kind in 1970, the Advisory Council on the Penal System suggested that they would appeal to sentencers with various penal philosophies:

> To some, it would be simply a more constructive and cheaper alternative to short sentences of imprisonment; by others it would be seen as introducing into the penal system a new dimension with an emphasis on reparation to the community; others again would regard it as a means of giving effect to the old adage that the punishment should fit the crime; while still others would stress the value of bringing offenders into close touch with those members of the community who are most in need of help and support.[117]

Perhaps it was this range of reparative, retributive, and rehabilitative functions which led to the swift adoption of community service orders into English sentencing practice. Since then they have undoubtedly become more onerous, and the 2003 Act raised the maximum from 240 to 300 hours. The choice of work, however, is for the probation service and not the courts; the organization of work placements and general supervision is subject to the National Standards. While the essence of the unpaid work requirement lies in its punitive function, in terms of the performance of hard work,[118] the other functions may nevertheless be achieved as by-products. In recent years the unpaid work requirement has come to be known as 'community payback', a reference to the element of symbolic reparation. In practical terms this means, first, that the unpaid work carried out by offenders on community sentences should be visible to members of the community (by using such indicators as plaques, badged supervisors and/or vehicles); and secondly, that local people and organizations should have a say in the projects to be carried out by offenders doing unpaid work.[119]

Unpaid work requirements were the single most used requirement in community orders in 2010, accounting for around a third of all orders. A similar proportion of orders had an element of supervision (33 per cent), but that was often combined with another requirement whereas unpaid work usually stood alone.[120] For what types of offender might unpaid work requirements be used? Evidence from Flood-Page and Mackie's survey in the mid-1990s suggests that magistrates made the choice between community service

---

[117] Advisory Council on the Penal System (1970), para. 33.
[118] This was the perception of offenders interviewed by Mair and Mills (2009).
[119] See the discussion by Bottoms (2008), pp. 151–2.
[120] Ministry of Justice (2008), Tables 3.9 and 3.10.

and probation on various grounds, often connected with their belief about the needs of the offender and the local organization of the two forms of sentence. Some said that unpaid work was more appropriate for unemployed offenders, since it might reintroduce them to a form of regular work, but the sentencing practices of magistrates in that study showed that a lower percentage of those on community service were unemployed compared with probation (65 per cent and 81 per cent respectively).[121] The same pattern was evident in the Crown Court cases (49 per cent and 83 per cent respectively). Fewer of those on community service had previous convictions (58 per cent, compared with 77 per cent for probation), and fewer stood convicted of more than one offence (31 per cent compared with 47 per cent for probation). As expected, fewer had problems of drug addiction, mental disorder, or stress.[122] In terms of ranking the various requirements, it may be argued that unpaid work could be less demanding than supervision; but, as we shall see below, supervision requirements have been abolished.

2. Rehabilitation activity requirement

Section 15 of the Offender Rehabilitation Act 2014 will, when brought into force, abolish the former 'activity requirement' and replace it with a 'rehabilitation activity requirement'. This is part of a strategy to ensure that all community orders are demanding, and it is combined with the abolition of the much-used supervision requirement – in a sense, severing the link with the longstanding welfarist concept of probation. The rehabilitation activity requirement will empower the supervising officer to instruct the offender to attend appointments, for the purpose of rehabilitation, and that comes close to the old form of probation work. But the requirement also empowers the officer to instruct the offender to attend accredited programmes or a 'restorative justice activity' (as defined in the Act). The former 'activity requirement' was not frequently used, accounting for some 6 per cent of requirements in community sentences in 2010, usually combined with supervision,[123] but the new format may prove more attractive to courts, especially since the supervision requirement is no longer available.

3. Programme requirement

Section 202 of the 2003 Act provides that an offender may be required to participate in an accredited programme for a specified number of days.[124] This requirement may only be imposed if a probation officer has recommended the programme as suitable for the offender and if the court is satisfied

---

[121] Flood-Page and Mackie (1998), pp. 37–8.   [122] Ibid., p. 102.
[123] Ministry of Justice (2011), Tables 3.9 and 3.10.
[124] For minor amendments, see the Legal Aid, Sentencing and Punishment of Offenders Act 2012, s. 70.

that a programme is available at the place specified. The legislation does not lay down a maximum period for this requirement: no doubt the length of the particular programme will be a factor here, but the need to observe proportionality constraints means that the courts should not simply make a programme requirement of whatever length is requested, without reference to the seriousness of the offence. Various types of programme have been accredited, including sex offender treatment programmes, general offender behaviour programmes (such as Reasoning and Rehabilitation and Think First), and others dealing with such problems as anger management and drink-impaired drivers.[125] Programme requirements were the third most frequently used requirement in 2010, made in some 10 per cent of community orders, often combined with supervision and/or another requirement.[126]

4. Prohibited activity requirement

Section 203 of the 2003 Act empowers a court to make a requirement prohibiting the offender from participating in specified activities on specified days or for a certain period. There is a duty to consult a probation officer before making this requirement. The section mentions the possibility of requiring that the offender does not possess, use, or carry a firearm; another possible prohibition would be from driving a motor vehicle. No maximum duration for this requirement is stated. This requirement has been little used, appearing in fewer than 1 per cent of orders in 2010.[127]

5. Curfew requirement

Section 204 of the Act[128] provides that a court may require an offender to remain, for periods specified in the relevant order (not less than 2 nor more than 16 hours per day), at a place so specified. The requirement may last for a maximum period of 12 months, and before making it the court must obtain and consider information about the place at which the offender is to remain under curfew. A court that decides on a curfew requirement must also impose an electronic monitoring requirement, unless an exception applies. One exception is where the consent of another person is needed and it is not forthcoming (s. 215(2)); another is where the court has not been notified that arrangements for electronic monitoring are available in the area (s. 218(4)); and a third is where 'in the particular circumstances of the case' the court considers it inappropriate to require electronic monitoring (s. 177(3)(b)). In 2010 a curfew requirement was included in 7 per cent of community orders.[129]

Experiments with electronic monitoring began in 1990, the then government declaring that 'the criminal justice system should take advantage of

---

[125] Rex, Lieb, Bottoms and Wilson (2003).   [126] Ministry of Justice (2011), Table 4.   [127] Ibid.
[128] As amended by the Legal Aid, Sentencing and Punishment of Offenders Act 2012, s. 71.
[129] Ibid.

modern technology when it is sensible and practical to do so'.[130] Some have argued that electronic monitoring is not acceptable because it breaches an offender's human rights: requiring an offender to wear an electronic anklet may be held incompatible with Article 3 of the Convention (no inhuman or degrading punishment) or with Article 8 (right to respect for private life), but there has not been a successful challenge on these grounds. Interviews of magistrates and probation officers suggested that tagging was thought particularly useful to disrupt 'pattern offending', such as shoplifting, night-time burglary, or public order offences on Friday and Saturday nights.[131] Indeed, curfew orders may be seen as creating a 'virtual prison' for an offender, by placing strong restrictions on movement for certain periods;[132] but those restrictions do not prevent offending, as the self-report study by Anthea Hucklesby suggests,[133] and so curfews are not truly incapacitative. Hucklesby's small study argues that a curfew (especially if combined with a supervision requirement) has considerable rehabilitative potential, even for offenders who are substance misusers, in that it may help offenders to disengage from certain habits and criminal networks, and may enable some offenders to generate stronger personal relationships (by staying at home rather than going out). Of course there were negative aspects, such as the problems of aligning curfews with employment hours, and many of those placed on a curfew had various personal problems and several previous convictions, which put them at considerable risk of reoffending.

6. Electronic monitoring requirement

Amendments to the 2003 Act made by Schedule 16, Part 4 of the Crime and Courts Act 2013 establish the electronic monitoring requirement as a requirement in its own right. The 2003 Act's provisions on curfews empowered courts to add an electronic monitoring requirement to other requirements so long as all the necessary conditions were fulfilled (s. 177(4)), but the government wished to see wider use of the technology of electronic monitoring, not merely to enforce curfews but to help with the enforcement of other requirements in community sentences.[134]

7. Exclusion requirement

Section 205 of the Act empowers a court to prohibit an offender from entering a specified place for a specified period of up to two years. The order may limit the prohibition to certain hours, or to different places for different times. This power was first introduced in 2000, and it is similar in some ways to the anti-social behaviour order, which could also be used to prohibit a person from

---

[130] Home Office (1990), para. 4.22.   [131] Mortimer, Pereira and Walter (1999), p. 3.
[132] See Roberts (2004).   [133] Hucklesby (2008), pp. 59–60.
[134] Ministry of Justice (2012), paras. 42–60.

going to certain places (although ASBOs had to be for a minimum of two years).[135] Exclusion requirements were little used in 2010, appearing in fewer than 1 per cent of orders.[136]

8. Residence requirement

Section 206 of the Act provides that a court may make a requirement that the offender should reside, for a specified period, at a certain place. The court is required to consider the offender's home surroundings, and only to specify a hostel or other institution as the place of residence if so recommended by a probation officer. Much depends on the availability of hostel accommodation and the assessed suitability of the offender for a particular hostel. However, it will be noted that the residence requirement does not have to relate to a hostel: an offender may be required to reside at his home, or with a relative, for example. In appropriate cases this requirement could be combined with others, such as supervision or curfew; but in 2010 fewer than 1 per cent of orders included a residence requirement.[137]

9. Mental health treatment requirement

Sections 207 and 208 of the Act provide that a court may require the offender to submit to treatment by or under the direction of a registered medical practitioner. Like the residence condition, this is a longstanding requirement that was formerly added to a probation order in appropriate cases, and that may be used for offences that normally attract a substantial custodial sentence.[138] It will be discussed further in Chapter 12.3 below.

10. Drug rehabilitation requirement

Sections 209–211[139] provide that a court may require an offender to submit to drug treatment and testing for a specified period. The court first has to be satisfied that the offender is dependent on, or has a propensity to misuse, drugs; that this may be susceptible to treatment; and that arrangements can be made for treatment, either as a resident or as a non-resident. This requirement may only be made if the offender consents. There are provisions for courts to review the offender's progress (s. 210) and to make changes to the requirement (s. 211), somewhat along the lines of 'drug courts' in the United States, and the 'drug court' model has been piloted in this country. The requirement replaces the DTTO (drug treatment and testing order), introduced in 2000 in order to provide a measure aimed directly at tackling the link between drugs and crime. As the name suggested, the two elements were that the offender should

---

[135] For further discussion, see ch. 6.5 above and ch. 11.5.8 below.
[136] Ministry of Justice (2011), Table 4.   [137] Ibid.
[138] E.g. *Attorney General's Reference No. 37 of 2004 (Dawson)* [2005] 1 Cr App R (S) 295.
[139] As amended by the Legal Aid, Sentencing and Punishment of Offenders Act 2012, s. 74.

undergo a programme of treatment and that during that programme he should be subjected to periodic testing to see whether he was still taking drugs.

The DTTO had a broadly favourable reception in the courts:[140] many sentencers have welcomed a measure that tackles addiction and welcomed the court's role in monitoring progress, but one frequently heard complaint was that the resources were not available for a sufficient number of orders (and indeed some areas ran out of earmarked funds).[141] Enthusiasm for these orders is sometimes tempered by the frequency with which offenders lapse or fail to complete them, an expected outcome given the chaotic and troubled lives of most of the offenders involved.[142] 'Relapse emerges as a regular feature along the road to abstinence.'[143]

Drug treatment requirements formed part of 5 per cent of community orders in 2010, often combined with a supervision requirement.[144] Their positioning in the sentencing hierarchy has given rise to differences of opinion. In an attempt to summarize the relevant Court of Appeal decisions in eight propositions in *Woods and Collins* (2006),[145] Hughes J made it clear that such an order should not be made for very serious offences, but could be suitable for a prolific offender if there were a positive recommendation and if the judge regarded the prospects of rehabilitation as good. In that case the offence was a single burglary of a petrol station, and an order was considered appropriate in the case of the second offender (the first being sentenced to 20 months). Other decisions suggest that significant violence would rule out a community order with drug treatment requirement, and that an offence 'worth' more than three years could rarely be considered appropriate for such an order.[146] However, guidelines from the Sentencing Council have included the following paragraph at Step Two:

> Where the defendant is dependent on or has a propensity to misuse drugs and there is sufficient prospect of successs, a community order with a drug rehabilitation requirement under section 209 of the Criminal Justice Act 2003 can be a proper alternative to a short or moderate length custodial sentence.[147]

This demonstrates that rehabilitation may trump proportionate punishment in cases of moderate seriousness, but that much is left to the court's judgment

---

[140] See e.g. Darbyshire (2011), p. 207.   [141] See Hough et al. (2003), p. 49.

[142] See Sparrow and McIvor (2013), p. 304, reporting that between 2003 and 2009 the completion rate increased from 28 to 47 per cent, although the authors suggest that the greater use of shorter orders might have explained part of this change.

[143] Sparrow and McIvor (2013), p. 308, commenting on research findings.

[144] Ministry of Justice (2011).   [145] [2006] 1 Cr App R (S) 477.

[146] Cf. *Attorney General's Reference No. 82 of 2005* [2006] 1 Cr App R (S) 679 (order upheld for three non-violent robberies by man with 54 previous convictions) with *Attorney General's Reference No. 114 of 2005* [2006] 2 Cr App R (S) 595 (order for robbery involving hammer and knife increased to 4 years' imprisonment).

[147] Sentencing Council, *Burglary Offences Definitive Guideline* (2011), p. 8; *Drug Offences Definitive Guideline* (2012), p. 12.

of whether there is a 'sufficient prospect of success' and, if so, whether this alternative is 'proper'.

11. Alcohol treatment requirement

Section 212 of the Act empowers a court to impose a requirement that the offender submits to treatment with a view to the reduction or elimination of the offender's dependency on alcohol. This requirement does not include submission to testing, but otherwise it has similar conditions to the drug rehabilitation requirement – the court must be satisfied that the offender is dependent on alcohol; that this may be susceptible to treatment; that arrangements can be made for treatment, either as a resident or as a non-resident; and that the offender consents. Alcohol treatment requirements formed part of 3 per cent of orders in 2010.[148] Given the high rate of alcohol misuse by offenders this is a lower figure than one might expect. The National Audit Office found that, because alcohol treatment programmes are largely funded by the National Health Service, they were either not available or used only patchily in many areas.[149] Clearly there is a need for improved organization and planning here.

12. Alcohol abstinence and monitoring requirement

Section 76 of the Legal Aid, Sentencing and Punishment of Offenders Act 2012 inserts into the community sentence provisions of the 2003 Act an alcohol abstinence and monitoring requirement. This requires the offender to abstain from alcohol, or to ensure that his alcohol level does not exceed a specified level, for a period of not more than 120 days. The requirement may only be made if alcohol consumption was an element in the offence of conviction (such as drunk driving) or a contributory factor in the commission of the offence or an associated offence. This requirement, which may not be made at the same time as an alcohol treatment requirement, is intended as part of a strategy to tackle the connection between alcohol and crime,[150] and it is being introduced on a pilot basis initially.

13. Foreign travel prohibition requirement

Section 72 of the Legal Aid, Sentencing and Punishment of Offenders Act 2012 inserts into the community sentence provisions of the 2003 Act a new form of requirement. The foreign travel prohibition requirement prohibits the offender from travelling, on days or for a period specified in the order, to any country outside the UK or to any country other than one or ones specified in the order. The maximum duration is 12 months. This is intended as a punitive restriction.

---

[148] Ministry of Justice (2008), Tables 3.9 and 3.10.   [149] National Audit Office (2008).
[150] Ministry of Justice (2010), pp. 28–9 and 60.

14. Attendance centre requirement

Section 214 provides that a court may require an offender to attend at an attendance centre for between 12 and 36 hours, so long as local arrangements are available. Attendance centres were developed primarily for young offenders, and are discussed further in Chapter 12 below. Section 177(1) provides that this requirement cannot be made unless the offender is aged under 25 at the time. In 2010 this was the least used of all requirements.

10.6.4 The choice of requirement(s)

Assuming that the statutory test of seriousness for a community sentence (considered in part 10.6.2 above) has been satisfied, the court's next step is to choose which requirement(s) is(are) appropriate in the particular case. The relevant statutory provisions are in s. 148(2) as amended:

> Where a court passes a community sentence which consists of or includes a community order –
>
> (a) the particular requirement or requirements forming part of the community order must be such as, in the opinion of the court, is, or taken together are, the most suitable for the offender, and
> (b) the restrictions on liberty imposed by the order must be such as in the opinion of the court are commensurate with the seriousness of the offence, or the combination of the offence and one or more offences associated with it.

This subsection must now be read subject to the new s. 177(2A), inserted by Schedule 16, Part 1 of the Crime and Courts Act 2013. This states that:

> Where the court makes a community order, the court must –
>
> (a) Include in the order at least one requirement imposed for the purpose of punishment, or
> (b) Impose a fine for the offence in respect of which the community order is made, or
> (c) Comply with both of paragraphs (a) and (b).

A new s. 177(2B) states that s. 177(2A) does not apply where there are exceptional circumstances which make it unjust for the court to comply with it. This new provision is discussed below after the elements of s. 148(2) have been examined.

The structure of s. 148(2) builds on suggestions made by Bottoms (1989) and particularly by Wasik and von Hirsch in 1988, demonstrating how the desert rationale might be applied to non-custodial sentencing. Those authors sketched a model based on the 'limited substitutability' of sanctions of roughly the same degree of severity,[151] and the statutory test goes some way in this

---

[151] Wasik and von Hirsch (1988), p. 561.

direction – prescribing not only that the particular order(s) 'must be ... the most suitable for the offender' but also that the community orders must be commensurate with the seriousness of the offence. The statutory formula in s. 148(2) is therefore designed to ensure that measures to reduce reoffending are taken within the framework of a proportionate sentence.

Three aspects of the statutory framework call for discussion here – a) determining suitability for the offender; b) ensuring that the restrictions on liberty are commensurate with the seriousness of the offence(s); and c) including a punitive element.

a) *Determining suitability for the offender:* a pre-sentence report from the Probation Service (see Chapter 13.4 below) will in many cases be influential in the decision whether to make a community sentence rather than an alternative disposal. However, the SGC's guideline also states that, once a court has decided on a community sentence, it should ask for a pre-sentence report specific to the issues in the particular case.[152] The pre-sentence report will be crucial in advising courts of the programmes available to allow them to deal suitably with the particular offender. In deciding on the particular requirements to impose, the court must also have regard to the factors in b) and c) below.

b) *Ensuring that the restrictions on liberty are commensurate with the serious-ness of the offence:* as s. 148(2)(b) states and as the SGC's guideline emphasizes, the court must preserve proportionality between the restrictions on liberty entailed by the requirement(s) and the seriousness of the offence(s). The SGC's guideline set out three ranges of sentence within community orders, graduated according to the degree of restriction they impose. Courts are required by the guideline to indicate, when they ask for a pre-sentence report on this point, 'which of the three sentencing ranges is relevant and the purpose(s) of sentencing that the package of requirements is required to fulfil'.[153]

The three sentence ranges set out in the SGC's guideline are Low, Medium, and High.[154] The Low range may include 40–80 hours of unpaid work, a curfew requirement 'for a few weeks', a prohibited activity requirement (no maximum duration is mentioned), or an attendance centre requirement (for which the maximum is 36 hours). Community orders in this range are said to be suitable for offences below the community sentence thresh-old,[155] and for lesser offences of possession of class C drugs with intent

---

[152] Section 161 of the 2003 Act also empowers a court to make a pre-sentence drug testing order, for the purpose of ascertaining whether an offender has any specified Class A drug in his body.

[153] SGC, *New Sentences: Criminal Justice Act 2003*, para. 1.1.16.

[154] The Sentencing Advisory Panel approached this issue, in its advice to the SGC, on the basis of the indications given in Halliday (2001), pp. 40–1.

[155] I.e. offenders sentenced under s. 151 (see part 10.6.2 above), who have been fined three times but whose offence is not serious enough to meet the threshold for a community sentence.

to supply.[156] The Medium range may include a greater number of hours of unpaid work (e.g. 80–150), an activity requirement of 20–30 days, a curfew requirement lasting 2–3 months, or an exclusion requirement of around 6 months.[157] Community sentences in this band might be appropriate for handling stolen goods (less than £1,000 if for resale; more if for personal use), and for level 3 burglaries of commercial premises.[158] The High range includes unpaid work of 150–300 hours, activity requirements up to the 60-day maximum, curfew orders lasting for 4–6 months, and so forth. Such orders should be made in cases which are just short of satisfying the custody test, where the court decides that a community sentence is appropriate, for example level 3 offences of domestic burglary.[159] These 'non-exhaustive descriptions of examples of requirements that may be appropriate for each level' are printed in an Annex to the Council's definitive guidelines, but they now have to be read subject to the changed list of requirements (e.g. activity requirements no longer exist, whereas foreign travel prohibitions and rehabilitation activity requirements have been introduced); and, of course, subject to the new s. 177 (2A), which remains to be discussed.

c) *Including a punitive element*: as explained above, a 2013 amendment imposes on courts the (qualified) duty to ensure that every community sentence includes 'at least one requirement imposed for the purpose of punishment'. The reasoning behind this new duty was somewhat strange. The Ministry of Justice stated that community orders can be more effective than custodial sentences, with over 8 per cent fewer reconvictions.[160] It went on to say that community sentences 'are not currently as effective a response as they could be' because they 'do not include a clear punitive element alongside other requirements aimed at rehabilitation and reparation'. No evidence is produced for this assertion (and what does the word 'effective' mean here?), and it is further weakened by the statement that 'all community orders involve some restriction of the offender's liberty and in that respect they can all be regarded as punitive to some degree'.[161] However, the government's aim is to require courts 'to select a requirement which has punishment as its primary purpose' – community payback, an electronically monitored curfew, or a fine. The terms of s. 177(2A) do not bear this out, since the obligation is only to include at least one requirement imposed for the purpose of punishment, not for the *primary* purpose of punishment. Unless the intention is that new Council guidelines steer the courts towards requirements that are intended to be primarily punitive, the new provision is likely to have little effect.[162] Moreover, there is an

[156] Sentencing Council, *Drug Offences Definitive Guideline* (2012), p. 13.
[157] Cf. Hucklesby (2008) on the positioning of curfew orders; also Harrison (2006).
[158] Sentencing Council, *Burglary Offences Definitive Guideline* (2011), p. 13.   [159] Ibid., p. 9.
[160] Ministry of Justice (2012), para. 33.   [161] Ibid., para. 38.
[162] Wasik (2014), p. 485, suggests that it may be 'ignored in practice'.

'escape clause', and the government accepted that an explicitly punitive requirement would not be suitable for some offenders, such as those with mental health problems. This reference to suitability is a reminder that the statutory framework in s. 148(2) remains in place, so that even if the court does decide to include a punitive element, it must be the most suitable for the offender and the whole order must be commensurate with the seriousness of the offence.

Once the court has decided that the statutory conditions of suitability and proportionality in s. 148(2) are satisfied, it must then ensure that due credit has been given for any time spent in custody on remand. This would be a routine matter if a custodial sentence were imposed, and courts must take care not to overlook the same principle of fairness in cases where they decide on a community sentence. The guideline indicates how courts should approach this issue, particularly in cases around the custody threshold where there may be a choice between imposing a custodial sentence that (in fact) enables immediate release, and imposing a community sentence that is reduced in its onerousness to take account of the time spent on remand.[163]

The SGC's guideline is absolutely clear that there is no obstacle to an offender's being given two or three successive community sentences under the 2003 Act. Thus, the fact that there is only one form of community sentence in law

> does not mean that offenders who have completed a community sentence and have then reoffended should be regarded as ineligible for a second community sentence on the basis that this has been tried and failed. Further community sentences, perhaps with different requirements, may well be justified.[164]

In order to ensure that relevant information is properly transmitted, however, courts are urged to record their community sentences in terms of the purpose of the order and the range (low, medium, or high) in which the sentence was placed.

10.6.5 Enforcement and breach

While a requirement is in force, the Offender Manager should monitor, review, and evaluate the offender's progress and, if necessary, consider an appropriate form of response – which may be early revocation for good progress, or taking action for breach (see below). The general approach to supervision is much more controlling than a decade or two ago, and it is certainly fair to conceptualize the supervision requirement as a restriction on liberty.[165] However, there remains a commitment to rehabilitative techniques, thus ensuring that supervision requirements continue to fall within Francis

---

[163] SGC, above n. 153, paras. 1.1.37–1.1.40.   [164] Ibid., para. 1.1.34.   [165] Harrison (2006).

Allen's definition of rehabilitation – 'effect[ing] changes in the characters, attitudes and behaviour of convicted offenders'.[166]

Section 179 states that Schedule 8 to the 2003 Act governs the breach, revocation, and amendment of community orders. The Schedule confers on the 'responsible officer' a discretion in relation to the first breach of a requirement without reasonable excuse, either to give a warning or to initiate breach proceedings; in relation to the second breach, however, the responsible officer must bring the offender back to court in breach proceedings. The National Standards set out the approach that an Offender Manager should take in cases of unexplained failure to attend appointments and other breaches of requirements.[167] The court's powers on breach are tough, and differ according to whether the breach is a failure to comply or the commission of a further offence, but the SGC's guideline is designed to ensure that 'the primary objective' of the court's response to breach proceedings is to ensure 'that the requirements of the sentence are finished'. Thus paragraphs 9 and 10 of Schedule 8 state that a court that finds a failure to comply without reasonable excuse must either amend the terms of the community order 'so as to impose more onerous requirements' or revoke the order and deal with the offender as for the original offence. A magistrates' court also has the option of fining the offender and leaving the order in place. If the court finds that 'the offender has wilfully and persistently failed to comply with the requirements of the order', it must impose a prison sentence of up to 51 weeks.[168] However, the court must take account of the extent to which the offender has complied with the requirements of the order, and give any credit for 'part performance'; it should also take account of 'the reasons for the breach'.[169] In many cases, an appropriate response may be to lengthen the order or to include an extra requirement in it. However, the Council's guideline warns that imposing extra requirements should not be allowed to make compliance with the terms of the order less likely, and that imposing a custodial sentence may be out of proportion to the original sentence. Indeed, on the use of custody for breach, the Council takes a strong line:

> Custody should be the last resort, reserved for those cases of deliberate and repeated breach where all reasonable efforts to ensure that the offender complies have failed.[170]

Nonetheless, the wording of Schedule 8 remains severe, and, as noted above, custody is permitted in all breach cases and is required where there is 'wilful and persistent' breach, even in cases where the original offence was

---

[166] Allen (1981), p. 2.   [167] NOMS (2007), pp. 45–9.

[168] This power extends to cases where the original offence was non-imprisonable: Sch. 8, paras. 9 (1)(c) and 10(1)(c).

[169] SGC, above n. 153, para. 1.1.46; *Poulton* [2013] EWCA Crim 1453.

[170] SGC, ibid., para. 1.1.47.

non-imprisonable. This is another example of breach being punished more severely than the original offence, the court thereby regarding defiance of authority as a particularly serious wrong. As argued in Chapter 6.3.1 above, the reasons for breach may be much more complex and decisions on the appropriate response require flexibility.

10.7 Deferment of sentence

To the great surprise of many, the power to defer sentence – on the statute book since 1972 and hardly ever used – was retained and slightly revived in the 2003 Act. Thus s. 278 of the Act introduced Schedule 23, which replaced ss. 1 and 2 of the Powers of Criminal Courts (Sentencing) Act 2000 with substituted sections. A court is empowered to defer sentence for up to six months if 'the offender undertakes to comply with any requirements as to his conduct during the period of deferment that the court considers it appropriate to impose'. Courts can therefore impose conditions relating to attendance at a course of treatment, or relating to residence in a particular place, or whatever they think appropriate. There is now a specific provision for courts to include a requirement to participate in 'restorative justice activities'.[171] If the offender fails to comply with one or more of the requirements, the court may deal with the offender before the end of the deferment period and may pass sentence for the original offence – and also for any offence committed within the period of deferment. The court may appoint a supervisor for the period of deferment, who will usually be a probation officer.

The idea of deferment is to allow the court to test the offender's resolve and intentions, and perhaps also to enable the offender to have a positive influence over the sentence ultimately imposed. The SGC's guideline provides that:

> The use of deferred sentences should be predominantly for a small group of cases close to a significant threshold where, should the defendant be prepared to adapt his behaviour in a way clearly specified by the sentencer, the court may be prepared to impose a lesser sentence.[172]

It seems that most of these cases will be on the cusp of custody, where a community sentence might be considered in favourable circumstances; but the Council also contemplates that there may be cases that pass the test for a community sentence but where a discharge or fine might be imposed if the conditions of the deferment are fulfilled. In the earlier leading case of *George*,[173] the Court of Appeal held that at the end of the deferment period the sentencer should 'determine if the defendant has substantially conformed or attempted to conform with the proper expectations of the deferring court ... If he has, then the defendant may legitimately expect that an

---

[171] Section 1ZA of the 2000 Act, inserted by Pt 2 of Sch. 16 to the Crime and Courts Act 2013.
[172] SGC, n. 153 above, para. 1.2.7.   [173] (1984) 6 Cr App R (S) 211.

immediate custodial sentence will not be imposed'. Although the use of deferment has risen in recent years, the total number of cases in 2011 was only 2,000.

10.8 Conclusions

We have seen in this chapter that there is a wide range of non-custodial sentences available to the courts. And yet, the use of custody remains high. There is broad agreement about what happened in English sentencing in the ten years prior to the 2003 Act: the use of imprisonment increased sharply, many of those who would previously have received a community sentence or a suspended sentence were sent to custody, and many of those who would previously have been fined (and, latterly, some of those who would have received a conditional discharge) were given community sentences. There was, in other words, a ratcheting-up of sentence severity, a gradual up-tariffing of offenders with increases in the use of both custody and community sentences.

The decade since the implementation of the 2003 Act has seen few major changes, taking full account of the complexity of sentencing and the difficulties of interpreting the statistics. The most obvious change is that some 41,000 more suspended sentences were passed on adults in 2013 than in 2004.[174] The displacement appears to have been mostly from community sentences (down 32,000), but also from fines, immediate custody and other measures. Thus what appears to have happened is another ratcheting effect: some 32,000 offenders who would previously have received community sentences have been given suspended sentence orders – an utterly predictable malfunction, and the fourth edition of this work made the point clearly.[175] The 2003 Act provided statutory threshold tests, as we have seen, and these were refined more closely in the SGC's guidelines. But there is little evidence of those guidelines being consulted and followed by sentencers: it seems possible that offence guidelines are noticed much more than general or overarching guidelines.

One fundamental error was the peremptory abolition of unit fines in 1993. The scheme had several faults, but the proper approach would have been to remedy those faults. By giving way to a press campaign and to a small minority of magistrates, and preferring political kudos to sound policy, the Home Secretary of the time squandered the opportunity to make financial penalties fairer and returned the fine to its previous chaos. The obvious deleterious consequences – that fewer offenders would be fined, and that the poor would receive higher fines – have followed, as demonstrated in part 10.5 above. Subsequent developments on fines have been positive – the sharp decline in

---

[174] See the discussion of suspended sentence orders in ch. 9.4.5 above.
[175] 4th edn (2005), pp. 274–7, 330–1.

committals to prison for default, and the substantial increase in the percentage of fines paid – but they have not succeeded in restoring the attraction of fines for sentencers. How can this trend be reversed? To bring offenders down-tariff is much more difficult than to take them up-tariff, and it means unravelling practices developed over a decade or so. The 2003 Act makes it clear that the fine does not always stand beneath community sentences in order of 'penal bite', and that substantial fines may be used for offenders who are close to satisfying the custody test. But that change is only likely to affect a small number of cases; and in any event it raises fairness problems, which may undermine the principle of equality before the law (Chapter 7, above). Despite recommendations in the 2003 Carter Report and the Coulsfield Report of 2004, among others, no government appears to have had an appetite for the major reversal of policy that would be required if we were to return to a system based on day fines or unit fines. Yet only such a system can deliver a reasonably fair and just system across all levels of financial resources, and even then it would require measures to give compensation orders and fines a more prominent place in sentencing.

A restless decade for penal policy since 2003 is now giving way to new initiatives and new objectives. The coalition government has proclaimed a 'rehabilitation revolution', which takes the form of the Transforming Rehabilitation programme. This has six points:

i) Creating a new public sector National Probation Service to work with the most high-risk offenders.
ii) Forming 21 new Community Rehabilitation Companies to turn round the lives of medium- and low-risk offenders.
iii) Giving statutory supervision and rehabilitation in the community to every offender released from custody, including those sentenced to less than 12 months' imprisonment.
iv) Establishing a nationwide 'through the prison gate' resettlement service to give most offenders continuity of support from custody into the community.
v) Opening up the market to a diverse range of new rehabilitation providers 'to get the best out of the public, voluntary and private sectors and giving them the flexibility to do what works'.
vi) Only paying providers in full for real reductions in offending.

Much could be said about these initiatives, and a few comments will be ventured here. Most important is the context of these reforms: as seen in 10.6.4 above, the government is still pursuing a punitive agenda for community sentences, and it remains committed to a high prison population. Any improvements in reducing reoffending that flow from Transforming Rehabilitation will be welcome but must be viewed in this wider and distinctly less optimistic context.

While the creation of a market is an objective of the government reforms, as it was for prison privatization, public sector providers are to retain responsibility for high-risk offenders, as an extension of the MAPPA arrangements (see 10.6.1 above). Behind the drive to market testing for 'rehabilitation providers' is not just value for money but also the hope that new rehabilitative methods can be trialled by voluntary and private sector providers, at their own cost (in the sense that there will not be full payment if results do not follow as specified). This gives a new twist to the dalliance with the What Works movement in the early 2000s: the then government's over-enthusiastic and rapid roll-out of 'what works' programmes, encouraged by the Halliday Report, did not have the significant benefits expected. The reconviction rates of those who completed these programmes were generally not superior to the rates of those who experienced other measures. [176] Most criminologists would not be surprised, since, even if reconvictions are an acceptable measure of success, the best that could be expected would be that some forms of intervention work more effectively with some forms of offender. James McGuire, perhaps the leader of the What Works movement in this country, has insisted that overall reductions in reconviction rates can be produced, but that this can only occur if the various programmes and interventions are properly designed and delivered.[177] In practice there have often been problems of both design and delivery in this country, some resulting from underfunding and some from overambitious government targets. Whether the search for more effective ways of reducing reoffending will be enhanced by opening the field to competition from voluntary sector and private sector providers remains to be seen, but a great deal of planning and investment is necessary if the desired results are to be achieved.

It may prove to be points iii) and iv) of the Transforming Rehabilitation programme that have the longest-lasting effects. The absence of a supervision requirement for offenders serving prison sentences of under 12 months has been a longstanding anomaly, not least because this group has the highest reconviction rate on release from prison. The Labour government proposed to tackle it through the Custody Plus sentence for which the Criminal Justice Act 2003 made provision, but the government got cold feet about the probable overuse of the measure and the resultant expense, and it was never brought into force.[178] Now the coalition's policy of reducing reoffending has led to the passage of the Offender Rehabilitation Act 2014, s. 2 of which inserts a new s. 256AA into the 2003 Act so as to impose a 12-month supervision period on all offenders released from prison after serving a sentence of between 1 day and 2 years. The supervision of these offenders will be under contract, just like community orders, and the offender manager may therefore be a probation officer or an officer of a voluntary association or private company, as part of a system of payment by results (known as PbR).[179]

---

[176] See Bottoms (2004), pp. 61–3; Raynor (2012); Harper and Chitty (2005).
[177] McGuire (2002).   [178] See 4th edn of this work at pp. 277–8; 5th edn at p. 295.
[179] Ministry of Justice (2012), paras. 150–4.

At the same time, the coalition government has shown recognition of the particular problems of certain groups of offenders with special needs, notably women offenders and drug offenders. For women the government has promised at least six women's community centres offering selected community payback schemes for women, and also at least four women-only 'intensive treatment-based alternatives to custody'. These and other initiatives are long overdue as part of the unduly slow response to the recommendations in the Corston Report (2007).[180] Similarly, the government has outlined new initiatives to tackle drugs and alcohol in relation to offending.[181] If these initiatives are known to be successful and are available to courts, there remain the problems of increasing the confidence of sentencers in community orders, and also of devising and enforcing guidelines on the use of types of sentence. The Sentencing Council has not yet tackled this problem, but it seems that the SGC's guideline on *New Sentences: Criminal Justice Act 2003* was either rejected or ignored by many sentencers. No doubt it was integrated into magistrates' training, but it seems not to have been an effective vehicle for shaping judicial approaches to suspended sentences, community sentences, and related measures. In the meantime, the Probation Service is undergoing its most radical reshaping for decades, with only around 30 per cent of staff likely to be retained and the remainder expected to be taken on by private contractors whose bids are successful under the CRC initiative. While the extension of supervision to offenders imprisoned for under 12 months is a welcome step, the future of community sentences and of supervision in the community seems uncertain.

---

[180] Ibid., paras. 159–60; see ch. 7.3 above, and Malloch and McIvor (2011).
[181] Cf. Sparrow and McIvor (2013).

11

Ancillary orders and civil preventive orders

This chapter sets out to discuss the ever-expanding range of ancillary orders available to courts at the sentencing stage, and to explore the also expanding range of civil preventive orders, breach of which may constitute a serious criminal offence. The chapter begins with a summary of the current sentencing framework, before going on to examine the range of privatory orders, reparative orders, and preventive orders that courts may make. The rationale for the various orders is then reassessed, before a concluding section on sentencing for breach of an order.[1]

11.1 The statutory sentencing framework

The framework of sentencing established by the Criminal Justice Act 2003 (as amended) has been much discussed in Chapters 9 and 10 above, and the present summary eschews detailed statutory references in order to convey the essence of the decision-making scheme in respect of adult offenders, as set down in the legislation. The following sequence begins with the least onerous sentence and ends with the most onerous.

> Is an absolute or conditional discharge sufficient?
> Is the case suitable for a fine (which may be substantial enough to satisfy the community order threshold or come close to the custody threshold)?

---

[1] In previous editions this chapter also dealt with procedural issues in sentencing, but they now form the subject matter of a new ch. 13 below.

Is the case serious enough to warrant a community sentence?

Is the offence so serious that neither a fine alone nor a community sentence can be justified, and therefore a custodial sentence is unavoidable?

If the case passes the custody threshold test, are there factors indicating that the sentence may be suspended or a community sentence given?

If neither of those alternatives is possible and an immediate custodial sentence is unavoidable, is the case one to which a minimum sentence applies, or is the case one in which it is appropriate to impose a dangerous offender sentence (life imprisonment or an extended sentence)?

If not, what is the shortest term commensurate with the seriousness of the offence?

This is a simplified version. It is phrased in terms of sentencing for a single offence, and we saw in Chapter 8 that sentencing for more than one offence brings various other complications. The framework leaves out of account the court's duty to consider making a compensation order (see Chapter 10.4 above), and also various duties relating to the ancillary orders, such as the duty to initiate the procedure for confiscation (see part 11.5.1 below.) It also takes no account of the statutory requirements on aggravating and mitigating factors, examined in Chapters 5 and 6 above.

As is apparent from earlier chapters, the sentencing guidelines now steer the court towards a particular starting point and range for each category of offence. However, in theory it is the legislation that takes priority, and this is recognized in the text of guidelines such as that on non-domestic burglary, which directs the court to what it terms the 'custody threshold' (for category 2 or 3 offences) and the 'community order threshold' (for category 3 offences), drawing attention to the statutory tests.[2] The nine-step decision sequence, which is a familiar feature of Council guidelines, includes at Step Seven, 'Compensation and ancillary orders', and states: 'In all cases, courts should consider whether to make compensation and/or other ancillary orders.'[3] Those orders are discussed in 11.3, 11.4, and 11.5 below; but first, a brief discussion of the impact of the distinction between punishment and prevention.

11.2 Preventive and punitive orders

Most of the orders discussed in this chapter may be described as 'preventive'. However, in the context of the European Convention on Human Rights it is often important to determine whether a particular order amounts to a penalty (i.e. a punishment) or is *merely* preventive. If an order has a significant punitive element (even though it is also to some extent preventive), it must comply with certain human rights standards. In particular, it must not operate retrospectively (Art. 7), its ambit must be clear (Art. 7), and it must only be imposed after

---

[2] Sentencing Council, *Burglary Offences: Definitive Guideline* (2011), p. 13.   [3] Ibid., p. 14.

all the safeguards appropriate to a criminal charge have been observed
(Art. 6(3)). Thus in *Welch* v. *UK* (1995)[4] the European Court of Human Rights
held that the confiscation procedures of the Drug Trafficking Act 1986 violated
Article 7 of the Convention by imposing a retrospective penalty on the
offender. Section 38(4) of the Act did expressly give retroactive effect to
the powers of confiscation, provided the defendant had been charged after
the Act came into force. The key question was therefore whether a confiscation
order was a 'penalty'. In deciding that it was, the Court noted that the measure
had punitive as well as preventive and reparative aims; that the order was
calculated by reference to 'proceeds' rather than profits; that the amount of the
order could take account of culpability; and that the order was enforceable by a
term of imprisonment in default. These factors, in combination, led the Court
to conclude that the measure was in substance punitive, even though its aim
was said to be preventive. In *Ibbotson* v. *UK* (1997),[5] by contrast, the European
Commission on Human Rights held that the notification requirement under
the Sex Offenders Act 1997 was not a 'penalty', since it was much less severe
than confiscation, there was no provision for imprisonment in default
(a separate prosecution would have to be brought), and it was preventive
'in the sense that the knowledge that a person has been registered with the
police may dissuade him from committing further offences'.

When the Court of Appeal came to tackle this issue, in the context of the
(now repealed) order disqualifying an offender from working with children,
they had to decide whether this was merely a preventive order (which could
operate retrospectively) or whether in substance it was a penalty (which
could not, because of Article 7, operate retrospectively). In determining that
it was merely preventive in *Field and Young* (2003),[6] the Court laid considerable weight on the fact that the order applied both where a person is convicted
and where a person is found to be either unfit to plead or not guilty by reason
of insanity. However, the reasoning is flawed. The Court appeared to think
that it would be difficult to regard the order as preventive if it could only be
made after a conviction, but it was easier to regard it as preventive because it
could also be made after a finding of insanity or disability in relation to the
trial. This is manifestly unsatisfactory: the whole point of that provision is to
treat the severely mentally disordered (for these purposes) as if they had been
convicted, rather than to suggest that these orders can be made generally on
persons who have not been convicted. The Court of Appeal placed form above
substance, and it seems highly unlikely that the Strasbourg Court would yield
to a device which, if approved, could be deployed widely by draftsmen to
transform truly punitive orders into preventive orders. Is it really suggested
that, if the Drug Trafficking Act 1986 had provided for the making of
confiscation orders not only on conviction but also after a finding of insanity

---

[4] (1995) 20 EHRR 247.   [5] (1999) 27 EHRR CD 332.   [6] [2003] 2 Cr App R (S) 175.

or unfitness to plead, the Court in *Welch*[7] would have reached a different conclusion and found the orders to be non-punitive? More will be said below about the punitive/preventive distinction and its implications in the context of particular ancillary orders.[8]

11.3 Punitive privatory orders

The two forms of order discussed here are punitive in intent, and should therefore be taken into account in calculating the overall proportionality of the sentence to the offence(s) of which the offender is convicted. (Other privatory orders, such as confiscation orders and forfeiture orders, are discussed in 11.5.1 and 11.5.12 below.)

11.3.1 Deprivation orders

Section 143 of the PCCS Act 2000 empowers a court to make an order depriving the offender of any property used (or intended for use) in committing or facilitating the commission of the offence, which was lawfully seized from the offender or under his control at the time of arrest or summons.[9] Subsections (6) and (7) make it clear that a number of motoring offences fall within the rubric of 'facilitating the commission of the offence', and so a court may order that the offender be deprived of a car for the offence of driving whilst disqualified. However, as the Divisional Court held in *Highbury Corner Stipendiary Magistrate, ex p. DiMatteo* (1990),[10] the court must also request or receive information about the financial impact on the offender before making the order. The decision also emphasizes the importance of regarding the order as part of the total sentence on the offender, which ought not to be out of proportion with the seriousness of the offence(s).[11] In *Ball* (2003)[12] the Court of Appeal quashed a deprivation order in respect of a Mercedes car with a personalized number plate, used in facilitating theft, on the grounds that the judge had failed to give counsel the opportunity to address the court in relation to a forfeiture order and its possible effects, and failed to follow the statutory requirement to make an estimate of the value of the property before deciding whether to make the order.

11.3.2 Disqualification from driving

Sections 146–147 of the Powers of Criminal Courts (Sentencing) Act 2000 empower courts to disqualify from driving any person who uses a vehicle

---

[7] Above, n. 4.   [8] See Ashworth and Zedner (2014), chs. 1 and 4.
[9] This does not apply if the property (a car) belongs to another, such as a hire purchase company: *Kearney* [2011] 2 Cr App R (S) 608.
[10] (1990) 12 Cr App R (S) 263.   [11] See also *Lee* [2013] 2 Cr App R (S) 79, upholding the order.
[12] [2003] 2 Cr App R (S) 92.

for the purposes of crime, or any person convicted of an offence. The Act does not require any connection between the nature of the offence and the making of the order, but in *Cliff* (2005)[13] the Court of Appeal held that there must be 'sufficient reason' for using the power. Such a reason was found in *Bowling* (2009),[14] where the offender had exposed himself to children from his car; but the Court of Appeal was concerned that the duration of the order might prevent him from finding work on release from prison, and therefore reduced it. The rationale of this power seems to be punitive rather than preventive, and so the court should take it into account when assessing the overall proportionality of the sentence.

11.4 Reparative orders

The most frequently used order of this kind is the compensation order, which was discussed in detail in Chapter 10.4 above. It is important to note that the compensation order has priority over a fine and over any order for payment of costs. Three other forms of reparative order may be mentioned briefly: the purpose of all four orders is to make reparation to the victim, and therefore they should be left out of account when assessing whether the sentence is proportionate.

11.4.1 Restitution orders

Section 148 of the Powers of Criminal Courts (Sentencing) Act 2000 empowers a court to make an order, on conviction for a theft offence (or where one is taken into consideration on another charge), requiring the offender to restore to the victim the property stolen, or goods representing that property, or a sum equivalent to the value of the stolen property that was taken from the offender's possession on arrest. It will be seen that the conditions for making this order are precise, and it is relatively rare for courts to make restitution orders (81 in 2012).

11.4.2 Reparation orders

The reparation order is a form of community sentence available only when sentencing offenders under 18. It will therefore be dealt with in Chapter 12.1 below.

11.4.3 Victim surcharge

The victim surcharge was introduced by the Criminal Justice Act 2003 as a £15 surcharge on all offenders, the proceeds to be used to fund various victim

---

[13] [2005] 2 Cr App R (S) 22.   [14] [2009] 1 Cr App R (S) 122.

services, raising about £10 million per year. Since October 2012 the victim surcharge is levied on a graduated scale, from 10 per cent of a fine, through £60 for offenders sentenced to a community sentence, to £100 for those sentenced to 6–24 months' imprisonment and £120 for those sentenced to longer terms. The surcharge must be imposed, unless the court makes a compensation order and the offender has insufficient means to pay both the surcharge and appropriate compensation.

11.5 Preventive orders

The discussion now moves to the ever-lengthening list of preventive orders, some 18 of which are set out below. The government has increased the number and range of these orders under the banner of public protection, but it is important to recognize that this has been done in order to avoid some of the procedural requirements of sentences. By terming these orders 'preventive' and making many of them available to a court without conviction (e.g. simply on application), recent governments have insisted that this avoids the procedural protections that go with sentences of the court – such as the need to observe the various 'fair trial' requirements relevant to a criminal charge in Article 6 of the Convention, and the non-retrospectivity principle enshrined in Article 7, and so forth.[15] Whether it has successfully avoided these safeguards remains to be tested at the European level; but it is important to recall that the Strasbourg Court held in *Welch* v. *United Kingdom*[16] that a sentence which was preventive in intent may still be regarded as punitive in substance. This applies to confiscation orders, and may apply to other preventive orders.

11.5.1 Confiscation orders[17]

The principal statute, replacing earlier legislation, is the Proceeds of Crime Act 2002 (POCA). This statute is extensive and detailed, and it suffices here to mention the principal provisions of Part 2 of the Act. Where an offender has been convicted in the Crown Court, the judge must initiate the confiscation procedure if there is an application from the prosecution[18] or the judge believes that it is appropriate to do so (s. 6). The next step depends on whether the judge decides that the offender has a 'criminal lifestyle' or not. Section 75 sets out the elements of a 'criminal lifestyle', in terms of being convicted of one of a listed group of offences, or of 'conduct forming part of a course of criminal activity'. If the court decides that the offender has a 'criminal lifestyle', it must make certain assumptions about property possessed by the offender in the previous six years (s. 10). If the court decides that the

---

[15] See further Ashworth and Zedner (2014), ch. 4; Ramsay (2012).
[16] Above, n. 4 and accompanying text.   [17] For thoughtful analysis, see Alldridge (2003).
[18] There is no discretion if such an application is made: *Hockey* [2008] 1 Cr App R (S) 279.

offender does not have a 'criminal lifestyle', it must decide whether he has benefited from the particular criminal conduct in the case – not using the assumptions in s. 10, but possibly requiring the offender to furnish information on pain of adverse inferences (s. 18). Section 7 prescribes the way in which the court should arrive at the 'recoverable amount', and s. 9 prescribes what deductions and additions may be made. The court may then make an order, and must at the same time fix a term of imprisonment in default of payment. Where a court makes a confiscation order, it must take account of that order before it imposes a fine, deprivation order, or any other order requiring the offender to make a payment (other than a compensation order). However, it should not take the confiscation order into account otherwise in determining the appropriate sentence.[19]

What is the justification for such extensive powers of confiscation? This must be located in a version of the principle that it is wrong to allow an offender to profit from her or his crime. In theory, this principle should operate separately from the sentencing process, although we have seen that where an offender has limited resources the confiscation order is given priority over a fine. The separateness of confiscation orders is therefore parallel to the separateness of compensation to the victim. Both may be seen as forms of corrective justice, rather than as punishments. That, however, is the position in theory. In practice, as explained in 11.2 above, the European Court of Human Rights has ruled that confiscation orders, which give the judge extensive powers to reach back into the offender's property and which provide for substantial terms of imprisonment in default of payment, are in substance 'penalties' within the meaning of Article 7 of the Convention and therefore cannot be allowed to operate retrospectively.[20]

To characterise confiscation orders as a form of corrective justice raises difficult questions, however. It is one thing to deprive an offender of the economic benefits of the crime. It is another thing to provide – as do the POCA provisions on offenders deemed to have a 'criminal lifestyle' – for 'extended confiscation' that reaches further than the profits of the crime of which the offender has been convicted, and aims at depriving the offender of what are termed the 'proceeds' of crime.[21] This may go beyond the 'profits' of the crime, and therefore cannot be rested on that moral principle. It seems that at this point a vague notion of deterrence takes over: the extended confiscation regime is defended as a deterrent to crime, as removing assets so that they cannot be laundered or otherwise used in criminal activities, and as preventing the distortion of markets. However, as with other assertions about deterrence (see 3.3.2 above), there is a lack of empirical evidence on its working and its effectiveness.

---

[19] Proceeds of Crime Act 2002, s. 13.   [20] *Welch* v. *UK*, above n. 4.
[21] For detailed discussion of the issues, see Alldridge (2003) and (2011), and Boucht (2013).

While the senior judiciary continues to emphasise a deterrent rationale for the confiscation regime,[22] and to refer to effectiveness as the first principle,[23] the relevance of the right to property in Article 1 of Protocol 1 to the Convention has also been recognised. The confiscation order and its provision of imprisonment in default must remain proportionate, that is, the means employed to deprive the offender of assets must be proportionate to the legitimate aim pursued.[24] This does not rule out the joint and several liability of co-offenders,[25] but it does prevent an order being made in respect of sums that have been repaid in compensation,[26] or in respect of expenses that are not truly a 'benefit',[27] or imposed upon 'mere couriers or custodians or other very minor contributors to an offence, rewarded by a specific fee'.[28] This confiscation regime is far-reaching, and it is hardly surprising that most of the sentencing cases heard in the House of Lords or Supreme Court have concerned issues relating to confiscation. There are issues of substantive and procedural justice here which have received insufficient critical discussion in this country.

11.5.2 Disqualification from driving

Although treated as an ancillary order, the court's power to disqualify road traffic offenders from driving may be regarded by many recipients as the primary penalty.[29] The detailed rules may be found in the Road Traffic Act 1988. Disqualification from driving for at least 12 months is mandatory following the offences of driving with excess alcohol, failure to provide a sample for testing, and causing death by driving. Only in cases where 'special reasons' are found can the mandatory period of disqualification be avoided. Disqualification also ensues when an offender accumulates 12 penalty points as a result of 2 or more offences, and it is a discretionary penalty for various offences connected with motoring, such as taking a car without the owner's consent. The rationale for this power is said to be preventive/protective, and therefore the length of disqualification should be influenced less by proportionality to the current offence than by proportionality to the probable danger, to which the offender's driving record as a whole is relevant.[30] However, it is established that account should be taken, when setting a lengthy period of disqualification, of the effect on the offender's future prospects of employment

---

[22] E.g. *Waya* [2013] 2 Cr App R (S) 87, at [2].   [23] *Castillo* [2012] 2 Cr App R (S) 201, at [13].

[24] *Jahn v. Germany* (2006) 42 EHRR 1084, cited in *Waya* [2013] 2 Cr App R (S) 87 at [12].

[25] *May* [2009] 1 Cr App R (S) 162; *Lambert and Walding* [2012] 2 Cr App R (S) 535.

[26] *Jawad* [2014] 1 Cr App R (S) 85.   [27] *Ahmad and Ahmed* [2012] 2 Cr App R (S) 491.

[28] *May* [2009] 1 Cr App R (S) at p. 182, applied in *Revenue and Customs Prosecution Office v. Mitchell* [2009] Crim LR 469.

[29] Disqualification from driving under ss. 146–147, a punitive order, was discussed at 11.3.2 above.

[30] 'Public protection' from dangerous drivers was the preventive rationale in *Backhouse et al.* [2010] EWCA Crim 1111.

and therefore of law-abidance.[31] If the person breaches the order, there is a separate offence of driving whilst disqualified, an offence triable summarily with a maximum sentence of 6 months' imprisonment.

11.5.3 Disqualification from acting as a company director

The power to disqualify a person from acting as a director of a company was granted by the Company Directors Disqualification Act 1986. Civil courts use the power in around 1,000 cases per year, but the criminal courts invoke it in around 100 cases per year, most frequently in cases involving fraudulent trading or similar offences. Orders of over 10 years up to the maximum of 15 years should be reserved for very serious cases, with orders in the 6–10 year range more appropriate for offences committed over a shorter period of time and yielding less money.[32] 'The rationale behind the power to disqualify is the protection of the public' from dishonest or incompetent directors,[33] but the order does not disqualify the person from being an employee, only a manager or promoter of a company.

11.5.4 Other orders for disqualification

Courts have other forms of disqualification order available to them in particular types of case. One order that has been abolished is disqualification from working with children or vulnerable adults:[34] there is now a system of automatic and discretionary disqualifications, managed by the Disclosure and Barring Service.[35] Following a conviction under the Dangerous Dogs Act 1991, a court is empowered to disqualify the offender from having custody of a dog for a specified period.[36] There is a wider power of disqualification from keeping an animal, exercisable under s. 34 of the Animal Welfare Act 2006 on conviction for one of several animal welfare offences. The rationale for these orders is the prevention of further similar offences.

11.5.5 Binding-over orders

Probably the longest-standing preventive order available to the courts is the power to bind over an offender or other person, outlined in Chapter 10.3 above. Such a person may be bound over to keep the peace, and the prohibitions in the order must attain a sufficient level of precision and certainty.[37]

---

[31] E.g. *Doick* [2004] 2 Cr App R (S) 203.
[32] For a review of the authorities, see *Cadman* [2012] 2 Cr App R (S) 525.
[33] *Edwards* [1998] 2 Cr App R (S) 213, at 215–6.   [34] See 5th edn of this work, pp. 364–5.
[35] Safeguarding Vulnerable Groups Act 2006, amended by the Protections of Freedoms Act 2012.
[36] See e.g. Sentencing Council, *Dangerous Dog Offences: Definitive Guideline* (2012), p. 6.
[37] *Hashman and Harrup* v. *UK* (2000) 30 EHRR 241.

11.5.6 Orders under the Family Law Act

Two kinds of order made under provisions in the Family Law Act 1996 now take the same form as the civil preventive orders discussed in 11.5.7 and 11.5.8 below. Thus if a family court makes a non-molestation order under s. 42 of the Act – and some 19,000 were made in 2012, more than any other form of civil preventive order – s. 42A provides that breach of the order is a criminal offence with a maximum sentence of 5 years' imprisonment. Similarly, s. 63C provides for the making of a forced marriage protection order, breach of which is also a criminal offence with a maximum penalty of 5 years' imprisonment. Sentencing for these offences is regulated by the guideline on 'Breach of a Protective Order', discussed in 11.7 below.

11.5.7 Restraining orders

Section 5 of the Protection from Harassment Act 1997 empowers a court, on conviction of an offender for an offence of harassment, to make an order restraining the offender from conduct that amounts to harassment or will cause a fear of violence. Section 5A, inserted by the Domestic Violence, Crime and Victims Act 2004, empowers a court to make such a restraining order after an acquittal of a harassment offence: the court must make it clear that the civil standard of proof has been attained.[38] The purpose of a s. 5 restraining order is that of 'protecting the victim of the offence'; s. 5A 'addresses a future risk, the evidential basis for such an assessment being the conduct of the defendant'.[39] Breach of a restraining order is a criminal offence with a maximum sentence of 5 years' imprisonment. Sentencing for this offence is regulated by the general guideline on 'Breach of a Protective Order',[40] discussed in 11.7 below.

11.5.8 Anti-social behaviour orders, IPNAs and CBOs

Probably the broadest and certainly the most notorious of the courts' powers to impose preventive restrictions was the anti-social behaviour order, introduced by the Crime and Disorder Act 1998 and abolished by the Anti-Social Behaviour, Crime and Policing Act 2014. As outlined in Chapter 6.6 above, the ASBO is replaced by two orders – a civil injunction for the prevention of nuisance and annoyance (IPNA), enforceable through ordinary powers of contempt of court;[41] and a criminal behaviour order (CBO) made on conviction and the breach of which constitutes a criminal offence with a maximum sentence of 5 years' imprisonment. As argued in Chapter 6.6 above, the IPNA is very broad

---

[38] *Major* [2011] 2 Cr App R (S) 139; *McDermott et al.* [2014] 1 Cr App R (S) 1.
[39] *Major* [2011] 2 Cr App R (S) 139, at [16].
[40] SGC, *Breach of a Protective Order: Definitive Guideline* (2006).
[41] On which see *Baird* [2011] 2 Cr App R (S) 451.

in its scope, and the CBO is open to many of the objections against the ASBO. The breach rate for ASBOs was around 42 per cent, and the maximum penalty for breach (5 years) is much higher than is available for many criminal offences. The SGC guideline stated that 'where breach of an ASBO also constitutes another offence with a lower maximum penalty than that for breach of the order, this penalty is an element to be considered in the interests of proportionality, although the court is not limited by it'.[42] In practice, a custodial sentence may be imposed for breach of an ASBO when the prohibition broken is one from which Parliament has withdrawn the sanction of imprisonment, such as begging or soliciting for prostitution. Judgments such as that in *Fagan*,[43] upholding a sentence of 20 months' imprisonment for repeated breach of an ASBO prohibiting begging, demonstrate that sentencing for preventive orders appears to be as much about punishing defiance of the law as about protecting the public from significant harassment, alarm, or distress.

11.5.9 Banning orders

Two different forms of banning order are available. Section 14A of the Football Spectators Act 1989 (as amended by the Football (Disorder) Act 2000) provides that, on conviction of a relevant football-related offence,[44] a court must make a banning order in respect of designated football matches if it is satisfied that this would help to prevent violence and disorder in connection with regulated football matches. If the court is not so satisfied, it must state this in open court and give its reasons: it must bear in mind that the order is a ban on attendance at all regulated football matches, and that it must endure for certain minimum periods (depending on the sentence imposed for the conviction: if immediate imprisonment is imposed, the order must be between 6 and 10 years, but in other cases it must be between 3 and 5 years).[45] A sentencer may impose a lesser ban by means of a community order with a prohibited activity requirement.[46] A banning order is not a penalty but is merely a preventive order, although it has been held that the standard of proof should be equivalent to that in criminal proceedings.[47] Banning orders may also be imposed by magistrates on application from the police (s. 14B). Whether the substantial number of banning orders made in this decade (about 700 per year) and the declining incidence of football-related violence are cause and effect is difficult to assess, not least because many other factors are relevant to a proper evaluation.[48] The second form of banning order is the drinking banning order, introduced by s. 1 of

---

[42] SGC, *Breach of an Anti-Social Behaviour Order* (2008), p. 5.   [43] [2011] 1 Cr App R (S) 619.
[44] The sentencer must make a finding that the offence was 'related to football matches': *Doyle* [2013] 1 Cr App R (S) 197, *Irving and Irving* [2014] 2 Cr App R (S) 32.
[45] For an example of a three-year order, see *O'Keefe* [2004] 1 Cr App R (S) 404.
[46] On which see *Boggild et al.* [2012] 1 Cr App R (S) 459, per Hughes LJ.
[47] *Gough* v. *Chief Constable of Derbyshire* [2002] QB 459.   [48] Stott and Pearson (2006).

the Violent Crime Reduction Act 2006 but abolished by the Anti-Social Behaviour, Crime and Policing Act 2014 in favour of the IPNA (see 11.5.7 above). The order prohibited the offender from doing specified acts, in order to protect people from criminal or disorderly conduct by him while he was affected by alcohol.

11.5.10 Exclusion from licensed premises orders

Under the Licensed Premises (Exclusion of Certain Persons) Act 1980 a court which is dealing with an offence committed on licensed premises which involved the use or threat of violence may make an exclusion order, excluding the offender from certain premises for a period of between 3 months and 2 years. The power should generally not be used for isolated incidents, but reserved for persistent nuisances,[49] and the court must specify the premises from which the offender is excluded.[50] Breach of the order is a summary offence with a maximum of 1 month's imprisonment. The Violent Crime Reduction Act 2006 provided for the repeal of this preventive order in favour of the drinking banning order, but now that is to be repealed in favour of the IPNA. It remains to be seen what happens.

11.5.11 Financial reporting orders

Section 76 of the Serious Organised Crime and Police Act 2005 introduced the power to make a financial reporting order for certain offences under the Theft Act and Fraud Act, where the court believes there is a high risk of the offender committing another such offence. Since the orders have been held to be preventive, i.e. to protect the public from such offences by requiring the offender to make regular reports on certain aspects of his or her financial affairs to a named person, it has been assumed that they do not amount to a penalty under Article 7 of the Convention and may therefore be imposed retrospectively.[51] The order requires the offender to report specified transactions; breach is a summary offence with a maximum sentence of 6 months' imprisonment.

11.5.12 Forfeiture orders

Section 27 of the Misuse of Drugs Act 1971 empowers a court to order the forfeiture of anything shown to the satisfaction of the court to relate to the drug offence(s) of which the offender stands convicted.

---

[49] *Grady* (1990) 12 Cr App R (S) 152.   [50] *Arrowsmith* [2003] 2 Cr App R (S) 301.
[51] *Adams* [2008] EWCA Crim 914, at [25]; cf. the discussion in 11.2 above.

11.5.13 Sexual offences prevention orders

Section 104 of the Sexual Offences Act 2003 empowers a court which has convicted an offender of a listed offence to make a sexual offences prevention order, if it is satisfied that this is necessary for the purpose of protecting one or more others from 'serious sexual harm', a phrase that sets the threshold high.[52] The terms of the order may prohibit an offender from doing 'anything described in the order' for a period of at least 5 years (s. 107). It is also possible for the court to make such an order outside criminal proceedings, on application by the police.[53] In formulating guidance on the use of SOPOs, Hughes LJ in *Smith* (2012) emphasised that the order must be necessary, proportionate, and clearly drafted.[54] The contents of a SOPO are entirely negative or preventive, and may include a prohibition on making any contact or communication with a person under 16 and not residing in a private dwelling where there is a child under 16.[55] In cases of child pornography, a total ban on internet use would be disproportionate, but it may be fruitful to require the offender to retain a readable internet history for inspection.[56] Breach of a SOPO is an offence carrying a maximum sentence of 5 years' imprisonment: repeated and brazen flouting of an order may justify a term of 5 years.[57] The SOPO will be repealed by Schedule 5 of the Anti-Social Behaviour, Crime and Policing Act 2014, and a new Sexual Harm Prevention Order will take its place (and that of foreign travel orders, below, too). The SHPO is broader in ambit, since its aim is to prevent sexual harm (s. 103A2(b)), not 'serious sexual harm' as in the SOPO, but its features are otherwise similar.

11.5.14 Risk of sexual harm orders

Section 123 of the Sexual Offences Act 2003 empowers a magistrates' court to make a risk of sexual harm order on application from the police, in respect of a person who has on two or more occasions engaged in sexually explicit conduct or communication with children. The police may apply for this order in respect of someone who has a conviction or a person without any conviction. The court must only make an order if satisfied that it is necessary to protect one or more children from physical or psychological harm. The essence of the order is a prohibition on 'doing anything described in the order' for at least 2 years. This is a particularly controversial power because it applies equally in respect of persons who have never been convicted, so long as the court receives

---

[52] *Rampley* [2007] 1 Cr App R (S) 542, and Sexual Offences Act 2003, s. 106(3).
[53] For commentary on this and the other preventive orders in sexual cases, see Shute (2004).
[54] [2012] 1 Cr App R (S) 470, at [3–5].
[55] Cf. *Pilling* [2014] 2 Cr App R (S) 16, quashing an order in respect of girls under 18.
[56] *Smith* [2012]1 Cr App R (S) 470, at [20]. 'Inspection', not 'removal': *Kimpriktzis* [2014]1 Cr App R (S) 23.
[57] *David E.* [2012] 1 Cr App R (S) 338 (consecutive sentences amounting to 6 years for continual breaches reduced to 5 years).

evidence satisfying it as to the past conduct and future danger to children.[58] Breach of an RSHO is an offence carrying a maximum of 5 years' imprisonment. The RSHO will be repealed by Schedule 5 of the Anti-Social Behaviour, Crime and Policing Act 2014 and replaced by a Sexual Risk Order. The SRO differs in two main respects: the requirement of 'two or more occasions' is reduced to one, and the purpose may be to protect the public or children or vulnerable persons, not merely children.

11.5.15 Foreign travel orders

Section 114 of the Sexual Offences Act 2003 empowers a magistrates' court to make an FTO on application from the police, in respect of a person who has been convicted or cautioned for a qualifying offence, if an order is necessary for the protection of children from serious sexual harm. As explained at the end of 11.5.13, the 2014 Act will absorb the FTO into the new and broader Sexual Harm Prevention Order.

11.5.16 Travel restriction orders

Section 33 of the Criminal Justice and Police Act 2001 requires courts to consider making a travel restriction order whenever they sentence an offender to 4 years or more for a drug trafficking offence. Guidance on the proper use of the power was given in *Mee* (2004),[59] where the Court of Appeal recognized that if the offence appeared to be opportunistic rather than part of a pattern, it might not be necessary to make an order.[60] The order prohibits the offender from leaving the UK for a minimum of 2 years after release from prison. Breach is an offence with a maximum sentence of 5 years' imprisonment.

11.5.17 Serious crime prevention orders

Part 1 of the Serious Crime Act 2007 permits the Crown Court, on application by the police, to make a serious crime prevention order with a view to disrupting the activities of someone convicted of serious offences. Sitting as a civil court, the judge may make the order if there are reasonable grounds to believe that it would protect the public by 'preventing, restricting or disrupting' involvement by the defendant in serious crime.[61] Examples might be restrictions on financial, property or business dealings that impinge on working arrangements, locations, communications with others, travel, and so

---

[58] See Shute (2004), p. 431.   [59] [2004] 2 Cr App R (S) 434.
[60] Such circumstances were found in *Fuller* [2006] 1 Cr App R (S) 52, where the Court of Appeal quashed a 5-year order on a drug courier who had previous good character; also *Onung* [2007] 2 Cr App R (S) 9.
[61] Guidance may be found in the judgment of Hughes LJ in *Hancox and Duffy* [2010] 2 Cr App R (S) 484. For legislative amendments, see Serious Crime Act 2015, ss. 45–51.

forth. Once again, the potential width of the requirements is enormous, and courts will be expected to justify the order and its contents as a proportionate interference with the subject's right to respect for his private life. Breach is an offence carrying a maximum of 5 years' imprisonment.[62]

11.5.18 Violent offender orders

Under ss. 98–106 of the Criminal Justice and Immigration Act 2008, a magistrates' court may (on application by the police) make a violent offender order. The defendant must have a qualifying conviction, and the court should be satisfied that D has acted in a way that makes it necessary to make a VOO for the purpose of protecting the public from the risk of serious violent harm caused by D. To this end, the order may contain one or more suitable prohibitions, e.g. exclusion from a particular area or from contact with a particular person, for between 2 and 5 years. Breach is an offence carrying a maximum of 5 years' imprisonment.

11.6 Revisiting the nature of the orders

The title of this chapter refers to ancillary orders and to civil preventive orders. Parts 3, 4, and 5 of the chapter have revealed a long list of varied orders, with few unifying themes. Does 'ancillary' have any meaning other than to refer to orders that accompany the main disposal and are in some way subordinate to it? Does 'civil preventive order' refer to an established category, or to a technique used to different extents in different orders?

We may begin by dividing orders into purely civil or free-standing orders, orders dependent on a criminal conviction, and dual orders which may be imposed in civil proceedings or may be imposed on conviction:

i) *Purely civil orders:* non-molestation orders and forced marriage protection orders, injunctions to prevent nuisance or annoyance (IPNA), serious crime prevention orders (SCPO), violent offender orders (VOO), and the new sexual risk orders (SRO, replacing RSHO).

ii) *Orders following criminal conviction:* deprivation orders, restitution orders, the victim surcharge, disqualification from driving, disqualifications from keeping dogs or animals, confiscation orders, criminal behaviour orders (CBO), exclusion from licensed premises orders, financial reporting orders, forfeiture orders, and (not hitherto mentioned) hygiene prohibition orders under the Food Hygiene (England) Regulations 2013.

iii) *Dual orders, available on conviction or in purely civil proceedings:* disqualification of company directors, binding over to keep the peace, restraining orders, football banning orders (FBO), and the new sexual harm prevention orders (SHPO, replacing the SOPO and foreign travel orders).

---

[62] Cf. *Koli* [2013] 1 Cr App R (S) 39 on the relevance of reasons for, and consequences of, breach.

Most of these can be regarded as preventive in purpose, and so the relevant issues concern risk of future harm and how proportionately to make a preventive order that protects the public without unduly restricting the activities of the defendant. Some of the orders are plainly punitive, such as deprivation orders and disqualification from driving when ordered for a non-driving offence (11.3.2 above). Some of the orders which are preventive in purpose have been held to be punitive in substance, notably confiscation orders (11.2 above), and other orders may be similarly classified,[63] the consequence of which is that Article 7 of the Convention (no retrospectivity) and related human rights are applicable. Leaving aside the punitive orders, some of the others are reparative (see 11.3 above), and then the remainder can be described as preventive, in the sense that their rationale is to prevent future harm. They may be experienced as punitive – this is certainly true of some disqualifications, and may be true of the prohibitions in many other orders – but they may fairly be regarded as preventive.

Punitive orders should be taken into account as part of the sentence: when the court is determining whether the sentence is proportionate to the offence(s) committed, account must be taken of the privative order as part of the whole. This is not, however, true of reparative orders: reparation to the victim is separate from punishment, and should not therefore be regarded as part of the sentence. This strand of reasoning is also applied to preventive orders. A preventive order is not part of the sentence, but rather a restrictive measure calculated to reduce future risk. Thus, the fact that many of these orders can be made only in civil proceedings (list i), or can be made in civil or criminal proceedings (list iii), tends to testify to their preventive and non-punitive character.[64] More ambiguous are orders in list ii, which may only be made on conviction but which are claimed to be preventive in purpose and not punitive. In principle, preventive orders are not part of the sentence and should therefore be left out of account when overall proportionality is considered.[65] Otherwise put, a court's function post-conviction is not only to pass sentence for the offence(s) but also to consider what preventive orders are necessary to enhance public protection from future harm that might be caused by this offender.

The next question is whether the restrictions imposed by these preventive measures are justifiable, and this raises two sets of considerations – the broad issue of the collateral consequences of conviction, and the more specific issue of whether the form in which most of these civil preventive measures are created is defensible. First, a few words about the collateral consequences of conviction. While the focus in this chapter has been on orders that may be made by a court, there are also statutory schemes not involving the courts – for

---

[63] Cf. financial reporting orders, in 11.5.11 above.
[64] So long as they are not held to be punitive in substance: see 11.2 above.
[65] See further Wasik and von Hirsch (1997).

example, the notification provisions that apply to sex offenders under Part 2 of the Sexual Offences Act 2003, and the disqualifications imposed by the Disclosure and Barring Service.[66] Orders of these kinds call for justification on grounds of public protection, as do several of the preventive orders made by the courts. In the United States it is more common for states to have a range of 'collateral sanctions' attending conviction, including civil prohibitions on voting, holding public office, sitting on a jury, and so forth; indeed, some states make a felony conviction grounds for divorce.[67] In England and Wales the focus of debate on civil and political consequences of conviction is the prohibition on voting that applies to all prisoners.[68] More broadly, the rationale for most preventive orders (including statutory schemes such as sex offender notification) must be found in public protection, a rationale that could lead to over-broad restrictions if not restrained by some proportionality standards (see next paragraph). However, there is a countervailing argument based on the importance of ensuring that offenders can be successfully reintegrated into society. Thus, underlying legislation such as the Rehabilitation of Offenders Act 1974 is the belief that convicted offenders should not bear the burden of their criminal record indefinitely, that barriers should not be placed for too long in the way of social reintegration, and thus that the rules for disclosure of criminal convictions should be graduated according to the seriousness of the offence.[69] Insofar as this legislation upholds the principle of offender reintegration, that principle should also operate to restrain the 'public protection' rationale of the preventive orders.

Turning now to the *form* of the civil preventive orders, the basic model is the two-step order: a court acting under civil procedure draws up prohibitions that are regarded as necessary or appropriate (according to the legislation) to ensure public protection, and then any breach of that prohibitive order amounts to a criminal offence, often with a substantial maximum penalty of 5 years' imprisonment. When these orders are described as *civil* preventive orders, the emphasis is placed on the mode and place of their creation, without referring to the criminal nature of the potential consequences. The reality, as Hughes LJ remarked, is that in many of these orders 'each of its prohibitions creates for the defendant a new and personal criminal offence carrying up to five years' imprisonment for breach', which is 'likely to remain with the defendant for many years after the end of the principal sentence imposed, whether custodial or otherwise'.[70] These remarks are applicable to non-molestation orders, restraining orders, criminal behaviour orders (formerly ASBOs), sexual harm prevention orders, sexual risk orders, travel restriction orders, serious crime prevention orders, and violent offender orders, all of

---

[66] See n. 35 above and accompanying text.   [67] See further Buckler and Travis (2003).

[68] *Hirst v. United Kingdom* (2006) 42 EHRR; see further Easton (2011).

[69] For analysis of the shortcomings of the rules in England and Wales, see Larrauri (2014).

[70] In *Smith* [2012] 1 Cr App R (S) 470, at [3].

which have a 5-year maximum penalty for breach. Before we consider six arguments against civil preventive orders, a few words should be devoted to purely civil orders.

The IPNA, already discussed in Chapter 6.6 and part 11.5.8 of this chapter, is essentially a civil injunction, granted by a civil court applying the civil standard of proof (balance of probabilities), and enforced through proceedings for contempt of court that may lead to imprisonment of up to 2 years. Civil injunctions can be used to prevent various infringements of rights: in November 2014 Birmingham City Council obtained injunctions against 10 men, prohibiting them from approaching a particular 17 year-old girl and also from approaching any girl under 18. The High Court was satisfied that the injunctions were necessary to protect vulnerable children from exploitation.[71] Mention should also be made of the statutory procedure for 'gang injunctions', under s. 47 of the Policing and Crime Act 2009. The police or local authority can apply for an injunction if they can satisfy the court that a defendant has engaged in, encouraged or assisted in gang-related violence. The injunction will typically include a range of prohibitions, such as associating with named persons, going to particular areas (exclusion zones), or wearing gang colours, and may include some specified activities such as attending anger management courses or mediation sessions. Enforcement is through proceedings for contempt of court.[72]

These purely civil orders are very different from the kinds of civil preventive orders set out in 11.5 above, most of which are enforced through a criminal offence with a 5-year maximum penalty. What are the objections to civil preventive orders? Six criticisms may be listed.[73] First, even where the legislation requires a court to impose prohibitions that are 'necessary' for the given purpose, they tend to cover a wider range of activities than the order is targeting, such as excluding the defendant from a place from which the harm-to-be-prevented can be perpetrated. Second, courts are given lawmaking powers normally confined to the legislature in a democracy: this is the implication of Hughes LJ's reference to each prohibition creating a new criminal offence for this defendant. Third, it is wrong that a court may include in a prohibition conduct that Parliament has decided should not attract a custodial penalty (as with begging and soliciting for prostitution), when the effect of so including it is that imprisonment becomes available for breach of the civil order. Fourth, many of the orders have lengthy minimum periods for which they must run (e.g. at least 3 years for football banning orders; at least 2 years for criminal behaviour orders and for sexual risk orders), which inhibits the court from ensuring proportionality. Fifth, the maximum penalty of 5 years' imprisonment is higher than that for many criminal offences, and must be considered in relation to the significance of the breach (e.g. defiance of

---

[71] *The Guardian*, 19 November 2014.   [72] Home Office (2011).
[73] For elaboration, see Ashworth and Zedner (2014), pp. 84–9.

the law, or causing the harm-to-be-prevented). And sixth, the procedural implications of the orders are confused and questionable. The government's aim is often to ensure that the measure does not involve criminal procedure and the various human rights entailed, partly to avoid having to rely on witnesses who are in fear. For some civil preventive measures the court has insisted that the standard of proof should be equivalent to that required in criminal proceedings,[74] largely because of the drastic consequences of breach. Generally speaking, however, there are few procedural constraints and entitlements if criminal procedure is not applicable. In this respect, preventive measures fall into a jurisprudential black hole.[75]

11.7 Sentencing for breach of a preventive order

It is manifest from part 5 above that the range of preventive orders is wide, and that they are capable of being very restrictive. They are entirely negative in content, and none of them provides for support during the period of the prohibitions. Yet the penalties for breach are high, many of them having a maximum sentence of 5 years for breach. As already stated, this maximum is often higher than would be available if a substantive offence were charged.

The SGC issued two sets of relevant guidelines. The guideline on *Breach of a Protective Order* is chiefly concerned with restraining orders under the Protection from Harassment Act 1997 and non-molestation orders under ss. 42 and 42A of the Family Law Act 1996, both having maximum sentences of 5 years for breach. The main aim of sentencing for breach 'should be to obtain future compliance with that order', taking account of the nature and context of the originating conduct and of the nature and context of the conduct that caused the breach.[76] In relation to anti-social behaviour orders (and, presumably, their replacement – criminal behaviour orders), the same main aim is articulated – 'to achieve the purpose of the order'. The originating conduct is relevant, but the chief determinant of sentence should be the degree of harassment, alarm, or distress caused by the breach. The guideline provides that the custody threshold may be passed by cases of moderate harm inflicted and intended (e.g. lesser degrees of threats or intimidation, the use of seriously abusive language, or causing more than minor damage to property).[77] There is a range of other relevant factors, such as the persistence of the breach and the previous record of the offender. The guideline restates the protection of the public as the rationale for creating many of the orders listed in 11.5 above, and thus sentencing for breach should be concerned with reinforcing that

---

[74] The leading case is *R (McCann)* v. *Crown Court at Manchester* [2003] 1 AC 787, but see also n. 47 above.
[75] Ashworth and Zedner (2014), pp. 260–2.
[76] SGC, *Breach of a Protective Order* (2006), part E.
[77] SGC, *Breach of an Anti-Social Behaviour Order* (2008), pp. 8–9.

protection, but doing so proportionately. Much depends on the fairness of the prohibitions originally imposed: the imposition of multiple conditions is inappropriate, especially on young offenders,[78] and particularly without an element of supervision. It is, in truth, setting a person up to fail.

Sentences close to the 5-year maximum have been approved in cases of repeated breaches involving violence or the threat of violence.[79] A single breach of a restraining order involving a threat of violence has been held to justify a sentence of 2 years,[80] whereas persistent breaches not involving any threat were held to justify custody.[81] One of the most important decisions is that in *Lamb* (2006),[82] holding that repeated breaches of an ASBO that involved the commission of no crime nor any harassment or distress could not justify a sentence as long as 22 months' detention; the court held that 2 months was more proportionate.

---

[78] The use of ASBOs for mentally disturbed people is also a matter of concern, not least because of the absence of support as part of the order: see the Bradley Report (2009), ch. 2.

[79] *Todd* [2013] 1 Cr App R (S) 479, 4 years upheld for persistent flouting of restraining order, causing fear; cf. *Richardson* [2014] 2 Cr App R (S) 21, 3 years upheld for persistent breaches by woman.

[80] *McDonald* [2013] 1 Cr App R (S) 21.

[81] *Moore* [2013] 2 Cr App R (S) 527 (3 months, plus activation of two 3-month suspended sentences).

[82] [2006] 2 Cr App R (S) 84.

12

Special sentencing powers

Contents

This chapter deals with three sets of sentencing powers for particular groups of offender. It begins with the sentencing of young offenders under the age of 18, deals briefly with young adult offenders aged from 18 to 21, and then concludes with the various powers for dealing with mentally disordered offenders. In respect of each group, we will consider the justifications for separate sentencing powers, and the extent to which the rationale for special powers carries through into sentencing practice.

12.1 Young offenders

For over a century there have been different sentencing procedures for younger offenders. Those aged under 18 (before the Criminal Justice Act 1991, under 17) have been dealt with in different courts, formerly called juvenile courts and then renamed 'youth courts'. There is a considerable literature about the development of sentencing policy in respect of young offenders,[1] whereas the discussion here is necessarily briefer.

12.1.1 A short history of juvenile justice

Ever since 1933, the law has laid down that, in dealing with a juvenile offender, a court 'shall have regard to the welfare of the child or young person'.[2] This welfare ideology reached its apotheosis in the Children and Young Persons Act 1969, which sought to 'decriminalize' the juvenile court by

---

[1] For an overview, see Morgan and Newburn (2012); see also Fionda (2005) and Muncie (2015).
[2] Children and Young Persons Act 1933, s. 44(1).

regarding the commission of an offence as merely one way in which the court's powers to intervene for the welfare of the child could be activated. The legislation contemplated that children under 14 would be dealt with outside the criminal courts, and those aged 14–16 would only rarely be taken to court.[3] The 1969 Act failed, however, to resolve the longstanding tension between the welfare ideology and the tougher, punitive approach. In 1970 there was a change of government, and some sections of the 1969 Act (notably the increase in the age of criminal responsibility from 10 to 14) were never implemented. In practice, the 1970s was a decade in which two apparently contradictory developments took place: the cautioning of young offenders increased, but so did the use of custodial sentences.

The 1980s began with tough talking about juvenile offenders, but perhaps the most significant provision in the Criminal Justice Act 1982 was the introduction of restrictions on custodial sentences for young offenders, inserted by way of backbench amendment rather than government policy. This, together with the expansion of cautioning for young offenders, meant that the 1980s turned out to be a decade of decreasing severity in the approach to young offenders. A government-funded initiative to expand schemes of 'intermediate treatment' gathered momentum, and the number of juveniles sentenced to custody, which had risen steeply in the 1970s, fell spectacularly in the 1980s, from a peak of 7,900 in 1981 to merely 1,600 in 1991. The Criminal Justice Act 1991 replaced the juvenile court with the youth court, and expanded its jurisdiction to cover all defendants aged under 18. Subsequently the punitive turn in criminal justice, coinciding with the appointment of Michael Howard as Home Secretary in 1993, affected young offenders too, with a restriction on the use of cautions for youth offenders.[4]

The change of government in 1997 brought an even tougher policy, as is evident from the title of the White Paper *No More Excuses*.[5] The resulting legislation, in the Crime and Disorder Act 1998 and the Youth Justice and Criminal Evidence Act 1999, introduced a more managerial approach to youth justice through the Youth Justice Board (YJB) and local authorities, and it also formalized and toughened the system for cautioning young offenders and produced increases in the use of custody in the first decade of the twenty-first century. However, from 2007 the YJB was given various targets, and the youth justice system was reshaped by a series of amendments in Part 1 of the Criminal Justice and Immigration Act 2008, which will be discussed below. Most importantly, the YJB tackled its targets with spectacular successes in two out of three. Thus the number of first-time entrants into the youth justice system declined from over 100,000 in 2007 to around 20,000 in 2013, due to youth crime prevention initiatives, restorative justice schemes and other diversionary developments.[6] The number of young people under 18 in custody

---

[3] Bottoms (1974).   [4] Home Office circular 18/1994.   [5] Home Office (1997).
[6] Youth Justice Board (2014), p. 8.

plummeted from 3,200 in 2002 to 1,100 in 2014, largely through the success of the youth rehabilitation order (see below) and local schemes. Only the third target, reducing youth reoffending, has proved difficult, and significant improvements have not been seen.[7] In large measure, then, the youth justice system can claim to have successfully implemented the principles and policies of restraint set out in Chapter 3.4.

12.1.2 Responsibility and young offenders[8]

The minimum age of criminal responsibility in England and Wales is 10, much lower than that in most other European countries (e.g. France 13, Germany 14, Nordic countries 15, Spain and Portugal 16). The low minimum age has been subjected to considerable international criticism,[9] but there is no proposal to alter it. This low minimum age makes it all the more urgent to consider the extent to which young offenders are less responsible than adults, and should therefore be treated differently by the criminal justice system. Franklin Zimring has advanced three reasons why children are less responsible: first, their cognitive abilities are not fully developed, so that they do not always recognize the implications of their acts; secondly, their control mechanisms are underdeveloped, and it is in the teenage years that self-control is learned; thirdly, young people have an underdeveloped capacity to resist peer pressure, which is important when so many offences are committed in groups or to impress others.[10]

The next step, as Andrew von Hirsch argues,[11] is to explain why this diminished culpability should lead to a different sentencing approach. This is because the state is not justified in expecting children to behave as adults: the state ought to recognize that it is not reasonable to expect full cognitive abilities, self-control, and resistance to peer pressure from young people whose characters are necessarily at the stage of development, and indeed that the state's responsibility should be to ensure that children have support by reinforcing institutions (such as the family) that should provide support. Thus it is right that the youth justice system should have a different, more constructive, and caring approach than the adult criminal justice system, with a reduced level of penal response.

12.1.3 Rationales for sentencing the young

For about a century it has been accepted that young defendants should, in principle, be dealt with in separate courts. The vast majority of young

---

[7] Ibid., p. 9.   [8] See von Hirsch, Ashworth and Roberts (2009), ch. 7, for selected readings.
[9] E.g. UN Committee on the Rights of the Child (2008).
[10] Zimring, excerpted in von Hirsch, Ashworth and Roberts (2009), pp. 316–22.
[11] Von Hirsch, excerpted in ibid., pp. 323–9.

defendants appear in the youth court (much less formal than an adult court), where the tribunal consists of specially trained magistrates or a District Judge (Magistrates' Courts), and which has powers of sentence up to 2 years' detention (compared with a maximum of 6 months for adult magistrates' courts). Only around 3 per cent of young defendants are tried in the Crown Court, usually where they are accused of murder, manslaughter, or another very serious offence, or where they are charged jointly with an adult. The Crown Court is required to adapt its procedure to the age and maturity of the defendant, so as to ensure that he or she is capable of understanding and participating in the proceedings.[12]

What rationale for sentencing should a court adopt? Section 142A of the Criminal Justice Act 2003, inserted by s. 9 of the Criminal Justice and Immigration Act 2008, is intended to restate the purposes of sentencing in relation to young offenders. It requires a court dealing with an offender under 18 to have regard to: (a) the principal aim of the youth justice system, which is the prevention of offending and reoffending;[13] (b) the welfare of the child, a longstanding requirement;[14] and (c) 'the purposes of sentencing'. Those purposes are fourfold:

(i) the punishment of offenders;
(ii) the reform and rehabilitation of offenders;
(iii) the protection of the public; and
(iv) the making of reparation by offenders to persons affected by the offence.

Those requirements follow the example of s. 142 of the Criminal Justice Act 2003 for adults, in setting out a number of (often conflicting) purposes to which a court is expected to 'have regard'. Indeed, in relation to sentencing young offenders the position is even more difficult for the conscientious sentencer. The prevention of offending by children and young persons remains the principal aim of the youth justice system as a whole. Usually that will point in the same direction as 'the welfare of the child', a phrase that implies an objective judgment by the court (taking account of the views of professionals contained in, for example, a pre-sentence report) of what will be in the best interests of this child.[15] The list of four purposes, (i) to (iv), brings in different considerations. Whether 'punishment' should be a sole and sufficient purpose for sentencing the young may be debated; but it certainly has a role, as Article 40.4 of the United Nations Convention on the Rights of the Child recognizes, in ensuring that all penal responses to the young should be proportionate, whatever other purpose is being pursued. Reform and

---

[12] *V and T* v. *United Kingdom* (2000) 30 EHRR 121, *SC* v. *United Kingdom* (2005) 40 EHRR 226.
[13] Originating in s. 37 of the Crime and Disorder Act 1998.
[14] Originating in s. 44 of the Children and Young Persons Act 1933.
[15] Article 3 of the UN Convention on the Rights of the Child states that 'the best interests of the child' should be 'a primary consideration in all actions concerning children'.

rehabilitation as purposes seem congruent with the prevention of offending and the best interests of the child. Public protection may be seen as an exception confined to a few serious cases, and it would have been preferable if it had been phrased as 'the protection of the public from serious harm' or something similar. The making of reparation may be seen as a particularly important objective in dealing with young offenders, not least because (as suggested earlier) many of them fail to see the full implications of their offences. Indeed, it may be thought surprising that the purpose of 'restorative justice' is not found on this statutory list, given its relevance to referral orders (and to pre-court diversion) for young offenders.

Why should priority be given to purposes such as rehabilitation and reparation when dealing with young offenders? The reasons, surely, are as stated above by Zimring and by von Hirsch. The state has a special responsibility towards the young, largely because they have underdeveloped faculties which the state ought to assist in developing. As the Sentencing Advisory Panel recognized,[16] young people who offend tend to have a number of social and personal disadvantages, including higher rates of exclusion from school, of placement in care, of substance misuse, of Attention Deficit Hyperactivity Disorder, of mental disorder, and of low IQ. The state must take steps to prepare such young people for full citizenship, and this means more supportive sentences for those who offend.[17]

Notably absent from the list of purposes for sentencing young offenders, when compared with the list for adults, is 'the reduction of crime (including its reduction by deterrence)'. One might argue that 'the reduction of crime' generally is encompassed by the principal aim of the youth justice system, 'the prevention of offending'. But is the implication that deterrent sentences, whether for the purpose of deterring the individual offender or for the purposes of deterring potential imitators,[18] are not lawful for young offenders? In principle there is a strong argument in favour of this interpretation: s. 37 of the Crime and Disorder Act 1998, declaring 'the prevention of offending' as the principal aim, was not aimed at producing deterrent sentences, and suspended sentences have never been extended to young offenders on the basis that their deterrent impact is unlikely to be as effective, given the diminished controls of the young. Section 142A creates specific exceptions for the two minimum sentences that apply to young offenders as well as to adults (under s. 51A(2) of the Firearms Act 1968 and s. 29(6) of the Violent Crime Reduction Act 2006), those exceptions being focused on deterrence as a purpose. It is therefore submitted that, apart from these exceptional cases, s. 142A(3) would render it unlawful for a court to impose a higher sentence on

[16] SAP, *Sentencing Principles – Youths* (2009), para. 48.

[17] The *Youth Crime Action Plan 2008* recognized that the most prolific young offenders 'typically exhibit a complexity of personal and family risk factors from early childhood' (p. 31).

[18] See the discussion of these two rationales in ch. 3.3.2 above.

a youth for reasons of deterrence. This submission gains strength from the decision of the Supreme Court of Canada in *B. W. P.* (2006),[19] where the Court held unanimously that, since the Canadian statute mentions deterrence as a sentencing purpose for adults but does not include it in the list of purposes for sentencing young offenders, the correct conclusion is that neither general nor specific deterrence is a proper basis for imposing a sentence on a young offender. However, in this country when bringing the youth justice provisions of the Criminal Justice and Immigration Act 2008 into force, the government omitted from the commencement order the list of purposes for sentencing young offenders set out in the new s. 142A(3). In *Smickele et al.* (2013)[20] Hughes LJ concluded that 'it is not the law that deterrence can play no part in the sentencing of young offenders'. Thus the prevention of offending and reoffending remains the principal aim of the youth justice system, and it seems that deterrence forms part of that.[21]

The SGC's guideline on *Sentencing Principles – Youths* (2009) attempts to reinterpret the multiplicity of statutory purposes so as to identify some practical objectives for sentencers. Beginning with the principle that the sentence should be no more restrictive of liberty than is proportionate to the seriousness of the offence, it refers to such objectives as 'confronting young offenders with the consequences of their offending' and 'helping them to develop a sense of personal responsibility', tackling the personal and social factors that led to the offending and strengthening the 'protective factors', encouraging reparation and reinforcing the responsibilities of parents. While there are some examples of the Court of Appeal applying the SGC's principles with care, there are rather too many Court of Appeal judgments that make no reference to the youth sentencing guidelines.[22]

12.1.4 The structure of the youth justice system

The principal agency is the Youth Justice Board, created by s. 41 of the 1998 Act, with the tasks of monitoring the operation of the youth justice system, and advising the government on how the aims of the system might be pursued most effectively, for example by promoting good practice and commissioning research. In practice the Board has achieved great successes in shaping youth justice towards its declared goals, as we noted at the end of 12.1.1. Beneath the Board, each local authority must establish a youth offending team (s. 39 of the 1998 Act). These 150 or more teams (or YOTs, as they are known) draw from at least five local agencies: probation, social work, police, health,

---

[19] 2006 SCC 27.   [20] [2013] 1 Cr App R (S) 354, at pp. 359–60.

[21] See also Lord Thomas CJ in *Gomes Monteiro* [2014] 2 Cr App R (S) 483 on deterrence and knives.

[22] E.g. *L* [2013] 1 Cr App R (S) 317; *Attorney General's Reference No. 47 of 2012* [2013] 2 Cr App R (S) 12. The Sentencing Council is reviewing the guideline on youth sentencing.

and education. Their main tasks are to coordinate youth justice services, to carry out functions assigned to them under local youth justice plans, and to arrange youth offender panels (YOPs) for offenders referred to them under the 1999 Act (see below). Youth offender panels consist of lay people, dealing with individual youth offenders within the framework of the legislation, and supported by YOT members. The youth justice system relies quite heavily on the idea of expert diagnosis of a young offender's predicament: all children entering the youth justice system undergo an ASSET assessment, looking particularly at risk factors, and this is applied so as to produce a 'scaled approach' to intervention.[23]

Also within the YOTs are various schemes for 'early prevention', encouraged by the YJB. For example, there are now considerable numbers of Youth Inclusion Panels (YIPs), identifying those young people considered to be at the greatest risk of offending and engaging them in positive and supportive activities; and also Youth Inclusion and Support Panels (YISPs), focused on children aged 8–13 identified as being at risk of offending. Early prevention is closely connected with the YJB's target of reducing the number of first-time entrants to the youth justice system. The Bradley Report recommended that each YOT should contain a mental health professional, in order to ensure that early prevention schemes and other YOT activities can make appropriate referrals.[24]

Once a child becomes such a first-time entrant, diversion from the courts retains a prominent place in youth justice policy.[25] Sections 65 and 66 of the Crime and Disorder Act 1998 created a system of reprimands and warnings, stating that no young offender should receive more than one reprimand and one warning; and, if the offence was too serious for a mere reprimand, the police must proceed straight to a warning. These two measures were abolished by the Legal Aid, Sentencing and Punishment of Offenders Act 2012,[26] and replaced by youth cautions and youth conditional cautions, which have the same elements as the corresponding adult cautions. The 'cautioning rate' (as defined in Table 14) declined significantly towards the end of the first decade in this century but appears to have steadied since then. The explanation is probably that more cases are being diverted at an early stage rather than being brought into the formal system,[27] and therefore that some cases that would previously have received a reprimand, warning, or caution are being winnowed out into other schemes such as restorative justice. There is, however, evidence to suggest that there may be some unfair treatment at the diversion stage in respect of looked-after children, and of racial origin.

[23] On the development of ASSET, see Baker (2004); cf. Bateman (2011) for a critique.
[24] Bradley (2009), para. 10.
[25] For discussion of such policies and practices across Europe, see Jehle, Lewis and Sobota (2008).
[26] Inserting a new s. 66ZA into the Crime and Disorder Act 1998.
[27] House of Commons Justice Committee (2013), [7], noting the abolition of police targets for 'bringing offences to justice' and the subsequent diversion of relatively minor offences.

Some looked-after children are brought to court for offences that would not be treated so seriously if occurring in a family home.[28] On racial origin, Feilzer and Hood found that 'the odds of a case involving a mixed-parentage youth being prosecuted was 2.7 times that of a white youth with similar case characteristics', whereas the odds for a black youth were only slightly higher than for a white youth.[29] The YJB has announced a three-year strategy to address the over-representation of black and minority ethnic young people in the youth justice system.[30]

12.1.5 Sentencing powers

If a young defendant is taken to court, the youth court is required to make a referral order wherever a young offender who has not previously been convicted by a court pleads guilty to an offence, unless a custodial sentence is justified;[31] the court also has a discretion to make a referral order in other cases. The order may be for a period, to be specified, between 3 and 12 months: the SGC's guideline states that courts should be prepared to use all the gradations within the 12-month period (not just 3, 6, 9, and 12), and that orders of 10–12 months should only be made for the more serious offences.[32] The referral is to the local YOT, which is then bound to establish a youth offender panel for the offender, with a view to drawing up a programme of behaviour to which the offender is invited to agree. There will be an ASSET assessment, on the basis of which the youth offender panel should propose a contract, making certain requirements of the offender, of which 'the aim (or principal aim) is the prevention of reoffending by the offender'.[33] This procedure must involve the offender's parent or guardian, but may not involve a legal representative. The programme may involve the payment of financial compensation to the victim, attendance at a restorative justice conference with the victim, the performance of unpaid work in the community, participation in certain activities, and so forth. If the offender agrees, this becomes a 'youth offender contract', with provisions for a return to court in the event of breach. If the offender does not agree, the case is returned to the youth court and it is supposed to proceed to deal with the offender as normal. A substantial proportion of these contracts include an element of reparation and/or a restorative justice component. Although it seems that a majority of these contracts are fulfilled to the satisfaction of victims, there remain questions about their role in an essentially punitive framework.[34] However, the study of referral orders by Newburn, Crawford and others showed that the system was welcomed by all groups of participants:

---

[28] House of Commons Justice Committee (2013), [12–16], citing broken crockery.
[29] Feilzer and Hood (2003), p. ix.　　[30] Youth Justice Board (2014), p. 11.
[31] Section 16 of the PCCS Act 2000.　　[32] SGC, *Sentencing Principles – Youths* (2009).
[33] Section 8(1) of the 1999 Act.　　[34] See Ball (2000).

Within a relatively short period of time the panels have established themselves as constructive, deliberative and participatory forums in which to address young people's offending behaviour. The informal setting of youth offender panels would appear to allow young people, their parents/carers, victims (where they attend), community panel members and YOT advisers opportunities to discuss the nature and consequences of a young person's offending, as well as how to respond to this in ways which seek to repair the harm done and to address the causes of the young person's offending behaviour. This view is echoed by all participants in panels ...[35]

The same study reported that apology and reparation were recurrent features of the contracts resulting from the panel meetings. One early criticism of the referral order system was that its mandatory nature meant that many relatively minor cases were receiving undue attention, and in 2003 the youth court was given a discretion not to make a referral order in minor cases. Some 30 per cent of all court orders for young offenders in 2006 were referral orders, and the reoffending rate was lower than for other measures.[36]

Subject to the making of referral orders for first offenders pleading guilty, the framework of what are sometimes termed 'first-tier' sentences for youths is similar to that for adults, in the sense that the power to make an absolute discharge, conditional discharge, bind-over, compensation order, and fine remain available in most cases.[37] If a financial penalty is imposed, the parents may be ordered to pay if the offender is aged 16 or 17, and they must be ordered to pay if the offender is aged under 16. The parents have a right to be heard before being ordered to pay, and it is their means that should be taken into account. Although fining is not a common response to juvenile offending, reconviction figures suggest that it is relatively effective, as is the conditional discharge.[38]

Indeed, when dealing with offenders under 16, the youth court's powers and duties extend to the parents of the offender. Thus, a youth court is required to order parents to attend court if their child is being prosecuted, unless it would be unreasonable to require this. There is also a presumption that a court should bind over the parents of a child aged under 16 to exercise proper care and control over the child: if it declines to do so, it should state its reasons. There is a further power to bind over the parents of a child who is placed on a community sentence, requiring them to ensure that the child completes it. The general theme of encouraging greater parental responsibility is undoubtedly right, insofar as family units are critical to much social behaviour. But a more constructive approach than court orders, threats, and coercion would be

---

[35] Newburn, Crawford et al. (2002), p. 62.
[36] SAP, *Sentencing Principles – Youths, Consultation Paper* (2008). Sections 43–45 of the Criminal Justice and Courts Act 2015 give courts greater flexibility when dealing with breach of a referral order.
[37] For further discussion of these measures see ch. 10 above.
[38] Mair (2004), p. 151, with qualifications.

to provide greater support for parents through local authority social workers and parental support groups. Thus the Children Act 1989 provides for local authorities to provide support and assistance to parents based on assessment of the needs of the child, without resort to care proceedings and without any attribution of blame. Often the situation is far more complex than simply locating blame with the parents, especially when courts are often dealing with 'vulnerable and needy families'.[39] However, parents may have other duties imposed on them, such as that of attending all meetings of a young offender panel relating to their child, where a referral order has been made. Indeed, ss. 8–10 of the Crime and Disorder Act 1998 also empower a court to make a parenting order, requiring a parent to attend guidance sessions and so on as specified. The question of the appropriate degree of coercion on parents of offending children remains controversial, and the parenting order has not been a conspicuous success.[40]

The youth court may also make certain civil or ancillary orders, of which the *anti-social behaviour order* was the most prominent. We have seen that ASBOs have now been replaced by civil Injunctions for the Prevention of Nuisance and Annoyance (IPNAs) and by Criminal Behaviour Orders (CBOs),[41] but it is important to note that around half of all ASBOs were made against persons under 18 – even though the government stated during the parliamentary debates that ASBOs were not intended for the young. The possibility of imposing these orders – or any of the many other civil preventive orders set out in Chapter 11.5 above – on young people who then breach them and may be sent into custody, with all the procedural imperfections outlined earlier,[42] remains a serious problem. It does not sit well with the orientation of other aspects of the youth justice system, which is probably why the government originally stated that the ASBO was not intended for the young.

Moving up from 'first-tier' orders, the next tier of youth sentencing is now occupied by a measure introduced by s. 1 of the Criminal Justice and Immigration Act 2008, the youth rehabilitation order (YRO). This is somewhat similar in conception to the community order for adults under the Criminal Justice Act 2003, but there are some noteworthy differences. The similarity of conception is that the YRO is a single order with a multiplicity of separate requirements, of which the court may specify 1 or more. There are 15 standard requirements, more than the 14 available for adults, and the list for youths includes a local authority residence requirement, a drug-testing requirement, an intoxicating substances treatment requirement, and an education requirement. The unpaid work requirement is only available where the young offender is aged 16 or 17. As with the community order for adults, a court may not make a YRO unless it is satisfied that the offence is serious enough to warrant that; and the court must ensure that the requirements are those most

---

[39] Arthur (2005).   [40] Burney and Gelsthorpe (2008).   [41] See ch. 11.5.8 above.
[42] See ch. 6.6 above.

suitable for the offender, and are proportionate to the seriousness of the offence(s). The YRO may be for up to 3 years, but many of the requirements may only run for a shorter period, the supervision requirement being the main exception.

Judgments of suitability should be assisted by a pre-sentence report, which should include an ASSET assessment of the young offender.[43] Judgments of proportionality depend not just on the seriousness of the offence but also on the relative restrictiveness of the particular requirement(s). The YJB has developed what it calls a 'scaled approach' to YRO requirements: this identifies three levels of intervention – the standard intervention level for those with low likelihood of reoffending and low risk of causing serious harm, the enhanced intervention level for those with a medium risk of reoffending or of causing serious harm, and the intensive intervention level for those with a high likelihood of reoffending or of causing serious harm.[44] The scaled approach then indicates the degree and kind of intervention that will be appropriate at each level. The SGC's guideline recognizes the helpfulness of the scaled approach, but emphasizes the overriding proportionality principle and also the important distinction between requirements that are rehabilitative, protective of the public, or punitive.

A significant difference between the community order for adults and the YRO is that there is a more intensive version of the YRO, aimed particularly at young offenders who would otherwise go into custody. This is the YRO with intensive supervision and surveillance, or the YRO with a fostering require-ment. The fostering requirement must only be imposed if the court is satisfied that a significant factor in the offence was the circumstances in which the defendant was living, and that the order will assist rehabilitation. The require-ment of intensive supervision and surveillance builds on the experience of the Intensive Supervision and Surveillance Programme (ISSP), which attempted to combine the supervision of difficult and often troubled persistent offenders with surveillance of them. The Audit Commission commended ISSPs as 'a more constructive and cheaper option for persistent young offenders than a spell in custody'.[45] An evaluation by an Oxford University team showed some variation in the delivery of ISSP, with standards not uniformly high, and some evidence of improved reconviction rates.[46]

These two enhanced versions of the YRO are combined with stiff statutory criteria that are distinctly more restrictive than those for YROs in general. Thus s. 1(4) of the Criminal Justice and Immigration Act 2008 states that a YRO with either of these enhanced requirements (the two cannot be imposed

---

[43] See n. 23 above.

[44] The latest version of *Youth Justice: The Scaled Approach. A Framework for Assessment and Intervention* may be found at www.gov.uk/government/organisations/youth-justice-board-for-england-and-wales; for critique, see Bateman (2011).

[45] Audit Commission (2004).   [46] Moore et al. (2004).

together) may only be made if (i) the offence is imprisonable, and (ii) the offence is so serious that, but for the availability of an enhanced YRO, a custodial sentence would be appropriate for the offender, and (iii) (where the offender is under 15) the offender is a persistent offender. Moreover, where a custodial sentence is imposed on a person under 18, the court is required to state why one of these enhanced YROs cannot be justified.[47] The SGC's guideline reinforces the statutory criteria, and the government should receive credit for imposing such tough restrictions.

The court has extensive powers when a young offender breaches a requirement of a YRO: it may impose a fine, amend the order, or revoke the order and re-sentence the offender. However, it is not obliged to make any order, and is not obliged to make the order more onerous than it is. The SGC recommends that a court should regard its primary objective, when sentencing for breach, as that of ensuring that the offender completes the order. It emphasizes the need for the court to receive information explaining the reasons for the breach, so as to enable it to fulfil the primary objective or at least to ensure that its response is properly informed. The court has extra powers where it is proved that the young offender has 'wilfully and persistently' breached the order, including the making of a YRO with intensive supervision and surveillance even if the original offence would not have justified this.

The statistics demonstrate a reorientation of youth sentencing in recent years, in the context of an overall decline in young offenders dealt with. The years 1997–2007 showed an enormous increase in community sentences for offenders aged 10–17, from 26,000 to 66,000 per year. During the same period the use of custody declined slightly from 7,000 to 5,800 per year. The disposals that declined more sharply were the fine and the conditional discharge.[48] However, since 2008 there has been a continuing emphasis on community sentences and a remarkable decline in the use of custody: in the year 2012–13 some 43,601 young offenders were sentenced (and a further 33,661 dealt with out of court, mostly by reprimands, warnings, and conditional cautions). Of the 43,601 sentenced, some 29,343 received youth rehabilitation orders, 2,780 were sent into custody, and the remaining 11,478 received other disposals such as fines or discharges.[49] This suggests that the welfare principle is playing a strong role in youth sentencing.[50]

The custodial sentence for offenders aged 10–17 is the detention and training order (DTO), the statutory provisions on which are to be found in the Powers of Criminal Courts (Sentencing) Act 2000. Section 100 provides that no such order may be made unless the statutory test for custody is satisfied.[51] The 2008 Act raised the bar further, stating that a court that

---

[47] Sch. 4, para. 80(3) of the Criminal Justice and Immigration Act 2008.
[48] Ministry of Justice (2008), Table 1.5.
[49] Ministry of Justice (2013), 'Youth Justice Sentencing'.
[50] Burnett and Appleton (2004) and Field (2007).   [51] See ch. 9.4.1 above.

imposes custody must explain why a YRO with intensive supervision and surveillance or with a fostering requirement is not appropriate, and that custody should be used only 'as a last resort'.[52] The Youth Crime Action Plan 2008 emphasized the expectation that 'most young offenders can be punished and dealt with effectively in the community'. The youth court sentencing statistics quoted in the previous paragraph indicate a strong move away from custody. However, the Chief Inspector's 2014 report – while welcoming the closure of several young offender units because of the decline in numbers – records that safety levels at some young offender institutions are unacceptably low.[53] Sections 38–40 introduce a new form of youth detention with a focus on education, called 'secure colleges'.

Where the young offender is aged under 15, the court may only impose custody if it is of the opinion that he is a 'persistent offender': that term is not defined in the legislation, but the SGC guideline suggests that a clear case would be where the offender has had 3 official responses to offending in the previous 12 months.[54] Additionally, a court may only impose a DTO on an offender aged 10 or 11 if of the opinion 'that only a custodial sentence would be adequate to protect the public from further offending by him'. Section 101 of the 2000 Act provides that a DTO may only be for one of the specified lengths – 4, 6, 8, 10, 12, 18, or 24 months. Not surprisingly, this restriction has been criticized for distorting the courts' attempts to reflect differences in culpability between offenders, and mitigating factors such as a plea of guilty. The SGC's guideline suggests that, in calculating the appropriate length of detention, the court should make deductions from the relevant offence guideline for adults. Those deductions should be age related, subject to the court's judgment of the young offender's maturity and other relevant factors. Thus the starting point for an offender aged 15 to 17 might be half to three-quarters of that which would have been selected for an adult, always depending on maturity.[55] Custody for offenders under 15 should be rare: statute allows this where the child under 15 is a 'persistent offender', but the guideline suggests that this exception should be used sparingly.[56] Under a DTO the young offender serves half the sentence in a young offender institution and is then released under supervision for the remainder of the sentence.

Section 91 of the Powers of Criminal Courts (Sentencing) Act 2000 provides for the long-term detention of young offenders for serious offences. The power

---

[52] For reflections on this formula, see ch. 9.3 above.   [53] HMCI Prisons (2014), pp. 65–6.

[54] The SGC's formulation refers to a previous contact with authority in which the offending behaviour has been challenged: cf. where one of the previous offences was merely theft of a cycle, DTO quashed in favour of a YRO (*L* [2013]1 Cr App R (S) 317, not referring to the SGC guidelines); cf. the case of a young offender with no previous convictions who is convicted of multiple offences on his first court appearance, classed as a 'persistent offender' in *AS* [2001] 1 Cr App R (S) 62.

[55] See *Walsh* [2014] 2 Cr App R (S) 468 for discussion of the guideline.

[56] SGC, *Sentencing Principles – Youths* (2009).

may only be exercised where the offender is convicted of an offence with a maximum penalty of 14 years, or of a few listed offences. Guidelines on the proper use of the s. 91 power were laid down in *Mills* (1998),[57] where Lord Bingham CJ emphasized that no young offender should be given a custodial sentence unless absolutely necessary, and then for no longer than is necessary. The length of sentence should be calculated in a way that makes allowance for the offender's youth and for any plea of guilty. However the *Mills* judgment suggested that sentences as low as 2 years might be imposed under the s. 91 power, whereas the SGC's guideline is that the circumstances must justify a sentence substantially above 2 years before this power is invoked. Severe sentences are imposed on very young offenders from time to time, such as the 3-year sentence of long-term detention imposed on a boy of 11 for causing grievous bodily harm to a younger boy when he was 10.[58]

Alongside the s. 91 sentence are various powers for dealing with 'dangerous' young offenders, somewhat analogous to the powers for adults discussed in Chapter 6.8 above. There is provision in the Criminal Justice Act 2003, as amended by the Legal Aid, Sentencing and Punishment of Offenders Act 2012, for a discretionary sentence of detention for life, and an extended sentence of detention. At a minimum the sentencing court will have to find that the young offender presents a significant risk of serious harm to others.

12.2 Young adult offenders

Offenders aged 18, 19, and 20 are tried and sentenced in adult courts, but there is some difference in the orders available to the court. There is a lengthy tradition of separate custodial institutions for offenders aged under 21 – formerly known as borstals, detention centres, or youth custody centres, and now known as young offender institutions. The reasoning is partly to prevent the 'contamination' of young offenders by older and more experienced criminals, and partly to enable more constructive regimes with a greater emphasis on education and on industrial training. The Younger Report justified special attention to this group thus:

> This is a highly delinquent group making a major demand on the penal system. While offenders in the group often have records of serious delinquency behind them, many are not yet set in their ways. They may be failures of the school system or immature in other respects, and the few years after leaving school may offer a last chance of helping them to make good the ground they have lost. A special concentration of public effort upon this group of young adults, who are in danger of going on to long and costly criminal careers, is a sensible investment by society at a time when resources, both human and material, are too scarce to allow a similar degree of attention to be paid to all age groups.[59]

[57] [1998] 1 Cr App R (S) 128.   [58] *Jamie Craig W.* [2003] 1 Cr App R (S) 502.
[59] Advisory Council on the Penal System (1974), para. 9.

The 'special concentration' for which the Younger Report argued has dropped down the order of penal priorities since then, although there have been a few relevant initiatives in recent years. The Barrow Cadbury Trust funded a review in 2004, and the government's Social Exclusion Unit's report on *Transitions – Young Adults with Complex Needs* (2005) made important recommendations for policy initiatives for vulnerable members of this age group. The Sheffield desistance study focused on this age group, demonstrating the complexity of their behaviour patterns and the fragility of efforts to desist.[60] Some continental European systems allow special procedures for young adults if they are still at the developmental stage of a juvenile and are therefore thought suitable for an educational rather than punitive sentence.[61]

12.2.1 Cautioning young adults

The high rate of cautioning for juveniles has never been matched by a similar rate for young adults. Initiatives were begun in the late 1980s to increase the cautioning rate for young adults, with considerable success. For young adult males the cautioning rate for indictable offences was 34 per cent in 1998, declined to 28 per cent in 2001, and then rose to 37 per cent in 2007; for young adult females there was also an increase in cautioning, with a trajectory from 46 per cent in 1998, through 41 per cent in 2001, to 57 per cent in 2007 – a rate considerably higher than that for young men.[62] The overall figures sit comfortably between the rates for 15–17 year-olds and the rates for adults aged 21 and over, suggesting a gradual transition rather than the abrupt decline in cautioning that used to follow attainment of the age of 18. The cautioning rate for all age groups has fallen considerably in the last five years, but there remains some differentiation for young adults. Research by Roger Evans showed that, as with many other decisions in criminal justice, much depends on the ground-level views of those who decide whether or not to caution: in one of the two police divisions he studied, there was a distinct uneasiness about a higher use of cautions for young adults,[63] and there is still considerable variation across the country. Some of the reluctance may stem from the fact that 18 is now the peak age of offending for males, but it can be pointed out that the peak age was previously 16 and the expansion of juvenile cautioning took place nevertheless.

12.2.2 Sentencing young adults

The sentencing framework for young adults is largely that for adults, with a few exceptions. It was noted in Chapter 10.6.3.14 that one form of requirement

---

[60] Bottoms and Shapland (2011).
[61] See e.g. Bohlander (2012), pp. 10–13, on the German system.
[62] Ministry of Justice (2008), Table 1.5.   [63] Evans (1993).

in a community sentence, the attendance centre order, is available only up to the age of 25. So far as custodial sentences are concerned, since 1982 custody for young adults has not been imprisonment but detention in a young offender institution, preserving the segregation that has long been a feature of the system. There is a legislative provision (in s. 61 of the Criminal Justice and Court Services Act 2000) that will reverse this policy and assimilate offenders in this age group into adult prisons, but successive governments have declined to implement this change. Instead, the focus has been on various initiatives for the management of offenders in this age group, both in custody and in the community;[64] and there are some appellate judgments recognizing that young adult offenders may properly be accorded mitigation on account of their age.[65] Indeed, the CCSS shows that the second most powerful mitigating factor in 2013 burglary cases was 'age/lack of maturity affecting responsibility',[66] and this factor is explicitly linked to the young adult age group.[67]

As Tables 4 and 5 in Appendix B show, the use of custody for this age group has fallen substantially since its peak in the years 2004–08 (for young men) and in the years 2000–02 (for young women). Thus for young men the number sentenced to immediate custody in 2013 was 7,612, less than half that in 2007 and the previous years. For young women the number sentenced to immediate custody in 2013 was 327, less than half the number for 2010 and about a third of the numbers for previous years. There have been overall reductions in the number of young adults for sentence, but they do not account fully for declining use of detention in a young offender institution. Suspended sentence orders became available for this age group (as for all adults) in 2005: for young women the SSSO was used in 2013 more than immediate custody (see Table 5), whereas for young men the rise in SSSOs seems to have taken away from both detention and community sentences. Fines have declined in this age category as in all others. Sentencing guidelines do not make separate provision for this age group and, at present, do not contain any discussion of the approach to sentencing young adults, apart from the general injunction to have regard to the age and maturity of each offender.

12.3 Mentally disordered offenders[68]

It is generally accepted that people who commit offences while mentally disordered, or who are mentally disordered at the time of trial, should not be dealt with in the same way as other offenders. The criminal law provides a procedural bar to trial, unfitness to plead, and also a defence of insanity,[69] and if either is upheld the court has a discretion in the order it may make: Criminal Procedure (Insanity and Unfitness to Plead) Act 1991. The test of

---

[64] Allen (2007).   [65] E.g. *Fadairo* [2013] 1 Cr App R (S) 371.   [66] CCSS (2014), p. 28.
[67] E.g. Sentencing Council, *Theft Offences Guideline Consultation* (2014), p. 25.
[68] For fuller discussion, see Peay (2011).   [69] See Ashworth and Horder (2013), pp. 139–46.

unfitness to stand trial relates to the defendant's ability to follow the proceedings and to instruct counsel: around 100 defendants a year are found unfit to plead.[70] The legal requirements of the defence of insanity are still restrictive and, despite the flexibility of powers on a verdict of insanity, its use since the 1991 Act remains low.[71] Most of those who are mentally disordered tend not to plead insanity, but instead acquiesce in conviction and seek a medical disposal at the sentencing stage. This means that sentencers have to deal with far more people in this category than they would need to if there were proper adherence to the principle that persons whose responsibility was significantly affected at the time of the offence should not be subjected to criminal conviction.

At the sentencing stage there is a long tradition of regarding (some) mentally disordered offenders as either requiring treatment instead of punishment, or deserving of mitigation. Indeed, the SGC guideline's list of mitigating factors states that 'mental illness or disability' is a factor indicating 'significantly lower culpability'.[72] This approach can be rationalized on the basis that such offenders may not have sound powers of reasoning or control, and may therefore not understand the significance of punishment or may not deserve it. Sentencing has a communicative element, which cannot be realized where it is the offender's understanding that is impaired.[73] However, not all mentally disordered people lack understanding: some suffer affective disorders, which reduce their ability to control their behaviour and thus supply a different ground for doubting that punishment is deserved.

Insofar as the orientation of sentencing for mentally disordered offenders has been towards treatment and rehabilitation, this raises its own difficulties. If there is no proportionality constraint, the compulsory treatment may endure far longer than any compulsory powers taken against a non-disordered offender. Moreover, treatment may bestow far more discretion on the psychiatrist or hospital than would be acceptable in most sentences. This makes it important to ensure that there is a proportionality constraint upon the duration of compulsory powers in the name of criminal justice, and also to ensure that the rights of mentally disordered offenders are respected and not subjugated to assumptions about dangerousness. The recent trend to phrase a more repressive policy towards mentally disordered offenders in terms of risk and public protection fails, as Jill Peay strongly argues,[74] to place a proper interpretation on the empirical foundations and normative implications of assessments of dangerousness.

The Mental Health Act 1983, which provides the legislative framework on mental health issues, has now been substantially amended (but not replaced)

---

[70] Mackay (2011); Peay (2011), ch. 17.
[71] Mackay (2012), reporting some 20–30 insanity pleas per year between 2008 and 2011; see also Peay (2011) ch. 19.
[72] SGC, *Overarching Principles – Seriousness* (2004), p. 7.   [73] Duff (1986).   [74] Peay (2012).

by the Mental Health Act 2007. Since then, Lord Bradley's report on *People with Mental Health Problems or Learning Disabilities in the Criminal Justice System* has been published,[75] as was a government reply that accepted most of Bradley's recommendations,[76] although implementation has been very slow.[77]

12.3.1 Diversion of mentally disordered offenders

The police have long had the power to remove to a place of safety any person who appears to be suffering from mental disorder and to be in need of care and control. The power, in s. 136 of the Mental Health Act 1983,[78] is used in over 14,000 cases each year,[79] more in some areas than others. However, in many cases the 'place of safety' is a police station, which is often an unsuitable place to hold such a person. The Bradley Report recommended local protocols to identify mental health facilities that could serve as 'places of safety'.[80] If a mentally disordered person is arrested in the normal way, the disorder may be regarded as a reason for cautioning the offender or as a reason for discontinuing a prosecution, under the Code for Crown Prosecutors. Home Office circular 60/1990, *Provision for Mentally Disordered Offenders*, encourages the diversion of mentally disordered offenders away from the criminal justice system where possible, and Corston (2007) made a particular recommendation in respect of women. There are many diversion schemes across the country, either at police stations or at courts, which draw upon mental health professionals in order to assess and, where appropriate, divert mentally disordered people from the formal criminal process.[81] There remain difficulties of achieving this in practice, however. The Bradley Report called for improved identification of mentally disordered people, and the availability of screening services at police stations.[82] Geoffrey Pearson and Elizabeth Burney, in their study of one such scheme, demonstrated that other problems bulk large in many of these cases – notably accommodation needs, the overlap between mental health problems and substance abuse, and the over-representation of black people with psychotic illness – and that their solution requires considerable inter-agency co-operation and financial resources.[83] Moreover, the schemes do not cover all areas, and there is no requirement on courts to consider the effect of a custodial remand on a defendant's mental health.[84] In 2014 the government announced an additional £25m of funding for liaison and diversion schemes.[85]

---

[75] Bradley (2009).   [76] Ministry of Justice (2009).
[77] House of Commons Justice Committee (2014), [86].   [78] As amended by s. 44 of the 2007 Act.
[79] HSCIC (2013), Figure 8.   [80] Bradley (2009), ch. 2.
[81] Lennox et al. (2009); Peay (2011), pp. 161–2.   [82] Bradley (2009), ch. 4.
[83] Burney and Pearson (1995).   [84] See Cavadino (1999).
[85] House of Commons Justice Committee (2014), [86].

12.3.2 Special orders for the mentally disordered

Absolute or conditional discharges may be appropriate in some cases where the offender is suffering from mental disorder. Beyond that, the courts have special orders available for the mentally disordered. If the offence is of sufficient seriousness, the court may consider a community sentence with a mental health treatment requirement, a guardianship order or a hospital order. The gateway to these powers is a finding of mental disorder: s. 1 of the Mental Health Act 2007 sweeps away the previous definitions of four types of disorder and states that mental disorder 'means any disorder or disability of the mind'. There are, however, two exclusions from this broad 'definition', relating to those with learning disability (s. 2) and to dependence on alcohol or drugs (s. 3).

The powers in the Mental Health Act 1983 were intended to enhance the possibility of treatment, but it is important to signal at the outset a major difference between medical and penal disposals. The prisons cannot refuse to accept persons sentenced to imprisonment, but psychiatrists and the hospitals can and do refuse to accept people on whom the criminal courts might wish to make a particular order. The availability of a place remains a precondition of all the orders discussed below.

Section 35 of the 1983 Act permits remand to hospital for the preparation of a report for the court, but many psychiatric reports for the courts are still prepared when the defendant is in prison, which may be a manifestly unsuitable environment. Since few of these defendants present a danger to the public, it seems unnecessary to remand them to prison, but at present it is doubtful whether the mental hospitals could cope with the large numbers of people on whom the courts want reports. There are court-based assessment schemes in some areas, enabling a psychiatric assessment to be carried out promptly without the need for a remand, and the power under s. 35 is relatively little used.[86]

Section 36 provides for remand to hospital for treatment, and s. 38 creates the interim hospital order. Again, these have not been greatly used, and this may stem partly from the difficulties over hospital beds and admission policies, discussed below. An example of the operation of these powers is provided by *Attorney General's Reference (No. 34 of 1992)* (1993).[87] The offender pleaded guilty to wounding with intent and was remanded to prison for psychiatric reports. Four months later, on considering the reports, the court made an interim hospital order and the offender was admitted to Broadmoor Hospital under s. 38: the purpose was to see whether he was susceptible to treatment that would justify the making of a hospital order. Five months later, the psychiatrist reported to the court that, although treatment was exceedingly difficult, it would be appropriate to make a full hospital order with restrictions. However, the defendant then changed his plea and, by the time the case ultimately came to

---

[86] For a recent example, see *Catchpole* [2014] 2 Cr App R (S) 516.
[87] (1993) 15 Cr App R (S) 167.

court for sentence a further twelve months later, two psychiatrists reported that the defendant's condition was not susceptible to treatment.

Turning to special sentences for the mentally disordered, a court may make a community order with a mental health treatment requirement under ss. 207–208 of the Criminal Justice Act 2003.[88] This is subject to all the conditions that must be fulfilled if a community sentence is to be imposed.[89] Before making this particular requirement the court must receive a report from a duly qualified medical practitioner, and must satisfy itself that the offender's mental condition requires and may be susceptible to treatment, and that it is not such as to warrant the making of a hospital order or guardianship order. The treatment prescribed may be as a resident at a specified hospital or as an outpatient, or by or under the direction of a specified doctor or chartered psychologist, and the offender must consent to it. The requirement was formerly subject to a maximum of 1 year, but that limit has now been removed and it is for the court to specify the duration of the requirement. This form of sentence was for many years the most frequently used of the special orders, averaging around 1,000 cases per year. However, recent figures show a decline, with some 600 mental health treatment requirements in community orders in 2012–13 and a further 200 attached to suspended sentence orders.[90] These orders may occasionally be made in a case that might otherwise justify a substantial custodial sentence, as where an offender suffering from a depressive illness was sentenced for attempting to rob a post office using a sawn-off air pistol.[91]

Guardianship orders are rarely used: they place an offender under the guardianship of a local authority or a person approved by such an authority, and might be suitable for mentally impaired people who would benefit from occupational training and other guidance. Hospital orders are made more frequently, although in lower numbers than in previous decades. Before making a hospital order under s. 37 of the Mental Health Act 1983, the court must have evidence from two qualified practitioners, of whom one is approved under s. 13 of the 1983 Act, to the effect that the offender is suffering from a mental disorder which makes detention for medical treatment appropriate.[92] An order cannot be made unless a hospital has signified its willingness to admit the offender for treatment. There are two main reasons why hospital orders cannot be made on more mentally disordered offenders: first, the 1983 Act (as amended by ss. 4 and 5 of the 2007 Act) includes a treatability condition, so that the court must be satisfied that 'appropriate medical

---

[88] On which see Seymour and Rutherford (2008).   [89] See ch. 10.6 above.

[90] Ministry of Justice (2014), Table 4.4.

[91] *Attorney General's Reference No. 37 of 2004 (Dawson)* [2005] 1 Cr App R (S) 295: the Court refused the reference and thus the community sentence stood.

[92] In *Nafei* [2005] Crim LR 409 the Court of Appeal reiterated that s. 37 confers a power. In a case where psychiatrists recommended a hospital order for a man who was not suffering from mental disorder at the time of the offence but was at the time of sentence, the Court upheld a sentence of 12 years' imprisonment for drug importation.

treatment is available', and that includes 'psychological intervention and specialist mental health habilitation, rehabilitation or care', designed to alleviate or prevent the worsening of the condition. The definition of treatment is now broadened, but the treatment requirement will still rule out the admission of some mentally disordered people. Secondly, some local mental hospitals tend to pursue fairly restrictive criteria for admission, and offender-patients are sometimes refused admission on the basis that they are likely to disrupt the regime. In the debates on the legislation that became the 1983 Act the government resisted an amendment that would have required hospitals to accept offender-patients sent by the courts: s. 39 of the Act requires regional hospital authorities to respond to requests from courts for information on hospital accommodation in their area, but this is merely a prompting device. The effect of a s. 37 hospital order is that the patient may be detained for 6 months initially, and this is renewable for a further 6 months and then for 1 year at a time. If the offender-patient is not discharged by the hospital, the case will be reviewed periodically by a Mental Health Review Tribunal.

For some mentally disordered offenders, a hospital order is not considered sufficient, because local hospitals can provide little security and the offender is regarded as a danger to others. In this sphere there is often a casual mixture of fact and fiction. It is sometimes assumed that mentally disordered offenders pose greater dangers than others because of their disorder. Jill Peay counters this:

> It is particularly galling to those involved in treating the mentally disordered that such concerns persisted despite repeated demonstrations that 'reoffending rates are in fact no higher than for any other class of offender'; that the trend was in the direction of mentally ill people committing fewer homicides than mentally ordered people; and the fact that when psychiatric patients killed, they were much more likely to kill themselves than others. Finally, there is good evidence that those restricted patients discharged from hospital pose a much lower risk of serious reoffending than comparable offenders released from prison.[93]

This is not to deny that there are mentally disordered offenders who appear dangerous. But it is necessary to warn against the too-ready progression from mental disorder, to unpredictability, to danger, and to long-term detention (whether for 'treatment' or not).

This brings us to the strongest of measures available for mentally disordered offenders: the Crown Court has the power to add to a hospital order a restriction order, under s. 41 of the 1983 Act. A restriction order is without limit of time,[94] and the release conditions are stringent (see below). Before adding a restriction order, the court must have heard oral evidence from at

---

[93] Peay (2007), p. 500.
[94] The 2007 Act abolished the little-used power to make a s. 41 order for a determinate number of years.

least one of the medical practitioners, and it must be satisfied that a restriction order is necessary for the protection of the public from serious harm – a formula subsequently used in the dangerousness provisions of the Criminal Justice Act 2003.[95] In *Kearney* (2003)[96] the Court of Appeal quashed a restriction order in a case where the judge had not addressed himself to the phrase 'necessary for the protection of the public from serious harm', and where the facts and the psychiatrists' reports were equivocal on this. Some general considerations for the making of restriction orders were set out by Mustill LJ in *Birch* (1989).[97] Where the potential harm from further offences is serious, a low risk of repetition might be sufficient; a high probability of the recurrence of relatively minor offences should not suffice, but there may be evidence that, say, a propensity to burgle might well lead to violence.[98] In recent years the courts have tended to make around 250–350 restriction orders per year (the figure for 2008 was 343).[99] Research by Street into the imposition of restriction orders found that 77 per cent were diagnosed as suffering from mental illness, and 13 per cent as psychopathic; that some 69 per cent had been psychiatric in-patients before; and that 20 per cent were black (compared with 1.6 per cent of the general population).[100]

In some cases, either a hospital place is unavailable or the court decides that imprisonment is necessary. In *Vowles et al.* (2015)[101] the Court of Appeal has laid down guidance on how a judge should proceed in these cases. First, a court must not feel circumscribed by the psychiatric opinions. Even if two psychiatric opinions recommend a hospital order, as required under s. 37/41, this is not a sufficient reason on its own for a medical disposal: the court's duty under s. 37(2)(b) is to consider whether a hospital order is the most suitable method of dealing with the case.

Secondly, the court must consider a) the extent to which D needs treatment for the mental disorder from which he or she suffers; b) the extent to which the offending is attributable to the mental disorder, or whether D's responsibility was 'diminished' but not wholly extinguished;[102] and c) the extent to which punishment is required.

Thirdly, and also in relation to suitability, the court must have regard to the protection of the public, and must pay very careful attention to the different processes for deciding release and to the different effect in each case of the conditions applicable after release.[103]

Fourthly, in a case where the medical evidence suggests that D is suffering from a mental disorder, that the offending is wholly or in significant part

---

[95] See ch. 6.9 above.   [96] [2003] 2 Cr App R (S) 85.   [97] (1989) 11 Cr App R (S) 202.
[98] *Golding* [2007] 1 Cr App R (S) 486, upholding a s. 41 order on a persistent burglar with paranoid schizophrenia but no history of violence.
[99] Ministry of Justice (2010), Table 6.   [100] Street (1998), s. 1.   [101] [2015] EWCA Crim 45.
[102] E.g. *Welsh* [2011] 2 Cr App R (S) 399; *Attorney General's Reference No. 54 of 2011* [2012] 1 Cr App R (S) 637.
[103] *Drew* [2003] UKHL 25; for research on release decisions, see Boyd-Caine (2012).

attributable to that disorder, and that treatment is available, and where the court considers that a hospital order with or without restrictions may be appropriate, it must address the issues in the following order:

i) the court must consider whether the mental disorder can be appropriately dealt with by a hospital and limitation direction, under the terms of the amended s. 45A;

ii) if it can, and if D was aged 21 at the time of conviction, it should make such a direction under s. 45A;

iii) If not, it should consider whether the medical evidence fulfils the requirements for a hospital order under s. 37(2)(a), and (where applicable) for a restriction order under s. 41, and should consider whether such an order is the 'most suitable method of disposing of the case' under s. 37(2)(b).

iv) The wording of s. 37(2)(b) requires a court, when deciding on suitability, to have regard to 'other available methods of dealing with' D. Relevant to this is the power to transfer an offender from prison to hospital for treatment, under s. 47 of the 1983 Act.

This new guidance reverses the statutory order of priority and emphasizes punishment. It attempts to revive the provisions in s. 45A of the Mental Health Act 1983, the little-used 'hospital and limitation' direction whereby the court is satisfied that D needs hospital treatment for a mental disorder but wishes to ensure that release is effected only by the Parole Board. Rather than imposing a prison sentence and hoping that the Secretary of State uses the power to transfer D to hospital, the judge is able to direct that D be admitted to hospital (a place being available) within the overall framework of a prison sentence, which may be determinate or may be a life sentence.[104] The hospital and limitation direction in its original form was given a critical reception,[105] and even since it was broadened in 2007 the annual number of cases has averaged only about 16.[106]

12.3.3 Prisons and the mentally disordered

The previous paragraphs disclose at least some explanations of the process by which mentally disordered offenders come to be sent to prison. First, if the treatability requirement ('appropriate medical treatment is available') is not fulfilled, a hospital order becomes impossible and the court might feel that prison is the only alternative. This has often been the outcome for offenders diagnosed as suffering from psychopathic disorder, as it is rare for such a person to be regarded as treatable. Second, even where the treatability requirement is fulfilled, no hospital place may be available. Thus, every year, numerous offenders suffering from mental disorder are given custodial sentences.

---

[104] As in *Jenkin* [2013] 2 Cr App R (S) 63.   [105] Eastman and Peay (1998).
[106] The statistics are set out in *Vowles* [2015] EWCA Crim 45, at [20].

As we saw in Chapter 9.7.4, studies suggest that around one-third of all convicted prisoners and almost two-thirds of remand prisoners have some form of mental disorder. A substantial proportion of those mentally disordered prisoners have problems of substance abuse: although that cannot be the sole diagnosis (since dependence on alcohol and drugs is excluded from the definition of mental disorder by s. 3 of the 2007 Act), there is a considerable problem presented by these 'dual diagnosis' cases, as the Bradley Report recognized.[107] A third and related point is that there is simply not enough accommodation available: with only around 3,500 beds in high-security hospitals and medium-secure units, and relatively few available for offender-patients in local mental hospitals, the numbers in prison could not be accommodated. This shows that the matter is largely one of allocation of resources: the community care policy must be enhanced, but there will still be cases where the practical choice lies between hospital and prison. Since it is widely accepted that prison is unsuitable for people suffering from mental disturbance, it is unjust to send them there. It remains a fact, however, that mentally disordered offenders are being sent to prison and will continue to be sent there. Concerns about the inadequacy of prison medical care for the mentally disordered were recorded by the Joint Committee on a previous Mental Health Bill, referring to 'an over-reliance on medication and no therapy available'.[108]

A possibility in some cases is to have a prisoner transferred to mental hospital, under Mental Health Act powers that treat him or her as a restricted patient. Although the number of transfers remains fairly low compared with the number of mentally disordered offenders in prison, it has increased significantly in the last decade. The number of sentenced prisoners transferred from prison to hospital under s. 47 averaged 450 from 2010–13, significantly more than the annual number of hospital orders (some 300 per year).[109] In their study of remand prisoners transferred under s. 49 Mackay and Machin found that transfers were both humane and in some cases useful in testing the treatability of mental conditions.[110] They also found that some 19 per cent of those transferred were black.[111] These transfers mark an overdue recognition of the inappropriateness of prison for the mentally disordered, but in turn they create further pressure on beds in medium-secure units and high-security hospitals – as noted by the Joint Committee.[112] The fact that many transfers take place towards the end of a prison sentence suggests that they may be motivated by risk-based concerns rather than by the need for treatment.[113] The Bradley Report called for prompter recognition of mental disorder and swifter transfers.[114]

---

[107] Bradley (2009), ch. 4; see also ch. 9.7.4 above.
[108] Joint Committee on the Draft Mental Health Bill (2005), para. 256; cf. Peay (2014).
[109] The statistics are set out in *Vowles* [2015] EWCA Crim 45, at [20].
[110] Mackay and Machin (2000).   [111] Cf. the similar finding of Street, n. 100 above.
[112] Joint Committee on the Draft Mental Health Bill (2005), para. 256.   [113] Peay (2007), p. 510.
[114] Bradley (2009), ch. 4.

In cases where custody is being contemplated, s. 157 of the Criminal Justice Act 2003 imposes a duty to obtain and consider a medical report before passing any custodial sentence on a person who appears to be mentally disordered (although s. 157(2) qualifies that duty), and also requires the court to consider any other information bearing on the offender's mental condition and the likely effect of a custodial sentence on that condition and on any possible treatment for it.[115] This is a necessary provision, but a similar section has been in force for over a decade and its effects are difficult to discern. However, there are provisions to ensure that the possibility of making a hospital order or a guardianship order is preserved in spite of certain mandatory provisions: in the case of an offence for which sentence would fall to be imposed under s. 51A of the Firearms Act 1968 (mandatory minimum of 5 years for possessing firearm), or under ss. 110 or 111 of the Powers of Criminal Courts (Sentencing) Act 2000 (minimum sentences for third class A drug dealing or third domestic burglary), or under ss. 225–228 of the Criminal Justice Act 2003 (as amended: see Chapter 6.8), 'nothing in these provisions shall prevent a court from making an order . . . for the admission of the offender to a hospital'.

12.3.4 Conclusions

The proper approach to the sentencing of mentally disordered offenders remains a matter of controversy. There has tended to be a major division of policy between mentally disordered and other offenders: for the former, a treatment approach must be available, but increasingly an approach based on risk and public protection is providing the framework for the sentence, even if treatment is provided within it. A better approach is to recognize that both the treatment approach and the risk-based approach lend the awesome authority of the criminal justice system to wide therapeutic discretion, and that respect for the rights of the mentally disordered means that they should not be compulsorily detained under 'criminal' powers beyond the point at which a non-disordered offender would be released from prison.[116] It is therefore important that proportionality of sentence should be reasserted as a constraint on sentencing the mentally disordered, no less than in respect of sentencing generally.

The controversy over the proper response to mentally disordered offenders is evident from various sets of proposals issued in recent years. The Richardson Report, reviewing the Mental Health Act 1983, was chiefly concerned with the civil powers over mentally disordered people. It did not examine closely the response to mentally disordered offenders, but it recognized that treatment

---

[115] The section re-enacts s. 4 of the Criminal Justice Act 1991; see also s. 166(5) of the 2003 Act, preserving the courts' power to mitigate sentence in the case of mentally disordered offenders.
[116] See Gostin (1977), p. 96.

ought to be given priority over punishment, as the 1983 Act requires. It made a number of recommendations, insisting (inter alia) that prisoners should have a right to a mental health assessment, and that there should be no compulsory treatment in prisons – only in hospitals.[117] The subsequent Bradley Report accepted that public protection remains a priority, but proposed a range of measures to ensure that many mentally disordered offenders are diverted from the criminal justice system and that, when they are prosecuted and convicted, prison is used sparingly for them. 'Custody can exacerbate mental health problems, heighten vulnerability and increase the risk of self-harm and suicide.'[118]

The government's focus on risk and public protection led it to construct a category of Dangerous People with Severe Personality Disorder (DSPD), and to develop a particular risk-based response to such offenders.[119] Having made extravagant claims about some 2,000 offenders in this category who posed a risk to the public, the then government subsequently decided to go ahead with a pilot scheme with four units (two in prisons, two in hospitals) for some 300 persons placed in this category. As Seddon demonstrates, the definition of the category is highly contestable; the motivation of the policy is political, emotive, and (allegedly) instrumental; and the only positive aspect is that there is an attempt to provide treatment for these people and to gather evidence on the success or otherwise of that treatment.[120] However, the then government went ahead without a firm evidential foundation for the policy, and the tendency to over-predict dangerousness is so well known[121] as to undermine justification for this curtailment of individuals' rights.

---

[117] Richardson (1999), chs. 15 and 16.   [118] Bradley (2009), ch. 1.   [119] See Peay (2011), ch. 11.
[120] Seddon (2008).   [121] See ch. 6.8 above.

13

Procedural issues at sentencing

Contents

This chapter examines several procedural issues that arise at the sentencing stage at the Crown Court or in a magistrates' court. Other types of court do exist or have existed, but without insisting on full procedural formality. For example, the North Liverpool Community Justice Centre opened in 2005 to provide a local focus to justice, combining the jurisdiction of a magistrates' court, youth court, and Crown Court in combination with local problem-solving services. An evaluation found that, despite the extra resources at its disposal, the court did not reduce reoffending rates, although there was a higher proportion of drug offenders than at other courts.[1] The Centre is due to close. There have also been six pilot Dedicated Drug Courts (DDC) across the country. These have the jurisdiction of a magistrates' court and try to achieve continuity of the bench. However, an evaluation found that they were not more effective in reducing reoffending, and that much depended on the availability of good local services.[2]

This chapter considers general issues in sentencing procedure. Before sentence is passed in any case other than a minor summary one, there will usually be either a trial or, if the plea was guilty, a prosecution statement of facts. In some cases these provide the court with an insufficient basis on which to pass sentence: what is to be done? Again, what is the role of advocates for prosecution and defence in relation to sentencing, and what role should they play? When should pre-sentence reports be relied upon by sentencers?

---

[1] Booth et al. (2012).   [2] Kerr et al. (2011).

What are the various obligations on sentencers to give reasons for sentence, and to explain the effect of sentences? What place do victims have in the sentencing process, and what role should they have?

13.1 The factual basis for sentencing

Even after a full trial on a not guilty plea, the court may not have heard sufficient evidence on certain points to provide a proper factual basis on which to pass sentence. A carefully controlled trial will concentrate on the legal points at issue: if the offence is defined broadly by the law, some points relevant to sentence (e.g. provocation, knowledge of the class of drug possessed) might not be fully dealt with during the trial. However, difficulties of this kind are much more likely to occur on a guilty plea, after which the prosecution may state the facts in one way and the defence may advance a different version. In a system of criminal law which includes many broadly defined offences, these difficulties are likely to be perpetuated. Yet the implications for offenders are considerable, sometimes amounting to the gulf between a custodial and a non-custodial sentence, or between a long or a shorter term of imprisonment. It is surely wrong that defendants should suffer a disadvantage simply because the legal system happens to assign certain issues to the sentencing stage rather than to the trial process. Issues which can affect sentence substantially and which are disputed should, as a matter of principle, be resolved only after a procedurally fair examination of the evidence which accords proper safeguards to the defendant. This proposition derives support from the general right to a fair trial in Article 6.1 of the European Convention on Human Rights, although the Strasbourg jurisprudence on this aspect of sentencing remains underdeveloped.[3] How do the rules and procedures evolved by the Court of Appeal measure up to principles of fairness?

13.1.1 Interpreting a jury verdict

The general principle is that the judge must base the sentence on a version of the facts which is consistent with the verdict. Occasionally, cases arise in which a crucial issue (e.g. whether the offender's acts were intentional or merely reckless; whether he was the perpetrator or a mere accomplice) is likely to be left unclear when the jury gives its verdict, because the definition of the crime charged does not draw the necessary distinction. Judges are discouraged from asking the jury for a special verdict in these circumstances, but they may do so. As the Court of Appeal explained in *Cawthorne* (1996):[4]

---

[3] Cf. *De Salvador Torres v. Spain* (1997) 23 EHRR 601, where the Court found no violation but where the Commission discussed the application of the right to have adequate time and facilities for the preparation of a defence (Art. 6.3(b)) in relation to statutory aggravating factors.

[4] [1996] 2 Cr App R (S) 445, at p. 450.

> Whether or not the judge asks the jury to indicate to him the basis of their verdict is entirely a matter for the judge's discretion. In many cases the judge will not wish to do so, and doing so will throw an unnecessary additional burden upon the jury. In a case such as the present . . . there are grave dangers in asking juries how they have reached a particular verdict. For example, they may not all have reached it by precisely the same route.

In that case it was unclear whether the manslaughter verdict was based on lack of intent, provocation, or gross negligence. The judge's duty is to reach a conclusion on the basis of the facts proved during the trial.[5] If the judge is left unsure, then the sentence should be based on the version of facts more favourable to the offender. In *McGlade* (1990)[6] D had been convicted of the buggery of a young woman on charges of rape and buggery. At this time (i.e. before 1994) the offence of buggery of a woman was committed whether or not she consented, and in this case it was unclear from the jury's verdict whether they concluded that she had or had not consented. The judge sentenced D to 5 years' imprisonment on the basis that she had not consented. The Court of Appeal held that this was proper: 'the learned judge, having heard all the evidence himself in the course of the trial, is free and, indeed, it is his duty to come to a conclusion, if he can, upon where the truth lies'. In this case the finding made the difference between 5 years' imprisonment and a short, even perhaps a non-custodial sentence. In principle, an issue not concluded by the verdict (and not relevant to the definition of the offence) should be explored after conviction and before sentence, in an adversarial proceeding. It appears from *Finch* (1993)[7] that a judge is not allowed to reject a version of facts accepted by the jury without holding a post-conviction hearing (see part 13.1.2 below for *Newton* hearings); but where the verdict is equivocal, as in *Cawthorne* and in *McGlade*, it seems that no *Newton* hearing is required. However, in those circumstances the judge must take care to give a reasonably full explanation of the conclusions reached on the evidence heard.[8] Where there has been a trial and the jury has convicted only on the lesser charge, it is clear that the judge should not pass sentence on a basis that presupposes the truth of the rejected evidence.[9]

13.1.2 Interpreting a guilty plea

Where an offender pleads guilty, the judge does not have the opportunity to hear the evidence. All that is provided are the case papers, the prosecution's statement of facts, and perhaps a defence 'basis of plea'. The prosecution

---

[5] E.g. *Griffin* [2008] 2 Cr App R (S) 357.   [6] (1990) 12 Cr App R (S) 105.
[7] (1993) 14 Cr App R (S) 226.
[8] *Byrne* [2003] 1 Cr App R (S) 338, where the jury's manslaughter verdict was equivocal between provocation and lack of intent.
[9] *Gillespie* [1999] 2 Cr App R (S) 61.

statement may disclose that the offence had particularly serious consequences, to the extent that a higher offence might have been charged, and surprisingly the court is entitled to sentence on that basis unless there is a defence challenge.[10] On the other hand, the Court of Appeal has laid down that 'the prosecution should not lend itself to any agreement whereby a case is presented to a sentencing judge to be dealt with ... on an unreal and untrue set of facts'.[11] In practice it is not uncommon for a defendant to submit a written basis of plea, when pleading guilty.[12] If the prosecution accepts this statement, the judge is bound by it for sentencing purposes.[13] If it is not accepted, the judge should hold a *Newton* hearing in order to determine the facts.[14] In health and safety cases, it is normal for the agreed basis of plea to set out the aggravating and mitigating factors.[15] If D is seeking a *Goodyear* indication of sentence in advance of plea, the basis of plea must be agreed before this can be done.[16]

The approach is different if the parties do not agree, as Lord Bingham CJ stated in *Tolera* (1999):[17]

> If the defendant wishes to ask the court to pass sentence on any other basis than that disclosed in the Crown case, it is necessary for the defendant to make that quite clear. If the Crown does not accept the defence account, and if the discrepancy between the two accounts is such as to have a potentially significant effect on the level of sentence, then consideration must be given to the holding of a *Newton* hearing to resolve the issue. The initiative rests with the defence ...

This may occur, for example, where there is a disagreement about the extent of a defendant's involvement in a crime,[18] or where criminal liability is strict (i.e. no proof of culpability is required), and where the defence contend that the crime was committed inadvertently.[19] If the defence advance in mitigation

---

[10] *R* v. *Nottingham Crown Court, ex p. DPP* [1996] 1 Cr App R (S) 283 (plea of guilty to common assault, papers disclosed injuries serious enough to justify charge of assault occasioning actual bodily harm).

[11] *Beswick* [1996] 1 Cr App R (S) 343, at p. 346.

[12] For examples see *Attorney General's Reference No. 70 of 2003* [2004] 2 Cr App R (S) 254, at p. 256, and *Dudley* [2012] 2 Cr App R (S) 61, at [16].

[13] *May* [2005] 2 Cr App R (S) 408, at p. 427, and *Rattu* [2012] 1 Cr App R (S) 10. Lord Judge CJ has stated that a plea agreement between prosecution and defence that presents the court with an 'agreed package' of facts and sentence is not recognised in this country: *Dougall* [2011] 1 Cr App R (S) 227, at [19].

[14] *Elicin and Moore* [2009] 1 Cr App R (S) 561 (basis of plea found to be untrue, credit for guilty plea withheld); cf. *SW* [2013] 2 Cr App R (S) 549 (judge failed to invite submissions before deciding point inconsistently with basis of plea).

[15] *Friskies Pet Care Ltd* [2000] 2 Cr App R (S) 401, applied in *AGC Automotive Ltd* [2008] 2 Cr App R (S) 146.

[16] *Asiedu* [2009] 1 Cr App R (S) 420, discussing the procedural aspects of *Goodyear* indications.

[17] [1999] 1 Cr App R (S) 25, at p. 29, reaffirmed by Leveson LJ in *Cairns* [2013] 2 Cr App R (S) 474.

[18] *Anderson* [2003] 1 Cr App R (S) 421; *Dudley* [2012] 2 Cr App R (S) 61.

[19] *Lester* (1975) 63 Cr App R 144.

a version of the facts which seems to lack foundation, it is the judge's duty to examine the allegedly mitigating material in order to form of a view about it: this has often occurred in drugs cases, where the offender alleges that all the drugs were for personal use only.[20] It appears that the judge may reject the defence version without hearing evidence if that version is 'manifestly false' and 'incredible', but the normal practice would be for the judge to call upon the defence to adduce some evidence on the matter, if only the defendant's testimony, and this evidence should be tested in the normal way.[21] (These requirements only apply on a plea of guilty: where there has been a trial, the judge is empowered to reject a subsequent basis of plea tendered by the defence without holding a *Newton* hearing, so long as the parties are put on notice, allowed to make submissions, and given a reasoned decision.)[22]

The most significant procedural development in recent years has been the spread of so-called '*Newton* hearings'. Again, the crime which produced the procedural problem in *Newton* (1982)[23] was buggery of a woman, in this case Newton's wife. Newton pleaded guilty, but he contended that his wife had consented, whereas the prosecution's version of the facts was that there were threats of violence and no consent. (The offence of buggery with consent in private was abolished in 1994.) In the Court of Appeal, Lord Lane CJ held that there are two alternative ways of resolving such a conflict. One is for the judge to hear no evidence but to invite submissions from counsel and then form a conclusion. If this approach is taken, and the submissions are substantially in conflict, the judge's duty is to accept the defence version.[24] 'The second method which could be adopted by the judge in these circumstances is himself to hear the evidence on one side and another, and come to his own conclusion, acting so to speak as his own jury on the issue which is the root of the problem.' In the case of *Newton* the sentence of 8 years' imprisonment was quashed because the judge had adopted the first approach, but without concluding in favour of the defence. It is the second approach which is now favoured in these cases, and a considerable jurisprudence has developed. Thus, where the defence contend that an attack was provoked and the prosecution maintain that there was no provocation, the judge ought to hold a *Newton* hearing before passing sentence.[25] Similarly, where the defence contend that the offender believed the drug was cannabis not cocaine, the judge should hold a *Newton* hearing – always subject to the judge's right to decide the issue if the defence version is considered incapable of belief.[26]

---

[20] See *Ribas* (1976) 63 Cr App R 14 and many subsequent decisions.
[21] As set out in *Tolera* (above n. 17) and *Anderson* (above n. 18).
[22] *Taylor* [2007] 2 Cr App R (S) 129, at p. 134; *Stevens* [2011] 2 Cr App R (S) 591, at [18].
[23] (1982) 4 Cr App R (S) 388.
[24] *Tovey* (1993) 14 Cr App R (S) 766; *Stevens* [2011] 2 Cr App R (S) 591.
[25] *Costley* (1989) 11 Cr App R (S) 357.   [26] *Broderick* (1993) 15 Cr App R (S) 476.

13.1.3 Towards procedural fairness

The advent of *Newton* hearings marked an important step forward in procedural fairness where facts are disputed after a guilty plea: bearing in mind the great effect on sentence which such issues may have, they ought properly to be resolved according to rules of evidence no less fair than those applicable at the trial.[27] However, as we saw in Chapter 5 above, aggravating and mitigating factors – some of them statutory – may also have a significant effect on the severity of the sentence. It is established that, if there is a dispute, the prosecution must establish aggravating or other offence-related factors to the criminal standard of proof,[28] whereas the defence need only establish mitigating factors and other 'extraneous' factors to the civil standard.[29] However, in the United States there has been constitutional debate about whether the defendant should have a right to trial by jury on such matters, rather than simply a bench trial or (in English terms) a *Newton* hearing. In *Apprendi* v. *New Jersey* (2000)[30] the Supreme Court held that:

> Other than the fact of a prior conviction, any fact that increases the penalty for a crime beyond the prescribed statutory maximum must be submitted to a jury, and proved beyond a reasonable doubt.

That decision related to an offence with a maximum of 10 years, but which could have an enhanced maximum of 20 years if committed with a purpose to intimidate because of race, colour, gender, disability, and so forth. It was held that the defendant had a right to jury trial on the issue of intimidation for discriminatory purposes. In *Blakely* v. *Washington* (2004)[31] this principle was extended by interpreting the 'maximum sentence' so as to include the maximum set by the applicable guideline, but its impact is still limited.[32] If the principle were to be applied to English law, that would mean that any judge who decided that the facts of the case took it outside the applicable category range specified in a definitive guideline – because the aggravating factors were so powerful, for example – should offer the defendant the opportunity of a jury trial on those issues. However, juries are typically not involved in sentencing in England and Wales, and procedural propriety would surely be satisfied by a *Newton* hearing with the burden of proof beyond reasonable doubt on the prosecution. Decisions of this nature are important because of the great effect that certain factors may have on sentence (e.g. whether the offender knew that the victim was elderly, or disabled). A fair procedure should require the right to an adversarial hearing on the issue, and English law falls short of that

---

[27] *McGrath and Casey* (1983) 5 Cr App R (S) 460.

[28] Particularly important when those factors determine the starting point for calculating the minimum term for murder: *Davies* [2009] 1 Cr App R (S) 79.

[29] *Guppy and Marsh* (1995) 16 Cr App R (S) 25; *Lashari* [2011] 1 Cr App R (S) 439.

[30] (2000) 120 S. Ct. 2348.   [31] (2004) 124 S. Ct. 2531, discussed in ch. 2.2 above.

[32] Reitz (2011), pp. 231–5.

insofar as it allows the court to dismiss without further enquiry any defence submissions it regards as 'incredible' or 'manifestly false'.

The general principle should be that sentencing decisions are part of the criminal trial and, as such, should remain subject to normal criminal procedure. This has been the position under the European Convention on Human Rights since 1972:

> The Commission considers that complaints concerning proceedings on sentence, even after a plea of guilty, could raise issues under Article 6 of the Convention, so that for example a defendant should have the opportunity of being represented where the prosecution gives evidence in relation to sentence. In the opinion of the Commission, the determination of a criminal charge, within the meaning of Article 6(1) of the Convention, includes not only the determination of the guilt or innocence of the accused, but also in principle the determination of his sentence; and the expression 'everyone charged with a criminal offence' in Article 6(3) includes persons who, although already convicted, have not been sentenced. The Commission observes that questions of sentence may be closely related to questions of guilt or innocence, and that in the criminal procedure of many states parties to the Convention, they cannot be separated at this stage in the proceedings.[33]

This position has been maintained by the European Court of Human Rights in relation to the Article 6(3) rights and other Article 6 rights such as the right to trial (and sentence) within a reasonable time.[34] But what about the presumption of innocence in Article 6(2)? It would seem elementary that a person who has been convicted of the offence charged cannot be presumed innocent. The European Court of Human Rights has found this issue difficult, and there are conflicting statements. Whereas the Court in *Minelli* v. *Switzerland*[35] declared that 'Article 6(2) governs criminal proceedings in their entirety', the Court in *Phillips* v. *United Kingdom*[36] held by a majority that the presumption of innocence in Article 6(2) is not applicable to confiscation orders, which are sentences. Part of the difficulty is that the Court's jurisprudence on Article 6(2) is weak: it does not insist on placing the burden of proof on the prosecution, and allows presumptions of fact or law so long as account is taken of 'the importance of what is at stake'.[37] This enabled the Court in *Phillips* to conclude that, even if Article 6(2) were applicable, the presumptions that lead to confiscation orders were justifiable on public interest grounds.[38] A preferable approach would be to accept that the presumption of innocence

---

[33] *X* v. *United Kingdom* (1972) 2 Digest 766 (European Commission on Human Rights).
[34] See e.g. *V and T* v. *United Kingdom* (2000) 30 EHRR 121; *Cuscani* v. *United Kingdom* (2003) 36 EHRR 2.
[35] (1983) 5 EHRR 554.   [36] [2001] Crim LR 817.
[37] *Salabiaku* v. *France* (1991) 13 EHRR 379; for discussion, see Emmerson, Ashworth and Macdonald (2012), pp. 670–4.
[38] See also the Supreme Court's decision in *Gale* v. *Serious Organised Crime Agency* [2011] UKSC 49, on which see King (2014).

cannot apply to the sentencing stage as such, but to argue that where liberty is at stake (and also large sums of money) there is a powerful argument for placing on the prosecution a burden of proving issues beyond a reasonable doubt. The argument would therefore rest on the importance of the human rights that might be taken away or diminished by the proceedings, e.g. the right to personal liberty if a prison sentence is under consideration, or (less weighty) the right to property if a confiscation order is being contemplated.[39]

13.2 Police antecedents statements

The Criminal Practice Direction requires the provision of a statement in the following format:[40] first, 'personal details and a summary of convictions and cautions', in the form of the Police National Computer (PNC) Court/Defence/ Probation Summary sheet; secondly, 'previous convictions' in the form of the full PNC printout; and thirdly, 'recorded cautions' in the form of a full PNC printout. Both the second and third items should be supplemented by the police if they know of other convictions and cautions. In the Crown Court there should additionally be information on the circumstances of the last three similar convictions and, if the case involves breach of a community order, the circumstances of the offence for which that order was given. The Practice Direction allocates to the prosecutor the duty of ensuring that the PNC documents presented to the court are up to date, and that any changes are drawn to the court's attention.

13.3 The role of the prosecution

Where there is a guilty plea, the prosecution is expected to state the facts of the case. The process of constructing this statement depends on the police and on the Crown Prosecution Service. There has been evidence that some defendants believe that the prosecution has given an unjustifiably serious impression of the facts of their case, whereas others acknowledge that certain inaccuracies in the statement militated in their favour.[41] Sometimes the statement represents the outcome of a compromise in relation to plea; for example the prosecution may agree not to mention a certain factor in return for the defendant's changing his plea from not guilty to guilty.[42] We saw in part 13.1 above that if the defence wish to dispute the prosecution's version, there are various procedural methods at their disposal. It is equally true that the prosecution

---

[39] For elaboration of this argument for procedural protections, see Ashworth and Zedner (2014), pp. 258–62.
[40] *Criminal Practice Directions* [2013] EWCA Crim 1631, Preliminary Proceedings, Part 10A.2.
[41] Baldwin and McConville (1978), pp. 545–6.
[42] Cf. *Beswick*, above n. 11, deploring prosecution acquiescence in an untrue version of the facts.

may, and indeed should, challenge any statement made by the defence in mitigation which it believes to be unjustifiable.

How far beyond presenting the facts of the case might the prosecution go? The English tradition, represented by the Bar's Code of Conduct, is that the prosecutor 'should not attempt by advocacy to influence the court in regard to sentence'. The 2004 version of the Code for Crown Prosecutors set out the prosecutor's principal duties, and although this passage does not appear in the 2013 version (7th edn), it bears repetition here:

Crown prosecutors should draw the court's attention to

- any aggravating or mitigating factors disclosed by the prosecution case;
- any victim personal statement;
- where appropriate, evidence of the impact of the offending on the community;
- any statutory provisions or sentencing guidelines which may assist;
- any relevant statutory provisions relating to ancillary orders (such as anti-social behaviour orders).[43]

As appears from this passage, the notion that the prosecutor should play no part in sentencing is no longer true (if it ever was). The change was encouraged by Lord Bingham as Lord Chief Justice, when he urged judges to 'invite assistance from prosecuting counsel' and expressed the hope 'that judges will not be affronted if prosecuting counsel do offer to give guidance to the relevant provisions and appropriate authorities' in a case.[44] None of this detracts from the proposition that a prosecutor should not urge a particular sentence. It remains important that greater prosecutorial involvement be encased within a clear ethical framework: prosecutors should act in the spirit of a Minister of Justice, not striving for severity but adopting a balanced view in the public interest.[45] This requires both familiarity and sympathy with the aims of sentencing policy. The leading case lays down that the prosecutor 'should always be ready to assist the court by drawing attention to any statutory provisions that govern the court's sentencing powers', in order to prevent the passing of an unlawful sentence. The prosecutor should also draw to the court's attention any relevant guidelines.[46] Indeed, English judges may enter into discussion with counsel for both sides about the appropriate category range for the case, and the appropriate starting point.[47] The High Court of Australia has rightly emphasized that a prosecutor's submissions as to sentence are merely opinions, which cannot bind the judge; but it is doubtful whether the Court was right to go on to hold that it is not procedurally unfair for the judge to decline to hear from the prosecution on sentence.[48]

---

[43] Crown Prosecution Service (2004), para. 11.1.
[44] *Attorney General's Reference No. 7 of 1997 (Fearon)* [1998] 1 Cr App R (S) 268, at pp. 272–3.
[45] See Blake and Ashworth (1998).   [46] Per Lord Phillips CJ in *Cain* [2007] 2 Cr App R (S) 135.
[47] Padfield (2013), pp. 46–7.   [48] *Barbaro and Zirilli* v. *R.* [2014] HCA 2.

13.4 Pre-sentence reports

In 1960 the Streatfeild Committee declared that 'our cardinal principle throughout is that sentences should be based on reliable, comprehensive information relevant to what the court is seeking to do'.[49] The next three decades saw great increases in the supply of social inquiry reports to courts, but there was frequent debate about the contents of the reports. In the 1970s, Thorpe found a tendency of probation officers to omit certain details when they might tell against the recommendation which the writer wished to make. Sentencers voiced various criticisms of reports – of the social work jargon in which they were sometimes written; of the gullibility of some probation officers in accepting the defendant's claims without checking them; and of the 'unrealistic' nature of some of the recommended sentences. Loraine Gelsthorpe and Peter Raynor reported on the variation in quality of pre-sentence reports and the need for tighter quality control procedures; but their research, which also contains interesting judicial reflections on reports, relates to a pilot study carried out in the months after the enactment of the 1991 Act.[50] Michael Cavadino reported on a 'before and after' study of reports immediately before the 1991 Act and in 1993, after the introduction of the Act. His research suggested a more positive attitude among report writers, and a strong change towards focusing on the seriousness of the offence and on the offending behaviour, although he also found that the quality of reports was variable.[51]

In some cases a court may adjourn the case before sentence to allow for the preparation of a pre-sentence report, for example where the defendant had pleaded not guilty and no pre-sentence report had been prepared. The principle is that, if the court adjourns the case specifically in order to have the offender's suitability for a certain sentence assessed, and the report confirms suitability, it is then wrong for the court to impose a custodial sentence. In the leading case of *Gillam* (1980),[52] the case had been adjourned to assess suitability for community service, but the judge then imposed custody despite a favourable report. As Watkins LJ held,

> when a judge in these circumstances purposely postpones sentence so that an alternative to prison can be examined, and that alternative is found to be a satisfactory one in all respects, the court ought to adopt the alternative. A feeling of injustice is otherwise aroused.

A judicious court should make it clear, when asking for a report, that all options remain open. Otherwise, if the court appears to go back on a reasonable expectation it created, the *Gillam* principle will lead to the quashing of the subsequent custodial sentence.[53]

---

[49] Streatfeild (1960), para. 336.   [50] Gelsthorpe and Raynor (1995).   [51] Cavadino (1997).
[52] (1980) 2 Cr App R (S) 267.   [53] E.g. *Waterton* [2003] 1 Cr App R (S) 606.

Section 156 of the Criminal Justice Act 2003 requires courts to obtain and consider a pre-sentence report (PSR) before imposing a community sentence, and before forming an opinion that the case passes the custody threshold, before deciding what is the shortest term commensurate with the seriousness of the offence, and before determining that an offender is 'dangerous' for the purposes of the dangerousness provisions. However, if the court is of the opinion that it is unnecessary to obtain a PSR in any of the stated circumstances, it need not do so; failure to obtain a report does not invalidate the sentence.

The form and contents of pre-sentence reports are governed by the *National Standards for the Management of Offenders* (2011). In outline, a standard delivery PSR should contain:

a) Basic facts about the offender and the sources used to prepare the report;
b) An offence analysis;
c) An assessment of the offender;
d) An assessment of the risk of harm to the public and the likelihood of re-offending;
e) A sentencing proposal.[54]

A major part of the risk assessment process is the use of a full OASys assessment.[55] There is also provision for a fast delivery PSR, usually requested where there has been a conviction after a plea of not guilty. Fast delivery reports should be available within 24 hours, but are not recommended where a custodial sentence or a high community order is being considered.[56] Cooper has noted the increased tendency of PSRs to be victim-centred, and argues that this prevents them from giving proper weight to rehabilitative and other individualized objectives.[57]

There always seems to have been a tension between those who write and those who receive PSRs. The findings of Scottish research suggest that a major barrier to communication between the two groups is the firm judicial insistence on their 'ownership' of sentencing.[58] This not only means that many judges are unhappy to see anything so bold as a recommendation for a particular form of sentence in a PSR, but that they are also resistant to what might be termed 'gentler persuasion'. Thus the Scottish research suggests that, important as it is to improve the quality of PSRs, little progress towards influencing sentencers is likely to occur so long as the sentencing process is thought to belong to the courts. Moreover, there is bound to be tension between the 'external context' in the PSR, recognizing (for example) the offender's social disadvantage, and the more rationalistic legal model of behaviour.[59]

Nonetheless, the practice of passing sentence without a pre-sentence report ought to be reappraised. We have noted that the Criminal Justice Act

---

[54] SGC, *Magistrates' Court Sentencing Guidelines* (2008), p. 190.
[55] See Merrington (2004), and for research on the operation of OASys see Debidin (2009).
[56] SGC, *Magistrates' Court Sentencing Guidelines* (2008), p. 190.   [57] Cooper (2013), p. 162.
[58] Tata et al. (2008), on this point in accord with Cavadino (1997), pp. 545–6.
[59] See further Field and Tata (2010), introducing a special comparative issue on PSRs.

2003 allows this, as previous legislation did. Yet when courts pass sentence without obtaining a report, they often do so on the spurious basis that they have learnt quite enough about the offender and his background from the trial. In view of the legislation it seems wrong for a judge to conclude that simply because an immediate custodial sentence is deemed inevitable there is no need for a pre-sentence report.[60] Indeed, Lord Judge CJ emphasised the value of a PSR before passing sentence in serious sexual cases, as a means of assessing the offender's motivation and dangerousness.[61] Moreover, one obvious danger – that more black offenders will be sent to custody, because more black offenders plead not guilty and are therefore unlikely to have pre-sentence reports prepared[62] – requires greater attention than it has received. Indeed, even where a PSR is prepared on a defendant from an ethnic minority, there are opportunities for discriminatory forces to have an impact.[63]

13.5 Defence speech in mitigation

In contrast to the prosecution statement of facts, the 'plea in mitigation' by the defence advocate has traditionally been allowed to range over the facts of the offence, the background and characteristics of the offender, and the suitability of possible sentences. If the defence advocate makes factual points, they must be proved to the civil standard (not reasonable doubt, as for the prosecutor).[64] Recent research by Jacobson and Hough (2007) demonstrates the wide range of factors used for mitigating purposes, from the offender's role in the crime, to the immediate antecedents or circumstances of the offence, to the defendant's situation at the time, and the defendant's response to the offence and the prosecution, the defendant's past, the defendant's future prospects, and so forth.[65] Joanna Shapland found that the best speeches in mitigation tended to be constructed in a way which appeared to show 'realism', by recognizing the gravity of the offence and any other factors against the offender. Thus a common approach was for the advocate to acknowledge each aggravating factor but to qualify it immediately by reference to a mitigating factor. As Shapland commented,

> this would seem to be one effective method of both being seen to be realistic and dealing with the [versions of the] offences given by the prosecution and the police, so turning them to the benefit of the offender.[66]

---

[60] Cf. *Lawrence* [2012] 2 Cr App R (S) 243 (no PSR, decision acceptable if taken judicially) with *Milhailsens* [2010] EWCA Crim 2545 (judge said report would be 'waste of money', wrong approach); the relevant legislation on the test for custody and for community sentences is set out in App. A.

[61] *Attorney General's References Nos. 73 and 75 of 2010, and No. 3 of 2011* [2011] 2 Cr App R (S) 555, at [7].

[62] See Hood (1992), p. 156, showing a strong association between custody for blacks and the absence of a social inquiry report. See generally ch. 7.2 above.

[63] Hudson and Bramhall (2005).   [64] See the authorities at n. 29 above.

[65] Jacobson and Hough (2007), ch. 2.   [66] Shapland (1981), p. 82.

Such an approach would have been welcome to the judges interviewed in the Oxford pilot study, who stressed the importance of 'realism, in terms of pitching sentencing suggestions at an appropriate level; ready support for factual assertions, such as an employer's letter to confirm the availability of a job; and sound knowledge of the purpose and availability of the various sentences'. This kind of realism is related very much to the individual judge's view of the case, and requires counsel to modify the mitigating strategy according to indications from the judge.

There is some evidence that judges may value the speech in mitigation more highly than a PSR, for two reasons. First, it tends to be more up to date, whereas a PSR may have been written some weeks before the hearing.[67] Secondly, the mitigating speech may be more realistic in its proposals, not least because it is delivered 'live'. On the other hand, a speech in mitigation is less likely to be based on direct and probing interviews by a trained case-worker, although the defence advocate can incorporate comments from the pre-sentence report into the speech. In terms of reliability, both the probation officer and the defence advocate often have nothing more than the offender's word on which to base their submissions. However, the defence advocate has the great advantage of being in court and able to respond to any indications from the bench as to whether a certain line of argument is worth pursuing or not. In that way, the defence advocate may be able to change tack in response to something as apparently slender as the eyebrow movements of the judge.[68]

It is well established that the judge should give notice to defence counsel of an intention to impose certain types of sentence, in order to give counsel the opportunity to address the court on the issue – in particular severe sentences such as discretionary life imprisonment or an extended sentence, and also sentences that might be unexpected, such as disqualification from driving in a case where it is merely a discretionary penalty (e.g. for taking a car without consent).[69] A defence advocate is expected to give notice to the court of an intention to dispute the prosecution's version of the facts, on a guilty plea.[70] Defence advocates have the same duties to the court as prosecutors in relation to the avoidance of errors: they should be ready to draw a court's attention to any relevant law and guidelines affecting a case.[71]

13.6 The obligation to give reasons for sentence

It is a fundamental tenet of natural justice that decision-makers should give reasons for their decisions, and the argument is surely at its strongest where the decisions affect the liberty of the subject. The case for reasoned decisions

---

[67] Oxford Pilot Study (1984), pp. 43–4.
[68] Oxford Pilot Study (1984), p. 44; see also Mackenzie (2005), pp. 22–3.
[69] *Ireland* (1988) 10 Cr App R (S) 474.   [70] *Gardener* (1994) 15 Cr App R (S) 667.
[71] See nn. 44–6 above and accompanying text.

in sentencing is therefore unanswerable in principle,[72] and is now reinforced by Article 6 of the Convention as a result of the Human Rights Act 1998. Offenders should be able to know the reasons for sentences imposed upon them, and victim(s) and the wider public also have an interest in knowing. The duty to give reasons may conduce to decisions which are more considered and more consonant with legal principle. And the giving of reasons enables appellate courts better to assess the appropriateness of a sentence which has been challenged on appeal.

What counts as a reason for sentence? Clearly, a kind of moral expostulation about the offence, 'one of the worst of its kind', 'a dreadful and brutal attack', is hardly enough on its own. To amount to a 'reason', the sentencer's remarks must surely link the sentence to the relevant sentencing guideline (notably to the offence category and the starting point) or, for those rare offences without a guideline, to general levels of sentence for that kind of offence. Reasons will also be required for significant aggravating and mitigating factors and other general principles. As the Council of Europe's 1992 recommendation on *Consistency in Sentencing* proposed:

E.1 Courts should, in general, state concrete reasons for imposing sentences. In particular, specific reasons should be given when a custodial sentence is imposed. Where sentencing orientations or starting points exist, it is recommended that courts give reasons when the sentence is outside the indicated range of sentence.

E.2 What counts as a 'reason' is a motivation which relates the particular sentence to the normal range of sentences for the type of crime and to the declared rationales of sentencing.

Along these lines are the current statutory provisions on the duty to give reasons for, and explain the effect of, sentences: s. 174(5) of the Criminal Justice Act 2003 as amended. The essence of these provisions is that, except in relation to mandatory or prescribed minimum sentences, a sentencer 'must state in open court, in ordinary language and in general terms, its reasons for deciding on the sentence passed', and must explain to the offender the effect of the sentence in ordinary language. The precise requirements differ according to whether the sentence is custodial, or is a community sentence, or is a fine or discharge. For example, if the sentence is custodial, the court must firstly comply with the statutory test for passing a custodial sentence;[73] must identify any definitive sentencing guideline relevant to the case, and must explain how the court has met the requirements set out in s. 125 of the Coroners and Justice Act 2009; must, if the sentence has been reduced on account of a plea of guilty, state that it has so reduced the sentence; must, if the offence is racially or religiously aggravated or aggravated by reference to the victim's sexual

---

[72] Thomas (1963).

[73] Section 152(2) of the Criminal Justice Act 2003, discussed in ch. 9.4.1 above.

orientation or disability, state that that has been treated as an aggravating factor; mention any other aggravating factors or mitigating factors that the court has regarded as being of particular importance. Additionally, there are duties to explain the effect of the sentence: if the sentence is custodial, the court must explain the rules on release and licence. Finally, the court has duties to state the reason for not making certain ancillary orders if it so decides, for example a compensation order,[74] a football banning order (where there is a conviction of a football-related offence),[75] failure to activate a suspended sentence in full,[76] and so on.

The obligations thus imposed on magistrates and judges are extensive. There are occasional examples of a judicial failure even to refer to the relevant guideline, let alone to provide detailed reasons as required.[77] The complexity of sentencing law is often criticised, and there is plenty to object to in the frequent legislative tinkering with provisions for political reasons, and the failure to consolidate sentencing provisions or to place a premium on clarity. However, some degree of complexity is hardly surprising in a modern sentencing system, and the task of explaining the effect of a given sentence remains an important social function. Whatever meaning is assigned to the nebulous concept of 'public confidence', it is surely right that a court should give reasons for its sentence and explain its effect openly and clearly.

Should courts go further than this, and set out the main elements in their calculation of the sentence? There are now some circumstances in which courts have to be more explicit about the calculations that lead them to a particular sentence – particularly in respect of custodial sentences, but not exclusively so. Thus the guideline judgment on sentencing in cases of racial aggravation states that courts 'should say, publicly, what the appropriate sentence would have been for the offence without the racial aggravation',[78] thereby making it clear what was added to take account of the aggravating factor. Similarly, the SGC guideline on the guilty plea discount goes further than s. 174(2), mentioned above, by recommending that 'the court should usually state what the sentence would have been if there had been no reduction as a result of the guilty plea'.[79] This applies to all courts and to all forms of sentence. Whether obligations of this kind will be imposed more widely remains to be seen, but even these two obligations are significant steps in the direction of transparency in sentencing, with benefits both to the public and to counsel and appellate tribunals.

---

[74] On which see ch. 10.4 above.   [75] On which see ch. 11.5.9 above.

[76] On which see ch. 9.4.5 above.

[77] See ch. 1.5.2(a) above, and e.g. *Adcock* [2010] 2 Cr App R (S) 643.

[78] *Kelly and Donnelly* [2001] 2 Cr App R (S) 341, at p. 347. The judgment presumably applies to religious aggravation, and also to aggravation related to disability or sexual orientation.

[79] SGC, *Reduction in Sentence for a Guilty Plea: Revised Guideline* (2007), para. 3.1.

13.7 The role of the victim

As already noted,[80] there has been increasing recognition of the rights of
victims of crime in England and Wales. Victim Support provides support
and advice for victims after the crime, and the Domestic Violence, Crime and
Victims Act 2004 required the creation of the Victims' Code of Practice.
The current version[81] imposes obligations on several agencies within the
criminal justice system, enforceable in the first place by complaint to the
relevant agency and, in the absence of satisfaction, by way of complaint to
the Parliamentary Commissioner for Administration (the Ombudsman). The
2004 Act also created the office of Commissioner for Victims, and the current
Commissioner has committed herself to ensuring compliance by the relevant
agencies with the Code's provisions.[82] The Sentencing Council has a duty to
have regard to 'the impact of sentencing decisions on victims of offences',[83]
and one way in which it discharges this duty is to commission research into
victims' experiences and views before drawing up guidelines.

Victims' rights may be divided, somewhat crudely, into rights to services
and procedural rights.[84] The Victims' Code of Practice is the main source of
rights to services, in the sense that it sets out the obligations of the various
service providers. The police are required, among other things, to inform the
victim if a suspect has been arrested and then released on bail; if an offender
has been given a caution, reprimand or warning; if no arrest has been made, to
provide monthly updates on progress; if a date has been set for court proceedings; and if court proceedings have been concluded, to inform the victim of the
outcome. The police also have a duty to pass on details of relevant cases to the
local Victim Support group within two days, unless the victim asks the police
not to do so. And, when taking statements from victims, the police must
inform them of their right to make a victim personal statement. The Crown
Prosecution Service is required to tell the victim when charges have been
dropped or altered, and to give an explanation for that outcome; to have in
place a system for taking account of the contents of victim personal statements; and to ensure, so far as possible, that the prosecuting lawyer meets the
victim before the start of any court hearing. However, the duty to take account
of the victim's views must be set against the prosecutor's duty to 'form an
overall view of the public interest'.[85] Obligations are imposed on Victim
Support to provide various contracted services, and also to provide the
Witness Service at courts in accordance with the standards agreed. Courts
have various obligations to liaise with other agencies and to provide appropriate facilities, and so forth. Although recent years have seen rather more

[80] In ch. 10.4 above.   [81] *Code of Practice for Victims of Crime* (3rd edn, 2013).
[82] Commissioner for Victims and Witnesses (2014), p. 10.
[83] Coroners and Justice Act 2009, s. 120(11)(c); see further Edwards (2013).
[84] See the informative discussion by Hoyle (2012), and more specifically Edwards (2004).
[85] *Code for Crown Prosecutors* (7th edn, 2013), para. 4.12c.

promises than delivery in respect of victim services, especially in terms of keeping victims informed of events in 'their' case, the Code of Practice is to be welcomed as a major step in the formalization of victim services.

Whether victims should be granted procedural rights at the sentencing stage is a different question. Much depends, of course, on the rationale for sentencing and on its social and constitutional function. There are good principled and pragmatic reasons for reserving the functions of trial and sentencing to an impartial and independent judiciary – for example, only public condemnation after a trial according to settled principles can convey the appropriate censure of an offender; victims cannot be expected to be impartial or independent in matters of sentencing; and the state should retain a monopoly of force, not only as part of the assurance of citizens that others will abide by the rules, but also to prevent vigilantism.[86] More could be said about the tendency of governments to use the rhetoric of 'rebalancing the criminal justice system' in favour of victims,[87] but the focus here is on two possible victims' rights: a victim's right to convey to the court information about the offence and its impact, and a victim's right to voice an opinion on the sentence to be imposed.

13.7.1 Information from victims

Victim Personal Statements (VPS) were introduced to England and Wales in October 2001.[88] The police should inform the victim of the possibility of making a VPS. Making a statement provides victims with the opportunity to describe how the crime has affected them – an 'explanatory and appreciative description' of facts and emotions.[89] Victims who make a VPS have the right to update it at any time before the trial. When a VPS is presented to a court, the proper approach is set out in the current Criminal Practice Direction:[90]

(a) The Victim Personal Statement and any evidence in support should be considered and taken into account by the court prior to passing sentence.
(b) Evidence of the effects of an offence on the victim contained in the Victim Personal Statement or other statement must be in proper form, that is a S9 witness statement or an expert's report and served upon the defendant's solicitor or the defendant if he is not represented, prior to sentence. Except where inferences can properly be drawn from the nature of or circumstances surrounding the offence, a sentencer must not make assumptions unsupported by evidence about the effects of an offence on the victim.

---

[86] See further Matravers (2010).   [87] See further Walklate (2012).
[88] Many other jurisdictions, particularly within the Commonwealth, have similar schemes. For that in Victoria, introduced after three official reports recommending against it, see Fox and Freiberg (1999), pp. 165–75. See also O'Malley (2006), ch. 9, on the reception of victim impact statements in Ireland.
[89] See Bottoms (2010) on the court's 'duty to understand'.
[90] *Practice Direction (Criminal Proceedings: Consolidation)* Part III.28 (2013), elaborated on by Lord Judge CJ in *Perkins* [2013] 2 Cr App R (S) 460.

(c) The court must pass what it judges to be the appropriate sentence having regard to the circumstances of the offence and of the offender taking into account, so far as the court considers it appropriate, the impact on the victim. The opinions of the victim or the victim's close relatives as to what the sentence should be are therefore not relevant, unlike the consequences of the offence on them. Victims should be advised of this. If, despite the advice, opinions as to sentence are included in the statement, the court should pay no attention to them.

(d) The court should consider whether it is desirable in its sentencing remarks to refer to the evidence provided on behalf of the victim ...

The requirements in paragraph (b) are a response to the difficulties arising from unsubstantiated claims about the effects of crime: if the effect on the victim is relevant, and therefore is capable of amounting to an aggravating factor in sentencing, it is right that it should be proved in the normal way.[91] Similarly, just as it is unfair on victims that they should have their character or conduct attacked in the defence speech in mitigation, without an opportunity for the prosecutor to challenge what has been said, so it is unfair on an offender if unsubstantiated allegations are made by the victim without a proper opportunity to challenge them.[92]

From the court's point of view, a VPS may provide helpful information to 'complete the picture' of the offence, but this raises the deeper question of the relevance of this information. Insofar as it refers to the after-effects of an offence, should it be relevant at all? Why should the offender's sentence vary according to the chance circumstance of whether a particular victim suffers an impact that is unusually great or unusually small? The general question of liability for unforeseen consequences was aired in Chapter 4 above:[93] Lord Judge CJ has pointed out that s. 143(1) of the 2003 Act requires courts to have regard to 'any harm the offence caused',[94] but those words only form part of that subsection and it is quite clear that culpability as well as harm should be integral to the court's assessment.[95] Particularly controversial are cases such as *Hind* (1994),[96] where there was evidence that the victim of a rape, the offender's former lover, had not suffered much trauma as a result of the offence. The Court of Appeal held that this might be accepted as a factor reducing the seriousness of the offence. The guidelines on rape, it will be recalled, provide that particularly great trauma resulting from the offence is an aggravating factor.[97]

From the victim's point of view, is the VPS scheme a positive development? A recent study by Julian Roberts and Marie Manikis found that only 43 per cent of victims recalled being offered the opportunity to make a VPS; of those,

[91] The early decision in *Hobstaff* (1993) 14 Cr App R (S) 605 made this point.
[92] See *McDermott* [2014] 1 Cr App R (S) 1.   [93] See particularly ch. 4.4.4 above.
[94] In *Perkins* [2013] 2 Cr App R (S) 460, at [2].   [95] Edwards (2013), p. 83.
[96] (1994) 15 Cr App R (S) 114; see also *Hutchinson*, ibid., 134.
[97] Ch. 4.4.7 above; see also *Gardner* [2011] 1 Cr App R (S) 65, on harassment.

some 55 per cent went on to make a VPS; and of those, some 68 per cent believed that their statement had been considered fully, or to some degree, by the court.[98] There was considerable local area variation in the making of VPSs: London had the lowest percentage of victims making a VPS, at some 15 per cent.[99] One possible disadvantage of victim statements is that they may create or increase the fear of reprisals from the offender's family or associates. In an early English survey a substantial minority of the 70 per cent of victims who declined to make a statement did so for fear of the offender's reaction if it became known to him.[100] However, a more recent Scottish survey is more positive: although a mere 15 per cent of victims took the opportunity to make a statement, some 61 per cent of those who did make a statement said that it made them feel better.[101] Since only around half of the Scottish makers of statements knew whether their statement had been taken into account in sentencing, it seems that this was not the main priority for those victims. The results accord with the argument of Edna Erez and Julian Roberts that the value of VPSs should be judged not on the instrumental model of effect on the sentencing decision but rather in terms of facilitating an expressive communication by the victim. They point out that, in surveys conducted by Erez and by others, victims who made a statement found that a positive experience.[102]

13.7.2 Family impact statements

Family Impact Statements are the equivalent of the VPS in homicide cases. Almost all the above comments on the VPS apply no less to Family Impact Statements.[103] It may be expected that the research findings would be similar.[104]

13.7.3 Community impact statements

The *Criminal Practice Directions* also provide for a community impact statement to be prepared and submitted by the police in appropriate cases. The purpose is 'to make the court aware of particular crime trends in the local area and the impact of these on the local community'.[105] It should be in the form of a witness statement and supported by evidence, a requirement that was interpreted somewhat loosely in *Wicks* (2014).[106] In that case some statistical

---

[98] Roberts and Manikis (2013), referred to in *Perkins* [2013] 2 Cr App R (S) 460, at [8].
[99] Roberts and Manikis (2013), p. 257.
[100] Hoyle et al. (1998), a study of the 1990s pilot scheme.
[101] Chalmers, Duff and Leverick (2007), also a study of a pilot scheme.
[102] Roberts and Erez (2010); Erez (1999), pp. 550–4.
[103] *Perkins* [2013] 2 Cr App R (S) 460, at [6].   [104] For a small early study, see Rock (2010).
[105] For a possible application, see Sentencing Council, *Theft Offences Guideline Consultation* (2014), p. 23.
[106] [2014] 1 Cr App R (S) 355; cf. now *Skelton* [2015] 1 Cr App R (S) 265.

support was produced on appeal, but in many other respects the statement rested on unsupported police assertions. This highlights a particular danger of such statements, not least if they are to be relied upon to increase the sentence level.[107]

13.7.4 Victim's opinion on sentence

Some of the jurisdictions which make formal provision for victim impact statements also allow the VPS to include an expression of opinion on the appropriate sentence. Some states in the United States go further and provide victims with a 'right of allocution', allowing a victim to make a statement in court in relation to the sentence.[108] From the victim's point of view, this may have even stronger advantages (possibility of real influence) and disadvantages (fear of ostracism or retaliation) than merely making a factual statement. But what are the implications of such statements for the aims and purposes of sentencing? If the primary aim of sentencing is restorative,[109] then one possible route to the achievement of restorative justice might be to allow the individual victim to play a part in the determination of the sentence – provided that it must be a restorative sentence, not a purely punitive one, and provided that the individual victim does not decide what is necessary for the restoration of the community (an essential aspect of most modern restorative theories), since that ought to be the task of community representatives too. Thus, in the Family Group Conferences in New Zealand, convened to decide on the response to a young offender's crime, the conference includes not only the offender and family and the victim and family, but also a police officer and (in some cases) a social worker.[110]

In the context of a sentencing system whose primary aim is not restorative,[111] however, there must be grave doubts about allowing a victim to voice an opinion as to sentence. It is unfair and wrong that an offender's sentence should depend on whether the victim is vindictive or forgiving: in principle, the sentence should be determined according to the normal effects of a given type of crime, without regard to the disposition of the particular victim.[112] As Victim Support has asserted, 'the rule of law demands that victims do not dictate justice or sentencing'.[113] If it is then said that allowing the victim to make a statement on sentence is not the same as allowing the victim to determine the sentence, one wonders about the point of the exercise. Victims' expectations might be unfairly raised and then dashed if a court

---

[107] On local prevalence as an aggravating factor, see SGC, *Overarching Principles: Seriousness* (2004), p. 9.

[108] See Doak (2008).   [109] See ch. 3.3.7 above; Hoyle (2012), pp. 414–19.

[110] See Morris, Maxwell and Robertson (1993), Morris and Maxwell (2000).

[111] Cf. Edwards (2004) on other ways of conceptualizing the issue.

[112] See Matravers (2010) and Bottoms (2010) for fuller discussion.

[113] Victim Support (2010), p. 1.

declines to follow the suggestions made, and the whole process might appear to victims as a cruel pretence.

The English courts have now reached some such position, although not without some deviations. There are several cases in which victims and/or their families have written to the court to plead for mercy, to express forgiveness or otherwise to suggest that a lenient sentence is appropriate. In *Buchanan* (1980)[114] the Court of Appeal referred to a 'long and loving' letter from the victim, pleading for the offender's release so that she could live with him again, but the court held that he must receive the proper sentence for the offence. In *Darvill* (1987)[115] the Court of Appeal was equivocal, affirming that the offender must be sentenced for the offence he has committed but adding that 'forgiveness can in many cases have an effect, albeit an indirect effect, on the task of the sentencing judge. It may reduce the possibility of reoffending, it may reduce the danger of public outrage which sometimes arises when a defendant has been released into the community unexpectedly early ...'. This theme was taken up in *Attorney General's Reference (No. 18 of 1993)* (1994),[116] where the offender struck a pregnant woman and a child with an iron bar. The sentencer was shown a letter from the then-pregnant victim and others from her family, stating that the offender had been forgiven and had been punished sufficiently by being remanded in custody pending trial. A probation order was made. The Court of Appeal, considering whether the sentence was unduly lenient, had received another letter from the victim. Referring to the 'very exceptional circumstances', the court did not alter the sentence, and clearly paid some attention to the forgiveness expressed by the victim and the family.

The leading decision is *Nunn* (1996),[117] where a young man had caused the death by dangerous driving of a close friend. The mother and sister of the victim wrote to the court to say that, distressed as they were by their loss, the fact that the offender (a friend of the family) was in prison was also a continuing source of grief. The purport of their representations was that the sentence of 4 years should be reduced. Judge LJ said this:

> We mean no disrespect to the mother and sister of the deceased, but the opinions of the victim, or the surviving members of the family, about the appropriate level of sentence do not provide any sound basis for reassessing a sentence. If the victim feels utterly merciful towards the criminal, and some do, the crime has still been committed and must be punished as it deserves. If the victim is obsessed with vengeance, which can in reality only be assuaged by a very long sentence, as also happens, the punishment cannot be made longer by the court than would otherwise be appropriate. Otherwise cases with

[114] (1980) 2 Cr App R (S) 13.   [115] (1987) 9 Cr App R (S) 225.
[116] (1994) 15 Cr App R (S) 800.
[117] [1996] 2 Cr App R (S) 136, endorsed by Lord Bingham CJ in *Roche* [1999] 2 Cr App R (S) 105 and incorporated into more general guidance in *Perks* [2001] 1 Cr App R (S) 66.

identical features would be dealt with in widely differing ways, leading to improper and unfair disparity . . .

In this case the court did reduce the sentence from 4 to 3 years, but it did so in response to the evidence that its length was adding to the grief of the victim's family, and not in response to their views on the appropriate sentence. Indeed, as Judge LJ pointed out, in this case the other two members of the deceased's family (his father and brother) did not share the views of the mother and sister.

In a system that treats proportionality to the seriousness of the offence as the primary determinant of sentence, this is clearly the right approach. The court's first duty is to impose the proper sentence for the case, by reference to the law and the guidelines, as the Criminal Practice Direction states.[118] The only exception for which there is authority is where some reduction in sentence is appropriate in order to mitigate the suffering of the victim's family. Thus in *Robinson* (2003),[119] the Court took note of the serious effects of the offender's imprisonment on the victim's family (who were close friends) and reduced a manslaughter sentence from 4 years to 18 months. Exceptional cases apart, the general approach in *Nunn* is consistent with that taken under the European Convention on Human Rights: in *McCourt* v. *United Kingdom* (1993)[120] a murdered woman's mother alleged a breach of Article 8 on the ground that she was denied the right to participate in the process of sentencing the convicted offender, to be informed of the date of his release, and to express her views to those who decided on release. The European Commission on Human Rights noted that the Home Office does accept submissions from victims' families and places them before the Parole Board, and also has a practice of ensuring that victims' families are informed of any impending release of the offender. However, the Commission accepted that it would be inappropriate to recognize any role for the victim's family in setting the tariff period for the offender, since they would lack the requisite impartiality. The Commission concluded that the application disclosed no interference with the victim's family's right to respect for family life under Article 8.

---

[118] Set out at the beginning of 13.7.1 above; see the discussion by Edwards (2013), pp. 79–80.

[119] [2003] 2 Cr App R (S) 515; cf. *Attorney General's Reference No. 77 of 2002 (Scotney)* [2003] 1 Cr App R (S) 564, where the Court of Appeal, in a judgment delivered by Judge LJ (who also gave the leading judgment in *Nunn*), held that a community punishment order was not unduly lenient for causing death by careless driving while intoxicated in a case where the impact of the death on the offender and the victim's family (who were close) was so exceptional that a merciful course was justified.

[120] (1993) 15 EHRR CD 110.

14

Sentencing, guidelines
and the punitive state

Contents

The purpose of this chapter is to draw together various themes emerging from the topics examined in the 13 substantive chapters, and to offer some concluding reflections. The chapter begins by returning to a fundamental issue – the role that sentencing should be expected to fulfil in criminal justice. The second topic is the relationship between rule-of-law principles and the sentencing process, examining the interplay between guidelines and judicial discretion in England and Wales and in some other jurisdictions. From this we move to the third topic of guidelines and penal moderation. Fourthly, we return to the struggle between the proportionality principle and the increasing reliance on the rhetoric of protection and risk and the proliferation of preventive orders in sentencing. In the fifth part, entitled 'Stepping back from the punitive state', the chapter concludes with a brief reassessment of the prospects for significant changes in the direction of sentencing policy in England and Wales.

14.1 The responsibility of sentencing

There is no doubt that the task of sentencing imposes a great burden on magistrates and judges. Many of them say that it is the hardest and most disturbing of judicial tasks. Given the momentous consequences it may have for offenders, in terms of deprivations or restrictions on liberty, that is as it should be. In the present context, however, a more significant question is what sentencers and sentencing should be held responsible *for*. Given the place of sentencers in the criminal process, would it be fair to assume that they are responsible for crime rates in society, or for the subsequent conduct of offenders?

The first part of an answer to this question must emphasize the limited role that sentencers play in the criminal justice system. The cases that come before them have already been shaped and filtered by other processes and other actors. It is not just that some crimes are never reported or, if reported, are not traced to a suspect. We have also seen that many cases are dealt with by 'out-of-court penalties' of various kinds, and thus never come before a court for sentence. The police, the Crown Prosecution Service and the various inspectorates and agencies with a power to prosecute make choices about whether it is in the public interest to bring a case to court. When a case does come to court, it will often be the subject of some negotiation by the prosecutor and the defence in relation to the plea: the 'basis of plea' on which a plea of guilty is tendered may shape the 'facts of the case' in a particular way. Thus, by the time a case comes before the court for sentence, it has been the subject of various processes of selection and refinement. Sentencers have some powers to override such negotiations but do not often do so.

The sentencing decision itself may be shaped by submissions from the prosecution and the defence, and by the contents of a pre-sentence report. The impact of the sentence on the offender is likely to depend on decisions taken by other actors in the criminal justice system – most obviously the Parole Board in relation to release from indeterminate, extended or very long sentences, but also the prison service in deciding on Home Detention Curfew, decisions by the Probation Service as to the form of the requirements added to a community order or suspended sentence order, and decisions on the response to breach of a requirement, decisions on fine enforcement made by courts administrators, and so forth. As Padfield, Morgan and Maguire argue, such decisions:

> raise important questions about the transparency, fairness and accountability of the quasi-judicial decisions that significantly affect the lives of both offenders and victims. They also raise questions about the extent to which different kinds of offence, suspect or offender are, or should be, treated differently in terms of the locus of decisions made about them and the safeguards that surround the process.[1]

Moreover, there are advantages in thinking about sentencing as a process rather than as a single, one-off decision. But it must then be seen as a process shared with other decision-makers, not necessarily in the formal sense of having a separate *juge d'application des peines* as in France (dealing with the execution of the sentence pronounced by the court and empowered to make substitutions),[2] but in a looser sense in which other agents become significant decision-makers in relation to the precise form of what is imposed on the offender.

---

[1] Padfield, Morgan and Maguire (2012), p. 956.   [2] See Hodgson (2005).

The above observations indicate one reason why the sentencer (alone) cannot be held responsible for the crime rate or for an offender's reoffending, but there are other considerations too. As argued in Chapter 1.4, the very concept of 'the crime rate' is a difficult one, although the counting methods of the Crime Survey for England and Wales have been deployed for over 30 years now. By this measure crime rates have declined in this country since the late 1990s, as in most other European countries. Improved crime prevention measures may well have played a part in bringing down property crimes, but on the other hand the willingness of victims to report certain crimes (serious sexual offences, 'domestic' violence) may have increased, as a result of initiatives within criminal justice. What we do know (as explained in Chapter 1.4 above) is that such a low proportion of crimes are reported to the police and recorded by the police, and such a low proportion of those are detected (around a quarter), that the criminal justice system makes a formal response to only around 3 per cent of offences committed in any one year. Of those about a third (or 1 per cent) receive a caution, reprimand, or warning. This means that the courts sentence only around 2 per cent of offenders. The idea that sentencing policy in respect of this 2 per cent – which is admittedly higher in some categories, such as serious violence (10 per cent), but not so as to weaken the argument here – can have a significant effect on the overall crime rate is difficult to sustain. There is a whole range of broader social factors that may have an impact on offending rates, such as drugs, alcohol, poverty, and the availability of readily stealable items such as mobile phones. Thus simplistic ideas about marginal deterrence – the assumption that increasing sentences will have a kind of hydraulic effect in reducing criminality – are unsustainable. As we saw in Chapter 3.3 above, the evidence on deterrence and incapacitation does not bear this out.[3] Some judges seem either to be unaware of this or to doubt it, since general deterrent rhetoric remains common when justifying sentences.[4] Some politicians, especially ministers, must be aware of the evidence, since there is ample support for it in research conducted or commissioned by government. But by setting over-ambitious targets for sentencing and by subscribing to a notion of 'public confidence' that too readily dissolves into beliefs about sentence severity (and may be influenced by media representations anyway), the government goes against the evidence that it possesses.[5]

On this first issue, then, the conclusion is that too much should not be expected of sentencing. It should aim to be fair and proportionate, and within those parameters should strive for constructive goals such as rehabilitation and reparation. To exceed the proportionate sentence would call for strong

---

[3] See further the brief but penetrating analysis by Bottoms (2004), pp. 60–72.
[4] See ch. 3.3.2 and 3.5.
[5] For the fragile relationships between public opinion and public assessments of the sentencing system, see Hough and Roberts (1998) and Hough et al. (2003).

principled arguments supported by evidence-based justifications. Sentencing is a form of public censure, and the sentences imposed should convey the relative degree of censure for the particular offence(s). It is true that punishment levels are far more controllable by the state than crime levels, and so governments in certain types of political system are tempted to announce expressive policies.[6] But the fact is that sentencing is merely a small part of criminal justice policy, and it is wrong to treat it as a primary form of crime prevention: there are several other kinds of initiative that have a greater crime-preventive potential than modifications of sentencing levels, although it is of course necessary to have in existence a sentencing system that operates so as to exert an overall or underlying preventive effect.

14.2 Rule-of-law values, discretion and guidelines

Sentencing decisions are of great significance to the public (insofar as they convey the degree of censure of the offender for the offence(s)), to victims, and to the offenders themselves. These decisions may involve considerable deprivation of liberty, restrictions on liberty, or deprivation of money or other assets. Both the element of public censure and the potential loss of fundamental rights render it imperative that the rule of law should apply to such decisions so far as possible: although the sentencing decision will always require an element of judgment, that judgment should be exercised within a framework of law, applying principles and standards set out in advance. The purpose of rule-of-law values such as these is to facilitate the guidance of individuals by the law, and to provide for clear, consistent, and transparent court decisions.

These rule-of-law propositions, powerful as their constitutional roots undoubtedly are, remain controversial. Some sentencers will argue that rules, principles, and guidelines can only take the process so far. Beyond that, given the diversity of fact situations, everything turns on 'the facts of the case', and 'no two cases are alike'. This line of argument is a plea for ample discretion for sentencers, to allow them to take account of the varying combinations of facts and to individualize the sentence. Strongly inimical to this are mandatory sentences. Thus English law mandates a sentence of life imprisonment for the crime of murder, although it makes provisions for the court to set the minimum term to be served.[7] English law also contains some mandatory minimum sentences that can only be avoided if the court finds 'exceptional circumstances':[8] such sentences constrain judicial discretion severely, preventing the sentencer from taking account of many factors that would normally mitigate the offence. English law also contains some weaker mandatory minimum sentences, termed 'presumptive sentences', which must be imposed

---

[6] Cf. Garland (2000) with Lacey (2008).
[7] This is a simplification: the details may be found in ch.4.4.1 above.
[8] For examples and discussion, see ch. 3.5.1.

unless it is not 'in the interests of justice' to do so.[9] The 'interests of justice' exception is more flexible than 'exceptional circumstances', and it is for discussion whether it prevents sentencers from taking account of factors that would normally mitigate sentence. If we leave out this last, weak form of mandatory sentence, then we can focus on mandatory sentences and mandatory minimum sentences with an 'exceptional circumstances' clause, and we can advance the preliminary conclusion that such laws take the rule-of-law approach too far in that they unduly inhibit the courts from taking account of individual factors relevant to the sentence.

The Australian courts have espoused an extreme version of what may be termed the 'individualization thesis' by promoting a sentencing approach that they call 'instinctive synthesis'. One of its foremost advocates, McHugh J, sought to explain thus the contrast between instinctive synthesis and other ('two-tier') approaches:

> By two-tier sentencing I mean the method of sentencing by which a judge first determines a sentence by reference to the 'objective circumstances' of the case. This is the first tier of the process. The judge then increases or reduces this hypothetical sentence incrementally or decrementally by reference to other factors, usually, but not always, personal to the accused. This is the second tier. By instinctive synthesis, I mean the method of sentencing by which the judge identifies all the factors that are relevant to the sentence, discusses their significance and then makes a value judgment as to what is the appropriate sentence given all the factors of the case. Only at the end of the process does the judge determine the sentence.
>
> The two-tier sentencer contends that using the instinctive synthesis is inimical to the judicial process and is an exercise of arbitrary judicial power, unchecked by the giving of reasons. The two-tier sentencer claims ... that, where the sentence is the result of an instinctive synthesis, it makes one 'wonder whether figures have not just been plucked out of the air'. The instinctive synthesizer, on the other hand, contends that the two-tier sentencer mistakes an illusion of exactitude for the reality of sentencing, because there is no method of sequential arithmetical reasoning that produces the correct sentence for any case. A sentence can only be the product of human judgment, based on all the facts of the case, the judge's experience, the data derived from comparable sentences and the guidelines and principles authoritatively laid down in statutes and authoritative judgments ... The circumstances of criminal cases are so various that they cannot be the subject of mathematical equations ...[10]

---

[9] See further ch. 6.7.

[10] Per McHugh J in *Markarian* v. *R.* [2005] HCA 25, at [51–52]. Other judges have expressed themselves more moderately: thus Gleeson CJ accepted the approach of instinctive synthesis but stated that 'the law strongly favours transparency. Accessible reasoning is necessary in the interests of victims, of the parties, appeal courts and the public. There may be some occasions when some indulgence in an arithmetical process will better serve these ends. This case was not however one of them because of the number and complexity of the considerations which had to be weighed by the trial judge': ibid., at [39].

The logic of this passage is not perfect.[11] In the penultimate sentence McHugh J cites 'guidelines ... laid down in ... authoritative judgments', a concession that seems to acknowledge the role that guidelines could play. The reference in the final sentence to 'mathematical equations' is unconvincing hyperbole. Nonetheless, there are two powerful concerns about justice underlying the instinctive synthesis argument: that discretion is necessary so that the facts of individual cases can be reflected by the sentencer, and that guideline systems are unlikely to specify the weight to be given to all the relevant factors. The first of those points is a strong argument against mandatory sentences. The more pressing question is whether the rule of law requires common starting points and sentence ranges of the kind that guideline systems aim to provide.

The various guideline systems that are in force across the world vary considerably in their effects on judicial discretion. For many years the US federal sentencing guidelines were the most strongly binding, requiring the court to locate the crime within one of 43 'severity levels' and to move a certain number of levels upwards or downwards to take account of other significant factors, then to assess the offender's 'criminal history score', the result of which would be to place the sentence within a fairly narrow range.[12] There is a whole variety of state guideline systems in the United States, but perhaps the best known is that in Minnesota.[13] The Minnesota guidelines divide all offences into just 11 severity levels, and then have 7 criminal history scores (from 0–6), resulting in a grid that resembles a road mileage chart. The sentencer identifies the relevant severity band for this offence, and the relevant criminal history score for this offender, and then finds the square in the grid where they intersect. That is the presumptive sentencing range, from which the court may depart on giving reasons that are open to appellate scrutiny. The legislation allows the judge to depart only on finding 'substantial and compelling' circumstances, but in practice the system is more flexible and some categories have departure rates of around 50 per cent.[14] Thus the Minnesota grid itself looks restrictive and forbidding, but in fact there is considerable room for judicial discretion. Ostensibly less restrictive are the many advisory or voluntary guideline systems in the US in states such as Maryland, Delaware, and Virginia. Many such states have a sentencing grid, but its voluntary status makes ample allowance for judicial discretion. Nevertheless, it appears that compliance rates in some of those states are no lower than for presumptive

---

[11] See also Tonry (1996), pp. 178–9.
[12] As a result of the US Supreme Court's ruling in *United States* v. *Booker* (2005) 543 US 220, the federal guidelines are now advisory only. For discussion, see Stith and Cabranes (1998) and Barkow (2005).
[13] The Minnesota model has been adopted more or less in Kansas, North Carolina, Washington, and Oregon: for analysis, see Frase (2013), ch. 3.
[14] Reitz (2013), p. 194, adding that similar frameworks in Washington and Oregon have also been applied flexibly.

guidelines.[15] Undoubtedly the most significant step in bringing rule-of-law values into sentencing in recent years has been the revision of the sentencing provisions of the Model Penal Code. Under the guiding hand of Kevin Reitz as Reporter, the MPC sets out a principled and integrated set of standards for sentencing, standards that should serve as a reference point for sentencing reforms across the world.[16]

When the question of revising the English approach to guidelines was debated in 2008, the Gage Report was clear from the outset that a grid-style approach, along the lines of many US jurisdictions, would not be considered suitable for use in England and Wales.[17] As noted in Chapter 1.5 above, the narrative style of guidelines was developed in England and Wales by the Court of Appeal, when giving guideline judgments, and was adapted by the Sentencing Guidelines Council in its definitive guidelines. The approach of the Sentencing Council, under the framework of the Coroners and Justice Act 2009, continues to be based on the narrative approach but is veering towards a grid-based structure. There is to be no general sentencing grid covering the major offences, like those in the US federal guidelines or Minnesota. But sentencing for each offence or group of offences is often represented in a form that resembles a grid, and the stepwise approach lends a certain structure of its own to the sentencing exercise. The structure of the post-2010 English guidelines was explained in Chapter 1.5, and will not be set out in full here. Readers will recall that at Step One the court must assess harm and culpability factors so as to place the offence in one of (usually) three categories; at Step Two account should be taken of aggravating factors (including previous convictions) and also personal mitigating factors; subsequent steps involve adjustments for a guilty plea, for totality, and for other factors.

Many of those (particularly judges)[18] who reject the very notion of sentencing guidelines will point to the structure whereby the factors to be taken into account at Step One are exhaustively listed, and the relevant starting point is then indicated by the guideline. They will argue that such a mandatory structure crosses the line by restricting judicial discretion unduly, thus (almost as with mandatory minimum sentences) preventing the court from adjusting the sentence to the facts of the particular case. Against this, it can be argued that the English guidelines incorporate so much flexibility as to take insufficient account of rule-of-law values. Four points may be made briefly in support of this assessment. First, although the Gage Report recommended a

---

[15] Frase (2005), pp. 1198–9, reports that in Virginia trial judges are subject to reappointment by the legislature, and that a high rate of departure from the guidelines is thought to weigh against reappointment.

[16] American Law Institute (2014).

[17] Reitz (2013), pp. 193–6, suggests that this was based, in part at least, on over-reactions to the appearance of the grid rather than on understanding. For a recent overview of US guideline systems, see Frase (2013).

[18] E.g. in Australia (see n. 10 above) and in Scotland (see Tata (2013), pp. 240 and 250).

form of words that would impose on sentencers a duty to follow the guidelines, the Coroners and Justice Act 2009 dilutes that duty almost to vanishing point by applying it to the whole sentence range rather than to the relevant offence category.[19] Secondly, at Step Two the guidelines provide for sentencers to reflect previous convictions, but say absolutely nothing about the way in which the criminal record should be assessed (repeating but not elaborating on the contested concept of 'relevance'). This leaves English sentencers with little guidance: one need not go so far as the 'criminal history scores' used in many US guideline systems, but attention should be paid to the New Zealand guidelines, which are more explicit about the effect of previous convictions on sentence for some crimes.[20] Thirdly, Step Six enshrines the totality principle, when sentencing for multiple offences, but the 'guideline' on totality does little more than state that the overall sentence must be 'just and proportionate'.[21] This leaves courts with considerable discretion. Fourthly, at Step Two there is provision for the courts to take account of aggravating and mitigating factors, including personal mitigation, but nothing is said about the weight to be assigned to these factors. It is no answer to state that the weight must vary according to the facts of the case: that may be conceded, but the point is that courts may vary in their assessment of how much a particular factor should count, taking different views on the relevance to sentence of intoxication in different circumstances, employment history, caring responsibilities, and so forth. These are questions of principle, to be resolved before one reaches the facts of the particular case.[22]

The Gage Report recognized these deficiencies, but concluded in relation to the last three issues that 'no attempt should be made to quantify the weight to be given as this will vary from case to case'. Further guidance is needed, but it 'should be in narrative form'.[23] That recommendation did too little to emphasize the issues of principle involved, and the consequence is that the English guidelines have a considerable degree of built-in flexibility, which sentencers may exploit in order to ensure that the sentence is tailored to the individual case. Whatever restrictions there may be at Step One, in relation to the exhaustive list of factors indicating a particular starting point, those restrictions quickly dissipate at Step Two and onwards. The fear of the Australian judges, particularly McHugh J,[24] that an English-style approach would deprive them of the discretion to do individualized justice is simply not borne out by the guidelines in practice. Indeed, given the absence of principled guidance on the issues set out above, it is rule-of-law values that are compromised, not judicial discretion. The English guidelines provide sentencers

---

[19] For further explanation, see ch. 1.5 above.
[20] The New Zealand sentencing guidelines were drafted in 2008 but have not been implemented: see Young and King (2013).
[21] For further explanation, see ch. 8.3.4.   [22] For further discussion, see ch. 5.6.
[23] Gage Report (2008), p. 24.   [24] Above, n. 10 and accompanying text.

with some orientation at Step One, and that can be claimed to deliver some consistency of approach. But the four points made in the previous paragraph identify considerable weaknesses in the English approach. If one adds to this the great breadth of the category ranges in many of the English guidelines (e.g. for causing grievous bodily harm with intent, 3–5 years, 5–9 years, and 9–16 years),[25] the degree of constraint exerted by the guidelines is considerably muted.

Judicial concern about the possible loss of their discretion to do individualized justice has nonetheless led to strong rearguard actions in several countries. The very idea of guidelines has been regarded as an unwelcome and even unconstitutional intrusion into judicial discretion in many continental European countries,[26] although the first steps towards judge-made sentencing guidelines have recently been taken by the Court of Criminal Appeal in Ireland.[27] In other jurisdictions, calls for sentencing guidelines have been met by different proposals to increase consistency in sentencing. Thus in Scotland, when the introduction of mandatory minimum sentences was being discussed, it was the judges who gave their support instead to the development of a Sentencing Information System.[28] This system categorized information about sentencing practices across Scotland, with a view to informing judges of sentences in similar types of case. Unfortunately, owing to certain controversies, it has been allowed to wither on the vine. Subsequently the judges have given some support to the creation of an Advisory Panel on Sentencing in Scotland, a body designed to conduct research, to consult widely, and to come up with proposed guidelines; but it is clear that the senior judiciary retains the decision-making power in relation to any guidance or guidelines.[29] In Australia, too, calls for greater consistency have been met with the creation of sentencing commissions with an advisory function. The Judicial Commission of New South Wales had some such function for many years, and that state created a Sentencing Council in 2008 with an advisory role. Victoria has a Sentencing Advisory Council tasked with research and the making of recommendations, but there has been only one proposal for a guideline judgment in the last decade which has been referred (as statutorily required) to the SAC for advice. Tasmania also has a Sentencing Advisory Council. These bodies typically make recommendations to the relevant state's Court of Appeal,

---

[25] Sentencing Council, *Assault: Definitive Guideline* (2011), p. 5; in contrast, the ranges in US guideline systems are typically much narrower.

[26] Ashworth (2002), pp. 220–3.

[27] *People (DPP)* v. *Ryan* [2014] IECCA 11, esp. at para. 7.16; *People (DPP)* v. *Fitzgibbon* [2014] IECCA 12, esp. at para. 8.10, and *People (DPP)* v. *Z.* [2014] IECCA 13, all judgments handed down on the same day.

[28] Tata (2013), pp. 244–8. A somewhat similar system had been operating for some years in New South Wales, and is still operating. See generally Miller (2004).

[29] Tata (2013), pp. 249–50.

which may have a statutory power to lay down guidelines and which retains control over the decision-making power.[30]

While the strong judicial concern about loss of discretion has led to this patchwork of other expedients in Scotland and Australia, it appears to have become almost a complete barrier to any similar developments in Canada and in New Zealand. The Canadian judiciary was vocal in rejecting proposals for a sentencing commission to create guidelines in 1988–90, and that remains the situation.[31] In New Zealand, too, the judiciary has played its part: the fact that the guidelines have not yet been implemented is 'testament to the strength of judicial and political views that sentencing is an ad hoc and individualized enterprise which ought to have relatively few systemic constraints'.[32] Given this strong judicial insistence on discretion, why has the English judiciary 'allowed' guidelines to take root? Why have the English judiciary and magistracy – not noted for their reticence, and often powerful in blocking unwanted initiatives – not taken the same course as their common law colleagues? A full answer to this question would involve many details and some conjecture, but four elements will surely be prominent.

First, the judiciary has retained ownership of the guidelines, through its standing majority on the Sentencing Council. The senior judiciary is in a position to ensure that nothing that is too challenging to the traditions of judicial sentencing is endorsed by the Council. After all, it was the English Court of Appeal that pioneered guideline judgments, and judges have had many decades to recognize that narrative guidelines may structure but do not eliminate judicial discretion. Likewise, senior magistrates played a leading role in drafting the guidelines for the lower courts. *Secondly*, the judiciary and magistracy did bring pressure to bear when Parliament was discussing the departure test for the Council's guidelines, and this explains why the relevant provisions in the Coroners and Justice Act 2009 apply only to the broad offence range and not to the specific category range.[33] *Thirdly*, English judges recognize the flexibility inherent in the type of guideline system that started with guideline judgments and now takes the form of definitive guidelines. It is no accident that there is little principled guidance on aggravation and mitigation, on previous convictions, and the totality of sentences. This leaves ample room for the exercise of discretion and individualized justice, subject to appellate control. And *fourthly*, sentencing guidance in England and Wales remains a loose partnership between the Sentencing Council and the Court of Appeal. While the Council issues its guidelines after due consultation and research, the Court of Appeal in occasional judgments continues to give guidance on aspects of sentencing not covered by definitive guidelines.[34]

---

[30] See Freiberg and Gelb (2008), ch. 1, and Freiberg (forthcoming, 2016) for full details.
[31] Doob and Webster (forthcoming, 2016).   [32] Young and King (2013), p. 217; see also p. 209.
[33] See ch. 2.2 above.   [34] See ch.1.5.3(b) for recent examples.

The strong judicial presence described in this paragraph suggests that the fears of the judiciary in other common law countries are exaggerated.

That leads us back to the issues raised earlier. If the English guidelines really are so flexible, do they measure up to rule-of-law values? The answer to this must be in the negative. This is not to doubt the value of the nine-step process established by the Sentencing Council as a means of ensuring commonality of approach. But it is to suggest that the paucity of principled guidance on aggravating and mitigating factors, on previous conviction, and on totality of sentence, allows the Council guidelines to fall below an acceptable level of clarity and consistency. Little better is the neglect of general principles relating to different types of sentence: there is guidance on community sentences, suspended sentence orders, and a number of other forms of sentence, but it is very rarely referred to. The approach to sentencing set out by the Council finds no place for the existing guidelines on general principles. Even its own guideline on totality of sentences is frequently not cited by the Court of Appeal, let alone by trial judges. This leads on to the related question about judicial training. The guidelines and their methodology should be central to the training of judges, as they are for magistrates;[35] this does not seem to be the case. Moreover, there is a need for further research if practical sentencing is to be aligned with rule-of-law values, as well as allowing sufficient discretion. Research that involves observing judges and discussing their approach to particular cases is needed[36] (as well as reversal of the decision to discontinue the CCSS). Two such studies have been started, a Cambridge study – halted in 2008 ostensibly because of data unavailability,[37] and an Oxford study – halted by the then Lord Chief Justice in 1981 on the basis that it would not yield useful information.[38] Research on aggravation and mitigation shows the benefits of this kind of research.[39] It is vital that there should now be a commitment on all sides to see through a broad-based enquiry into sentencing practices, so that a proper understanding of sentencers' behaviour can be obtained. This would help discussions of the most appropriate adjustment between rule-of-law principles and judicial discretion.

14.3 Guidelines and penal moderation

Sentencing guidelines are a tool. They may be used to take sentence levels up or down. Legislative starting points for minimum terms were used by the British Parliament to raise sentence levels for murder in 2003.[40] Many state guideline systems in the USA include an obligation to adjust the guidelines to reflect penal capacity or other restraining factors. This was true of the

---

[35] Cf. Padfield (2013), p. 49.   [36] See ch. 2.2 above.   [37] Dhami and de Souza (2008).
[38] Oxford Pilot Study (1984).   [39] Jacobson and Hough (2007).
[40] See ch. 4.4.1 above. In 2013 the government of Macedonia organised consultations on guidelines as a way of increasing sentence levels in that country.

Minnesota guidelines in the early 1980s: not only did the Sentencing Commission have to take account of prison capacity and correctional resources, but it also had a mandate to reduce imprisonment for property offences and enhance it for violent offences.[41] Other states adopting guidelines have imposed prison capacity constraints. At one stage this was an aspiration for the new Sentencing Council in England and Wales,[42] but the Gage Report considered it and rejected it on grounds of practicability.[43] It is possible that, with improved sentencing statistics of the kind that the (recently abolished) CCSS was providing, any problems of practicability would be overcome. In principle, however, the use of a capacity constraint to control sentence levels is no more than half a loaf. It would certainly be important as a means of eliminating prison overcrowding, with its consequential implications for human rights. But prison capacity can be changed; more prisons can be constructed; and, if that occurs, the total numbers imprisoned could increase.

Given the overuse of imprisonment in England and Wales as compared with its European neighbours, the Council ought to be tasked with a decremental strategy, lowering sentence levels gradually.[44] Its current approach is to try to reproduce existing sentence levels, save in the occasional limited respect in which it tries to lower a sentence level (e.g. for drug mules).[45] In practical terms, however, it is uncertain whether the judicial majority on the Council would be enthusiastic about any such mandate. Under the 2009 Act the Council has the statutory duty to take account of the costs and effectiveness of different forms of sentence: that might lead it to reconsider the length of the sentences handed down, but there is little evidence of this duty being taken seriously.

14.4 Risk, prevention and public protection

While the proportionality principle is said to underlie the sentencing guidelines, based on a reading of s. 143(1) of the Criminal Justice Act 2003, recent years have seen an increasing emphasis on the risk that offenders of certain kinds are believed to present. It can be argued that the state has a duty to protect its citizens and others within its boundaries, and that this duty is heightened where there is a danger to life.[46] The spread of preventive measures has been evident at several points during the chapters of this book, and three examples of the 'preventive state' may be drawn together here – civil preventive orders and similar ancillary orders; the sentencing of recidivists; and indeterminate sentences.

We saw in Chapter 11 that several civil preventive orders are available to courts, both on conviction and (in some instances) without a conviction.

---

[41] Frase (2005). [42] Carter (2007) was attracted to this approach.
[43] Gage Report (2008), p. 28. [44] See further ch. 9.3.1. [45] See ch. 4.4.5.
[46] See further Ashworth and Zedner (2014), ch. 1.

While the ASBO attracted the greatest public and scholarly attention before its replacement by two other orders,[47] measures such as the Sexual Harm Prevention Order[48] and the Sexual Risk Order[49] are among many orders with a similar structure, the former being available only on conviction and the latter being available when a court is persuaded that there is sufficient evidence of risk. Public protection is the rationale for such measures, but major issues of justice and fairness are raised by their format. Their designation as civil orders is intended to reduce procedural protection for persons made subject to them; the prohibitions they contain may be wide-ranging, and may go beyond the evidence provided; and both these elements must be viewed in the context of the criminalization of breach, with a penalty that for many orders is up to 5 years' imprisonment. It is undoubtedly important for the public to be adequately protected, but in view of what is at stake for those made subject to the orders the procedural protections should be no less than those for criminal sentencing.

The legislation on persistent offenders, discussed in Chapter 6.3 above, urges courts to treat each recent and relevant previous conviction as an aggravating factor when sentencing for the current offence. It is one thing to make longer sentences available for repeat sexual and violent offenders.[50] It is quite another thing to allow disproportionate sentences for persistent minor offenders – notably property offenders such as shop thieves, handbag thieves, and pickpockets. It is questionable whether these offences are serious enough in the scale of things to warrant sentences of 3, 4, or 5 years' imprisonment, often accompanied by a vague description such as 'professional' or 'career criminal'. As mentioned in Chapter 6, current guidelines do not take the matter much further. Thus the draft guidelines on theft offences include the following statement:

> In particular, relevant recent convictions may justify an upward adjustment, including outside the category range. In cases involving significant persistent offending, the community and custody thresholds may be crossed even though the other characteristics of the offence would otherwise warrant a lesser sentence.[51]

This wording would allow a court to sentence a repeat thief outside the otherwise appropriate category, without offering any guidance on the features of the criminal record needed to justify this departure from proportionality or on the magnitude of the permissible departure. This is a (lack of) policy that urgently needs to be reconsidered.

---

[47] See ch. 11.5.8 for explanation.   [48] A new order to replace the SOPO: see ch. 11.5.13.

[49] A new order to replace the RSHO: see ch. 11.5.14.

[50] This has been the trend in many jurisdictions: for the Nordic countries, see Lappi-Seppala (forthcoming, 2016); for France, see Hodgson and Soubise (forthcoming, 2016).

[51] Sentencing Council, *Theft Offences Guideline: Consultation* (2014), p. 22.

Provisions on dangerous offenders form a part of many sentencing systems across the world, despite the well-documented problems of identifying the dangerous and the poor prediction rates revealed by almost all studies.[52] What has been different about the English provisions on indeterminate sentences has been their breadth, resulting in a prison population 19 per cent of which consists of prisoners on indeterminate sentences. These numbers are well beyond those of our European neighbours. We noted in Chapter 6.8 above that part of the problem lay in the sentence of imprisonment for public protection (IPP): this sentence was abolished in 2012 and replaced by substantially less extensive measures, but some 5,000 IPP prisoners remain in prison, awaiting release. This is not just a question of prison numbers;[53] it is also a matter of fairness and proportionality. A related cause for concern is the length of minimum terms for murder, which has grown considerably since 2003.[54] Judgments about the need for public protection from a particular individual are being made on speculative bases, and are resulting in incarceration well beyond what our European neighbours would consider appropriate.

A further objection to these three elements of the risk-based penal strategy is that they, like most other severe elements in the criminal justice system, are likely to impinge disproportionately on offenders from disadvantaged backgrounds.[55] In all the debate about sentencing and criminal justice policy in the last few years, the impacts on members of ethnic minorities, on the unemployed, and on the addicted have received little attention; and although the treatment of mentally disordered offenders and of women offenders has received discussion, there has been little by way of concrete changes of approach. Some general points were made on race, poverty, and gender in Chapter 7 above and on mental disorder in Chapter 9.7 and 12.3 above, but one salient feature is the extent to which these and other disadvantaged categories overlap. The criminal justice system, and particularly the prison system, contains a disproportionate number of people with not just one but more than one of these characteristics. Thus black people may be over-represented among the mentally disordered; a high proportion of mentally disordered offenders are unemployed and without settled accommodation; many women offenders are also very poor and/or have a drug or alcohol problem; and so forth. These facts, as well known to the government as to criminologists, have been marginalized in policy-making and debate, probably because they do not have the vote-winning potential of the dangerousness sentences or the approach to persistent offenders.

---

[52] See generally ch. 6.8 above.
[53] Strong criticisms were voiced by the Chief Inspector of Prisons: see ch. 9.6 above.
[54] See ch. 4.4.1 above.
[55] See Bateman (2011), cited in ch. 12.1 in relation to ASSET assessments.

14.5 Stepping back from the punitive state

Two of the major themes running through this book are the importance of bringing rule-of-law values further into sentencing and the need to question the relatively high use of imprisonment in sentencing in England and Wales. Most of the emphasis in this chapter so far has been on rule-of-law values, but parts 14.3 and 14.4 have begun to raise questions about penal excesses and penal moderation.[56] The use of imprisonment in England and Wales is pro rata around double that in Germany, the Netherlands, and the Nordic countries, and there would seem to be no persuasive criminological reason for that. How could English sentence levels be brought closer to the levels in those neighbouring countries?

It has been argued that one reason for the high use of custody in UK jurisdictions is the nature of our political system. As argued in Chapter 9.2.1 above, there is a difference between social democratic systems and neo-liberal systems in relation to penal policy. The work of Cavadino and Dignan,[57] Lacey[58] and Lappi-Seppala[59] emphasizes the social and political locus of criminal justice in general and sentencing in particular. However, this focus on the broad socio-economic, cultural, and political conditions only takes the analysis so far. Account should also be taken of the 'different institutional structures [that] affect the way in which popular conceptions [of deserved punishment] feed into the development and implementation of policy'.[60] It is not only that the corporatist/social democratic approach in Germany means that there is little political or legal discussion of sentencing reform. There are also important institutional features such as the form of German legal education (inculcating certain values) and the selection of career judges from the top law school graduates.[61] Thus Garland argues that, in explaining penal trends and possible futures, more attention should be paid to the institutions of the 'penal state', particularly the policy-making processes in a particular jurisdiction. It seems quite possible that the career judiciary in many continental European systems is a force for moderation, perhaps because the judges accept the idea of education and training to a much greater extent than their English counterparts, who come to the judiciary with many years of experience in the courts and tend to be somewhat resistant to the idea of further 'education'. However, this is likely to be no more than a single element in a complex explanation that might include the acceptance in government circles of the belief that the declining crime rate is attributable to harsher sentencing,[62] and the prevalence of a belief that any attempt to scale back penalties would be politically disastrous, a belief so strong that even in times of austerity the

---

[56] See further Loader (2010).   [57] Cavadino and Dignan (2006).   [58] Lacey (2008).
[59] Lappi-Seppala (2013).   [60] Lacey (2008), p. 19.   [61] Hoernle (2013).
[62] Cf. Garland (2014), p. 68, where it is argued that crime rates and punishment levels are not unconnected, even if they do not stand in a hydraulic relationship.

economic arguments for reducing the costs of imprisonment have been restricted to making prisons cheaper rather than reducing the lengths of prison sentences and the numbers imprisoned.[63]

The unavoidable complexity of the explanatory framework is illustrated by the story of youth sentencing in the last decade, outlined in Chapter 12.1. Going against all that has happened in adult imprisonment, it has proved possible to reduce the use of custody for youths to around one-third of its level seven or eight years ago. Various influences have been suggested – the decision of the Youth Justice Board to target high-custody areas in order to demonstrate the benefits of community sentences, a provision in the Criminal Justice and Immigration Act 2008 requiring a court to give reasons for not imposing a youth rehabilitation order before it sends the young person to custody, and the moderate SGC guidelines on youth sentencing and their use in training magistrates. There is no definitive explanation, but perhaps the most important element is 'the dog that did not bark'. The media seem not to have noticed this dramatic reduction, and have not publicized it. One cannot imagine a similar reduction in adult imprisonment occurring without a furore in the press. Moreover, such a sharp reduction in custody was not part of a concerted policy involving the relevant government departments, the Youth Justice Board, and sentencers. It is consistent with the longstanding policy of the YJB, a key institution of the English penal state, but the precise mechanics remain obscure.

---

[63] Cf. some jurisdictions in the USA, particularly California, where considerations of cost have been invoked in order to drive prison numbers down from their previous heights: Reitz (2013), pp. 188–9.

Appendix A
Selected Statutory Provisions

Criminal Justice Act 2003:

s. 143 *Determining the seriousness of an offence*

(1) In considering the seriousness of any offence, the court must consider the offender's culpability in committing the offence and any harm which the offence caused, was intended to cause or might foreseeably have caused.

(2) In considering the seriousness of an offence ('the current offence') committed by an offender who has one or more previous convictions, the court must treat each previous conviction as an aggravating factor if (in the case of that conviction) the court considers that it can reasonably be so treated having regard, in particular, to:

(a) the nature of the offence to which the conviction relates and its relevance to the current offence, and

(b) the time that has elapsed since the conviction . . .

s. 144 *Reduction in sentences for guilty pleas*

(1) In determining what sentence to pass on an offender who has pleaded guilty to an offence in proceedings before that or another court, a court must take into account –

(a) the stage in the proceedings for the offence at which the offender indicated his intention to plead guilty, and

(b) the circumstances in which this indication was given.

(2) In the case of an offence the sentence for which falls to be imposed under subsection (2) of section 110 or 111 of the Sentencing Act, nothing in that subsection prevents the court, after taking into account any matter referred to in subsection (1) of this section, from imposing any sentence which is not less than 80 per cent of that specified in that subsection . . .

s. 148 *Restrictions on imposing community sentences*

(1) A court must not pass a community sentence on an offender unless it is of the opinion that the offence, or the combination of the

offence and one or more offences associated with it, was serious enough to warrant such a sentence.

(2) Where a court passes a community sentence which consists of or includes a community order –

   (a) the particular requirement or requirements forming part of the community order must be such as, in the opinion of the court, is, or taken together are, the most suitable for the offender, and

   (b) the restrictions on liberty imposed by the order must be such as in the opinion of the court are commensurate with the seriousness of the offence, or the combination of the offence and one or more offences associated with it . . .

s. 152 *General restrictions on imposing discretionary custodial sentences*

(1) This section applies where a person is convicted of an offence punishable with a custodial sentence other than one –

   (a) fixed by law, or

   (b) [falling to be imposed as a mandatory or prescribed sentence].

(2) The court must not pass a custodial sentence unless it is of the opinion that the offence, or the combination of the offence and one or more offences associated with it, was so serious that neither a fine alone nor a community sentence can be justified for the offence . . .

s. 153 *Length of discretionary custodial sentences: general provision*

(1) This section applies where a court passes a custodial sentence other than one fixed by law or falling to be imposed under section 225 or 226.

(2) [Subject to the provisions for mandatory and prescribed sentences], the custodial sentence must be for the shortest term (not exceeding the permitted maximum) that in the opinion of the court is commensurate with the seriousness of the offence, or the combination of the offence and one or more offences associated with it . . .

Coroners and Justice Act 2009:

s. 120 *Sentencing guidelines*

(3) The Council must prepare –

   (a) sentencing guidelines about the discharge of a court's duty under section 144 of the Criminal Justice Act 2003 (reduction in sentences for guilty pleas), and

   (b) sentencing guidelines about the application of any rule of law as to the totality of sentences . . .

(11) When exercising functions under this section, the Council must have regard to the following matters—

(a) the sentences imposed by courts in England and Wales for offences;

(b) the need to promote consistency in sentencing;

(c) the impact of sentencing decisions on victims of offences;

(d) the need to promote public confidence in the criminal justice system;

(e) the cost of different sentences and their relative effectiveness in preventing re-offending;

(f) the results of monitoring carried out under section 128 ...

s. 125 *Sentencing guidelines: duty of court*

(1) Every court –

(a) must, in sentencing an offender, follow any guidelines which are relevant to the offender's case, and

(b) must, in exercising any other functions relating to the sentencing of offenders, follow any sentencing guidelines which are relevant to the exercise of the function

unless the court is satisfied that it would be contrary to the interests of justice to do so ...

(3) The duty imposed on a court by subsection (1)(a) to follow any sentencing guidelines which are relevant to the offender's case includes –

(a) in all cases, a duty to impose on P, in accordance with the offence-specific guidelines, a sentence which is within the offence range, and

(b) where the offence-specific guidelines describe categories of case in accordance with section 121(2), a duty to decide which of the categories most resembles P's case in order to identify the sentencing starting point in the offence range;

but nothing in this section imposes on the court a separate duty, in a case within paragraph (b), to impose a sentence which is within the category range.

(4) Subsection 3(b) does not apply if the court is of the opinion that, for the purpose of identifying the sentence within the offence range which is the appropriate starting point, none of the categories sufficiently resembles P's case.

. . .

s. 128 *Monitoring*

(1) The Council must –

(a) monitor the operation and effect of its sentencing guidelines, and

(b) consider what conclusions can be drawn from the information obtained by virtue of paragraph (a).

(2) The Council must, in particular, discharge its duty under subsection (1)(a) with a view to drawing conclusions about –

(a) the frequency with which, and extent to which, courts depart from sentencing guidelines;

(b) the factors which influence the sentences imposed by courts;

(c) the effect of the guidelines on the promotion of consistency in sentencing;

(d) the effect of the guidelines on the promotion of public confidence in the criminal justice system . . .

Appendix B:
Statistical Tables

Table 1 *Summary of criminal justice statistics, 1951, 1961, 1971, 1981, 1991, 2001, 2007, 2013*

	1951	1961	1971	1981	1991	2001[7]	2007[7]	2013
England and Wales					(000)			
Crime measured by British Crime Survey	[1]	[1]	[1]	11,046	15,125	13,037	10,143	7,333
Notifiable offences								
– offences recorded by the police[2]	525	807	1,666[3]	2,794	5,075	5,525	4,951	3,507
– offences detected	247	361	775[3]	1,056	1,479	1,291	1,374	–
– detection rate (percentage)	47	45	45[3]	38	29	23	28	–
Number of offenders cautioned[4]	[6]	70	109	154	279	230	363	176
of which Indictable offences[5]	[6]	25	77	104	180	144	205	91
Defendants proceeded against at magistrates' courts	736	1,161	1,796	2,294	1,985	1,838	1,733	1,407
of which Indictable offences[5]	122	159	374	523	510	501	–	362
Defendants found guilty at magistrates' courts	705	1,121	1,648	2,042	1,438	1,293	1,351	1,091
of which Indictable offences[5]	115	151	282	402	269	270	252	225
Defendants sentenced at the Crown Court after summary convictions	3	4	14	14	7	16	5	18
Defendants tried at the Crown Court	20	34	48	79	100	77	83	83
Defendants found guilty at the Crown Court	18	31	40	63	81	56	65	68
Total offenders found guilty at both courts	723	1,152	1,688	2,105	1,519	1,350	1,416	1,172
of which Indictable offences[5]	133	182	342	465	347	324	313	294
Total offenders found guilty or cautioned[4]	723[6]	1,222	1,797	2,259	1,796	1,580	1,489	1,353
of which Indictable offences[5]	133[6]	207	419	568	527	468	473	388

[1] The British Crime Survey did not commence until 1982, where interviews were based on the previous year's experience of crime.
[2] Excluding other criminal damage of value £20 and under. Includes estimates for criminal damage over £20 for Merseyside and Metropolitan Police. Figures were affected by the new counting rules from 1998 onwards and by the NCRS from 2001–2 onwards.
[3] Adjusted to take account of the Criminal Damage Act 1971.
[4] Cautions, written warnings and all fixed penalties for summary motoring offences are not covered in this volume but are published in the Home Office Statistical Bulletin 'Motoring offences and breath tests'.
[5] Indictable offences include those triable either way.
[6] Cautions figures were not collected until 1954.
[7] Both British Crime Survey data and notifiable offences data are for the financial years, i.e. 2001–2 and 2007–8.
Source: Criminal Statistics 2003, 2007, 2014 Table 1.1.

Table 2 *Male offenders aged 21 and over sentenced by disposals, 1997–2013*

| | All Courts | | | | | | | |
	Absolute discharge	Conditional discharge	Fine	Suspended sentence order	Community sentence	Immediate custody	Otherwise dealt with	Total offenders sentenced
MALES								
1997	12,694	54,022	721,349	2,747	76,877	66,417	13,510	947,616
1998	12,373	55,627	761,907	2,664	79,966	70,966	14,415	997,918
1999	10,808	54,559	716,102	2,403	78,831	73,527	15,284	951,514
2000	10,206	52,383	703,703	2,355	77,459	73,995	14,603	934,704
2001	9,777	53,169	642,609	2,115	79,646	74,183	15,520	877,019
2002	10,026	55,994	674,684	1,889	87,962	79,600	17,654	927,810
2003	9,322	60,266	731,687	2,093	92,670	78,619	20,405	994,992
2004	8,303	56,812	766,673	2,083	98,923	77,870	25,532	1,036,196
2005	7,115	53,796	716,021	7,526	98,178	74,092	24,166	980,894
2006	6,284	50,309	665,665	25,253	88,192	69,397	26,332	931,432
2007	5,670	54,010	643,216	30,538	88,472	68,563	23,425	913,894
2008	4,825	49,802	583,620	30,073	87,863	73,160	27,279	856,622
2009	4,476	47,113	594,104	33,638	94,053	74,114	16,015	863,513
2010	4,291	51,614	559,550	36,104	96,192	76,644	19,573	843,968
2011	4,194	49,931	526,067	36,025	91,502	81,848	19,874	809,441
2012	3,951	47,724	496,414	33,101	81,984	77,571	18,582	759,327
2013	4,102	45,797	477,613	37,264	69,590	75,362	21,453	731,181

Source: Sentencing Statistics (Ministry of Justice 2008) Table 1.5; *Sentencing Statistics Supplementary Tables* (Ministry of Justice 2014) Table A5.1.

Table 3 *Female offenders aged 21 and over sentenced by disposals, 1997–2013*

| | All Courts | | | | | | | |
	Absolute discharge	Conditional discharge	Fine	Suspended sentence order	Community sentence	Immediate custody	Otherwise dealt with	Total offenders sentenced
FEMALES								
1997	2,610	15,842	151,441	744	13,188	4,556	1,830	190,211
1998	2,469	16,485	163,568	784	14,642	5,380	2,114	205,442
1999	2,455	15,871	147,790	758	15,245	6,123	2,449	190,700
2000	2,644	15,946	182,300	717	15,608	6,337	2,362	225,914
2001	2,501	16,226	163,376	640	16,124	6,546	2,698	208,111
2002	2,592	17,420	180,061	630	17,628	7,228	3,203	228,763
2003	2,219	18,544	180,329	624	17,418	7,413	3,675	230,222
2004	1,921	17,788	196,500	772	18,411	7,491	5,160	248,043
2005	1,719	16,636	200,782	1,499	18,207	6,898	4,386	250,127
2006	1,589	15,452	195,988	4,069	16,268	6,540	5,102	245,008
2007	1,436	16,610	204,612	5,042	16,631	6,522	4,378	255,231
2008	1,338	16,179	198,590	5,377	17,431	7,124	7,475	253,514
2009	1,277	16,075	225,465	6,203	19,227	6,913	3,235	278,395
2010	1,279	17,448	216,940	6,420	20,026	7,199	3,463	272,775
2011	1,260	17,164	214,714	6,851	19,431	7,562	3,455	270,437
2012	1,215	16,021	219,411	6,447	17,226	7,015	3,306	270,641
2013	1,210	15,429	214,639	6,745	15,194	6,681	4,126	264,024

Source: Sentencing Statistics (Ministry of Justice 2008) Table 1.5; *Sentencing Statistics Supplementary Tables* (Ministry of Justice 2014) Table A5.1.

Table 4 *Male offenders aged 18-20 sentenced by disposals, 1997-2013*

				All Courts				
	Absolute discharge	Conditional discharge	Fine	Suspended sentence order	Community sentence	Immediate custody	Otherwise dealt with	Total offenders sentenced
MALES								
1997	1,630	12,535	86,085	–	20,714	15,143	3,022	139,129
1998	1,606	13,282	90,942	–	22,730	16,152	3,156	147,868
1999	1,419	13,684	87,676	–	23,557	17,048	3,619	147,003
2000	1,377	12,605	84,999	–	23,101	17,324	3,418	142,824
2001	1,251	12,755	82,122	–	23,115	16,882	3,794	139,919
2002	1,332	12,630	83,401	–	23,443	16,290	3,818	140,914
2003	1,340	12,963	87,255	–	23,491	14,465	3,851	143,365
2004	1,022	11,818	82,262	–	24,260	13,817	4,553	137,732
2005	958	10,901	73,613	567	23,676	13,351	4,236	127,302
2006	839	10,686	68,859	3,740	22,089	13,046	4,401	123,660
2007	767	11,807	63,208	4,597	22,462	13,487	4,442	120,770
2008	689	10,334	60,414	4,973	21,155	12,622	4,393	114,580
2009	621	9,861	61,493	4,610	22,693	13,155	3,251	115,684
2010	644	10,295	53,884	4,807	21,629	12,442	3,956	107,657
2011	522	8,949	47,888	4,496	19,284	11,655	3,771	96,565
2012	485	7,953	39,253	4,308	14,907	9,385	2,515	78,806
2013	406	6,942	33,200	3,755	11,476	7,612	2,028	65,419

Source: Sentencing Statistics (Ministry of Justice 2008) Table 1.5. *Sentencing Statistics Supplementary Tables* (Ministry of Justice 2014) Table A5.1.

Table 5 *Female offenders aged 18-20 sentenced by disposals, 1997-2013*

				All Courts				
	Absolute discharge	Conditional discharge	Fine	Suspended sentence order	Community sentence	Immediate custody	Otherwise dealt with	Total offenders sentenced
FEMALES								
1997	201	2,887	10,650	–	2,681	642	269	17,330
1998	–	3,098	11,648	–	3,109	851	332	19,254
1999	216	3,052	10,416	–	3,377	963	385	18,409
2000	168	3,048	11,162	–	3,398	1,117	373	19,266
2001	146	2,848	10,328	–	3,253	1,066	347	17,988
2002	172	2,787	10,711	–	3,300	1,073	427	18,470
2003	–	2,751	11,386	–	2,989	973	428	18,702
2004	130	2,542	11,401	–	3,213	819	562	18,667
2005	141	2,345	11,738	71	3,080	880	494	18,749
2006	132	2,174	12,051	447	2,790	851	589	19,034
2007	144	2,346	12,328	510	2,852	804	522	19,506
2008	127	2,236	13,699	582	2,988	789	709	21,130
2009	112	2,247	15,891	553	3,289	806	430	23,328
2010	111	2,356	13,777	636	3,011	739	489	21,119
2011	121	2,092	13,688	551	2,621	587	497	20,157
2012	101	1,602	11,994	471	2,078	512	343	17,101
2013	104	1,438	9,721	432	1,613	327	253	13,888

Source: Sentencing Statistics (Ministry of Justice 2008) Table 1.5; *Sentencing Statistics Supplementary Tables* (Ministry of Justice 2014) Table A5.1.

Table 6 *Male offenders aged 10–17 sentenced by disposals, 1997–2013*

					All Courts			
	Absolute discharge	Conditional discharge	Fine	Suspended sentence order	Community sentence	Immediate custody	Otherwise dealt with	Total offenders sentenced
MALES								
1997	770	20,149	16,627	–	23,619	6,775	1,707	69,647
1998	703	21,640	18,659	–	25,640	6,881	1,973	75,496
1999	639	22,144	18,861	–	27,076	7,244	3,298	79,262
2000	923	18,066	19,680	–	31,353	6,968	3,580	80,570
2001	1,200	13,526	20,325	–	37,117	7,147	4,772	84,087
2002	4,191	8,183	14,077	–	46,677	6,886	3,172	83,186
2003	4,979	7,328	12,630	–	46,975	5,776	3,150	80,838
2004	2,935	7,975	14,712	–	48,983	5,881	2,927	83,413
2005	2,574	7,671	13,113	–	51,005	5,512	2,587	82,465
2006	2,467	7,384	10,900	–	51,163	5,730	2,492	80,136
2007	2,438	7,798	9,629	–	54,873	5,361	2,519	82,619
2008	2,126	7,067	8,107	–	49,274	5,030	2,417	74,021
2009	1,840	6,416	7,091	–	45,757	4,532	2,205	67,841
2010	1,943	6,553	5,742	–	39,361	3,935	4,611	62,145
2011	1,578	5,820	4,649	–	34,561	3,905	3,087	53,600
2012	1,281	4,464	3,321	–	26,728	2,862	1,686	40,342
2013	818	4,030	2,465	–	19,999	2,196	1,062	30,570

Source: Sentencing Statistics (Ministry of Justice 2008) Table 1.5. *Sentencing Statistics Supplementary Tables* (Ministry of Justice 2014) Table A5.1.

Table 7 *Female offenders aged 10–17 sentenced by disposals, 1997–2013*

					All Courts			
	Absolute discharge	Conditional discharge	Fine	Suspended sentence order	Community sentence	Immediate custody	Otherwise dealt with	Total offenders sentenced
FEMALES								
1997		4,108	1,833	–	2,911	308	194	9,445
1998		4,420	2,391	–	3,301	336	244	10,798
1999		4,582	–	–	3,547	409	427	10,898
2000		3,559	1,711	–	4,619	446	477	10,910
2001	136	2,648	–	–	5,742	449	709	11,398
2002	519	1,294	1,043	–	7,510	530	466	11,362
2003	614	1,195	878	–	8,138	424	444	11,693
2004	473	1,300	954	–	9,156	444	448	12,775
2005	489	1,321	941	–	10,101	503	383	13,738
2006	439	1,351	699	–	10,335	453	393	13,670
2007	531	1440	824	–	11,134	469	370	14,768
2008	470	1,249	801	–	10,390	446	338	13,694
2009	404	1,289	720	–	9,906	381	392	13,092
2010	389	1,167	606	–	8,143	258	637	11,200
2011	322	1,004	484	–	6,748	269	444	9,271
2012	263	763	316	–	4,894	182	232	6,650
2013	159	694	265	–	3,761	117	117	5,113

Source: Sentencing Statistics (Ministry of Justice 2008) Table 1.5. *Sentencing Statistics Supplementary Tables* (Ministry of Justice 2014) Table A5.1.

Table 8 Male population in prison establishments and police cells; by type of custody, sentence length and age group. England and Wales, 30 June, 2002–2013

	2002	2003	2004	2005	2006	2007	2008	2009	2010	2011	2012	2013
Total population in **prison and police cells**, of which	66,824	69,062	70,036	71,676	73,519	75,451	78,689	79,084	80,735	81,189	81,925	83,842
Remand	12,083	12,001	11,544	11,863	12,165	11,953	12,566	12,463	12,218	11,717	10,691	10,971
Untried	7,351	7,339	7,198	7,536	7,554	7,795	8,177	8,208	7,981	7,796	7,212	7,743
Convicted unsentenced	4,732	4,662	4,346	4,327	4,611	4,158	4,389	4,255	4,237	3,921	3,479	3,228
Under sentence	53,967	55,962	57,523	58,780	59,981	62,250	64,699	65,133	67,561	68,542	70,085	70,913
Fine defaulter	31	43	48	77	83	62	99	86	111	118	109	132
Less than or equal to 6 months	5,032	5,479	5,286	5,518	5,467	4,699	5,321	4,648	4,820	4,939	4,504	4,643
Greater than 6 months to less than 12 months	2,155	2,037	2,110	2,038	2,273	2,250	2,600	2,238	2,303	2,162	2,264	2,153
12 months or less than 4 years	20,466	19,994	20,103	20,337	20,327	21,601	22,326	19,201	19,698	19,203	20,122	19,373
4 years or more (excluding Indeterminate)	21,301	23,155	24,564	25,113	24,783	24,456	23,318	21,407	22,706	23,406	24,520	26,322
Indeterminate sentences	4,982	5,254	5,412	5,697	7,048	9,182	11,035	11,813	12,753	13,267	13,360	13,182
Recalls	–	–	–	–	–	–	–	5,740	5,170	5,447	5,206	5,108
Non-criminal prisoners	774	1,099	969	1,033	1,373	1,248	1,424	1,488	956	930	1,149	1,958
Total adult population in **prison**, of which	55,873	58,577	59,764	61,372	62,818	64,064	67,812	68,616	70,902	72,041	73,511	76,704
Remand	9,558	9,765	9,273	9,598	9,714	9,539	10,141	10,062	9,951	9,665	8,970	9,526
Untried	5,905	5,982	5,825	6,162	6,049	6272	6,720	6,671	6,471	6,457	6,054	6,728
Convicted unsentenced	3,653	3,783	3,448	3,436	3,665	3267	3,421	3,391	3,480	3,208	2,916	2,798
Under sentence	45,599	47,798	49,598	50,844	51,845	53,351	56,363	57,171	60,057	61,506	63,479	65,353
Fine defaulter	31	40	43	75	79	58	93	83	106	112	105	129
Less than or equal to 6 months	3,776	4,190	4,068	4,242	4,209	3,387	4,047	3,681	3,875	4,051	3,747	4,069
Greater than 6 months to less than 12 months	1,456	1,467	1,467	1,459	1,670	1,608	1,933	1,684	1,778	1,700	1,838	1,871
12 months to less than 4 years	15,813	15,626	16,020	16,177	16,069	17,016	18,044	15,486	16,104	15,904	16,857	16,605
4 years or more (excluding Indeterminate)	19,688	21,380	22,741	23,375	23,142	22,766	21,898	19,870	21,166	21,858	23,058	24,924
Indeterminate sentences	4,835	5,095	5,259	5,516	6,676	8,517	10,348	11,253	12,315	12,922	13,074	12,956
Recalls	–	–	–	–	–	–	–	5,114	4,713	4,959	4,800	4,799
Non-criminal prisoners	716	1,014	893	930	1,259	1,174	1,308	1,383	894	870	1,062	1,825

Table 8 (*cont.*)

	2002	2003	2004	2005	2006	2007	2008	2009	2010	2011	2012	2013
Remand	2,035	1,784	1,780	1,794	1,896	1,889	1,846	1,899	1,801	1,629	1,444	1,261
Untried	1,142	1,041	1,051	1,048	1,138	1162	1,097	1,184	1,143	1,014	936	870
Convicted unsentenced	893	743	729	746	758	727	749	715	658	615	508	391
Under sentence	6,382	6,440	6,219	6,156	6,322	7,072	6,460	6,401	6,342	5,902	5,627	4,879
Fine defaulter	0	3	5	2	4	4	6	3	5	6	4	3
Less than or equal to 6 months	843	887	802	795	790	856	806	650	710	655	569	443
Greater than 6 months to less than 12 months	418	319	379	326	349	385	390	340	361	298	293	207
12 months to less than 4 years	3,548	3,445	3,212	3,274	3,347	3,662	3,376	2,976	3,042	2,760	2,762	2,404
4 years or more (excluding Indeterminate)	1,454	1,641	1,684	1,595	1,503	1,570	1,276	1,383	1,409	1,425	1,347	1,309
Indeterminate sentences	120	144	138	164	329	596	606	505	387	307	255	208
Recalls	–	–	–	–	–	–	–	544	428	451	397	305
Non-criminal prisoners	57	85	75	100	113	72	115	105	62	59	85	132
Total 15–17-year-olds in **prison**, of which	2,477	2,176	2,198	2,254	2,370	2,354	2,456	2,063	1,628	1,558	1,258	866
Remand	490	452	491	471	555	525	580	502	466	423	277	184
Untried	304	316	322	326	367	361	360	353	367	325	222	145
Convicted unsentenced	186	136	169	145	188	164	219	149	99	98	55	39
Under sentence	1,986	1,724	1,706	1,780	1,814	1,827	1,876	1,561	1,162	1,134	979	681
Fine defaulter	0	0	0	0	0	0	0	0	0	0	0	0
Less than or equal to 6 months	413	401	416	481	468	457	467	317	235	233	188	131
Greater than 6 months to less than 12 months	282	251	265	254	254	258	277	214	164	164	133	75
12 months to less than 4 years	1,105	923	871	886	911	923	906	739	552	539	503	364
4 years or more (excluding Indeterminate)	159	134	139	143	138	120	144	154	131	123	115	89
Indeterminate sentences	27	15	15	17	43	69	81	55	51	38	31	18
Recalls	–	–	–	–	–	–	–	82	29	37	9	4
Non-criminal prisoners	1	0	1	3	1	2	1	0	0	1	2	1

Source: Offender Management Statistics (Ministry of Justice 2008), Table 7.1; Offender Management Statistics (Ministry of Justice 2014), Table A1.1.

Table 9 Female population in prison establishments and police cells; by type of custody, sentence length and age group. England and Wales, 30 June, 2002-2013

	2002	2003	2004	2005	2006	2007	2008	2009	2010	2011	2012	2013
Total population in **prison and police cells**, of which	4,394	4,595	4,452	4,514	4,463	4,283	4,505	4,307	4,267	4,185	4,123	3,853
Remand	998	1,072	951	1,001	902	891	874	813	786	747	633	601
Untried	526	557	518	548	510	592	573	522	506	503	459	451
Convicted unsentenced	472	515	433	453	392	299	301	291	280	244	174	150
Under sentence	3,339	3,477	3,453	3,477	3,512	3,351	3,535	3,427	3,439	3,422	3,477	3,214
Fine defaulter	3	3	4	1	6	6	11	13	18	11	18	20
Less than or equal to 6 months	415	490	466	492	492	466	552	483	523	502	499	442
Greater than 6 months to less than 12 months	194	172	195	186	252	211	266	195	199	211	209	152
12 months to less than 4 years	1,392	1,384	1,333	1,291	1,292	1,239	1,306	1,161	1,159	1,189	1,182	1,044
4 years or more (excluding Indeterminate)	1,170	1,261	1,273	1,322	1,243	1,130	1,053	988	979	933	964	940
Indeterminate sentences	165	167	182	185	227	299	347	369	381	377	394	403
Recalls	–	–	–	–	–	–	–	218	180	199	211	213
Non-criminal prisoners	57	46	48	36	49	41	96	67	42	16	13	38
Total adult population in **prison**, of which	3,735	4,038	3,936	4,018	3,986	3,787	4,030	3,883	3,866	3,825	3,812	3,657
Remand	832	915	822	866	770	756	767	708	696	662	566	558
Untried	437	488	442	471	428	513	503	453	449	448	411	417
Convicted unsentenced	395	427	380	395	342	243	264	255	247	214	155	141
Under sentence	2,852	3,078	3,067	3,122	3,173	2,992	3,175	3,110	3,130	3,147	3,233	3,063
Fine defaulter	3	3	4	1	5	6	11	12	18	11	18	20
Less than or equal to 6 months	324	419	384	421	429	367	460	408	460	451	451	407
Greater than 6 months to less than 12 months	141	142	167	161	227	192	233	175	178	192	188	139
12 months to less than 4 years	1,139	1,171	1,142	1,110	1,112	1,079	1,153	1,039	1,021	1,060	1,079	993
4 years or more (excluding Indeterminate)	1,093	1,184	1,198	1,256	1,187	1,065	990	929	928	887	921	909
Indeterminate sentences	152	159	172	173	213	283	329	358	365	364	380	394
Recalls	–	–	–	–	–	–	–	189	160	182	196	201
Non-criminal prisoners	51	45	47	30	43	39	88	65	40	16	13	36
Total young adults in **prison**, of which	544	479	439	424	407	421	405	367	373	337	287	188
Remand	153	137	111	120	113	116	93	93	85	78	59	43
Untried	84	57	66	66	68	65	64	59	53	50	42	34

Table 9 (*cont.*)

	2002	2003	2004	2005	2006	2007	2008	2009	2010	2011	2012	2013
Convicted unsentenced	69	80	44	54	45	51	29	34	32	28	17	9
Under sentence	384	342	328	300	289	303	303	272	286	259	228	143
Fine defaulter	0	0	0	0	1	0	0	1	0	0	0	0
Less than or equal to 6 months	70	60	62	49	50	78	72	62	58	50	47	34
Greater than 6 months to less than 12 months	33	26	20	23	19	17	26	15	17	17	18	10
12 months to less than 4 years	198	177	166	151	151	134	129	106	128	122	95	48
4 years or more (excluding Indeterminate)	72	73	70	65	55	61	58	52	51	43	40	31
Indeterminate sentences	12	7	10	12	13	13	18	9	13	10	14	8
Recalls	–	–	–	–	–	–	–	27	19	17	14	12
Non-criminal prisoners	6	0	0	4	6	2	8	2	2	0	0	2
Total 15–17-year-olds in **prison**, of which	115	78	77	72	70	75	70	57	28	23	24	8
Remand	13	20	18	15	19	19	14	12	5	7	8	0
Untried	5	12	10	11	14	14	6	10	4	5	6	0
Convicted unsentenced	8	8	9	4	5	5	8	2	1	2	2	0
Under sentence	103	57	58	55	50	56	57	45	23	16	16	8
Fine defaulter	0	0	0	0	0	0	0	0	0	0	0	0
Less than or equal to 6 months	22	11	19	21	13	20	20	13	5	1	1	1
Greater than 6 months to less than 12 months	20	4	9	3	6	3	7	5	4	2	3	3
12 months to less than 4 years	55	37	25	30	29	26	24	16	10	7	8	3
4 years or more (excluding Indeterminate)	5	4	5	1	1	4	6	7	0	3	3	0
Indeterminate sentences	1	1	0	0	1	3	0	2	3	3	0	1
Recalls	–	–	–	–	–	–	–	2	1	0	0	0
Non-criminal prisoners	0	1	1	2	0	0	0	0	0	0	0	0

Source: Offender Management Statistics (Ministry of Justice 2008), Table 7.1; *Offender Management Statistics* (Ministry of Justice 2014), Table A1.1.

Table 10 *Empirical, Recommended and Expected Reductions, CCSS*[1]

	⅓ or greater	21–32%	11–20%	1–10%	Nil	Recommended	Expected Reduction
Early plea cases	89%	9%	2%	<.05%	<.5%	33%	32%
Inter-mediate cases	37%	34%	22%	6%	1%	25%	23%
Late plea cases	12%	9%	24%	49%	6%	10%	13%

[1] Roberts (2013), p. 116.

Table 11 *Persons sentenced for indictable offences by previous convictions (percentages)*[2]

No. of convictions	2006	2007	2008	2009	2010	2011	2012	2013
0	21	21	20	20	20	19	17	17
1–2	18	18	17	17	17	17	16	15
3–6	19	19	18	18	18	17	17	17
7–10	12	12	12	11	11	11	11	11
11–14	9	8	9	8	8	8	8	8
15+	23	23	25	26	26	28	31	33

[2] Ministry of Justice (2014), Table A6.2.

Table 12 *Offenders aged 21 and over, selected sentences 2005-2013*

	Magistrates' courts			Crown Court		
	Community sentence	Suspended sentence	Immediate custody	Community sentence	Suspended sentence	Immediate custody
Male						
2005	83,799	5,671	41,290	14,379	1,855	32,802
2007	79,415	19,702	36,316	9,057	10,836	32,247
2009	83,843	19,663	34,999	10,210	13,975	39,115
2010	83,780	20,544	36,363	12,412	15,560	40,281
2011	80,422	20,688	38,317	11,080	15,337	43,531
2012	72,343	18,626	37,486	9,641	14,475	40,085
2013	62,008	20,683	35,922	7,582	16,581	39,440
Female						
2005	15,390	881	4,251	2,817	618	2,647
2007	14,837	2,835	3,860	1,794	2,207	2,662
2009	17,163	3,251	3,838	2,064	2,952	3,075
2010	17,568	3,360	4,218	2,458	3,060	2,981
2011	17,173	3,671	4,248	2,258	3,180	3,314
2012	15,256	3,492	4,205	1,970	2,955	2,810
2013	13,690	3,790	4,122	1,504	2,955	2,559

Source: Sentencing Statistics Supplementary Tables (Ministry of Justice 2014), Table A5.2.

Table 13 *Prison population: offenders under immediate custodial sentences*

Offence	Males				Females			
	1997	2002	2007	2014	1997	2002	2007	2014
Violence	10,033	11,674	16,929	18,694	391	538	687	902
Sexual offences	4,069	5,270	7,287	11,100	8	23	48	92
Burglary	7,976	8,917	7,723	6,926	101	239	197	215
Robbery	6,277	7,208	8,437	8,210	161	314	311	297
Theft etc.	3,929	4,278	3,332	3,852	334	461	374	525
Drugs	6,483	8,749	9,569	9,866	691	1,317	1,044	440
Sentenced total	46,611	53,936	62,188	68,163	2,063	3,336	3,345	3,198

Source: Based on Ministry of Justice 2008, Table 7.2; Ministry of Justice 2014, *Offender Management Statistics Quarterly: April to June 2014, Prison Population 2014*, Table A1.4.

Table 14 *Cautioning rate for young offenders, given as a percentage of offenders found guilty or receiving a reprimand or final warning*

	Boys			Girls		
	10–11	12–14	15–17	10–11	12–14	15–17
1992	96	86	59	99	96	81
1997	93	74	49	98	89	68
2002	83	63	41	94	84	62
2007	87	68	46	94	84	62
2010	84	54	34	94	72	52
2013	84	56	38	90	68	52

Source: *Criminal Justice Statistics 2002*, Table 2.3; *Criminal Justice Statistics 2007*, Table 3.5; *Criminal Justice Statistics 2010*, Table A2.2; *Criminal Justice Statistics 2013*, Table 2.1.

Appendix C
Selected Sentencing Council Guidelines

Guideline for offences of drug importation, from Sentencing Council, Drug Offences Definitive Guideline (2012):

Step One

Determining the offence category

The court should determine the offender's culpability (role) and the harm caused (quantity) with reference to the tables below.

In assessing culpability, the sentencer should weigh up all the factors of the case to determine role. Where there are characteristics present which fall under different role categories, the court should balance these characteristics to reach a fair assessment of the offender's culpability.

In assessing harm, quantity is determined by the weight of the product. Purity is not taken into account at step 1 but is dealt with at step 2.

Where the operation is on the most serious and commercial scale, involving a quantity of drugs significantly higher than category 1, sentences of 20 years and above may be appropriate, depending on the role of the offender.

Culpability demonstrated by offender's role

One or more of these characteristics may demonstrate the offender's role. These lists are not exhaustive.

(cont.)

LEADING role:

- directing or organising buying and selling on a commercial scale;
- substantial links to, and influence on, other in a chain;
- close links to original source;
- expectation of substantial financial gain;
- uses business as cover;
- abuses a position of trust or responsibility.

SIGNIFICANT role:

- operational or management function within a chain;
- involves others in the operation whether by pressure, influence, intimidation or reward;
- motivated by financial or other advantage, whether or not operating alone;
- some awareness and understanding of scale of operation.

LESSER role:

- performs a limited function under direction;
- engaged by pressure, coercion, intimidation;
- involvement through naïvety/exploitation;
- no influence on those above in a chain;
- very little, if any, awareness or understanding of the scale of operation;
- if own operation, solely for own use (considering reasonableness of account in all the circumstances).

Category of harm

Indicative quantity of drug concerned (upon which the starting point is based):

Category 1

- heroin, cocaine – 5kg;
- ecstasy – 10,000 tablets;
- LSD – 250,000 squares;
- amphetamine – 20kg;
- cannabis – 200kg;
- ketamine – 5kg.

(*cont.*)

Category 2

- heroin, cocaine – 1kg;
- ecstasy – 2,000 tablets;
- LSD – 250,000 squares;
- amphetamine – 4kg;
- cannabis – 40kg;
- ketamine – 1kg.

Category 3

- heroin, cocaine – 150kg;
- ecstasy – 300 tablets;
- LSD – 2,500 squares;
- amphetamine – 750g;
- cannabis – 6kg;
- ketamine – 150kg.

Category 4

- heroin, cocaine – 5g;
- ecstasy – 20 tablets;
- LSD – 170 squares;
- amphetamine – 20g;
- cannabis – 100g;
- ketamine – 5g.

Step Two

Starting point and category range

Having determined the category, the court should use the corresponding starting point to reach a sentence within the category range below. The starting point applies to all offenders irrespective of plea or previous convictions. The court should then consider further adjustments within the category range for aggravating or mitigating features, set out over the page. In cases where the offender is regarded as being at the very top of the 'leading' role it may be justifiable for the court to depart from the guideline.

Where the defendant is dependent on or has a propensity to misuse drugs and there is sufficient prospect of success, a community order with a drug rehabilitation requirement under section 209 of the Criminal Justice Act 2003 can be a proper alternative to a short or moderate length custodial sentence.

For **class A** cases, section 110 of the Powers of Criminal Courts (Sentencing) Act 2000 provides that a court should impose a minimum sentence of at least seven years' imprisonment for a third class A trafficking offence except where the court is of the opinion that there are particular circumstances which (a) relate to any of the offences or to the offender; and (b) would make it unjust to do so in all the circumstances.

The table below contains a **non-exhaustive** list of additional factual elements providing the context of the offence and factors relating to the offender. Identify whether any combination of these, or other relevant factors, should result in an upward or downward adjustment from the starting point. In some cases, having considered these factors, it may be appropriate to move outside the identified category range.

For appropriate **class C** ranges, consider the custody threshold as follows:

- has the custody threshold been passed?
- if so, is it unavoidable that a custodial sentence be imposed?
- if so, can that sentence be suspended?

Factors increasing seriousness

Statutory aggravating factors:

Previous convictions, having regard to a) nature of the offence to which conviction relates and relevance to current offence; and b) time elapsed since conviction (see box above if third drug trafficking conviction)

Offender used or permitted a person under 18 to deliver a controlled drug to a third person

Offence committed on bail

Other aggravating factors include:

Sophisticated nature of concealment and/or attempts to avoid detection

Attempts to conceal or dispose of evidence, where not charged separately

Exposure of others to more than usual danger, for example drugs cut with harmful substances

Presence of weapon, where not charged separately

High purity

Failure to comply with current court orders

Offence committed on licence

CLASS A	Leading role	Significant role	Lesser role
Category 1	**Starting point** 14 years' custody	**Starting point** 10 years' custody	**Starting point** 8 years' custody
	Category range 12–16 years' custody	**Category range** 9–12 years' custody	**Category range** 6–9 years' custody
Category 2	**Starting point** 11 years' custody	**Starting point** 8 years' custody	**Starting point** 6 years' custody
	Category range 9–13 years' custody	**Category range** 6 years 6 months' – 10 years' custody	**Category range** 5–7 years' custody
Category 3	**Starting point** 8 years 6 months' custody	**Starting point** 6 years' custody	**Starting point** 4 years 6 months' custody
	Category range 6 years 6 months' – 10 years' custody	**Category range** 5–7 years' custody	**Category range** 3 years 6 months' – 5 years' custody
Category 4	Where the quantity falls below the indicative amount set out for category 4 on the previous page, first identify the role for the importation offence, then refer to the starting point and ranges for possession or supply offences, depending on intent. Where the quantity is significantly larger than the indicative amounts for category 4 but below category 3 amounts, refer to the category 3 ranges above.		

CLASS B	Leading role	Significant role	Lesser role
Category 1	**Starting point** 8 years' custody	**Starting point** 5 years 6 months' custody	**Starting point** 4 years' custody
	Category range 7–10 years' custody	**Category range** 5–7 years' custody	**Category range** 2 years 6 months' – 5 years' custody
Category 2	**Starting point** 6 years' custody	**Starting point** 4 years' custody	**Starting point** 2 years' custody
	Category range 4 years 6 months' – 8 years' custody	**Category range** 2 years 6 months' – 5 years' custody	**Category range** 18 months' – 3 years' custody
Category 3	**Starting point** 4 years' custody	**Starting point** 2 years' custody	**Starting point** 1 year's custody
	Category range 2 years 6 months' – 5 years' custody	**Category range** 18 months' – 3 years' custody	**Category range** 12 weeks' – 18 months' custody
Category 4	Where the quantity falls below the indicative amount set out for category 4 on the previous page, first identify the role for the importation offence, then refer to the starting point and ranges for possession or supply offences, depending on intent. Where the quantity is significantly larger than the indicative amounts for category 4 but below category 3 amounts, refer to the category 3 ranges above.		

CLASS C	Leading role	Significant role	Lesser role
Category 1	**Starting point** 5 years' custody **Category range** 4–8 years' custody	**Starting point** 3 years' custody **Category range** 2–5 years' custody	**Starting point** 18 months' custody **Category range** 1–3 years' custody
Category 2	**Starting point** 3 years 6 months' custody **Category range** 2–5 years' custody	**Starting point** 18 months' custody **Category range** 1–3 years' custody	**Starting point** 26 weeks' custody **Category range** 12 weeks' – 18 months' custody
Category 3	**Starting point** 18 months' custody **Category range** 1–3 years' custody	**Starting point** 26 weeks' custody **Category range** 12 weeks' – 18 months' custody	**Starting point** High level community order **Category range** Medium level community order – 12 weeks' custody
Category 4	Where the quantity falls below the indicative amount set out for category 4 on the previous page, first identity the role for the importation offence, then refer to the starting point and ranges for possession or supply offences, depending on intent. Where the quantity is significantly larger than the indicative amounts for category 4 but below category 3 amounts, refer to the category 3 ranges above.		

Factors reducing seriousness or reflecting personal mitigation

Lack of sophistication as to nature of concealment

Involvement due to pressure, intimidation or coercion falling short of duress, except where already taken into account at step 1

Mistaken belief of the offender regarding the type of drug, taking into account the reasonableness of such belief in all the circumstances

Isolated incident

Low purity

No previous convictions **or** no relevant or recent convictions

Offender's vulnerability was exploited

Remorse

Good character and/or exemplary conduct

Determination and/or demonstration of steps having been taken to address addiction or offending behaviour

Serious medical conditions requiring urgent, intensive or long-term treatment

Age and/or lack of maturity where it affects the responsibility of the offender

Mental disorder or learning disability

Sole or primary carer for dependent relatives

Step Three

Consider any factors which indicate a reduction, such as assistance to the prosecution
The court should take into account sections 73 and 74 of the Serious Crime and Police Act 2005 (assistance by defendants: reduction or review of sentence) and any other rule of law by virtue of which an offender may receive a discounted sentence in assistance given (or offered) to the prosecutor or investigator.

Step Four

Reduction for guilty pleas
The court should take account of any potential reduction for a guilty plea in accordance with section 144 of the Criminal Justice Act 2003 and the *Guilty Plea* guideline.

For class A offences, where a minimum mandatory sentence is imposed under section 110 Powers of Criminal Courts (Sentencing) Act, the discount for an early guilty plea must not exceed 20 per cent.

Step Five

Totality principle
If sentencing an offender for more than one offence, or where the offender is already serving a sentence, consider whether the total sentence is just and proportionate to the offending behaviour.

Step Six

Confiscation and ancillary orders
In all cases, the court is required to consider confiscation where the Crown invokes the process or where the court considers it appropriate. It should also consider whether to make ancillary orders.

Step Seven

Reasons
Section 174 of the Criminal Justice Act 2003 imposes a duty to give reasons for, and explain the effect of, the sentence.

Step Eight

Consideration for remand time
Sentencers should take into consideration any remand time served in relation to the final sentence at this final step. The court should consider whether to give credit for time spent on remand in custody or on bail in accordance with sections 240 and 240A of the Criminal Justice Act 2003.

Bibliography

Advisory Council on the Penal System (1970), *Non-Custodial and Semi-Custodial Penalties*, London: HMSO.

Advisory Council on the Penal System (1974), *The Young Adult Offender*, London: HMSO.

Advisory Council on the Penal System (1977), *The Length of Prison Sentences*, London: HMSO.

Advisory Council on the Penal System (1978), *Sentences of Imprisonment: A Review of Maximum Penalties*, London: HMSO.

Alldridge, P. (2003), *Money Laundering Law*, Oxford: Hart.

Alldridge, P. (2011), 'The Limits of Confiscation', *Criminal Law Review*, 827.

Allen, F. (1981), *The Decline of the Rehabilitative Ideal*, New Haven: Yale University Press.

Allen, R. (2007), *Lost in Transition: Three Years On*, London: Barrow Cadbury Trust.

ALRC, Australian Law Reform Commission (2006), *Same Crime, Same Time: Sentencing of Federal Offenders*, ALRC No. 103, Sydney: Law Reform Commission.

American Law Institute (2014), *Model Penal Code: Sentencing, Tentative Draft No. 3*, Philadelphia: American Law Institute.

Angiolini, E. (2012), *Report of the Commission on Women Offenders*, Edinburgh: Scottish Executive.

Appleton, C. (2010), *Life after Life Imprisonment*, Oxford: Oxford University Press.

Arthur, R. (2005) 'Punishing Parents for the Crimes of their Children', *Howard Journal of Criminal Justice*, 44: 235.

Ashworth, A. (2002), 'European Sentencing Traditions: Accepting Divergence or Aiming for Convergence?', in C. Tata and N. Hutton (eds.), *Sentencing and Society*, Aldershot: Ashgate.

Ashworth, A. (2002a), 'Robbery Reassessed', *Criminal Law Review*, 851.

Ashworth, A. (2002b), 'Rights, Responsibilities and Restorative Justice', *British Journal of Criminology*, 42: 578.

Ashworth, A. (2003), 'Sentencing and Sensitivity', in L. Zedner and A. Ashworth (eds.), *The Criminological Foundations of Penal Policy: Essays in Honour of Roger Hood*, Oxford: Oxford University Press.

Ashworth, A. (2004), 'Social Control and Anti-Social Behaviour: The Subversion of Human Rights?', *Law Quarterly Review*, 120: 263.

Ashworth, A. (2010), 'Sentencing Guidelines and the Sentencing Council,' *Criminal Law Review*, 389.

Ashworth, A. (2011b), 'Re-evaluating the Justifications for Aggravation and Mitigation at Sentencing', in J. V. Roberts (ed.), *Mitigation and Aggravation in Sentencing*, Cambridge: Cambridge University Press.

Ashworth, A. (2013a), 'The Struggle for Supremacy in Sentencing', in A. Ashworth and J. V. Roberts (eds.), *Sentencing Guidelines: Exploring the English Model*, Oxford: Oxford University Press.

Ashworth, A. (2013b), *What if Imprisonment were Abolished for Property Offences?* London: Howard League for Penal Reform.

Ashworth, A. and Horder, J. (2013), *Principles of Criminal Law*, 7th edn, Oxford: Oxford University Press.

Ashworth, A. and Player, E. (1998), 'Sentencing, Equal Treatment and the Impact of Sanctions', in A. Ashworth and M. Wasik (eds.), *Fundamentals of Sentencing Theory*, Oxford: Oxford University Press.

Ashworth, A. and Redmayne, M. (2010), *The Criminal Process*, 4th edn, Oxford: Oxford University Press.

Ashworth, A. and Zedner, L. (2014), *Preventive Justice*, Oxford: Oxford University Press.

Audit Commission (2004), *Youth Justice 2004*, London: Audit Commission.

Auld, Lord Justice (2001), *Review of the Criminal Courts of England and Wales*, London: The Stationery Office.

Bagaric, M. (2001), *Punishment and Sentencing: A Rational Approach*, London: Cavendish.

Bagaric, M. and Alexander, T. (2011), '(Marginal) General Deterrence Doesn't Work – and What it Means for Sentencing', *Criminal Law Journal*, 35: 269.

Baker, E. (2013), 'Sentencing Guidelines and European Union Law', in A. Ashworth and J. V. Roberts (eds.), *Sentencing Guidelines: Exploring the English Model*, Oxford: Oxford University Press.

Baker, K. (2004), 'Is Asset Really an Asset?', in R. Burnett and C. Roberts (eds.), *What Works in Probation and Youth Justice*, Cullompton: Willan.

Baldock, J. C. (1980), 'Why the Prison Population Has Grown Larger and Younger', *Howard Journal of Criminal Justice*, 19: 142.

Baldwin, J. and McConville, M. (1978), 'Sentencing Problems Raised by Guilty Pleas', *Modern Law Review*, 41: 544.

Ball, C. (2000), 'A Significant Move towards Restorative Justice, or a Recipe for Unintended Consequences?', *Criminal Law Review*, 211.

Banks, R. and Harris, L. (2014), *Banks on Sentencing, vols. I and II*, Etchingham, Sussex: Banks.

Barkow, R. (2005), 'Administering Crime', *UCLA Law Review*, 52: 715.

Bateman, T. (2011), 'Punishing Poverty: the Scaled Approach and Youth Justice Practice', *Howard Journal of Criminal Justice*, 50: 171.

Bennett, C. (2010), 'More to Apologize For', in J. V. Roberts and A. von Hirsch (eds.), *Previous Convictions at Sentencing*, Oxford: Hart.

Bennett, T. and Wright, R. (1984), *Burglars on Burglary*, London: Gower.

Bentham, J. (1948 [1789]), *Principles of Morals and Legislation*, Oxford: Blackwell.

Berman, G. and Dar, A. (2013), *Prison Population Statistics*, London: House of Commons Library.

Bingham, T. (1996), 'The Courts and the Constitution', *King's College Law Journal*, 7: 12.

Blake, M. and Ashworth, A. (1998), 'Some Ethical Issues in Defending and Prosecuting Criminal Cases', *Criminal Law Review*, 16.

Blumstein, A. et al. (1986), *Criminal Careers and Career Criminals*, Washington: National Institute of Justice.

Bohlander, M. (2012), *Principles of German Criminal Procedure*, Oxford: Hart.

Booth, L. et al. (2012), *North Liverpool Community Justice Centre: Analysis of Re-offending Rates and Efficiency of Court Processes*, London: Analytical Services, Ministry of Justice.

Bottomley, A. K. and Coleman, C. (1981), *Understanding Crime Rates*, London: Saxon House.

Bottoms, A. E. (1973), 'The Efficacy of the Fine: The Case for Agnosticism', *Criminal Law Review*, 543.

Bottoms, A. E. (1974), 'On the Decriminalisation of the Juvenile Court', in R. Hood (ed.), *Crime, Criminology and Public Policy*, London: Heinemann.

Bottoms, A. E. (1981), 'The Suspended Sentence in England', *British Journal of Criminology*, 21: 1.

Bottoms, A. E. (1987), 'Limiting Prison Use: Experience in England and Wales', *Howard Journal of Criminal Justice*, 26: 177.

Bottoms, A. E. (1995), 'The Philosophy and Politics of Punishment and Sentencing', in C. Clarkson and R. Morgan (eds.), *The Politics of Sentencing Reform*, Oxford: Oxford University Press.

Bottoms, A. E. (1998), 'Five Puzzles in von Hirsch's Theory of Punishment', in A. Ashworth and M. Wasik (eds.), *Fundamentals of Sentencing Theory*, Oxford: Oxford University Press.

Bottoms, A. E. (2004), 'Empirical Research Relevant to Sentencing Frameworks', in A. Bottoms, S. Rex and G. Robinson (eds.), *Alternatives to Prison: Options for an Insecure Society*, Cullompton: Willan.

Bottoms, A. E. (2008), 'The Community Dimension of Community Penalties', *Howard Journal of Criminal Justice*, 47: 146.

Bottoms, A. E. (2010), 'The Duty to Understand', in A. E. Bottoms and J. V. Roberts (eds.), *Hearing the Victim*, Oxford: Hart.

Bottoms, A. E. and Brownsword, R. (1982), 'The Dangerousness Debate after the Floud Report', *British Journal of Criminology*, 22: 229.

Bottoms, A. E., Rex, S. and Robinson, G. (2004), 'How Did We Get Here?', in A. Bottoms, S. Rex and G. Robinson (eds.), *Alternatives to Prison: Options for an Insecure Society*, Cullompton: Willan.

Bottoms, A. E. and Shapland, J. (2011), 'Steps towards Desistance in Young Adult Male Offenders', in S. Farrall, M. Hough, S. Maruna and R. Sparks (eds.), *Escape Routes: Contemporary Perspectives on Life after Punishment*, Abingdon: Routledge.

Bottoms, A. E. and von Hirsch, A. (2010), 'The Crime-Preventive Impact of Penal Sanctions', in P. F. Cane and H. M. Kritzer (eds.), *Oxford Handbook of Empirical Legal Research*, Oxford: Oxford University Press.

Bottoms, A. E. and Wilson, A. (2004), 'Attitudes to Crime in Two High-Crime Communities', in A. Bottoms, S. Rex and G. Robinson (eds.), *Alternatives to Prison: Options for an Insecure Society*, Cullompton: Willan.

Boucht, J. (2013), 'Extended Confiscation and the EU', *European Journal of Crime, Criminal Law and Criminal Justice*, 21: 127.

Bowling, B. and Phillips, C. (2002), *Racism, Crime and Justice*, Harlow: Longman.

Boyd-Caine, T. (2012), *Protecting the Public? Detention and Release of Mentally Disordered Offenders*, Abingdon: Routledge.

Bradley, Lord (2009), *Report on People with Mental Health Problems or Learning Disabilities in the Criminal Justice System*, London: Ministry of Justice.

Braithwaite, J. and Pettit, P. (1990), *Not Just Deserts*, Oxford: Oxford University Press.

Bridge, Lord Justice (1978), *Report of the Working Party on Judicial Studies and Information*, London: HMSO.

British Academy (2014), *A Presumption against Imprisonment: Social Order and Social Values*, London: British Academy.

Brody, S. R. (1976), *The Effectiveness of Sentencing*, Home Office Research Study 35, London: HMSO.

Brody, S. and Tarling, R. (1981), *Taking Offenders out of Circulation*, Home Office Research Study 64, London: HMSO.

Brooke, D., Taylor, C., Gunn, J. and Maden, A. (1996) 'Point Prevalence of Mental Disorder in Unconvicted Male Prisoners', *British Medical Journal*, 313: 1524.

Brooks, T. (2013), *Punishment*, Abingdon: Routledge.

Brown, M. (1998), 'Serious Violence and Dilemmas of Sentencing', *Criminal Law Review*, 710.

Brown, M. and Pratt, J. (2000), *Dangerous Offenders: Punishment and Social Control*, London: Routledge.

Brownlee, I. (2004), 'The Statutory Charging Scheme in England and Wales', *Criminal Law Review*, 896.

Buckler, K. G. and Travis, L. F. (2003), 'Reanalyzing the Prevalence and Social Context of Collateral Consequence Statutes', *Journal of Criminal Justice*, 31:435.

Burnett, R. (1994), *Recidivism and Imprisonment*, Home Office Research Bulletin 36: 19.

Burnett, R. and Appleton, C. (2004), 'Joined-Up Services to Tackle Youth Crime: A Case-Study in England', *British Journal of Criminology*, 44: 34.

Burnett, R. and Maruna, S. (2004), 'So Prison Works, Does It?', *Howard Journal of Criminal Justice*, 43: 390.

Burnett, R. and Maruna, S. (2006), 'The Kindness of Prisoners: Strengths-Based Resettlement in Theory and Practice', *Criminology and Criminal Justice*, 6: 83.

Burney, E. and Gelsthorpe, L. (2008), 'Do We Need a Naughty Step? Rethinking the Parenting Order after 10 Years', *Howard Journal of Criminal Justice*, 47: 470.

Burney, E. and Pearson, G. (1995), 'Mentally Disordered Offenders: Finding a Focus for Diversion', *Howard Journal of Criminal Justice*, 34: 291.

Canadian Sentencing Commission (1987), *Sentencing Reform: A Canadian Approach*, Ottawa: Ministry of Supply and Services.

Canton, R. (2013), 'The Point of Probation: On Effectiveness, Human Rights and the Virtue of Obliquity', *Criminology and Criminal Justice*, 13: 577.

Carter Review (2003), *Managing Offenders, Reducing Crime*, London: Home Office.

Carter Review (2007), *Securing the Future*, London: Ministry of Justice.

Cavadino, M. (1997), 'Pre-Sentence Reports: The Effects of Legislation and National Standards', *British Journal of Criminology*, 37: 529.

Cavadino, M. (1999), 'Diverting Mentally Disordered Offenders from Custody', in D. Webb and R. Harris (eds.), *Managing People Nobody Owns*, London: Routledge.

Cavadino, M. and Dignan, J. (2006), *Penal Systems: A Comparative Approach*, London: Sage.

Cavadino, M., Dignan, J. and Mair, G. (2013), *The Penal System*, 5th edn, London: Sage.

CCSS (2014), *Crown Court Sentencing Survey, Annual Publication 2013*, London: Sentencing Council.

Chalmers, J., Duff, P. and Leverick, F. (2007), 'Victim Impact Statement: Can Work, Do Work (for those who bother to make them)', *Criminal Law Review*, 360.

Chaplin, R., Flatley, J and Smith, K. (2011) *Crime in England and Wales 2010–11*, Statistical Bulletin 10/11, London: Home Office.

Charman, E., Gibson, B., Honess, T. and Morgan, R. (1996), *Fine Impositions and Enforcement Following the Criminal Justice Act 1993*, Home Office Research Findings 36, London: Home Office.

Clarke, A., Moran-Ellis, J. and Sleny, J. (2002), *Attitudes to Date Rape and Relationship Rape*, Guildford: Department of Sociology, University of Surrey.

Clayton, R. and Murphy, C. (2014), 'The Emergence of the EU Charter of Fundamental Rights in UK Law', *European Human Rights Law Review*, 469.

Commissioner for Victims and Witnesses (2014), *Report for the Secretary of State for Justice 2013–14*, London: Commissioner for Victims and Witnesses.

Cook, D. and Hudson, B. (eds.) (1993), *Racism and Criminology*, London: Sage.

Cooke, R. K. (1987), 'The Practical Problems of the Sentencer', in D. Pennington and S. Lloyd-Bostock (eds.), *The Psychology of Sentencing*, Oxford: Centre for Socio-Legal Studies.

Cooper, J. (2013), 'Nothing Personal: The Impact of Personal Mitigation at Sentencing', in A. Ashworth and J. V. Roberts (eds.), *Sentencing Guidelines: Exploring the English Model*, Oxford: Oxford University Press.

Corbett, C. (1987), 'Magistrates' and Court Clerks' Sentencing Behaviour: An Experimental Study', in D. Pennington and S. Lloyd-Bostock (eds.), *The Psychology of Sentencing*, Oxford: Centre for Socio-Legal Studies.

Cornford, A. (2012), 'Criminalising Anti-Social Behaviour', *Criminal Law and Philosophy*, 6: 1.

Cornish, D. B. and Clarke, R. (1986), *The Reasoning Criminal: Rational Choice Perspectives on Offending*, New York: Springer-Verlag.

Corston, Baroness (2007), *Review of Women with Particular Vulnerabilities in the Criminal Justice System*, London: Home Office.

Coulsfield, Lord (2004), *Crime, Courts and Confidence: Report of an Independent Inquiry into Alternatives to Prison*, London: Esmee Fairbairn Foundation.

Council of Europe (1976), *Alternative Measures to Imprisonment*, Recommendation R (76) 10, Strasbourg: Council of Europe.

Council of Europe (1984), *Convention on Compensation for the Victims of Violent Crime*, Strasbourg: Council of Europe.

Council of Europe (1987), *The Simplification of Criminal Justice*, Strasbourg: Council of Europe.

Council of Europe (1992), *European Rules on Community Sanctions and Measures*, Recommendation R (92) 16, Strasbourg: Council of Europe.

Council of Europe (1993), *Consistency in Sentencing*, Recommendation R (92) 17, Strasbourg: Council of Europe.

Cox, E. (1984 [1877]), *The Principles of Punishment*, London: Garland.

CPT (2001), *European Committee for the Prevention of Torture and Inhuman or Degrading Punishment, Report of Inspection of English Prisons*, Strasbourg: Council of Europe.

Crawford, A. and Evans, K. (2012), 'Crime Prevention and Community Safety', in M. Maguire, R. Morgan and R. Reiner (eds.), *Oxford Handbook of Criminology*, 5th edn, Oxford: Oxford University Press.

Crow, I. and Simon, F. (1989), *Unemployment and Sentencing*, London: NACRO.

Crown Prosecution Service (2004), *Code for Crown Prosecutors*, London: Crown Prosecution Service.

Crown Prosecution Service (2010), *Code for Crown Prosecutors*, www.cps.gov.uk

Crown Prosecution Service (2013), *Annual Report 2012–13*, www.cps.gov.uk

Cunningham, S. (2007), 'Punishing Drivers who Kill: Putting Road Safety First?', *Legal Studies*, 27: 288.

Dagger, R. (2008), 'Punishment as Fair Play', *Res Publica*, 14: 259.

Darbyshire, P. (1984), *The Justices' Clerk*, Chichester: Barry Rose.

Darbyshire, P. (1997a), 'An Essay on the Importance and Neglect of the Magistracy', *Criminal Law Review*, 627.

Darbyshire, P. (1997b), 'For the New Lord Chancellor – Some Causes for Concern about Magistrates', *Criminal Law Review*, 861.

Darbyshire, P. (2000), 'The Mischief of Plea Bargaining and Sentence Rewards', *Criminal Law Review*, 894.

Darbyshire, P. (2006), 'Transparency in getting the Accused to Plead Guilty Early', *Cambridge Law Journal*, 48.

Darbyshire, P. (2011), *Sitting in Judgment: The Working Lives of Judges*, Oxford: Hart.

Davies, M. and Tyrer, J. (2003), '"Filling in the Gaps" – A Study of Judicial Culture', *Criminal Law Review*, 243.

Dawes, W. et al. (2011), *Attitudes to Guilty Plea Sentence Reductions*, London: Sentencing Council.

de Keijser, J. (2014), 'Penal Theory and Popular Opinion: The Deficiencies of Direct Engagement', in J. Ryberg and J. V. Roberts (eds.), *Popular Punishment*, New York: Oxford University Press.

Debidin, M. (ed.) (2009), *A Compendium of Research and Analysis on OASys 2006–09*, MoJ Research Series 16/09, London: Ministry of Justice.

Dhami, M. (2013), 'A "Decision Science" Perspective on the Old and New Sentencing Guidelines in England and Wales', in A. Ashworth and J. V. Roberts (eds.), *Sentencing Guidelines: Exploring the English Model*, Oxford: Oxford University Press.

Dhami, M., Belton, I. and Goodman-Delahunty, J. (2015), 'Quasirational Models of Sentencing', *Journal of Applied Research on Memory and Cognition* (forthcoming).

Dhami, M. and Souza, K. A. (2008), *Study of Sentencing and its Outcomes: Pilot Report*, MoJ Research Series 2/09, London: Ministry of Justice.

Diamond, S. S. (1981), 'Exploring Sources of Sentencing Disparity', in B. Sales (ed.), *The Trial Process*, New York: Plenum.

Dignan, J. (2005), *Understanding Victims and Restorative Justice*, Maidenhead: Open University Press.

Dingwall, G. (2006), *Alcohol and Crime*, Cullompton: Willan.

Dingwall, G. and Koffman, L. (2008), 'Determining the Impact of Intoxication in a Desert-Based Sentencing Framework', *Criminology and Criminal Justice*, 8: 335.

Doak, J. (2008), *Victims' Rights, Human Rights and Criminal Justice*, Oxford: Hart.

Doob, A. and Webster, C. (2003), 'Sentence Severity and Crime: Accepting the Null Hypothesis', *Crime and Justice: A Review of Research*, 30: 143.

Dove-Wilson (1932), *Report of the Departmental Committee on Persistent Offenders*, London: HMSO.

Dowds, L. and Hedderman, C. (1997), 'The Sentencing of Men and Women', in C. Hedderman and L. Gelsthorpe (eds.), *Understanding the Sentencing of Women*, Home Office Research Study 170, London: Home Office.

Downes, D. (1988), *Contrasts in Tolerance*, Oxford: Oxford University Press.

Downes, D. and Morgan, R. (2007), 'No Turning Back: The Politics of Law and Order into the Millenium', in M. Maguire, R. Morgan and R. Reiner (eds.), *Oxford Handbook of Criminology*, 4th edn, Oxford: Oxford University Press.

Duff, R. A. (1986), *Trials and Punishments*, Cambridge: Cambridge University Press.

Duff, R. A. (2001), *Punishment, Communication and Community*, New York: Oxford University Press.

Duff, R. A. (2013), 'Pre-Trial Detention and the Presumption of Innocence', in A. Ashworth, L. Zedner and P. Tomlin (eds.), *Prevention and the Limits of the Criminal Law*, Oxford: Oxford University Press.

Durlauf, S. and Nagin, D. (2011), 'Imprisonment and Crime: Can Both be Reduced?', *Criminology and Public Policy*, 10: 13.

Eastman, N. and Peay, J. (1998), 'Sentencing Psychopaths', *Criminal Law Review*, 93.

Easton, S. (2008), 'Dangerous Waters: Taking Account of Impact in Sentencing', *Criminal Law Review*, 105.

Easton, S. (2011), *Prisoners' Rights: Principles and Practice*, Abingdon: Routledge.

Eaton, M. (1986), *Justice for Women?* Milton Keynes: Open University Press.

Edwards, I. (2004), 'An Ambiguous Participant: The Victim and the Criminal Justice System', *British Journal of Criminology*, 44: 967.

Edwards, I. (2013), 'Victims, Sentencing Guidelines and the Sentencing Council', in A. Ashworth and J. V. Roberts (eds.), *Sentencing Guidelines: Exploring the English Model*, Oxford: Oxford University Press.

Elliott, R., Airs, J. and Webb, S. (1999), *Community Penalties for Fine Default and Persistent Petty Offending*, Home Office Research Findings 98, London: Home Office.

Emmerson, B., Ashworth, A. and Macdonald, A. (eds.) (2012), *Human Rights and Criminal Justice*, 3rd edn, London: Sweet & Maxwell.

Erez, E. (1999), 'Who's Afraid of the Big, Bad Victim?', *Criminal Law Review*, 545.

Evans, R. (1993), 'Evaluating Young Adult Cautioning Schemes', *Criminal Law Review*, 490.

Fairhead, S. (1981), *Persistent Petty Offenders*, Home Office Research Study 66, London: HMSO.

Farrall, S. and Calverley, A. (2006), *Understanding Desistance from Crime*, Maidenhead: Open University Press.

Farrall, S., Hough, M., Maruna, S. and Sparks, R. (eds.) (2011), *Escape Routes: Contemporary Perspectives on Life after Punishment*, Abingdon: Routledge.

Farrington, D. (1997), 'Human Development and Criminal Careers', in M. Maguire, R. Morgan and R. Reiner (eds.), *Oxford Handbook of Criminology*, 2nd edn, Oxford: Oxford University Press.

Farrington, D. (2007), 'Childhood Risk Factors and Risk-Based Prevention', in M. Maguire, R. Morgan and R. Reiner (eds.), *Oxford Handbook of Criminology*, 4th edn, Oxford: Oxford University Press.

Farrington, D. and Langan, P. (1992), 'Changes in Crime and Punishment in England and America in the 1980s', *Justice Quarterly*, 9: 5.

Farrington, D. and Morris, A. (1983), 'Sex, Sentencing and Reconvictions', *British Journal of Criminology*, 23: 229.

Fawcett Society (2007), *Women and Justice: Third Annual Review of the Commission on Women and the Criminal Justice System*, London: Fawcett Society.

Feeley, M. and Simon, J. (1994) 'Actuarial Justice: The Emerging New Criminal Law', in D. Nelken (ed.), *The Futures of Criminology*, London: Sage.

Feilzer, M. and Hood, R. (2003), *Minority Ethnic Young People in the Youth Justice System*, London: Youth Justice Board.

Field, S. (2007), 'Practice Cultures and the "New" Youth Justice in (England and) Wales', *British Journal of Criminology*, 47: 311.

Field, S. and Tata, C. (2010), 'Connecting Legal and Social Justice in the Neo-Liberal World? The Construction, Interpretation and Use of Pre-Sentence Reports', *Punishment and Society*, 12: 235.

Fionda, J. (2005), *Devils and Angels: Youth Policy and Crime*, Oxford: Hart.

Fitzgerald, M. (1993), *Ethnic Minorities and the Criminal Justice System*, Royal Commission on Criminal Justice Research Study 21, London: HMSO.

Fitz-Gibbon, K. (2013), 'The Mandatory Life Sentence for Murder: An Argument for Judicial Discretion in England', *Criminology and Criminal Justice*, 13: 506.

Fitzmaurice, C. and Pease, K. (1986), *The Psychology of Judicial Sentencing*, Manchester: Manchester University Press.

Fletcher, G. P. (1978), *Rethinking Criminal Law*, Boston: Little, Brown.

Flood-Page, C. and Mackie, A. (1998), *Sentencing Practice: An Examination of Decisions in Magistrates' Courts and the Crown Court in the mid-1990s*, Home Office Research Study 180, London: Home Office.

Floud, J. and Young, W. (1981), *Dangerousness and Criminal Justice*, London: Heinemann.

Flynn, A. (2011), 'Fortunately We in Victoria are not in that UK Position: Australian and United Kingdom Perspectives on Plea Bargaining Reform', *Deakin Law Review*, 16: 361.

Folkard, S. (1976), *IMPACT volume II*, Home Office Research Study 36, London: HMSO.

Fox, R. and Freiberg, A. (1999), *Sentencing: State and Federal Law in Victoria*, 2nd edn, Melbourne: Oxford University Press.

Frase, R. (2005), 'State Sentencing Guidelines: Diversity, Consensus, and Unresolved Policy Issues', *Columbia Law Review*, 105: 1190.

Frase, R. (2013), *Just Sentencing: Principles and Procedures for a Workable System*, New York: Oxford University Press.

Freiberg, A. and Gelb, K. (eds.) (2008), *Penal Populism, Sentencing Councils and Sentencing Policy*, Cullompton: Willan.

Freiberg, A. and Murray, S. (2012), 'Constitutional Perspectives on Sentencing: Some Challenging Issues', *Criminal Law Journal*, 36: 335.

Gage Report (2008), *Sentencing Guidelines in England and Wales: An Evolutionary Approach*, London: Sentencing Commission Working Group.

Galligan, D. (1987), 'Regulating Pre-Trial Decisions', in I. Dennis (ed.), *Criminal Law and Criminal Justice*, London: Sweet & Maxwell.

Gardner, J. (1998), 'Crime: In Proportion and in Perspective', in A. Ashworth and M. Wasik (eds.), *Fundamentals of Sentencing Theory*, Oxford: Oxford University Press.

Gardner, J. and Shute, S. (2000), 'The Wrongness of Rape', in J. Horder (ed.), *Oxford Essays in Jurisprudence: Fourth Series*, Oxford: Oxford University Press.

Garland, D. (1990), *Punishment and Modern Society*, Oxford: Oxford University Press.

Garland, D. (2000), *The Culture of Control*, Oxford: Oxford University Press.

Garland, D. (2014), 'Cultures of Control and Penal States', in *Beyond Punitiveness: Crime and Crime Control in Europe in a Comparative Perspective*, Proceedings of Criminology No. 73, Budapest: Hungarian Society of Criminologists.

Gelsthorpe, L. and Loucks, N. (1997), 'Magistrates' Explanations of Sentencing Decisions', in C. Hedderman and L. Gelsthorpe (eds.), *Understanding the Sentencing of Women*, Home Office Research Study 170, London: Home Office.

Gelsthorpe, L. and Padfield, N. (eds.) (2003), *Exercising Discretion: Decision-Making in the Criminal Justice System and Beyond*, Cullompton: Willan.

Gelsthorpe, L. and Raynor, P. (1995), 'Quality and Effectiveness in Probation Officers' Reports', *British Journal of Criminology*, 35: 188.

Gibson, B. (1990), *Unit Fines*, Winchester: Waterside Press.

Goodman-Delahunty, J. and Sporer, S. L. (2010), 'Unconscious Influences in Sentencing Decisions: A Research Review of Psychological Sources of Disparity,' *Australian Journal of Forensic Sciences*, 42: 9.

Goold, B. J. and Neyland, P. (eds.) (2009), *New Directions in Surveillance and Privacy*, Cullompton: Willan.

Gostin, L. (1977), *A Human Condition*, vol. II, London: MIND.

Greene, J. (1998), 'The Unit Fine: Monetary Sanctions Apportioned to Income', in A. von Hirsch and A. Ashworth (eds.), *Principled Sentencing*, Oxford: Hart Publishing.

Greenwood, P. (1982), *Selective Incapacitation*, Santa Barbara: RAND.

Guldenmund, B., Harding, C. and Sherlock, J. (1995), 'Sentencing and EU Law', in C. Harding et al., *Criminal Justice in Europe*, Oxford: Oxford University Press.

Gunn, J., Maden, A. and Swinton, M. (1991), 'Treatment Needs of Prisoners with Psychiatric Diagnoses', *British Medical Journal*, 303: 338.

Hadden, T. (1968), 'Offences of Violence: The Law and the Facts', *Criminal Law Review*, 521.

Halliday (2001), *Making Punishments Work: Report of a Review of the Sentencing Framework for England and Wales*, London: Home Office.

Hammond, W. H. and Chayen, E. (1963), *Persistent Offenders*, London: HMSO.

Harcourt, B. (2007), *Against Prediction: Profiling, Policing and Punishing in an Actuarial Age*, Chicago: University of Chicago Press.

Harding, R. (1990), 'Rational-Choice Gun Use in Armed Robbery', *Criminal Law Forum*, 1: 427.

Harper, G. and Chitty, C. (2005), *The Impact of Corrections on Offending: A Review of What Works*, Home Office Research Study 291, London: Home Office.

Harris, J. and Grace, S. (1999), *A Question of Evidence? Investigating and Prosecuting Rape in the 1990s*, Home Office Research Study 196, London: Home Office.

Harrison, K. (2006), 'Community Punishment or Community Rehabilitation: Which Is the Highest in the Sentencing Tariff?', *Howard Journal of Criminal Justice*, 45: 141.

Hart, H. L. A. (2008), *Punishment and Responsibility*, Oxford: Oxford University Press.

Hawkins, K. (2003), *Law as Last Resort*, Oxford: Oxford University Press.

Hedderman, C. (1990), *The Effect of Defendants' Demeanour on Sentencing in Magistrates' Courts*, Home Office Research Bulletin 29, London: Home Office.

Hedderman, C. and Gelsthorpe, L. (1997), *Understanding the Sentencing of Women*, Home Office Research Study 170, London: Home Office.

Hedderman, C. and Hough, M. (1994), *Does the Criminal Justice System Treat Men and Women Differently?* Home Office Research Findings 10, London: Home Office.

Hedderman, C. and Moxon, D. (1992), *Magistrates' Courts or Crown Courts? Mode of Trial Decisions and Sentencing*, Home Office Research Study 125, London: HMSO.

Heidensohn, F. and Silvestri, M. (2012), 'Gender and Crime', in M. Maguire, R. Morgan and R. Reiner (eds.), *Oxford Handbook of Criminology*, 5th edn, Oxford: Oxford University Press.

Henham, R. (1991), *Sentencing Principles and Magistrates' Sentencing Behaviour*, Aldershot: Avebury.

Hessick, J. and Hessick, A. (2011), 'Constitutional Rights at Sentence', *California Law Review*, 99: 47.

Hirst, M. (2008), 'Causing Death by Driving and other Offences: A Question of Balance', *Criminal Law Review*, 339.

HM Chief Inspector of Prisons (2009), *Her Majesty's Chief Inspector of Prisons, Report 2007–08*, London: The Stationery Office.

HM Chief Inspector of Prisons (2014), *Annual Report 2013–14*, HC 680, London: The Stationery Office.

HM Inspectorate of Constabulary/HM Crown Prosecution Service Inspectorate (2011), *Exercising Discretion: The Gateway to Justice*, London: Criminal Justice Joint Inspection.

Hodgson, J. (2005), *French Criminal Justice*, Oxford: Hart.

Hoernle, T. (2013), 'Moderate and Non-Arbitrary Sentencing without Guidelines: The German Experience', *Law and Contemporary Problems*, 76: 189.

Hogarth, J. (1971), *Sentencing as a Human Process*, Toronto: University of Toronto Press.

Home Office (1965), *The Adult Offender*, London: HMSO.

Home Office (1977), *Prisons and the Prisoners*, London: HMSO.

Home Office (1990), *Crime, Justice and Protecting the Public*, London: HMSO.

Home Office (1996), *Protecting the Public: The Government's Strategy on Crime*, Cm 3190, London: HMSO.

Home Office (1997), *No More Excuses: A New Approach to Tackling Youth Crime in England and Wales*, Cm 3089, London: The Stationery Office.

Home Office (2001), *Criminal Justice: The Way Ahead*, London: The Stationery Office.

Home Office (2002), *Justice for All*, Cm 5563, London: The Stationery Office.

Home Office (2004), *Reducing Crime, Changing Lives*, London: Home Office.

Home Office (2011), *Statutory Guidance: Injunctions to Prevent Gang-Related Violence*, London: the Stationery Office.

Home Office (2014), *Review of the Operation of Injunctions to Prevent Gang-Related Violence*, London: Home Office.

Hood, R. (1962), *Sentencing in Magistrates' Courts*, London: Tavistock.

Hood, R. (1972), *Sentencing the Motoring Offender*, London: Heinemann.

Hood, R. (1992), *Race and Sentencing*, Oxford: Oxford University Press.

Hood, R. and Shute, S. (1996), 'Protecting the Public: Automatic Life Sentences, Parole and High Risk Offenders', *Criminal Law Review*, 788.

Hood, R., Shute, S., Feilzer, M. and Wilcox, A. (2002), 'Sex Offenders Emerging from Long-Term Imprisonment', *British Journal of Criminology*, 42: 371.

Hood, R., Shute, S. and Seemungal, F. (2003), *Ethnic Minorities in the Criminal Courts: Perceptions of Fairness*, Oxford: Centre for Criminology.

Hough, M., Jacobson, J. and Millie, A. (2003), *The Decision to Imprison: Sentencing and the Prison Population*, London: Prison Reform Trust.

Hough, M. and Roberts, J. (1998), *Attitudes to Punishment: Findings from the British Crime Survey*, Home Office Research Study 179, London: Home Office.

Hough, M. and Roberts, J. V. (2012), 'Public Opinion, Crime and Criminal Justice', in M. Maguire, R. Morgan and R. Reiner (eds.), *Oxford Handbook of Criminology*, 5th edn, Oxford: Oxford University Press.

House of Commons (2004), Draft Sentencing Guidelines 1 and 2, Home Affairs Committee, Fifth Report of Session 2003–04, HC 1207, London: HMSO.

House of Commons (2008), *Towards Effective Sentencing*, Report of the Justice Committee, London: The Stationery Office.

House of Commons Expenditure Committee (1978), *The Reduction of Pressure on the Prison System*, London: HMSO.

House of Commons Home Affairs Committee (2013), session 2012–13, *The Draft Anti-Social Behaviour Bill: Pre-Legislative Scrutiny*, London: House of Commons.

House of Commons Justice Committee (2014), *Crime Reduction Policies – a Co-ordinated Approach?* First Report of Session 2014–15, London: Stationery Office.

House of Lords (2003), *Criminal Justice Bill*, Select Committee on the Constitution, London: The Stationery Office.

Hoyle, C. (2012), 'Victims, the Criminal Process and Restorative Justice', in M. Maguire, R. Morgan and R. Reiner (eds.), *Oxford Handbook of Criminology*, 5th edn, Oxford: Oxford University Press.

Hoyle, C. and Cuneen, C. (2009), *Restorative Justice: For and Against*, Abingdon: Routledge.

Hoyle, C. and Young, R. (2003), 'New, Improved, Police-Led Restorative Justice?', in A. von Hirsch, J. Roberts et al. (eds.), *Restorative Justice and Criminal Justice*, Oxford: Hart.

Hoyle, C. et al. (1998), *Evaluation of the One-Stop Shop and Victim Statement Pilots*, London: Home Office.

HSCIC (2013), *Health and Social Care Information Centre*, www.hscic.gov.uk

Hucklesby, A. (2008), 'Vehicles of Desistance: The Impact of Electronically Monitored Curfew Orders', *Criminology and Criminal Justice*, 8: 51.

Hudson, B. (1994), 'Punishing the Poor: A Critique of the Dominance of Legal Reasoning in Penal Policy and Practice', in A. Duff et al. (eds.), *Penal Theory and Practice*, Manchester: Manchester University Press.

Hudson, B. (1995), 'Beyond Proportionate Punishment: Difficult Cases', *Crime, Law and Social Change*, 22: 59.

Hudson, B. (1998), 'Doing Justice to Difference', in A. Ashworth and M. Wasik (eds.), *Fundamentals of Sentencing Theory*, Oxford: Oxford University Press.

Hudson, B. and Bramhall, G. (2005), 'Assessing the "Other": Constructions of "Asian-ness" in Risk Assessments by Probation Officers', *British Journal of Criminology*, 45: 721.

Hutton, N. (1999), 'Sentencing in Scotland', in P. Duff and N. Hutton (eds.), *Criminal Justice in Scotland*, Aldershot: Ashgate.

Hutton, N. (2013), 'The Definitive Guideline on Assault Offences: The Performance of Justice', in A. Ashworth and J. V. Roberts (eds.), *Sentencing Guidelines: Exploring the English Model*, Oxford: Oxford University Press.

Jacobson, J. and Hough, M. (2007), *Mitigation: The Role of Personal Factors in Sentencing*, London: The Prison Reform Trust.

Jacobson, J. and Hough, M. (2011), 'Personal Mitigation: An Empirical Analysis in England and Wales', in J. V. Roberts (ed.), *Mitigation and Aggravation at Sentencing*, Cambridge: Cambridge University Press.

Jacobson, J., Kirby, A. and Hough, M. (2011), *Public Attitudes to the Sentencing of Drug Offenders*, London: Sentencing Council.

James Committee (1975), *Report of the Committee on the Distribution of Criminal Business between the Crown Court and the Magistrates' Courts*, London: HMSO.

Jareborg, N. (1995), 'The Swedish Sentencing Reform', in C. Clarkson and R. Morgan (eds.), *The Politics of Sentencing Reform*, Oxford: Oxford University Press.

Jareborg, N. (1998), 'Why Bulk Discounts in Multiple Sentencing?', in A. Ashworth and M. Wasik (eds.), *Fundamentals of Sentencing Theory*, Oxford: Oxford University Press.

Jehle, J.-M., Lewis, C. and Sobota, P. (2008), 'Dealing with Juvenile Offenders in the Criminal Justice System', *European Journal of Criminal Policy Research*, 14: 237.

Jennings, W. I. (1959), *The Law and the Constitution*, London: University of London Press.

Jeremy, D. (2010), 'Sentencing Policy or Short-Term Expediency?'*Criminal Law Review*, 593.

Joint Committee on the Draft Mental Health Bill (2005), *First Report*, Session 2004–5, HL 79-1, HC 95-1, London: The Stationery Office.

Joint Inspection Report (2004), *Joint Inspection Report into Persistent and Prolific Offenders*, London: Home Office.

Jones, P. (2002), 'The Halliday Report and Persistent Offenders', in S. Rex and M. Tonry (eds.), *Reform and Punishment: The Future of Sentencing*, Cullompton: Willan.

Jones, S. (2011), 'Under Pressure: Women who Plead Guilty to Crimes they have not Committed', *Criminology and Criminal Justice*, 11: 77.

Judicial College of Victoria (2014), *Sentencing Manual*, Melbourne: Judicial College of Victoria.

Judicial Studies Board (2007), *ASBOs: A Guide for the Judiciary*, www.jsboard.co.uk

Justice Committee (2013), *Women Offenders after the Corston Report*, 2nd report of session 2013–14, London: House of Commons.

Justice Committee (2013a), *13th Report: Women Offenders – Follow-Up*, HC 314, London: The Stationery Office.

Kadish, S. (1987), *Blame and Punishment*, New York: Macmillan.

Kazemian, L. and Farrington, D. (2006), 'Exploring Residual Career Length and Residual Number of Offenses for Two Generations of Repeat Offenders', *Journal of Research in Crime and Delinquency*, 43: 89.

Kemshall, H. (2008), *Understanding the Community Management of High Risk Offenders*, Maidenhead: Open University Press.

Kerr, J. et al. (2011), *The Dedicated Drug Courts Pilot Evaluation Process Study*, MoJ Research Series 1/11, London: Ministry of Justice.

Kershaw, C. et al. (2008), *Crime in England and Wales 2007/08*, London: Home Office.

King, C. (2014), 'Civil Forfeiture and Article 6 of the ECHR', *Legal Studies*, 34: 371.

Kleck, G. (2003), 'Constricted Rationality and the Limits of General Deterrence', in T. Blomberg and S. Cohen (eds.), *Punishment and Social Control*, New York: Aldine de Gruyter.

Kleinig, J. (1998), 'The Hardness of Hard Treatment', in A. Ashworth and M. Wasik (eds.), *Fundamentals of Sentencing Theory*, Oxford: Oxford University Press.

Knowles, D. (2010), *Political Obligation: A Critical Introduction*, Abingdon: Routledge.

Kolber, A. (2009) 'The Subjective Experience of Punishment', *Columbia Law Review*, 109: 182.

Kurki, L. (2001), 'Restorative and Community Justice in the United States', *Crime and Justice: A Review of Research*, 26: 355.

Lacey, N. (1988), *State Punishment*, London: Routledge & Kegan Paul.

Lacey, N. (1998), *Unspeakable Subjects*, Oxford: Hart.

Lacey, N. (2008), *The Prisoners' Dilemma: Political Economy and Punishment in Contemporary Democracies*, Cambridge: Cambridge University Press.

Lacey, N., Wells, C. and Quick, O. (2003) *Reconstructing Criminal Law*, London: Butterworths.

Lappi-Seppala, T. (2001), 'Sentencing and Punishment in Finland', in M. Tonry and R. Frase (eds.), *Sentencing and Sanctions in Western Countries*, New York: Oxford University Press.

Lappi-Seppala, T. (2013), 'Imprisonment and Penal Demands: Exploring the Dimensions and Drivers of Systemic and Attitudinal Punitivity', in S. Body-Gendrot, M. Hough, R. Levy and S. Snacken (eds.), *European Handbook of Criminology*, Abingdon: Routledge.

Larrauri, E. (2014), 'Criminal Record Disclosure and the Right to Privacy', *Criminal Law Review*, 723.

Law Commission (1994), *Binding Over*, Law Com. No. 222, London: HMSO.

Law Commission (2014), *Hate Crime: Should the Current Offences be Extended?* Law Com. No. 348, London: the Law Commission.

Lee, Y. (2009), 'Recidivism as Omission: A Relational Account', *Texas Law Review*, 87: 571.

Lemon, N. (1974), 'Training, Personality and Attitudes as Determinants of Magistrates' Sentencing', *British Journal of Criminology*, 14: 34.

Lennox, C., Senior, J. and Shaw, J. (2009), *Offender Health: Scoping Review and Research Priorities*, Manchester: Department of Health, University of Manchester.

Leverick, F. (2014), 'Sentence Discounting for Guilty Pleas: An Argument for Certainty over Discretion', *Criminal Law Review*, 338.

Levi, M. (2012), 'Organized Crime and Terrorism', in M. Maguire, R. Morgan and R. Reiner (eds.), *Oxford Handbook of Criminology*, 5th edn, Oxford: Oxford University Press.

Liberty (2013), *Committee Stage Briefing on the Anti-Social Behaviour, Crime and Policing Bill in the House of Commons*, London: Liberty.

Liebling, A. and Arnold, M. (2004), *Prisons and their Moral Performance*, Oxford: Oxford University Press

Liebling, A. and Crewe, B. (2012), 'Prison Life, Penal Power and Prison Effects', in M. Maguire, R. Morgan and R. Reiner (eds.), *Oxford Handbook of Criminology*, 5th edn, Oxford: Oxford University Press.

Lippke, R. (2007), *Rethinking Imprisonment*, Oxford: Oxford University Press.

Livingstone, S., Owen, T. and Macdonald, A. (2008), *Prison Law*, London: Sweet & Maxwell.

Lloyd, C., Mair, G. and Hough, M. (1994), *Explaining Reconviction Rates*, Home Office Research Study 135, London: HMSO.

Loader, I. (2010), 'For Penal Moderation: Notes towards a Public Philosophy of Punishment', *Theoretical Criminology*, 14: 349.

Lovegrove, A. (1997), *The Framework of Judicial Sentencing*, Cambridge: Cambridge University Press.

Lovegrove, A. (2004), *Sentencing the Multiple Offender: Judicial Practice and Legal Principle*, Canberra: Australian Institute of Criminology.

Macdonald, S. (2006), 'The Principle of Composite Sentencing: Its Centrality to, and Implications for, the ASBO', *Criminal Law Review*, 791.

Mackay, R. (2011), 'Unfitness to Plead: Some Observations on the Law Commission's Consultation Paper', *Criminal Law Review*, 433.

Mackay, R. (2012), 'Ten More Years of the Insanity Defence', *Criminal Law Review*, 946.

Mackay, R. and Machin, D. (2000), 'The Operation of Section 48 of the Mental Health Act 1983', *British Journal of Criminology*, 40: 727.

Mackenzie, D. L. (2006), 'Reducing the Criminal Activities of Known Offenders and Delinquents', in L. W. Sherman et al. (eds.), *Evidence-Based Crime Prevention*, London: Routledge.

Mackenzie, G. (2005), *How Judges Sentence*, Sydney: Federation Press.

Maguire, M. (1982), *Burglary in a Dwelling*, London: Heinemann.

Maguire, M. (2004), 'The Crime Reduction Programme in England and Wales: Reflections on the Vision and the Reality', *Criminal Justice*, 4: 213.

Mair, G. (2004), 'Diversionary and Non-Supervisory Approaches to Dealing with Offenders', in A. Bottoms, S. Rex and G. Robinson (eds.), *Alternatives to Prison: Options for an Insecure Society*, Cullompton: Willan.

Mair, G. and Mills, H. (2009), *The Community Order and the Suspended Sentence Order Three Years On*, London: Centre for Crime and Justice Studies.

Malloch, M. and McIvor, G. (2011), 'Women, Drugs and Community Intervention', in R. Sheehan, G. McIvor and C. Trotter (eds.), *Working with Women Offenders in the Community*, Cullompton: Willan.

Manson, A., Healy, P. et al. (2008), *Sentencing and Penal Policy in Canada*, 2nd edn, Toronto: Emond Montgomery.

Martinson, R. (1979), 'New Findings, New Views: A Note of Caution Regarding Sentencing Reform', *Hofstra Law Review*, 7: 242.

Martinson, R. et al. (1974), 'What Works? Questions and Answers about Prison Reform', *The Public Interest*, 22.

Maruna, S. (2001), *Making Good: How Ex-Convicts Reform and Rebuild their Lives*, Washington: American Psychological Association.

Maslen, H. and Roberts, J. V. (2013), 'Remorse and Sentencing: An Analysis of Sentencing Guidelines and Sentencing Practice', in A. Ashworth and J. V. Roberts (eds.), *Sentencing Guidelines*, Oxford: Oxford University Press.

Mason, A. (2001), 'Mandatory Sentencing: Implications for Judicial Independence', *Australian Journal of Human Rights*, 7: 21.

Mathiesen, T. (1990), *Prison on Trial*, London: Sage.

Matravers, M. (2010), 'Victim, State and Civil Society', in A. E. Bottoms and J. V. Roberts (eds.), *Hearing the Victim*, Oxford: Hart.

McBarnet, D. (1981), *Conviction: Law and State*, Oxford: Martin Robertson.

McConville, M. and Bridges, L. (1993), 'Convicting the Innocent', *New Law Journal*, 160.

McConville, M. and Marsh, L. (2014), *Criminal Judges*, Cheltenham: Edward Elgar.

McGuire, J. (ed.) (2002), *Offender Rehabilitation and Treatment*, Chichester: Wiley.

McNeill, F. (2006), 'The Desistance Paradigm for Offender Management', *Criminology and Criminal Justice*, 6: 39.

Merrington, S. (2004), 'Assessment Tools in Probation', in R. Burnett and C. Roberts (eds.), *What Works in Probation and Youth Justice*, Cullompton: Willan.

Miers, D. (2014), 'Compensating Deserving Victims of Violent Crime: The Criminal Injuries Compensation Scheme 2012', *Legal Studies*, 34: 242.

Miller, M. (2004), 'Sentencing Reform: The Sentencing Information System Alternative to Guidelines', in M. Tonry (ed.), *The Future of Imprisonment*, New York: Oxford University Press.

Miller, M. (2005), 'A Map of Sentencing and a Compass for Judges: Sentencing Information Systems, Transparency, and the Next Generation of Reform', *Columbia Law Review*, 105: 1351.

Millie, A., Tombs, J. and Hough, M. (2007), 'Borderline Sentencing: A Comparison of Sentencers' Decision-Making in England and Wales, and Scotland', *Criminology and Criminal Justice*, 7: 243.

Ministry of Justice (2007), *The Government's Response to the Report by Baroness Corston*, Cm 7621, London: The Stationery Office.

Ministry of Justice (2008), *Punishment and Reform: Our Approach to Managing Offenders*, London: Ministry of Justice.

Ministry of Justice (2008), *Sentencing Statistics 2007, England and Wales*, London: Ministry of Justice.

Ministry of Justice (2009), *Lord Bradley's Review of People with Mental Health Problems in the Criminal Justice System: The Government's Response*, London: The Stationery Office.

Ministry of Justice (2010), *Breaking the Cycle*, London: Ministry of Justice.

Ministry of Justice (2011), *Offender Management Statistics 2011*, www.gov.uk/government/statistics/offender-management-statitsics-quarterly

Ministry of Justice (2012), *Breaking the Cycle: Government Response*, London: Ministry of Justice.

Ministry of Justice (2013), *Prison Population Figures 2013*, www.gov.uk/government/statistics/prison-population-figures

Ministry of Justice (2013), *Story of the Prison Population 1993–2012*, London: Ministry of Justice.

Ministry of Justice (2014), *Sentencing Statistics 2013, England and Wales*, London: Ministry of Justice.

Mitchell, B. (1998), 'Public Perceptions of Homicide and Criminal Justice', *British Journal of Criminology*, 38: 453.

Mitchell, B. (2009), 'More Thoughts about Unlawful Act Manslaughter and the One-Punch Killer', *Criminal Law Review*, 502.

Mitchell, B. (2013), 'Sentencing Guidelines for Murder', in A. Ashworth and J. Roberts (eds.), *Sentencing Guidelines: Exploring the English Model*, Oxford: Oxford University Press.

Mitchell, B. and Roberts, J. V. (2012), *Exploring the Mandatory Life Sentence for Murder*, Oxford: Hart.

Monahan, J. (2004), 'The Future of Violence Risk Management', in M. Tonry (ed.), *The Future of Imprisonment*, New York: Oxford University Press.

Moore, M. (1988), 'The Moral Worth of Retribution', in F. Schoemann (ed.), *Responsibility, Character and the Emotions*, Cambridge: Cambridge University Press.

Moore, R. (2003), 'The Use of Financial Penalties and the Amounts Imposed: The Need for a New Approach', *Criminal Law Review*, 13.

Moore, R. (2004), 'The Methods for Enforcing Financial Penalties: The Need for a Multi-Dimensional Approach', *Criminal Law Review*, 728.

Moreno, Y. and Hughes, P. (2009), *Effective Prosecution*, Oxford: Oxford University Press.

Morgan, R. (2003), 'Thinking about the Demand for Probation Services', *Probation Journal*, 50: 7.

Morgan, R. and Newburn, T. (2012), 'Youth Justice', in M. Maguire, R. Morgan and R. Reiner (eds.), *Oxford Handbook of Criminology*, 5th edn, Oxford: Oxford University Press.

Morris, A. (2002), 'Critiquing the Critics', *British Journal of Criminology*, 42: 596.

Morris, A. and Maxwell, G. (2000), 'Restorative Conferencing', in G. Bazemore and M. Schiff (eds.), *Restorative and Community Justice*, Cincinnati: Anderson Publishing.

Morris, A., Maxwell, G. M. and Robertson, J. P. (1993), 'Giving Victims a Voice: The New Zealand Experience', *Howard Journal of Criminal Justice*, 32: 304.

Morris, N. (1974), *The Future of Imprisonment*, Chicago: University of Chicago Press.

Morris, N. and Tonry, M. (1990), *Between Prison and Probation*, New York: Oxford University Press.

Morse, S. (2000), 'Deprivation and Desert', in W. C. Heffernan and J. Kleinig (eds.), *From Social Justice to Criminal Justice*, New York: Oxford University Press.

Mortimer, E., Pereira, E. and Walter, I. (1999), *Making the Tag Fit*, Home Office Research Findings 105, London: Home Office.

Moxon, D. (1988), *Sentencing Practice in the Crown Court*, Home Office Research Study 103, London: HMSO.

Moxon, D. (1998), 'The Role of Sentencing Policy', in C. Nuttall (ed.), *Reducing Offending: An Assessment of Research Evidence on Ways of Dealing with Offending Behaviour*, Home Office Research Study 187, London: Home Office.

Moxon, D., Sutton, M. and Hedderman, C. (1990), *Unit Fines: Experiments in Four Courts*, Research and Planning Unit Paper 59, London: Home Office.

Moxon, D. and Whittaker, C. (1996), *Imprisonment for Fine Default*, Home Office Research Findings 35, London: Home Office.

Muncie, J. (2015), *Youth and Crime*, 4th edn, London: Sage.

Munro, C. (1992), 'Judicial Independence and Judicial Functions', in M. Wasik and C. Munro (eds.), *Sentencing, Judicial Discretion and Judicial Training*, London: Sweet & Maxwell.

Myhill, A. and Allen, J. (2002), *Rape and Sexual Assault of Women*, Home Office Research Study 237, London: Home Office.

Nagin, D. (1998), 'Criminal Deterrence Research at the Outset of the 21st Century', *Crime and Justice: A Review of Research*, 23: 51.

Nagin, D., Cullen, F. T. and Johnson, C. L. (2009), 'Imprisonment and Reoffending', in M. Tonry (ed.), *Crime and Justice: A Review of Research*, vol. xxxviii, New York: Oxford University Press.

Narayan, U. (1993), 'Appropriate Responses and Preventive Benefits: Justifying Censure and Hard Treatment in Legal Punishment', *Oxford Journal of Legal Studies*, 13: 166.

National Audit Office (2008), *National Probation Service: The Supervision of Community Orders in England and Wales*, London: The Stationery Office.

New South Wales Law Reform Commission (2013), *Encouraging Appropriate Early Guilty Pleas: Models for Discussion*, Consultation Paper 15, Sydney: NSW Law Reform Commission.

New South Wales Sentencing Council (2011), *Suspended Sentences*, Sydney: NSW Sentencing Council.

Newburn, T., Crawford, A. et al. (2002), *The Introduction of Referral Orders into the Youth Justice System*, Home Office Research Study 242, London: Home Office.

NOMS (2007), *National Standards for the Supervision of Offenders*, www.justice.gov.uk

NOMS (2011), *National Standards for the Management of Offenders*, www.justice.gov.uk

Norrie, A. (2014), *Crime, Reason and History*, 3rd edn, Cambridge: Cambridge University Press.

Nuttall, C. and Pease, K. (1994), 'Changes in the Use of Imprisonment in England and Wales', *Criminal Law Review*, 316.

O'Malley, P. (2009), *The Currency of Justice*, London: Routledge.

O'Malley, T. (2006), *Sentencing Law and Practice*, 2nd edn, Dublin: Round Hall.

O'Malley, T. (2013), 'Living without Guidelines', in A. Ashworth and J. V. Roberts (eds.), *Sentencing Guidelines: Exploring the English Model*, Oxford: Oxford University Press.

Office for National Statistics (2014), *Crime in England and Wales, Year ending March 2014*, London: ONS.

Oxford Pilot Study (1984), *Sentencing in the Crown Court: Report of an Exploratory Study*, by A. Ashworth, E. Genders, G. Mansfield, J. Peay and E. Player, Oxford: University of Oxford Centre for Criminology.

Padfield, N. (2008), *Text and Materials on the Criminal Justice Process*, 4th edn, Oxford: Oxford University Press.

Padfield, N. (2009), 'Parole and Early Release: The Criminal Justice and Immigration Act 2008 Changes in Context', *Criminal Law Review*, 166.

Padfield, N. (2011), 'Intoxication as a Sentencing Factor: Mitigation or Aggravation?', in J. V. Roberts (ed.), *Mitigation and Aggravation at Sentencing*, Cambridge: Cambridge University Press.

Padfield, N. (2013), 'Exploring the Success of Sentencing Guidelines', in A. Ashworth and J. V. Roberts (eds.), *Sentencing Guidelines: Exploring the English Model*, Oxford: Oxford University Press.

Padfield, N. and Maruna, S. (2006), 'The Revolving Door at the Prison Gate', *Criminology and Criminal Justice*, 6: 329.

Padfield, N., Morgan, R. and Maguire, M. (2012), 'Out of Court, Out of Sight? Criminal Sanctions and Non-Judicial Decision-Making', in Maguire, M., Morgan, R. and Reiner, R. (eds.), *Oxford Handbook of Criminology*, 5th edn, Oxford: Oxford University Press.

Parker, H., Sumner, M. and Jarvis, G. (1989), *Unmasking the Magistrates*, Milton Keynes: Open University Press.

Parole Board (2014), *Annual Report and Accounts 2013–14*, London: Stationery Office.

Pease, K. (1988), *The Seriousness of Offences: Findings from the 1988 British Crime Survey*, London: Home Office.

Peay, J. (2007), 'Mentally Disordered Offenders, Mental Health and Crime', in M. Maguire, R. Morgan and R. Reiner (eds.), *Oxford Handbook of Criminology*, 4th edn, Oxford: Oxford University Press.

Peay, J. (2011), *Mental Health and Crime*, Abingdon: Routledge.

Peay, J. (2012), 'Mentally Disordered Offenders, Mental Health and Crime', in M. Maguire, R. Morgan and R. Reiner (eds.), *Oxford Handbook of Criminology*, 5th edn, Oxford: Oxford University Press.

Peay, J. (2014), *Imprisoning the Mentally Disordered – A Manifest Injustice?* LSE Law Working Papers Series 07/2014, London: LSE.

Phillips, C. and Bowling, B. (2012), 'Ethnicities, Racism, Crime and Justice', in M. Maguire, R. Morgan and R. Reiner (eds.), *Oxford Handbook of Criminology*, 5th edn, Oxford: Oxford University Press.

Pina-Sanchez, J. and Linacre, R. (2013), 'Sentence Consistency in England and Wales: Evidence from the Crown Court Sentencing Survey', *British Journal of Criminology*, 53: 1118.

Player, E. (2005), 'The Reduction of Women's Imprisonment in England and Wales', *Punishment and Society*, 7: 419.

Player, E. (2012), 'Sentencing Women: Towards Gender Equality', in L. Zedner and J. V. Roberts (eds.), *Principles and Values in Criminal Law and Criminal Justice*, Oxford: Oxford University Press.

Pratt, J. (2007), *Penal Populism*, London: Routledge.

Prison Reform Trust (2000), *Justice for Women: The Need for Reform*, London: Prison Reform Trust.

Prison Reform Trust (2013), *Bromley Briefings Prison Factfile*, Autumn 2013, London: Prison Reform Trust.

Quirk, H. (2013), 'Sentencing White Coat Crime', *Criminal Law Review*, 871.

Radzinowicz, L. and Hood, R. (1979), 'Judicial Discretion and Sentencing Standards', *University of Pennsylvania Law Review*, 1288.

Radzinowicz, L. and Hood, R. (1980), 'Incapacitating the Habitual Criminal: The English Experience', *Michigan Law Review*, 1305.

Radzinowicz, L. and Hood, R. (1986), *The Emergence of Penal Policy in Victorian and Edwardian England*, London: Stevens.

Raine, J. and Dunstan, E. (2009), 'How Well do Sentencing Guidelines Work? Equity, Proportionality and Consistency in the Determination of Fine Levels', *Howard Journal of Criminal Justice*, 48: 13.

Raine, J., Dunstan, E. and Mackie, A. (2004), 'Financial Penalties: Who Pays, Who Doesn't, and Why Not?', *Howard Journal of Criminal Justice*, 43: 518.

Ramsay, P. (2012), *The Insecurity State*, Oxford: Oxford University Press.

Ranyard, R., Hebenton, B. and Pease, K. (1994), 'An Analysis of a Guideline Case as Applied to Rape', *Howard Journal of Criminal Justice*, 33: 203.

Raynor, P. (2012), 'Community Penalties: Probation, and Offender Management', in M. Maguire, R. Morgan and R. Reiner (eds.), *Oxford Handbook of Criminology*, 5th edn, Oxford: Oxford University Press.

Raynor, P. and Robinson, G. (2009), *Rehabilitation, Crime and Justice*, 2nd edn, Basingstoke: Palgrave Macmillan.

Raz, J. (1979), *The Authority of Law*, Oxford: Oxford University Press.

Reitz, K. (2010), 'The Illusion of Proportionality: Desert and Repeat Offenders', in J. V. Roberts and A. von Hirsch (eds.), *Previous Convictions at Sentencing*, Oxford: Hart.

Reitz, K. (2011), 'Proof of Aggravating and Mitigating Facts at Sentence', in J. V. Roberts (ed.), *Mitigation and Aggravation in Sentencing*, Cambridge: Cambridge University Press.

Reitz, K. (2013), 'Comparing Sentencing Guidelines: Do US Systems have Anything Worthwhile to Offer England and Wales?', in A. Ashworth and J. V. Roberts (eds.), *Sentencing Guidelines: Exploring the English Model*, Oxford: Oxford University Press.

Rex, S. (1998), 'Applying Desert Principles to Community Sentences', *Criminal Law Review*, 381.

Rex, S., Lieb, R., Bottoms, A. and Wilson, L. (2003), *Accrediting Offender Programmes*, Home Office Research Study 273, London: Home Office.

Richardson, G. (1999), *Review of the Mental Health Act 1983: Report of the Expert Committee*, London: Department of Health.

Riley, D. (1985), 'Drinking Drivers: The Limits to Deterrence', *Howard Journal of Criminal Justice*, 24: 241.

Riley, D. and Vennard, J. (1988), *Triable-Either-Way Cases: Crown Court or Magistrates' Court*, Home Office Research Study 98, London: HMSO.

Roberts, C. (2004), 'Offending Behaviour Programmes: Emerging Evidence and Implications for Practice', in R. Burnett and C. Roberts (eds.), *What Works in Probation and Youth Justice*, Cullompton: Willan.

Roberts, J. (2003), 'Evaluating the Pluses and Minuses of Custody', *Howard Journal of Criminal Justice*, 42: 229.

Roberts, J. (2004), *The Virtual Prison*, Cambridge: Cambridge University Press.

Roberts, J. (2008a), *Punishing Persistent Offenders*, Oxford: Oxford University Press.

Roberts, J. (2008b), 'Aggravating and Mitigating Factors at Sentencing: Towards Greater Consistency of Application', *Criminal Law Review*, 264.

Roberts, J. V. (2009), 'Revisiting the Recidivist Sentencing Premium', in A. von Hirsch, A. Ashworth and J. V. Roberts (eds.), *Principled Sentencing*, 3rd edn, Oxford: Hart Publishing.

Roberts, J. (2011), 'The Future of State Punishment: The Role of Public Opinion in Sentencing', in M. Tonry (ed.), *Retributivism Has a Past – Has it a Future?*, New York: Oxford University Press.

Roberts, J. V. (ed.) (2011a), *Mitigation and Aggravation at Sentencing*, Cambridge: Cambridge University Press.

Roberts, J. V. (2011b), 'Sentencing Guidelines and Judicial Discretion: Evolution of the Duty of Courts to Comply in England and Wales', *British Journal of Criminology*, 51: 997.

Roberts, J. V. (2012), 'Points of Departure: Reflections on Sentencing outside the Definitive Guideline Ranges', *Criminal Law Review*, 439.

Roberts, J. V. (2013), 'Complying with Sentencing Guidelines', in A. Ashworth and J. V. Roberts (eds.), *Sentencing Guidelines: Exploring the English Model*, Oxford: Oxford University Press.

Roberts, J. and Erez, J. (2010), 'Communication in Sentencing', in A. E. Bottoms and J. V. Roberts (eds.), *Hearing the Victim*, Oxford: Hart.

Roberts, J., Hough, M. et al. (2008), 'Public Attitudes to the Sentencing of Offences Involving Death by Driving', *Criminal Law Review*, 525.

Roberts, J. V., Hough, M., Jacobson, J. and Moon, N. (2009), 'Public Attitudes to Sentencing Purposes and Sentencing Factors: An Empirical Analysis', *Criminal Law Review*, 771.

Roberts, J. V. and Manikis, M. (2013), 'Victim Personal Statements in England and Wales', *Criminology and Criminal Justice*, 13: 245.

Roberts, J. V. and Pina-Sanchez, J. (2014), 'Previous Convictions at Sentencing: Exploring Empirical Trends in the Crown Court', *Criminal Law Review*, 575.

Roberts, J. V. and Rafferty, A. (2011), 'Sentencing Guidelines in England and Wales: Exploring the New Format', *Criminal Law Review*, 681.

Roberts, J. and Stalans, L. J. (1997), *Public Opinion, Crime and Criminal Justice*, Boulder: Westview.

Robinson, G. (2008), 'Late-Modern Rehabilitation: The Evolution of a Penal Strategy', *Punishment and Society*, 8: 429.

Robinson, G. and Shapland, J. (2008), 'Reducing Recidivism: A Task for Restorative Justice', *British Journal of Criminology*, 48: 337.

Robinson, P. and Darley, J. (1995), *Justice, Liability and Blame*, Boulder: Westview.

Rock, P. (1990), *Helping Victims of Crime*, Oxford: Oxford University Press.

Rock, P. (2010), 'Hearing Victims of Crime', in A. E. Bottoms and J. V. Roberts (eds.), *Hearing the Victim*, Oxford: Hart.

Roording, J. (1996), 'The Punishment of Tax Fraud', *Criminal Law Review*, 240.

Royal Commission on Criminal Justice (1993), *Report*, London: HMSO.

Ryan, A. (2011), 'Hobbes' Political Philosophy', in T. Sorell (ed.), *The Cambridge Companion to Hobbes*, Cambridge: Cambridge University Press.

Ryberg, J. (2010), 'Recidivism, Retributivism and the Lapse Theory of Previous Convictions', in J. V. Roberts and A. von Hirsch (eds.), *Previous Convictions at Sentencing*, Oxford: Hart.

Ryberg, J. and Roberts, J. V. (2014), *Popular Punishment*, New York: Oxford University Press.

Scotland's Choice (2008), *Report of the Scottish Prisons Commission*, Edinburgh: Scottish Executive.

Scottish Government (2012), *Prison Statistics Scotland 2011–2012*, Edinburgh: Scottish Executive.

SCWG Survey (2008), *Crown Court Sentencing Survey*, Sentencing Commission Working Group, London: Ministry of Justice.

Sebba, L. (1980), 'Is Mens Rea a Component of Perceived Offense Seriousness?', *Journal of Criminal Law and Criminology*, 71: 124.

Seddon, T. (2008), 'Dangerous Liaisons: Personality Disorder and the Politics of Risk', *Punishment and Society*, 8: 301.

Sellin, T. and Wolfgang, M. (1978), *The Measurement of Delinquency*, New York: Wiley.

Sentencing Advisory Council of Victoria (2012), *Community Attitudes to Offence Seriousness*, Melbourne: Sentencing Advisory Council.

Sentencing Advisory Panel (2010), *Overarching Principles of Sentencing: Advice to the Sentencing Guidelines Council*, London: Sentencing Advisory Panel.

Sentencing Council (2011), *Drug Offences: Analysis and Research Bulletin*, London: Sentencing Council.

Sentencing Council (2014), *Crown Court Sentencing Survey Annual Publication 2013*, London: Sentencing Council for England and Wales.

Seymour, L. and Rutherford, M. (2008), *The Community Order and the Mental Health Treatment Requirement*, London: Sainsbury Centre for Mental Health.

Shapland, J. (1981), *Between Conviction and Sentence*, London: Routledge and Kegan Paul.

Shapland, J. (2011), 'Personal Mitigation and Assumptions about Offending and Desistance', in J. V. Roberts (ed.), *Mitigation and Aggravation at Sentencing*, Cambridge: Cambridge University Press.

Shapland, J., Willmore, J. and Duff, P. (1985), *Victims in the Criminal Justice System*, London: Heinemann.

Shaw, S. (1989), 'Monetary Penalties and Imprisonment', in P. Carlen and D. Cook (eds.), *Paying for Crime*, Milton Keynes: Open University Press.

Shute, S. (2004), 'The New Civil Preventative Orders', *Criminal Law Review*, 417.

Simester, A. and von Hirsch, A. (2011), *Crimes, Harms and Wrongs*, Oxford: Hart.

Singer, R. (1979), *Just Deserts: Sentencing Based on Equality and Desert*, New York: Ballinger.

Singleton, N., Meltzer, H. and Gatward, R. (1998), *Psychiatric Morbidity among Prisoners in England and Wales*, London: HMSO.

Skeem, J. and Monahan, J. (2011), 'Current Directions in Violence Risk Assessment', *Current Directions in Psychological Science*, 21: 38.

Smith, A. T. H. (1983), 'The Prerogative of Mercy', *Public Law*, 203.

Smith, D. J. (2007), 'Crime and the Life Course', in M. Maguire, R. Morgan and R. Reiner (eds.), *Oxford Handbook of Criminology*, 4th edn, Oxford: Oxford University Press.

Social Exclusion Task Force (2009), *Reaching Out: An Action Plan on Social Exclusion*, London: Cabinet Office.

Social Exclusion Unit (2002), *Crime and Social Exclusion*, London: Office of the Deputy Prime Minister.

South African Law Commission (2000), *Report on a New Sentencing Framework*, Pretoria: South African Law Commission.

Sparks, R., Bottoms, A. E. and Hay, W. (1996), *Prisons and the Problem of Order*, Oxford: Clarendon Press.

Sparrow, P. and McIvor, G. (2013), 'Sentencing Drug Offenders under the 2003 Criminal Justice Act: Challenges for the Probation Service', *Criminology and Criminal Justice*, 13: 298.

Spohn, C. (2002), *How Do Judges Decide? The Search for Fairness and Justice in Punishment*, London: Sage.

Sprack, J. (2012), *A Practical Approach to Criminal Procedure*, 13th edn, Oxford: Oxford University Press.

Steiker, C. S. (2013), 'Proportionality as a Limit on Preventive Justice: Promises and Pitfalls', in A. Ashworth, L. Zedner and P. Tomlin (eds.), *Prevention and the Limits of the Criminal Law*, Oxford: Oxford University Press.

Stenning, P. and Roberts, J. V. (2001), 'Empty Promises: Parliament, the Supreme Court and the Sentencing of Aboriginal Offenders', *Saskatchewan Law Review*, 64: 137.

Stephen, J. F. (1885), 'Sentencing', *The Nineteenth Century*, 17: 795.

Stevens, R. (1993), *The Independence of the Judiciary*, Oxford: Clarendon Press.

Stith, K. and Cabranes, J. A. (1998), *Fear of Judging*, Chicago: University of Chicago Press.

Stott, C. and Pearson, G. (2006), 'Football Banning Orders, Proportionality and Public Order Policing', *Howard Journal of Criminal Justice*, 45: 241.

Streatfeild, Mr Justice (1960), *Report of the Interdepartmental Committee on the Business of the Criminal Courts*, London: HMSO.

Street, R. (1998), *The Restricted Hospital Order*, Home Office Research Study 186, London: Home Office.

Tague, P. (2006), 'Tactical Reasons for Recommending Trials rather than Guilty Pleas in the Crown Court', *Criminal Law Review*, 23.

Tague, P. (2007), 'Barristers' Selfish Incentives in Counselling Defendants over Choice of Plea', *Criminal Law Review*, 3.

Tarling, R. (1979), *Sentencing Practice in Magistrates' Courts*, Home Office Research Study 56, London: HMSO.

Tarling, R. (2006), 'Sentencing Practice in Magistrates' Courts Revisited', *Howard Journal of Criminal Justice*, 45: 29.

Tata, C. (1997), 'Conceptions and Representations of the Sentencing Decision Process', *Journal of Law and Society*, 24: 395.

Tata, C. (2013), 'The Struggle for Sentencing Reform: Will the English Sentencing Guidelines Model Spread?', in A. Ashworth and J. V. Roberts (eds.), *Sentencing Guidelines: Exploring the English Model*, Oxford: Oxford University Press.

Tata, C. et al. (2008), 'Assisting and Advising the Sentencing Decision Process: The Pursuit of "Quality" in Pre-Sentence Reports', *British Journal of Criminology*, 48: 835.

Taylor, Lord (1996), 'Continuity and Change in the Criminal Law', *King's College Law Journal*, 7: 1.

Thomas, D. A. (1963), 'Sentencing – The Case for Reasoned Decisions', *Criminal Law Review*, 243.

Thomas, D. A. (1970), *Principles of Sentencing*, London: Heinemann

Thomas, D. A. (1974), 'The Control of Discretion in the Administration of Criminal Justice', in R. Hood (ed.), *Crime, Criminology and Public Policy*, London: Heinemann.

Thomas, D. A. (1978), *The Penal Equation*, Cambridge: Institute of Criminology.

Thomas, D. A. (1979), *Principles of Sentencing*, 2nd edn, London: Heinemann.

Thomas, D. A. (1997), 'Sentencing Legislation – The Case for Consolidation', *Criminal Law Review*, 406.

Thorburn, M. (2012), 'Proportionate Sentencing and the Rule of Law', in L. Zedner and J. V. Roberts (eds.), *Principles and Values in Criminal Law and Criminal Justice*, Oxford: Oxford University Press.

Tonry, M. (1994), 'Proportionality, Parsimony and Interchangeability of Punishments', in A. Duff et al., *Penal Theory and Practice*, Manchester: Manchester University Press.

Tonry, M. (1996), *Sentencing Matters*, New York: Oxford University Press.

Tonry, M. (2004), *Punishment and Politics*, Cullompton: Willan.

Tonry, M. (2009), 'The Mostly Unintended Consequences of Mandatory Penalties: Two Centuries of Consistent Findings', *Crime and Justice: A Review of Research*, Chicago: University of Chicago Press, 65.

Tonry, M. (2010), 'The Questionable Relevance of Previous Convictions to Punishment for Later Crimes', in J. V. Roberts and A. von Hirsch (eds.), *Previous Convictions at Sentencing*, Oxford: Hart.

Tonry, M. (2011), *Punishing Race: A Continuing American Dilemma*, New York: Oxford University Press.

Travis, J., Western, B. and Redburn, S. (eds.) (2014), *The Growth of Incarceration in the United States: Exploring the Causes and Consequences*, National Academies Press.

Tyler, T. (2006), *Why People Obey the Law*, rev. edn, Princeton: Princeton University Press.

United Nations (1990), *The United Nations and Crime Prevention and Criminal Justice*, New York: United Nations.

United Nations Committee on the Rights of the Child (2008), *Report on United Kingdom*, at www.ohchr.org

Van Zyl Smit, D. and Ashworth, A. (2004), 'Disproportionate Sentences as Human Rights Violations', *Modern Law Review*, 67: 541.

Van Zyl Smit, D. and Dünkel, F. (2001), *Imprisonment Today and Tomorrow*, 2nd edn, The Hague: Kluwer.

Victim Support (2010), *Victims Justice? What Victims and Witnesses Really Want from Sentencing*, London: Victim Support.

Von Hirsch, A. (1986), *Past or Future Crimes*, Manchester: Manchester University Press.

Von Hirsch, A. (1993), *Censure and Sanctions*, Oxford: Oxford University Press.

Von Hirsch, A. and Ashworth, A. (2005), *Proportionate Sentencing*, Oxford: Oxford University Press.

Von Hirsch, A., Ashworth, A. and Roberts, J. V. (eds.) (2009), *Principled Sentencing: Readings on Theory and Policy*, 3rd edn, Oxford: Hart.

Von Hirsch, A., Bottoms, A. E., Burney, E. and Wikstrom, P.-O. (1999), *Criminal Deterrence: An Analysis of Recent Research*, Oxford: Hart.

Von Hirsch, A., Garland, D. and Wakefield, A. (2000), *Ethical and Social Perspectives on Situation Crime Prevention*, Oxford: Hart.

Von Hirsch, A. and Jareborg, N. (1989), 'Sweden's Sentencing Statute Enacted', *Criminal Law Review*, 275.

Von Hirsch, A. and Jareborg, N. (1991), 'Gauging Criminal Harm: A Living Standard Analysis', *Oxford Journal of Legal Studies*, 11: 1.

Walen, A. (2011), 'A Punitive Precondition for Preventive Detention', *San Diego Law Review*, 48: 1229.

Walker, N. (1982), 'Unscientific, Unwise, Unprofitable or Unjust?', *British Journal of Criminology*, 22: 276.

Walker, N. (1991), *Why Punish?*, Oxford: Oxford University Press.

Walklate, S. (2012), 'Courting Compassion', *Howard Journal of Criminal Justice*, 51: 109.

Walmsley, R. (1986), *Personal Violence*, Home Office Research Study 89, London: HMSO.

Walmsley, R. (2013), *World Prison Population List*, 10th edn, Colchester: International Centre for Prison Studies.

Wandall, R. (2008), *Decisions to Imprison*, Aldershot: Ashgate.

Warner, K. (2007), 'Mandatory Sentencing and the Role of the Academic', *Criminal Law Forum*, 18: 321.

Warner, K. (2011), 'Equality Before the Law: Racial and Social Background Factors as Sources of Mitigation at Sentencing', in J. V. Roberts (ed.), *Mitigation and Aggravation at Sentencing*, Cambridge: Cambridge University Press.

Warner, K. (2012), 'Equality Before the Law and Equal Impact of Sanctions', in L. Zedner and J. V. Roberts (eds.), *Principles and Values in Criminal Law and Criminal Justice*, Oxford: Oxford University Press.

Wasik, M. (1982), 'Partial Excuses in the Criminal Law', *Modern Law Review*, 45: 515.

Wasik, M. (1983), 'Excuses at the Sentencing Stage', *Criminal Law Review*, 450.

Wasik, M. (1985), 'The Grant of an Absolute Discharge', *Oxford Journal of Legal Studies*, 5: 211.

Wasik, M. (1998), 'Crime Seriousness and the Offender-Victim Relationship in Sentencing', in A. Ashworth and M. Wasik (eds.), *Fundamentals of Sentencing Theory*, Oxford: Oxford University Press.

Wasik, M. (2000), 'Sentencing in Homicide', in A. Ashworth and B. Mitchell (eds.), *Rethinking English Homicide Law*, Oxford: Oxford University Press.

Wasik, M. (2008), 'Sentencing Guidelines in England and Wales – State of the Art?', *Criminal Law Review*, 253.

Wasik, M. (2010), 'Dimensions of Criminal History: Reflections on Theory and Practice', in J. V. Roberts and A. von Hirsch (eds.), *Previous Convictions at Sentencing*, Oxford: Hart.

Wasik, M. (2012), 'Concurrent and Consecutive Sentences Revisited', in L. Zedner and J. V. Roberts (eds.), *Principles and Values in Criminal Law and Criminal Justice*, Oxford: Oxford University Press.

Wasik, M. (2014), 'Sentencing: The Last Ten Years', *Criminal Law Review*, 477.

Wasik, M. and von Hirsch, A. (1988), 'Non-Custodial Penalties and the Principles of Desert', *Criminal Law Review*, 555.

Wasik, M. and von Hirsch, A. (1997), 'Civil Disqualifications Attending Conviction', *Cambridge Law Journal*, 599.

Weatherburn, D. and Moffatt, S. (2011), 'The Specific Deterrent Effect of Higher Fines on Drink-Driving Offenders', *British Journal of Criminology*, 51: 789.

Webster, C. and Doob, A. (2012), 'Searching for Sasquatch: Deterrence of Crime through Sentence Severity', in J. Petersilia and K. Reitz (eds.), *Oxford Handbook of Sentencing and Corrections*, New York: Oxford University Press.

Wells, M. (1992), *Sentencing for Multiple Offences in Western Australia*, Perth: University of Western Australia Crime Research Centre.

West, D. (1963), *The Habitual Prisoner*, London: Heinemann.

Whittaker, C. and Mackie, A. (1997), *Enforcing Financial Penalties*, Home Office Research Study 165, London: Home Office.

Wilkinson, J. (2005), 'Evaluating Evidence for the Effectiveness of the Reasoning and Rehabilitation Programme', *Howard Journal of Criminal Justice*, 44: 70.

Willcock, H. D. and Stokes, J. (1963), *Deterrents and Incentives to Crime among Youths Aged 15–21 Years*, London: HMSO.

Windlesham, Lord (1996), *Responses to Crime: vol. III*, Oxford: Oxford University Press.

Wintemute, R. (2004), 'Filling the Article 14 Gap', *European Human Rights Law Review*, 484.

Woolf, Lord Justice (1991), *Prison Disturbances, April 1990: Report of an Inquiry*, London: HMSO.

Young, P. (1989), *Punishment, Money and the Legal Order*, Edinburgh: Edinburgh University Press.

Young, W. and Browning, C. (2008), 'New Zealand's Sentencing Council', *Criminal Law Review*, 287.

Young, W. and King, A. (2013), 'The Origins and Evolution of Sentencing Guidelines: A Comparison of England and Wales and New Zealand', in A. Ashworth and J. V. Roberts (eds.), *Sentencing Guidelines: Exploring the English Model*, Oxford: Oxford University Press.

Youth Justice Board (2002), *Annual Review 2002*, London: Youth Justice Board.

Youth Justice Board (2014), *Annual Report and Accounts 2013–14*, London: Ministry of Justice.

Zander, M. and Henderson, P. (1993), *Crown Court Study*, Royal Commission on Criminal Justice Research Study 19, London: HMSO.

Zedner, L. (1994), 'Reparation and Retribution: Are They Reconcilable?', *Modern Law Review*, 57: 228.

Zedner, L. (2002), 'Dangers of Dystopias in Criminal Theory', *Oxford Journal of Legal Studies*, 22: 341.

Zedner, L. (2009), *Security*, Abingdon: Routledge.

Zeisel, H. and Diamond, S. S. (1977), 'The Search for Sentencing Equity', *American Bar Foundation Research Journal*, 881.

Zimring, F. and Hawkins, G. (1995), *Incapacitation: Penal Confinement and the Restraint of Crime*, New York: Oxford University Press.

Zimring, F., Hawkins, G. and Kamin, J. (2001), *Punishment and Democracy: Three Strikes and You're Out in California*, New York: Oxford University Press.

Index